Libraries and Information Services in the United Kingdom and the Republic of Ireland 2010–2011

Libraries and Information Services in the United Kingdom and the Republic of Ireland 2010–2011

facet publishing

© CILIP: the Chartered Institute of Library and Information Professionals 2011

Published by Facet Publishing
7 Ridgmount Street, London WC1E 7AE
www.facetpublishing.co.uk

Facet Publishing is wholly owned by CILIP: the Chartered Institute of Library and Information Professionals.

First published as *Libraries in the United Kingdom and the Republic of Ireland* by The Library Association, 1960 and thereafter annually.

Twenty-ninth edition published as *Libraries and Information Services in the United Kingdom and the Republic of Ireland* by Facet Publishing, 2002. This thirty-seventh edition 2011

ISBN 978-1-85604-708-1
ISSN 1741-7120

Mixed Sources
Product group from well-managed forests and other controlled sources
www.fsc.org Cert no. SA-COC-1565
© 1996 Forest Stewardship Council

Text printed on FSC accredited material.

This thirty-seventh edition has been compiled by Lin Franklin and June York.

Typeset in 9/11pt Humanist 521 by Facet Publishing.
Printed and bound in Great Britain by MPG Books Group Ltd, Bodmin, Cornwall.

CONTENTS

Preface   vii

Public Libraries in the United Kingdom   I
England   3
Northern Ireland   129
Scotland   131
Wales   171
Crown Dependencies   187

Public Libraries in the Republic of Ireland   189

Libraries in Academic Institutions in the United Kingdom   217

Selected Government, National and Special Libraries in the United Kingdom   317

Selected Academic, National and Special Libraries in the Republic of Ireland   391

Schools and Departments of Information and Library Studies in the United Kingdom and the Republic of Ireland   403

The Regions of England   411

Name and place index   413

How this book is organized

Libraries and Information Services in the United Kingdom and the Republic of Ireland is published annually, and is a listing of organizations falling into the five categories below.

I Public library authorities

■ All public library authorities in the UK and the Republic of Ireland, arranged under home countries
- Public Libraries in England, Northern Ireland, Scotland, Wales and Crown Dependencies
- Public Libraries in the Republic of Ireland

Service managers and officers, including those for children's services, are listed, as supplied by the individual authorities.

It is clearly impossible to list here all branch libraries, mobile bases and so on, so each entry includes headquarters/central library details, together with major branches and area/regional/group libraries, as supplied by each individual library. Libraries in this section are arranged by name of authority.

A listing of the nine Government regions in England, indicating which public library authorities fall in their areas, is given on page 411.

2 Academic libraries (arranged by name of institution)

■ University libraries in the UK and the Republic of Ireland, together with major department and site/campus libraries
■ College libraries at the universities of Oxford, Cambridge and London
Please note: potential users of the Oxford and Cambridge libraries should be aware that their use is restricted to members of the college, and to bona fide scholars on application to the Librarian; any additional information about their use is given with each entry.
■ The university-equivalent colleges in the Republic of Ireland
■ Other degree-awarding institutions in the UK
All colleges of higher education funded by HEFCE, SHEFC and HEFCW are included.

3 Selected government, national and special libraries in the UK and the Republic of Ireland

■ Special libraries are included if they are one of the main libraries or organizations in their subject field. For example, the British Architectural Library at the Royal Institute of

British Architects is included for architecture, the Institution of Civil Engineers for civil engineering.

Many of the libraries in this section require a prior appointment to be made before visiting.

4 Schools and departments of information and library studies

■ Each academic institution offering courses in information and library studies, with full contact details of the departments concerned.

5 Index

■ Organizations are fully indexed by name and place.

Updating Libraries and Information Services in the UK

The directory is compiled by mailing questionnaires or entries for updating to libraries already listed in this book, and to others that have been suggested for inclusion. We would like to thank all the libraries for taking the time to reply to yet another mailing. With their assistance we received a 100% return rate. This means that every entry has been approved by the institution concerned.

We are dependent upon libraries to keep us informed of changes throughout the year. In this way we shall be able to ensure that our mailing label service is as current as possible. Libraries will, of course, be contacted afresh for the preparation of the next edition.

Please help us to improve this directory

Any comments about additions or other changes to *Libraries and Information Services in the United Kingdom and the Republic of Ireland* will be welcomed. Please address them to:

The Editor, Libraries and Information Services in the UK, Facet Publishing, 7 Ridgmount Street, London WC1E 7AE

Tel: 020 7255 0590
e-mail: info@facetpublishing.co.uk

Mailing list

The data in this directory is also available to rent in a variety of formats including .csv files* via e-mail or on disk/CD, or as laser-quality adhesive labels. Visit the Facet Publishing website at www.facetpublishing.co.uk/listrental.shtml for further information.

Full set
Named Chief Librarian   ISBN 978 1 85604 026 6
Acquisitions Librarian   ISBN 978 1 85604 198 0

Public libraries (main headquarters)
Named Chief Librarian   ISBN 978 0 85365 587 9
Acquisitions Librarian   ISBN 978 1 85604 199 7

Public libraries (main headquarters and branches)
Named Chief Librarian   ISBN 978 1 85604 025 9

Academic and special libraries
Named Chief Librarian   ISBN 978 0 85365 959 4
Acquisitions Librarian   ISBN 978 1 85604 201 7

* For single use only within 30 days by a third-party mailing house.

Public Libraries in the United Kingdom, the Channel Islands and the Isle of Man

England
Northern Ireland
Scotland
Wales
Crown Dependencies

Service managers and officers, including those for children's services, are listed, as supplied by the individual authorities

BARKING AND DAGENHAM

Authority: London Borough of Barking and Dagenham

Library Services HQ, 18 Muirhead Quay, Highbridge Road, Barking, Essex IG11 7BG
☎020 8724 8530 (enquiries and administration)
Fax 020 8594 8489
e-mail: libraries@lbbd.gov.uk
url: www.lbbd.gov.uk/4-libraries/libraries-menu.html
Group Manager – Libraries Zoinul Abidin (e-mail: zoinul.abidin@lbbd.gov.uk)
Service Development Manager Mrs Susan Leighton MA MCLIP (e-mail: susan.leighton@lbbd.gov.uk)
Customer Services Manager Ms Vashti Thorne BA MCLIP (e-mail: vashti.thorne@lbbd.gov.uk)

Central/largest library

Barking Library, BLC, 2 Town Square, Barking, Essex IG11 7NB
☎020 8724 8725

Community libraries

Castle Green Library, Gale Street, Dagenham, Essex RM9 4UN
☎020 8270 4166

Fanshawe Library, Fanshawe Community Centre, Barnmead Road, Dagenham, Essex RM9 5DX
☎020 8270 4244

Marks Gate Library, Rose Lane, Chadwell Heath, Essex RM6 5NJ
☎020 8270 4165

Markyate Library, Markyate Road, Dagenham, Essex RM8 2LD
☎020 8270 4137

Rectory Library, Rectory Road, Dagenham, Essex RM10 9SA
☎020 8270 6233

Robert Jeyes Library, High Road, Chadwell Heath, Essex RM6 6AS
☎020 8270 4305

Rush Green Library, Dagenham Road, Rush Green, Essex RM7 0TL
☎020 8270 4304

Thames View Library, Bastable Avenue, Barking, Essex IG11 0LG
☎020 8270 4164

Valence Library, Becontree Avenue, Dagenham, Essex RM8 3HS
☎020 8270 6864

Wantz Library, Rainham Road North, Dagenham, Essex RM10 7DX
☎020 8270 4169

BARNET
Authority: London Borough of Barnet

Resources – Libraries, Museums & Local Studies, Building 4, North London Business Park, Oakleigh Road South, London NII INP
☎020 8359 7770
Fax 0870 889 6804
url: www.barnet.gov.uk/libraries
Head of Libraries, Museums & Local Studies Tom Pike (e-mail: tom.pike@barnet.gov.uk)
Divisional Manager: Library Operations Ms Gill Harvey BSc(Hons) MCLIP (e-mail: gill.harvey@barnet.gov.uk)
Divisional Manager: Adults Mike Fahey (e-mail: mike.fahey@barnet.gov.uk)
Divisional Manager: Children and Young People Ms Hannah Richens BA(Hons) DipILM MCLIP (e-mail: hannah.richens@barnet.gov.uk)

Lending libraries

Burnt Oak Library, Watling Avenue, Edgware, Middlesex HA8 0UB
☎020 8359 3880
e-mail: burnt.oak.library@barnet.gov.uk
Library Customer Service Manager Ms Emma Martin (e-mail: emma.martin@barnet.gov.uk), Steve Saunders (e-mail: steve.saunders@barnet.gov.uk) (job share)

Childs Hill Library, 320 Cricklewood Lane, London NW2 2QE
☎020 8359 3900
e-mail: childshill.library@barnet.gov.uk
Assistant Library Customer Service Manager Mrs Nathalie Pease (e-mail: nathalie.pease@barnet.gov.uk), Keith Meyer (e-mail: keith.meyer@barnet.gov.uk) (job share)

Chipping Barnet Library, 3 Stapylton Road, Barnet, Herts EN5 4QT
☎020 8359 4040
e-mail: chipping.barnet.library@barnet.gov.uk
Library Customer Service Manager Robert Prosser (e-mail: robert.prosser@barnet.gov.uk)

Church End Library, 24 Hendon Lane, Finchley, London N3 ITR
☎020 8359 3800
e-mail: church.end.library@barnet.gov.uk
Library Customer Service Manager Ms Paula Pendred (e-mail: paula.pendred@barnet.gov.uk)

East Barnet Library, 85 Brookhill Road, East Barnet, Herts EN4 8SG
☎020 8359 3860
e-mail: east.barnet.library@barnet.gov.uk
Library Customer Service Manager Ms Liz Clifford (e-mail: liz.clifford@barnet.gov.uk)

East Finchley Library, 226 High Road, London N2 9BB
☎020 8359 3815
e-mail: east.finchley.library@barnet.gov.uk

Library Customer Service Manager Ms Sarah Green (e-mail: sarah.green@barnet.gov.uk)

Edgware Library, Hale Lane, Edgware, Middlesex HA8 8NN
☎020 8359 2626
e-mail: edgware.library@barnet.gov.uk
Library Customer Service Manager David Izzard

Friern Barnet Library, Friern Barnet Road, London N11 3DS
☎020 8359 3895
e-mail: friern.barnet.library@barnet.gov.uk
Assistant Library Customer Service Manager Ms Tracey Lowe (e-mail: tracey.lowe@barnet.gov.uk), Ms Amanda Heather (e-mail: amanda.heather@barnet.gov.uk) (job share)

Golders Green Library, 156 Golders Green Road, London NW11 8HE
☎020 8359 2060
e-mail: golders.green.library@barnet.gov.uk
Library Customer Service Manager Ms Lucy Mukuru

Grahame Park Library, The Concourse, London NW9 5XL
☎020 8359 3930
e-mail: grahame.park.library@barnet.gov.uk
Assistant Library Customer Service Manager Ms Nati Lamela (e-mail: nati.lamela@barnet.gov.uk)

Hampstead Garden Suburb Library, 15 The Market Place, London NW11 6LB
☎020 8359 3915
e-mail: hampstead.garden.library@barnet.gov.uk
Assistant Library Customer Service Manager Ms Wynn Quek (e-mail: wynn.quek@barnet.gov.uk)

Hendon Library, The Burroughs, London NW4 4BQ
☎020 8359 2628
e-mail: hendon.library@barnet.gov.uk
Library Customer Service Manager Ms Anne Messere (e-mail: anne.messere@barnet.gov.uk)

Mill Hill Library, Hartley Avenue, London NW7 2HX
☎020 8359 3830
e-mail: mill.hill.library@barnet.gov.uk
Library Customer Service Manager Ms Dawn Andrews (e-mail: dawn.andrews@barnet.gov.uk)

North Finchley Library, Ravonsdale Avenue, North Finchley, London N12 9HP
☎020 8359 3845
e-mail: north.finchley.library@barnet.gov.uk
Library Customer Service Manager Ms Fiona Page-Roberts

Osidge Library, Brunswick Park Road, London N11 1EY
☎020 8359 3920
e-mail: osidge.library@barnet.gov.uk
Library Customer Service Manager Steve Saunders (e-mail: steve.saunders@barnet.gov.uk)

South Friern Library, Colney Hatch Lane, London N10 1HD
☎020 8359 3946
e-mail: south.friern.library@barnet.gov.uk
Assistant Library Customer Service Manager Sim Branaghan (e-mail: sim.branaghan@barnet.gov.uk)

BARNSLEY
Authority: Barnsley Metropolitan Borough Council

Central Library, Shambles Street, Barnsley S70 2JF
☎(01226) 773911/30 (enquiries), (01226) 773926 (administration)
Fax (01226) 773955
e-mail: barnsleylibraryenquiries@barnsley.gov.uk
url: www.barnsley.gov.uk/libraries
Chief Libraries Officer Mrs Kathryn Green BA(Hons) MCLIP DMS
Libraries Operations Officer Ms Wendy Mann BSc(Hons) MCLIP
Information and Resources Officer Ms Jane Lee BA(Hons) MCLIP DMS
Archives and Local Studies Officer Paul Stebbing BA(Hons) MARM RMSA

Central/largest library

Central Library, Shambles Street, Barnsley, Barnsley, South Yorks S70 2JF
☎(01226) 773940 (enquiries)
Fax (01226) 773955

BATH AND NORTH EAST SOMERSET
Authority: Bath and North East Somerset Council

HQ Customer Service, Libraries and Information, Bath Central Library, 19a The Podium, Northgate Street, Bath BA1 5AN
☎(01225) 394041
url: www.bathnes.gov.uk/libraries
Library Services Manager Mrs June Brassington MCLIP (01225 396424; e-mail: june_brassington@bathnes.gov.uk)

Central/largest library

Bath Library and Information Centre, 19a The Podium, Northgate Street, Bath BA1 5AN
☎(01225) 394041 (enquiries)
e-mail: libraries@bathnes.gov.uk
SMS (text): (07797) 806545
Libraries Development Manager Ms Julia Burton BLib MCLIP (01225 396078; e-mail: julia_burton@bathnes.gov.uk)
Libraries Operational and Staff Development Manager Mrs Helen Chamberlain BA MCLIP MCMI (e-mail: helen_chamberlain@bathnes.gov.uk)
Libraries Customer Services Manager Peter Moth MCMI (e-mail: peter_moth@bathnes.gov.uk)

Group libraries

Keynsham Library, The Centre, Keynsham, Bristol BS31 1ED
☎(01225) 394041

Midsomer Norton Library, 119 High Street, Midsomer Norton, Bath BA3 2DA
☎(01225) 394041

BEDFORD
Authority: Bedford Borough Council

Libraries, Bedford Central Library, Harpur Street, Bedford MK40 IPG
☎(01234) 718178
Fax (01234) 342163
url: www.bedford.gov.uk
Head of Libraries Ms Jenny Poad BA DMS MCLIP (e-mail: jenny.poad@bedford.gov.uk)

Central/largest library

Central Library, Harpur Street, Bedford MK40 1PG
☎(01234) 718178
Fax (01234) 342163
e-mail: bedford.library@bedford.gov.uk
Central Library Manager Ms Joanne Smith

Area libraries

Kempston Library, Halsey Road, Kempston, Bedford MK42 8AU
☎(01234) 276453
Fax (01234) 841476
e-mail: kempston.library@bedford.gov.uk
Library Manager Ms Ros Willis

Putnoe Library, Library Walk, Putnoe, Bedford MK41 8HQ
☎(01234) 276462
Fax (01234) 272833
e-mail: putnoe.library@bedford.gov.uk
Library Manager Ms Coral Clarke

BEXLEY
Authority: London Borough of Bexley

Directorate of Social and Community Services, Libraries and Community Information, Ground Floor, Footscray Offices, Maidstone Road, Sidcup, Kent DA14 5HS
☎020 8303 7777
Fax 020 8309 4142
url: www.bexley.gov.uk
Head of Libraries, Arts and Archives Ms Judith Mitlin BSc PLD DMS (020 8309 4131; e-mail: judith.mitlin@bexley.gov.uk)
Development Manager (Libraries) H C M Paton BA DipLib MCLIP (020 8309 4134; e-mail: hugh.paton@bexley.gov.uk)
Operations Manager Philip Ware BA MCLIP (020 8309 4166; e-mail: philip.ware@bexley.gov.uk)
Borough Archivist Simon McKeon BA MA (020 8303 7777 ext 3470; e-mail: simon.mckeon@bexley.gov.uk)

Central/largest library

Central Library, Townley Road, Bexleyheath, Kent DA6 7HJ
☎020 8303 7777
Fax 020 8304 7058
Group Manager Ms Caroline Duckworth DipLib MCLIP (e-mail:
caroline.duckworth@bexley.gov.uk)

BIRMINGHAM
Authority: Birmingham City Council

Central Library, Chamberlain Square, Birmingham B3 3HQ
☎0121 303 4511 (enquiries), 0121 303 2449 (management)
Fax 0121 233 9695 (enquiries), 0121 303 2861 (management)
e-mail: libraries@birmingham.gov.uk
url: www.birmingham.gov.uk
Assistant Director, Culture Brian Gambles MA (e-mail:
brian.gambles@birmingham.gov.uk)
Head of Library Services Mrs Linda Butler BA MBA MCLIP
(e-mail: linda.butler@birmingham.gov.uk)
Head of Central Library Geoff Mills BA MSc DipLib MCLIP
(e-mail: geoff.mills@birmingham.gov.uk)
Head of Archives and Heritage Paul Hemmings BLib MCLIP
(e-mail: paul.hemmings@birmingham.gov.uk)
Head of Reading and Children's Services Mrs Patsy Heap BA MCLIP
(e-mail: patsy.heap@birmingham.gov.uk)

BLACKBURN WITH DARWEN
Authority: Blackburn with Darwen Borough Council

Central Library, Town Hall Street, Blackburn, Lancashire BB2 IAG
☎(01254) 661221 (enquiries), 01254 587902 (facilities)
Fax (01254) 678898
url: www.blackburn.gov.uk/libraries
Head of Library and Information Services Mrs Kath Sutton BA MCLIP (01254 587907;
e-mail: kath.sutton@blackburn.gov.uk)
Principal Librarian: Customer Services Ms Adele Karwat BA MCLIP (01254 587954;
e-mail: adele.karwat@blackburn.gov.uk)
Principal Librarian: Literacy Development and Stock Miss Jean Gabbatt BLib MCLIP
(01254 587937; e-mail: jean.gabbatt@blackburn.gov.uk)
Senior Librarian: Literacy Development Mrs Geraldine Wilson MCLIP (01254 587236;
e-mail: geraldine.wilson@blackburn.gov.uk)

BLACKPOOL
Authority: Blackpool Borough Council

Cultural Services, Progress House, Clifton Road, Blackpool, Lancs FY4 4US
☎(01253) 478080 (enquiries), 01253 478105 (administration)
Fax (01253) 478059
url: www.blackpool.gov.uk

Assistant Director, Cultural Services Ms P Hamilton (e-mail:
polly.hamilton@blackpool.gov.uk)
Head of Libraries Mrs A Ellis BA MCLIP DMS (e-mail: anne.ellis@blackpool.gov.uk)
Head of Arts Ms Carolyn Primett BA MA (e-mail: carolyn.primett@blackpool.gov.uk)
Head of Heritage Ms Heather Morrow (e-mail: heather.morrow@blackpool.gov.uk)

Central/largest library

Central Library, Queen Street, Blackpool, Lancs FYI IPX
☎(01253) 478080
Fax (01253) 478082

BOLTON
Authority: Bolton Metropolitan Borough Council

Central Library, Le Mans Crescent, Bolton, Lancs BLI ISE
☎(01204) 333173
Fax (01204) 332225
e-mail: central.library@bolton.gov.uk
url: www.bolton.gov.uk
Assistant Director, Adult Services (Adult and Community Services) Mrs Stephanie
Crossley BA(I Ions) DipLIS MCLIP (e-mail: stephanie.crossley@bolton.gov.uk)
Head of Library Service Mrs Julie Spencer MBE BA(Hons) MBA MCLIP
(e-mail: julie.spencer@bolton.gov.uk)
Knowledge and E-Services Manager Mrs Ann Melmoth BA MBA MCLIP
(e-mail: ann.melmoth@bolton.gov.uk)
Communities and Learning Manager Ms Mary Keane BA(Hons) DipLib MCLIP
(e-mail: mary.keane@bolton.gov.uk)
Customer Services Manager Mrs Judith Rudd MCLIP (e-mail:
judith.rudd@bolton.gov.uk)

BOURNEMOUTH
Authority: Bournemouth Borough Council

**Bournemouth Libraries, Information, Community and Culture, Town Hall, Bourne
Avenue, Bournemouth BH2 6DY**
☎(01202) 454848 (general enquiries)
Fax (01202) 454830
e-mail: bournemouth@bournemouthlibraries.org.uk
url: www.bournemouth.gov.uk/libraries
Service Director Ms Sue Bickler (01202 454966; e-mail:
sue.bickler@bournemouth.gov.uk)
Service and Strategy Manager: Bournemouth Libraries Ms Medi Bernard BA DipLib
MCLIP (01202 454618; e-mail: medi.bernard@bournemouthlibraries.org.uk)

Central/largest library

The Bournemouth Library, 22 The Triangle, Bournemouth BH2 5RQ
☎(01202) 454848
Area Manager Graham Brown BA(Hons) MCLIP (01202 454841; e-mail:
graham.brown@bournemouthlibraries.org.uk)

BRACKNELL FOREST

Authority: Bracknell Forest Borough Council

Environment, Culture and Communities, Time Square, Market Street, Bracknell, Berks RG12 1JD
☎(01344) 423149
Fax (01344) 411392
e-mail: bracknell.library@bracknell-forest.gov.uk
url: www.bracknell-forest.gov.uk/libraries
Head of Libraries, Arts and Heritage Ms Ruth Burgess BLib MCLIP (01344 351315; e-mail: ruth.burgess@bracknell-forest.gov.uk)

Central/largest library

Bracknell Library, Town Square, Bracknell, Berks RG12 1BH
☎(01344) 423149
Fax (01344) 411392
e-mail: bracknell.library@bracknell-forest.gov.uk
url: www.bracknell-forest.gov.uk/libraries
Community Services Manager Mrs Fiona Atkinson BA(Hons) MA MCLIP (e-mail: fiona.atkinson@bracknell-forest.gov.uk)

BRADFORD

Authority: City of Bradford Metropolitan District Council

Central Library, Prince's Way, Bradford BD1 1NN
☎(01274) 433600
Fax (01274) 395108
e-mail: public.libraries@bradford.gov.uk
url: www.bradford.gov.uk
Strategic Director, Culture, Tourism & Sport Ms Jane Glaister OBE BA FMA PGDipLib (01274 432647; e-mail: jane.glaister@bradford.gov.uk)
Acting Head of Libraries Ms Jane Heap BA(Hons) MCLIP (01274 434681; e-mail: jane.heap@bradford.gov.uk)

Branch libraries

Branch libraries, c/o Central Library, Prince's Way, Bradford BD1 1NN
☎(01274) 433600
Fax (01274) 395108
e-mail: public.libraries@bradford.gov.uk
Principal Libraries Officer: Operations North Ms Jackie Kitwood BA DipLib MCLIP (01274 437152; e-mail: jackie.kitwood@bradford.gov.uk)

BRENT

Authority: London Borough of Brent

Environment and Culture Directorate, Ground Floor, Brent House, 349-357 High Road, Wembley, Middlesex HA9 6BZ
☎020 8937 3144
Fax 020 8937 3008

url: www.brent.gov.uk
Director of Environment and Culture Richard Saunders
Assistant Director (Culture) Ms Sue Harper (020 8937 5192; e-mail:
sue.harper@brent.gov.uk)
Head of Libraries, Arts and Heritage Ms Susan McKenzie BA DAA (020 8937 3149;
e-mail: susan.mckenzie@brent.gov.uk)

Area libraries

Barham Park Library, Harrow Road, Sudbury, Middlesex HA0 2HB
☎020 8937 3550
Fax 020 8937 3553

Cricklewood Library, 152 Olive Road, Cricklewood, London NW2 6UY
☎020 8937 3540
Fax 020 8937 3579

Ealing Road Library, Coronet Parade, Wembley, Middlesex HA0 4BR
☎020 8937 3560
Fax 020 8937 3568

Harlesden Library, Craven Park Road, Harlesden, London NW10 8SE
☎020 8965 7132
Fax 020 8937 3570

Kensal Rise Library, Bathurst Gardens, Harlesden, London NW10 5JA
☎020 8937 3660
Fax 020 8937 3664

Kilburn Library, 42 Salusbury Road, Kilburn, London NW6 6NN
☎020 8937 3530
Fax 020 8937 3537

Kingsbury Library Plus, 522–524 Kingsbury Road, London NW9 9HE
☎020 8937 3520
Fax 020 8937 3523

Neasden Library Plus, 277 Neasden Lane, London NW10 1QJ
☎020 8937 3580
Fax 020 8937 3588

Preston Library, Carlton Avenue East, Wembley, Middlesex HA9 8PL
☎020 8937 3510
Fax 020 8937 3535

Stock Support and Interlibrary loans, 2–12 Grange Road, Willesden, London NW10 2QY
☎020 8937 3416
Fax 020 8937 3471

Tokyngton Library, Monks Park, Wembley, Middlesex HA9 6JE
☎020 8937 3590
Fax 020 8937 3595

Town Hall Library, Brent Town Hall, Forty Lane, Wembley, Middlesex HA9 9HV
☎020 8937 3500
Fax 020 8937 3504

Willesden Green Library Centre, 95 High Road, Willesden, London NW10 2SF
☎020 8937 3400
Fax 020 8937 3401

BRIGHTON AND HOVE
Authority: Brighton and Hove City Council

Royal Pavilion Libraries and Museums Divisions, Cultural Services, Jubilee Library, Jubilee Street, Brighton BN1 IGE
☎(01273) 290800 (general); (01273) 296930 (administration)
Fax (01273) 296976
url: www.citylibraries.info
Head of Libraries and Information Services Ms Sally McMahon BA DipLib MCLIP
(e-mail: sally.mcmahon@brighton-hove.gov.uk)
Neighbourhood and Enterprise Manager Alan Issler BA MCLIP (e-mail:
alan.issler@brighton-hove.gov.uk)
Jubilee and Central Services Manager Ms Kate Rouse MSc (e-mail:
kate.rouse@brighton-hove.gov.uk)

Central libraries

Jubilee Library, Jubilee Street, Brighton BN1 IGE
☎(01273) 290800

Hove Library, 182-186 Church Road, Hove, East Sussex BN3 2EG
☎(01273) 290700

BRISTOL
Authority: Bristol City Council

Central Library, College Green, Bristol BS1 5TL
☎0117 903 7200 (all enquiries)
Fax 0117 922 1081
e-mail: bristol.library.service@bristol.gov.uk
url: www.bristol.gov.uk
Head of Libraries Ms Kate Murray (e-mail: k.murray@bristol.gov.uk)
Service Development Manager Ms Janet Bremner BA MCLIP (e-mail:
janet.bremner@bristol.gov.uk), Ms Julie Bowie BA MCLIP (e-mail:
julie.bowie@bristol.gov.uk)
Building Development Manager Ms Julie York BA MCLIP (e-mail:
julie.york@bristol.gov.uk)
Young People's Manager Mrs Janet Randall BA MCLIP (e-mail:
janet.randall@bristol.gov.uk), Mrs Julia E Ball BLib MCLIP (e-mail: julia.ball@bristol.gov.uk)
(job-share)
Customer Services Manager Ms Emelli Doran BSc (e-mail: emelli.doran@bristol.gov.uk)

BROMLEY
Authority: London Borough of Bromley

Central Library, High Street, Bromley, Kent BR1 IEX
☎020 8460 9955 (enquiries and administration)

Fax 020 8313 9975
e-mail: reference.library@bromley.gov.uk
url: www.bromley.gov.uk
Head of Library, Archive and Museum Services David Brockhurst BA (e-mail:
david.brockhurst@bromley.gov.uk)
Assistant Head of Library, Archive and Museum Services Tim Woolgar MCLIP
(e-mail: tim.woolgar@bromley.gov.uk)

Central/largest library

Central Library, High Street, Bromley, Kent BR1 1EX
☎Tel/fax etc. as HQ

District libraries

Beckenham Library, Beckenham Road, Beckenham, Kent BR3 4PE
☎020 8650 7292/3

Orpington Library, The Priory, Church Hill, Orpington, Kent BR6 0HH
☎(01689) 831551

BUCKINGHAMSHIRE
Authority: Buckinghamshire County Council

Culture and Learning, County Hall, Walton Street, Aylesbury, Bucks HP20 1UU
☎(0845) 370 8090; 230 3232
e-mail: library@buckscc.gov.uk
url: www.buckscc.gov.uk/libraries
Head of Culture and Learning Services Mrs Paula Buck (01296 382986)
Service Delivery Manager David Jones (01296 382254; fax: 01296 382259;
e-mail: c-dajones@buckscc.gov.uk)

Main group libraries

(telephone number for the following libraries is ☎(0845) 230 3232

Amersham Library, Chiltern Avenue, Amersham, Bucks HP6 5AH
Library Manager Ms Glenys Brown

Aylesbury Central Library, Walton Street, Aylesbury, Bucks HP20 1UU
Library Manager Ms Sarah Townsend PGDipIM MCLIP

Beaconsfield Library, Reynolds Road, Beaconsfield, Bucks HP9 2NJ
Library Manager Ms Michelin Katts BA PGDipLIS

Buckingham Library, Verney Close, Buckingham MK18 1JP
Library Manager Ms Steph Gassor MCLIP

Chesham Library, Elgiva Lane, Chesham, Bucks HP5 2JD
Library Manager Ms Marinella Sinagoga BA(Hons) MA

Hazlemere Library, 312 Amersham Road, Hazlemere, Bucks HP15 7PY
Fax (01494) 816621
Library Manager Ms Janet Webb

High Wycombe Library, Queen Victoria Road, High Wycombe, Bucks HP11 1BD
Fax (01494) 533086
Library Manager Ms Helen Goreham BLib MCLIP

Marlow Library, Institute Road, Marlow, Bucks SL7 1BL
Library Manager Ms Harlene Semmens

BURY
Authority: Bury Metropolitan Borough Council

Arts, Libraries and Adult Learning, 3 Knowsley Place, Duke Street, Bury, Lancs BL9 0EJ
☎0161 253 5861 (administration)
e-mail: information@bury.gov.uk
url: www.bury.gov.uk/culture.htm
Assistant Director (Arts, Libraries and Adult Learning) Mrs Diana Sorrigan BA
MCLIP (0161 253 5900; e-mail: d.sorrigan@bury.gov.uk)
Libraries and Adult Learning Manager (Central Services and Social Inclusion)
Mrs Lesley Kelly BA MA (0161 253 7579; e-mail: s.l.kelly@bury.gov.uk)
Libraries and Adult Learning Manager (Branches/Centres and Staff Development)
Ms Jane Barkess BA MA (0161 253 6142; e-mail: j.e.barkess@bury.gov.uk)

Central/largest library

Central Library, Manchester Road, Bury, Lancs BL9 0DG
☎0161 253 5873
Fax 0161 253 5857
e-mail: information@bury.gov.uk
Library Supervisors Ms Barbara Markuss, Ms Carol McLoone, Stephen Stretton

Branch libraries

Prestwich Library & Adult Learning Centre, Longfield Centre, Prestwich, Manchester
M25 1AY
☎0161 253 7214/7216
Fax 0161 798 9981
e-mail: prestwich.lib@bury.gov.uk
Library & Adult Learning Centre Supervisors Ms Joan Watkiss BA DipLib (0161 253
7219), David Galloway BA DipLib (0161 253 7219)

Radcliffe Library, Stand Lane, Radcliffe, Manchester M26 1NW
☎0161 253 7161
Fax 0161 724 6087
e-mail: radcliffe.lib@bury.gov.uk
Library Supervisor Vacant

Ramsbottom Library & Adult Learning Centre, Carr Street, Ramsbottom, Bury, Lancs
BL0 9AE
☎0161 253 5352/5425
e-mail: ramsbottom.lib@bury.gov.uk
Library & Adult Learning Centre Supervisor Ms Deborah Smith NEBS

Tottington Library, Market Street, Tottington, Bury, Lancs BL8 3LN
☎0161 253 6652

Fax (01204) 886517
e-mail: tottington.lib@bury.gov.uk
Library Supervisors Mrs Lynsay Snape NEBS, Mrs Stephanie Lamb NEBS (part-time)

Unsworth Library, Sunnybank Road, Unsworth, Bury, Lancs BL9 8ED
☎0161 253 7560
Fax 0161 272 1931
e-mail: unsworth.lib@bury.gov.uk
Library Supervisor Mrs Stephanie Lamb NEBS (part-time)

Whitefield Library & Adult Learning Centre, Pinfold Lane, Whitefield, Manchester M45 7NY
☎0161 253 5548
Fax 0161 796 1780
e-mail: whitefield.lib@bury.gov.uk
Library & Adult Learning Centre Supervisor Mrs Janet Moores

Outreach libraries

Ainsworth Library, Church Street, Ainsworth, Lancs BL2 5RP
☎0161 253 5886
e mail: ainsworth.lib@bury.gov.uk

Brandlesholme Community Library, 375 Brandlesholme Road, Bury, Lancs BL8 1HS
☎0161 764 2731

Castle Sport and Leisure Library, Castle Leisure Centre, Bolton Street, Bury, Lancs BL9 0EZ
☎0161 253 5560
e-mail: castle.llb@bury.gov.uk

Moorside Community Library, St John's Church Hall, Parkinson Street, Bury, Lancs BL9 6NY
☎0161 253 6471
e-mail: moorside.lib@bury.gov.uk

New Kershaw Centre, Deal Street, Bury, Lancs BL9 7PZ
☎0161 253 6400
e-mail: kershaw.lib@bury.gov.uk

Sedgeley Park Community Library, St Gabriel's Community Rooms, Bishops Road,
Prestwich, Manchester M25 0HT
☎0161 798 9420

South Cross Street Community Library, 90 South Cross Street, Bury, Lancs BL9 0RS
☎0161 253 6079

Topping Fold Library, Topping Fold Road, Bury, Lancs BL9 7NG
☎0161 253 6361
e-mail: topping.lib@bury.gov.uk

CALDERDALE
Authority: Calderdale Metropolitan Borough Council

Central Library, Northgate, Halifax, Yorks HX1 1UN
☎(01422) 392630 (enquiries), 392605 (administration)
Fax (01422) 392615
e-mail: libraries@calderdale.gov.uk

url: www.calderdale.gov.uk
Head of Cultural Services Gary Borrows MCLIP
Collections and Service Development Manager David Duffy BA MCLIP
(01422 392602; e-mail: david.duffy@calderdale.gov.uk)
Operations and Customer Services Manager Ms Carole Heaton MA MCLIP
(01422 392623; e-mail: carole.heaton@calderdale.gov.uk)

CAMBRIDGESHIRE
Authority: Cambridgeshire County Council

Cambridgeshire Libraries, Archives and Information, ET1042, A0005 Castle Court, Shire Hall, Cambridge CB3 0AP
☎(01223) 703520 (administration)
e-mail: your.library@cambridgeshire.gov.uk
url: www.cambridgeshire.gov.uk/library
Acting Head of Libraries, Archives and Information Mrs Christine May BA MCLIP
(01223 703521; e-mail: christine.may@cambridgeshire.gov.uk)
Head of Policy, Planning and Culture Chris Heaton MA MCLIP (01223 703519; e-mail: chris.heaton@cambridgeshire.gov.uk)

Central/largest library

Central Library, 7 Lion Yard, Cambridge CB2 3QD
☎0345 045 5225

Hub libraries

Ely Library, 6 The Cloisters, Ely, Cambs CB7 4ZH
☎0345 045 5225
Fax (01353) 616164

Huntingdon Library and Archive, Princes Street, Huntingdon, Cambs PE29 3PA
☎0345 045 5225
Fax (01480) 372729

March Library, City Road, March, Cambs PE15 9LT
☎0345 045 5225
Fax (01354) 754760

St Ives Library, Station Road, St Ives, Cambs PE27 5BW
☎0345 045 5225
Fax (01480) 375496

St Neots Library, Priory Lane, St Neots, Cambs PE19 2BH
☎0345 045 5225
Fax (01480) 396006

Wisbech Library, 5 Ely Place, Wisbech, Cambs PE13 1EU
☎0345 045 5225
Fax (01945) 589240

CAMDEN
Authority: Camden Council

Libraries, Information and Community Learning, Culture and Environment Directorate, 7th Floor, Town Hall Extension, Argyle Street, London WCIH 8EQ
☎020 7974 4001
Fax 020 7974 4801
url: www.camden.gov.uk
Head of Library Customer Services Mike Clarke BA MCLIP (020 7974 4058; e-mail: mike.clarke@camden.gov.uk)
Senior Delivery Manager, Camden Information Services Steve Lack BA(Hons) DipLib MCLIP (e-mail: steve.lack@camden.gov.uk)
Senior Delivery Manager, Learning and Reading Ms Lottie Collins (e-mail: lottie.collins@camden.gov.uk)
Senior Delivery Manager, Bibliographic Services Gordon Keys (e-mail: gordon.keys@camden.gov.uk)

Central/largest library

Swiss Cottage Library, 88 Avenue Road, London NW3 3IIA
☎020 7974 4001 (general enquiries)
e-mail: swisscottagelibrary@camden.gov.uk
Senior Officer Chris Davies BA MCLIP

Libraries

(telephone numbers for the following libraries are the same as for HQ)

Belsize Library, Antrim Road, London NW3 4XN
e-mail: belsizelibrary@camden.gov.uk
Senior Officer Ms Yasmin Hounsell

Camden Town Library, Crowndale Centre, 218 Eversholt Street, London NW1 1BD
e-mail: camdentownlibrary@camden.gov.uk
Senior Officer Michael Dempsey

Chalk Farm Library, Sharpleshall Street, London NW1 8YN
e-mail: chalkfarmlibrary@camden.gov.uk
Senior Officer Damian Mansi

Heath Library, Keats Grove, London NW3 2RR
e-mail: heathlibrary@camden.gov.uk
Senior Officer Ms Caroline Spencer

Highgate Library, Chester Road, London N19 5DH
e-mail: highgatelibrary@camden.gov.uk
Senior Officer Ms Joanna Birch

Holborn Library, 32-38 Theobalds Road, London WC1X 8PA
e-mail: holbornlibrary@camden.gov.uk
Senior Delivery Manager Steve Lack BA(Hons) DipLib MCLIP (e-mail: steve.lack@camden.gov.uk)

Kentish Town Library, 262-266 Kentish Town Road, London NW5 2AA

e-mail: kentishtownlibrary@camden.gov.uk
Senior Officer Nicky Amboule

Kilburn Library Centre, 12-22 Kilburn High Road, London NW6 5UH
e-mail: kilburnlibrarycentre@camden.gov.uk
Senior Officer Ms Raheel Mapara

Queens Crescent Library, 165 Queens Crescent, London NW5 4HH
e-mail: queenscrescentlibrary@camden.gov.uk
Senior Officer Colin Carsten

Regents Park Library, Compton Close, off Robert Street, London NW1 3QT
e-mail: regentsparklibrary@camden.gov.uk
Senior Officer Nick Durant

St Pancras Library, Camden Town Hall Extension, Argyle Street, London WC1H 8NN
e-mail: stpancraslibrary@camden.gov.uk
Senior Officer Ms Diane Bowman

West Hampstead Library, Dennington Park Road, London NW6 1AU
e-mail: westhampsteadlibrary@camden.gov.uk
Senior Officer Ms Mary Holden

Other services

Access and Inclusion, Highgate Library, Chester Road, London N19 5DH
e-mail: highgatelibrary@camden.gov.uk
Library Manager, Mobile Services Tony May

Camden Local Studies and Archives Centre, Holborn Library, 32–38 Theobalds Road,
London WC1X 8PA
e-mail: localstudies@camden.gov.uk
Senior Archivist Tudor Allen
Senior Officer, Local Studies Aiden Flood

Schools Library Service, Swiss Cottage Central Library, 88 Avenue Road, London NW3 3HA
e-mail: sls@camden.gov.uk
Senior Officer Ms Jean Aston (e-mail: jean.aston@camden.gov.uk)

CENTRAL BEDFORDSHIRE
Authority: Central Bedfordshire Council

Libraries Operations, Dunstable Library, Vernon Place, Dunstable, Beds LU5 4HA
☎0300 300 8060
url: www.centralbedfordshire.gov.uk
Interim Library Services Manager Ms Nicola Avery BAHons) MCLIP

Largest libraries

Dunstable Library, Vernon Place, Dunstable, Beds LU5 4HA
☎0300 300 8056
Fax (01582) 471290
e-mail: dunstable.library@centralbedfordshire.gov.uk
Library Manager Ms Carly Levingstone

Leighton Buzzard Library, Lake Street, Leighton Buzzard, Beds LU7 1RX
☎0300 300 8059
Fax (01525) 815368
e-mail: leightonbuzzard.library@centralbedfordshire.gov.uk
Library Manager Ms Hazel Kerr

Area libraries

Biggleswade Library, Chestnut Avenue, Biggleswade, Beds SG18 0LL
☎0300 300 8055
Fax (01767) 601802
e-mail: biggleswade.library@centralbedfordshire.gov.uk
Library Manager Ms Sue Townsend

Flitwick Library, Conniston Road, Flitwick, Beds MK45 1QJ
☎0300 300 8057
Fax (01525) 713897
e-mail: flitwick.library@centralbedfordshire.gov.uk
Library Manager John Booth

Houghton Regis Library, Bedford Square, Houghton Regis, Beds LU5 5ES
☎(01582) 865473
Fax (01582) 868466
e-mail: houghtonregis.library@centralbedfordshire.gov.uk
Library Manager Ms Sue Styvant

Shefford Library, High Street, Shefford, Beds SG17 5DD
☎0300 300 8067
Fax (01462) 639071
e-mail: shefford.library@centralbedfordshire.gov.uk
Library Manager Ms Carol Forse

CHESHIRE EAST
Authority: Cheshire East Council

Libraries and Cultural Services, Health and Wellbeing, Westfields, Middlewich Road, Sandbach, Cheshire CW11 1HZ
☎(0300) 123 5500
e-mail: librarynotifications@cheshireeast.gov.uk
url: www.cheshireeast.gov.uk/leisure_and_culture/libraries.aspx
Libraries and Cultural Services Manager Ms Linda Morris DipLib (01244 976024; e-mail: linda.morris@cheshireeast.gov.uk)
Group Librarian Mrs Lynda Cotterill BA MCLIP (01270 375285; e-mail: lynda.cotterill@cheshireeast.gov.uk)
Reading & Learning Resources Manager Roy Walker DLIS (01244 976023; e-mail: roy.walker@cheshireeast.gov.uk)

Group HQs

Business Information Service, Ellesmere Port Library, Civic Way, Ellesmere Port, Cheshire CH65 0BG
☎0151 337 4693/4695

Fax 0151 355 6849
e-mail: bisep@cheshiresharedservices.gov.uk
url: www.cheshirewestandchester.gov.uk/business/business_support/business_information_
service.aspx
Business Librarians Ms Lynn Wilkinson, Ms Linda Bennett

Congleton Library, Market Square, Congleton, Cheshire CW12 1BU
☎(01260) 375550
Fax (01260) 375551
e-mail: congleton.infopoint@cheshireeast.gov.uk
Area Librarian Vacant

Crewe Library, Prince Albert Street, Crewe, Cheshire CW1 2DH
☎(01270) 375250
Fax (01270) 375293
e-mail: crewe.infopoint@cheshireeast.gov.uk
Area Librarian Vacant

Macclesfield Library, 2 Jordangate, Macclesfield, Cheshire SK10 1EE
☎(01625) 374000
Fax (01625) 612818
e-mail: macclesfield.infopoint@cheshireeast.gov.uk
Group Librarian Paul Everitt MCLIP (e-mail: paul.everitt@cheshireeast.gov.uk)

Wilmslow Library, South Drive, Wilmslow, Cheshire SK9 1NW
☎(01625) 374060
Fax (01625) 374065
e-mail: wilmslow.infopoint@cheshireeast.gov.uk
Area Librarian Paul Everitt MCLIP (e-mail: paul.everitt@cheshireeast.gov.uk)

CHESHIRE WEST AND CHESTER
Authority: Cheshire West and Chester Council

Culture and Recreation HQ, 58 Nicholas Street, Chester CH1 2NP
☎(0300) 123 8123
e-mail: librarynotifications@cheshirewestandchester.gov.uk
url: www.cheshirewestandchester.gov.uk/libraries
Senior Manager, Culture and Tourism Jason Doherty (e-mail:
jason.doherty@cheshirewestandchester.gov.uk)

Chester Library, Northgate Street, Chester CH1 2EF
☎(01244) 972612
Fax (01244) 315534
e-mail: chester.infopoint@cheshirewestandchester.gov.uk
Area Librarian: Chester/Ellesmere Port Mrs Rachel Foster BA(Hons) MCLIP
(e-mail: rachel.foster@cheshirewestandchester.gov.uk)

Ellesmere Port Library, Civic Way, Ellesmere Port, Cheshire L65 0BG
☎0151 337 4689
e-mail: eport.infopoint@cheshirewestandchester.gov.uk
Manager Library Services Ms Shan Wilkinson BA MCLIP (01606 867652; e-mail:
shan.wilkinson@cheshirewestandchester.gov.uk)

Northwich Library, Witton Street, Northwich, Cheshire CW9 5DR
☎(01606) 44221
Fax (01606) 48396
e-mail: northwich.infopoint@cheshirewestandchester.gov.uk
Area Librarian: Vale Royal Ms Caroline Rowland BA MA MCLIP, Mrs Kit Syder BA
MCLIP (e-mail: rowland/syder@cheshirewestandchester.gov.uk)

Cheshire Libraries Shared Services

Business Information Service, Ellesmere Port Library, Civic Way, Ellesmere Port, Cheshire
CH65 0BG
☎0151 337 4693/4695
Fax 0151 355 6849
e-mail: bisep@cheshiresharedservices.gov.uk
url: www.cheshirewestandchester.gov.uk/business/business_support/business_information_
service.aspx
Libraries Shared Services Manager Ms Sue Eddison (e-mail:
sue.eddison@cheshirewestandchester.gov.uk)
Business Librarians Ms Lynn Wilkinson, Ms Linda Bennett

CORNWALL
Authority: Cornwall Council

Cultural Services Department, Room 429, County Hall, Truro, Cornwall TR1 3AY
☎0300 123 4111 (enquiries)
Fax (01872) 223509
e-mail: enquirycentre@cornwall.gov.uk
url: www.cornwall.gov.uk
Head of Libraries and Historic Collections Paul Brough

Additional libraries

*(telephone numbers for the following libraries (with the exception of the Cornish Studies Library)
are the same as for HQ)*

Bodmin Library, Lower Bore Street, Bodmin, Cornwall PL31 2LX

Bude Library, The Wharf, Bude, Cornwall EX23 8LG

Callington Library, Coronation Road, Callington, Cornwall PL17 7DR

Camborne Library, The Cross, Camborne, Cornwall TR14 8HA

Camelford Library, Town Hall, Market Place, Camelford, Cornwall PL32 9PD

Cornish Studies Library, Alma Place, Redruth, Cornwall TR15 2AT
☎(01209) 216760
e-mail: cornishstudies.library@cornwall.gov.uk

Falmouth Library, The Moor, Falmouth, Cornwall TR11 3QA

Fowey Library, Caffa Mill House, 2 Passage Lane, Fowey, Cornwall PL23 1JS

Hayle Library, Commercial Road, Hayle, Cornwall TR27 4DE

Helston Library, Trengrouse Way, Helston, Cornwall TR13 8AG

Launceston Library, Bounsalls Lane, Launceston, Cornwall PL15 9AB

Liskeard Library, Barras Street, Liskeard, Cornwall PL14 6AB

Looe Library, Millpool, West Looe, Cornwall PL13 2AF

Lostwithiel Library, Taprell House, North Street, Lostwithiel, Cornwall PL22 0BL

Newquay Library, Marcus Hill, Newquay, Cornwall TR7 1BD

Padstow Library, The Core Building, The Lawns, Hill Street, Padstow, Cornwall PL28 8EB

Par Library, Hamley's Corner, Eastcliffe Road, Par, Cornwall PL24 2AH

Penryn Library, St Thomas Street, Penryn, Cornwall TR10 8JN

Penzance Library, Morrab Road, Penzance, Cornwall TR18 4EY

Perranporth Library, Oddfellows Hall, Ponsmere Road, Perranporth, Cornwall TR6 0BW

Redruth Library, Clinton Road, Redruth, Cornwall TR15 2QE

Reference and Information Library, Union Place, Truro, Cornwall TR1 1EP

St Agnes Library, The Car Park, St Agnes, Cornwall TR5 0TP

St Austell Library, 2 Carlyon Road, St Austell, Cornwall PL25 4LD

St Columb Library, The Town Hall, St Columb, Cornwall TR9 6AN

St Dennis Library, St Dennis CP School, Carne Hill, St Dennis, Cornwall PL26 8AY

St Ives Library, Gabriel Street, St Ives, Cornwall TR26 2LU

St Just Library, Market Street, St Just, Cornwall TR19 7HX

St Keverne Library, St Keverne CP School, School Hill, St Keverne, Cornwall TR12 6NQ

Saltash Library, Callington Road, Saltash, Cornwall PL12 6DX

Torpoint Library, Fore Street, Torpoint, Cornwall PL11 2AG

Truro Library, Pydar Street, Truro, Cornwall TR1 1EP

Upton Cross Library, Upton Cross School, Liskeard, Cornwall PL14 5AX

Wadebridge Library, Southern Way, Wadebridge, Cornwall PL27 7BX

COVENTRY
Authority: Coventry City Council

Coventry Libraries and Information Services, 2nd Floor, West Orchard House, 28-34 Corporation Street, Coventry CV1 1GF
☎024 7683 1579
Fax 024 7683 2470
url: www.coventry.gov.uk
Head of Cultural Services Ms Alice Davey
Service Manager, Library and Information Services Mrs Carmel Reed BA DMS MCLIP
(024 7683 1579; fax: 024 7683 2470; e-mail: carmel.reed@coventry.gov.uk)
Operations Manager Colin Scott (024 7683 2457; fax: 024 7683 2470; e-mail:

colin.scott@coventry.gov.uk)
Resources Development Manager Dave Lloyd (024 7683 2086; fax: 024 7683 2470;
e-mail: dave.lloyd@coventry.gov.uk)
Access Development Manager Ms Dawn Beaumont (024 7683 2317; fax: 024 7683
2470; e-mail: dawn.beaumont@coventry.gov.uk)

Central/largest library

Central Library, Smithford Way, Coventry CV1 1FY
☎024 7683 2314 (enquiries), 024 7683 2321 (library office)
Fax 024 7683 2440 (enquiries), 024 7683 2315 (library office)
e-mail: central.library@coventry.gov.uk (enquiries)

East Area Libraries

Aldermoor Library, Aldermoor Farm School, Pinley Fields, Stoke Aldermoor, Coventry
CV3 1DD
☎024 7644 2840
Fax 024 7644 2840
e-mail: aldermoorfarm.library@coventry.gov.uk

Arena Park Library, Coventry Arena Shopping Park, Classic Drive, Rowley's Green,
Coventry CV6 6AГ
☎024 7678 5181
Fax 024 7670 0329
e-mail: arenapark.library@coventry.gov.uk

Bell Green Library and Learning Centre, 17-23 Riley Square, Bell Green, Coventry CV2 1LS
☎024 7668 8986
Fax 024 7666 3468
e-mail: bellgreen.library@coventry.gov.uk

Caludon Castle School and Community Library, Axholme Road, Coventry CV2 5BD
☎024 7678 8300
Fax 024 7663 6282
e-mail: caludon.library@coventry.gov.uk

Cheylesmore Community Library, Poitiers Road, Cheylesmore, Coventry CV3 5JX
☎024 7650 2106
Fax 024 7650 5287
e-mail: cheylesmore.library@coventry.gov.uk

Foleshill Library, Broad Street, Foleshill, Coventry CV6 5BG
☎024 7668 9154
Fax 024 7666 7461
e-mail: foleshill.library@coventry.gov.uk

Hillfields Community Library, St Peter's Centre, Charles Street, Coventry CV1 5NP
☎024 7663 3878
Fax 024 7623 1970
e-mail: library.hillfields@coventry.gov.uk

Stoke Library, Kingsway, Stoke, Coventry CV2 4EA
☎024 7645 2059

Fax 024 7645 2567
e-mail: stoke.library@coventry.gov.uk

Willenhall Library, 106 Remembrance Road, Willenhall, Coventry CV3 3DN
☎024 7630 2383
Fax 024 7630 2151
e-mail: willenhall.library@coventry.gov.uk

West Area Libraries

Allesley Park Community Library, St John's School, Winsford Avenue, Allesley Park,
Coventry CV5 9HZ
☎(07903) 749521

Canley Library, Prior Deram Walk, Canley, Coventry CV4 8FT
☎024 7667 3041
Fax 024 7671 7361
e-mail: canley.library@coventry.gov.uk

Coundon Library, Moseley Avenue, Radford, Coventry CV6 1HT
☎024 7659 3496
Fax 024 7659 8768
e-mail: coundon.library@coventry.gov.uk

Earlsdon Library, Earlsdon Avenue North, Earlsdon, Coventry CV5 6FZ
☎024 7667 5359
Fax 024 7671 7958
e-mail: earlsdon.library@coventry.gov.uk

Finham Library, Droylsdon Park Road, Finham, Coventry CV3 6EQ
☎024 7641 4050
Fax 024 7641 9524
e-mail: finham.library@coventry.gov.uk

Jubilee Library, Jubilee Crescent, Radford, Coventry CV6 3EX
☎024 7659 6762
Fax 024 7659 5728
e-mail: jubileecrescent.library@coventry.gov.uk

Tile Hill Library, Jardine Crescent, Tile Hill, Coventry CV4 9PL
☎024 7646 4994
Fax 024 7669 5774
e-mail: tilehill.library@coventry.gov.uk

CROYDON
Authority: Croydon Council

Central Library, Croydon Clocktower, Katharine Street, Croydon CR9 1ET
☎020 8726 6900
Fax 020 8253 1004
e-mail: libraries@croydon.gov.uk
url: www.croydon.gov.uk
Head of Libraries Ms Aileen T Cahill BSocSc DipLib MCLIP

Customer Services Manager Ms Andrea Hurren BA(Hons) (e-mail: andrea.hurren@croydon.gov.uk)

Branch libraries

Ashburton Library, Ashburton Learning Village, Oasis Academy Shirley, Shirley Road, Addiscombe, Croydon CR9 7AL
☎020 8726 6900
e-mail: ashburton@croydon.gov.uk

Bradmore Green Library, Bradmore Way, Coulsdon, Croydon CR5 1PE
☎020 8726 6900
e-mail: bradmoregreen@croydon.gov.uk

Broad Green Library, 89 Canterbury Road, Croydon CR0 3HH
☎020 8726 6900
e-mail: broadgreen@croydon.gov.uk

Coulsdon Library, Brighton Road, Coulsdon, Croydon CR5 2NH
☎020 8660 6900
e-mail: coulsdon@croydon.gov.uk

New Addington Library, Central Parade, New Addington, Croydon CR0 0JB
☎020 8726 6900
e-mail: newaddington@croydon.gov.uk

Norbury Library, Beatrice Avenue, Norbury, Croydon SW16 4UW
☎020 8726 6900
e-mail: norbury@croydon.gov.uk

Purley Library, Banstead Road, Purley, Croydon CR8 3YH
☎020 8726 6900
e-mail: purley@croydon.gov.uk

Sanderstead Library, Farm Fields, South Croydon, Croydon CR2 0HL
☎020 8726 6900
e-mail: sanderstead@croydon.gov.uk

Selsdon Library, Addington Road, Selsdon, Croydon CR2 8LA
☎020 8726 6900
e-mail: selsdon@croydon.gov.uk

Shirley Library, Wickham Road/Hartland Way, Shirley, Croydon CR0 8BH
☎020 8726 6900
e-mail: shirley@croydon.gov.uk

South Norwood Library, Lawrence Road, South Norwood, Croydon SE25 5AA
☎020 8726 6900
e-mail: southnorwood@croydon.gov.uk

Thornton Heath Library, 190 Brigstock Road, Thornton Heath, Croydon CR7 7JE
☎020 8726 6900
e-mail: thorntonheath@croydon.gov.uk

CUMBRIA
Authority: Cumbria County Council

Adult and Local Services, Arroyo Block, The Castle, Carlisle CA3 8UR
☎(01228) 227295
Fax (01228) 607299
url: www.cumbria.gov.uk/libraries/
Assistant Director, Local Services Jim Grisenthwaite (01228 227282; e-mail:
jim.grisenthwaite@cumbriacc.gov.uk)
County Manager - Library Services Ms Lorraine Arnold
Principal Administrative Officer Paul Graham (01228 227294; e-mail:
paul.graham@cumbriacc.gov.uk)

Group libraries

Barrow-in-Furness Library, Ramsden Square, Barrow-in-Furness, Cumbria LA14 1LL
☎(01229) 407370
Fax (01229) 894371
e-mail: barrow.library@cumbriacc.gov.uk
Area Library Manager Ms Bernadette Maine MCLIP

Carlisle Library, 11 Globe Lane, Carlisle CA3 8NX
☎(01228) 227310
Fax (01228) 607333
e-mail: carlisle.library@cumbriacc.gov.uk
Area Library Manager Mike Lister MCLIP

Daniel Hay Library, Lowther Street, Whitehaven, Cumbria CA28 7QZ
☎(01946) 506400
Fax (01946) 852911
e-mail: whitehaven.library@cumbriacc.gov.uk
Area Library Manager Mrs Alayne Cowling MCLIP

Kendal Library, Stricklandgate, Kendal, Cumbria LA9 4PY
☎(01539) 713520
Fax (01539) 773544
e-mail: kendal.library@cumbriacc.gov.uk
Area Library Manager Tom Holliday MCLIP

Penrith Library, St Andrews Churchyard, Penrith, Cumbria CA11 7YA
☎(01768) 812100
Fax (01768) 242101
e-mail: penrith.library@cumbriacc.gov.uk
Area Library Manager Mike Lister MCLIP

Workington Library, Vulcans Lane, Workington, Cumbria CA14 2ND
☎(01900) 706170
Fax (01900) 325181
e-mail: workington.library@cumbriacc.gov.uk
Area Library Manager Mrs Alayne Cowling MCLIP

DARLINGTON
Authority: Darlington Borough Council

Central Library, Crown Street, Darlington DLI IND
☎(01325) 462034 (enquiries)
Fax (01325) 381556
e-mail: crown.street.library@darlington.gov.uk
url: www.darlington.gov.uk/library
Head of Libraries and Community Learning Mrs Ruth Bernstein
Media and Information Manager Mrs Lynne Litchfield
Lending Services Manager Mrs Margaret Wood
Senior Community Engagement Officer Mrs Jeannie Bishop
Local Studies Librarian Miss Katherine Williamson
Stock Services Librarian Mrs Jean Longstaff

Branch library

Cockerton Library, Cockerton Green, Darlington DL3 9AA
☎(01325) 461320
Library Manager Ms Carole Houghton MA MCLIP

DERBY
Authority: Derby City Council

Derby City Libraries, Neighbourhoods, Roman House, Friar Gate, Derby DEI IXB
☎(01332) 641723
Fax (01332) 715549
e-mail: libraries@derby.gov.uk
url: www.derby.gov.uk/libraries
Head of Library Services David Potton MA DipLib MCLIP (01332 641719; e-mail: david.potton@derby.gov.uk)
Assistant Head of Library Services (Resources and Learning) Mark Elliott BLib(Hons) MCLIP PGC(Man) (01332 641725; e-mail: mark.elliott@derby.gov.uk)
Assistant Head of Library Services (Operations and Community) Ms Fran Renwick MA MCLIP (01332 641726; e-mail: fran.renwick@derby.gov.uk)

Central/largest library

Central Library, The Wardwick, Derby DEI IHS
☎(01332) 641702 (enquiries), 641700 (renewals)
Fax (01332) 369570
Operations Manager (Central Library Services) Ms Julie Topham (01332 641703; e-mail: julie.topham@derby.gov.uk)

DERBYSHIRE
Authority: Derbyshire County Council

Cultural and Community Services Department, County Hall, Matlock, Derbyshire DE4 3AG
☎(01629) 536590 (enquiries and administration)
Fax (01629) 536522

e-mail: derbyshire.libraries@derbyshire.gov.uk
url: www.derbyshire.gov.uk
Strategic Director of Cultural and Community Services Martin Molloy OBE BA
DipLib MCLIP (e-mail: martin.molloy@derbyshire.gov.uk)
**Deputy Director of Cultural and Community Services and Head of Libraries and
Heritage Division** Miss Jaci Brumwell MCLIP (e-mail: jaci.brumwell@derbyshire.gov.uk)
Assistant Director, Policy, Information and Partnership Robert Gent BA DMS MIMgt
MCLIP (e-mail: robert.gent@derbyshire.gov.uk)
Assistant Director of Libraries and Heritage Divison Don Gibbs BA MCLIP (e-mail:
don.gibbs@derbyshire.gov.uk)
Operations Manager (North Area) Martyn Shaw BA DipLib MCLIP (e-mail:
martyn.shaw@derbyshire.gov.uk)
Operations Manager (South Area) Mrs Carol Brooks BA FCLIP (e-mail:
carol.brooks@derbyshire.gov.uk)
Operations Manager (West Area) Mrs Ann Ainsworth BA MCLIP (e-mail:
ann.ainsworth@derbyshire.gov.uk)

Central/largest library (North Area)

Chesterfield Library, New Beetwell Street, Chesterfield, Derbyshire S40 1QN
☎(01629) 533400
Fax (01246) 209304
e-mail: chesterfield.library@derbyshire.gov.uk
Senior Librarian Ms Janet Scott BA MA MCLIP (e-mail: janet.scott@derbyshire.gov.uk)

North Area

Chesterfield Library, New Beetwell Street, Chesterfield, Derbyshire S40 1GN
☎(01629) 533400
Fax (01246) 209304
Principal Librarian Mrs Julie Potton BA MCLIP (e-mail: julie.potton@derbyshire.gov.uk)

South Area

Ilkeston Library, Market Place, Ilkeston, Derbyshire DE7 5RN
☎0115 930 1104
Fax 0115 944 1226
e-mail: ilkeston.library@derbyshire.gov.uk
Principal Librarian Ms Rosina Peberdy BA MSc(Econ) MCLIP (e-mail:
rosina.peberdy@derbyshire.gov.uk)

West Area

Buxton Library, Kents Bank Road, Buxton, Derbyshire SK17 9HJ
☎(01629) 533460
Fax (01298) 73744
e-mail: buxton.library@derbyshire.gov.uk
Principal Librarian Ms Catherine Mills BA(Hons) MA MCLIP (e-mail:
catherine.mills@derbyshire.gov.uk)

DEVON
Authority: Devon County Council

Devon Libraries, Great Moor House, Bittern Road, Sowton, Exeter, Devon EX2 7NL
☎(01392) 384315
Fax (01392) 384316
e-mail: devlibs@devon.gov.uk
url: www.devon.gov.uk/libraries
Head of Libraries Ms Ciara Eastell BA(Hons) MA MCLIP (e-mail:
ciara.eastell@devon.gov.uk)
Service Support Manager Mike Skinner BLS DipHE (e-mail:
mike.skinner@devon.gov.uk)
Operations Manager Ms Liz Alexander MCLIP (e-mail: liz.alexander@devon.gov.uk)

Central/largest libraries

Barnstaple Library, Tuly Street, Barnstaple, Devon EX31 1EL
☎(01271) 388619 (tel/fax)
e-mail: barnstaple.library@devon.gov.uk
Library Manager Geoff King

Exeter Central Library, Castle Street, Exeter, Devon EX4 3PQ
☎(01392) 384222
Fax (01392) 384228
e-mail: exeter.library@devon.gov.uk
Library Manager Andrew Davey BSc MCLIP

Larger branch libraries

Bideford Library, 6 New Road, Bideford, Devon EX39 2HR
☎(01237) 476075 (tel/fax)
Librarian i/c Mrs Rose Arno, Mrs Margaret Shambrook

Exmouth Library, 40 Exeter Road, Exmouth, Devon EX8 1PS
☎(01395) 272677
Fax (01395) 271426
Librarian i/c Kelvin Crook MCLIP

Honiton Library, 48 New Street, Honiton, Devon EX14 1BS
☎(01404) 42818
Fax (01404) 45326
Librarian i/c Miss Jenny Wood MBE

Kingsbridge Library, Ilbert Road, Kingsbridge, Devon TQ7 1EB
☎(01548) 852315
Fax (01548) 857210
Librarian i/c Mrs Wendy Bloomer

Newton Abbot Library, Market Street, Newton Abbot, Devon TQ12 2RJ
☎(01626) 206420
Fax (01626) 206425
Librarian i/c Mrs Linda Roland-Howe

St Thomas Library, Cowick Street, Exeter, Devon EX4 1AF
☎(01392) 252783
Librarian i/c Mrs Jill Hughes

Sidmouth Library, Blackmore Drive, Sidmouth, Devon EX10 8LA
☎(01395) 512192
Librarian i/c Mrs Gill Spence

Tavistock Library, The Quay, Plymouth Road, Tavistock, Devon PL19 8AB
☎(01822) 612218
Fax (01822) 610690
Librarian i/c Mrs Jude Jeal

Teignmouth Library, Fore Street, Teignmouth, Devon TQ14 8DY
☎(01626) 774646
Fax (01626) 870155
Librarian i/c Mrs Pauline Anderson MCLIP

Tiverton Library, Phoenix House, Phoenix Lane, Tiverton, Devon EX16 6SA
☎(01884) 244644
Fax (01884) 244645
Librarian i/c Vacant

(Note: This is not the full list of branch libraries)

DONCASTER
Authority: Doncaster Metropolitan Borough Council

Central Library, Waterdale, Doncaster DN1 3JE
☎(01302) 734305
Fax (01302) 734302
e-mail: reference.library@doncaster.gov.uk
url: www.doncaster.gov.uk/library
Head of Library and Information Services Vacant
Library Stock Manager John Seeley BEd MCLIP (01302 573081)
Community Development Manager Ms Clare A. E. O'Brien BA(Hons) (01302 734298)

DORSET
Authority: Dorset County Council

County Library HQ, Colliton Park, Dorchester, Dorset DT1 1XJ
☎(01305) 225000 (enquiries)
Fax (01305) 224344 (administration)
e-mail: dorsetlibraries@dorsetcc.gov.uk
url: www.dorsetforyou.com/libraries
Head of Cultural Services Paul Leivers BA MBA MCLIP (e-mail:
p.leivers@dorsetcc.gov.uk)
Dorset Library Services Manager Mrs Tracy Long BA(Hons) MCLIP (01305 224458;
e-mail: t.long@dorsetcc.gov.uk)
Senior Manager, Customer Services Mrs Elaine Arthur BA(Hons) MCLIP DMS (e-mail:
seniormanagercustomerservices@dorsetcc.gov.uk), Mrs Linda Constable BA(Hons) MCLIP
PGDip(Res)

Senior Manager, Reading and Learning Sharon Kirkpatrick BLS MCLIP (01305 228529; e-mail: s.d.kirkpatrick@dorsetcc.gov.uk)
Business Support Manager Lynne Jordan (01305 224449)

DUDLEY
Authority: Dudley Metropolitan Borough Council

Directorate of Adult, Community and Housing Services, Ednam House, St James's Road, Dudley, West Midlands DY1 3JJ
☎(01384) 812295 (administration)
Fax (01384) 811995
url: www.dudley.gov.uk/libraries
Assistant Director of Libraries, Archives and Adult Learning Mrs Kate Millin BLib MCLIP (01384 812295; e-mail: kate.millin@dudley.gov.uk)

Libraries - Heads of Service

Dudley Library, St James's Road, West Midlands DY1 1HR
Head of Service - Library Strategy and Development Mrs Jayne Wilkins BA(Hons) MCLIP (01384 812680; fax: 01384 815543; e-mail: jayne.wilkins@dudley.gov.uk)
Head of Service - Library Operations Mrs Jen Beardsmore BA MCLIP (01384 815551; fax: 01384 815543; e-mail: jen.beardsmore@dudley.gov.uk)

Locality libraries

Brierley Hill Library, High Street, Brierley Hill, West Midlands DY5 3ET
☎(01384) 812865
Fax (01384) 812866
e-mail: bhilllib.ed@dudley.gov.uk
Locality Librarian Ms Louise Clark BA MCLIP

Dudley Library, St James's Road, West Midlands DY1 1HR
☎(01384) 815560
Fax (01384) 815543
e-mail: dudlibref.ed@dudley.gov.uk
Locality Librarian Mrs Sharon Whitehouse BA MCLIP

Halesowen Library, Queensway Mall, The Cornbow, Halesowen, West Midlands B63 4AJ
☎(01384) 812980
Fax (01384) 812981
e-mail: hallib.ed@dudley.gov.uk
Locality Librarian Ms Sandra Francis

Sedgley Library, Ladies Walk Centre, Ladies Walk, Sedgley, West Midlands DY3 3UA
☎(01384) 812790
e-mail: sedglib.ed@dudley.gov.uk
Locality Librarian Mrs Annette Templar BA(Hons)

Stourbridge Library, Crown Centre, Crown Lane, Stourbridge, West Midlands DY8 1YE
☎(01384) 812945
Fax (01384) 812946
e-mail: stourlibref.ed@dudley.gov.uk
Locality Librarian Ms Angela Horton

Archives and Local History Service

Mount Pleasant Street, Coseley, Dudley, West Midlands WV14 9JR
☎(01384) 812770 (tel/fax)
Borough Archivist Miss Gillian Roberts BA DAA (e-mail: gillian.roberts@dudley.gov.uk)

DURHAM
Authority: Durham County Council

**Libraries, Learning and Culture, Adults, Wellbeing and Health, Sevenhills, Unit I
Greenhills Business Park, Enterprise Way, Spennymoor, Co Durham DLI6 6JB**
☎0191 383 6543
Fax 0191 383 4182
url: www.durham.gov.uk
Head of Libraries, Learning and Culture Ms Rosemary Laxton MCLIP (e-mail:
rosemary.laxton@durham.gov.uk)
Strategic Manager – Libraries Ms Anne Davison BA MCLIP (e-mail:
anne.davison@durham.gov.uk)
Strategic Manager – Heritage and Culture Neil Hillier (e-mail:
neil.hillier@durham.gov.uk)
Team Manager – Heritage and Culture Ms Julie Biddlecome (e-mail:
julie.biddlecombe@durham.gov.uk)
Strategic Manager – Learning and Outreach Ms Sheila Owens BA MCLIP (e-mail:
sheila.owens@durham.gov.uk)
Team Manager – Marketing and Information Ms Carol Smith (e-mail:
carol.smith@durham.gov.uk)
Team Manager – Lifelong Learning Ms Jeanette Stephenson MCLIP (e-mail:
jeanette.stephenson@durham.gov.uk)
Team Manager – Support Services Andy Raine MCLIP (e-mail:
andy.raine@durham.gov.uk)
Team Area Manager – West Peter Burns MCLIP (e-mail: peter.burns@durham.gov.uk)
Team Area Manager – East Ms June Gowland BA(Hons) MCLIP DipMgt (e-mail:
june.gowland@durham.gov.uk)

Central/largest library

Durham Clayport Library, Millennium Place, Durham DH1 1WA
☎0191 386 4003
Fax 0191 386 0379
e-mail: durhamclayportlibrary@durham.gov.uk
Manager Geoff Pratt

EALING
Authority: Ealing Council

**Library Administrative Office, Ist Floor SW, Perceval House, I4–I6 Uxbridge Road, London
W5 2HL**
☎020 8825 5600
Fax 020 8825 5553
e-mail: libuser@ealing.gov.uk
url: www.ealing.gov.uk/libraries/index.htm

Assistant Director, Arts, Heritage and Libraries Ms Carole Stewart
(e-mail: cstewart@ealing.gov.uk)
Principal Library Manager Ms Heather Farrar BLS MCLIP (e-mail:
hfarrar@ealing.gov.uk)

Central/largest library

Ealing Central Library, 103 Ealing Broadway Centre, London W5 5JY
☎020 8825 9278
e-mail: centlib@ealing.gov.uk

Main libraries

Acton Library, High Street, Acton, London W3 6NA
☎020 8825 7622
e-mail: actolib@ealing.gov.uk

Greenford Library, Oldfield Lane South, Greenford, Middlesex UB6 9LG
☎020 8825 7227
e-mail: greelib@ealing.gov.uk

Southall Library, Osterley Park Road, Southall, Middlesex UB2 4BL
☎020 8825 7259
e-mail: soutlib@ealing.gov.uk

EAST RIDING OF YORKSHIRE
Authority: East Riding of Yorkshire Council

East Riding Libraries, Council Offices, Main Road, Skirlaugh, East Riding of Yorks
HU11 5HN
☎(01482) 392702
Fax (01482) 392711
url: www.eastriding.gov.uk
Acting Libraries, Arts and Heritage Group Manager Mrs Libby Herbert (01482
392701; e-mail: libby.herbert@eastriding.gov.uk)

EAST SUSSEX
Authority: East Sussex County Council

Library and Information Service, G-Floor, Centre Block, County Hall, St Anne's Crescent,
Lewes, East Sussex BN7 1UE
☎(01273) 481870 (administration)
Fax (01273) 481716
url: www.eastsussex.gov.uk
Assistant Director, Libraries and Culture Dr Irene Campbell MA DipLib MCLIP FRSA
(01273 481347; e-mail: irene.campbell@eastsussex.gov.uk)
Assistant Head of Library and Information Services: Strategy and Performance
Ms Rhona Drever MA(Hons) DipLib MCLIP (01273 481329; e-mail:
rhona.drever@eastsussex.gov.uk)
Assistant Head of Library and Information Services: Customer Services
Mrs Valerie Wright MCLIP (01273 482129; e-mail: valerie.wright@eastsussex.gov.uk)

Area offices

(the telephone number for the following libraries is ☎(0345) 6080196)

East Area

Hastings Library, Brassey Institute, 13 Claremont, Hastings, East Sussex TN34 1HE
Fax (01424) 443289
Area Manager Mick Bacon MCLIP (01424 420501; e-mail: mick.bacon@eastsussex.co.uk)

South Area

Eastbourne Library, Grove Road, Eastbourne, East Sussex BN21 4TL
Fax (01323) 649174
Area Manager Ms Alison Cairns BA(Hons) DipLib DMS MCLIP (01323 434203; e-mail:
alison.cairns@eastsussex.gov.uk)

West Area

Lewes Library, Styles Field, Friars Walk, Lewes, East Sussex BN7 2LZ
Fax (01273) 477881
Area Manager Ms Laura Chrysostomou (e-mail: laura.chrysostomou@eastsussex.gov.uk)

North Area

Uckfield Library, Library Way, High Street, Uckfield, East Sussex TN22 1AR
Fax (01825) 769762
Area Manager Mrs Joss Makin MCLIP (01825 769761; e-mail:
joss.makin@eastsussex.gov.uk)

Branch libraries

(the telephone number for the following libraries is ☎(0345) 6080196)

Battle Library, 7 Market Square, Battle, East Sussex TN33 0XA
e-mail: library.battle@eastsussex.gov.uk

Bexhill Library, Western Road, Bexhill-on-Sea, East Sussex TN40 1DY
e-mail: library.bexhill@eastsussex.gov.uk

Crowborough Library, Pine Grove, Crowborough, East Sussex TN6 1DH
e-mail: library.crowborough@eastsussex.gov.uk

Eastbourne Library, Grove Road, Eastbourne, East Sussex BN21 4TL
e-mail: library.eastbourne@eastsussex.gov.uk

Forest Row Library, The Community Centre, Hartfield Road, Forest Row, East Sussex
RH18 5DZ
e-mail: library.forestrow@eastsussex.gov.uk

Hailsham Library, Western Road, Hailsham, East Sussex BN27 3DN
e-mail: library.hailsham@eastsussex.gov.uk

Hampden Park Library, Brodrick Close, Hampden Park, Eastbourne, East Sussex
BN22 9NQ
e-mail: library.hampdenpark@eastsussex.gov.uk

Hastings Children's Library, Robertson Passage, off Robertson Street, Hastings, East Sussex TN34 1HL
e-mail: hastings.children@eastsussex.gov.uk

Hastings Library, Brassey Institute, 13 Claremont, Hastings, East Sussex TN34 1HE
e-mail: library.hastings@eastsussex.gov.uk

Heathfield Library, 21 High Street, Heathfield, East Sussex TN21 8LU
e-mail: library.heathfield@eastsussex.gov.uk

Hollington Library, 96 Battle Road, St Leonards on Sea, East Sussex TN37 7AG
e-mail: library.hollington@eastsussex.gov.uk

Langney Library, Unit 3, The Shopping Centre, 110 Kingfisher Drive, Langney, Eastbourne, East Sussex BN23 7RT
e-mail: library.langney@eastsussex.gov.uk

Lewes Library, Styles Field, Friars Walk, Lewes, East Sussex BN7 2LZ
e-mail: library.lewes@eastsussex.gov.uk

Mayfield Library, Mayfield CE School, Fletching Street, Mayfield, East Sussex TN20 6TA
e-mail: library.mayfield@eastsussex.gov.uk

Newhaven Library, 16 High Street, Newhaven, East Sussex BN9 9PD
e-mail: library.newhaven@eastsussex.gov.uk

Ore Library, Old London Road, Ore, Hastings, East Sussex TN35 5BP
e-mail: library.ore@eastsussex.gov.uk

Peacehaven Library, Meridian Centre, Peacehaven, East Sussex BN10 8BB
e-mail: library.peacehaven@eastsussex.gov.uk

Pevensey Bay Library, Wallsend House, Richmond Road, Pevensey Bay, East Sussex BN24 6AU
e-mail: library.pevenseybay@eastsussex.gov.uk

Polegate Library, Windsor Way, Polegate, East Sussex BN26 6QF
e-mail: library.polegate@eastsussex.gov.uk

Ringmer Library, Cecil Gates Room, The Village Hall, Lewes Road, Ringmer, Lewes, East Sussex BN8 5QH
e-mail: library.ringmer@eastsussex.gov.uk

Rye Library, Lion Street, Rye, East Sussex TN31 7LB
e-mail: library.rye@eastsussex.gov.uk

Seaford Library, 17 Sutton Park Road, Seaford, East Sussex BN25 1QX
e-mail: library.seaford@eastsussex.gov.uk

Uckfield Library, Library Way, High Street, Uckfield, East Sussex TN22 1AR
e-mail: library.uckfield@eastsussex.gov.uk

Wadhurst Library, The Institute, High Street, Wadhurst, East Sussex TN5 6AP
e-mail: library.wadhurst@eastsussex.gov.uk

Willingdon Library, Coppice Avenue, Lower Willingdon, Eastbourne, East Sussex BN20 9PN
e-mail: library.willingdon@eastsussex.gov.uk

Bibliographic Services

Bibliographic Services, Brooks Road, Lewes, East Sussex BN7 2BY
Head of Information and Local Studies Ms Noreen Finn MCLIP (01273 335381;
e-mail: noreen.finn@eastsussex.gov.uk)
Manager of Young People's Services Mrs Greta Paterson MA DipLib MCLIP DMS
(01273 335382; e-mail: greta.paterson@eastsussex.gov.uk)
Reader Development Manager Chris Desmond (01273 481537;
e-mail: chris.desmond@eastsussex.gov.uk)
Manager, Equal Access Services Ms Abigail Luthmann (01273 335383;
e-mail: abigail.luthmann@eastsussex.gov.uk)

Schools Library Service

Hammonds Drive, Lottbridge Drove, Hampden Park, Eastbourne, East Sussex BN23 6PW
Head of Schools Library and Museum Service Ms Michele Eaton BA(Hons) MCLIP
(01323 416324; e-mail: michele.eaton@eastsussex.gov.uk)

ENFIELD
Authority: London Borough of Enfield

Leisure, Culture and Youth, PO Box 58, Civic Centre, Enfield, Middlesex EN1 3XJ
☎020 8379 3747 (enquiries and administration)
Fax 020 8379 3777
url: www.enfield.gov.uk
Head of Libraries and Museums Ms Julie Gibson MA MCLIP (020 8379 3749;
e-mail: julie.gibson@enfield.gov.uk)
Libraries Strategy and Resources Manager Mrs Madeline Barratt BA MCLIP DipLaw
(e-mail: madeline.barratt@enfield.gov.uk)
Development and Operational Manager, Adult and Community Services
Ms Pam Tuttiett BA MCLIP (e-mail: pam.tuttiett@enfield.gov.uk)
Development and Operational Manager, Children and Young People Ms Lucy Love
BA(Hons) DipLib MCLIP (e-mail: lucy.love@enfield.gov.uk)
Information and Digital Citizenship Manager Peter Brown BA MCLIP
(e-mail: peter.brown@enfield.gov.uk)

Enfield North Area: Main library

Enfield Town Library, 66 Church Street, Enfield, Middlesex EN2 6AX
☎020 8379 8341
Fax 020 8379 8331

Enfield South Area: Main library

Edmonton Green Library, 36/44 South Mall, London N9 0NX
☎020 8379 2600
Fax 020 8379 2615

ESSEX
Authority: Essex County Council

Adults, Health and Community Wellbeing, Goldlay Gardens, Chelmsford, Essex CM2 0EW

☎(01245) 284981
Fax (01245) 492780
e-mail: essexlib@essexcc.gov.uk
url: www.essexcc.gov.uk/libraries
Director: Adult Learning and Libraries Mrs Susan Carragher BA(Hons) MCLIP
(e-mail: susan.carragher@essexcc.gov.uk) (based at County Hall, PO Box 47, Chelmsford,
Essex CM2 6WN)
Principal Ofcer: Libraries Martin Palmer BA MBA MCLIP MCMI (01245 244954;
e-mail: martin.palmer@essexcc.gov.uk)
Service Development Manager Ms Elaine Adams BA MCLIP DMS (e-mail:
elaine.adams@essexcc.gov.uk)
Library Locality Manager – North Ms Jenny Salisbury BLib(Hons) MCLIP
(e-mail: jenny.salisbury@essexcc.gov.uk)
Library Locality Manager – South Ms Liz Malone LLB(Hons) DipLIS MCLIP
(e-mail: liz.malone@essex.gov.uk)

Major libraries

Chelmsford Library, PO Box 882, Market Road, Chelmsford, Essex CM1 1LH
☎(01245) 492758
Fax (01245) 492536
e-mail: chelmsford.library@essexcc.gov.uk

Colchester Library, Trinity Square, Colchester, Essex CO1 1JB
☎(01206) 245900
Fax (01206) 245901
e-mail: colchester.library@essexcc.gov.uk

GATESHEAD
Authority: Gateshead Metropolitan Borough Council

**Libraries and Arts Service, Central Library, Prince Consort Road, Gateshead, Tyne and
Wear NE8 4LN**
☎0191 433 8400
Fax 0191 477 7454
e-mail: libraries@gateshead.gov.uk
url: www.gateshead.gov.uk/libraries
Head of Libraries and Arts Ms Ann Borthwick BA MCLIP (0191 433 6929; e-mail:
annborthwick@gateshead.gov.uk) (located at Libraries and Arts Service, Old Town Hall,
West Street, Gateshead, Tyne and Wear NE8 1HE)
Principal Libraries Manager Stephen Walters BSc MCLIP (e-mail:
stephenwalters@gateshead.gov.uk)
Libraries Operations Manager Ms Angela Lingwood MCLIP (e-mail:
angelalingwood@gateshead.gov.uk)

GLOUCESTERSHIRE
Authority: Gloucestershire County Council

Libraries and Information Service, Quayside House, Shire Hall, Gloucester GL1 2HY
☎0845 230 5420 (general enquiries), (01452) 425048 (management)
Fax (01452) 425042

e-mail: libraryhelp@gloucestershire.gov.uk
url: www.gloucestershire.gov.uk/libraries
Head of Libraries and Information David Paynter MCLIP
(e-mail: david.paynter@gloucestershire.gov.uk)
Assistant Heads of Libraries and Information Ms Sue Laurence BA(Hons) DipLib
MCLIP (e-mail: sue.laurence@gloucestershire.gov.uk), Ms Jo Hand BA DipLib MCLIP
(e-mail: jo.hand@gloucestershire.gov.uk)
Team Leader (Stock and Information) Mrs Katie Smith BA(Hons) MA MCLIP
(e-mail: katie.a.smith@gloucestershire.gov.uk)
Team Leader (Development and Access) Mrs Jill Barker BA DipLib MCLIP
(e-mail: jill.barker@gloucestershire.gov.uk)
Team Leader (Business Operations) Ms Jacqui Brading
(e-mail: jacqui.brading@gloucestershire.gov.uk)
Stock Manager Miss Kate Aston (e-mail: kate.aston@gloucestershire.gov.uk)

Central/largest libraries

Cheltenham Library, Clarence Street, Cheltenham, Glos GL50 3JT
☎(01242) 532688/532685
Fax (01242) 532684
Library Manager Ms Jane Allen

Gloucester Library, Brunswick Road, Gloucester GL1 1HT
☎(01452) 426973/426977
Fax (01452) 521468
Library Manager Peter Clark

Area libraries

Cheltenham, Tewkesbury and Cotswolds. Based at Cheltenham Library, Clarence Street,
Cheltenham, Glos GL50 3JT
☎(01242) 532678
Fax (01242) 532673
Team Leader: Cheltenham, Tewkesbury and Cotswold Area Ms Kathleen Sullivan BA
MA (e-mail: kathleen.sullivan@gloucestershire.gov.uk)

Gloucester, Forest and Stroud. Based at Gloucester Library, Brunswick Road, Gloucester
GL1 1HT
☎(01452) 426976
Fax (01452) 521468
Team Leader: Gloucester, Forest and Stroud Area Ms Christiane Nicholson BA
MCLIP (e-mail: christiane.nicholson@gloucestershire.gov.uk)

Selected branch libraries

Cirencester Bingham Library, The Waterloo, Cirencester, Glos GL7 2PZ
☎(01285) 659813
Library Manager Ms Jackie Belcher, Ms Rachel Philips

Tewkesbury Library, Sun Street, Tewkesbury, Glos GL20 5NX
☎(01684) 293086
Fax (01684) 290125
Library Manager Ms Janet Thomson

GREENWICH
Authority: Greenwich Council

Culture and Community Services, Library Support Services, Plumstead Library, 232 Plumstead High Street, London SE18 1JL
☎020 8317 4466
Fax 020 8317 4868
e-mail: libraries@greenwich.gov.uk
url: www.greenwich.gov.uk/libraries
Head of Community Services Ms Julia Newton MCLIP

District libraries

Blackheath Library, 17-23 Old Dover Road, London SE3 7BT
☎020 8858 1131

Eltham Library, Archery Road, London SE9 1HA
☎020 8921 3456

Woolwich Library, Calderwood Street, London SE18 6QZ
☎020 8921 5750
Senior Librarian, Children and Young People Ms Katy Taylor

HACKNEY
Authority: London Borough of Hackney

Strategic Leadership Team, Hackney Service Centre, 2nd Floor - South Zone, 1 Hillman Street, London E8 1DY
☎020 8356 1694
Fax 020 8356 1693
e-mail: libraries@hackney.gov.uk; info@hackney.gov.uk
url: www.hackney.gov.uk
Head of Libraries, Archives and Information Services Edward Rogers (020 8356 4782; e-mail: edward.rogers@hackney.gov.uk)
Interim Archives and Information Manager, Libraries Gerard Robson BSc(Hons) PGDip RM (020 8356 7571; e-mail: gerard.robson@hackney.gov.uk)
Development Manager, Libraries Ms Anita Kane BA DipLib MCLIP (020 8356 1696; e-mail: anita.kane@hackney.gov.uk)
Operations Manager, Libraries John Holland (020 8356 1695; e-mail: john.holland@hackney.gov.uk)

Central/largest library

Hackney Central Library, Technology and Learning Centre, 1 Reading Lane, London E8 1GQ
☎020 8356 5239
Fax 020 8356 2531
Library Manager Ms Sue Comitti (020 8356 2562; e-mail: sue.comitti@hackney.gov.uk)

Information Services, Technology and Learning Centre, 1 Reading Lane, London E8 1GQ
☎020 8356 4358
e-mail: reference.library@hackney.gov.uk
Knowledge Manager Cyprian Marah BA(Hons) DipEd DipLib MA (020 8356 2568; e-mail: cyprian.marah@hackney.gov.uk)

Town centre libraries

C L R James Library, 24-30 Dalston Lane, London E8 3AZ
☎020 8356 1962
Fax 020 7254 4655
Library Manager Ms Eileen Cannon (e-mail: eileen.cannon@hackney.gov.uk)

Clapton Library, Northwold Road, London E5 8RA
☎020 8356 1620
Fax 020 8806 7849
Library Manager Ms Christiana Ikeogu (e-mail: christiana.ikeogu@hackney.gov.uk)

Community Library Service, c/o Stoke Newington Library, Church Street, London N16 0JS
☎020 8356 5238
Fax 020 8356 5234
e-mail: homevisitservice.library@hackney.gov.uk
Manager Christopher Garnsworthy (e-mail: christopher.garnsworthy@hackney.gov.uk)

Hackney Archives, 43 De Beauvoir Road, London N1 5SQ
☎020 7241 2886
Fax 020 7241 6688
e-mail: archives@hackney.gov.uk
url: www.hackney.gov.uk/archives
Principal Archivist Ms Libby Adams (e-mail: libby.adams@hackney.gov.uk)

Homerton Library, Homerton High Street, London E9 6AS
☎020 8356 1963
Fax 020 8356 7945
Manager Ms Marcia Charles (e-mail: marcia.charles@hackney.gov.uk)

Shoreditch Library, 80 Hoxton Street, London N1 6LP
☎020 8356 5236/2542
Fax 020 8356 4353
Library Manager Ms Sarah Fletcher (e-mail: sarah.fletcher@hackney.gov.uk)

Stamford Hill Library, Portland Avenue, London N16 6SB
☎020 8356 1964
Fax 020 8356 1709
Library Manager Ms Margaret Sinn (e-mail: margaret.sinn@hackney.gov.uk)

Stoke Newington Library, Church Street, London N16 0JS
☎020 8356 5235/5230
Fax 020 8356 5234
Library Manager Ms Jackie Obeney-Williams (020 8356 5238; e-mail: jackie.obeney-williams@hackney.gov.uk)

Woodberry Down Community Library, Robin Redmond Centre, 440 Seven Sisters Road, London N4 2RD
☎020 8356 1965

(Please note: Woodberry Down Community Library is run by local volunteers)

HALTON
Authority: Halton Borough Council

Halton Lea Library, Halton Lea, Runcorn, Cheshire WA7 2PF
☎(01928) 704455
url: www.halton.gov.uk/libraries
Library Services Manager Mrs Paula Reilly-Cooper BSc DipLib MCLIP (0303 333 4300
ext 4096; e-mail: paula.reilly-cooper@halton.gov.uk) (Based at Runcorn Town Hall, Heath
Road, Runcorn, Cheshire WA7 5TD)
Operational Manager Miss Siobhan Kirk BA(Hons) MCLIP (01928 704455; e-mail:
siobhan.kirk@halton.gov.uk), Ms Julie Griffiths BA(Hons) (e-mail:
julie.griffiths@halton.gov.uk)

Contacts for Central/Largest and Area Libraries
Stock Specialist Officer Mrs Trudy Jones BA(Hons) MCLIP (e-mail:
trudy.jones@halton.gov.uk), Ms Alison Russell (e-mail: alison.russell@halton.gov.uk) (Based
at Runcorn Library, Egerton Street, Runcorn, Cheshire WA7 1JL)
Reference and Information Officer Mrs Jean Bradburn MCLIP (e-mail:
jean.bradburn@halton.gov.uk) (Based at Runcorn Library, Egerton Street, Runcorn,
Cheshire WA7 1JL)
Systems Officer Ms Catherine Jones BA(Hons) MA (e-mail:
catherine.jones@halton.gov.uk) (Based at Runcorn Library, Egerton Street, Runcorn,
Cheshire WA7 1JL)
Young Persons Officer Mrs Allyson Watt BA(Hons) MCLIP (e-mail:
allyson.watt@halton.gov.uk), Mrs Jennie Archer MCLIP (e-mail:
jennie.archer@halton.gov.uk) (Based at Runcorn Library, Egerton Street, Runcorn,
Cheshire WA7 1JL)
Reader Development Officer Ms Janette Fleming (e-mail: janette.fleming@halton.gov.uk)
(Based at Runcorn Library, Egerton Street, Runcorn, Cheshire WA7 1JL)
Bibliographical Services Officer Mrs Geraldine Kane BA(Hons) MCLIP

Central/largest library

Halton Lea Library, Halton Lea, Runcorn, Cheshire WA7 2PF
☎Tel/fax etc. as HQ

Area libraries

Ditton Library, Queens Avenue, Ditton, Widnes, Cheshire WA8 8HR
☎0151 424 2459

Runcorn Library, Egerton Street, Runcorn, Cheshire WA7 1JL
☎(01928) 574495

Widnes Library, Kingsway Learning Centre, Victoria Square, Widnes, Cheshire WA8 7QY
☎0151 907 8383
Fax 0151 907 8384

HAMMERSMITH AND FULHAM
Authority: London Borough of Hammersmith and Fulham

Hammersmith Library, Shepherds Bush Road, London W6 7AT

☎020 8753 2400 (24-hr information phoneline), 020 8753 3827 (enquiries), 020 8753 3813 (administration)
Fax 020 8753 3815
url: www.lbhf.gov.uk
Head of Libraries, Events and Registration Ms Donna Pentelow (020 8735 2358; e-mail: donna.pentelow@lbhf.gov.uk)
Deputy Head of Libraries Christopher Lloyd BA(Hons) MA (020 8753 3811; e-mail: chris.lloyd@lbhf.gov.uk)
Borough Archivist and Local History Manager Ms Jane Kimber BA(Hons) DAA MSc (020 8741 5159; e-mail: jane.kimber@lbhf.gov.uk)
Children & Young People's Librarian Vacant

Area libraries

Fulham Library, 598 Fulham Road, London SW6 5NX
☎020 8753 3877
Library Manager Ms Ann Cooper

Hammersmith Library, Shepherds Bush Road, London W6 7AT
☎020 8753 3823
Library Manager Ms Clare Edgson

Shepherds Bush Library, 7 Uxbridge Road, London W12 8LJ
☎020 8753 3842
Fax 020 8740 1712
Library Manager Ben Walsh

Branch libraries

Askew Road Library, 87/91 Askew Road, London W12 9AS
☎020 8753 3863

Barons Court Library, North End Crescent, London W14 8TG
☎020 8753 3888

Sands End Library, The Community Centre, 59-61 Broughton Road, London SW6 2LE
☎020 8753 3885

Housebound Readers Service
☎020 7610 4251

HAMPSHIRE
Authority: Hampshire County Council

Library and Information Service, Library HQ, Units 5/6 Moorside Place, Moorside Road, Winnall Industrial Estate, Winchester, Hants SO23 7RX
☎(01962) 826688
Fax (01962) 856615
url: www.hants.gov.uk/library
Assistant Director (Libraries and Information) Ms Nicola Horsey BA MSc (01962 845423; fax: 01962 850667; e-mail: nicola.horsey@hants.gov.uk) (located at Recreation and Heritage Department, Room 104, Mottisfort Court, High Street, Winchester, Hants SO23 8ZF)

Head of Operations Alec Kennedy BA(Hons) DMS MCLIP (01962 826681; e-mail: alec.kennedy@hants.gov.uk)

Personalisation Programme Manager Ms Julie Edyvean (01962 826618; e-mail: julie.edyvean@hants.gov.uk)

Group Manager East Ms Helen Bryant (07912 341075; e-mail: helen.bryant@hants.gov.uk) (based at Waterlooville Library)

Group Manager West Ms Jane Selby (07912 341072; e-mail: jane.selby@hants.gov.uk) (based at Romsey Library)

Group Manager, Discovery Centres Tim Wills (01962 826685; e-mail: tim.wills@hants.gov.uk)

Childrens and Schools Services Manager Anne Marley BA MCLIP (01962 826658; e-mail: anne.marley@hants.gov.uk)

Stock Manager Stephen Edwards BA MCLIP (Mobile 07590 774511; e-mail: stephen.edwards@hants.gov.uk)

Planning and Performance Manager Ms Kathy Allen (01962 826607; e-mail: kathy.allen@hants.gov.uk)

HARINGEY

Authority: London Borough of Haringey

Haringey Library Services, Central Library, High Road, Wood Green, London N22 6XD
☎020 8489 2780
Fax 020 8489 2722
url: www.haringey.gov.uk

Assistant Director, Culture, Libraries and Learning Ms Diana Edmonds MBE FRSA FCLIP BA DipLib (e-mail: diana.edmonds@haringey.gov.uk)

Library Service Delivery and Development Manager Ms Maria Stephanou BSc(Hons) (020 8489 2736; e-mail: maria.stephanou@haringey.gov.uk)

Central Library

Wood Green Central Library, High Road, Wood Green, London N22 6XD
☎020 8489 2780
Fax 020 8489 2555

Area libraries

Hornsey Library, Haringey Park, London N8 9JA
☎020 8489 1118
Library Manager Ms Sian Segel BA(Hons)

Marcus Garvey Library, Tottenham Green Leisure Centre, 1 Philip Lane, London N15 4JA
☎020 8489 5309
Library Manager Ms Anne Doherty BSc(Hons)

HARROW

Authority: Harrow Council

Civic Centre Library, PO Box 4, Civic Centre, Station Road, Harrow, Middlesex HA1 2UU
☎020 8424 1055/6 (enquiries), 020 8424 1059/1970 (administration)
Fax 020 8424 1971

e-mail: library@harrow.gov.uk
url: www.harrow.gov.uk/library
Head of Service - Libraries and Culture John Pennells MCLIP DMS (e-mail:
john.pennells@harrow.gov.uk)
Service Manager (Stock and Support Services) Ms Nikki Copleston BA MCLIP
(020 8424 1046; e-mail: nikki.copleston@harrow.gov.uk)
Principal Librarian (Reference and Information Services) Paul Lane MA DipLib
MCLIP (020 8424 1055; e-mail: paul.lane@harrow.gov.uk)
Interim Service Manager (Libraries, Lending Services) Tim Bryan BA DipLib MCLIP
(020 8416 8639; e-mail: tim.bryan@harrow.gov.uk)
Interim Principal Librarian (Young People's Services and Lifelong Learning) Simon
Smith BA(Hons) MCLIP (020 8424 1052; e-mail: simon.smith@harrow.gov.uk)

Central/largest library

Gayton Library, 5 St John's Road, Harrow, Middlesex HA1 2EE
☎020 8427 6012/8986
Interim Senior Lending Librarian Ms Fiona Mehta (e-mail: fiona.mehta@harrow.gov.uk)

HARTLEPOOL
Authority: Hartlepool Borough Council

Central Library, 124 York Road, Hartlepool TS26 9DE
☎(01429) 272905
Fax (01429) 283400
e-mail: infodesk@hartlepool.gov.uk
url: www.hartlepool.gov.uk/libraries
Borough Librarian Graham Jarritt BA(Hons) (e-mail: graham.jarritt@hartlepool.gov.uk)

Resources and Development

Resources and Development Section, Carnegie Building, Northgate, Hartlepool TS24 0LT
☎(01429) 523644
Fax (01429) 275665
Resources and Development Officer Mrs Kay Tranter BA(Hons) (e-mail:
kay.tranter@hartlepool.gov.uk)

HAVERING
Authority: London Borough of Havering

Central Library, St Edwards Way, Romford, Essex RM1 3AR
☎(01708) 432389 (enquiries); (01708) 434924 (library marketing)
e-mail: libraryservices@havering.gov.uk
url: www.anywhere.me/havering
Library Services Manager Ms Ann Rennie (01708 434922; e-mail:
ann.rennie@havering.gov.uk)
Reader Development Manager Mrs Ruth Gedalovitch BA(Hons) MCLIP (01708 434930;
e-mail: ruth.gedalovitch@havering.gov.uk)
Frontline Services Manager Ms Nicky Dunne (01708 434930; e-mail:
nicky.dunne@havering.gov.uk)

HEREFORDSHIRE
Authority: Herefordshire Council

Herefordshire Libraries, Shirehall, Hereford HRI 2HY
☎(01432) 261556
Fax (01432) 260744
url: www.herefordshire.gov.uk/libraries
Assistant Cultural Services Manager Michael Ligema BA(Hons) (01432 260631;
e-mail: mligema@herefordshire.gov.uk)
Principal Libraries Officer Jon Chedgzoy BA(Hons) DipLib MCLIP (01432 260557;
e-mail: jchedgzoy@herefordshire.gov.uk)
Senior Stock Librarian Ms Carolyn Huckfield BA(Hons) MCLIP (01432 261570;
e-mail: chuckfield@herefordshire.gov.uk)

Central library

Hereford Library, Broad Street, Hereford HR4 9AU
☎(01432) 383600
Fax (01432) 383607

Largest libraries

Leominster Library, 8 Buttercross, Leominster, Herefordshire HR6 8BN
☎(01432) 383290
Fax (01568) 616025

Ross-on-Wye Library, Cantilupe Road, Ross-on-Wye, Herefordshire HR9 7AN
☎(01432) 383280
Fax (01432) 383282

HERTFORDSHIRE
Authority: Hertfordshire County Council

Libraries, Culture and Learning, New Barnfield, Travellers Lane, Hatfield, Herts AL10 8XG
☎0300 123 4049 (enquiries)
url: www.hertsdirect.org/libraries
Head of Libraries, Culture and Learning Ms Glenda Wood BA(Hons) DipLib MCLIP
(01707 281584; e-mail: glenda.wood@hertscc.gov.uk)
Head of Operations, Planning and Performance Derek Knight MCLIP (01707 281584;
e-mail: derek.knight@hertscc.gov.uk)
Head of Stock, Reader Development and Customer Service Ms Sue Valentine
BA(Hons) MCLIP (01707 281584; e-mail: sue.valentine@hertscc.gov.uk)
Head of Information Services and Lifelong Learning Andrew Bignell BA DipLib
(01707 281584; e-mail: andrew.bignell@hertscc.gov.uk)
Head of Young People, Schools and Equalities Ms Michele Murphy BA(Hons) MCLIP
(01707 281630; e-mail: michele.murphy@hertscc.gov.uk)
Head of Logistics and Continuity Ms Jean Holmes BA MCLIP (01707 281584; e-mail:
jean.holmes@hertscc.gov.uk)
Mobile Services Manager Neil Baxter (01438 737333; e-mail:
neil.baxter@hertscc.gov.uk)

Central/largest library

Central Resources Library, New Barnfield, Travellers Lane, Hatfield, Herts AL10 8XG
☎0300 123 4049
e-mail: centralresources.library@hertscc.gov.uk
Central Resources Librarian Ms Myra Campbell MA MCLIP

District libraries

(telephone numbers for the following libraries is the same as for HQ and Central/largest)

Bishop's Stortford Library, 6 The Causeway, Bishop's Stortford, Herts CM23 2EJ
e-mail: bishopsstortford.library@hertscc.gov.uk
District Librarian (East Herts and Broxbourne Districts) Ms Rachel Bilton

St Albans Library, The Maltings, St Albans, Herts AL1 3JQ
e-mail: st.albans.library@hertscc.gov.uk
District Librarian (Dacorum and St Albans Districts) Russel Barrow BA(Hons)

Stevenage Library, Southgate, Stevenage, Herts SG1 1HD
e-mail: stevenage.library@hertscc.gov.uk
District Librarian (Stevenage and North Herts Districts) Ms Claire Barraclough BA
MCLIP

Watford Library, Hempstead Road, Watford, Herts WD1 3EU
e-mail: watford.library@hertscc.gov.uk
District Librarian (Three Rivers and Watford Districts) Ms Marie Staunton BA DipLib
MCLIP

Welwyn Garden City Library, Campus West, Welwyn Garden City, Herts AL8 6AJ
e-mail: wgc.library@hertscc.gov.uk
District Librarian (Welwyn, Hatfield and Hertsmere Districts) Jim Macrae MA
MCLIP

HILLINGDON
Authority: London Borough of Hillingdon

Central Library, 14 High Street, Uxbridge, Middlesex UB8 1HD
☎(01895) 250600 (enquiries), (01895) 250713 (administration)
Fax (01895) 811164
e-mail: librarycontact@hillingdon.gov.uk
url: www.hillingdon.gov.uk/libraries
Interim Head of Sport, Culture and Leisure Alan Dalton (e-mail:
adalton@hillingdon.gov.uk)
Senior Library Manager Daniel Waller BA(Hons) (e-mail: dwaller@hillingdon.gov.uk)

Central/largest library

Central Library, 14 High Street, Uxbridge, Middlesex UB8 1HD
☎(01895) 250600
Fax (01895) 811164
e-mail: librarycontact@hillingdon.gov.uk
Central Library Manager Ms Zoe Iggulden

HOUNSLOW

Authority: London Borough of Hounslow

Hounslow Libraries, CentreSpace, Treaty Centre, High Street, Hounslow, Middlesex TW3 IES
☎0845 456 2800 (enquiries), 0845 456 2930 (administration)
Fax 0845 456 2965
e-mail: hounslow-info@laing.com
url: www.hounslow.info
Operations Manager Mrs Elaine Collier BSc DipLib MCLIP (e-mail:
elaine.collier@laing.com)
Service Development Manager Ms Elizabeth Lee BA(Hons) MCLIP (e-mail:
elizabeth-lee@laing.com)

Central/largest library

Hounslow Library, CentreSpace, Treaty Centre, High Street, Hounslow, Middlesex TW3 IES
☎0845 456 2800
Fax 0845 456 2965

Branch libraries

Beavers Library @ The Hub, 103 Salisbury Road, Hounslow, Middlesex TW4 7NW
☎020 8572 6995

Bedfont Library, Staines Road, Bedfont, Middlesex TW14 8BD
☎020 8890 6173

Brentford Library, Boston Manor Road, Brentford, Middlesex TW8 8DW
☎020 8560 8801

Chiswick Library, Duke's Avenue, Chiswick, London W4 2AB
☎020 8994 1008

Cranford Library, Bath Road, Cranford, Middlesex TW5 9TL
☎020 8759 0641

Feltham Library, The Centre, High Street, Feltham, Middlesex TW13 4GU
☎020 8890 3506

Hanworth Library, 2-12 Hampton Road West, Feltham, Middlesex TW13 6AW
☎020 8898 0256

Heston Library, New Heston Road, Heston, Middlesex TW5 0LW
☎020 8570 1028

Isleworth Library, Twickenham Road, Isleworth, Middlesex TW7 7EU
☎020 8560 2934

Osterley Library, St Mary's Crescent, Osterley, Middlesex TW7 4NB
☎020 8560 4295

ISLE OF WIGHT
Authority: Isle of Wight Council

Library Headquarters, 5 Mariners Way, Somerton Industrial Estate, Cowes, Isle of Wight PO31 8PD
☎(01983) 203880 (enquiries and administration)
Fax (01983) 203899
url: www.iwight.com/living_here/libraries
Libraries Officer Rob Jones BA MCLIP CertEd (e-mail: rob.jones@iow.gov.uk)
Development Librarian – Operations Andrew Walker BA MCLIP (e-mail: andrew.walker@iow.gov.uk)
Development Librarian – Stock and Information John English BLib DMS MCLIP (e-mail: john.english@iow.gov.uk)
Development Librarian – Young People and Lifelong Learning Mrs Elspeth Jackson BA(Hons) DipLIS MCLIP (e-mail: elspeth.jackson@iow.gov.uk)

Central/largest library

Lord Louis Library, Orchard Street, Newport, Isle of Wight PO30 1LL
☎(01983) 527655 (enquiries and administration)
Fax (01983) 825972

Area libraries

Bembridge Library, Church Road, Bembridge, Isle of Wight PO35 5NA
☎(01983) 873102 (tel/fax)

Brighstone Library, New Road, Brighstone, Newport, Isle of Wight PO30 4BB
☎(01983) 740150 (tel/fax)

Cowes Library, Beckford Road, Cowes, Isle of Wight PO31 7SG
☎(01983) 293341 (tel/fax)

East Cowes Library, The York Centre, 11 York Avenue, East Cowes, Isle of Wight PO32 6QY
☎(01983) 293019 (tel/fax)

Freshwater Library, School Green Road, Freshwater, Isle of Wight PO35 5NA
☎(01983) 752377 (tel/fax)

Niton Library, High Street, Niton, Isle of Wight PO38 2AZ
☎(01983) 730863 (tel/fax)

Ryde Library, George Street, Ryde, Isle of Wight PO33 2JE
☎(01983) 562170
Fax (01983) 615644

Sandown Library, High Street, Sandown, Isle of Wight PO36 8AF
☎(01983) 402748 (tel/fax)

Shanklin Library, Victoria Avenue, Shanklin, Isle of Wight PO37 6PG
☎(01983) 863126 (tel/fax)

Ventnor Library, High Street, Ventnor, Isle of Wight PO38 1LX
☎(01983) 852039 (tel/fax)

ISLINGTON
Authority: London Borough of Islington

Library and Heritage Services, Central Library, 2 Fieldway Crescent, London N5 IPF
☎020 7527 6900 (enquiries), 020 7527 6905 (administration)
Fax 020 7527 6906
e-mail: hlcs@islington.gov.uk
url: www.islington.gov.uk/libraries
Head of Library and Heritage Services Ms Rosemary Doyle MCLIP MBA (020 7527 6903; e-mail: rosemary.doyle@islington.gov.uk)
Assistant Head of Library and Heritage Services Ms Michelle Gannon BSc(Hons) (020 7527 6907; e-mail: michelle.gannon@islington.gov.uk)
Children and Young People's Services Manager Geoff James BA(Hons) DipLib MCLIP (020 7527 6997; e-mail: geoff.james@islington.gov.uk)

Central/largest library

Central Library, 2 Fieldway Crescent, London N5 IPF
☎020 7527 6900
Fax 020 7527 6902
Customer Services Manager Ms Teresa Gibson (020 7527 6950; e-mail: teresa.gibson@islington.gov.uk)

Other libraries

Archway Library, Hamlyn House, Highgate Hill, London N19 5PH
☎020 7527 7820
Fax 020 7527 7833
e-mail: archway.library@islington.gov.uk
Person in charge Ms Kate Tribe, Ms Tracey Clark-Edwards

Finsbury Library, 245 St John Street, London EC1V 4NB
☎020 7527 7960
Fax 020 7527 7998
e-mail: finsbury.library@islington.gov.uk
Person in charge Ms Pamela Quantrill

John Barnes Library, 275 Camden Road, London N7 0JN
☎020 7527 7900
Fax 020 7527 7907
e-mail: johnbarnes.library@islington.gov.uk
Person in charge Nick Tranmer

Lewis Carroll Library, Copenhagen Street, London N1 0ST
☎020 7527 7936
Fax 020 7527 7935
e-mail: lewiscarroll.library@islington.gov.uk
Person in charge Ms Marcia Ludlow

Mildmay Library, 21-23 Mildmay Park, London N1 4NA
☎020 7527 7880
Fax 020 7527 7898
e-mail: mildmay.library@islington.gov.uk

Person in charge Ms Carol Roberts

N4 Library, 26 Blackstock Road, London N4 2DW
☎020 7527 7800
Fax 020 527 7808
e-mail: n4.library@islington.gov.uk
Person in charge Chris Millington

North Library, Manor Gardens, London N7 6JX
☎020 7527 7840
Fax 020 7527 7854
e-mail: north.library@islington.gov.uk
Person in charge Ms Carole Levy

South Library, 115-117 Essex Road, London N1 2SL
☎020 7527 7860
Fax 020 7527 7869
e-mail: south.library@islington.gov.uk
Person in charge Cuneyt Yilmaz

West Library, Bridgeman Road, London N1 1BD
☎020 7527 7920
Fax 020 7527 7929
e-mail: west.library@islington.gov.uk
Person in charge Ms Marcia Ludlow

KENSINGTON AND CHELSEA
Authority: Royal Borough of Kensington and Chelsea

Central Library, Phillimore Walk, London W8 7RX
☎020 7361 3010 (general enquiries), 020 7361 3058 (management)
Fax 020 7361 2976
e-mail: headoflibraryservice@rbkc.gov.uk
url: www.rbkc.gov.uk/libraries
Head of Library Service Ms J E Battye BA MCLIP
Assistant Head of Libraries – Service Delivery & Development Miss Elizabeth Hibbs
BA DipLib MCLIP

Main libraries

Brompton Library, 210 Old Brompton Road, London SW5 0BS
☎020 7361 3010

Central Library, Hornton Street, London W8 7RX
☎020 7361 3010
Fax 020 7361 2976

Chelsea Library, The Old Town Hall, Kings Road, London SW3 5EZ
☎020 7361 3010

North Kensington Library, 108 Ladbroke Grove, London W11 1PZ
☎020 7361 3010

KENT
Authority: Kent County Council

Libraries and Archives, Springfield, Maidstone, Kent ME14 2LH
☎(01622) 696505
Fax (01622) 696450
e-mail: libraries@kent.gov.uk
url: www.kent.gov.uk/libs
Head of Libraries and Archives Ms Cath Anley
Business Support Manager Ms Diane Chilmaid
Strategic Manager (Projects) Ms Lesley Spencer
Strategic Manager (Innovation) Mrs Gill Bromley
Strategic Manager (Modernisation) Ms Susan Sparks
Strategic Manager (Operations) Ms Lynn Catt
Stock Services Manager Ken Jarvis

Ask-a-Kent Librarian

County Central Library, Springfield, Maidstone, Kent ME14 2LH
☎(01622) 696438
Fax (01622) 696494
e-mail: libraries.informationservices.kent.gov.uk
url: www.kent.gov.uk/onlinelibrary
Information Services Manager Ms Christel Pobgee

Main district libraries

Ashford Library, 15 Park Mall, Ashford, Kent TN24 8RY
☎(01233) 620649
Fax (01233) 620295
e-mail: ashfordlibrary@kent.gov.uk
District Manager Mrs Heather Hilton

Canterbury Library, 35 Pound Lane, Canterbury, Kent CT1 2JF
☎(01227) 463608
Fax (01227) 768338
e-mail: canterburylibrary@kent.gov.uk
District Manager Mrs Sally Reeve

County Central Library, Springfield, Maidstone, Kent ME14 2LH
☎(01622) 696511
Fax (01622) 696464
District Manager Ms Shirley Sheridan

Dartford Library, Central Park, Dartford, Kent DA1 1EU
☎(01322) 221133
Fax (01322) 278271
e-mail: dartfordlibrary@kent.gov.uk
District Manager Christoph Bull

Dover Discovery Centre, Market Square, Dover, Kent CT16 1PB
☎(01304) 204241
Fax (01304) 225914

e-mail: doverlibrary@kent.gov.uk
District Manager Ms Jackie Taylor-Smith

Gravesend Library, 21-22 St George's Square, St George's Shopping Centre, Gravesend,
Kent DA11 0TB
☎(01474) 352758
Fax (01474) 320284
e-mail: gravesendlibrary@kent.gov.uk
District Manager Christoph Bull

Maidstone Library, St Faith's Street, Maidstone, Kent ME14 1LH
☎(01622) 752344
Fax (01622) 754980
e-mail: maidstonelibrary@kent.gov.uk
District Manager Ms Shirley Sheridan

Sevenoaks Kaleidoscope, Buckhurst Lane, Sevenoaks, Kent TN13 1LQ
☎(01732) 453118
Fax (01732) 457468
e-mail: sevenoakslibrary@kent.gov.uk
District Manager Ms Fiona Dutton

Shepway - Folkestone Library, 2 Grace Hill, Folkestone, Kent CT20 1HD
☎(01303) 850123
Fax (01303) 242907
e-mail: folkestonelibrary@kent.gov.uk
District Manager Mrs Sally Reeve

Swale - Sittingbourne Library, Central Avenue, Sittingbourne, Kent ME10 4AH
☎(01795) 476545
Fax (01795) 428376
e-mail: sittingbournelibrary@kent.gov.uk
District Manager Christoph Bull

Thanet - Margate Library, Cecil Street, Margate, Kent CT9 1RE
☎(01843) 223626
Fax (01843) 293015
District Manager Ms Jackie Taylor-Smith

Tonbridge Library, Avebury Avenue, Tonbridge, Kent TN9 1TG
☎(01732) 352754
Fax (01732) 358300
e-mail: tonbridgelibrary@kent.gov.uk
District Manager Ms Fiona Dutton

Tunbridge Wells Library, Mount Pleasant Road, Tunbridge Wells, Kent TN1 1NS
☎(01892) 522352
Fax (01892) 514657
e-mail: tunbridgewellslibrary@kent.gov.uk
District Manager Mrs Heather Hilton

Note: Ashford, Gravesend and Canterbury libraries will be moving premises during 2011 -
please refer to website for details

KINGSTON UPON HULL
Authority: Kingston upon Hull City Council

Central Library, Albion Street, Kingston upon Hull HUI 3TF
☎(01482) 210000 (enquiries), (01482) 616822 (administration)
Fax (01482) 616827
url: www.hullcc.gov.uk
Assistant Head of Service – Libraries Ms Michelle Alford BA(Hons)

Area libraries

Anlaby Park Library, The Greenway, Anlaby High Road, Kingston upon Hull HU4 6TX
☎(01482) 614483

Avenues Library, 76 Chanterlands Avenue, Kingston upon Hull HU5 3TS
☎(01482) 331280

Bransholme Library, District Centre, Goodhart Road, Bransholme, Kingston upon Hull
HU7 4EF
☎(01482) 331234

Fred Moore Library, Wold Road, Derringham Bank, Kingston upon Hull HU5 5UN
☎(01482) 331239

Freedom Centre Library, 95 Preston Road, Kingston upon Hull HU9 5QB
☎(01482) 710100

Gipsyville Library, 728-730 Hessle High Road, Kingston upon Hull HU4 6JA
☎(01482) 616973

Greenwood Avenue Library, Greenwood Avenue, Kingston upon Hull HU6 9RU
☎(01482) 331257

Holderness Road Customer Service Centre and Library, I The Mount, Holderness Road,
Kingston upon Hull HU9 2BN
☎(01482) 318830

Ings Customer Service Centre and Library, Savoy Road, Kingston upon Hull HU8 0TY
☎(01482) 331250

Longhill Library, 162 Shannon Road, Kingston upon Hull HU8 9RW
☎(01482) 331530

Marfleet Library, Marfleet Primary Health Care Centre, Preston Road, Kingston upon Hull
HU9 5UZ
☎(01482) 331264

Stadium Library, The Learning Zone, KC Stadium, Walton Street, Kingston upon Hull
HU3 6HU
☎(01482) 381947

Walker Street Customer Service Centre, The Octagon, Walker Street, Kingston upon Hull
HU3 2RA
☎(01482) 318845

Western Library, The Boulevard, Hessle Road, Kingston upon Hull HU3 3ED
☎(01482) 331217

KINGSTON UPON THAMES
Authority: Royal Borough of Kingston upon Thames

Kingston Library, Fairfield Road, Kingston upon Thames, Surrey KT1 2PS
☎020 8547 6413 (administration)
Fax 020 8547 6426
url: www.kingston.gov.uk
Strategic Manager: Library and Heritage Service Ms Grace McElwee BA(Hons)
DipLib MCLIP (020 8547 6423; e-mail: grace.mcelwee@rbk.kingston.gov.uk)
ICT Development Manager M O'Brien (020 8547 6420; e-mail:
mike.obrien@rbk.kingston.gov.uk)
Reading Resources Manager Ms Alison Townsend BA MA MCLIP (020 8547 6494;
e-mail: alison.townsend@rbk.kingston.gov.uk)

Branch libraries

Community Library, Surbiton Library Annexe, Ewell Road, Surbiton, Surrey KT6 6AG
☎020 8547 6453
Fax 020 8339 9805
Library Manager P Tanter (e-mail: paul.tanter@rbk.kingston.gov.uk)

Hook and Chessington Library, Hook Road, Chessington, Surrey KT9 1EJ
☎020 8547 6480
Fax 020 8547 6483
Library Manager Ms M Newman (e-mail: michaela.newman@rbk.kingston.gov.uk)

Kingston Library, Fairfield Road, Kingston upon Thames, Surrey KT1 2PS
☎020 8547 6400
Fax 020 8547 6401
Library Manager Alan Gale (e-mail: alan.gale@rbk.kingston.gov.uk)

New Malden Library, Kingston Road, New Malden, Surrey KT3 3LY
☎020 8547 6490
Fax 020 8547 6495
Library Manager Adam Moore (e-mail: adam.moore@rbk.kingston.gov.uk)

Old Malden Library, Church Road, Worcester Park, Surrey KT4 7RD
☎020 8547 6467
Fax 020 8547 6469
Library Manager Adam Moore (e-mail: adam.moore@rbk.kingston.gov.uk)

Surbiton Library, Ewell Road, Surbiton, Surrey KT6 6AG
☎020 8547 6444
Fax 020 8547 6449
Library Manager Ms Carolyn Roberts (e-mail: carolyn.roberts@rbk.kingston.gov.uk)

Tolworth Community Library and IT Learning Centre, The Broadway, Tolworth, Surbiton,
Surrey KT6 7DJ
☎020 8547 6470
Fax 020 8547 6471
e-mail: tolworth.library@rbk.kingston.gov.uk
Library Manager Ms Carolyn Roberts (e-mail: carolyn.roberts@rbk.kingston.gov.uk)

Tudor Drive Library, Tudor Drive, Kingston upon Thames, Surrey KT2 5QH

☎020 8547 6457
Fax 020 8547 6459
Library Manager Alan Gale (e-mail: alan.gale@rbk.kingston.gov.uk)

KIRKLEES
Authority: Kirklees Council

Kirklees Customer & Exchequer Services, Red Doles Lane, Huddersfield, West Yorks HD2 IYF
☎(01484) 226300
Fax (01484) 226342
url: www.kirklees.gov.uk
Assistant Director, Customer & Exchequer Services Ms Jane Brady (01484 221193;
e-mail: jane.brady@kirklees.gov.uk) (based at 3rd Floor, Civic Centre 1, Huddersfield,
West Yorks HD1 2NF
Assistant Head of Service (Frontline Services) Dave Thompson (01484 226303;
e-mail: dave.thompson@kirklees.gov.uk)

Central/largest library

Huddersfield Library & Information Centre, Princess Alexandra Walk, Huddersfield, West
Yorks HD1 2SU
☎(01484) 221951
Fax (01484) 221952
Chief Librarian & Manager i/c Ms Jan Clark BA MCLIP (e-mail:
jan.clark@kirklees.gov.uk)

Area libraries and information centres

Area East. Dewsbury Library & Information Centre, Railway Street, Dewsbury, West Yorks
WF12 8EQ
☎(01924) 325080
Manager I/c Ms Alison Peaden BA MCLIP (e-mail: alison.peaden@kirklees.gov.uk)

Area North. Cleckheaton Library & Information Centre, Whitcliffe Road, Cleckheaton,
West Yorks BD19 3DX
☎(01274) 335169
Manager i/c Ms Janet Pearson BSc(Hons) PGDipInfStud PGCentMgt (e-mail:
janet.pearson@kirklees.gov.uk)

Area South. Shepley Library & Information Centre, Marsh Lane, Shepley, Huddersfield,
West Yorks HD8 8AE
☎(01484) 222728
Manager i/c Ms Kathryn Harrison BA(Hons) PGDipLib MCLIP (e-mail:
kathryn.harrison@kirklees.gov.uk)

Area West. Holmfirth Library & Information Centre, 47 Huddersfield Road, Holmfirth,
West Yorks HD9 3JH
☎(01484) 222430
Manager i/c Ms Carol Stump (e-mail: carol.stump@kirklees.gov.uk)

Mobiles and Home Service, Customer & Exchequer Services, Library and Information
Centres HQ, Red Doles Lane, Huddersfield, West Yorks HD2 IYF

☎(01484) 226350
Manager i/c Ms Jan Clark BA MCLIP (e-mail: jan.clark@kirklees.gov.uk)

KNOWSLEY

Authority: Knowsley Metropolitan Borough Council

Huyton Library, Civic Way, Huyton, Merseyside L36 9GD
☎0151 443 3628
Fax 0151 443 3739
url: www.knowsley.gov.uk/residents/libraries.aspx
Head of Libraries Peter Marchant MA BA(Hons) DipLib DM MCLIP (e-mail:
peter.marchant@knowsley.gov.uk)

Central/largest library

Huyton Library, Civic Way, Huyton, Merseyside L36 9GD
☎0151 443 3734
Fax 0151 443 3739
e-mail: huyton.library.dlcs@knowsley.gov.uk
Library Managers Ms Phyl Carolan, Brian Lester

Branch libraries

Halewood Library, The Halewood Centre, Roseheath Drive, Halewood, Knowsley,
Merseyside L26 0TS
☎0151 443 2086
Fax 0151 443 2088
e-mail: halewood.library.dlcs@knowsley.gov.uk

Kirkby Library, Newtown Gardens, Kirkby, Merseyside L32 8RR
☎0151 443 4290
Fax 0151 546 1453
e-mail: kirkby.library.dlcs@knowsley.gov.uk

Page Moss Library, Stockbridge Lane, Huyton, Merseyside L36 3SA
☎0151 489 9814
Fax 0151 480 9284
e-mail: page.moss.library.dlcs@knowsley.gov.uk

Prescot Library, High Street, Prescot, Merseyside L34 3LD
☎0151 426 6449
Fax 0151 430 7548
e-mail: prescot.library.dlcs@knowsley.gov.uk

Stockbridge Village Library, Unit 12, The Croft, Stockbridge Village, Merseyside L28 1NR
☎0151 480 3925 (tel/fax)
e-mail: stockbridge.library.dlcs@knowsley.gov.uk

Whiston Library, Dragon Lane, Whiston, Merseyside L35 3QW
☎0151 426 4757
Fax 0151 493 0191
e-mail: whiston.library.dlcs@knowsley.gov.uk

LAMBETH
Authority: London Borough of Lambeth

Lambeth Libraries and Archives Headquarters, 1st Floor, Blue Star House, 234–244 Stockwell Road, London SW9 9SP
☎020 7926 0750 (enquiries); 020 7926 1000 (switchboard)
Fax 020 7926 0751
url: www.lambeth.gov.uk
Head of Libraries and Archives Ms Sandra Goodwin BSc (e-mail: sgoodwin@lambeth.gov.uk)
Acting Deputy Head of Libraries and Archives Ms Marcia Bogle-Mayne (e-mail: mboglemayne@lambeth.gov.uk), Michel Merson (e-mail: mmerson@lambeth.gov.uk)
Development Manager, Learning and Access Ms Susan Doyle MCLIP (e-mail: sdoyle@lambeth.gov.uk)
Development Manager, Information and ICT Vacant
Support Services Manager Vacant

Lambeth Archives and Minet Library

Minet Library, 52 Knatchbull Road, London SE5 9QY
☎020 7926 6076
Fax 020 7926 6080
e-mail: minetlibrary@lambeth.gov.uk/archives@lambeth.gov.uk
Manager Jon Newman MA DAA (e-mail: jnewman@lambeth.gov.uk), Len Reilly BA DipLib MCLIP (e-mail: ljreilly@lambeth.gov.uk)

North Area

Clapham Library, 1 Northside, Clapham Common, London SW4 0QW
☎020 7926 0717
Fax 020 7926 4859
e-mail: claphamlibrary@lambeth.gov.uk
Area Library Manager Michel Merson (e-mail: mmerson@lambeth.gov.uk)

Durning Library, 167 Kennington Lane, London SE11 4HF
☎020 7926 8682/3
Fax 020 7926 8685
e-mail: durninglibrary@lambeth.gov.uk

South Lambeth Library, 180 South Lambeth Road, London SW8 1QP
☎020 7926 0705/0710
Fax 020 7926 0708
e-mail: southlambethlibrary@lambeth.gov.uk

Waterloo Library, 114–118 Lower Marsh, London SE1 7AG
☎020 7926 8750/1
Fax 020 7926 8749
e-mail: waterloolibrary@lambeth.gov.uk

Central Area

Brixton Library, Brixton Oval, London SW2 1JQ
☎020 7926 1056

Fax 020 7926 1070
e-mail: brixtonlendinglibrary@lambeth.gov.uk
Area Library Manager Vacant

Carnegie Library, 188 Herne Hill Road, London SE24 0AG
☎020 7926 6050
Fax 020 7926 6072
e-mail: carnegielibrary@lambeth.gov.uk

South Area

Streatham Library, 63 Streatham High Road, London SW16 1PL
☎020 7926 6768
Fax 020 7926 5804
e-mail: streathamlibrary@lambeth.gov.uk
Area Library Manager Ms Marcia Bogle-Mayne (e-mail: mboglemayne@lambeth.gov.uk)

West Norwood Library, Norwood High Street, London SE27 9JX
☎020 7926 8092
Fax 020 7926 8032
e-mail: westnorwoodlibrary@lambeth.gov.uk

Support Services

Children and Young People Services, Brixton Library, Brixton Oval, London SW2 1JQ
☎020 7926 1104
Fax 020 7926 1070
Senior Children and Young People Librarian Ms Sandra Davidson (e-mail: sdavidson@lambeth.gov.uk)

Literacy Development, Brixton Library, Brixton Oval, London SW2 1JQ
☎020 7926 1103
Fax 020 7926 1070
Literacy Development Librarian Abibat Olulode (e-mail: aolulode@lambeth.gov.uk)

Reader Development, Brixton Library, Brixton Oval, London SW2 1JQ
☎020 7926 1105
Fax 020 7926 1070
Reader Development Officer Tim O'Dell (e-mail: todell@lambeth.gov.uk)

Stock Services, 188 Herne Hill Road, London SE24 0AG
☎020 7926 6069
Fax 020 7926 6072
e-mail: stocksupportservices@lambeth.gov.uk
Stock Services Manager Ms Clare Stockbridge Bland BA MCLIP (e-mail: cstockbridgebland@lambeth.gov.uk)

LANCASHIRE
Authority: Lancashire County Council

Adult and Community Services Directorate, County Library and Information Services, East Cliff, PO Box 162, Preston, Lancs PR1 3EA
☎(01772) 534008

Fax (01772) 534880
e-mail: library@lancashire.gov.uk
url: www.lancashire.gov.uk/libraries
Acting Head of Library and Information Services Mrs Julie Bell BA(Hons) MCLIP
(01772 534010; e-mail: julie.bell@lancashire.gov.uk)
Strategic Manager – Support David Blackett BA MCLIP (01772 534091; e-mail:
david.blackett@lancashire.gov.uk)
Strategic Manager – Planning Ms Ann Marsh BLib MCLIP (01772 536727; e-mail:
ann.marsh@lancashire.gov.uk)

District libraries

Accrington Library, St James' Street, Accrington, Lancs BB5 1NQ
☎(01254) 872385
Fax (01254) 301066

Burnley Library, Grimshaw Street, Burnley, Lancs BB11 2BD
☎(01282) 437115
Fax (01282) 452869

Chorley Library, Union Street, Chorley, Lancs PR7 1EB
☎(01257) 277222
Fax (01257) 231730

Clitheroe Library, Church Street, Clitheroe, Lancs BB7 2DG
☎(01200) 428788
Fax (01200) 443203

Fleetwood Library, North Albert Street, Fleetwood, Lancs FY7 6AJ
☎(01253) 775800
Fax (01253) 775804

Harris Library, Market Square, Preston, Lancs PR1 2PP
☎(01772) 532676
Fax (01772) 555527

Lancaster Library, Market Square, Lancaster, Lancs LA1 1HY
☎(01524) 580700
Fax (01524) 580709

Leyland Library, Lancastergate, Leyland, Preston, Lancs PR25 1EX
☎(01772) 432804
Fax (01772) 456549

Morecambe Library, Central Drive, Morecambe, Lancs LA4 5DL
☎(01524) 415215
Fax (01524) 415008

Nelson Library, Market Square, Nelson, Lancs BB9 7PU
☎(01280) 692511
Fax (01282) 449584

Rawtenstall Library, Queen's Square, Rawtenstall, Lancs BB4 6QU
☎(01706) 227911
Fax (01706) 217014

Skelmersdale Library, Southway, Skelmersdale, Lancs WN8 6NL
☎(01695) 720312
Fax (01695) 558627

St Anne's Library, 254 Clifton Drive South, Lytham St Anne's, Lancs FY8 1NR
☎(01253) 643900
Fax (01253) 643909

LEEDS
Authority: Leeds City Council

City Development Department, 7th Floor (West), No 110 Merrion Centre, Merrion House, Leeds LS2 8DT
☎0113 247 8330 (management enquiries)
Fax 0113 247 6044
url: www.leeds.gov.uk
Chief Libraries, Arts and Heritage Officer Ms Catherine Blanshard BA MCLIP
(e-mail: catherine.blanshard@leeds.gov.uk)

Library headquarters

Library Headquarters, 1 Bowcliffe Road, Off Gibraltar Island Road, Hunslet, Leeds LS10 1HB
☎0113 395 2311/3 (general enquiries)
Fax 0113 395 2362/3

Central/largest library

Central Library, Municipal Buildings, Calverley Street, Leeds LS1 3AB
☎0113 247 8274
Fax 0113 247 8268
url: www.leeds.gov.uk
Library Service Delivery Manager Ms Bev Rice BA (e-mail: bev.rice@leeds.gov.uk)

LEICESTER
Authority: Leicester City Council

Culture, 12th Floor, Block A, New Walk Centre, Welford Place, Welford Road, Leicester LE1 6ZG
☎0116 252 6762 (administration)
Fax 0116 285 4698
e-mail: libraries@leicester.gov.uk
url: www.leicester.gov.uk/libraries
Head of Libraries and Information Services Adrian Wills BA DMS MCLIP
(0116 252 7327; e-mail: adrian.wills@leicester.gov.uk)
Performance and Project Manager Lee Warner BA(Hons) (0116 252 7306;
e-mail: lee.warner@leicester.gov.uk)
Service Delivery Manager Ms Sally Mitchell (e-mail: sally.mitchell@leicester.gov.uk)
Library Services Manager – Children and Young People Paul Gobey BA DipLib
MCLIP (0116 225 4997; e-mail: paul.gobey@leicester.gov.uk)

Central/largest libraries

Central Library – Learning and Information, Bishop Street, Leicester LE1 6AA
☎0116 299 5401
Fax 0116 299 5444
e-mail: central.reference@leicester.gov.uk

Central Library – Lending, 54 Belvoir Street, Leicester LE1 6QL
☎0116 299 5402 (enquiries)
Fax 0116 299 5434
e-mail: central.lending@leicester.gov.uk
Senior Manager - Central Libraries Michael Lewis

LEICESTERSHIRE
Authority: Leicestershire County Council

Library Services, County Hall, Glenfield, Leicester LE3 8TD
☎0116 305 7015 (enquiries), 0116 305 7363 (administration)
Fax 0116 305 7370
e-mail: libraries@leics.gov.uk
url: www.leics.gov.uk/libraries
Head of Library Services Ms Margaret Bellamy DMS MBA MCLIP
(e-mail: mbellamy@leics.gov.uk)
Service Delivery Manager Nigel Thomas BLib(Hons) MCLIP DPLM
(e-mail: nthomas@leics.gov.uk)
Development Manager: Special Projects Steve Kettle (0116 305 3801;
e-mail: steve.kettle@leics.gov.uk)
Development Manager Mrs Glenys Willars MA MCLIP (0116 305 3808;
e-mail: glenys.willars@leics.gov.uk)

Main library group HQs

Loughborough Library, Granby Street, Loughborough, Leics LE11 3DZ
☎(01509) 212985/266436
Fax (01509) 610594
Area Manager Ms Gill Loveridge BA MBA MCLIP (e-mail: gloveridge@leics.gov.uk)
Area Community Manager Ms Lesley Bowell BA MCLIP (e-mail: lbowell@leics.gov.uk)

Wigston Library, Bull Head Street, Wigston, Leicester LE18 1PA
☎0116 305 3689
Fax 0116 281 2985
Area Manager Mrs Lorraine Selby (e-mail: lselby@leics.gov.uk)
Area Community Manager Mrs Hilary Ward BA(Hons) PGDipLib MCLIP
(e-mail: hward@leics.gov.uk)

Market town libraries

Coalville Library, High Street, Coalville, Leics LE67 3EA
☎0116 305 3565
Fax (01530) 832019
Area Community Manager Ms Liz Evans (e-mail: levans@leics.gov.uk)

Hinckley Library, Lancaster Road, Hinckley, Leics LE10 0AT
☎(01455) 635106
Fax (01455) 251385
Area Community Manager Ms Tracey Beighton (e-mail: tbeighton@leics.gov.uk)

Melton Mowbray Library, Wilton Road, Melton Mowbray, Leics LE13 0UJ
☎0116 305 3646
Fax (01664) 410199
Area Community Managers Ms Ruth Pointer BA MCLIP (e-mail: rpointer@leics.gov.uk),
Mrs Jackie Knight MCLIP (e-mail: jknight@leics.gov.uk)

Pen Lloyd Library, Adam & Eve Street, Market Harborough, Leics LE16 7LT
☎0116 305 3627
Fax (01858) 821265
Area Community Managers Ms Ruth Pointer BA MCLIP (e-mail: rpointer@leics.gov.uk),
Mrs Jackie Knight MCLIP (e-mail: jknight@leics.gov.uk)

LEWISHAM
Authority: London Borough of Lewisham

Community Services, 2nd Floor, Laurence House, 1 Catford Road, London SE6 4RU
☎020 8314 8024 (enquiries)
Fax 020 8314 3229
url: www.lewisham.gov.uk
Library and Information Service Manager Dr Antonio Rizzo BA(Hons) MA(ISM)
(020 8314 8025; e-mail: antonio.rizzo@lewisham.gov.uk)
Service Manager Vacant
Children and Young Persons Librarian Ms Joanne Moulton BA DipIM MCLIP
(020 8314 7189; e-mail: joanne.moulton@lewisham.gov.uk)'

Central/largest library

Lewisham Library, 199-201 Lewisham High Street, London SE13 6LG
☎020 8314 9800
Fax 020 8297 1169
Central Librarian Victor Chapman BLib(Hons) MCLIP (e-mail:
victor.chapman@lewisham.gov.uk)

LINCOLNSHIRE
Authority: Lincolnshire County Council

**Community Services (Culture and Adult Education), County Offices, Newland, Lincoln
LN1 1YL**
☎(01522) 553207
Fax (01522) 552811
url: www.lincolnshire.gov.uk
Head of Libraries and Inclusion John Pateman BA DipLib MBA FCLIP (e-mail:
john.pateman@lincolnshire.gov.uk)
Network Manager East Gary Porter (01522 552831; e-mail:
gary.porter@lincolnshire.gov.uk)
Network Manager West Mike Cavanagh (01522 552839; e-mail:
mike.cavanagh@lincolnshire.gov.uk)

Central/largest libraries

Lincoln Central Library, Free School Lane, Lincoln LN2 1EZ
☎(01522) 782010
Fax (01522) 575011
e-mail: lincoln_library@lincolnshire.gov.uk

Mobile Library Services, Eastgate Centre, 105 Eastgate, Sleaford, Lincs NG34 7EN
☎(01522) 550361
Fax (01522) 550372

LIVERPOOL

Authority: Liverpool City Council

Liverpool Libraries and Information Services, Municipal Buildings, Dale Street, Liverpool L2 2DH
☎0151 233 6346
Fax 0151 233 6399
url: www.liverpool.gov.uk
Head of Libraries and Information Services Miss Joyce Little BA(Hons) MBA MCLIP
(e-mail: joyce.little@liverpool.gov.uk)
Manager, Information and Digital Services Alan Metcalf BSc DipLib MCLIP (0151 233 5808; e-mail: alan.metcalf@liverpool.gov.uk)
Manager, Learning and Diversity John Keane BA(Hons) MCLIP (0151 233 5833; e-mail: john.keane@liverpool.gov.uk)
Manager, Books and Lending Kenneth Kay BA(Hons) DipLib MCLIP (0151 233 5847; e-mail: kenneth.kay@liverpool.gov.uk)

Central/largest library

Central Library, William Brown Street, Liverpool L3 8EW
☎0151 233 5858 (enquiries), 0151 233 5851 (administration)
Fax 0151 233 5886 (enquiries), 0151 233 5824 (administration)
e-mail: refbt.central.library@liverpool.gov.uk

Other large libraries

Allerton Library, Liverpool L18 6HG
☎0151 233 3333
e-mail: allerton.library@liverpool.gov.uk

Childwall Fiveways Library, Liverpool L15 6QR
☎0151 722 3214
e-mail: childwall.library@liverpool.gov.uk

Norris Green Library, Townsend Avenue, Liverpool L11 5AF
☎0151 233 1090
e-mail: norrisgreen.library@liverpool.gov.uk

LONDON, CITY OF

Authority: City of London

Libraries, Archives and Guildhall Art Gallery, Aldermanbury, London EC2V 7HH

☎020 7332 1852
Fax 020 7600 3384
url: www.cityoflondon.gov.uk
Director David Pearson MA FCLIP FSA (e-mail: david.pearson@cityoflondon.gov.uk)
Assistant Director (Heritage) Dr Deborah Jenkins (e-mail:
deborah.jenkins@cityoflondon.gov.uk)
Assistant Director (Libraries) Barry Cropper MA DipLib MCLIP MCMI HonFCLIP
(e-mail: barry.cropper@cityoflondon.gov.uk)

Central/largest libraries

Barbican Library, Barbican Centre, Silk Street, London EC2Y 8DS
☎020 7638 0569
Fax 020 7638 2249
Librarian i/c John Lake BA MCLIP (e-mail: john.lake@cityoflondon.gov.uk)

Guildhall Library, Aldermanbury, London EC2V 7HH
☎020 7332 1868/1870
Fax 020 7600 3384
Librarian i/c Andrew Harper BA MCLIP (e-mail: andrew.harper@cityoflondon.gov.uk)

Regional/district libraries

Camomile Street Library, 12-20 Camomile Street, London EC3A 7EX
☎020 7247 8895
Fax 020 7377 2972
Librarian i/c Malcolm Key BA MCLIP (e-mail: malcolm.key@cityoflondon.gov.uk)

City Business Library, Aldermanbury, London EC2V 7HH
☎020 7332 1812
Fax 020 7332 1847
Librarian i/c Ms Goretti Considine MCLIP (e-mail: goretti.considine@cityoflondon.gov.uk)

Shoe Lane Library, Hill House, Little New Street, London EC4A 3JR
☎020 7583 7178
Fax 020 7353 0884
Librarian i/c Leslie King BA MCLIP (e-mail: leslie.king@cityoflondon.gov.uk)

LUTON
Authority: Luton Culture Services Trust for Luton Borough Council

Libraries Service, Central Library, St George's Square, Luton, Beds LU1 2NG
☎(01582) 547418 (enquiries)
Fax (01582) 547461
e-mail: lendinglibrary@lutonculture.com
url: www.lutonlibraries.co.uk
Director of Libraries Ms Jean George BA DMS MCLIP (01582 547422; e-mail:
jean.george@lutonculture.com)
Adult Services Manager Ms Fiona Marriott BA MCLIP (01582 547417; e-mail:
fiona.marriott@lutonculture.com)
Information Services and Electronic Delivery Manager Mrs Lucy Cross BLib MCLIP
(01582 547439; e-mail: lucy.cross@lutonculture.com)

Central/largest library

Central Library, St George's Square, Luton, Beds LU1 2NG
☎(01582) 547418
Library Manager Ms Julie Devine, Ms Sarah Barry (01582 547424) (job share)

Branch libraries

Leagrave Library and Luton Mobile Library Service, Marsh Road, Luton, Beds LU3 2NL
☎(01582) 556650
Fax (01582) 556651
Library Manager Mrs Claire Dimmock

Lewsey Library, Landrace Road, Luton, Beds LU4 0SW
☎(01582) 696094
Library Manager Mrs Julie Kelly

Marsh Farm Library and Luton Home Library Service, Purley Centre, Luton, Beds LU3 3SR
☎(01582) 574803/491428 (Home Library Service)
e-mail: homelibraryservice@lutonculture.com
Library Manager Ms Zoe Ayres

Stopsley Library, Hitchin Road, Luton, Beds LU2 7UG
☎(01582) 706368
Library Manager Mrs Pip Hipwell

Sundon Park Library, Hill Rise, Luton, Beds LU3 3EE
☎(01582) 574573
Library Manager Mrs Ann Soan

Wigmore Library, Wigmore Lane, Luton, Beds LU3 8DJ
☎(01582) 706340
Library Manager Mrs Jane Wigley

MANCHESTER
Authority: Manchester City Council

City Library, Elliot House, 151 Deansgate, Manchester M3 3WD
☎0161 234 1900
Fax 0161 274 7053
e-mail: libraries@manchester.gov.uk
url: www.manchester.gov.uk/libraries
Head of Library and Information Service Neil MacInnes
(e-mail: n.macinnes@manchester.gov.uk)
Head of Library Operations Mrs Eunice Long
Head of Children, Learning and Access Ms Wendy Broadbent BA MCLIP
(e-mail: w.broadbent@manchester.gov.uk), Ms Jill Sharp BA DipLib MCLIP
(e-mail: j.sharp@manchester.gov.uk)
Head of Information Services Ms Linda Dawes BA MCLIP
(e-mail: l.dawes@manchester.gov.uk)
Service Improvement Manager Paul Wright (e-mail: p.wright@manchester.gov.uk)
City Library Manager Steve Willis BA DipLib MCLIP (e-mail: s.willis@manchester.gov.uk)

Library Operations

Chorlton Group, Chorlton Library, Manchester Road, Chorlton, Manchester M21 9PN
☎0161 227 3700
Group Manager David Green (e-mail: d.green1@manchester.gov.uk)

Crumpsall Group, Crumpsall Library, Abraham Moss Centre, Manchester M8 5UF
☎0161 227 3777
Group Manager Ms Louise Cunningham (e-mail: l.cunningham@manchester.gov.uk)

Didsbury Group, Didsbury Library, 692 Wilmslow Road, Didsbury, Manchester M20 2DN
☎0161 277 3755
Group Manager Ms Gail Mallet (e-mail: g.mallet@manchester.gov.uk)

Forum Group, Forum Library, The Forum, Forum Square, Manchester M22 5RX
☎0161 277 3700
Group Manager Ms Fran Goddard (e-mail: f.goddard@manchester.gov.uk)

Longsight Group, Longsight Library, 519 Stockport Road, Manchester M12 4NE
☎0161 277 3706
Group Managers Ms Helen Blagborough BSc DipLib MCLIP (e-mail:
h.blagborough@manchester.gov.uk), Ms Sue Moores (e-mail:
s.moores@manchester.gov.uk)

Miles Platting Group, East City Library, Whitworth House, Ashton Old Road, Manchester
M11 2WH
☎0161 234 7021
Group Manager Ms Maxine Goulding (e-mail: m.goulding@manchester.gov.uk)

Mobile Services, Hammerstone Road Depot, Gorton, Manchester M18 8EQ
☎0161 227 3800
Group Manager Paul Fear (e-mail: p.fear@manchester.gov.uk)

MEDWAY
Authority: Medway Council

Chatham Library, Gun Wharf, Dock Road, Chatham, Kent ME4 4TX
☎(01634) 337799
Fax (01634) 337800
e-mail: chatham.library@medway.gov.uk/libraries
url: www.medway.gov.uk/libraries
Strategic Librarian Duncan Mead BA MCLIP (01634 337282; e-mail:
duncan.mead@medway.gov.uk), Ms Lyn Rainbow BA(Hons) MCLIP (01634 338736)

Central/largest libraries

Chatham Library, Gun Wharf, Dock Road, Chatham, Kent ME4 4TX
☎(01634) 337799
Fax (01634) 337800
e-mail: chatham.library@medway.gov.uk

Gillingham Library, High Street, Gillingham, Kent ME7 1BG
☎(01634) 337340
Fax (01634) 283805

Strood Library, 32 Bryant Road, Strood, Rochester, Kent ME2 3EP
☎(01634) 335890
Fax (01634) 297919

MERTON
Authority: London Borough of Merton

Libraries and Heritage Services, Merton Civic Centre, London Road, Morden, Surrey SM4 5DX
☎020 8545 3783
Fax 020 8545 3237
url: www.merton.gov.uk
Head of Libraries and Heritage Services Ms Ingrid Lackajis BA DipLib (020 8545 3770; e-mail: ingrid.lackajis@merton.gov.uk)
Libraries Performance and Operations Manager Anthony Hopkins (020 8545 4101; e-mail: anthony.hopkins@merton.gov.uk)
Services Manager Ms Annette Acquah (020 8545 4089; e-mail: annette.acquah@merton.gov.uk)

Main libraries

Mitcham Library, London Road, Mitcham, Surrey CR4 7YR
☎020 8274 5745
Fax 020 8646 6360
e-mail: mitcham.library@merton.gov.uk
Library Manager Vacant

Morden Library, Civic Centre, London Road, Morden, Surrey SM4 5DX
☎020 8545 4040
Fax 020 8545 4037
e-mail: morden.library@merton.gov.uk
Library Manager Ms Sarah Azhar

Wimbledon Library, Wimbledon Hill Road, London SW19 7NB
☎020 8274 5757/8 (reference); 020 8274 5759 (renewals)
Fax 020 8944 6804
e-mail: wimbledon.library@merton.gov.uk
Library Manager Vacant

Branch libraries

Aragon Library, Aragon School, Aragon Road, Morden, Surrey SM4 4QU
☎020 8274 5715
e-mail: aragon.library@merton.gov.uk
Information Officer Colin Robinson

Donald Hope Library (Colliers Wood), Cavendish House, High Street, London SW19 2HR
☎020 8274 5757
Fax 020 8543 9767
e-mail: donaldhope.library@merton.gov.uk
Library Manager Ms Chrysella Holder

Pollards Hill Library, South Lodge Avenue, Mitcham, Surrey CR4 1LT

☎020 8274 5745
Fax 020 8765 0925
e-mail: pollardshill.library@merton.gov.uk
Library Manager Vacant

Raynes Park Library, Approach Road, London SW20 8BA
☎020 8274 5718
Fax 020 8542 1893
e-mail: raynespark.library@merton.gov.uk
Library Manager Ms Chandra Kargupta

West Barnes Library, Station Road, New Malden, Surrey KT3 6JF
☎020 8274 5789
Fax 020 8336 0554
e-mail: westbarnes.library@merton.gov.uk
Library Manager Vacant

MIDDLESBROUGH
Authority: Middlesbrough Borough Council

Libraries and Information, Central Library, Victoria Square, Middlesbrough TS1 2AY
☎(01642) 729416 (administration)
Fax (01642) 729953
url: www.middlesbrough.gov.uk
Library Services Manager Mrs Jen Brittain BA (e-mail:
jen_brittain@middlesbrough.gov.uk)

Central/largest library

Central Library, Victoria Square, Middlesbrough TS1 2AY
☎(01642) 729002 (enquiries), (01642) 729416 (administration)
Fax (01642) 729953
Resources Manager Ms Julie Tweedy BA MCLIP (e-mail:
julie_tweedy@middlesbrough.gov.uk)
Operations Manager Mrs Diane Fleet (e-mail: diane_fleet@middlesbrough.gov.uk)

MILTON KEYNES
Authority: Milton Keynes Council

Central Library, 555 Silbury Boulevard, Milton Keynes MK9 3HL
☎(01908) 254050
Fax (01908) 254089
e-mail: central.library@milton-keynes.gov.uk
url: www.milton-keynes.gov.uk/libraries
Principal Librarian (Projects and Development) Ms Sally Elson BA DipLib MCLIP
Principal Librarian (Central Library Services) Dave Quayle BA MCLIP (01908 254068;
e-mail: dave.quayle@milton-keynes.gov.uk)
Principal Librarian (Reference and Information) Ms Helen Bowlt BA(Hons) MCLIP
(01908 254078; e-mail: helen.bowlt@milton-keynes.gov.uk), Mrs Michelle Herriman BA
DipLib MCLIP (e-mail: michelle.herriman@milton-keynes.gov.uk) (job-share)
Senior Librarian (Children and Young People) Mrs Emma Carrick BA MCLIP

(01908 254081; e-mail: emma.carrick@milton-keynes.gov.uk)
Learning and Skills Manager Ms Deborah Cooper (01908 254074; e-mail:
deborah.cooper@milton-keynes.gov.uk)

Community library

Bletchley Library, Westfield Road, Bletchley, Milton Keynes MK2 2RA
☎(01908) 372797
Fax (01908) 645562
Library Manager (Community Libraries) Ms Michelle Thomas BA DipLib MCLIP
(e-mail: michelle.thomas@milton-keynes.gov.uk)

NEWCASTLE UPON TYNE
Authority: Newcastle upon Tyne City Council

**Newcastle Libraries and Information Services, City Library, The Charles Avison Building,
33 Newbridge Street West, PO Box 88, Newcastle upon Tyne NEI 8AX**
☎0191 277 4100 (enquiries), 0191 277 4140 (administration)
Fax 0191 277 4137
e-mail: info@newcastle.gov.uk
url: www.newcastle.gov.uk/libraries
Head of Culture, Libraries and Lifelong Learning Tony Durcan BLib MCLIP (e-mail:
tony.durcan@newcastle.gov.uk)
City Libraries' Manager David Fay BA MCLIP (e-mail: david.fay@newcastle.gov.uk)
Libraries Development Manager: City Ms Angela Forster (0191 277 4148; e-mail:
angela.forster@newcastle.gov.uk)
Libraries Development Manager: Communities Mrs Janice Hall MCLIP (0191 277
4175; e-mail: janice.hall@newcastle.gov.uk)
Systems Manager Andrew Scrogham BA MCLIP (e-mail:
andrew.scrogham@newcastle.gov.uk)
Facilities and Buildings Manager Mark Thurston (0191 277 4167; e-mail:
mark.thurston@newcastle.gov.uk)

NEWHAM
Authority: London Borough of Newham

Customer Services, Northern Dockside, 1000 Dockside Road, London E16 2QU
☎020 8430 2000 (Council switchboard)
url: www.newham.gov.uk
Divisional Director of Customer Services Robert Caister (ext 31062)
Customer Service Managers Ms Angelina Leatherbarrow (ext 33610), Tony Farrell
(ext 31745), Ron Springer (ext 33510), Franklin Ushedo (ext 37215)
Customer Service Support Manager Mrs Alexis Wainwright (ext 37215)

Largest library

Stratford Library, 3 The Grove, Stratford, London E15 1EL
☎020 3373 0826 (Main), 020 3373 6881 (Archives & Local Studies)
Customer Service Manager Ron Springer

Branch libraries

Beckton Globe Library, 1 Kingsford Way, London E6 5JQ
☎020 3373 0853
Customer Service Manager Tony Farrell

Canning Town Library, Barking Road, Canning Town, London E16 4HQ
☎020 3373 0854
Customer Service Manager Tony Farrell

Custom House Library, Prince Regent Lane, London E16 3JJ
☎020 3373 0855
Customer Service Manager Tony Farrell

East Ham Library, High Street South, London E6 6EL
☎020 3373 0827
Customer Service Manager Ms Angelina Leatherbarrow

Green Street Library, 337–341 Green Street, Upton Park, London E13 9AR
☎020 3373 0857
Customer Service Manager Franklin Ushedo

Library @ The Gate, 4–20 Woodgrange Road, Forest Gate, London E7 0QH
☎020 3373 0856
Customer Service Manager Ron Springer

Manor Park Library, Romford Road, Manor Park, London E12 5JY
☎020 3373 0858
Customer Service Manager Ms Angelina Leatherbarrow

North Woolwich Library, 5 Pier Parade, North Woolwich, London E16 2LJ
☎020 3373 0843
Customer Service Manager Tony Farrell

Plaistow Library, North Street, Plaistow, London E13 9HL
☎020 3373 0859
Customer Service Manager Franklin Ushedo

NORFOLK
Authority: Norfolk County Council

Library and Information Service, County Hall, Martineau Lane, Norwich NR1 2UA
☎(01603) 222049
Fax (01603) 222422
e-mail: libraries@norfolk.gov.uk
url: www.library.norfolk.gov.uk
Head of Libraries and Assistant Director Community Services (Cultural Services and Libraries) Mrs Jennifer Holland BA(Hons) MCLIP MCMI (01603 222272; e-mail: jennifer.holland@norfolk.gov.uk)
Finance and Business Support Manager John Perrott DMF (01603 222054; e-mail: john.perrott@norfolk.gov.uk)
Assistant Heads of Service – Localities Ms Sarah Hassan BA(Hons) MA MCLIP (01362 656976; e-mail: sarah.hassan@norfolk.gov.uk), Ms Jan Holden BA(Hons) DipLib MA (01603 774701; e-mail: janet.holden@norfolk.gov.uk)

Assistant Head of Service – Development Mrs Lorna Payne MA MCLIP (01603 222273; e-mail: lorna.payne@norfolk.gov.uk)

Central/largest libraries

Dereham Library, 59 High Street, Dereham, Norfolk NR19 1DZ
☎(01362) 693184
Fax (01362) 691891
e-mail: dereham.lib@norfolk.gov.uk
Assistant Head of Service Ms Sarah Hassan BA(Hons) MA MCLIP (e-mail: sarah.hassan@norfolk.gov.uk)

Gorleston Library, Lowestoft Road, Gorleston, Norfolk NR31 6SG
☎(01493) 662156
Fax (01493) 446010
e-mail: gorleston.lib@norfolk.gov.uk
Assistant Head of Service Ms Jan Holden BA(Hons) DipLib MA (e-mail: janet.holden@norfolk.gov.uk)

Great Yarmouth Library, Tolhouse Street, Great Yarmouth, Norfolk NR30 2SH
☎(01493) 844551
Fax (01493) 857628
e-mail: yarmouth.lib@norfolk.gov.uk
Assistant Head of Service Ms Jan Holden BA(Hons) DipLib MA (e-mail: janet.holden@norfolk.gov.uk)

King's Lynn Library, London Road, King's Lynn, Norfolk PE30 5EZ
☎(01553) 772568
Fax (01553) 769832
e-mail: kings.lynn.lib@norfolk.gov.uk
Assistant Head of Service Ms Sarah Hassan BA(Hons) MA MCLIP (e-mail: sarah.hassan@norfolk.gov.uk)

Norfolk and Norwich Millennium Library, The Forum, Millennium Plain, Norwich NR2 1AW
☎(01603) 774774
Fax (01603) 774705
e-mail: millennium.lib@norfolk.gov.uk
Assistant Head of Service Ms Jan Holden BA(Hons) DipLib MA (e-mail: janet.holden@norfolk.gov.uk)

Thetford Library, Raymond Street, Thetford, Norfolk IP24 2EA
☎(01842) 752048
Fax (01842) 750125
e-mail: thetford.lib@norfolk.gov.uk
Assistant Head of Service Ms Sarah Hassan BA(Hons) MA MCLIP (e-mail: sarah.hassan@norfolk.gov.uk)

Area library HQs

North, South and West Area HQ, Dereham Library, 59 High Street, Dereham, Norfolk NR19 1DZ
☎(01362) 693184
Fax (01362) 691891

e-mail: dereham.lib@norfolk.gov.uk
Assistant Head of Service Ms Sarah Hassan BA(Hons) MA MCLIP (e-mail: sarah.hassan@norfolk.gov.uk)

Norwich and East Area HQ, Norfolk and Norwich Millennium Library, The Forum, Millennium Plain, Norwich NR2 1AW
☎(01603) 774774
Fax (01603) 774705
e-mail: millennium.lib@norfolk.gov.uk
Assistant Head of Service Ms Jan Holden BA(Hons) DipLib MA (e-mail: janet.holden@norfolk.gov.uk)

NORTH EAST LINCOLNSHIRE
Authority: North East Lincolnshire Council

Central Library, Town Hall Square, Grimsby, North East Lincs DN31 1HG
☎(01472) 323600 (enquiries), (01472) 323617 (administration)
Fax (01472) 323618
e-mail: librariesandmuseums@nelincs.gov.uk
url: www.nelincs.gov.uk
Head of Cultural Services Steve Hipkins BA(Hons) MA DipLib MCLIP (01472 323611; e-mail: steve.hipkins@nelincs.gov.uk)
Principal Librarian (Customer Services) Mrs Joan Sargent BA DipLib (01472 323614; e-mail: joan.sargent@nelincs.gov.uk)
Principal Librarian (Strategy) Ms Anna Worrall (01472 323612; e-mail: anna.worrall@nelincs.gov.uk)

Branch libraries

Cleethorpes Library, Alexandra Road, Cleethorpes, North East Lincs DN35 8LG
☎(01472) 323648/323650
Fax (01472) 323652

Grant Thorold Library, Durban Road, Grimsby, North East Lincs DN32 8BX
☎(01472) 323631
Fax (01472) 323816

Humberston Library, Church Lane, Humberston, North East Lincs DN36 4HT
☎(01472) 323682

Immingham Library, Civic Centre, Pelham Road, Immingham, North East Lincs DN40 1QF
☎(01469) 516050
Fax (01469) 516051

Laceby Library, The Stanford Centre, Cooper Lane, Laceby, North East Lincs DN37 7AX
☎(01472) 323684

Nunsthorpe Library, Grimsby Institute of Further and Higher Education, Nunsthorpe, Community Campus, Sutcliffe Avenue, Grimsby, North East Lincs DN33 1AW
☎(01472) 323636

Scartho Learning Centre and Library, St Giles Avenue, Grimsby, North East Lincs DN33 2HB
☎(01472) 323638

Waltham Library, High Street, Waltham, North East Lincs DN37 0LL
☎(01472) 323656

Willows Library, Binbrook Way, Grimsby, North East Lincs DN37 9AS
☎(01472) 323679

NORTH LINCOLNSHIRE
Authority: North Lincolnshire Council

Scunthorpe Central Library, Carlton Street, Scunthorpe, North Lincs DN15 6TX
☎(01724) 860161 (tel/fax)
e-mail: ref.library@northlincs.gov.uk
url: www.northlincs.gov.uk/library/
Head of Library and Information Services Ms Helen Rowe BA DipLib MCLIP (e-mail: helen.rowe@northlincs.gov.uk)
Assistant Library Manager (Children and Young People Services) Colin Brabazon
BA DipLib MCLIP (e-mail: colin.brabazon@northlincs.gov.uk)

NORTH SOMERSET
Authority: North Somerset Council

Libraries Office, The Winter Gardens, Royal Parade, Weston-super-Mare, Somerset BS23 1AQ
☎(01934) 426658
Fax (01934) 427230
url: www.librarieswest.org.uk (online catalogue); www.n-somerset.gov.uk/leisure/libraries
Library and Information Service Manager Andy Brisley BLib MCLIP (e-mail: andy.brisley@n-somerset.gov.uk)

Largest library

Weston Library, The Boulevard, Weston-super-Mare, Somerset BS23 1PL
☎(01934) 426010
Fax (01934) 426956
e-mail: weston.library@n-somerset.gov.uk
Customer Services Manager Ms Mary Lamb MCLIP (e-mail: mary.lamb@n-somerset.gov.uk)

NORTH TYNESIDE
Authority: North Tyneside Council

Central Library, Northumberland Square, North Shields, Tyne and Wear NE30 1QU
☎0191 643 5270
Fax 0191 200 6118
e-mail: central.library@northtyneside.gov.uk
url: www.northtyneside.gov.uk/libraries
Senior Manager, Serving Communities Delivery Team Mrs Julia Stafford BA MCLIP
(e-mail: julia.stafford@northtyneside.gov.uk)
Area Manager, North East (Whitley Bay) Ms Andrea Stephenson BA MCLIP (e-mail: andrea.stephenson@northtyneside.gov.uk)

Area Manager, North West (Killingworth) Ms Paula Harvey BA(Hons) ILM BSc CBIS MCLIP (e-mail: paula.harvey@northtyneside.gov.uk)
Area Manager, South East (North Shields) Mrs Gayle Taylor BSc(Hons) MCLIP (e-mail: gayle.taylor@northtyneside.gov.uk)
Area Manager, South West (Wallsend) Ms Yvonne Gorgon BA(Hons) PGCE (e-mail: yvonne.gorgon@northtyneside.gov.uk)

Main libraries

Killingworth Library, White Swan Centre, Citadel East, Killingworth, Tyne and Wear NE12 6SS
☎(0191) 643 2040
Fax (0191) 643 8536
e-mail: killingworth.library@northtyneside.gov.uk

Wallsend Library, Ferndale Avenue, Wallsend, Tyne and Wear NE28 7NB
☎0191 643 2075
Fax 0191 643 5839
e-mail: wallsend.library@northtyneside.gov.uk

Whitley Bay Library, Park Road, Whitley Bay, Tyne and Wear NE26 1EJ
☎0191 200 8500
Fax 0191 200 8536
e-mail: whitleybay.library@northtyneside.gov.uk

NORTH YORKSHIRE
Authority: North Yorkshire County Council

Adult and Community Services (Library and Community Services), Library HQ, 21 Grammar School Lane, Northallerton, North Yorks DL6 1DF
☎(01609) 533800 (enquiries and administration)
Fax (01609) 780793
e-mail: libraries@northyorks.gov.uk
url: www.northyorks.gov.uk/libraries
Assistant Director (Library and Community Services) Ms Julie Blaisdale BA(Hons) MCLIP (e-mail: julie.blaisdale@northyorks.gov.uk)
General Manager: Archives, Registrations and Coroners Services Ms Lesley Willetts BA DipLib MCLIP (e-mail: lesley.willetts@northyorks.gov.uk)
General Manager: Libraries Ms Chrys Mellor BSc(Econ) DipLib MCLIP (e-mail: chrys.mellor@northyorks.gov.uk)
Management Co-ordinators Miss Barbara Poole BA MCLIP (e-mail: barbara.poole@northyorks.gov.uk), Mrs Judith Walsh (e-mail: judith.walsh@northyorks.gov.uk), Lee Taylor BA(Hons) MA MCLIP (e-mail: lee.taylor@northyorks.gov.uk)
Manager: Children and Schools Mrs Brenda Hooper BSc MCLIP (e-mail: brenda.hooper@northyorks.gov.uk)

Larger libraries

Harrogate Library and Information Centre, Victoria Avenue, Harrogate, North Yorks HG1 1EG
☎0845 034 9520 (Lending), 0845 034 9521 (Reference)

Fax (01423) 523158
e-mail: harrogate.library@northyorks.gov.uk
url: www.northyorks.gov.uk/libraries/branches/harrogate.shtm

Scarborough Library and Information Centre, Vernon Road, Scarborough, North Yorks
YO11 2NN
☎0845 034 9516 (Lending), 0845 034 9517 (Reference)
Fax (01723) 353893
e-mail: scarborough.library@northyorks.gov.uk
url: www.northyorks.gov.uk/libraries/branches/scarborough.shtm
Principal Officer Lee Taylor BA(Hons) MA MCLIP (01609 533588; e-mail:
lee.taylor@northyorks.gov.uk)

(Note: These do not represent the full list of Library and Information Centres. Please see
website for more details: www.northyorks.gov.uk/libraries)

NORTHAMPTONSHIRE
Authority: Northamptonshire County Council

Libraries HQ, Customer and Cultural Services, PO Box 216, John Dryden House,
8-10 The Lakes, Northampton NN4 7DD
☎(01604) 236236
Fax (01604) 237937
e-mail: nlis@northamptonshire.gov.uk
url: www.northamptonshire.gov.uk
Customer and Library Service Manager Ms Grace Kempster OBE BA(Hons) MLib
MCLIP FRSA (e-mail: gkempster@northamptonshire.gov.uk)

Area libraries

Central Library, Abington Street, Northampton NN1 2BA
☎(01604) 462040
Fax (01604) 462055
Principal Librarian Ms Barbara Leigh (e-mail: bleigh@northamptonshire.gov.uk)

Daventry Library, North Street, Daventry, Northants NN11 4GH
☎(01327) 703130
Fax (01327) 300501
Principal Librarian Ms Robyn Davison (e-mail: rdavison@northamptonshire.gov.uk)

Kettering Library, Sheep Street, Kettering, Northants NN16 0AY
☎(01536) 512315
Fax (01536) 411349
Principal Librarian Mrs Anne Lovely BA(Hons) MCLIP (e-mail:
alovely@northamptonshire.gov.uk)

NORTHUMBERLAND
Authority: Northumberland County Council

County Hall, Morpeth, Northumberland NE61 2EF
☎(0845) 600 6400
Fax (01670) 511413

e-mail: ask@northumberland.gov.uk
url: www.northumberland.gov.uk
County Heritage and Libraries Manager Ms Marguerite Gracey BA(Hons) DMS MCLIP
(e-mail: marguerite.gracey@northumberland.gov.uk)

Central/largest library

Morpeth Library, Gas House Lane, Morpeth, Northumberland NE61 1TA
☎(01670) 500390
Library Development and Resources Manager Ms Eileen Parker (01670 714371;
e-mail: eileen.parker@northumberland.gov.uk)
Library Operations Manager Mrs Ann Blakeley BA MCLIP DMS (e-mail:
ann.blakeley@northumberland.gov.uk)

Larger libraries

Alnwick Library, Green Batt, Alnwick, Northumberland NE66 1TU
☎(01665) 602689

Ashington Library, Kenilworth Road, Ashington, Northumberland NE63 8AA
☎(01670) 813245

Bedlington Library, Glebe Road, Bedlington, Northumberland NE22 6JX
☎(01670) 822056

Berwick Library, Walkergate, Berwick-upon-Tweed, Northumberland TD15 1DB
☎(01289) 334051

Blyth Library, Bridge Street, Blyth, Northumberland NE24 2DJ
☎(01670) 361352

Cramlington Library, Forum Way, Cramlington, Northumberland NE23 6QD
☎(01670) 714371

Hexham Library, Queen's Hall, Beaumont Street, Hexham, Northumberland NE46 3LS
☎(01434) 652488

Ponteland Library, Thornhill Road, Ponteland, Newcastle upon Tyne NE20 9PZ
☎(01661) 823594

Prudhoe Library, Front Street, Prudhoe, Northumberland NE42 5AA
☎(01661) 832540

NOTTINGHAM
Authority: City of Nottingham Council

Department of Communities, Libraries and Information Service, Loxley House, Station Street, Nottingham NG2 3NG
☎0115 915 2828
Fax 0115 915 8680
e-mail: enquiryline@nottinghamcity.gov.uk
url: www.mynottinghamcity.gov.uk/libraries
Joint Heads of Service, Libraries and Information Service Ms Christina Dyer BA
MCLIP (0115 876 4967; e-mail: christina.dyer@nottinghamcity.gov.uk), Ms Natalie Sellears
(0115 876 4968; e-mail: natalie.sellears@nottinghamcity.gov.uk)

Central/largest library

Nottingham Central Library, Angel Row, Nottingham NG1 6HP
☎0115 915 2828
Fax 0115 915 2850
e-mail: enquiryline@nottinghamcity.gov.uk
url: www.mynottinghamcity.gov.uk/libraries
Senior Library Manager Martin Willis (0115 915 2862; e-mail:
martin.willis@nottinghamcity.gov.uk)

NOTTINGHAMSHIRE
Authority: Nottinghamshire County Council

Communities Department, 4th Floor, County Hall, West Bridgford, Nottingham NG2 7QP
☎0115 977 4401
Fax 0115 977 2806
url: www.nottinghamshire.gov.uk/libraries
Head of Libraries, Archives and Information Peter Gaw BA MCLIP (0115 977 4201;
e-mail: peter.gaw@nottscc.gov.uk)
Assistant Head of Libraries Philip Marshall BA MCLIP (0115 982 9036; e-mail:
philip.marshall@nottscc.gov.uk) (based at Glaisdale Parkway)
Service Manager Libraries: Children, Youth and Inclusion Ms Carol Newman BA
MCLIP (e-mail: carol.newman@nottscc.gov.uk)
Service Manager Libraries: Customers, Staff and Development Mrs Kath Owen BA
MCLIP (0115 977 4437; e-mail: kath.owen@nottscc.gov.uk)
Service Manager Libraries: Information, Learning and Programmes Mrs Linda
Turner BA MCLIP (01777 708724; e-mail: linda.turner@nottscc.gov.uk)
Service Manager Libraries: Readers and Resources Ms Anne Corin BA MCLIP
(0115 982 9031; e-mail: anne.corin@nottscc.gov.uk), Ms Kirsty Blyth BA MCLIP (e-mail:
kirsty.blyth@nottscc.gov.uk) (job-share)
Service Manager Libraries: Systems and Performance Nick London BA MCLIP
(0115 982 9029; e-mail: nick.london@nottscc.gov.uk)

Central/largest library

Mansfield County Library, Four Seasons Centre, Westgate, Mansfield, Notts NG18 1NH
☎(01623) 627591
Fax (01623) 629276
e-mail: mansfield.library@nottscc.gov.uk

District libraries

Arnold County Library, Front Street, Arnold, Nottingham NG5 7EE
☎0115 920 2247
Fax 0115 967 3378
e-mail: arnold.library@nottscc.gov.uk

Beeston County Library, Foster Avenue, Beeston, Nottingham NG9 1AE
☎0115 925 5168
Fax 0115 922 0841
e-mail: beeston.library@nottscc.gov.uk

Mansfield County Library, Four Seasons Centre, Westgate, Mansfield, Notts NG18 1NH
☎(01623) 627591
Fax (01623) 629276
e-mail: mansfield.library@nottscc.gov.uk

Newark County Library, Beaumond Gardens, Baldertongate, Newark-on-Trent, Notts
NG24 1UW
☎(01636) 703966
Fax (01636) 610045
e-mail: newark.library@nottscc.gov.uk

Retford County Library, Churchgate, Retford, Notts DN22 6PE
☎(01777) 708724
Fax (01777) 710020
e-mail: retford.library@nottscc.gov.uk

Sutton in Ashfield Library, Idlewells Precinct, Sutton in Ashfield, Notts NG17 1BP
☎(01623) 556296
Fax (01623) 551962
e-mail: sutton.library@nottscc.gov.uk

West Bridgford Library, Bridgford Road, West Bridgford, Nottingham NG8 4GP
☎0115 981 6506
Fax 0115 981 3199
e-mail: westbridgford.library@nottscc.gov.uk

Other services

Support Services, Units 4-6, Glaisdale Parkway, Bilborough, Nottingham NG8 4GP
☎0115 985 4242
Fax 0115 928 6400

OLDHAM
Authority: Oldham Metropolitan Borough Council

Oldham Library, Cultural Quarter, Greaves Street, Oldham, Lancashire OL1 1AL
☎0161 770 8000 (general enquiries)
e-mail: oldham.library@oldham.gov.uk
url: www.oldham.gov.uk
Head of Heritage, Libraries and Arts Ms Sheena Macfarlane (0161 770 4664;
fax: 0161 770 4855; e-mail: sheena.macfarlane@oldham.gov.uk)

OXFORDSHIRE
Authority: Oxfordshire County Council

Social and Community Services, Community Services, Holton, Oxford OX33 1QQ
☎(01865) 810200
Fax (01865) 713927
url: www.oxfordshire.gov.uk/libraries
County Librarian Ms Caroline Taylor BA(Hons) DipLib MCLIP (01865 810212;
fax: 01865 713928; e-mail: carolinej.taylor@oxfordshire.gov.uk)

Central/largest library

Central Library, Westgate, Oxford OX1 1DJ
☎(01865) 815509
Fax (01865) 721694
e-mail: oxfordcentral.library@oxfordshire.gov.uk
Customer Service Manager Mrs Shirley Toase BA MCLIP (e-mail:
shirley.toase@oxfordshire.gov.uk)

Additional services

Strategy and Development, Social and Community Services, Community Services, Holton,
Oxford OX33 1QQ
☎(01865) 810203
Fax (01865) 713928
Assistant County Librarian Ms Jillian Southwell BA(Hons) DipLib MCLIP
(e-mail: jillian.southwell@oxfordshire.gov.uk)

Customer Services, Social and Community Services, Community Services, Banbury Library,
Marlborough Road, Banbury, Oxon OX16 5DB
☎(01295) 268249
Fax (01295) 264331
Assistant County Librarian Mrs Yvonne McDonald BA DMS DipLib MCLIP
(e-mail: yvonne.mcdonald@oxfordshire.gov.uk)

ICT and Service Support, Social and Community Services, Community Services, Holton,
Oxford OX33 1QQ
☎(01865) 810221
Fax (01865) 713928
Assistant County Librarian Charles Pettit MA MA(Lib) MCLIP
(e-mail: charles.pettit@oxfordshire.gov.uk)

PETERBOROUGH
Authority: Peterbrough Cultural and Leisure Trust trading as Vivacity

Central Library, Broadway, Peterborough PE1 1RX
☎(01733) 864280
Fax (01733) 319140
e-mail: libraries@vivacity-peterborough.com
url: www.vivacity-peterborough.com
Library and Customer Services Manager Ms Heather Walton BLS MCLIP (e-mail:
heather.walton@vivacity-peterborough.com)

District libraries

Bretton Library, Bretton Centre, Bretton, Peterborough PE3 8DS
☎(01733) 864280
e-mail: brettonlibrary@vivacity-peterborough.com

Orton Library, Orton Centre, Orton, Peterborough PE2 0RQ
☎(01733) 864280
e-mail: ortonlibrary@vivacity-peterborough.com

Werrington Library, Staniland Way, Werrington, Peterborough PE4 6JT
☎(01733) 864280
e-mail: werringtonlibrary@vivacity-peterborough.com

Community libraries

Dogsthorpe Library, Central Avenue, Dogsthorpe, Peterborough PE1 4LH
☎(01733) 864280
e-mail: dogsthorpelibrary@vivacity-peterborough.com

Eye Library, Crowland Road, Eye, Peterborough PE6 7TN
☎(01733) 864280
e-mail: eyelibrary@vivacity-peterborough.com

Hampton Library, Serpentine Green, Hampton, Peterborough PE7 8DR
☎(01733) 864280
e-mail: hamptonlibrary@vivacity-peterborough.com

Stanground Library, Southfields Avenue, Stanground, Peterborough PE2 8RZ
☎(01733) 864280
e-mail: stangroundlibrary@vivacity-peterborough.com

Thorney Library, Church Street, Thorney, Peterborough PE6 0QB
☎(01733) 864280
e-mail: thorneylibrary@vivacity-peterborough.com

Woodston Library, Orchard Street, Woodston, Peterborough PE2 9AL
☎(01733) 864280
e-mail: woodstonlibrary@vivacity-peterborough.com

PLYMOUTH
Authority: Plymouth City Council

Library and Information Services, Central Library, Drake Circus, Plymouth PL4 8AL
☎(01752) 305923 (enquiries and administration)
Fax (01752) 305929
e-mail: library@plymouth.gov.uk
url: www.plymouthlibraries.info; www.cyberlibrary.org.uk
City Librarian Alasdair MacNaughtan BA MCLIP DMS MCMI (01752 305901; e-mail: alasdair.macnaughtan@plymouth.gov.uk)
Resources Manager (Personnel & Finance) Frank Lowry MCLIP (01752 305911; e-mail: frank.lowry@plymouth.gov.uk)
Resources Manager (Stock & Services) Chris Goddard BMus DipLib MCLIP (01752 305900; e-mail: chris.goddard@plymouth.gov.uk)
Central Library Manager Shaun Standfield BSc (01752 306792; e-mail: shaun.standfield@plymouth.gov.uk)
Young People's Services Manager Ms Julia Hale BEd MA (01752 306799; e-mail: julia.hale@plymouth.gov.uk)

POOLE
Authority: Borough of Poole

Culture and Community Learning, Central Library, Dolphin Centre, Poole, Dorset BH15 1QE

☎(01202) 262400
Fax (01202) 262431
url: www.poole.gov.uk
Head of Culture and Community Learning Kevin McErlane BA(Hons) DipLib MBA
(e-mail: k.mcerlane@poole.gov.uk)
Library Services Development Manager John Lane MCLIP (01202 262433; e-mail:
john.lane@poole.gov.uk)
Library Services Operations Manager Chas Rowling (01202 262423; e-mail:
c.rowling@poole.gov.uk)

Central/largest library

Central Library, Dolphin Centre, Poole, Dorset BH15 1QE
☎(01202) 262424
e-mail: centrallibrary@poole.gov.uk
Librarian Mrs V Grier BA MCLIP (01202 262436; e-mail: v.grier@poole.gov.uk)

Healthpoint (health information centre also serving Dorset) e-mail:
healthpoint@poole.gov.uk

PORTSMOUTH
Authority: Portsmouth City Council

Library Service, Central Library, Guildhall Square, Portsmouth PO1 2DX
☎023 9268 8058
Fax 023 9283 9855
e-mail: library.admin@portsmouthcc.gov.uk
url: www.portsmouth.gov.uk/learning/29.html
Library Service Manager Mrs Lindy Elliott BA MCLIP (e-mail:
lindy.elliott@portsmouthcc.gov.uk)

School Library Service, Saxon Shore Infants School, Jubilee Avenue, Paulsgrove, Portsmouth
PO6 4QJ
☎023 9232 6612
e-mail: school.library@portsmouthcc.gov.uk

Branch libraries

Alderman Lacey Library, Tangier Road, Copnor, Portsmouth PO3 6HU
☎023 9282 3991 (tel/fax)
e-mail: alderman.library@portsmouthcc.gov.uk

Beddow Library, Milton Road, Milton, Portsmouth PO4 8PR
☎023 9273 1848 (tel/fax)
e-mail: beddow.library@portsmouthcc.gov.uk

Carnegie Library, Fratton Road, Fratton, Portsmouth PO1 5EZ
☎023 9282 2581
Fax 023 9273 9244
e-mail: carnegie.library@portsmouthcc.gov.uk

Cosham Library, Spur Road, Cosham, Portsmouth PO6 3ED

☎023 9237 6023
Fax 023 9237 1877
e-mail: cosham.library@portsmouthcc.gov.uk

Elm Grove Library, Elm Grove, Southsea, Portsmouth PO5 1LJ
☎023 9282 6058
e-mail: elmgrove.library@portsmouthcc.gov.uk

North End Library, Gladys Avenue, North End, Portsmouth PO2 9AX
☎023 9266 2651
Fax 023 9266 8151
e-mail: northend.library@portsmouthcc.gov.uk

Paulsgrove Library, Marsden Road, Paulsgrove, Portsmouth PO6 4JB
☎023 9237 7818 (tel/fax)
e-mail: paulsgrove.library@portsmouth.gov.uk

Portsea Library, St James Street, Portsea, Portsmouth PO1 3AP
☎023 9229 7072
e-mail: johnpounds.library@portsmouthcc.gov.uk

Community library services

Carnegie Library, Fratton Road, Fratton, Portsmouth PO1 5EZ
☎023 9275 1737
Fax 023 9273 9244
e-mail: community.library@portsmouthcc.gov.uk

READING
Authority: Reading Borough Council

Reading Central Library, Abbey Square, Reading RG1 3BQ
☎0118 901 5905/6
Fax 0118 901 5954
e-mail: info@readinglibraries.org.uk
url: www.readinglibraries.org.uk
Libraries and Resources Manager Ms Alison England BA(Hons) DipLib MCLIP
(0118 901 5970)
Resources Manager Ms Sara Walkinshaw
Support Staff Manager Ms Karen Eccles

Branch libraries

Battle Library, 420 Oxford Road, Reading RG3 1EE
☎0118 901 5100
Fax 0118 901 5101
Branch Manager Mrs Marjorie McClure

Caversham Library, Church Street, Caversham, Reading RG4 8AU
☎0118 901 5103
Fax 0118 901 5104
Branch Manager Ms Virginia Hobbs

Mobile Services, c/o Tilehurst Library, School Road, Tilehurst, Reading RG1 5AS

☎0118 901 5118
Manager Ms Dawn Littlefield

Palmer Park Library, St Bartholomew's Road, Reading RG1 3QB
☎0118 901 5106
Fax 0118 901 5107
Branch Manager Miss Christine Gosling

Southcote Library, Southcote Lane, Reading RG3 3BA
☎0118 901 5109
Fax 0118 901 5110
Branch Manager Mrs Eunice Long

Tilehurst Library, School Road, Tilehurst, Reading RG3 5AS
☎0118 901 5112
Fax 0118 901 5113
Branch Manager Andrew Mitchell

Whitley Library, Northumberland Avenue, Reading RG2 7PX
☎0118 901 5115
Fax 0118 901 5116
Branch Managers Mrs Caroline Kelly, Ms Jan Westall

REDBRIDGE
Authority: London Borough of Redbridge

Central Library, Clements Road, Ilford, Essex IG1 1EA
☎020 8478 7145
Fax 020 8708 2431
url: www.redbridge.gov.uk/libraries
Head of Cultural and Libraries Gareth Morley (e-mail:
gareth.morley@redbridge.gov.uk)
Library Services Manager Ms Anne Annison (e-mail: anne.annison@redbridge.gov.uk)
Principal Librarian: Customer Services and Staff Development Mrs Rosamund
Willis-Fear BA(Hons) MCLIP (e-mail: ros.willis-fear@redbridge.gov.uk)
Library Development Manager Ms Catherine Ball (e-mail:
catherine.ball@redbridge.gov.uk)
Principal Librarian, Young People and Schools Archie Black LLB DipLib MCLIP
(e-mail: archie.black@redbridge.gov.uk) (In charge of South Woodford, Wanstead,
Aldersbrook, Woodford Green Libraries and Schools Library Service)
Principal Librarian, Community and Reader Development Nick Dobson BA DipLib
(e-mail: nick.dobson@redbridge.gov.uk) (In charge of Fullwell Cross, Clayhall, Gants Hill,
Goodmayes and Hainault Libraries and Stock Services)
Senior Community Librarians Ms Rosemary Kennedy BA(Hons) MCLIP, Mrs Evelyn Reid
BA MCLIP (e-mail: evelyn.reid@redbridge.gov.uk), John Weeks MCLIP (e-mail:
john.weeks@redbridge.gov.uk), Ms Lesley Gould BA(Hons) MCLIP (e-mail:
lesley.gould@redbridge.gov.uk), Ms Jill Keeling (e-mail: jill.keeling@redbridge.gov.uk),
Archie Black LLB DipLib MCLIP (e-mail: archie.black@redbridge.gov.uk), Ms Elaine Sahlke
(e-mail: elaine.sahlke@redbridge.gov.uk), Ms Mina Rehman (e-mail:
mina.rehman@redbridge.gov.uk), Ms Rhonda Brooks (e-mail:
rhonda.brooks@redbridge.gov.uk)

Community Librarians Nick Spokes BA DipLib, Jon Woolf MA BA(Hons), Michael Fountain BA DipLib, Ms Alison Finch, Ms Donna Howells
Stock Services Manager Mrs Asifa Hussain (e-mail: asifa.hussain@redbridge.gov.uk)
Reference Librarian Joe Daggers (e-mail: joe.daggers@redbridge.gov.uk)
Assistant Reference Librarian Mrs Paula Wade (e-mail: paula.wade@redbridge.gov.uk)

Branch libraries

Aldersbrook Library, 2a Park Road, London E12 5HQ
☎020 8496 0006
Branch Manager Ms Alice Bird (e-mail: alice.bird@redbridge.gov.uk)

Clayhall Library, 1 Claybury Broadway, Clayhall, Ilford, Essex IG5 0LQ
☎020 8708 9340
Branch Manager James Fisher (e-mail: james.fisher@redbridge.gov.uk)
Senior Library Assistant Bill Foxwell (e-mail: bill.foxwell@redbridge.gov.uk)

Fullwell Cross Library, 140 High Street, Barkingside, Ilford, Essex IG6 2EA
☎020 8708 9281
Branch Manager James Fisher (e-mail: james.fisher@redbridge.gov.uk)

Gants Hill Library, 490 Cranbrook Road, Gants Hill, Ilford, Essex IG2 6LA
☎020 8708 9275
Branch Manager Ms Caroline Rudwick (e-mail: caroline.rudwick@redbridge.gov.uk)

Goodmayes Library, 76 Goodmayes Lane, Goodmayes, Ilford, Essex IG3 9QB
☎020 8708 7750
Branch Manager Matthew Alexander (e-mail: matthew.alexander@redbridge.gov.uk)

Hainault Library, 100 Manford Way, Chigwell, Essex IG7 4DD
☎020 8708 9206
Branch Manager Ms Laura Godfrey (e-mail: laura.godfrey@redbridge.gov.uk), Ms Anne Barrett (e-mail: anne.barrett@redbridge.gov.uk) (job share)

Keith Axon Centre, 160–170 Grove Road, Chadwell Heath, Essex RM6 4XB
☎020 8708 0790
Branch Manager Ms Pam Fleetwood (e-mail: pam.fleetwood@redbridge.gov.uk)

South Woodford Library, 116 High Road, London E18 2QS
☎020 8708 9067
Branch Manager Ms Barbara Dann (e-mail: barbara.dann@redbridge.gov.uk)

Wanstead Library, Spratt Hall Road, London E11 2RQ
☎020 8708 7400
Branch Manager Ms Alice Bird (e-mail: alice.bird@redbridge.gov.uk)

Woodford Green Library, Snakes Lane, Woodford Green, Essex IG8 0DX
☎020 8708 9055
Branch Manager Ms Sue Campbell (e-mail: susan.campbell@redbridge.gov.uk)

REDCAR AND CLEVELAND
Authority: Redcar and Cleveland Borough Council

Area Management Services, Redcar and Cleveland House, Kirkleatham Street, Redcar, Redcar and Cleveland TS10 1RT

☎(01642) 774774
Fax (01642) 444341
url: www.redcar-cleveland.gov.uk
Director of Area Management Services Simon Dale (e-mail:
simon_dale@redcar-cleveland.gov.uk)

Central/largest library

Central Library, Coatham Road, Redcar, Redcar and Cleveland TS10 1RP
☎(01642) 472162
Fax (01642) 492253
e-mail: redcar_library@redcar-cleveland.gov.uk
Libraries Officer Ian Wilson BA MCLIP (01642 444321; e-mail:
ian_wilson@redcar-cleveland.gov.uk)

RICHMOND UPON THAMES
Authority: London Borough of Richmond upon Thames

**Education, Children's and Cultural Services, Libraries Management, First Floor, Civic
Centre, 44 York Street, Twickenham, Middlesex TW1 3BZ**
☎020 8940 5529
Fax 020 8891 7714
e-mail: libraries@richmond.gov.uk
url: www.richmond.gov.uk/libraries
Head of Cultural Services Ian Dodds BSc(Hons) MA MCLIP
(e-mail: ian.dodds@richmond.gov.uk)
Operations and Performance Manager Ms Amanda Stirrup BA(Hons) MCLIP
(e-mail: amanda.stirrup@richmond.gov.uk)
Strategy and Development Manager Steve Liddle BA(Hons) DipLib
(e-mail: steven.liddle@richmond.gov.uk)

Central/largest library

Richmond Lending Library, Little Green, Richmond, Surrey TW9 1QL
☎020 8734 3330
Fax 020 8940 8030
e-mail: richmond.library@richmond.gov.uk
Customer Services Manager Leslie Cranfield MCLIP (e-mail:
l.cranfield@richmond.gov.uk)

Branch libraries

Castelnau Library, 75 Castelnau, Barnes, Middlesex SW13 9RT
☎020 8734 3350
e-mail: castelnau.library@richmond.gov.uk

East Sheen Library, Sheen Lane, London SW14 8LP
☎020 8734 3337
e-mail: eastsheen.library@richmond.gov.uk

Ham Library, Ham Street, Ham, Middlesex TW10 7HR
☎020 8734 3354

e-mail: ham.library@richmond.gov.uk

Hampton Hill Library, 68 High Street, Hampton Hill, Middlesex TW12 1NY
☎020 8734 3320
e-mail: hamptonhill.library@richmond.gov.uk

Hampton Library, Rosehill, Hampton, Middlesex TW12 2AB
☎020 8734 3347
e-mail: hampton.library@richmond.gov.uk

Reference Library, Old Town Hall, Whitaker Avenue, Richmond, Surrey TW9 1TP
☎020 8734 3308
Fax 020 8940 6899
e-mail: reference.services@richmond.gov.uk

Teddington Library, Waldegrave Road, Teddington, Middlesex TW11 8LG
☎020 8734 3304
e-mail: teddington.library@richmond.gov.uk

Twickenham Library, Garfield Road, Twickenham, Middlesex TW1 3JT
☎020 8734 3340
e-mail: twickenham.library@richmond.gov.uk

Whitton Library, 141 Nelson Road, Whitton, Middlesex TW2 7BB
☎020 8734 3343
e-mail: whitton.library@richmond.gov.uk

ROCHDALE
Authority: Rochdale Metropolitan Borough Council

Wheatsheaf Library, Wheatsheaf Shopping Centre, Baillie Street, Rochdale, Greater Manchester OL16 1JZ
☎(01706) 924900 (enquiries), (01706) 924911 (administration)
Fax (01706) 924992
url: www.rochdale.gov.uk/libraries
Area Librarian (Rochdale and Pennine) Mrs Julie Rees BA(Hons) DipLib (01706 924976; e-mail: julie.rees@rochdale.gov.uk)
Area Librarian (Heywood and Middleton) Mrs Janice Tod BSc(Hons) MCLIP (01706 924946; e-mail: janice.tod@rochdale.gov.uk)
E-Learning and Information Manager Ian Sutton BA MCLIP (01706 924989; e-mail: ian.sutton@rochdale.gov.uk)
Performance and Development Manager Philip Cooke BA(Hons) MA (01706 924889; e-mail: philip.cooke@rochdale.gov.uk)

Main libraries

Heywood Library, Church Street, Heywood, Greater Manchester OL10 1LL
☎0845 272 9260
Fax (01706) 368683

Middleton Library, Long Street, Middleton, Greater Manchester M24 6DU
☎0161 643 5228
Fax 0161 654 0745

ROTHERHAM

Authority: Rotherham Metropolitan Borough Council

Central Library, Walker Place, Rotherham, South Yorks S65 IJH
☎(01709) 823611 (enquiries), (01709) 823623 (management)
Fax (01709) 823650 (enquiries), (01709) 837649 (management)
e-mail: central.library@rotherham.gov.uk
url: www.rotherham.gov.uk
Cultural Services Manager Ms Elenore Fisher BA(Hons) DipLib MCLIP (e-mail:
elenore.fisher@rotherham.gov.uk)
Manager, Library and Information Service Bernard Murphy MA DipLib MCLIP

RUTLAND

Authority: Rutland County Council

Rutland County Library, Catmose Street, Oakham, Rutland LEI5 6HW
☎(01572) 722918 (enquiries)
Fax (01572) 724906 (enquiries)
e-mail: libraries@rutland.gov.uk
url: www,rutland.gov.uk/libraries
Head of Culture and Leisure Robert Clayton BA MA MCLIP (e-mail:
rclayton@rutland.gov.uk)

Community libraries

Ketton Library, High Street, Ketton, Rutland PE9 3TE
☎(01780) 720580

Ryhall Library, Coppice Road, Ryhall, Rutland PE9 4HY
☎(01780) 751726

Uppingham Library, Queen Street, Uppingham, Rutland LE15 9QR
☎(01572) 823218

ST HELENS

Authority: St Helens Council

Chief Executive's Department, Public Affairs Division, Chester Lane Centre and Library, Chester Lane, St Helens, Merseyside WA9 4DE
☎(01744) 677445 (Support Services)
Fax (01744) 677114
e-mail: keithpatterson@sthelens.gov.uk
url: www.sthelens.gov.uk
Head of Library Services Ms Kathy Johnson BA DipLib (e-mail:
kathrynjohnson@sthelens.gov.uk)
Community Development Manager (responsible for Children and Youth)
Ms Kathryn Boothroyd BA(Hons) MCLIP (01744 677486; e-mail:
kathrynboothroyd@sthelens.gov.uk)

Central/largest library

Central Library, The Gamble Building, Victoria Square, St Helens, Merseyside WA10 1DY

☎(01744) 676954
e-mail: centrallibrary@sthelens.gov.uk
Team Librarian Ms Jen Tapley (e-mail: jentapley@sthelens.gov.uk)

SALFORD
Authority: Salford Comunity Leisure

New Bridgewater House, 12 Bridgewater Road, Walkden, Salford, Manchester M28 3JE
☎0161 778 0770
e-mail: libraries@salford.gov.uk
url: www.salford.gov.uk/libraries
Libraries and Information Service Manager Ms Sarah Spence BA(Hons) MCLIP
(0161 778 0840; fax: 0161 745 9490; e-mail: sarah.spence@salford.gov.uk) (based at
Salford Museum and Art Gallery, Peel Park, The Crescent, Salford M5 4WU)
Children and Young People Library Service Manager Ms Pamela Manley BA MLS
PGDipLib MA(Ed) (0161 778 0842; e-mail: pamela.manley@salford.gov.uk)

Main libraries

Eccles Library, Eccles Gateway, 28 Barton Lane, Eccles, Manchester M30 0TU
☎0161 909 6528
Fax 0161 211 7002
Neighbourhood Library Manager Mrs Hannah Quinlan BA(Hons) MA MCLIP
(e-mail: hannah.quinlan@salford.gov.uk), Mrs Wendy Hilton BA MCLIP

Pendleton Library, Pendleton Gateway, 1 Broadwalk, Salford, Manchester M6 5FX
☎0161 909 6538
Fax 0161 211 7301
Neighbourhood Library Manager Vacant

Swinton Library, Chorley Road, Swinton, Salford, Manchester M27 4AE
☎0161 921 2360
Fax 0161 727 7071
Neighbourhood Library Manager Ms Carol Behrens BA DBA (e-mail:
carol.behrens@salford.gov.uk)

Walkden Library, Walkden Gateway, 2 Smith Street, Walkden, Manchester M28 3EZ
☎0161 909 6518
Fax 0161 211 7114
Neighbourhood Library Manager Chris Carson BA DMS MCLIP (e-mail:
chris.carson@salford.gov.uk)

SANDWELL
Authority: Sandwell Metropolitan Borough Council

**Sandwell Library and Information Service, Environment House, 2nd Floor, Lombard
Street, West Bromwich, West Midlands B70 8RU**
☎0121 569 4931
Fax 0121 569 4907
e-mail: information.service@sandwell.gov.uk
url: www.libraries.sandwell.gov.uk
Chief Librarian Barry Clark BLib MCLIP (e-mail: barry_clark@sandwell.gov.uk)

Central/largest library

Central Library, High Street, West Bromwich, West Midlands B70 8DZ
☎0121 569 4904
Fax 0121 525 9465

Additional services

Community History and Archives Service, Smethwick Library, High Street, Smethwick,
West Midlands B66 1AB
☎0121 558 2561
Fax 0121 555 6064
e-mail: archives.service@sandwell.gov.uk
Borough Archivist Ms Sarah Chubb UDIP RMSA (0121 558 2861; e-mail:
sarah_chubb@sandwell.gov.uk)

Community Libraries, c/o Central Library, High Street, West Bromwich, West Midlands
B70 8DZ
☎0121 569 4922
Fax 0121 525 9465
Principal Libraries Officer (Community Libraries) Ms Dawn Winter (0121 569 4922;
e-mail: dawn_winter@sandwell.gov.uk)

Library Support Services, Town Hall, High Street, West Bromwich, West Midlands B70 8DT
☎0121 569 4909
Fax 0121 569 4907
Principal Libraries Officer (Library Support Services) Ms Heather Vickerman
(0121 569 4906; e-mail: heather_vickerman@sandwell.gov.uk)

SEFTON
Authority: Sefton Council

**Leisure Services Department, 2nd Floor, Magdalen House, 30 Trinity Road, Bootle,
Liverpool L20 3NJ**
☎0151 934 2376
Fax 0151 934 2370
e-mail: library.service@leisure.sefton.gov.uk
url: www.sefton.gov.uk
Head of Library and Information Services Ms Christine Hall BA MCLIP (e-mail:
christine.hall@leisure.sefton.gov.uk)
Principal Development Manager – Stock and Reader Development David Eddy
(e-mail: david.eddy@leisure.sefton.gov.uk)
Principal Development Manager – Community Cohesion Ms Zoë Clarke BA MA
MCLIP (e-mail: zoe.clarke@leisure.sefton.gov.uk)
Principal Development Manager – Stock and Reader Development Andrew
Farthing (e-mail: andrew.farthing@leisure.sefton.gov.uk)

Central/largest libraries

Crosby Library, Crosby Road North, Waterloo, Liverpool L22 0LQ
☎0151 257 6400
Fax 0151 330 5770

Southport Library, Lord Street, Southport PR8 1DJ
☎0151 934 2118
Fax 0151 934 2115

SHEFFIELD
Authority: Sheffield City Council

Sheffield Libraries, Archives and Information Services, Central Library, Surrey Street, Sheffield S1 IXZ
☎0114 273 4712 (enquiries), 0114 205 3124 (library management)
Fax 0114 273 5009
e-mail: libraries@sheffield.gov.uk
url: www.sheffield.gov.uk/libraries
Head of Libraries, Archives and Information Martin Dutch BA(Hons) DipLib MCLIP
(0114 273 6998; e-mail: martin.dutch@sheffield.gov.uk)
Assistant Head of Service – Central Services David Isaac BA(Hons) DipLib DMS
MCLIP (0114 273 6959; e-mail: david.isaac@sheffield.gov.uk)
Assistant Head of Service – Communities Andrew Milroy BA DipLib (0114 273 4403;
e-mail: andrew.milroy@sheffield.gov.uk)
Archives and Local Studies Manager Peter Evans (0114 273 9395; e-mail:
pete.evans@sheffield.gov.uk)
Collections and Reader Development Manager Ms Alison Jobey BA MCLIP (0114 273
6499; e-mail: alison.jobey@sheffield.gov.uk)
ICT Manager John Murphy BSc(Hons) MA (0114 273 6645; e-mail:
john.murphy@sheffield.gov.uk)
Customer Standards and Performance Manager Ms Judith Adam MA(Hons) DipLib
MCLIP (0114 273 4254; e-mail: judith.adam@sheffield.gov.uk)
Marketing Officer Gurjit Bhachoo (0114 273 6942; e-mail:
gurjit.bhachoo@sheffield.gov.uk)
Community Libraries Manager Ms Lesley Gunter (0114 273 6642)

District libraries

Broomhill Library, Taptonville Road, Sheffield S10 5BR
☎0114 273 4276
e-mail: broomhill.library@sheffield.gov.uk

Burngreave Library, 179 Spital Hill, Sheffield S4 7LF
☎0114 203 9002
e-mail: burngreave.library@sheffield.gov.uk

Chapeltown Library, Nether Ley Avenue, Sheffield S35 1AE
☎0114 203 7000/1
e-mail: chapeltown.library@sheffield.gov.uk

Crystal Peaks Library, 1-3 Peak Square, Crystal Peaks Complex, Waterthorpe, Sheffield
S20 7PH
☎0114 293 0612/3
e-mail: crystalpeaks.library@sheffield.gov.uk

Darnall Library, Britannia Road, Sheffield S9 5JG
☎0114 203 7429

e-mail: darnall.library@sheffield.gov.uk

Ecclesall Library, Weetwood Gardens, Ecclesall Road South, Sheffield S11 9PL
☎0114 203 7222
Fax 0114 203 7227
e-mail: ecclesall.library@sheffield.gov.uk

Ecclesfield Library, High Street, Ecclesfield, Sheffield S35 9UA
☎0114 203 7013 (tel/fax)
e-mail: ecclesfield.library@sheffield.gov.uk

Firth Park Library, 443 Firth Park Road, Sheffield S5 6QQ
☎0114 203 7433
e-mail: firthpark.library@sheffield.gov.uk

Frecheville Library, Smalldale Road, Sheffield S12 4YD
☎0114 203 7817
e-mail: frecheville.library@sheffield.gov.uk

Gleadless Library, White Lane, Sheffield S12 3GH
☎0114 203 7804 (tel/fax)
e-mail: gleadless.library@sheffield.gov.uk

Greenhill Library, Hemper Lane, Sheffield S8 7FE
☎0114 203 7700
Fax 0114 293 0012
e-mail: greenhill.library@sheffield.gov.uk

Highfield Library, London Road, Sheffield S2 4NF
☎0114 203 7204
e-mail: highfield.library@sheffield.gov.uk

Hillsborough Library, Middlewood Road, Sheffield S6 4HD
☎0114 203 9529
e-mail: hillsborough.library@sheffield.gov.uk

Jordanthorpe Library, 15 Jordanthorpe Centre, Sheffield S8 8DX
☎0114 203 7701
Fax 0114 293 0388
e-mail: jordanthorpe.library@sheffield.gov.uk

Limpsfield Library, Limpsfield Middle School, Jenkin Avenue, Sheffield S9 1AN
☎0114 203 7430
Fax 0114 242 3808
e-mail: limpsfield.library@sheffield.gov.uk

Manor Library, Ridgeway Road, Sheffield S12 2SS
☎0114 203 7805
e-mail: manor.library@sheffield.gov.uk

Mobile Services, Staniforth Road Depot, Staniforth Road, Sheffield S9 3GZ
☎0114 273 4277

Newfield Green Library, Gleadless Road, Sheffield S2 2BT
☎0114 203 7818 (tel/fax)
e-mail: newfieldgreen.library@sheffield.gov.uk

Park Library, Duke Street, Sheffield S2 5QP
☎0114 203 9000 (tel/fax)
e-mail: park.library@sheffield.gov.uk

Parson Cross Library, Margetson Crescent, Sheffield S5 9ND
☎0114 203 9533
Fax 0114 203 9656
e-mail: parsoncross.library@sheffield.gov.uk

Southey Library, Moonshine Lane, Sheffield S5 8RB
☎0114 203 9531
Fax 0114 293 0024
e-mail: southey.library@sheffield.gov.uk

Stannington Library, Uppergate Road, Sheffield S6 8RB
☎0114 293 0489
Fax 0114 293 0488
e-mail: stannington.library@sheffield.gov.uk

Stocksbridge Library, Manchester Road, Stocksbridge, Sheffield S36 1DH
☎0114 273 4205
e-mail: stocksbridge.library@sheffield.gov.uk

Tinsley Library, Tinsley Shopping Centre, Bawtry Road, Sheffield S9 1UY
☎0114 203 7432
Fax 0114 293 0029
e-mail: tinsley.library@sheffield.gov.uk

Totley Library, 205 Baslow Road, Sheffield S17 4DT
☎0114 293 0406
e-mail: totley.library@sheffield.gov.uk

Upperthorpe Library, Upperthorpe Healthy Living Centre, 18 Upperthorpe, Sheffield S6 3NA
☎0114 270 2048
Fax 0114 276 2189
e-mail: upperthorpe.library@sheffield.gov.uk

Walkley Library, South Road, Sheffield S6 3TD
☎0114 203 9532 (tel/fax)
e-mail: walkley.library@sheffield.gov.uk

Woodhouse Library, Tannery Street, Sheffield S13 7JU
☎0114 269 2607 (tel/fax)
e-mail: woodhouse.library@sheffield.gov.uk

Woodseats Library, Chesterfield Road, Sheffield S8 0SH
☎0114 293 0411
e-mail: woodseats.library@sheffield.gov.uk

SHROPSHIRE
Authority: Shropshire County Council

Library and Information Services, Community Services Directorate, The Shirehall, Abbey Foregate, Shrewsbury, Shropshire SY2 6ND
☎(0345) 678 9034

Fax (01743) 255001
e-mail: libraries@shropshire-cc.gov.uk
url: www.shropshire-cc.gov.uk/library.nsf
Head of Libraries and Information Service James Anthony-Edwards MA MA MCMI
(e-mail: james.anthony-edwards@shropshire-cc.gov.uk)
Strategic Library Service Manager Don Yuile BA MCLIP (e-mail:
don.yuile@shropshire-cc.gov.uk)

Central/largest libraries

Castle Gates Library, Shrewsbury, Shropshire SY1 2AS
☎(0345) 678 9034
Fax (01743) 255309
Principal Librarian – Shrewsbury Ms Elaine Moss MCLIP (e-mail:
elaine.moss@shropshire-cc.gov.uk)

Reference and Information Service, 1a Castle Gates, Shrewsbury, Shropshire SY1 2AQ
☎(01743) 255380
Fax (01743) 255383
Strategic Library Service Manager – Central Ms Elaine Moss MCLIP (e-mail:
elaine.moss@shropshire-cc.gov.uk)

Area libraries

North Area. Oswestry Library, Arthur Street, Oswestry, Shropshire SY11 1JN
☎(0345) 678 9034
Fax (01691) 677399
Strategic Library Service Manager Ms Claire Cartlidge MCLIP (e-mail:
claire.cartlidge@shropshire-cc.gov.uk)

South Area. Bridgnorth Library, Listley Street, Bridgnorth, Shropshire WV16 4AW
☎(01746) 763358
Fax (01746) 766625
Strategic Library Service Manager Adrian Williams BA MCLIP (e-mail:
adrian.williams@shropshire-cc.gov.uk)

SLOUGH
Authority: Slough Borough Council

Slough Library, High Street, Slough SL1 1EA
☎(01753) 535166
Fax (01753) 825050
e-mail: library@slough.gov.uk
Head of Library Services Mrs Jackie Menniss BA(Hons) DipIM DipSM MCLIP
(01753 787506; e-mail: jackie.menniss@slough.gov.uk)
Assistant Head of Library Services Ms Liz McMillan MCLIP (e-mail:
liz.mcmillan@slough.gov.uk)

SOLIHULL
Authority: Solihull Metropolitan Borough Council

Central Library, Homer Road, Solihull, West Midlands B91 3RG

☎0121 704 6965 (public enquiries), 0121 704 6941 (administration)
Fax 0121 704 6991
e-mail: libraryarts@solihull.gov.uk
url: www.solihull.gov.uk
Head of Libraries Mrs Tracey Cox BLS(Hons) MCLIP (0121 704 6945; e-mail:
tcox@solihull.gov.uk)
Support Services Manager Ms Hilary Halliday BA MCLIP (0121 704 8227; e-mail:
hhalliday@solihull.gov.uk)
Children's, Family Learning and Schools Manager Vacant

Main area libraries

Central Library, Homer Road, Solihull, West Midlands B91 3RG
☎0121 704 6965
Fax 0121 704 6991
Central Area Manager Mrs Tracey Cox BLS(Hons) MCLIP (e-mail: tcox@solihull.gov.uk)

Chelmsley Wood Library, Stephenson Drive, Chelmsley Wood, Solihull, West Midlands
B37 5TA
☎0121 788 4380
Fax 0121 788 4381
Community Libraries Manager Ms Yvonne Negus BA MCLIP MISM (0121 704 6963;
e-mail: ynegus@solihull.org.uk)

SOMERSET
Authority: Somerset County Council

**Cultural Service, Administration Libraries Centre, Mount Street, Bridgwater, Somerset
TA6 3ES**
☎(01278) 451201
Fax (01278) 452787
e-mail: librec@somerset.gov.uk
url: www.somerset.gov.uk/libraries; www.librarieswest.org.uk
Helpline, Somerset Direct: 0845 345 9177
Group Manager – Cultural Services, Heritage and Libraries Tom Mayberry MA FSA
DAA
Libraries & Information Manager Philip Nichols BA MCLIP (01935 429614; e-mail:
penichols@somerset.gov.uk) (based at Yeovil Library)
Business Performance Manager Stephen G May (e-mail: sgmay@somerset.gov.uk)
Senior Librarian – Operations Mrs Sue Crowley BLib MCLIP (e-mail:
sacrowley@somerset.gov.uk)
Senior Librarian – Stock and Community Nigel J Humphrey BLib MA MCLIP (e-mail:
nhumphrey@somerset.gov.uk)
Senior Librarian – Service Development Ms Janet Blake BA MCLIP (e-mail:
jblake@somerset.gov.uk)
Consortium and Performance Manager Ms Kate Turner MA BLib MCLIP
Bibliographic Services Manager Miss Carol Gold (e-mail: cgold2@somerset.gov.uk)
Enquiry Centre Manager Mrs Jane Gill BA MCLIP (e-mail: jgill@somerset.gov.uk),
Mrs Maggie Harris MCLIP (e-mail: maharris@somerset.gov.uk)
Projects, Research and Marketing Officer Paul Smith BA(Hons) DipLib DMS MCLIP
(e-mail: psmith@somerset.gov.uk)

Manager, Resources for Learning Mrs Karen Horsfield BEd MSc MCLIP (e-mail: kahorsfield@somerset.gov.uk)

Group libraries

Mendip & Sedgemoor Group, Bridgwater Library, Binford Place, Bridgwater, Somerset TA6 3LF
☎(01278) 458373
Fax (01278) 451027

South Somerset Group, Yeovil Library, King George Street, Yeovil, Somerset BA20 1PY
☎(01935) 423144
Fax (01935) 431847

Taunton Deane & West Somerset Group, Taunton Library, Paul Street, Taunton, Somerset TA1 3XZ
☎(01823) 336334
Fax (01823) 340302

SOUTH GLOUCESTERSHIRE
Authority: South Gloucestershire Council

Library Service, PO Box 2078, Council Offices, Castle Street, Thornbury, South Glos BS35 9BJ
☎(01454) 865782
Fax (01454) 863309
e-mail: libraries@southglos.gov.uk
url: www.southglos.gov.uk/libraries
Head of Library and Information Service Martin Burton BA MCLIP
Team Manager (North) John Abraham MCLIP (01454 865664)
Team Manager (South) Michael Duffy MCLIP (01454 868450)

Central/largest library

Yate Library, 44 West Walk, Yate, South Glos BS37 4AX
☎(01454) 868006
Fax (01454) 865665
Group Librarian Neil Weston BA MCLIP

Group libraries

Bradley Stoke Library, Fiddlers Wood Lane, Bradley Stoke, South Glos BS32 9BS
☎(01454) 868006
Librarian Ms Catherine Whiteman MCLIP

Downend Library, Buckingham Gardens, Downend, South Glos BS16 5TW
☎(01454) 868006
Librarian Mrs Helen Egarr MCLIP

Kingswood Library, High Street, Kingswood, South Glos BS15 4AR
☎(01454) 868006
Librarian Ms Julie Barker

Thornbury Library, St Mary Street, Thornbury, South Glos BS35 2AA

☎(01454) 868006
Librarian Bob Filer BA MCLIP

SOUTH TYNESIDE
Authority: South Tyneside Council

South Tyneside Libraries, Central Library, Prince Georg Square, South Shields, Tyne and Wear NE33 2PE
☎0191 427 1818
Fax 0191 455 8085
e-mail: reference.library@southtyneside.gov.uk
url: www.southtyneside.info
Libraries Manager Mark C E Freeman BA(Hons) MCLIP (e-mail:
mark.freeman@southtyneside.gov.uk)
Development and Planning Co-ordinator David Whale MCLIP (e-mail:
david.whale@southtyneside.gov.uk)
Young People's Services Co-ordinator Ms Kathryn Armstrong MA MCLIP (e-mail:
kathryn.armstrong@southtyneside.gov.uk)
Information and Education Co-ordinator Ms Hildred Whale MCLIP (e-mail:
hildred.whale@southtyneside.gov.uk)
Community Development Co-ordinator Ms Lindsay Casselden BA(Hons) MA MCLIP
(e-mail: lindsay.casselden@southtyneside.gov.uk)

SOUTHAMPTON
Authority: Southampton City Council

City Libraries Service, Administration Office, Central Library, Civic Centre, Southampton SO14 7LW
☎023 8083 4645
Fax 023 8083 4483
e-mail: library@southampton.gov.uk
url: www.southampton.gov.uk/libraries
Libraries Manager David Baldwin BA MCLIP (023 8083 2219; e-mail:
david.baldwin@southampton.gov.uk)
Resources and Development Manager Mrs Elizabeth Whale MA (023 8083 2816;
e-mail: elizabeth.whale@southampton.gov.uk)
Neighbourhood Services Manager Ms Siobhan McGarrigle MA MCLIP (023 8083 2595;
e-mail: siobhan.mcgarrigle@southampton.gov.uk)

Central/largest library

Central Library, Civic Centre, Southampton SO14 7LW
☎023 8083 2664; mobile libraries 07768 541797
Fax 023 8033 6305
e-mail: library@southampton.gov.uk
Central Library Manager Richard Ashman (023 8083 2294; e-mail:
richard.ashman@southampton.gov.uk)
Supervisor Ms Kate Swindells (e-mail: kate.swindells@southampton.gov.uk)

Branch libraries

(telephone numbers and e-mail addresses same as for Central Library)

Bitterne Library, Bitterne Road East, Southampton SO18 5EG
Supervisor Ms Barbara McCaffrey (e-mail: barbara.mccaffrey@southampton.gov.uk)

Burgess Road Library, Burgess Road, Southampton SO16 3HF
Supervisor Ms Catherine Brear (e-mail: catherine.brear@southampton.gov.uk)

Cobbett Road Library, Cobbett Road, Southampton SO18 1HL
Supervisor Ms Jackie Sutton (e-mail: jackie.sutton@southampton.gov.uk)

Lordshill Library, District Centre, Lordshill, Southampton SO16 8HY
Supervisor Ms Lisa Dawbney (e-mail: lisa.dawbney@southampton.gov.uk)

Millbrook Library, 67 Cumbrian Way, Southampton SO16 4AT
Supervisor Mrs Angela Zabiela (e-mail: angela.zabiela@southampton.gov.uk)

Portswood Library, Portswood Road, Southampton SO17 2NG
Supervisor Ms Sara Goddard (e-mail: sara.goddard@southampton.gov.uk)

Shirley Library, Redcar Street, Southampton SO15 5LL
Supervisor Ms Judith O'Callaghan (e-mail: judith.ocallaghan@southampton.gov.uk)

Thornhill Library, 380 Hinkler Road, Southampton SO19 6DF
Supervisor Vacant

Weston Library, 6 Wallace Road, Weston, Southampton SO19 9GX
Supervisor Mrs Carolyn Taplin (e-mail: carolyn.taplin@southampton.gov.uk)

Woolston Library, Portsmouth Road, Southampton SO19 9AF
Supervisor Ms Jo Harley (e-mail: jo.harley@southampton.gov.uk)

SOUTHEND-ON-SEA
Authority: Southend-on-Sea Borough Council

Southend Central Library, Victoria Avenue, Southend-on-Sea, Essex SS2 6EX
☎(01702) 534100
Fax (01702) 469241
e-mail: library@southend.gov.uk
url: www.southend.gov.uk/library
Library Services Manager Simon May BSc MSc
Head of Information and Resources Chris Hayes BA DipLib

SOUTHWARK
Authority: London Borough of Southwark

**Environment and Housing, Culture, Libraries, Learning and Leisure, PO Box 64529,
London SE1 5LX**
☎020 7525 3719
Fax 020 7525 1568
e-mail: southwark.libraries@southwark.gov.uk
url: www.southwark.gov.uk
Head of Culture, Libraries and Learning Adrian Whittle BA (020 7525 1577; e-mail:
adrian.whittle@southwark.gov.uk)

Library Service Manager Ms Pam Usher BA(Hons) DMS MCLIP (020 7525 3918; e-mail: pam.usher@southwark.gov.uk)

Branch libraries

(telephone number is 020 7525 2000 for the following branch libraries)

Blue Anchor Library, Market Place, Southwark Park Road, London SE16 3UQ

Brandon Library, Maddock Way, Cooks Road, London SE17 3NH

Camberwell Library, 17-21 Camberwell Church Street, London SE5 8TR

Community Library Services, Rotherhithe Library, Albion Street, London SE16 1JA

Dulwich Library, 368 Lordship Lane, London SE22 8NB

East Street/Old Kent Road Library, 168-170 Old Kent Road, London SE1 5TY

Grove Vale Library, 25-27 Grove Vale, London SE22 8EQ

John Harvard Library, 211 Borough High Street, London SE1 1JA

Kingswood Library, Seeley Drive, London SE21 8QR

Local History Library, 211 Borough High Street, London SE1 1JA

Newington Library, 155 Walworth Road, London SE17 1RS

Nunhead Library, Gordon Road, London SE15 3RW

Peckham Library, 122 Peckham Hill Street, London SE15 5JR

Rotherhithe Library, Albion Street, London SE16 7HY

STAFFORDSHIRE
Authority: Staffordshire County Council

Library and Information Services, Culture and Libraries, Places Directorate, Tipping Street, Stafford ST16 2DH
☎(01785) 278312
Fax (01785) 278319
url: www.staffordshire.gov.uk
Assistant Director: Culture and Libraries Ms Janene Cox BLib MCLIP (01785 278368; e-mail: janene.cox@staffordshire.gov.uk)
Principal Librarian: Policy Development, Books, Reading and Learning
Mrs Catherine Mann BA(Hons) MCLIP (01785 278320; e-mail: catherine.mann@staffordshire.gov.uk)
Service Delivery Manager Mrs Elizabeth Rees-Jones BA(Hons) MCLIP (01785 278344; e-mail: elizabeth.rees-jones@staffordshire.gov.uk)
Principal Librarian: Policy Development, Community Engagement and Local Delivery Mrs Hilary Jackson BLib MCLIP (01785 278591; e-mail: hilary.jackson@staffordshire.gov.uk)
Library Operations Manager Mrs Alison Reynolds BA(Hons) MA MCLIP (01785 278353; e-mail: alison.reynolds@staffordshire.gov.uk)

Districts

Burton Library, Riverside, High Street, Burton-on-Trent, Staffs DE14 1AH
☎(01283) 239556
Fax (01283) 239571
e-mail: burton.library@staffordshire.gov.uk
District Manager Kevin Reynolds MCLIP (01283 239559; e-mail: kevin.reynolds@staffordshire.gov.uk)

Cannock Library, Manor Avenue, Cannock, Staffs WS11 1AA
☎(01543) 510365
Fax (01543) 510373
e-mail: cannock.library@staffordshire.gov.uk
District Manager Mrs Karen Yeomans BA(Hons) MCLIP (01543 510366; e-mail: karen.yeomans@staffordshire.gov.uk)

Leek Library, Nicholson Institute, Stockwell Street, Leek, Staffs ST13 6DW
☎(01538) 483209
e-mail: leek.library@staffordshire.gov.uk
District Manager Mrs Cathy Braddock BLib(Hons) MCLIP (01538 483206; e-mail: cathy.braddock@staffordshire.gov.uk)

Library and Information Service, Culture and Libraries, Places Directorate, Tipping Street, Stafford ST16 2DH
☎(01785) 278369
Fax (01785) 278309
Senior Librarian: Community Library Service Mrs Olwen Johnson MCLIP (01785 278317; e-mail: olwen.johnson@staffordshire.gov.uk)

Lichfield Library, The Friary, Lichfield, Staffs WS13 6QG
☎(01543) 510700
Fax (01543) 510716
e-mail: lichfield.library@staffordshire.gov.uk
District Manager Mrs Lorraine Riley BA(Hons) DipEd MA CBA MCLIP (01543 510702; e-mail: lorraine.riley@staffordshire.gov.uk)

Newcastle Library, Ironmarket, Newcastle, Staffs ST5 1AT
☎(01782) 297300
Fax (01782) 297323
e-mail: newcastle.library@staffordshire.gov.uk
District Manager Mrs Sam Mellenchip BA(Hons) PGDipLIS (01782 297305; e-mail: samantha.mellenchip@staffordshire.gov.uk)

Perton Library, Severn Drive, Perton, Staffs WV6 7QU
☎(01902) 755794
Fax (01902) 756123
e-mail: perton.library@staffordshire.gov.uk
District Manager Graham Riley MCLIP (01902 756123; e-mail: graham.riley@staffordshire.gov.uk)

Shire Hall Library, Market Street, Stafford ST16 2LQ
☎(01785) 278585
Fax (01785) 278599

District Manager Andrew Baker BA(Hons) MCLIP TSSF (01785 278335; e-mail: andrew.baker@staffordshire.gov.uk)

Tamworth Library, Corporation Street, Tamworth, Staffs B79 7DN
☎(01827) 475645
Fax (01827) 475658
e-mail: tamworth.library@staffordshire.gov.uk
District Manager Mrs Cathy Attwood MCLIP (01827 475651; e-mail: cathy.attwood@staffordshire.gov.uk)

Prison Library Service

Library and Information Services, Unit 4A & 4C, Drummond Road, Astonfields Industrial Estate, Stafford, Staffs ST16 3HJ
Senior Librarian: Prison Library Service Ms Lindsay Lorenz MCLIP (01785 278412; e-mail: lindsay.lorenz@staffordshire.gov.uk)

Children and Young People

Library and Information Services, Culture and Libraries, Places Directorate, Tipping Street, Stafford ST16 2DH
Service Development Officer: Children and Young People Mrs Sue Ball BA MCLIP (01785 854170; e-mail: sue.ball@staffordshire.gov.uk)

Schools Library Service

Kingston Centre, Fairway, Stafford ST16 3TW
☎(01785) 278346/278440/278340
e-mail: sls@staffordshire.gov.uk
Schools Library Service Development Manager Mrs Morna Williams MA(Hons) DipLib MCLIP (e-mail: morna.williams@staffordshire.gov.uk)

STOCKPORT
Authority: Stockport Metropolitan Borough Council

Communities, Regeneration and Environment Directorate, 6th Floor, Regal House, Duke Street, Stockport SK1 3DJ
☎0161 474 4445 (enquiries and administration)
e-mail: libraries@stockport.gov.uk
url: www.stockport.gov.uk/libraries
Head of Service: Libraries, Advice and Information John Condon (e-mail: john.condon@stockport.gov.uk)

Central/largest library

Central Library, Wellington Road South, Stockport SK1 3RS
☎0161 474 4530 (Local Heritage Library), 0845 644 4307 (all other library enquiries)
Fax 0161 474 7750
e-mail: lending.library@stockport.gov.uk; libraries@stockport.gov.uk

Library Operations and Support Services, Phoenix House, Bird Hall Lane, Stockport SK3 0RA
☎0161 474 5604
Fax 0161 491 6516

STOCKTON-ON-TEES

Authority: Stockton-on-Tees Borough Council

Children, Education and Social Care, Stockton Borough Libraries, Church Road, Stockton-on-Tees TS18 ITU
☎(01642) 526522
Fax (01642) 528078
url: www.stockton.gov.uk
Head of Culture and Leisure Reuben Kench (01642 527039;
e-mail: reuben.kench@stockton.gov.uk) (located at Municipal Buildings, Church Road,
Stockton-on-Tees TS18 1XE)
Library Development Officer Ms Emma Tennant MSc (01642 526520;
e-mail: emma.tennant@stockton.gov.uk) (also responsible for children's services)
Lending Services Officer Mrs Penny Slee (01642 526521; e-mail:
penny.slee@stockton.gov.uk)
Information Services Officer Ms Carole Wood (01642 528079;
e-mail: carole.wood@stockton.gov.uk)
Community Libraries Officer Ms Deb McDonagh (01642 526520;
e-mail: debbie.mcdonagh@stockton.gov.uk)
Libraries and Information Manager Ms Laurayne Featherstone (01642 526463;
e-mail: laurayne.featherstone@stockton.gov.uk)
Improvement Co-ordinator Mrs Sue Sneyd (01642 526472; e-mail:
sue.sneyd@stockton.gov.uk)
Reader Development Officer Mrs Claire Pratt BA MCLIP (01642 528041;
e-mail: claire.pratt@stockton.gov.uk)
Access to Digital Services Co-ordinator Steve Wild (01642 526501;
e-mail: steve.wild@stockton.gov.uk)
Stock Performance Officer Craig Peddie (01642 526998; e-mail:
craig.peddie@stockton.gov.uk)
Health and Wellbeing Librarian Ms Karen Morris (01642 524343;
e-mail: karen.morris@stockton.gov.uk)

Branch libraries

Billingham Branch Library, Bedale Avenue, Billingham, Stockton-on-Tees TS23 1AJ
☎(01642) 527895
e-mail: billingham.library@stockton.gov.uk
Branch Librarian Mrs Glynis Thirlaway

Egglescliffe Branch Library, Butterfield Drive, Orchard Estate, Egglescliffe, Stockton-on-Tees
TS16 0EL
☎(01642) 527958
e-mail: egglescliffe.library@stockton.gov.uk
Branch Librarian Miss Margaret Chapman MA(Lib)

Fairfield Branch Library, Fairfield Road, Stockton-on-Tees TS19 7AJ
☎(01642) 577962
e-mail: fairfield.library@stockton.gov.uk
Branch Librarian Richard Lacey MCLIP (e-mail: richard.lacey@stockton.gov.uk)

Ingleby Barwick Library, Ingleby Barwick Community Campus, Blair Avenue, Ingleby
Barwick, Stockton-on-Tees TS17 5BL

☎(01642) 750767
e-mail: inglebybarwick.library@stockton.gov.uk
Branch Librarian Mrs Cath Watkins

Norton Branch Library, 87 High Street, Norton, Stockton-on-Tees TS20 1AE
☎(01642) 528019
e-mail: norton.library@stockton.gov.uk
Branch Librarian Mrs Cath Maddison BSc DipLib

Roseberry Billingham Branch Library, The Causeway, Billingham, Stockton-on-Tees TS23 2LB
☎(01642) 528084
e-mail: roseberry.library@stockton.gov.uk
Branch Librarian Ivan Limon

Roseworth Branch Library, Redhill Road, Stockton-on-Tees TS19 9BX
☎(01642) 528098
Branch Librarian Mrs Jackie Fraser

Thornaby Central Branch Library, The Pavillion, New Town Centre, Thornaby, Stockton-on-Tees TS17 9EW
☎(01642) 528117
e-mail: thornaby.central.library@stockton.gov.uk
Branch Librarian Mrs Shelagh Freeman MCLIP

Thornaby Westbury Street Branch Library, Westbury Street, Thornaby, Stockton-on-Tees TS17 6PG
☎(01642) 528150
e-mail: thornaby.library@stockton.gov.uk
Branch Librarian Mrs Lucie Kirton

Yarm Branch Library, 41 High Street, Yarm, Stockton-on-Tees TS15 9BH
☎(01642) 528152
e-mail: yarm.library@stockton.gov.uk
Branch Librarian Mrs Wanda Sandham BA MCLIP

STOKE-ON-TRENT
Authority: Stoke-on-Trent City Council

Libraries and Archives, Community Services Division, Directorate of Adult Social Care, Health and Communities, City Central Library, Bethesda Street, Hanley, Stoke-on-Trent ST1 3RS
☎(01782) 238455 (enquiries); (01782) 238405 (administration)
Fax (01782) 238499
e-mail: stoke.libraries@stoke.gov.uk
url: www.stoke.gov.uk
Strategic Manager: Libraries Ms Janet Thursfield MCLIP (e-mail: janet.thursfield@stoke.gov.uk)
Principal Librarian: Service Development Mrs Anne Mackey BA MCLIP (e-mail: anne.mackey@stoke.gov.uk)
City Archivist Chris Latimer MA DAA (e-mail: chris.latimer@stoke.gov.uk)
Principal Librarians: Children's & Young People's Services Mrs Caroline Lovatt BA MCLIP (e-mail: caroline.lovatt@stoke.gov.uk), Ms Jayne Stanley BA DipLib (e-mail: jayne.stanley@stoke.gov.uk)

Stock and Resources Unit Manager Mrs Gill Taylor BA MCLIP (e-mail: gill.taylor@stoke.gov.uk)

SUFFOLK
Authority: Suffolk County Council

Adults and Communities Services, Endeavour House, Russell Road, Ipswich IP1 2BX
☎(01473) 264285 (enquiries and administration)
Fax (01473) 216847
e-mail: help@suffolklibraries.co.uk
url: www.suffolklibraries.co.uk
Service Director for Culture, Information, Inclusion and Learning Ms Guenever J Pachent BA DLIS MCLIP MILAM (01473 264672; e-mail: guenever.pachent@suffolk.gov.uk)
Head of Service Development, Information, Advice and Library Service Ms Alison Wheeler (01473 264611; e-mail: alison.wheeler@suffolk.gov.uk)
Head of Suffolk Libraries and Record Office Roger McMaster BA MA MCLIP (e-mail: roger.mcmaster@suffolk.gov.uk)
Adult Services Manager Stephen Taylor (01473 265309; e-mail: stephen.taylor@suffolk.gov.uk)
Children, Young People and Schools Library Service Manager Ms Helen Boothroyd BA MCLIP (01473 264623; e-mail: helen.boothroyd@suffolk.gov.uk)

Central/largest library

County Library, Northgate Street, Ipswich IP1 3DE
☎(01473) 583705 (reference); (01473) 583710 (lending)
Fax (01473) 583700
Area Manager (South) Mrs Lynda Farnworth BA DMA MCLIP (e-mail: lynda.farnworth@suffolk.gov.uk)
Assistant Manager Ms Marion Harvey (e-mail: marion.harvey@suffolk.gov.uk)

Area libraries

Bury St Edmunds Library, Sergeant's Walk, St Andrew's Street North, Bury St Edmunds, Suffolk IP33 1TZ
☎(01284) 352545
Area Manager (West) Ms Lisa Elmer (e-mail: lisa.elmer@suffolk.gov.uk)
Manager Neil Holmes (e-mail: neil.holmes@suffolk.gov.uk)

Lowestoft Library, Clapham Road South, Lowestoft, Suffolk NR32 1DR
☎(01502) 405342
Fax (01502) 405350
Area Manager (North) Paul Howarth (e-mail: paul.howarth@suffolk.gov.uk)
Manager Ms Tracy Etheridge (e-mail: tracy.etheridge@suffolk.gov.uk)

Selected branch libraries

Beccles Library, Blyburgate, Beccles, Suffolk NR34 9TB
☎(01502) 714073/716471
Library Manager Stephen Amer

Felixstowe Library, Crescent Road, Felixstowe, Suffolk IP11 7BY

☎(01394) 625766
Library Manager Mrs Lynne Gibbs

Hadleigh Library, 29 High Street, Hadleigh, Ipswich IP7 5AG
☎(01473) 823778
Library Manager Ms Sarah Hunt

Haverhill Library, Camps Road, Haverhill, Suffolk CB9 8HB
☎(01440) 702638
Library Manager Ms Sanphra Willmott (e-mail: sanphra.willmott@suffolk.gov.uk)

Mildenhall Library, Chestnut Close, Mildenhall, Bury St Edmunds, Suffolk IP28 7HL
☎(01638) 713558
Library Manager Ms Denise Gray

Newmarket Library, 1a The Rookery, Newmarket, Suffolk CB8 8EQ
☎(01638) 661216
Library Manager Mrs Grace Myers-Crump

Stowmarket Library, Milton Road North, Stowmarket, Suffolk IP14 1EX
☎(01449) 613143
Library Manager Ms Frances Law

Sudbury Library, Market Hill, Sudbury, Suffolk CO10 2EN
☎(01787) 296000
Library Manager Gareth Lewry (e-mail: gareth.lewry@suffolk.gov.uk)

Woodbridge Library, New Street, Woodbridge, Suffolk IP12 1DT
☎(01394) 625095
Library Manager Kevin Hartwell (e-mail: kevin.hartwell@suffolk.gov.uk)

SUNDERLAND
Authority: Sunderland City Council

City Library and Arts Centre, Fawcett Street, Sunderland SR1 1RE
☎0191 561 1235 (enquiries and administration)
Fax 0191 565 5950
e-mail: libraries@sunderland.gov.uk
url: www.sunderland.gov.uk
Assistant Head of Culture and Tourism (Libraries, Heritage, Events and Tourism)
Ms Jane F Hall BA(Hons) MCLIP (e-mail: Jane.Hall@sunderland.gov.uk)
Library Manager Mrs Allison Clarke BA (e-mail: allison.clarke@sunderland.gov.uk)
Principal Librarian (Development and Projects) Mrs Ann Scott MCLIP (e-mail:
ann.scott@sunderland.gov.uk)
Principal Librarian (Resources and Performance) Ms Julie McCann BA(Hons) MCLIP
(e-mail: julie.mccann@sunderland.gov.uk)
Principal Librarian (Reader Development) Mrs Joanne Parkinson BA(Hons) (e-mail:
joanne.parkinson@sunderland.gov.uk)
Principal Librarian (Library Development) Ms Vivienne Foster BA (e-mail:
vivienne.foster@sunderland.gov.uk)
Principal Librarian (Library Operations) Mrs Allison Clarke BA (e-mail:
allison.clarke@sunderland.gov.uk)

Area library

Washington Town Centre Library and Customer Service Centre, Independence Square, Washington, Tyne and Wear NE38 7RZ
☎0191 219 5611

SURREY

Authority: Surrey County Council

Libraries and Culture, Room 356, County Hall, Kingston upon Thames, Surrey KT1 2DN
☎08456 009009
Fax 020 8541 9447
url: www.surreycc.gov.uk/libraries
Head of Cultural Services Peter Milton (020 8541 7679; e-mail: peter.milton@surreycc.gov.uk)

Enquiries Direct

Enquiries Direct, c/o Guildford Library, 77 North Street, Guildford, Surrey GU1 4AL
☎(01483) 543599
Fax (01483) 543597
e-mail: libraries@surreycc.gov.uk

Senior Management Team

Mid-Surrey Area Office, (AO1), Opus II, Kingston Road, Leatherhead, Surrey KT22 7SY
☎07976 290762
Library Operations Manager Mrs Rose Wilson BA(Hons) (e-mail: r.wilson@surreycc.gov.uk)
Virtual Services Manager Mrs Hilary Ely MA MCLIP (07968 832419; e-mail: h.ely@surreycc.gov.uk)

East Surrey Area Office, (AO2) Omnibus, Lesbourne Road, Reigate, Surrey RH2 7JA
☎07968 832372
Library Sectors Manager Ms Sally Parker BA(Hons) FCLIP (e-mail: sally.p@surreycc.gov.uk)

Bourne Hall Library, Spring Street, Ewell, Surrey KT17 1UF
☎020 8786 7361
Property, Environment and Stock Manager John Case (e-mail: john.case@surreycc.gov.uk)

Woking Library, Gloucester Walk, Woking, Surrey GU21 1EP
☎(01483) 770591/2
Programme Manager Ms Janet Thomas BA(Hons) MCLIP (e-mail: janet.thomas@surreycc.gov.uk)

Guildford Library, 77 North Street, Guildford, Surrey GU1 4AL
☎0300 200 1001
Information Services Manager Mrs Sue Gent BSc(Hons) MCLIP (01483 543584; e-mail: sue.gent@surreycc.gov.uk)

The Drill Hall, Drill Hall Road, Off West Street, Dorking, Surrey RH4 1DD
☎(01306) 881499

Service Enabling Officer Mrs Christine Ganderton (e-mail:
christine.ganderton@surreycc.gov.uk)
Virtual Content Manager Ms Helen Leech (07792 225915; e-mail:
helen.leech@surreycc.gov.uk)

Library Sector Leads

Farnham Library, Vernon House, 28 West Street, Farnham, Surrey GU9 7DR
☎(01252) 716038
Library Sector Lead West Mrs Pauline Fella

Reigate Library, Bancroft House, Bancroft Road, Reigate, Surrey RH2 7RP
☎(01737) 244318
Library Sector Lead East Mrs Marion Saberi

Weybridge Library, Church Street, Weybridge, Surrey KT13 8DE
☎0300 200 1001
Library Sector Lead North Ms Crishna Simmons (01932 859713; e-mail:
chrisna.simmons@surreycc.gov.uk)

Main libraries

(All libraries in this section can be contacted on 0300 200 1001)

Addlestone Library, Runnymede Civic Centre, Station Road, Addlestone, Surrey K15 2AF

Ashford Library, Church Road, Ashford, Middlesex TW15 2XB

Banstead Library, The Horseshoe, Bolters Lane, Banstead, Surrey SM7 2AW

Camberley Library, Knoll Road, Camberley, Surrey GU15 3SY

Caterham Valley Library, Stafford Road, Caterham, Surrey CR3 6JG

Cranleigh Library, High Street, Cranleigh, Surrey GU6 8AE

Dittons Library, Mercer Close, Thames Ditton, Surrey KT7 0BS

Dorking Library, Pippbrook, Reigate Road, Dorking, Surrey RH4 1SL

Egham Library, High Street, Egham, Surrey TW20 9EA

Epsom Library, The Ebbisham Centre, 6 The Derby Square, Epsom, Surrey KT19 8AG

Esher Library, Old Church Path, Esher, Surrey KT10 9NS

Ewell Library, Bourne Hall, Spring Street, Ewell, Epsom, Surrey KT17 1UF

Farnham Library, Vernon House, 28 West Street, Farnham, Surrey GU9 7DR

Godalming Library, Bridge Street, Godalming, Surrey GU7 1HT

Guildford Library, 77 North Street, Guildford, Surrey GU1 4AL

Haslemere Library, 91 Wey Hill, Haslemere, Surrey GU27 1HP

Horley Library, Victoria Road, Horley, Surrey RH6 7AG

Leatherhead Library, The Mansion, Church Street, Leatherhead, Surrey KT22 8DP

Molesey Library, The Forum, Walton Road, West Molesey, Surrey KT8 2HZ

Oxted Library, 12 Gresham Road, Oxted, Surrey RH8 0BQ

Redhill Library, Warwick Quadrant, Redhill, Surrey RH1 1NN

Staines Library, Friends Walk, Staines, Middlesex TW18 4PG

Walton Library, 54 The Heart (off Hepworth Way), Walton on Thames, Surrey KT12 1GH

Weybridge Library, Church Street, Weybridge, Surrey KT13 8DE

Woking Library, Gloucester Walk, Woking, Surrey GU21 6EP

SUTTON
Authority: London Borough of Sutton

Sutton Central Library, St Nicholas Way, Sutton, Surrey SM1 1EA
☎020 8770 4700 (enquiries), 020 8770 4602 (administration)
Fax 020 8770 4777
e-mail: sutton.library@sutton.gov.uk
url: www.sutton.gov.uk
Executive Head of Leisure and Libraries Colin Beech (020 8770 4642; e-mail:
colin.beech@sutton.gov.uk)
Head of Libraries and Heritage Service Mrs Cathy McDonough BSc MCLIP (020 8770
4755; e-mail: cathy.mcdonough@sutton.gov.uk), Mrs Angela Fletcher BA(Hons) PGCE
(020 8770 4755; e-mail: angela.fletcher@sutton.gov.uk) (job-share)
Assistant Head of Libraries Jon Ward (020 8770 4708; e-mail: jon.ward@sutton.gov.uk)
Library Projects Manager Mrs Pauline Deakin BA MCLIP (020 8770 4772; e-mail:
pauline.deakin@sutton.gov.uk)
Facilities Manager (Libraries and Heritage) Jon Ward (020 8770 4708; e-mail:
jon.ward@sutton.gov.uk)

Main libraries

Carshalton Library, The Square, Carshalton, Surrey SM5 3BN
☎020 8647 1151
Library Manager Mrs Helen Viola

Cheam Library, Church Road, Cheam, Surrey SM3 8QH
☎020 8644 9377
Library Manager Ms Christine McCarthy

Wallington Library, Shotfield, Wallington, Surrey SM6 0HY
☎020 8770 4900
Library Manager Steve Winser

Worcester Park Library, Windsor Road, Worcester Park, Surrey KT4 8ES
☎020 8337 1609
Library Manager Ms Tracey Parker

SWINDON
Authority: Swindon Borough Council

Libraries, Housing, Leisure and Culture, Wat Tyler House East, Swindon SN1 2JH
☎(01793) 466035

url: www.swindon.gov.uk
Head of Libraries Ms Allyson Jordan MCLIP (e-mail: ajordan@swindon.gov.uk)

Central/largest library

Swindon Central Library, Regent Circus, Swindon SN1 1QG
☎(01793) 463238
Fax (01793) 541319
e-mail: central.library@swindon.gov.uk

Group libraries

Acquisitions Group. Library Support Unit, Liden Library, Barrington Close, Liden, Swindon SN3 6HF
☎(01793) 463510
Fax (01793) 463508
Acquisitions and Interlending Manager Adrian Peace (e-mail: apeace@swindon.gov.uk)

North and East Group Libraries. North Swindon Library, Orbital Shopping Park, Thamesdown Drive, Swindon SN25 4AN
☎(01793) 707120
Strategic Manager, Children and Young People's Services Mrs Mary Dawes (01793 707122; e-mail: mdawes@swindon.gov.uk)

Swindon Central Library, Regent Circus, Swindon SN1 1QG
☎(01793) 463238
Fax (01793) 541319
Strategic Manager, Information Services Mark Jones MCLIP (01793 463795; e-mail: markjones@swindon.gov.uk)

West and South Group Libraries. Liden Library, Barrington Close, Swindon SN3 6HF
☎(01793) 463504
Strategic Manager, Adult and Community Services Shaun Smith MCLIP (01793 466504; e-mail: ssmith@swindon.gov.uk)

TAMESIDE
Authority: Tameside Metropolitan Borough Council

Cultural and Customer Services, Council Offices, Wellington Road, Ashton-under-Lyne, Tameside OL6 6DL
url: www.tameside.gov.uk/libraries
Service Unit Manager Mrs Mandy Kinder (0161 342 2061; e-mail: mandy.kinder@tameside.gov.uk)
Service Delivery and Inclusion Manager Ms Judith Hall BLib MCLIP (e-mail: judith.hall@tameside.gov.uk)
Service Operations Manager Ms Denise Lockyer (0161 336 8234; e-mail: denise.lockyer@tameside.gov.uk)
Service Development Manager Philip Jones BA MCLIP (0161 342 2035; e-mail: philip.jones@tameside.gov.uk)

Central/largest library

Tameside Central Library, Old Street, Ashton-under-Lyne, Tameside OL6 7SG

☎0161 342 2029 (lending/enquiries), 0161 342 2037 (bibliographical enquiries),
0161 342 2031 (information)
Fax 0161 330 4762
e-mail: information.direct@tameside.gov.uk; central.library@tameside.gov.uk
Information Services Librarian Ms Karen Heathcote BA DipLIS MCLIP
Young People's Services Co-ordinator Mrs Ruth Lomas (0161 342 2664; e-mail:
ruth.lomas@tameside.gov.uk)

Other large library

Hyde Library, Union Street, Hyde, Cheshire SK14 1ND
☎0161 342 4450
Fax 0161 368 0909
e-mail: hyde.library@tameside.gov.uk

TELFORD AND WREKIN
Authority: Telford and Wrekin Council

Telford and Wrekin Libraries, Telford Library, St Quentin Gate, Telford, Shropshire TF3 4JG
☎(01952) 382915
Fax (01952) 382937
e-mail: telford.library@telford.gov.uk; libraryenquiries@telford.gov.uk
url: www.telford.gov.uk
Library Service Delivery Manager Ms Sharon Smith BA MCLIP
Senior Librarian, Information Services Mrs Helen Nahal BLib MCLIP
Library Services Development Manager Ms Marilyn Higson MA MCLIP

THURROCK
Authority: Thurrock Council

**Communities, Libraries and Cultural Services Department, Thameside Complex, Orsett
Road, Grays, Essex RM17 5DX**
☎(01375) 413976 (enquiries), (01375) 413963 (administration)
Fax (01375) 385504
e-mail: grays.library@thurrock.gov.uk
url: www.thurrock.gov.uk
Head of Communities, Libraries and Cultural Services Simon Black (01375 413962;
e-mail: sblack@thurrock.gov.uk)
Library Services Manager Mrs Ann Halliday BA(Hons) DipLIS MCLIP (01375 413972;
e-mail: ahalliday@thurrock.gov.uk)
Children's Services Manager Miss Rosalyn Jones BA(Hons) DipLib (01375 413969;
e-mail: rjones@thurrock.gov.uk)

Central/largest library

Grays Library, Thameside Complex, Orsett Road, Grays, Essex RM17 5DX
☎(01375) 413976
e-mail: grays.library@thurrock.gov.uk
Library Manager Ms Sue Pollett (e-mail: spollett@thurrock.gov.uk)

TORBAY
Authority: Torbay Council

Torquay Library, Lymington Road, Torquay, Devon TQI 3DT
☎(01803) 208300 (enquiries), (01803) 208310 (administration)
Fax (01803) 208311
url: www.torbay.gov.uk/libraries
Head of Library Services Miss Katie Lusty BA MCLIP (01803 208286; e-mail:
katie.lusty@torbay.gov.uk)
Resources and Technical Services Librarian Miss Elizabeth Kent BSc MCLIP (01803
208287; e-mail: liz.kent@torbay.gov.uk)
Community and Performance Librarian Nick Niles BA DipLib (01803 208288; e-mail:
nick.niles@torbay.gov.uk)
Community Librarian Mrs Angie Weatherhead BSc MA MSc (01803 208288; e-mail:
angie.weatherhead@torbay.gov.uk)

Branch libraries

Brixham Library, Market Street, Brixham, Devon TQ5 8EU
☎(01803) 853870
Branch Librarian Mrs Eleanor Moss MA

Churston Library, Broadsands Road, Paignton, Devon TQ4 6LL
☎(01803) 843757
Branch Librarian Mrs Susie Murr MCLIP

Paignton Library, Courtland Road, Paignton, Devon TQ3 2AB
☎(01803) 208321
Branch Librarian Mrs Rosie Corby BA MCLIP

TOWER HAMLETS
Authority: London Borough of Tower Hamlets

Shadwell Centre, 455 The Highway, London EIW 3HP
☎020 7364 5684
url: www.ideastore.co.uk
Head of Idea Stores Ms Judith St John (020 7364 5630; e-mail:
judith.st.john@towerhamlets.gov.uk)
Deputy Head of Idea Store Sergio Dogliani (020 7364 2649; e-mail:
sergio.dogliani@towerhamlets.gov.uk)
Access and Inclusion Manager Graham Pollard (020 7364 5091; e-mail:
graham.pollard@towerhamlets.gov.uk)
Library Development Adviser Ms Kate Pitman BA MCLIP (020 7364 5740; e-mail:
kate.pitman@towerhamlets.gov.uk)
Stock Development Manager Stephen Clarke BA MCLIP (020 7364 6794; e-mail:
steve.j.clarke@towerhamlets.gov.uk)

Largest idea store/library

Idea Store Whitechapel, 321 Whitechapel Road, London EI IBU
☎020 7364 4332
e-mail: ideastore@towerhamlets.gov.uk

Idea Store Manager Asab Ali (020 7364 1742; e-mail: asab.ali@towerhamlets.gov.uk)

Full-time idea stores/libraries

Bethnal Green Library, Cambridge Heath Road, London E2 0HL
☎020 8980 3902
e-mail: ideastore@towerhamlets.gov.uk
Idea Store Manager Ms Barbara Stretch (e-mail: barbara.stretch@towerhamlets.gov.uk)

Cubitt Town Library, Strattondale Street, London E14 3HG
☎020 7987 3152
e-mail: ideastore@towerhamlets.gov.uk
Idea Store Manager Ms Lisa Randall (020 7364 1260; e-mail:
lisa.randall@towerhamlets.gov.uk)

Idea Store Bow, 1 Gladstone Place, Roman Road, London E3 5ES
☎020 7364 4332
e-mail: ideastore@towerhamlets.gov.uk
Idea Store Manager Ms Barbara Stretch (020 7364 5775; e-mail:
barbara.stretch@towerhamlets.gov.uk)

Idea Store Canary Wharf, Churchill Place, Canary Wharf, London E14 5RB
☎020 7364 4332
e-mail: ideastore@towerhamlets.gov.uk
Idea Store Manager Ms Lisa Randall (020 7364 1260; e-mail:
lisa.randall@towerhamlets.gov.uk)

Idea Store Chrisp Street, 1 Vesey Path, East India Dock Road, London E14 6BT
☎020 8364 4332
e-mail: ideastore@towerhamlets.gov.uk
Idea Store Manager Shaw Rahman (020 7364 1502; e-mail:
shaw.rahman@towerhamlets.gov.uk)

Watney Market Library, 30-32 Watney Market, London E1 2PR
☎020 7790 4039
e-mail: ideastore@towerhamlets.gov.uk
Idea Store Manager Shaw Rahman (020 7364 1502; e-mail:
shaw.rahman@towerhamlets.gov.uk)

Local Studies and Archives

Bancroft Library, 277 Bancroft Road, London E1 4DQ
e-mail: localhistorylibrary@towerhamlets.gov.uk
Heritage Manager Ms Tamsin Bookey (020 7364 1293; e-mail:
tamsin.bookey@towerhamlets.gov.uk)
Borough Archivist Malcolm Barr-Hamilton BA DAS (020 7364 1289)

Part-time libraries

Dorset Library, Ravenscroft Street, London E2 7QX
☎020 7739 9489
Closed until further notice

TRAFFORD
Authority: Trafford Metropolitan Borough Council

Transformation and Resources, Access Trafford, Sale Library, Sale Waterside, Sale, Cheshire M33 7ZF
☎0161 912 2003 (enquiries and administration)
Fax 0161 912 3019
e-mail: libraries@trafford.gov.uk
url: www.trafford.gov.uk/libraries
Interim Head of Service, Access Trafford Ms Sharon Richardson

Main branch libraries

Altrincham Library, 20 Stamford New Road, Altrincham, Cheshire WA14 1EJ
☎0161 912 5920
Fax 0161 941 6452

Sale Library, Sale Waterside, Sale, Cheshire M33 7ZF
☎0161 912 3008
Fax 0161 912 3019

Stretford Library, Kingsway, Stretford, Manchester M32 8AP
☎0161 912 5150
Fax 0161 865 3835

Urmston Library, Unit 34, Golden Way, Urmston, Manchester M41 0NA
☎0161 912 2727
Fax 0161 912 2947

UPPER NORWOOD JOINT LIBRARY
Authority: Upper Norwood Joint Library

Upper Norwood Joint Library, 39–41 Westow Hill, Upper Norwood, London SE19 1TJ
☎020 8670 2551
Fax 020 8670 5468
e-mail: info@uppernorwoodlibrary.org
url: www.uppernorwoodlibrary.org
Chief Librarian Bradley Millington MCLIP (e-mail:
bmillington@uppernorwood.akhter.com)
Children's Librarian Ms Fiona Byers (e-mail: fbyers@uppernorwood.akhter.com)

WAKEFIELD
Authority: Wakefield Metropolitan District Council

Libraries and Information Services, Balne Lane, Wakefield, West Yorks WF2 0DQ
☎(01924) 302261 (enquiries and administration)
Fax (01924) 302245
e-mail: lib.admin@wakefield.gov.uk
url: www.wakefield.gov.uk/libraries
Libraries and Information Services Manager Ms Judith Walker
Library Managers Andrew Wright BMus(Hons) DipLib, Miss Helen Smithson, Tristan Bottom
Support Services Manager Matt Isherwood

WALSALL
Authority: Walsall Council

Libraries, Heritage and Arts, Tameway Tower, 6th Floor, 48 Bridge Street, Walsall, West Midlands WS1 IJZ
☎(01922) 650338
Fax (01922) 721682
e-mail: librarian@walsall.gov.uk
url: www.walsall.gov.uk/libraries
Head of Libraries, Heritage and Arts Mrs Sue Grainger MCLIP (e-mail: graingers@walsall.gov.uk)

Central/largest library

Central Library, Lichfield Street, Walsall, West Midlands WS1 1TR
☎(01922) 653121 (lending), (01922) 653110 (reference)
Fax (01922) 722687 (lending), (01922) 654013 (reference)
e-mail: centrallendinglibrary@walsall.gov.uk; reference@walsall.gov.uk
Central Library Manager Ms Denise Gold BA(Hons) (e-mail: goldd@walsall.gov.uk)
Strategic Manager - Development Ms Rita Mills
SLSS Manager Ms Louise Davies BA MCLIP (01922 724995; e-mail: davieslouise@walsall.gov.uk)

Area libraries

Aldridge Library, Rookery Lane, Aldridge, Walsall, West Midlands WS9 8NN
☎(01922) 655569
e-mail: aldridgelibrary@walsall.gov.uk

Beechdale Library, Beechdale Centre, Stephenson Square, Walsall, West Midlands WS2 7DX
☎(01922) 655890
e-mail: beechdalelibrary@walsall.gov.uk

Blakenall Library, Blakenall Village Centre, Thames Road, Blakenall, Walsall, West Midlands WS3 1LZ
☎(01922) 714967
e-mail: blakenalllibrary@walsall.gov.uk

Bloxwich Library, Elmore Row, Bloxwich, Walsall, West Midlands WS3 2HR
☎(01922) 655900
e-mail: bloxwichlibrary@walsall.gov.uk

Brownhills Library, Park View Centre, Chester Road North, Walsall, West Midlands WS8 7JB
☎(01922) 650730
e-mail: brownhillslibrary@walsall.gov.uk

Darlaston Library, 1 King Street, Darlaston, Walsall, West Midlands WS10 8DD
☎0121 526 4530
e-mail: darlastonlibrary@walsall.gov.uk

Local History Centre, Essex Street, Walsall, West Midlands WS2 7AS
☎(01922) 721305
Fax (01922) 634954
e-mail: localhistorycentre@walsall.gov.uk

Mobile and Home Library Service, Mobile Library Depot, Willenhall Lane, Bloxwich, Walsall, West Midlands WS3 2XN
☎(01922) 710625
e-mail: mobilelibrary@walsall.gov.uk

New Invention Library, The Square, Lichfield Road, Willenhall, Walsall, West Midlands WV12 5EA
☎(01922) 655570
e-mail: newinventionlibrary@walsall.gov.uk

Pelsall Library, High Street, Pelsall, Walsall, West Midlands WS3 4LX
☎(01922) 682212
e-mail: pelsalllibrary@walsall.gov.uk

Pheasey Library, Collingwood Centre, Collingwood Drive, Great Barr, Pheasey, Birmingham B43 7NE
☎(01922) 654865
e-mail: pheaseylibrary@walsall.gov.uk

Pleck Library, Darlaston Road, Pleck, Walsall, West Midlands WS2 9RE
☎(01922) 654860
e-mail: plecklibrary@walsall.gov.uk

Rushall Library, Pelsall Lane, Walsall, West Midlands WS4 1NL
☎(01922) 721310
e-mail: rushalllibrary@walsall.gov.uk

South Walsall Library, West Bromwich Road, Walsall, West Midlands WS5 4NW
☎(01922) 721347
e-mail: southwalsalllibrary@walsall.gov.uk

Streetly Library, Blackwood Road, Streetly, Birmingham B74 3PL
☎(01922) 654864
e-mail: streetlylibrary@walsall.gov.uk

Walsall Wood Library, Coppice Road, Walsall Wood, Walsall, West Midlands WS9 9BL
☎(01922) 655572
e-mail: walsallwoodlibrary@walsall.gov.uk

Willenhall Library, Walsall Street, Willenhall, Walsall, West Midlands WV13 2EX
☎(01902) 366513
e-mail: willenhalllibrary@walsall.gov.uk

WALTHAM FOREST
Authority: London Borough of Waltham Forest

Administrative Office, Silver Birch House, Uplands Business Park, Blackhorse Lane, Walthamstow, London E17 5SD
☎020 8496 3645
Fax 020 8496 3508
e-mail: wf.libs@walthamforest.gov.uk
url: www.walthamforest.gov.uk
Head of Libraries, Museum and Gallery Ms Lorna Lee BA(Hons) MA MSc (e-mail: lorna.lee@walthamforest.gov.uk)

Support & Development Manager Manny Manoharan BSc(Hons) PGDip (e-mail:
manny.manoharan@walthamforest.gov.uk)
Group Managers Paul Drumm BA(Hons) MA MSc (e-mail:
paul.drumm@walthamforest.gov.uk), Ms Caroline Rae BA(Hons) MA (e-mail:
caroline.rae@walthamforest.gov.uk)

Libraries

Hale End Library, Castle Avenue, Chingford, London E4 9QD
☎020 8496 1050 (voice and minicom)
Fax 020 8496 1055
e-mail: wf.libs@walthamforest.gov.uk

Harrow Green Library, Cathall Road, Leytonstone, London E11 4LF
☎020 8496 1063 (voice and minicom)
Fax 020 8496 1064
e-mail: wf.libs@walthamforest.gov.uk

Higham Hill Library, North Countess Road, Walthamstow, London E17 5HS
☎020 8496 1173 (voice and minicom)
Fax 020 8496 1172
e-mail: wf.libs@walthamforest.gov.uk

Lea Bridge Library, Lea Bridge Road, Leyton, London E10 7HU
☎020 8496 1152 (voice and minicom)
Fax 020 8496 1151
e-mail: wf.libs@walthamforest.gov.uk

Leyton Library, High Road, Leyton, London E10 5QH
☎020 8496 1090 (voice and minicom)
Fax 020 8496 1094
e-mail: wf.libs@walthamforest.gov.uk

Leytonstone Library, Church Lane, Leytonstone, London E11 1HG
☎020 8496 1190 (voice and minicom)
Fax 020 8496 1191
e-mail: wf.libs@walthamforest.gov.uk

North Chingford Library, The Green, Chingford, London E4 7EN
☎020 8496 1070 (voice and minicom)
Fax 020 8496 1069
e-mail: wf.libs@walthamforest.gov.uk

South Chingford Library, Hall Lane, Chingford, London E4 8EU
☎020 8496 1079 (voice and minicom)
Fax 020 8496 1080
e-mail: wf.libs@walthamforest.gov.uk

Walthamstow Library, High Street, Walthamstow, London E17 7JN
☎020 8496 5132 (voice and minicom)
Fax 020 8496 1172
e-mail: wf.libs@walthamforest.gov.uk

Wood Street Library, Forest Road, Walthamstow, London E17 4AA
☎020 8496 1156 (voice and minicom)

Fax 020 8496 1155
e-mail: wf.libs@walthamforest.gov.uk

WANDSWORTH
Authority: Wandsworth Council

Leisure and Amenity Services Department, Wandsworth High Street, London SW18 2PU
☎020 8871 6369 (enquiries and administration)
Fax 020 8871 7630
e-mail: libraries@wandsworth.gov.uk
url: www.wandsworth.gov.uk/libraries
Head of Library and Heritage Service Andrew Green BA(Hons) MLS MCLIP
Assistant Head of Library and Heritage Service Ms Meryl Jones MCLIP

Largest libraries

Balham Library, 16 Ramsden Road, London SW12 8QY
☎020 8871 7195
Fax 020 8675 4015

Battersea Library, 265 Lavender Hill, London SW11 1JB
☎020 8871 7466
Fax 020 7978 4376

Putney Library, 5/7 Disraeli Road, London SW15 2DR
☎020 8871 7090
Fax 020 8789 6175

Tooting Library, 75 Mitcham Road, London SW17 9PD
☎020 8871 7175
Fax 020 8672 3099

WARRINGTON
Authority: Warrington Borough Council

Central Library, Museum and Art Gallery, Museum Street, Cultural Quarter, Warrington, Cheshire WA1 1JB
☎(01925) 442889 (enquiries), (01925) 442733 (Divisional Support Team)
Fax (01925) 443257
e-mail: library@warrington.gov.uk
url: www.warrington.gov.uk/libraries
Head of Libraries, Heritage and Learning Martin Gaw BA DipLib MCLIP (01925 442733)
Principal Libraries Manager Ms Fiona Barry BA MCLIP (01925 442892)

Branch libraries

Birchwood Library, Brock Road, Warrington, Cheshire WA3 7PT
☎(01925) 827491 (tel/fax)

Burtonwood Library, Chapel Lane, Burtonwood, Warrington, Cheshire WA5 4PS
☎(01925) 226563 (tel/fax)

Culcheth Library, Warrington Road, Culcheth, Warrington, Cheshire WA3 5SL
☎(01925) 763293 (tel/fax)

Grappenhall Library, Victoria Avenue, Grappenhall, Warrington, Cheshire WA4 2PE
☎(01925) 262861 (tel/fax)

Great Sankey Library, Marina Avenue, Great Sankey, Warrington, Cheshire WA5 1JH
☎(01925) 231451 (tel/fax)

Lymm Library, Davies Way, Off Brookfield Road, Lymm, Warrington, Cheshire WA13 0QW
☎(01925) 754367 (tel/fax)

Orford Library, Poplars Avenue, Orford, Warrington, Cheshire WA2 9LW
☎(01925) 812821 (tel/fax)

Padgate Library, Insall Road, Padgate, Warrington, Cheshire WA2 0HD
☎(01925) 818096 (tel/fax)

Penketh Library, Honiton Way, Penketh, Warrington, Cheshire WA5 2EY
☎(01925) 723730
Fax (01925) 791264

Stockton Heath Library, Alexandra Park, Stockton Heath, Warrington, Cheshire WA4 2AN
☎(01925) 261148
Fax (01925) 267787

Westbrook Library, Westbrook Centre, Westbrook Crescent, Warrington, Cheshire WA5 5UG
☎(01925) 416561
Fax (01925) 230462

Woolston Library, Holes Lane, Woolston, Warrington, Cheshire WA1 3UJ
☎(01925) 816146 (tel/fax)

WARWICKSHIRE
Authority: Warwickshire County Council

Service, Communities and Wellbeing, Barrack Street, Warwick CV34 4TH
☎(01926) 412550 (enquiries and administration)
Fax (01926) 412471/412165
e-mail: librarieslearningandculture@warwickshire.gov.uk
url: www.warwickshire.gov.uk/libraries
Interim Head of Service, Communities and Wellbeing Simon Robson
Head of Library and Information Services (Strategy) Ayub Khan BA(Hons) FCLIP
(01926 412657; e-mail: ayubkhan@warwickshire.gov.uk)
Head of Library and Information Services (Operations) Ms Linda Smith MCLIP
(e-mail: lindasmith@warwickshire.gov.uk)
Service Improvement Manager Ms Liz Wood (01926 736360; e-mail:
lizwood@warwickshire.gov.uk)
Audience Development Manager Paul MacDermott BA DipLib MCLIP (e-mail:
paulmacdermott@warwickshire.gov.uk)
Network Information Access Manager Ms Sorrelle Clements (e-mail:
sorrelle.clements@warwickshire.gov.uk)

Divisional libraries

Central Warwickshire Division. Leamington Library (Central Divisional Library), Royal
Pump Rooms, The Parade, Leamington Spa, Warwicks CV32 4AA
☎(01926) 742721/742722
Fax (01926) 742749
e-mail: leamingtonlibrary@warwickshire.gov.uk
Divisional Librarian Ms Tracey Baker (e-mail: traceybaker@warwickshire.gov.uk)

North Warwickshire Division. Atherstone Library (North Divisional Library), Long Street,
Atherstone, Warwicks CV9 1AX
☎(01827) 712395/712034
Fax (01827) 720285
e-mail: atherstonelibrary@warwickshire.gov.uk
Divisional Librarian Ms Jayney Faulknall-Mills (e-mail:
jayneyfaulknall-mills@warwickshire.gov.uk)

Nuneaton and Bedworth Division. Nuneaton Library, Church Street, Nuneaton, Warwicks
CV11 4DR
☎024 7638 4027/024 7634 7006
Fax 024 7635 0125
e-mail: nuneatonlibrary@warwickshire.gov.uk
Divisional Librarian David Reed BA(Hons) MCLIP (e-mail:
davidreed@warwickshire.gov.uk)

South/East Division. Rugby Library (South Divisional Library), Little Elborow Street, Rugby,
Warwicks CV21 3BZ
☎(01788) 533250
Fax (01788) 533252
e-mail: rugbylibrary@warwickshire.gov.uk
Divisional Librarian Ms Corinne Harvey (e-mail: corinneharvey@warwickshire.gov.uk)

Stratford Library, Henley Street, Stratford-upon-Avon, Warwicks CV37 6PZ
☎(01789) 292209/296904
Fax (01789) 268554
e-mail: stratfordlibrary@warwickshire.gov.uk
Divisional Librarian Ms Tanya Butchers BA(Hons) MA MCLIP (e-mail:
tanyabutchers@warwickshire.gov.uk)

WEST BERKSHIRE
Authority: West Berkshire District Council

**Cultural Services, Council Offices, West Street House, West Street, Newbury, Berks
RG14 1BZ**
☎(01635) 519904
Fax (01635) 519811
e-mail: library@westberks.gov.uk
url: www.westberks.gov.uk
Library Services Manager Mrs Christine Owen BA(Hons) MCLIP (01635 519904; e-mail:
cowen@westberks.gov.uk)

Central/largest library

Newbury Central Library, The Wharf, Newbury, Berks RG14 5AU
☎(01635) 519900
Fax (01635) 519906
e-mail: newburylibrary@westberks.gov.uk
Newbury Branch Supervisor Mrs Sheila Ridley

WEST SUSSEX
Authority: West Sussex County Council

Library Service Administration Centre, 61 North Street, Chichester, West Sussex PO19 INB
☎(01243) 382541
Fax (01243) 382554
url: www.westsussex.gov.uk
BT Gold 74: SKK125
Service Manager – Libraries Mrs Lesley Sim BA(Hons) MCLIP (e-mail:
lesley.sim@westsussex.gov.uk)
(For management enquiries contact headquarters; for services contact one of the principal
libraries)

Principal libraries

Crawley Library, Southgate Avenue, Crawley, West Sussex RH10 6HG
☎(01293) 651751
Fax (01293) 511075
Area Librarian: Crawley Mrs Rita Lucas MCLIP (e-mail: rita.lucas@westsussex.gov.uk)

Worthing Library, Richmond Road, Worthing, West Sussex BN11 1HD
☎(01903) 704824
Fax (01903) 821902
Area Librarian: Worthing David Nye BA MCLIP (e-mail: david.nye@westsussex.gov.uk)

WESTMINSTER
Authority: Westminster City Council

**Westminster Libraries, Management Suite, 3rd Floor, Westminster Reference Library, 35
St Martin's Street, London WC2H 7HP**
☎020 7641 2496 (administration); all libraries: 020 7641 1300 (library enquiries), 020 7641
1400 (renewals)
url: www.westminster.gov.uk/libraries
Minicom: 020 7641 4879 (all libraries)
Director of Library Services David Ruse MCLIP MILAM (020 7641 2496; e-mail:
druse@westminster.gov.uk)
Customer Service Manager Tony Rice (020 7641 8970; e-mail:
trice@westminster.gov.uk)
Reading, Learning and Community Services Manager Ms Mary Enright BA DLIS MSc
(020 7641 1782; e-mail: menright@westminster.gov.uk)
Information and Archives Manager Ms Susanna Barnes (020 7641 5235; e-mail:
sbarnes2@westminster.gov.uk)

Development Manager – Stock Ms Anne Lewis-Lloyd (e-mail: alloyd@westminster.gov.uk)

Largest libraries

Charing Cross Library, 6 Charing Cross Road, London WC2H 0HF
☎020 7641 1300 (Chinese Community Librarian)
e-mail: charingcrosslibrary@westminster.gov.uk
Site Manager Ms Helen Rogers

Marylebone Library, 109 Marylebone Road, London NW1 5PS
e-mail: marylebonelibrary@westminster.gov.uk; (Marylebone Information Service): referencelibrarynw1@westminster.gov.uk
Site Manager Ms Anabel Lopez

Paddington Library, Porchester Road, London W2 5DU
e-mail: paddingtonlibrary@westminster.gov.uk
Site Manager Ms Elizabeth Williams BA MCLIP

Victoria Library, 160 Buckingham Palace Road, London SW1W 9UD
☎020 7641 1300 (Westminster Music Library)
e-mail: victorialibrary@westminster.gov.uk
Site Manager Ms Ann Farrell

Westminster Reference Library, 35 St Martin's Street, London WC2H 7HP
e-mail: referencelibrarywc2@westminster.gov.uk
Site Manager Ms Alexandra Buchholz

Community libraries

Church Street Library, Church Street, London NW8 8EU
e-mail: churchstreetlibrary@westminster.gov.uk
Site Manager Ms Michaela Hope (e-mail: mhope@westminster.gov.uk)

Maida Vale Library, Sutherland Avenue, London W9 2QT
e-mail: maidavalelibrary@westminster.gov.uk
Site Manager Tommy Hannover

Mayfair Library, 25 South Audley Street, London W1K 2PB
e-mail: mayfairlibrary@westminster.gov.uk
Site Managers Frederic Jardin, Ms Mary Houlihan

Pimlico Library, Rampayne Street, London SW1V 2PU
e-mail: pimlicolibrary@westminster.gov.uk
Site Manager Ms Sara Goward-Jones

Queen's Park Library, 666 Harrow Road, London W10 4NE
e-mail: queensparklibrary@westminster.gov.uk
Site Manager Hugh Thomas

St James's Library, 62 Victoria Street, London SW1E 6QP
e-mail: stjameslibrary@westminster.gov.uk
Site Manager Mark Tiller

St John's Wood Library, 20 Circus Road, London NW8 6PD

e-mail: stjohnswoodlibrary@westminster.gov.uk
Site Manager Vic Stewart

Other services

City of Westminster Archives Centre, 10 St Ann's Street, London SW1P 2DE
☎020 7641 5180
e-mail: archives@westminster.gov.uk
Archives and Local Studies Manager Adrian Autton (020 7641 5160; e-mail:
aautton@westminster.gov.uk)

WIGAN
Authority: Wigan Leisure and Culture Trust (on behalf of Wigan Council)

Libraries, Heritage and Arts, Redgate Road, South Lancs Industrial Estate, Bryn, Wigan WN4 8DT
☎(01942) 486980
e-mail: wiglib@wlct.org
url: www.wlct.gov.uk
Head of Libraries and Lifelong Learning Ms Taryn Pearson
Operations Business Manager Ms Wendy Heaton MCLIP
Customer Services Business Manager Andy Harrison
Children's and Information Services Manager Ms Jean Lamb

Central/largest libraries

Leigh Library, Turnpike Centre, Civic Square, Leigh, Lancs WN7 1EB
☎(01942) 404556 (lending), (01942) 404557 (information)
Fax (01942) 404567

Wigan Library, College Avenue, Wigan WN1 1NN
☎(01942) 827621 (lending), (01942) 827619 (information)
Fax (01942) 827640

WILTSHIRE
Authority: Wiltshire County Council

Library HQ, Bythesea Road, Trowbridge, Wilts BA14 8BS
☎(01225) 713700 (enquiries), (01225) 713727 (information)
Fax (01225) 713993
e-mail: libraryenquiries@wiltshire.gov.uk
url: www.wiltshire.gov.uk/libraries/
Head of Library & Information Services Geoff Langridge MA MLS MCLIP (e-mail:
geoff.langridge@wiltshire.gov.uk)
Customer Services Manager Ms Joan Davis BALib MCLIP (e-mail:
joan.davis@wiltshire.gov.uk)
Reading and Learning Services Manager Chris Moore BA(Hons) MSc MCLIP (e-mail:
chris.moore@wiltshire.gov.uk)
Stock Manager David Moger BA(Hons) DipLib MCLIP (e-mail:
david.moger@wiltshire.gov.uk)

District libraries

North and East Area. Chippenham Library, Timber Street, Chippenham, Wilts SN15 3EJ
☎(01249) 650536
Fax (01249) 553793
Area Manager (North & East) Ms Tessa Cozens BA(Hons) MCLIP (01249 445005;
e-mail: tessa.cozens@wiltshire.gov.uk)

South and West Area. Salisbury Library, Market Place, Salisbury, Wiltshire SP1 1BL
☎(01722) 324145
Fax (01722) 413214
Area Manager (South & West) Chris S Harling BA(Hons) MCLIP (01722 330606;
e-mail: chris.harling@wiltshire.gov.uk)

WINDSOR AND MAIDENHEAD
Authority: Royal Borough of Windsor and Maidenhead

Libraries, Arts and Heritage Service, Maidenhead Library, St Ives Road, Maidenhead, Berks SL6 1QU
☎(01628) 796969
Fax (01628) 796971
e-mail: maidenhead.library@rbwm.gov.uk
url: www.rbwm.gov.uk/web/onlinelibrary.htm
Head of Libraries, Arts & Heritage Mark Taylor BA MCLIP (01628 796989; fax: 01628
796986; e-mail: mark.taylor@rbwm.gov.uk)
Service Manager: Development Ms Sara Hudson BA DipLib MCLIP (01628 796742),
Richard Palfrey BSc MA MCLIP (e-mail: richard.palfrey@rbwm.gov.uk) (job-share)
Service Manager: Operations Mrs Angela Gallacher BA(Hons) AUDIS (01628 795641;
e-mail: angela.gallacher@rbwm.gov.uk)
Service Manager: Heritage & Arts Mrs Margaret Kirby BA(Hons) DipLib (01628 685811)

Central/largest library

Maidenhead Library, St Ives Road, Maidenhead, Berks SL6 1QU
☎(01628) 796968 (1st floor), 796969 (issue desk), 796985 (administration)
Fax (01628) 796971
e-mail: maidenhead.library@rbwm.gov.uk
Area Manager: North Mrs Avril Heaney (01628 796982)
Administration and Information Systems Officer Mrs Lisa Poole (01628 796985)

Other libraries

Ascot Durning Library, Ascot Racecourse, High Street, Ascot, Berks SL5 7JF
☎(01344) 630140

Cookham Library, High Road, Cookham Rise, Maidenhead, Berks SL6 9JF
☎(01626) 526147

Cox Green Library, Highfield Lane, Cox Green, Maidenhead, Berks SL6 3AX
☎(01628) 673942

Datchet Library, Village Hall, Horton Road, Datchet, Berks SL3 9HR
☎(01753) 545310

Dedworth Library, Dedworth County School, Smith's Lane, Windsor, Berks SL4 5PE
☎(01753) 868733

Eton Library, 136 High Street, Eton, Berks SL4 6LT
☎(01753) 860506

Eton Wick Library, Village Hall, Eton Wick, Berks SL4 6LT
☎(01753) 857933

Old Windsor Library, Memorial Hall, Straight Road, Windsor, Berks SL4 2JL
☎(01753) 852098

Sunninghill Library, Reading Room, School Road, Sunninghill, Berks SL5 7AD
☎(01344) 621493

Windsor Library, Bachelors Acre, Windsor, Berks SL4 1ER
☎(01753) 743940
Area Manager: South Paul Noakes (01753 743940)

Container Library operating at five sites. Contact number (☎01628 796555):
Holyport
Sunningdale
Woodlands Park
Wraysbury
Shifford Crescent

Mobile and Home Library Service operating through one vehicle (☎01628 796314)

WIRRAL
Authority: Metropolitan Borough of Wirral

Cultural Services, Westminster House, Hamilton Street, Birkenhead, Wirral, Cheshire CH41 5FN
☎0151 666 4717
url: www.wirral-libraries.net
Head of Libraries and Halls Ms Sue Powell BA MCLIP (e-mail:
suepowell@wirral.gov.uk)
Principal Librarian Mrs Julie Barkway BA DipLib MCLIP

Central/largest library

Birkenhead Central Library, Borough Road, Birkenhead, Wirral, Cheshire CH41 2XB
☎0151 652 6106 (enquiries), 0151 653 4700 (administration)
Fax 0151 653 7320
e-mail: co-ord@wirral.libraries.net
Principal Librarian, Operational Services Paul Irons BA MCLIP (e-mail:
paulirons@wirral-libraries.net)

Regional/district libraries

Bebington Central Library, Civic Way, Bebington, Wirral, Cheshire CH63 7PN
☎0151 643 7217
Fax 0151 643 7231

e-mail: bebington@wirral-library.net
Deputy Area Librarian Ms Claire Oxley

Wallasey Central Library, Earlston Road, Wallasey, Wirral, Cheshire CH45 5DX
☎0151 639 2334
Fax 0151 691 2040
e-mail: wallasey@wirral-library.net
Senior Library Managers Ms Clare Newton, Ms Kate Jones

West Kirby Library, The Concourse, West Kirby, Wirral, Cheshire CH48 4HX
☎0151 929 7808
Fax 0151 625 2558
e-mail: west.kirby@wirral-library.net
Senior Library Manager Mrs Julie Mann BA MCLIP

WOKINGHAM
Authority: Wokingham Borough Council

Libraries and Lifelong Learning, Wokingham Library, Denmark Street, Wokingham, Berks RG40 2BB
☎0118 978 1368
Fax 0118 929 1214
e-mail: libraries@wokingham.gov.uk
url: www.wokingham.gov.uk/libraries
Libraries Co-ordinator Richard Alexander (0118 974 6278; e-mail:
richard.alexander@wokingham.gov.uk)
Reader Development Officer, Young People and Families Ms Elizabeth McDonald
(e-mail: elizabeth.mcdonald@wokingham.gov.uk)
Reader Development Officer, Adults Ms Heather Dyson (e-mail:
heather.dyson@wokingham.gov.uk)
Branch Supervisor Ms Gill Cheale

WOLVERHAMPTON
Authority: Wolverhampton City Council

Adults and Community, Cultural Services Division, Libraries and Information Services, Central Library, Snow Hill, Wolverhampton WV1 3AX
☎(01902) 552025 (enquiries and administration)
Fax (01902) 552024
e-mail: libraries@wolverhampton.gov.uk
url: www.wolverhampton.gov.uk/libraries
City Librarian Mrs Karen Lees BA MCLIP (01902 552010; e-mail:
karen.lees@wolverhampton.gov.uk)
Assistant City Librarian Robert Johnson BA(Hons) (01902 552186; e-mail:
robert.johnson@wolverhampton.gov.uk)

Branch Libraries (East)

Ashmore Park Library, Griffiths Drive, Wednesfield, Wolverhampton WV11 2JW
☎(01902) 556296
e-mail: ashmorepark.library@wolverhampton.gov.uk

Branch Group Librarian Kevin Hudson BA (01902 556257)

Collingwood Community Library, 24 The Broadway, Bushbury, Wolverhampton WV10 8EB
☎(01902) 556302
e-mail: collingwood.library@wolverhampton.gov.uk

East Park Library, Hurstbourne Crescent, Eastfield, Wolverhampton WV1 2EE
☎(01902) 556257
e-mail: eastpark.library@wolverhampton.gov.uk

Long Knowle Library, Wood End Road, Wednesfield, Wolverhampton WV11 1YG
☎(01902) 556290
e-mail: longknowle.library@wolverhampton.gov.uk

Low Hill Library, Showell Circus, Low Hill, Wolverhampton WV10 9JJ
☎(01902) 556293
e-mail: lowhill.library@wolverhampton.gov.uk

Pendeford Library, Whitburn Close, Pendeford, Wolverhampton WV9 5NJ
☎(01902) 556250
e-mail: pendeford.library@wolverhampton.gov.uk

Wednesfield Library, 2 Well Lane, Wednesfield, Wolverhampton WV11 1XT
☎(01902) 556278
e-mail: wednesfield.library@wolverhampton.gov.uk

Branch Libraries (West)

Bilston Library, Mount Pleasant, Bilston, Wolverhampton WV14 7LU
☎(01902) 556253
e-mail: bilston.library@wolverhampton.gov.uk
Branch Group Librarian Ms Annie Owen BA (01902 556284)

Finchfield Library, White Oak Drive, Finchfield, Wolverhampton WV3 9AF
☎(01902) 556260
e-mail: finchfield.library@wolverhampton.gov.uk

Penn Library, Coalway Avenue, Penn, Wolverhampton WV3 7LT
☎(01902) 556281
e-mail: penn.library@wolverhampton.gov.uk

Spring Vale Library, Bevan Avenue, Wolverhampton WV4 6SG
☎(01902) 556284
e-mail: springvale.library@wolverhampton.gov.uk

Tettenhall Library, Upper Street, Tettenhall, Wolverhampton WV6 8QF
☎(01902) 556308
e-mail: tettenhall.library@wolverhampton.gov.uk

Warstones Library, Pinfold Grove, Warstone, Wolverhampton WV4 9PT
☎(01902) 556275
e-mail: warstones.library@wolverhampton.gov.uk

Whitmore Reans Library, Bargate Drive, Whitmore Reans, Wolverhampton WV6 0QW
☎(01902) 556269
e-mail: whitmorereans.library@wolverhampton.gov.uk

WORCESTERSHIRE
Authority: Worcestershire County Council

Libraries and Learning, Culture and Community Services, County Hall, Spetchley Road, Worcester WR5 2NP
☎(01905) 822819
Fax (01905) 766930
e-mail: librarieshq@worcestershire.gov.uk
url: www.worcestershire.gov.uk/libraries
Strategic Libraries and Learning Manager Ms Kathy Kirk (01905 766264; e-mail: kkirk@worcestershire.gov.uk)
Area Manager (North) Nigel Preedy BSc MCLIP (e-mail: npreedy@worcestershire.gov.uk)
Area Manager (South) Ms Sue Bulley (e-mail: sbulley@worcestershire.gov.uk)
Quality and Standards Manager Steve Mobley (01905 728884; e-mail: smobley@worcestershire.gov.uk)
Adult Learning Manager Colin Barnett (01905 766264; e-mail: cbarnett@worcestershire.gov.uk)
Literacy and Reading Manager Mrs Ruth Foster BA MCLIP MCMI (01905 427428; e-mail: rfoster@worcestershire.gov.uk)
Partnerships and Inclusion Manager Ms Annette Wright (01905 766969; e-mail: awright2@worcestershire.gov.uk)

Countywide Information Service (Intranet and Website), Information and Business Systems Division, County Hall, Spetchley Road, Worcester WR5 2NP
☎(01905) 766927
url: www.worcestershire.gov.uk
Web Manager Paul Taylor (e-mail: ptaylor@worcestershire.gov.uk)

Main libraries

Bromsgrove Library, Stratford Road, Bromsgrove, Worcs B60 1AP
☎(01905) 822722
Fax (01572) 765025
e-mail: bromsgrovelib@worcestershire.gov.uk
Bromsgrove Library Manager Ms Abigail Williams

Droitwich Library, Victoria Square, Droitwich, Worcs WR9 8DQ
☎(01905) 822722
Fax (01905) 797401
e-mail: droitwichlib@worcestershire.gov.uk
Droitwich Library Manager Ms Jacqueline Passey

Evesham Library, Oat Street, Evesham, Worcs WR11 4JP
☎(01905) 822722
Fax (01386) 765855
e-mail: eveshamlib@worcestershire.gov.uk
Evesham Library Manager Ms Janine Downes

Kidderminster Library, Market Street, Kidderminster, Worcs DY10 1PE
☎(01905) 822722
Fax (01562) 512907

e-mail: kidderminsterlib@worcestershire.gov.uk
Kidderminster Library Manager Kurt Sidaway BA(Hons) MCLIP

Malvern Library, Graham Road, Malvern, Worcs WR14 2HU
☎(01905) 822722
Fax (01684) 892999
e-mail: malvernlib@worcestershire.gov.uk
Malvern Library Manager Ms Carol Brown

Redditch Library, 15 Market Place, Redditch, Worcs B98 8AR
☎(01905) 822722
Fax (01527) 68571
e-mail: redditchlib@worcestershire.gov.uk
Redditch Library Manager Ms Angela Wright

Worcester Library, Foregate Street, Worcester WR1 1DT
☎(01905) 822722
Fax (01905) 765326
e-mail: worcesterlib@worcestershire.gov.uk
Worcester Librarian Ms Nicki Hitchcock BA DipILS MCLIP

YORK
Authority: City of York Council

Libraries and Heritage, 18 Back Swinegate, York YO1 8ZD
☎(01904) 553440
Fax (01904) 553378
Head of Libraries and Heritage Ms Fiona Williams BA(Hons) DipLib MCLIP (e-mail:
fiona.williams@york.gov.uk)
Business Support Manager Ms Diana Storey (e-mail: diana.storey@york.gov.uk)
Strategic Manager, Children, Young People and Families Ms Alison Jones BA(Hons)
DipInf (e-mail: alison.jones@york.gov.uk)
Strategic Manager: Reading and Information Ms Sarah Garbacz BA(Hons) MA(DipLib)
(e-mail: sarah.garbacz@york.gov.uk)

Central/largest library

Explore York Library Learning Centre, Museum Street, York YO1 7DS
☎(01904) 552828
e-mail: exploreyork@york.gov.uk/libraries
url: www.york.gov.uk/libraries
Central Library Manager Ms Marion Brookes

LIBRARIES NI (NORTHERN IRELAND LIBRARY AUTHORITY)

Authority: Northern Ireland Library Authority
Libraries NI, Unit 3A, The Sidings Office Park, Antrim Road, Lisburn, Co Antrim BT28 3RG
☎(028 92) 635322
Fax (028 92) 635329
e-mail: enquiries@librariesni.org.uk
url: www.librariesni.org.uk
Chief Executive Ms Irene Knox BA(Hons) MBA DipLib (e-mail: Irene.knox@librariesni.org.uk)
Director of Planning and Performance Mrs Anne Connolly BA(Hons) MA MBA (e-mail: anne.connolly@librariesni.org.uk)
Director of Service Delivery Ms Helen Osborn MLib MCLIP (e-mail: helen.osborn@librariesni.org.uk)
Director of Business Support Terry Heron BSc(Econ) Hons FCA (e-mail: terry.heron@librariesni.org.uk)

SCOTLAND

ABERDEEN

Authority: Aberdeen City Council

Aberdeen City Library and Information Services, Central Library, Rosemount Viaduct, Aberdeen AB25 1GW
☎(01224) 652500 (enquiries and administration)
Fax (01224) 641985
e-mail: CentralLibrary@aberdeencity.gov.uk
url: www.aberdeencity.gov.uk/libraries
Library and Information Services Manager Mrs Fiona Clark BA MCLIP (e-mail: fclark@aberdeencity.gov.uk)
Lending Services Manager John Grant BA MCLIP (01224 652521; e-mail: Jogrant@aberdeencity.gov.uk)
Information Services Manager Ms Susan Bell BA MCLIP (01224 652533; e-mail: sbell@aberdeencity.gov.uk)
Children's Services Manager Ms Helen Adair BA(Hons) MCLIP (e-mail: HAdair@aberdeencity.gov.uk)

ABERDEENSHIRE

Authority: Aberdeenshire Council

Library and Information Service, Meldrum Meg Way, Oldmeldrum, Aberdeenshire AB51 0GN
☎(01651) 872707 (enquiries and administration)
Fax (01651) 872142
e-mail: alis@aberdeenshire.gov.uk
url: www.aberdeenshire.gov.uk/libraries
Principal Libraries Officer Mrs Anne A M Harrison MCLIP (01651 871210; fax: 01651 872142; e-mail: anne.harrison@aberdeenshire.gov.uk)
Cultural Services Team Leaders Mrs Helen W Dewar MA MCLIP (01358 729208; fax: 01358 722864; e-mail: helen.dewar@aberdeenshire.gov.uk), Ms Hazel Weeks MCLIP (01771 623937; e-mail: hazel.weeks@aberdeenshire.gov.uk), Ms Geraldine Downie BA MCLIP (e-mail: geraldine.downie@aberdeenshire.gov.uk)

ANGUS

Authority: Angus Council

Cultural Services Department, William Wallace House, Forfar, Angus DD8 1WH
☎(01307) 461460
Fax (01307) 462590
e-mail: cultural.services@angus.gov.uk
url: www.angus.gov.uk
Senior Services Manager Cultural Services Norman K Atkinson DipEd AMA FMA
Libraries and Arts Manager Colin Dakers BA MCLIP

Central/largest library

Library Support Services, 50 West High Street, Forfar, Angus DD8 1BA
☎(01307) 466966
Fax (01307) 468451
e-mail: librarysupport.services@angus.gov.uk
Support Services Librarian Ms Vicky Fraser

Area libraries

Arbroath Library, Hill Terrace, Arbroath, Angus DD11 1AH
☎(01241) 872248
Fax (01241) 434396
e-mail: arbroath.library@angus.gov.uk
Librarian Henry Logan BA DipLib MCLIP

Brechin Library, 10 St Ninian's Square, Brechin, Angus DD9 7AA
☎(01356) 622687
e-mail: brechin.library@angus.gov.uk
Librarian Gavin Hunter MA MCLIP

Carnoustie Library, 21 High Street, Carnoustie, Angus DD7 6AN
☎(01241) 859620
e-mail: carnoustie.library@angus.gov.uk
Librarian Alasdair Sutherland BA MCLIP

Forfar Library, 50-56 West High Street, Forfar, Angus DD8 1BA
☎(01307) 466071
Fax (01307) 468451
e-mail: forfar.library@angus.gov.uk
Librarian Ms Fiona J. G. Dakers BA DipIM MCLIP

Kirriemuir Library, Town Hall, 28/30 Reform Street, Kirriemuir, Angus DD8 4BS
☎(01575) 572357
Librarian Ms Fiona J. G. Dakers BA DipIM MCLIP

Monifieth Library, High Street, Monifieth, Angus DD5 4AE
☎(01382) 533819
e-mail: monifieth.library@angus.gov.uk
Librarian Ms Hazel Cook BA MCLIP

Montrose Library, 214 High Street, Montrose, Angus DD10 8PH
☎(01674) 673256
e-mail: montrose.library@angus.gov.uk
Librarian Ms Christine Sharp BA MCLIP

ARGYLL AND BUTE
Authority: Argyll and Bute Council

**Library and Information Service HQ, Highland Avenue, Sandbank, Dunoon, Argyll
PA23 8QZ**
☎(01369) 703214
Fax (01369) 705797

url: www.argyll-bute.gov.uk
Culture and Libraries Manager Patrick McCann BA MCLIP (e-mail:
patrick.mccann@argyll-bute.gov.uk)
Youth Services Librarian Vacant

Area libraries

Campbeltown Library, Aqualibrium, Kinloch Road, Campbeltown, Argyll PA28 6EG
☎(01586) 555435
Fax (01586) 555438
Area Librarian Ms Sue Fortune MCLIP

Dunoon Library, 248 Argyll Street, Dunoon, Argyll PA23 7LT
☎(01369) 708682
Fax (01369) 701323
Area Librarian Ms Pauline Flynn BA MCLIP

Helensburgh Library, West King Street, Helensburgh, Dunbartonshire G84 8EB
☎(01436) 658833
Fax (01436) 679567
Senior Library Assistant Ms Fiona Sharkey

Oban Library, 77 Albany Street, Oban, Argyll PA34 4AL
☎(01631) 571444
Fax (01631) 571372
Area Librarian Kevin Baker BA DipLib MCLIP

Rothesay Library, Moat Centre, Stuart Street, Rothesay, Bute PA20 0BX
☎(01700) 503266
Fax (01700) 500511
Senior Library Assistant Ms Patricia McArthur

CLACKMANNANSHIRE
Authority: Clackmannanshire Council

**Clackmannanshire Libraries, Alloa Library, 26-28 Drysdale Street, Alloa,
Clackmannanshire FK10 1JL**
☎(01259) 722262
Fax (01259) 219469
e-mail: libraries@clacks.gov.uk
url: www.clacksweb.org.uk/dyna/library
Team Leader, Library Service John A Blake BSc DipLib MCLIP DipEdTech (ext 220)
Training and Stock Circulation Librarian Ms Tracy Docherty
Information Librarian and Archivist Ian D Murray MA DipLib MCLIP DAA

Branches within community access points

Alva Community Access Point, 153 West Stirling Street, Alva, Clackmannanshire FK12 2EL
☎(01259) 760652
Fax (01259) 760354
Senior Community Access Officer Ms N Foster (e-mail: nfoster@clacks.gov.uk)

Clackmannan Community Access Point, Main Street, Clackmannan FK10 4JA

☎(01259) 721579
Fax (01259) 212493
Senior Community Access Officer Ms J Laird (e-mail: jlaird@clacks.gov.uk)

Dollar Community Access Point, Dollar Civic Centre, Park Place, Dollar, Clackmannanshire
FK14 7AA
☎(01259) 743253
Fax (01259) 743328
Senior Community Access Officer Mrs K Waddell (e-mail: kwaddell@clacks.gov.uk)

Menstrie Community Access Point, The Dumyat Leisure Centre, Main Street East,
Menstrie, Clackmannanshire FK11 7BJ
☎(01259) 769439
Fax (01259) 762941
Senior Community Access Officer Mrs K Waddell (e-mail: kwaddell@clacks.gov.uk)

Sauchie Community Access Point, 42-48 Main Street, Sauchie, Clackmannanshire FL10 3JY
☎(01259) 721679
Fax (01259) 218750
Senior Community Access Officer Ms M Hunter (e-mail: mhunter@clacks.gov.uk)

Tillicoultry Branch Library, 99 High Street, Tillicoultry, Clackmannanshire FK13 6DL
☎(01259) 751685 (tel/fax)
Branch Library Co-ordinator Ms L Paterson (e-mail: lpaterson@clacks.gov.uk)

Tullibody Library, Leisure Centre, Abercromby Place, Tullibody, Clackmannanshire
FK10 2RS
☎(01259) 218725
Branch Library Co-ordinator Ms I Dykes (e-mail: idykes@clacks.gov.uk)

COMHAIRLE NAN EILEAN SIAR
Authority: Comhairle nan Eilean Siar

Public Library, 19 Cromwell Street, Stornoway, Isle of Lewis, Hebrides HS1 2DA
☎(01851) 708631
Fax (01851) 708676
e-mail: library.enquiries@cne-siar.gov.uk
url: www.cne-siar.gov.uk
Principal Officer, Cultural and Information Services Ms Trish Botten BA(Hons)
(e-mail: trish.botten@cne-siar.gov.uk)
Team Leader, Youth Services Ms Kathleen Milne BSocSci PGDipLIS MA MCLIP

Area libraries

Community Library, Castlebay Community School, Castlebay, Isle of Barra, Hebrides
HS9 5XD
☎(01871) 810124
Fax (01871) 810125
e-mail: castlebaylibrary@gnes.net
Senior Library Assistant Mrs Linda Mackinnon

Community Library, Daliburgh School, Daliburgh, Isle of South Uist, Hebrides HS8 5SS
☎(01878) 700882

Community Librarian Ms Felicity Bramwell (e-mail: fbramwell1a@gnes.net)

Community Library, Sgoil Lionacleit, Liniclate, Isle of Benbecula, Hebrides HS7 5PJ
☎(01870) 603532
Fax (01870) 602817
e-mail: lionacleitlibrary@gnes.net
Community Librarian Ms Felicity Bramwell (e-mail: fbramwell1a@gnes.net)

Community Library, Sgoil Shiaboist, Shawbost, Isle of Lewis, Hebrides HS2 9BQ
☎(01851) 710212
e-mail: shawlib@gnes.net
Library Assistant Mrs Catherine Campbell

Community Library, Sir E Scott School, Tarbert, Isle of Harris, Hebrides HS3 3BG
☎(01859) 502926
Library Assistant Mrs Fiona Morrison MA MCLIP (e-mail: fmmorrison1b@gnes.net)

DUMFRIES AND GALLOWAY
Authority: Dumfries and Galloway Council

Libraries, Information and Archives, Central Support Unit, Catherine Street, Dumfries DG1 1JB
☎(01387) 253820 (enquiries), 01387 252070 (administration)
Fax (01387) 260294
e-mail: yourlibrary@dumgal.gov.uk
url: www.dumgal.gov.uk
Principal Policy Officer: Libraries, Information and Archives J H Goldie BA DipLib MCLIP
Resources Development Manager Michael Russell
Section Librarian Young People Ms Christine Johnston MA(Hons) PGDip(Inf)

District libraries

Annan Library, Charles Street, Annan, Dumfries and Galloway DG12 5AG
☎(01461) 202809 (tel/fax)

Archive Centre, 33 Burns Street, Dumfries DG1 2PS
☎(01387) 269254
Fax (01387) 264126
e-mail: libarchive@dumgal.gov.uk

Castle Douglas Library, Market Hill, King Street, Castle Douglas, Dumfries and Galloway DG7 1AE
☎(01556) 502643 (tel/fax)

Dalbeattie Library, 23 High Street, Dalbeattie, Dumfries and Galloway DG5 4AD
☎(01556) 610898 (tel/fax)

Dalry Library, Main Street, Dalry, Castle Douglas, Dumfries and Galloway DG7 3UP
☎(01644) 430234 (tel/fax)

Eastriggs Library, Eastriggs Community School, Eastriggs, Annan, Dumfries and Galloway DG12 6PZ
☎(01461) 40844 (tel/fax)

Ewart Library, Catherine Street, Dumfries DG1 1JB
☎(01387) 253820
Fax (01387) 260294

Gatehouse Library, 63 High Street, Gatehouse of Fleet, Dumfries and Galloway DG7 2HS
☎(01557) 814646 (tel/fax)

Georgetown Library, Gillbrae Road, Georgetown, Dumfries DG1 4EJ
☎(01387) 256059 (tel/fax)

Gretna Library, The Richard Greenhow Centre, Central Avenue, Gretna, Dumfries and
Galloway DG16 5AQ
☎(01461) 338000 (tel/fax)

Kirkconnel Library, Greystone Avenue, Kelloholm, Dumfries and Galloway DG4 6RA
☎(01659) 67191 (tel/fax)

Kirkcudbright Library, Sheriff Court House, High Street, Kirkcudbright, Dumfries and
Galloway DG6 4JW
☎(01557) 331240 (tel/fax)

Langholm Library, Charles Street, Old Langholm, Dumfries and Galloway DG13 0AA
☎(01387) 380040 (tel/fax)

Lochmaben Library, Masonic Hall, High Street, Lochmaben, Lockerbie, Dumfries and
Galloway DG11 1NQ
☎(01387) 811865 (tel/fax)

Lochside Library, Lochside Road, Dumfries DG2 0LW
☎(01387) 268751 (tel/fax)

Lochthorn Library, Lochthorn, Dumfries DG1 1UF
☎(01387) 265780
Fax (01387) 266424

Lockerbie Library, 31ñ33 High Street, Lockerbie, Dumfries and Galloway DG11 2JL
☎(01576) 203380 (tel/fax)

Moffat Library, Town Hall, High Street, Moffat, Dumfries and Galloway DG10 9HF
☎(01683) 220952 (tel/fax)

Newton Stewart Library, Chuch Street, Newton Stewart, Dumfries and Galloway
DG8 6ER
☎(01671) 403450 (tel/fax)

Port William Library, Church Street, Port William, Newton Stewart, Dumfries and
Galloway DG8 9QJ
☎(01988) 700406 (tel/fax)

Sanquhar Library, 106 High Street, Sanquhar, Dumfries and Galloway DG4 6DZ
☎(01659) 50626 (tel/fax)

Stranraer Library, North Strand Street, Stranraer, Dumfries and Galloway DG9 7LD
☎(01776) 707400
Fax (01776) 703565

Thornhill Library, Townhead Street, Thornhill, Dumfries and Galloway DG3 5NW
☎(01848) 330654 (tel/fax)

Whithorn Library, St John's Street, Whithorn, Dumfries and Galloway DG8 8PF
☎(01988) 500406 (tel/fax)

Wigtown Library, County Buildings, Wigtown, Dumfries and Galloway DG8 9JH
☎(01988) 403329 (tel/fax)

DUNDEE
Authority: Dundee City Council

Leisure and Communities Department Head Office, Central Library Level 3, The Wellgate, Dundee DD1 1DB
☎(01382) 307462
Fax (01382) 307487
url: www.dundeecity.gov.uk/communities
Director of Leisure and Communities Department Stewart Murdoch MSc DPSE DipYCW (e-mail: stewart.murdoch@dundeecity.gov.uk)
Head of Libraries, Information and Cultural Services Mrs Moira Methven MCLIP (e-mail: moira.methven@dundeecity.gov.uk)

Central/largest library

Central Library, The Wellgate, Dundee DD1 1DB
☎(01382) 431500 (enquiries), (01382) 431501 (administration)
Fax (01382) 434642
url: www.dundeecity.gov.uk/library
Central Library Manager Mrs Judy Dobbie MA MCLIP (01382 431526; e-mail: judy.dobbie@dundeecity.gov.uk)
Section Leader (Reader Services) Ms Christine Ferguson MA MCLIP (01382 431549; e-mail: christine.ferguson@dundeecity.gov.uk)
Community Information Team Leader Mrs Frances Robertson MA MCLIP (01382 431533; e-mail: frances.robertson@dundeecity.gov.uk)
Reference Services Team Leader David Kett MCLIP (01382 431552; e-mail: david.kett@dundeecity.gov.uk)
Senior Library and Information Worker (Central Library) Ms Amina Shah MCLIP (01382 431523; e-mail: amina.shah@dundeecity.gov.uk)
Community Libraries and Learning Centres Manager Ms Frances Foster MCLIP (01382 436360; e-mail: frances.foster@dundeecity.gov.uk)
Community Outreach Team Ms Jayne Gair BA MCLIP (01382 438894; e-mail: jayne.gair@dundeecity.gov.uk)
Community Learning Team Ms Fiona Macpherson MA MCLIP (01382 438833; e-mail: fiona.macpherson@dundeecity.gov.uk)
Marketing and Promotion Team Ms Shona Donaldson BA(Hons) MCLIP (01382 438893; e-mail: shona.donaldson@dundeecity.gov.uk)
Stock Management Team Ms Janis Milne BA MCLIP (01382 431535; e-mail: janis.milne@dundeecity.gov.uk)
Staff Development Worker Mrs Frances Scott MCLIP (01382 438891; e-mail: frances.scott@dundeecity.gov.uk)
Senior Library and Information Worker (Schools Service) Ms Elaine Hallyburton MA(Hons) DipLib (01382 431546; e-mail: elaine.hallyburton@dundeecity.gov.uk)

Community libraries

Ardler Community Library, Ardler Complex, Turnberry Avenue, Ardler, Dundee
DD2 3TP
☎(01382) 432863
Fax (01382) 436446
e-mail: ardler.library@dundeecity.gov.uk
Library and Information Worker Ms Liz Young DipILS MCLIP

Arthurstone Community Library, Arthurstone Terrace, Dundee DD4 6RT
☎(01382) 438881
Fax (01382) 438886
e-mail: arthurstone.library@dundeecity.gov.uk
Library and Information Worker Mrs Shona Wood

Blackness Community Library, 225 Perth Road, Dundee DD2 1EJ
☎(01382) 435936
Fax (01382) 435942
e-mail: blackness.library@dundeecity.gov.uk
Library and Information Worker Ms Lorraine Andrews

Broughty Ferry Community Library, Queen Street, Broughty Ferry, Dundee DD5 2HN
☎(01382) 436919
Fax (01382) 436913
e-mail: broughty.library@dundeecity.gov.uk
Library and Information Worker Mrs Sandra Westgate, Mrs Lorraine Kell

Charleston Community Library, 60 Craigowan Road, Dundee DD2 4NL
☎(01382) 436639
Fax (01382) 436640
e-mail: charleston.library@dundeecity.gov.uk
Library and Community Centre Officer Ms Ailsa Caldwell

Coldside Neighbourhood Library, 150 Strathmartine Road, Dundee DD3 7SE
☎(01382) 432849
Fax (01382) 432850
e-mail: coldside.library@dundeecity.gov.uk
Library and Information Worker Ms Susan Ferguson

Douglas Community Library, Balmoral Place, Douglas, Dundee DD4 8SH
☎(01382) 436915
Fax (01382) 436922
e-mail: douglas.library@dundeecity.gov.uk
Library and Information Worker Ms Jill Reid

Fintry Community Library, Finmill Centre, Findcastle Street, Dundee DD4 9EW
☎(01382) 432560
Fax (01382) 432559
e-mail: fintry.library@dundeecity.gov.uk
Library and Information Worker Ms Barbara Cook

Hub Community Library and Learning Centre, Pitkerro Road, Dundee DD4 8ES
☎(01382) 438648
Fax (01382) 438627

e-mail: hub.library@dundeecity.gov.uk
Library and Information Worker Miss Karen Duffy

Kirkton Community Library, Derwent Avenue, Dundee DD3 0BW
☎(01382) 432851
Fax (01382) 432852
e-mail: kirkton.library@dundeecity.gov.uk
Library and Information Worker Mrs Ann Smith

Lochee Community Library, High Street, Lochee, Dundee DD2 3AU
☎(01382) 431835
Fax (01382) 431837
e-mail: lochee.library@dundeecity.gov.uk
Library and Information Worker Mrs Joan Rodger

Menzieshill Community Library, Orleans Place, Menzieshill, Dundee DD2 4BH
☎(01382) 432945
Fax (01382) 432948
e-mail: menzieshill.library@dundeecity.gov.uk
Library and Information Worker Mrs Irene Houston

Whitfield Community Library and Learning Centre, Whitfield Drive, Dundee DD4 0DX
☎(01382) 432561
Fax (01382) 432562
e-mail: whitfield.library@dundeecity.gov.uk
Library and Information Worker Mrs Ruth McDowall

EAST AYRSHIRE
Authority: East Ayrshire Council

Library, Registration and Information Services, Dick Institute, 14 Elmbank Avenue, Kilmarnock, Ayrshire KA1 3BU
☎(01563) 554300 (general enquiries)
Fax (01563) 554311
e-mail: libraries@east-ayrshire.gov.uk
url: www.east-ayrshire.gov.uk/thelibrary
Library, Registration and Information Services Manager Gerard Cairns BA DipLib MCLIP DMS (e-mail: gerard.cairns@east-ayrshire.gov.uk)
Senior Librarian Mrs Elaine Gray MA DipLib MCLIP (e-mail: elaine.gray@east-ayrshire.gov.uk)
Support Services Librarian Mrs Julia A Harvey MA(Hons) DipLib MCLIP (e-mail: julia.harvey@east-ayrshire.gov.uk)
Information Officer Ms Dawn Vallance BA(Hons) DipLib MCLIP (e-mail: dawn.vallance@east-ayrshire.gov.uk)
Community Librarian (Staff Development) Mrs Lynn Mee BA(Hons) MCLIP (e-mail: lynn.mee@east-ayrshire.gov.uk)
Service Development Manager Ms Dianne McGregor BA(Hons) (e-mail: dianne.mcgregor@east-ayrshire.gov.uk)
Community Librarian (Heritage Services) Mrs Anne Geddes MCLIP (e-mail: anne.geddes@east-ayrshire.gov.uk)
Community Librarian (Operations) Hugh MacLean MA(Hons) DipLib MCLIP (e-mail: hugh.maclean@east-ayrshire.gov.uk)

Service Development Officer Miss Pat Standen BA MCLIP (e-mail:
pat.standen@east-ayrshire.gov.uk), Mrs Margaret Patterson BA MCLIP (e-mail:
margaret.patterson@east-ayrshire.gov.uk) (job share)

EAST DUNBARTONSHIRE
Authority: East Dunbartonshire Council

**Corporate Directorate: Community Department: Community Services Section: Libraries
and Cultural Services, Library HQ, William Patrick Library, 2ñ4 West High Street,
Kirkintilloch, East Dunbartonshire G66 1AD**
☎0141 775 4501
Fax 0141 776 0408
e-mail: libraries@eastdunbarton.gov.uk
url: www.eastdunbarton.gov.uk
Area Operations Leader David Kenvyn BA MCLIP (0141 775 4519; e-mail:
david.kenvyn@eastdunbarton.gov.uk)
Support Services Librarian Ms Anne Murray BA MCLIP (0141 775 4511; e-mail:
anne.murray@eastdunbarton.gov.uk)
Assistant Manager, Children and Young People's Library Services Ms Frances
MacArthur MA MCLIP (0141 775 4526; e-mail: frances.macarthur@eastdunbarton.gov.uk)
Outreach Officer Ms Anne Kennedy (0141 775 4509; e-mail:
anne.kennedy@eastdunbarton.gov.uk)

Central/largest library

William Patrick Library, 2-4 West High Street, Kirkintilloch, East Dunbartonshire G66 1AD
☎0141 775 4524 (Lending Library)
Community Librarians Mrs Doreen Fergusson MA MCLIP (e-mail:
doreen.fergusson@eastdunbarton.gov.uk), Mrs Eryl Morris BA DipLib MCLIP (e-mail:
eryl.morris@eastdunbarton.gov.uk) (job-share)
Information and Local Studies Librarian Mrs Christine Miller BA DipLib MCLIP
(0141 775 4537; e-mail: christine.miller@eastdunbarton.gov.uk)
Assistant Information and Local Studies Librarian David Smith DipLib MCLIP
(0141 775 4541; e-mail: david.smith@eastdunbarton.gov.uk)
Archivist Ms Janice Miller (0141 775 4573; e-mail: janice.miller@eastdunbarton.gov.uk)
Freedom of Information Officer Stephen Armstrong (0141 775 4571; e-mail:
stephen.armstrong@eastdunbarton.gov.uk) (now based at Tom Johnston House)

Branch libraries

Bishopbriggs Library, 170 Kirkintilloch Road, Bishopbriggs, East Dunbartonshire G64 2LX
☎0141 772 4513
Fax 0141 762 5363
Community Librarian Mrs Fiona Warner BA MCLIP (e-mail:
fiona.warner@eastdunbarton.gov.uk)

Brookwood Library, 166 Drymen Road, Bearsden, Glasgow G61 3RJ
☎0141 942 6811
Fax 0141 943 1119
Community Librarian Ms Sandra Busby BA MCLIP (e-mail:
sandra.busby@eastdunbarton.gov.uk)

Lennoxtown Library, Main Street, Lennoxtown, East Dunbartonshire G65 7DG
☎(01360) 311436 (tel/fax)
Library Supervisor Ms Lesley Finlayson (e-mail: lesley.finlayson@eastdunbarton.gov.uk)

Lenzie Library, 13 Alexandra Avenue, Lenzie, East Dunbartonshire G66 5BG
☎0141 776 3021
Library Supervisor Neil Davidson (e-mail: neil.davidson@eastdunbarton.gov.uk),
Ms Naomi Niven (e-mail: naomi.niven@eastdunbarton.gov.uk) (job-share)

Milngavie Library, Community Centre, Allander Way, Milngavie, Glasgow G62 8PN
☎0141 956 2776
Fax 0141 570 0052
Community Librarian John Murray MCLIP (e-mail: john.murray@eastdunbarton.gov.uk)

Milton of Campsie Library, Craighead Road, Milton of Campsie, East Dunbartonshire
G65 8DL
☎(01360) 311925
Assistant in Charge Ms May Newton (e-mail: may.newton@eastdunbarton.gov.uk),
Ms Sandra Vernon (e-mail: sandra.vernon@eastdunbarton.gov.uk) (job-share)

Westerton Library, 82 Maxwell Avenue, Bearsden, Glasgow G61 1NZ
☎0141 943 0780
Library Supervisor Ms Elizabeth Bushfield (e-mail:
elizabeth.bushfield@eastdunbarton.gov.uk)
Area and Mobile Librarian Gerard Robertson (e-mail:
gerard.robertson@eastdunbarton.gov.uk) (responsible for Lennoxtown, Lenzie, Milton of
Campsie and Westerton Libraries)

EAST LOTHIAN
Authority: East Lothian Council

Library and Museum Headquarters, Dunbar Road, Haddington, East Lothian EH41 3PJ
☎(01620) 828205 (enquiries), (01620) 828200 (administration)
Fax (01620) 828201
e-mail: libraries@eastlothian.gov.uk (for general enquiries)
url: www.eastlothian.gov.uk
Principal Libraries Officer Ms Alison Hunter BA MCLIP
Senior Librarian, Adult Services Mrs Morag Tocher BA MA MCLIP
Senior Librarian, Computer Services Andy Holmes MA(Hons) DipLib
Senior Librarian, Young People's Services Ms Agnes Guyon MSc MCLIP
Records Manager Alex Fitzgerald PGDipARM
Archivist Ms Ruth Fyfe MA(Hons) DipArAd, Ms Frances Woodrow BSc(Hons) PGDipARM
(job-share)

Largest library

Musselburgh Library, 10 Bridge Street, Musselburgh, East Lothian EH21 6AG
☎0131 665 2183
e-mail: musselburgh.library@eastlothian.gov.uk
Area Librarian Mrs Dorothy Elliott MA DipLib

Branch libraries

Dunbar Library, Castellau, Belhaven Road, Dunbar, East Lothian EH42 1DA
☎(01368) 863521
e-mail: dunbar.library@eastlothian.gov.uk
Assistant i/c Mrs Anne Hampshire

East Linton Library, 60A High Street, East Linton, East Lothian EH40 3BX
☎(01620) 860015
e-mail: eastlinton.library@eastlothian.gov.uk
Assistant i/c Ms Carol Hastie

Gullane Library, East Links Road, Gullane, East Lothian EH31 2AF
☎(01620) 842073
e-mail: gullane.library@eastlothian.gov.uk
Assistant i/c Ms Avril Stevens

Haddington Library, Newton Port, Haddington, East Lothian EH41 3NA
☎(01620) 822531
e-mail: haddington.library@eastlothian.gov.uk
Area Librarian Ms Trina Gavan MCLIP

Longniddry Library, Church Way, Longniddry, East Lothian EH32 0LW
☎(01875) 852735
e-mail: longniddry.library@eastlothian.gov.uk
Assistant i/c Ms Anne Sturgeon

North Berwick Library, The Old School, School Road, North Berwick, East Lothian
EH39 4JU
☎(01620) 893470
e-mail: northberwick.library@eastlothian.gov.uk
Branch Librarian Miss Caroline Henley BA(Hons) MSc

Ormiston Library, 5A Meadowbank, Ormiston, East Lothian EH35 5LQ
☎(01875) 616675
e-mail: ormiston.library@eastlothian.gov.uk
Assistant i/c Bill Wilson BA(Hons)

Port Seton Library, Community Centre, South Seton Park, Port Seton, East Lothian
EH32 0BG
☎(01875) 811709
Fax (01875) 815177
e-mail: portseton.library@eastlothian.gov.uk
Assistant i/c Mrs Irene Muir

Prestonpans Library, West Loan, Prestonpans, East Lothian EH32 9NX
☎(01875) 810788
e-mail: prestonpans.library@eastlothian.gov.uk
Branch Librarian Ms Erica Thomson BA MCLIP

Tranent Library, 3 Civic Square, Tranent, East Lothian EH33 1LH
☎(01875) 610254
e-mail: tranent.library@eastlothian.gov.uk
Branch Librarian Ms Marjory Smith MCLIP

Wallyford Library, 3 Fa'side Buildings, Wallyford, East Lothian EH21 8BA
☎0131 653 2035
e-mail: wallyford.library@eastlothian.gov.uk
Assistant i/c Ms Wilma Porteous

Specialist library

Local History Centre, Newton Port, Haddington, East Lothian EH41 3NA
☎(01620) 823307
e-mail: localhistory@eastlothian.gov.uk
Local History Librarian Ms Sheila Millar BA(Hons) MSc MCLIP

EAST RENFREWSHIRE
Authority: East Renfrewshire Council

Library and Information Services, Church Road, Barrhead, East Renfrewshire G78 IFA
☎0141 577 3500 (enquiries)
Fax 0141 577 3501
url: www.eastrenfrewshire.gov.uk/libraries
Head of Education Services (Culture, Sport and Continuing Education)
Ken McKinlay MA(Hons) PGDipLib MCLIP (0141 577 3103; e-mail:
ken.mckinlay@eastrenfrewshire.gov.uk)
Arts, Learning and Libraries Manager Ms Claire Scott (0141 577 3531; e-mail:
claire.scott@eastrenfrewshire.gov.uk)
Learning Services Manager Ms Janice Weir BA MCLIP (0141 577 3516; e-mail:
janice.weir@eastrenfrewshire.gov.uk)
Systems Manager Scott Simpson BA PGDipIT MCLIP (0141 577 3509; e-mail:
scott.simpson@eastrenfrewshire.gov.uk)
Customer Services Manager John West BA(Hons) PGDipLib MCLIP (0141 577 3503;
e-mail: john.west@eastrenfrewshire.gov.uk)

Community libraries

Barrhead Community Library, Church Road, Barrhead, East Renfrewshire G78 IFA
☎0141 577 3518
e-mail: barrhead.library@eastrenfrewshire.gov.uk

Busby Community Library, Duff Memorial Hall, Main Street, Busby, East Renfrewshire
G76 8DX
☎0141 577 4971
Fax 0141 577 3768
e-mail: busby.library@eastrenfrewshire.gov.uk

Clarkston Community Library, Clarkston Road, Clarkston, East Renfrewshire
G76 8NE
☎0141 577 4972
Fax 0141 577 4973
e-mail: clarkston.library@eastrenfrewshire.gov.uk

Eaglesham Community Library, Montgomerie Hall, Eaglesham, Eaglesham, East
Renfrewshire G76 0LH
☎0141 577 3932

Fax 0141 577 3771
e-mail: eaglesham.library@eastrenfrewshire.gov.uk

Giffnock Community Library, Station Road, Giffnock, East Renfrewshire G46 6JF
☎0141 577 4976
Fax 0141 577 4978
e-mail: giffnock.library@eastrenfrewshire.gov.uk

Mearns Community Library, McKinley Place, Newton Mearns, East Renfrewshire G77 6EZ
☎0141 577 4979
Fax 0141 577 4980
e-mail: mearns.library@eastrenfrewshire.gov.uk

Neilston Community Library, Main Street, Neilston, East Renfrewshire G78 3NN
☎0141 577 4981
Fax 0141 577 4982
e-mail: neilston.library@eastrenfrewshire.gov.uk

Netherlee Community Library, Netherlee Pavilion, Linn Park Avenue, East Renfrewshire G44 3PH
☎0141 637 5102
e-mail: netherlee.library@eastrenfrewshire.gov.uk

Thornliebank Community Library, 1 Spiersbridge Road, Thornliebank, East Renfrewshire G46 7SJ
☎0141 577 4983
Fax 0141 577 4816
e-mail: thornliebank.library@eastrenfrewshire.gov.uk

Uplawmoor Community Library, Mure Hall, Tannoch Road, Uplawmoor, East Renfrewshire G78 4AF
☎(01505) 850564
e-mail: uplawmoor.library@eastrenfrewshire.gov.uk

EDINBURGH
Authority: City of Edinburgh Council

Headquarters, C3 Waverley Court, Level C3, 4 East Market Street, Edinburgh EH8 8BG
☎0131 529 7894
e-mail: eclis@edinburgh.gov.uk
url: http://yourlibrary.edinburgh.gov.uk
Head of Libraries and Information Services Mrs Liz McGettigan BA MCLIP (0131 529 7894; e-mail: liz.mcgettigan@edinburgh.gov.uk)
Commercial Manager Ms Sarah Forteath (0131 529 3961; e-mail: sarah.forteath@edinburgh.gov.uk)
Information and Digital Services Manager Jim Thompson (0131 529 7790; e-mail: jim.thompson@edinburgh.gov.uk)
Customer Services Manager Paul McCloskey (0131 529 6156; e-mail: paul.mccloskey@edinburgh.gov.uk)

Central/largest library
Central Library, George IV Bridge, Edinburgh EH1 1EG

Central Library and Information Services Managers Ms Hil Williamson (e-mail: hil.williamson@edinburgh.gov.uk), Ms Fiona Myles (e-mail: fiona.myles@edinburgh.gov.uk)

Community libraries

Balerno Library, 1 Main Street, Balerno, Edinburgh EH14 7EQ
☎0131 529 5500
Fax 0131 529 5502

Balgreen Library, 173 Balgreen Road, Edinburgh EH11 3AT
☎0131 529 5585
Fax 0131 529 5583
e-mail: balgreen.library@edinburgh.gov.uk

Blackhall Library, 56 Hillhouse Road, Edinburgh EH4 5EG
☎0131 529 5595
Fax 0131 336 5419
e-mail: blackhall.library@edinburgh.gov.uk

Colinton Library, 14 Thorburn Road, Edinburgh EH13 0BQ
☎0131 529 5603
Fax 0131 529 5607
e-mail: colinton.library@edinburgh.gov.uk

Corstophine Library, 12 Kirk Loan, Edinburgh EH12 7HD
☎0131 529 5506
Fax 0131 529 5508
e-mail: corstophine.library@edinburgh.gov.uk

Craigmillar Library, 7 Niddrie Marischal Gardens, Edinburgh EH16 4LX
☎0131 529 5597
Fax 0131 529 5601
e-mail: craigmillar.library@edinburgh.gov.uk

Currie Library, 210 Lanark Road, Edinburgh EH14 5NN
☎0131 529 5609
Fax 0131 529 5613
e-mail: currie.library@edinburgh.gov.uk

Fountainbridge Library, 137 Dundee Street, Edinburgh EH11 1BG
☎0131 529 5616
Fax 0131 529 5621
e-mail: fountainbridge.library@edinburgh.gov.uk

Gilmerton Library, 13 Newtoft Street, Edinburgh EH17 8RG
☎0131 529 5628
Fax 0131 529 5627
e-mail: gilmerton.library@edinburgh.gov.uk

Granton Library, Wardieburn Terrace, Edinburgh EH5 1DD
☎0131 529 5630
Fax 0131 529 5634
e-mail: granton.library@edinburgh.gov.uk

Kirkliston Library, 16 Station Road, Edinburgh EH29 9BE

☎0131 529 5510
Fax 0131 529 5514
e-mail: kirkliston.library@edinburgh.gov.uk

Leith Library, 28ñ30 Ferry Road, Edinburgh EH6 5AE
☎0131 529 5517
Fax 0131 554 2720
e-mail: leith.library@edinburgh.gov.uk

McDonald Road Library, 2 McDonald Road, Edinburgh EH7 4LU
☎0131 529 5652
Fax 0131 529 5646
e-mail: mcdonald.library@edinburgh.gov.uk

Moredun Library, 92 Moredun Park Road, Edinburgh EH17 7HL
☎0131 529 5652
Fax 0131 529 5651
e-mail: moredun.library@edinburgh.gov.uk

Morningside Library, 184 Morningside Road, Edinburgh EH10 4PU
☎0131 529 5654
Fax 0131 447 4685
e-mail: morningside.library@edinburgh.gov.uk

Muirhouse Library, 15 Pennywell Court, Edinburgh EH4 4TZ
☎0131 529 5528
Fax 0131 529 5532
e-mail: muirhouse.library@edinburgh.gov.uk

Newington Library, 17ñ21 Fountainhall Road, Edinburgh EH9 2LN
☎0131 529 5536
Fax 0131 667 5491
e-mail: newington.library@edinburgh.gov.uk

Oxgangs Library, 343 Oxgangs Road, Edinburgh EH13 9LY
☎0131 529 5549
Fax 0131 529 5554
e-mail: oxgangs.library@edinburgh.gov.uk

Piershill Library, 30 Piersfield Terrace, Edinburgh EH8 7BQ
☎0131 529 5685
Fax 0131 529 5691
e-mail: piershill.library@edinburgh.gov.uk

Portobello Library, 14 Rosefield Avenue, Edinburgh EH15 1AU
☎0131 529 5558
Fax 0131 669 2344
e-mail: portobello.library@edinburgh.gov.uk

Ratho Library, 6 School Wynd, Ratho, Edinburgh EH28 8TT
☎0131 333 5297 (tel/fax)
e-mail: ratho.library@edinburgh.gov.uk

Sighthill Library, 6 Sighthill Wynd, Edinburgh EH11 4BL
☎0131 529 5569

Fax 0131 529 5572
e-mail: sighthill.library@edinburgh.gov.uk

South Queensferry Library, 9 Shore Road, South Queensferry, Edinburgh EH30 9RD
☎0131 529 5576
Fax 0131 529 5578
e-mail: southqueensferry.library@edinburgh.gov.uk

Stockbridge Library, 11 Hamilton Place, Edinburgh EH3 5BA
☎0131 529 5665
Fax 0131 529 5681
e-mail: stockbridge.library@edinburgh.gov.uk

Wester Hailes Library, 1 Westside Plaza, Wester Hailes, Edinburgh EH14 2FT
☎0131 529 5667
Fax 0131 529 5671
e-mail: westerhailes.library@edinburgh.gov.uk

Access Services/Mobiles

Access Services, Access Services/Mobiles, 343 Oxgangs Road North, Edinburgh
EH13 9LY
☎0131 529 5683
Contact Ian Kirkby

FALKIRK
Authority: Falkirk Council

Library, Victoria Buildings, Queen Street, Falkirk FK2 7AF
☎(01324) 506800
Fax (01324) 506801
url: www.falkirk.gov.uk
Libraries Manager Vacant

Central/largest library

Falkirk Library, Hope Street, Falkirk FK1 5AU
☎(01324) 503605
Fax (01324) 503606
e-mail: falkirk.library@falkirk.gov.uk
Principal Librarian Ms Anna Herron MA DipLib MCLIP

Other libraries

Bo'ness Library, Scotland's Close, Bo'ness, Falkirk EH51 0AH
☎(01506) 778520
Fax (01506) 778521
e-mail: bo'ness.library@falkirk.gov.uk
Acting Librarian Ms Margaret Brodie BA MCLIP

Bonnybridge Library, Bridge Street, Bonnybridge, Falkirk FK4 1AA
☎(01324) 503295
Fax (01324) 503296

e-mail: bonnybridge.library@falkirk.gov.uk
Librarian Ms Naomi Kenny MA LPC LLB MSc MCLIP

Denny Library, 49 Church Walk, Denny, Falkirk FK6 6DF
☎(01324) 504242
Fax (01324) 504240
e-mail: denny.library@falkirk.gov.uk
Librarians Ms Vikki Ring BA MCLIP, Mrs Shona Hill BA MCLIP

Grangemouth Library, Bo'ness Road, Grangemouth, Falkirk FK3 8AG
☎(01324) 504690
Fax (01324) 504691
e-mail: grangemouth.library@falkirk.gov.uk
Senior Librarians Mrs Sharon Woodforde MCLIP, Mrs Rachel Williams BSc(Hons) DipLib

Larbert Library, 22 Hallam Road, Stenhousemuir, Larbert, Falkirk FK5 3JX
☎(01324) 503590
Fax (01324) 503592
e-mail: larbert.library@falkirk.gov.uk
Senior Librarians Mrs Karyn Jaffray BA MCLIP, Miss Tanya Milligan MA MCLIP, Ms Fiona Fraser BA MCLIP

Meadowbank Library, 2A Stevenson Avenue, Polmont, Falkirk FK2 0GU
☎(01324) 503870
Fax (01324) 503871
e-mail: meadowbank.library@falkirk.gov.uk
Librarians Mrs Lorraine Alexander BA MCLIP, Allan Wright MA MCLIP

Slamannan Library, The Cross, Slamannan, Falkirk FK1 3EX
☎(01324) 851373
Fax (01324) 851862
e-mail: slamannan.library@falkirk.gov.uk
Librarian Mrs Jane Humphreys MCLIP

FIFE
Authority: Fife Council

Libraries and Museums, Library and Museum Headquarters, East Fergus Place, Kirkcaldy, Fife KY1 1XT
☎(01592) 583204
e-mail: fife.libraries@fife.gov.uk
url: www.fifedirect.org.uk
Service Manager, Libraries, Arts and Museums Ms Dorothy Browse MBA MA MCLIP
(e-mail: dorothy.browse@fife.gov.uk)

Area library

Dunfermline Carnegie Library, Abbot Street, Dunfermline, Fife KY12 7NL
☎(01383) 602365

Group libraries

Cupar Library, 33-35 Crossgate, Cupar, Fife KY15 5AS
☎(01334) 659367

Glenwood Library, Glenwood Shopping Centre, Glenrothes, Fife KY6 1PA
☎(01592) 583205

Kirkcaldy Central Library, War Memorial Gardens, Kirkcaldy, Fife KY1 1YG
☎(01592) 583206

Leven Library, Durie Street, Leven, Fife KY8 4HE
☎(01334) 659373

St Andrews Library, Church Square, St Andrews, Fife KY16 9NN
☎(01334) 659378

GLASGOW
Authority: Glasgow City Council

Culture and Sport Glasgow, The Mitchell Library, North Street, Glasgow G3 7DN
☎0141 287 2999 (enquiries), 0141 287 2870 (service development)
Fax 0141 287 2815
e-mail: lil@csglasgow.org
url: www.csglasgow.org
Head of Libraries, Information and Learning Ms Karen Cunningham MA DipLib MCLIP
(0141 287 5114; fax: 0141 287 5151; e-mail: karen.cunningham@csglasgow.gov.uk)
(located at 20 Trongate, Glasgow G1 1LX)
Service Development Manager Gordon Anderson BA MCLIP (0141 287 2949; e-mail:
gordon.anderson@csglasgow.gov.uk)
Information Services Manager Ms Pamela Tulloch MA MBA DipLib MCLIP (0141 287
2862; e-mail: pamela.tulloch@csglasgow.gov.uk)
Community Libraries Network Manager Ms Wilma Moore MCLIP (0141 287 2806;
e-mail: wilma.moore@csglasgow.gov.uk)
Community Learning Manager Ms Jane Edgar DipYCW (0141 287 2881; e-mail:
jane.edgar@csglasgow.gov.uk)

Community libraries

Anniesland Library and Learning Centre, 833 Crow Road, Glasgow G13 1LE
☎0141 276 1622
Fax 0141 276 1623

Baillieston Library and Learning Centre, 141 Main Street, Glasgow G69 6AA
☎0141 276 0706
Fax 0141 276 0707

Barmulloch Library and Learning Centre, 46 Wallacewell Quadrant, Glasgow G21 3PX
☎0141 276 0875
Fax 0141 276 0876

Bridgeton Library and Learning Centre, 23 Landressy Street, Glasgow G40 1BP
☎0141 276 0870
Fax 0141 276 0871

Cardonald Library and Learning Centre, 1113 Mosspark Drive, Glasgow G52 3BU
☎0141 276 0880
Fax 0141 276 0881

Castlemilk Library and Learning Centre, 100 Castlemilk Drive, Glasgow G45 9TN
☎0141 276 0731
Fax 0141 276 0732

Couper Institute Library and Learning Centre, 84 Clarkston Road, Glasgow G44 3DA
☎0141 276 0771
Fax 0141 276 0772

Dennistoun Library and Learning Centre, 2a Craigpark, Glasgow G31 2NA
☎0141 276 0768
Fax 0141 276 0769

Drumchapel Library and Learning Centre, 65 Hecla Avenue, Glasgow G15 8LX
☎0141 276 1545
Fax 0141 276 1546

Elder Park Library and Learning Centre, 228a Langlands Road, Glasgow G51 3TZ
☎0141 276 1540
Fax 0141 276 1541

Gorbals Library and CybercafÈ and Learning Centre, 180 Crown Street, Glasgow G5 4XD
☎0141 429 0949
Fax 0141 429 0167

Govanhill Library and Learning Centre, Govanhill Neighbourhood Centre, 6 Daisy Street, Glasgow G42 8JL
☎0141 276 1550
Fax 0141 276 1551

Hillhead Library and Learning Centre, 348 Byres Road, Glasgow G12 8AP
☎0141 276 1617
Fax 0141 276 1618

Ibrox Library and Learning Centre, 1 Midlock Street, Glasgow G51 1SL
☎0141 276 0712
Fax 0141 276 0713

Knightswood Library and Learning Centre, 27 Dunterlie Avenue, Glasgow G13 3BB
☎0141 276 1555
Fax 0141 276 1556

Langside Library and Learning Centre, 2 Sinclair Drive, Glasgow G42 9QE
☎0141 276 0777
Fax 0141 276 0778

Leisure and Lifestyle at the Mitchell and Learning Centre, Granville Street, Glasgow G3 7DN
☎0141 287 2872

Library at the Bridge and Learning Centre, 1000 Westerhouse Road, Glasgow G34 9JW
☎0141 276 9712
Fax 0141 276 9711

Library@Goma and Learning Centre, Gallery of Modern Art, Queen Street, Glasgow G1 3AZ
☎0141 287 3010
Fax 0141 249 9943

Maryhill Library and Learning Centre, 1508 Maryhill Road, Glasgow G20 9AD
☎0141 276 0715
Fax 0141 276 0716

Milton Library and Learning Centre, Milton Community Campus, 204 Liddesdale Road,
Glasgow G22 7AR
☎0141 276 0885
Fax 0141 276 0886

Parkhead Library and Learning Centre, 64 Tollcross Road, Glasgow G31 4XA
☎0141 276 1530
Fax 0141 276 1531

Partick Library and Learning Centre, 305 Dumbarton Road, Glasgow G11 6AB
☎0141 276 1560
Fax 0141 276 1561

Pollok Library and Leisure Centre, 27 Cowglen Road, Glasgow G53 2EN
☎0141 276 6877

Pollokshaws Library and Learning Centre, 50-60 Shawbridge Street, Glasgow G43 1RW
☎0141 276 1535
Fax 0141 276 1536

Pollokshields Library and Learning Centre, 30 Leslie Street, Glasgow G41 2LF
☎0141 276 1685
Fax 0141 276 1686

Possilpark Library and Learning Centre, 127 Allander Street, Glasgow G22 5JJ
☎0141 276 0928
Fax 0141 276 0929

Riddrie Library and Learning Centre, 1020 Cumbernauld Road, Glasgow G33 2QS
☎0141 276 0690
Fax 0141 276 0691

Royston Library and Learning Centre, 67 Royston Road, Glasgow G21 2QW
☎0141 276 0890
Fax 0141 276 0891

Service Development and Learning Centre, The Mitchell Library, North Street, Glasgow
G3 7DN
☎0141 287 2870
Fax 0141 287 2815

Shettleston Library, 154 Wellshot Road, Glasgow G32 7AX
☎0141 276 1643
Fax 0141 276 1645

Springburn Library and Learning Centre, Kay Street, Glasgow G21 1JY
☎0141 276 1690
Fax 0141 276 1691

Whiteinch Library and Learning Centre, 14 Victoria Park Drive South, Glasgow G14 9RL
☎0141 276 0695
Fax 0141 276 0696

Woodside Library and Learning Centre, 343 St George's Road, Glasgow G3 6JQ
☎0141 276 1609
Fax 0141 276 1610

HIGHLAND
Authority: The Highland Council

Education, Culture and Sport Service, Glenurquhart Road, Inverness IV3 5NX
☎(01463) 702050
Fax (01463) 711177
Leisure and Learning Manager Graham Watson (e-mail:
graham.watson@highland.gov.uk)

Library Service HQ

Library Support Unit, 31A Harbour Road, Inverness IV1 1UA
☎(01463) 235713
Fax (01463) 236986
e-mail: libraries@highland.gov.uk
Principal Libraries Officer Ms Joyce Watson BA MCLIP ((01463) 251250; e-mail:
joyce.watson@highland.gov.uk)

Caithness, Sutherland, Ross-shire and Skye & Lochalsh

Area Support Base

Broadford Service Point and Library, Old Quarry Industrial Estate, Broadford, Isle of Skye
IV49 9AB
☎(01471) 820184
Fax (01471) 822588
Assistant Area Libraries Officer David Linton MCLIP (01471 820184; fax: 01471
822588; e-mail: david.linton@highland.gov.uk)

Carnegie Building, West End, Bonar Bridge, Sutherland IV24 3EA
☎(01863) 766709 (tel/fax)
Assistant Area Libraries Officer Ms Patricia Hannah MCLIP (e-mail:
patricia.hannah@highland.gov.uk)

Dornoch Library, Carnegie Building, High Street, Dornoch, Inverness IV25 3SH
☎(01862) 811585 (tel/fax)
Area Libraries Officer Mrs Alison Forrest BA DipLib MCLIP (e-mail:
alison.forrest@highland.gov.uk)

Area libraries

Achiltibuie Library, Coigach Community Hall, Achiltibuie, IV26 2YG
☎(01854) 622305 (tel/fax)
e-mail: achiltibuie.library@highland.gov.uk

Alness Library, Averon Centre, High Street, Alness, Highland IV17 0QB
☎(01349) 882674
Fax (01349) 883587
e-mail: alness.library@highland.gov.uk

Bettyhill Library, Naver Teleservice Centre, Bettyhill, Sutherland KW14 7SS
☎(01641) 521242 (tel/fax)
e-mail: bettyhill.library@highland.gov.uk

Bonar Bridge Library, Carnegie Building, West End, Bonar Bridge, Sutherland IV24 3EA
☎(01862) 811585 (tel/fax)
e-mail: bonarbridge.library@highland.gov.uk

Brora Library, Gower Street, Brora, Highland KW9 6PD
☎(01408) 621128
Fax (01408) 622064
e-mail: brora.library@highland.gov.uk

Cromarty Library, Hugh Miller Institute, Church Street, Cromarty, Ross & Cromarty,
IV11 8XA
☎(01381) 600318 (tel/fax)
e-mail: cromarty.library@highland.gov.uk

Dingwall Library, Dingwall Academy, Dingwall, Ross-shire IV15 9LT
☎(01349) 869869
Fax (01349) 869868
e-mail: dingwall.library@highland.gov.uk

Dornoch Library, Carnegie Building, High Street, Dornoch, Inverness IV25 3SH
☎(01862) 811079 (tel/fax)
e-mail: dornoch.library@highland.gov.uk

Fortrose Library, Fortrose Academy, Fortrose, Highland IV10 8TW
☎(01381) 622235 (tel/fax)
e-mail: fortrose.library@highland.gov.uk
Librarian Ms Sheena Paterson BA MCLIP (e-mail: sheena.paterson@highland.gov.uk)
(Joint school/community library)

Gairloch Library, Gairloch Community Library, Auchtercairn, Gairloch, IV21 2BP
☎(01445) 712469 (tel/fax)
e-mail: gairloch.library@highland.gov.uk
(Joint school/community library)

Golspie Library, Community Centre, Golspie High School, Sutherland KW10 6RA
☎(01408) 634084 (tel/fax)
e-mail: golspie.library@highland.gov.uk

Helmsdale Library, Community Centre, Dunrobin Street, Helmsdale, Sutherland KW8 6JX
☎(01431) 821742 (tel/fax)
e-mail: helmsdale.library@highland.gov.uk

Invergordon Library, High Street, Invergordon, Ross-shire IV18 0DG
☎(01349) 852698 (tel/fax)
e-mail: invergordon.library@highland.gov.uk

Kyle Service Point & Library, Main Street, Kyle of Lochalsh, Skye & Lochalsh, IV40 8AB
☎(01599) 534270
Fax (01599) 534562
e-mail: kyle.library@highland.gov.uk

Lairg Library, Main Street, Lairg, Sutherland IV27 4DD

☎(01549) 402577 (tel/fax)
e-mail: lairg.library@highland.gov.uk

Lochcarron Library, The Howard Doris Centre, Lochcarron, Ross & Cromarty, IV54 8UD
☎(01520) 722679 (tel/fax)
e-mail: lochcarron.library@highland.gov.uk

Muir of Ord Library, Tarradale School, Muir of Ord, Ross & Cromarty, IV6 7SU
☎(01463) 870196 (tel/fax)
e-mail: muiroford.library@highland.gov.uk

Plockton Library, Village Hall, Harbour Street, Plockton, Skye & Lochalsh, IV52 8TG
☎(01599) 544718 (tel/fax)

Portree Community Library, Viewfield Road, Portree, Isle of Skye IV51 9ET
☎(01478) 614823
Fax (01478) 614824
e-mail: portree.library@highland.gov.uk
(Joint school/community library)

Tain Library, Stafford Street, Tain, Highland IV19 1AZ
☎(01862) 892391 (tel/fax)
e-mail: tain.library@highland.gov.uk

Thurso Library, Davidson's Lane, Thurso, Caithness KW14 7AF
☎(01847) 893237
Fax (01847) 896114
e-mail: thurso.library@highland.gov.uk

Ullapool Library, Community High School, Mill Street, Ullapool, Highland IV26 2UN
☎(01854) 612543 (tel/fax)
e-mail: ullapool.library@highland.gov.uk
(Joint school/community library)

Wick Library, Carnegie Public Library, Sinclair Terrace, Wick, Caithness KW1 5AB
☎(01955) 602864
Fax (01955) 603000
e-mail: wick.library@highland.gov.uk

Inverness, Nairn, Badenoch & Strathspey and Lochaber

Area Support Base

The Highland Council, Education, Culture & Sport Office, 13 Ardross Street, Inverness
IV3 5NS
☎(01463) 663800
Fax (01463) 663839
Area Libraries Officer Mrs Charlotte E MacArthur BA(Hons) DipLib MCLIP (01463
663828; e-mail: charlotte.macarthur@highland.gov.uk)

Area libraries

Ardersier Library, Old School, Station Road, Ardersier, Inverness IV2 7SU
☎(01667) 462658 (tel/fax)
e-mail: ardersier.library@highland.gov.uk

Ardnamurchan Library, Sunart Centre, Strontian, Acharacle, PH36 4JA
☎(01397) 709226 (tel/fax)
e-mail: ardnamurchan.library@highland.gov.uk
(Joint school/community library)

Aviemore Library, Units 1 & 2, Market Hall, Aviemore, Badenoch & Strathspey, PH22 1RH
☎(01479) 811113 (tel/fax)
e-mail: aviemore.library@highland.gov.uk

Badenoch Library & Learning Centre, Spey Street, Kingussie, Highland PH21 1EH
☎(01540) 661596 (tel/fax)
e-mail: badenoch.library@highland.gov.uk

Beauly Library, Phipps Institute, Beauly, Inverness IV4 7EH
☎(01463) 782930 (tel/fax)
e-mail: beauly.library@highland.gov.uk

Caol Library, Glenkingie Street, Caol, Fort William, Lochaber, PH33 7DP
☎(01397) 702829 (tel/fax)
e-mail: caol.library@highland.gov.uk

Culloden Library, Keppoch Road, Culloden, Inverness IV2 7LL
☎(01463) 792531
Fax (01463) 793162
e-mail: culloden.library@highland.gov.uk
Librarian Ms Angela Donald MCLIP

Fort William Library, Education Culture and Sport Service, Airds Crossing, High Street,
Fort William, Lochaber, PH33 6EU
☎(01397) 703552
Fax (01397) 703538
e-mail: fortwilliam.library@highland.gov.uk

Glenurquhart Library, Pitkerrald Road, Drumnadrochit, Inverness IV63 6XA
☎(01456) 459223
e-mail: glenurquhart.library@highland.gov.uk
(Joint school/community library)

Grantown Library, YMCA Building, 20 High Street, Grantown-on-Spey, Badenoch &
Strathspey, PH26 3HB
☎(01479) 873175 (tel/fax)
e-mail: grantown.library@highland.gov.uk

Inshes Community Library, Inshes Primary School, Inshes Road, Inverness IV2 3RF
☎(01463) 725928 (tel/fax)
e-mail: inshes.library@highland.gov.uk
(Joint school/community library)

Inverness Library, Farraline Park, Inverness IV1 1NH
☎(01463) 236463
Fax (01463) 237001
e-mail: inverness.library@highland.gov.uk
Assistant Librarian Sam McDowell BA MCLIP (e-mail: sam.mcdowell@highland.gov.uk)
Reference Librarian Ms Edwina Burridge BA MCLIP (e-mail:
edwina.burridge@highland.gov.uk)

Kinlochleven Library, Riverside Road, Kinlochleven, PH50 4QH
☎(01855) 832047
Fax (01855) 832048
e-mail: kinlochleven.library@highland.gov.uk
(Joint school/community library)

Knoydart Library, The Store, Inverie, Knoydart, by Mallaig, PH41 4PL
☎(01687) 460253 (tel/fax)

Mallaig Library, Mallaig and Morar Community Centre, West Bay, Mallaig, PH41 4PY
☎(01687) 460097 (tel/fax)
e-mail: mallaig.library@highland.gov.uk

Nairn Library, 68 High Street, Nairn, Nairnshire IV12 4AU
☎(01667) 458506
Fax (01667) 458548
e-mail: nairn.library@highland.gov.uk
Librarian Mrs Jennifer Murdoch MCLIP BA (e-mail: jennifer.murdoch@highland.gov.uk)

INVERCLYDE
Authority: Inverclyde Council

Central Library, Clyde Square, Greenock, Renfrewshire PA15 INA
☎(01475) 712323
Fax (01475) 712339
e-mail: library.central@inverclyde.gov.uk
url: www.inverclyde.gov.uk/libraries
Libraries Manager Ms Alana Macmillan MA(Hons) (e-mail:
alana.macmillan@inverclyde.gov.uk)

MIDLOTHIAN
Authority: Midlothian Council

Library HQ, 2 Clerk Street, Loanhead, Midlothian EH20 9DR
☎0131 271 3980
Fax 0131 440 4635
e-mail: library.hq@midlothian.gov.uk
url: www.midlothian.gov.uk/library/
Library Services Manager Alan Reid MA MCLIP

Largest library

Penicuik Library, The Penicuik Centre, Carlops Road, Penicuik, Midlothian EH26 9EP
☎(01968) 664050
Fax (01968) 679408
e-mail: penicuik.library@midlothian.gov.uk
Senior Librarian Stephen Harris MA MSc

Branch libraries

Dalkeith Library, White Hart Street, Dalkeith, Midlothian EH22 1AE
☎0131 663 2083

Fax 0131 654 9029
e-mail: dalkeith.library@midlothian.gov.uk
Senior Librarian Thomas Regan BA MCLIP

Bonnyrigg Library, Polton Street, Bonnyrigg, Midlothian EH19 3HB
☎0131 663 6762
Fax 0131 654 9019
e-mail: bonnyrigg.library@midlothian.gov.uk
Senior Librarian David Stevenson BA MCLIP

Danderhall Library, 1A Campview, Danderhall, Midlothian EH22 1QD
☎0131 663 9293
e-mail: danderhall.library@midlothian.gov.uk
Assistant i/c Ms Rachel Archibald

Gorebridge Library, Hunterfield Road, Gorebridge, Midlothian EH23 4TT
☎(01875) 820630
Fax (01875) 823657
e-mail: gorebridge.library@midlothian.gov.uk
Assistant i/c Ms Janette Hamilton

Loanhead Library, George Avenue, Loanhead, Midlothian EH20 9HD
☎0131 440 0824
e-mail: loanhead.library@midlothian.gov.uk
Assistant i/c Vacant
Senior Support Assistant Ms Karen Cummings

Local Studies, 2 Clerk Street, Loanhead, Midlothian EH20 9DR
☎0131 271 3976
Fax 0131 440 4635
e-mail: local.studies@midlothian.gov.uk
Local Studies Officer Dr Kenneth Bogle MA MCLIP PhD

Mayfield Library, Stone Avenue, Mayfield, Dalkeith, Midlothian EH22 5PB
☎0131 663 2126
e-mail: mayfield.library@midlothian.gov.uk
Assistant i/c Ms Isobel Allen

Newtongrange Library, St Davids, Newtongrange, Midlothian EH22 4LG
☎0131 663 1816
Fax 0131 654 1990
e-mail: newtongrange.library@midlothian.gov.uk
Assistant i/c Ms Jacqueline Elliot

Roslin Library, 9 Main Street, Roslin, Midlothian EH25 9LD
☎0131 448 2781
e-mail: roslin.library@midlothian.gov.uk
Assistant i/c Ms Lorraine Martin

Woodburn Library, Dalkeith Comunity Centre, 6 Woodburn Road, Dalkeith, Midlothian
EH22 2AR
☎0131 654 4323
e-mail: woodburn.library@midlothian.gov.uk
Senior Librarian Thomas Regan BA MCLIP

MORAY
Authority: The Moray Council

Educational Services Department, Council Office, High Street, Elgin, Moray IV30 IBX
☎(01343) 562600 (enquiries), 01343 563398 (administration)
Fax (01343) 563478
url: www.moray.gov.uk
Libraries and Museums Manager G Alistair Campbell MA BCom MCLIP (e-mail: campbea@moray.gov.uk)

Central/largest library

Elgin Library, Cooper Park, Elgin, Moray IV30 IHS
☎(01343) 562600
Fax (01343) 562630
e-mail: elgin.library@moray.gov.uk
Principal Librarian (Central Services) Ms Sheila Campbell MCLIP (e-mail: sheila.campbell@moray.gov.uk)

Area libraries

Buckie Library, Cluny Place, Buckie, Banffshire AB56 IHB
☎(01542) 832121
Fax (01542) 835237
e-mail: buckie.library@moray.gov.uk
Senior Librarian (Buckie) Ms Eleanor Kidd MA MCLIP

Forres Library, Forres House, High Street, Forres, Moray IV36 IBU
☎(01309) 672834
Fax (01309) 675084
e-mail: forres.library@moray.gov.uk
Senior Librarian (Forres) Ms Jane Sandell MA MCLIP

Keith Library, Union Street, Keith, Banffshire AB55 5DP
☎(01542) 882223
Fax (01542) 882177
e-mail: keith.library@moray.gov.uk
Senior Librarian (Keith) Ms Susan Butts MA(Hons) MCLIP

NORTH AYRSHIRE
Authority: North Ayrshire Council

Library, 39-41 Princes Street, Ardrossan, Ayrshire KA22 8BT
☎(01294) 469137
Fax (01294) 604236
e-mail: libraryhq@north-ayrshire.gov.uk
url: www.north-ayrshire.gov.uk
Manager, Information and Culture Dr Audrey Sutton MA(Hons) DipLib PLD MCLIP (01294 212716; fax: 01294 222509; e-mail: asutton@north-ayrshire.gov.uk)
Assistant Manager, Information and Culture Ms Lesley Hamilton (01294 212716; fax: 01294 222509; e-mail: lhamilton@north-ayrshire.gov.uk)
Information and Culture Officer Paul Cowan BEd(Hons) DipLib MCLIP (01294 212716;

fax: 01294 222509; e-mail: pcowan@north-ayrshire.gov.uk)
Systems Support Officer Ms Alison McAllister BA(Hons) MCLIP (01294 212716; fax:
01294 222509; e-mail: amcallister@north-ayrshire.gov.uk)
Children and Families Officer Ms Melanie West BA DipLib MCLIP (01294 212716; fax:
01294 222509; e-mail: mwest@north-ayrshire.gov.uk)

Central/largest library

Irvine Library, 168 High Street, Irvine, Ayrshire KA12 8AN
☎(01294) 271295
Fax (01294) 313051
e-mail: irvinelibrary@north-ayrshire.gov.uk
Area Librarian Vacant

Area libraries

Largs Library, Allanpark Street, Largs, Ayrshire KA30 9AS
☎(01475) 673309 (tel/fax)
e-mail: largslibrary@north-ayrshire.gov.uk
Area Librarian Ms Eileen Vernon MA(Hons) DipLib MCLIP

Saltcoats Library, Springvale Place, Saltcoats, Ayrshire KA21 5LS
☎(01294) 469546 (tel/fax)
e-mail: saltcoatslibrary@north-ayrshire.gov.uk
Area Librarian Jim Macaulay MCLIP DipLib

NORTH LANARKSHIRE
Authority: North Lanarkshire Council

**Learning and Leisure Services, Municipal Buildings, Kildonan Street, Coatbridge, North
Lanarkshire ML5 3BT**
☎(01698) 332606
Fax (01698) 332624
url: www.northlan.gov.uk
Community Learning and Libraries Manager Ms Barbara Philliben
Bibliographic and Outside Services Manager James Lindsay BA MCLIP (e-mail:
lindsayj@northlan.gov.uk)
Acting Information Services Manager Jim Alexander (e-mail:
alexanderj@northlan.gov.uk)
Children and Young People's Library Services Manager Russell Brown BA(Hons)
MCLIP (e-mail: brownru@northlan.gov.uk)

South Area

Motherwell Library, 35 Hamilton Road, Motherwell, North Lanarkshire ML1 3BZ
☎(01698) 332626
Fax (01698) 332625
Lending Services Manager (South) Mrs Catriona Wales BA MCLIP (e-mail:
walesc@northlan.gov.uk)

North Area

Coatbridge Library, Buchanan Centre, 126 Main Street, Coatbridge, North Lanarkshire
ML5 3BG
☎(01236) 856444
Lending Services Manager (North) Mrs Wendy Bennett BA MCLIP (e-mail:
bennettw@northlan.gov.uk)

ORKNEY
Authority: Orkney Islands Council

The Orkney Library and Archive, 44 Junction Road, Kirkwall, Orkney KW15 1AG
☎(01856) 873166 (enquiries and administration)
Fax (01856) 875260
e-mail: general.enquiries@orkneylibrary.org.uk
url: www.orkneylibrary.org.uk
Library and Archive Manager Gary Amos (e-mail: gary.amos@orkneylibrary.org.uk)
Principal Librarian Ms Karen Walker BA (e-mail: karen.walker@orkneylibrary.org.uk)
Principal Archivist Ms Alison Fraser (e-mail: alison.fraser@orkneylibrary.org.uk)

PERTH AND KINROSS
Authority: Perth and Kinross Council

The A K Bell Library, York Place, Perth, Perthshire PH2 8EP
☎(01738) 444949
Fax (01738) 477010
e-mail: library@pkc.gov.uk
url: www.pkc.gov.uk/library
Community Libraries Manager Ms Helen Smout
Senior Children's Librarian Ms Morag Kelly MA DipLib MCLIP (e-mail:
makelly@pkc.gov.uk)

Area libraries

Auchterarder Library, Aytoun Hall, Chapel Wynd, Auchterarder, Perthshire PH3 1BL
☎(01764) 663850 (tel/fax)
e-mail: auchterarderlibrary@pkc.gov.uk
Community Librarian Mrs Kirsty Brown BA, Mrs Lesley Paul

Blairgowrie Library, 46 Leslie Street, Blairgowrie, Perthshire PH10 6AW
☎(01250) 871305
Fax (01250) 872905
e-mail: blairgowrielibrary@pkc.gov.uk
Community Librarian Simon McGowan MA

Loch Leven Community Library, Muirs, Kinross, Kinross-shire KY13 8FQ
☎(01577) 867205
e-mail: kinrosslibrary@pkc.gov.uk
Community Librarian Ms Sandra Birse

Scone Library, Sandy Road, Scone, Perth, Perthshire PH2 6LJ
☎(01738) 553029 (tel/fax)

e-mail: sconelibrary@pkc.gov.uk
Community Librarian Mrs Elaine Wallace BA, Ms Fiona Soutar

Strathearn Community Library, Strathearn Community Campus, Pittenzie Road, Crieff, Perthshire PH7 3RS
☎(01764) 657705
e-mail: criefflibrary@pkc.gov.uk
Community Librarian Ms Marilyn Gordon BA

Community libraries

Aberfeldy Library, Bank Street, Aberfeldy, Perthshire PH15 2BB
☎(01887) 820475
e-mail: aberfeldylibrary@pkc.gov.uk
Library Assistant in Charge Mrs Sue Bennett

Alyth Library, Airlie Street, Alyth, Blairgowrie, Perthshire PH11 8AH
☎(01828) 632731
e-mail: alythlibrary@pkc.gov.uk
Library Assistant in Charge Mrs Aileen Carnegie

Birnam Library, The Institute, Station Road, Birnam, Dunkeld, Perthshire PH8 0DS
☎(01350) 727971
e-mail: birnamlibrary@pkc.gov.uk
Library Assistant in Charge Mrs Margaret Quigley

Comrie Library, Drummond Street, Comrie, Perthshire PH6 2DS
☎(01764) 670273
e-mail: comrielibrary@pkc.gov.uk
Library Assistant in Charge Vacant

Coupar Angus Library, Town Hall, Union Street, Coupar Angus, Blairgowrie, Perthshire PH13 9AE
☎(01828) 627090
e-mail: couparanguslibrary@pkc.gov.uk
Library Assistant in Charge Mrs Shona Smith

North Inch Community Library, North Inch Campus, Gowans Terrace, Perth PH1 5BF
☎(01738) 454406
e-mail: northinchlibrary@pkc.gov.uk
Community Librarian Ms Elaine Blair

Pitlochry Library, 26 Atholl Road, Pitlochry, Perthshire PH16 5BX
☎(01796) 474635
e-mail: pitlochrylibrary@pkc.gov.uk
Library Assistant in Charge Mrs Grace Grant

West Mill Street Library, West Mill Street, Perth PH1 5QP
☎(01738) 638436
e-mail: westmillstreetlibrary@pkc.gov.uk
Library Assistants in Charge Mrs May Harris, Ms Elspeth Collier

RENFREWSHIRE

Authority: Renfrewshire Council

Library Services, Library Support Service, Netherhill Road, Gallowhill, Paisley, Renfrewshire PA3 4SF
☎0141 887 2723
Fax 0141 887 9557
e-mail: libraries@els.renfrewshire.gov.uk
url: www.renfrewshire.gov.uk
Libraries Manager Ms Jenifer McFarlane BA MCLIP (located at Paisley Museum, High Street, Paisley PA3 4SF)

Central/largest library

Central Library (Lending), 68 High Street, Paisley, Renfrewshire PA1 2BB
☎0141 887 3672
Fax 0141 887 6468
Librarian Ms Elaine Finlay BA(Hons) DipLib MCLIP

Central Library (Reference), 68 High Street, Paisley, Renfrewshire PA1 2BB
☎0141 889 2360
Fax 0141 887 6468
Librarian Ms Elaine Finlay BA(Hons) DipLib MCLIP

Community libraries

Bishopton Community Library, 11 Greenock Road, Bishopton, Renfrewshire PA7 5JW
☎(01505) 862136
Fax (01505) 862265
Librarian Ms Janet Clasper

Bridge of Weir Community Library, Main Street, Bridge of Weir, Renfrewshire PA11 3NR
☎(01505) 612220
Fax (01505) 615052
Librarians Ms Evelyn Gilchrist
Bryan Smith

Erskine Community Library, Bridgewater Place, Erskine, Renfrewshire PA8 7AA
☎0141 812 5331
Fax 0141 812 4977
Librarian Ms Alison Horsburgh BLib MCLIP

Ferguslie Park Community Library, Tannahill Centre, Blackstoun Road, Paisley, Renfrewshire PA3 1NT
☎0141 887 6404
Fax 0141 849 0003
Librarian Andrew Givan MA(Hons) MSc MCLIP

Foxbar Community Library, Ivanhoe Road, Paisley, Renfrewshire PA2 0JZ
☎(01505) 812353
Fax (01505) 816989
Librarian Ms Christine Storie BA MCLIP

Glenburn Community Library, Fairway Avenue, Paisley, Renfrewshire PA2 8DX

☎0141 884 2874
Fax 0141 884 5758
Librarian Ms Janis McIntyre DipHE MCLIP

Johnstone Community Library, Houston Court, Johnstone, Renfrewshire PA5 8DL
☎(01505) 329726
Fax (01505) 336657
e-mail: libraries.els@renfrewshire.gov.uk
Librarian Ms Jane Gourlay BA MCLIP

Linwood Community Library, Ardlamont Square, Linwood, Renfrewshire PA3 3DE
☎(01505) 325283
Fax (01505) 336150
Librarian Ms Linda Henderson MCLIP

Lochwinnoch Community Library, Old School, High Street, Lochwinnoch, Renfrewshire
PA12 4AB
☎(01505) 842305
Fax (01505) 843780
Librarian Ms Margaret Sweenie

Ralston Community Library, Community Centre, Allanton Avenue, Paisley, Renfrewshire
PA1 3BL
☎0141 882 1879
Fax 0141 882 2325
Contacts Ms Kay Wright, Ms Pauline Chisholm

Renfrew Community Library, Paisley Road, Renfrew, Renfrewshire PA4 8LJ
☎0141 886 3433
Fax 0141 886 1660
e-mail: libraries.els@renfrewshire.gov.uk
Librarian Ms Margaret Winters BA MCLIP

Toy Library, Foxbar Library, Ivanhoe Road, Paisley, Renfrewshire PA2 0JZ
☎(01505) 812353
Fax (01505) 816989
Librarian Ms Christine Storie BA MCLIP

Mobile Libraries, Glenburn Library, Fairway Avenue, Paisley, Renfrewshire PA2 8DX
☎0141 884 2874; 07770 366150/366151 (mobile tel nos)
Fax 0141 884 5758
e-mail: libraries.els@renfrewshire.gov.uk
Contact Ms Debbie McBride

SCOTTISH BORDERS
Authority: Scottish Borders Council

Scottish Borders Library Service, St Mary's Mill, Selkirk TD7 5EW
☎(01750) 20842
Fax (01750) 22875
url: www.scotborders.gov.uk
Head of Community Services Alan Hasson MA MBA DipLib MCLIP MIMgt
Library and Information Services Manager Ms Margaret Menzies BA MLib MCLIP

Community and Operations Librarian Keith Nairn MSc MCLIP
(e-mail: knairn@scotborders.gov.uk)
Information Systems Librarian Ms Sheena Milne MA MCLIP DipLib
Young People's Services Co-ordinator Ms Gill Swales BA MCLIP DipLib
(e-mail: gswales@scotborders.gov.uk)

Area libraries

Galashiels Library, Lawyer's Brae, Galashiels, Selkirkshire TD1 3JQ
☎(01896) 752512
Fax (01896) 753575
e-mail: libgalashiels@scotborders.gov.uk
Area Librarian Miss Caroline R Letton MA FSA(Scot) MCLIP DipLib

Hawick Library, North Bridge Street, Hawick, Roxburghshire TD9 9QT
☎(01450) 372637
Fax (01450) 370991
e-mail: libhawick@scotborders.gov.uk
Area Librarian John Beedle BA MCLIP

Peebles Library, Chambers Institute, High Street, Peebles, Peeblesshire EH45 8AG
☎(01721) 720123
Fax (01721) 724424
e-mail: libpeebles@scotborders.gov.uk
Area Librarian Paul Taylor BSc FSA MCLIP

Branch libraries

Coldstream Library, Gateway Centre, Coldstream, Scottish Borders TD12 4AE
☎(01890) 883314 (tel/fax)
e-mail: libcoldstream@scotborders.gov.uk
Branch Librarian Mrs Julia Townsend BA MCLIP
Library and Information Services Manager Ms Margaret Menzies BA MLib MCLIP

Duns Library, 49 Newtown Street, Duns, Berwickshire TD11 3AU
☎(01361) 882622
Fax (01361) 884104
e-mail: libduns@scotborders.gov.uk
Branch Librarian Ms Joan B Sanderson BA MCLIP

Earlston Library, High School, Earlston, Scottish Borders TD4 6ED
☎(01896) 849282
Fax (01896) 848918
e-mail: libearlston@scotborders.gov.uk
Branch Librarian Mrs Anne Taitt

Eyemouth Library, Manse Road, Eyemouth, Scottish Borders TD14 5JE
☎(01890) 750300
Fax (01890) 751633
e-mail: libeyemouth@scotborders.gov.uk
Branch Librarian Mrs Joan Thomas, Mrs Alison Fowler BA MCLIP

Innerleithen Library, Buccleuch Street, Innerleithen, Scottish Borders EH44 6LA
☎(01896) 830789 (tel/fax)

e-mail: libinnerleithen@scotborders.gov.uk
Branch Librarian Mrs Elaine Hogarth

Jedburgh Library, Castlegate, Jedburgh, Scottish Borders TD8 6AS
☎(01835) 863592 (tel/fax)
e-mail: libjedburgh@scotborders.gov.uk
Branch Librarian Miss Jennifer Coyle BSc(Hons) MSc
Library and Information Services Manager Ms Margaret Menzies BA MLib MCLIP

Kelso Library, Bowmont Street, Kelso, Roxburghshire TD5 7JH
☎(01573) 223171
Fax (01573) 226618
e-mail: libkelso@scotborders.gov.uk
Branch Librarian Mrs Ruth Holmes MSc MCLIP

Local Studies, St Mary's Mill, Selkirk TD7 5EW
☎(01750) 20842
Fax (01750) 22875
Librarian Miss Helen Darling BA(Hons) MCLIP (e-mail: hdarling@scotborders.gov.uk)

Melrose Library, 18 Market Square, Melrose, Scottish Borders TD6 9PN
☎(01896) 823052 (tel/fax)
e-mail: libmelrose@scotborders.gov.uk
Branch Librarian Mrs Mairi Wight

Selkirk Library, Ettrick Terrace, Selkirk TD7 4LF
☎(01750) 20267 (tel/fax)
e-mail: libselkirk@scotborders.gov.uk
Branch Librarian Ms Christine Johnston MA(Hons) PGDip(Inf)

SHETLAND ISLANDS
Authority: Shetland Islands Council

Shetland Library, Lower Hillhead, Lerwick, Shetland ZE1 0EL
☎(01595) 743868 (enquiries and administration)
Fax (01595) 694430
e-mail: shetlandlibrary@sic.shetland.gov.uk
Online catalogue: http://library.shetland.gov.uk/TalisPrism
Library and Information Services Manager Ms Silvija Crook BA MCLIP (e-mail:
silvija.crook@sic.shetland.gov.uk)
Support Services Librarian Douglas Garden (e-mail:
douglas.garden@sic.shetland.gov.uk)
Customer Services Librarian Ms Karen Fraser (e-mail: karen.fraser@sic.shetland.gov.uk)
Secretary/Administration Assistant Mrs Agnes Anderson (e-mail:
agnes.anderson@sic.shetland.gov.uk)
Administration Assistant Mrs Katrina Nicolson (e-mail:
katrina.nicolson@sic.shetland.gov.uk)
Systems Librarian Miss Aileen Paterson (e-mail: aileen.paterson@sic.shetland.gov.uk)
Young People's Services Librarian Mrs Morag Nicolson (e-mail:
morag.nicolson@sic.shetland.gov.uk)

SOUTH AYRSHIRE
Authority: South Ayrshire Council

Library HQ, 26 Green Street, Ayr KA8 8AD
☎(01292) 288820
Fax (01292) 619019
url: www.south-ayrshire.gov.uk
Libraries Manager Ms Jean Inness MA(Hons) DipLib MCLIP (e-mail:
jean.inness@south-ayrshire.gov.uk)

Central/largest library

Carnegie Library, 12 Main Street, Ayr KA8 8ED
☎(01292) 286385
Fax (01292) 611593
e-mail: carnegie.library@south-ayrshire.gov.uk

SOUTH LANARKSHIRE
Authority: South Lanarkshire Council

Libraries Service, Education Resources, Council Offices, Almada Street, Hamilton, South Lanarkshire ML3 0AA
☎(01698) 454545
Fax (01698) 454465
url: www.southlanarkshire.gov.uk
Libraries Manager Ms Diana Barr BA MCLIP MIMgt (01698 454412; e-mail:
diana.barr@southlanarkshire.gov.uk)
Information Services Co-ordinator John McGarrity BA MCLIP (01698 452220; e-mail:
john.mcgarrity@library.s-lanark.org.uk)
Service Development Co-ordinator Ms Frances Roberts BA MCLIP (01698 452144;
e-mail: frances.roberts@library.s-lanark.org.uk)

Central/largest library

East Kilbride Central Library, 40 The Olympia, East Kilbride, South Lanarkshire G74 1PG
☎(01355) 220046
Fax (01355) 229365
e-mail: libek@library.s-lanark.org.uk
Libraries Co-ordinator Ms Frances Roberts BA MCLIP (e-mail:
frances.roberts@library.s-lanark.org.uk)

STIRLING
Authority: Stirling Council

Library HQ, Springkerse Industrial Estate, Borrowmeadow Road, Stirling FK7 7TN
☎(01786) 432383 (enquiries/administration)
Fax (01786) 432395
e-mail: libraryheadquarters@stirling.gov.uk
url: www.stirling.gov.uk/community/libraries.htm
Head of Libraries, Learning, Communities and Culture Mrs Kathleen Taylor (01786
443388) (Based at Stirling Council, Viewforth, Stirling FK8 2ET)

Library and Archives Services Manager Robert Ruthven MA DipLIS MCLIP (01786 432380)

Central/largest library

Central Library, Corn Exchange Road, Stirling FK8 2HX
☎(01786) 432106 (reference), (01786) 432107 (lending), (01786) 432108 (administration)
Fax (01786) 473094
e-mail: centrallibrary@stirling.gov.uk
Community Librarian Ms Lindsay McKrell BA MSc PhD MCLIP

WEST DUNBARTONSHIRE
Authority: West Dunbartonshire Council

West Dunbartonshire Libraries, 19 Poplar Road, Dumbarton G82 2RJ
☎(01389) 608041 (enquiries and administration)
Fax (01389) 608044
url: www.wdcweb.info
Executive Director, Educational Services Terry Lanagan (based at Council Offices, Garshake Road, Dumbarton G82 3PU)
Manager, Lifelong Learning Ken Graham
Section Head, Libraries Miss Fiona MacDonald MA(Hons) DipLib MCLIP
Senior Officer, Young People's Services Ms Anne Louise Anglim BA(Hons) MCLIP
(e-mail: annelouise.anglim@west-dunbarton.gov.uk)

Area libraries

Clydebank Library, Dumbarton Road, Clydebank, Dumbarton G81 1XH
☎0141 962 2440 (enquiries)
Fax 0141 951 8275
Area Librarians Ms Maureen Lyden, Ms Laura Wilson BA(Hons) MCLIP

Dumbarton Library, Strathleven Place, Dumbarton G82 1BD
☎(01389) 608992 (enquiries), (01389) 608038 (administration)
Fax (01389) 607302
Area Librarian Ms Fiona Matheson MCLIP

WEST LOTHIAN
Authority: West Lothian Council

Library HQ, Connolly House, Hopefield Road, Blackburn, West Lothian EH47 7HZ
☎(01506) 776336 (enquiries), (01506) 776342 (administration)
Fax (01506) 776345
e-mail: library.info@westlothian.gov.uk
url: www.westlothian.gov.uk/libraries
Library Services Manager Mrs Jeanette Castle MA(Hons) DipILS MCLIP (e-mail: jeanette.castle@westlothian.gov.uk)
Support Services Manager Ms Anne Hunt MA(Hons) DipLib MCLIP (01506 776325; e-mail: anne.hunt@westlothian.gov.uk)

Development Managers Mrs Hilda Gibson ACLIP (01506 776350; e-mail:
hilda.gibson@westlothian.gov.uk), Mrs Mary Shelton MCLIP (01506 776350; e-mail:
mary.shelton@westlothian.gov.uk)

Central/largest library

Carmondean Library, Carmondean Centre, Livingston, West Lothian EH54 8PT
☎(01506) 777602 (enquiries)
e-mail: carmondean.lib@westlothian.gov.uk
Library Manager Ms Cathy MacIntyre BA MSc(Econ) MCLIP (e-mail:
cathy.macintyre@westlothian.gov.uk)

Branch libraries

Almondbank Library, The Mall, Craigshill, Livingston, West Lothian EH54 5EJ
☎(01506) 777500
e-mail: almondbank.lib@westlothian.gov.uk
Library Manager Thomas Connelly (e-mail: thomas.connelly@westlothian.gov.uk)

Armadale Library, West Main Street, Armadale, West Lothian EH48 3JB
☎(01501) 678400
e-mail: armadale.lib@westlothian.gov.uk
Library Manager Mrs Betty Hunter MCLIP (e-mail: betty.hunter@westlothian.gov.uk)

Bathgate Library, 66 Hopetoun Street, Bathgate, West Lothian EH48 4PD
☎(01506) 776400
e-mail: bathgate.lib@westlothian.gov.uk
Library Manager Mrs Anne Mackintosh BA MCLIP (e-mail:
anne.mackintosh@westlothian.gov.uk)

Blackburn Connected, Mill Centre, Blackburn, West Lothian EH47 7LQ
☎(01506) 776500
e-mail: blackburn.lib@westlothian.gov.uk
Library/Customer Services Manager Ms Marilyn James (e-mail:
marilyn.james@westlothian.gov.uk)

Blackridge Library, Craig Inn Centre, Blackridge, West Lothian EH48 3SP
☎(01501) 752396
e-mail: blackridge.lib@westlothian.gov.uk
Assistant in Charge Ms Moira McCabe (e-mail: moira.mccabe@westlothian.gov.uk)

Broxburn Library, West Main Street, Broxburn, West Lothian EH52 5RH
☎(01506) 775600
e-mail: broxburn.lib@westlothian.gov.uk
Library Manager Ms Catherine Lauriol MA MSc(Econ) MCLIP (e-mail:
catherine.lauriol@westlothian.gov.uk)

East Calder Library, Main Street, East Calder, West Lothian EH53 0EJ
☎(01506) 883633
e-mail: eastcalder.lib@westlothian.gov.uk
Library Manager Ms Gillian Downie BA MCLIP (e-mail:
gillian.downie@westlothian.gov.uk)

Fauldhouse Library, Lanrigg Road, Fauldhouse, West Lothian EH47 9JA

☎(01501) 770358
e-mail: fauldhouse.lib@westlothian.gov.uk
Library Manager Mrs Ann Beattie BA(Hons)

Lanthorn Library, Lanthorn Centre, Kenilworth Rise, Dedridge, Livingston, West Lothian
EH54 6NY
☎(01506) 777700
e-mail: lanthorn.lib@westlothian.gov.uk
Library Manager Ms Gillian Downie BA MCLIP (e-mail:
gillian.downie@westlothian.gov.uk)

Linlithgow Library, The Vennel, Linlithgow, West Lothian EH49 7EX
☎(01506) 775490
e-mail: linlithgow.lib@westlothian.gov.uk
Library Manager Mrs Kay Ali BA MCLIP (e-mail: kay.ali@westlothian.gov.uk)

Public Reference Library, West Lothian College, Almondvale Cresent, Livingston, West
Lothian EH54 7EP
☎(01506) 427601
Library Manager Ms Linda Hartley (e-mail: linda.hartley@west-lothian.ac.uk)

Pumpherston Library, Pumpherston Primary School, 18 Uphall Station Road, Pumpherston,
West Lothian FH53 0LP
☎(01506) 435837
e-mail: pumpherston.lib@westlothian.gov.uk
Assistant in Charge Ms Moira McHarg MIBiol (e-mail:
moira.mcharg@westlothian.gov.uk)

West Calder Library, Main Street, West Calder, West Lothian EH55 8BJ
☎(01506) 771631
e-mail: westcalder.lib@westlothian.gov.uk
Library Manager Ms Catherine Lauriol MA MSc(Econ) MCLIP (e-mail:
catherine.lauriol@westlothian.gov.uk)

Whitburn Library, Union Road, Whitburn, West Lothian EH47 0AR
☎(01501) 678050
e-mail: whitburn.lib@westlothian.gov.uk
Library Manager Ms Sandra Valaitis (e-mail: sandra.valaitis@westlothian.gov.uk)

WESTERN ISLES *see* COMHAIRLE NAN EILEAN SIAR

ANGLESEY, ISLE OF
Authority: Isle of Anglesey County Council

Department of Education and Leisure, Parc Mownt, Fford Glanhwfa, Llangefni, Ynys Môn LL77 7EY
☎(01248) 752095 (enquiries); (01248) 752900 (administration)
Fax (01248) 752999
url: www.ynysmon.gov.uk
Corporate Director: Education and Leisure Richard Parry Jones MA (e-mail: rpjed@ynysmon.gov.uk)
Head of Service: Lifelong Learning and Information John Rees Thomas BSc(Econ) DipLib MCLIP (e-mail: jrtlh@ynysmon.gov.uk)

Central/largest library

Llangefni Central Library, Lôn-y-Felin, Llangefni, Ynys Môn LL77 7RT
☎(01248) 752095
Fax (01248) 750197
Principal Librarian Ms Rachel Rowlands (e-mail: rfxlh@ynysmon.gov.uk)

Branch libraries

Amlwch Library, Lôn Parys, Amlwch, Ynys Môn LL68 9EA
☎(01407) 830145 (tel/fax)
e-mail: kbxlh@ynysmon.gov.uk
Library Manager Ms Rachel Rowlands (e-mail: rfxlh@ynysmon.gov.uk)

Archives, Shirehall, Glanhwfa Street, Llangefni, Ynys Môn LL77 7TW
☎(01248) 752080
Fax (01248) 751289
e-mail: archives@ynysmon.gov.uk
Archivist Ms Anne Venables BA DipAA (01248 752083; e-mail: avxed@ynysmon.gov.uk)

Holyhead Library, Newry Fields, Holyhead, Ynys Môn LL65 1LA
☎(01407) 762917
Fax (01407) 769616
e-mail: kpxlh@ynysmon.gov.uk
Library Manager Mrs Betsan Parri-Williams

Menai Bridge Library, Ffordd y Ffair, Menai Bridge, Ynys Môn LL59 5AS
☎(01248) 712706 (tel/fax)
e-mail: dbxlh@ynysmon.gov.uk
Library Manager Mrs Eluned Stephen

BLAENAU GWENT
Authority: Blaenau Gwent County Borough Council

Library Headquarters, Leisure Services, Anvil Court, Church Street, Abertillery, Blaenau Gwent NP13 1DB

url: www.blaenau-gwent.gov.uk
Principal Librarian Mrs Sue White MCLIP (01495 355950; e-mail: sue.white@blaenau-gwent.gov.uk)

Central/largest library

Ebbw Vale Library, 21 Bethcar Street, Ebbw Vale, Blaenau Gwent NP23 6HH
☎(01495) 303069
Fax (01495) 350547
e-mail: ebbw.vale.library@blaenau-gwent.gov.uk

Area libraries

Abertillery Library, Station Hill, Abertillery, Blaenau Gwent NP13 1TE
☎(01495) 355646
e-mail: abertillery.library@blaenau-gwent.gov.uk

Blaina Library, Reading Institute, High Street, Blaina, Blaenau Gwent NP13 3BN
☎(01495) 355609 (tel/fax)
Fax (01495) 290312
e-mail: blaina.library@blaenau-gwent.gov.uk

Brynmawr Library, Market Square, Brynmawr, Blaenau Gwent NP23 4AJ
☎(01495) 357743
Fax (01495) 357796
e-mail: brynmawr.library@blaenau-gwent.gov.uk

Cwm Library, Canning Street, Cwm, Blaenau Gwent NP23 7RW
☎(01495) 370454 (tel/fax)
e-mail: cwm.library@blaenau-gwent.gov.uk

Tredegar Library, The Circle, Tredegar, Blaenau Gwent NP22 3PS
☎(01495) 357869
Fax (01495) 355682
e-mail: tredegar.library@blaenau-gwent.gov.uk

BRIDGEND
Authority: Bridgend County Borough Council

Library and Information Service, Coed Parc, Park Street, Bridgend CF31 4BA
☎(01656) 754800
Fax (01656) 645719
e-mail: blis@bridgend.gov.uk
url: www.bridgend.gov.uk/libraries
Group Manager (Libraries, Adult Community Learning, Arts and Community Development) John C Woods BSc MCLIP (e-mail: john.woods@bridgend.gov.uk)
Principal Officer: Libraries Mrs Margaret Griffiths BLib MCLIP (e-mail: Margaret.Griffiths@bridgend.gov.uk)
Service Manager Richard Bellinger MSc MCLIP (e-mail: richard.bellinger@bridgend.gov.uk)
Resources Development Manager Mrs Claire Williams MSc(Econ) MCLIP (e-mail: claire.williams@bridgend.gov.uk)
Community Development Librarian Ms Helen Pridham BA DipIS MCLIP (e-mail:

helen.pridham@bridgend.gov.uk)
Children's Development Librarian Mrs Diana Apperley MA (e-mail:
diana.apperley@bridgend.gov.uk)

Central/largest libraries

Bridgend Lending Library, Wyndham Street, Bridgend CF31 1EF
☎(01656) 754830
Fax (01656) 754829
e-mail: bridgendlib@bridgend.gov.uk
Senior Site Manager Christopher Williams (e-mail:
christopher.williams@bridgend.gov.uk)

Maesteg Library, North's Lane, Maesteg, Glamorgan CF34 9AA
☎(01656) 754835
Fax (01656) 754834
e-mail: maestlib@bridgend.gov.uk
Branch Librarian John Robinson MA MCLIP (e-mail: john.robinson@bridgend.gov.uk)

Pencoed Library, Penybont Road, Pencoed, Glamorgan CF35 5RA
☎(01656) 754840
Fax (01656) 754842
e-mail: penclib@bridgend.gov.uk
Branch Librarian Mrs Pamela Grainger BA (e-mail: pamela.grainger@bridgend.gov.uk)

Porthcawl Library, Church Place, Porthcawl, Glamorgan CF36 3AG
☎(01656) 754845
Fax (01656) 754847
e-mail: porthcawllib@bridgend.gov.uk
Branch Librarian Mrs Elaine Winstanley BSc (e-mail: elaine.winstanley@bridgend.gov.uk)

Pyle Library, Pyle Life Centre, Helig Fan, Pyle, Glamorgan CF33 6BS
☎(01656) 754850
Fax (01656) 754852
e-mail: pylelib@bridgend.gov.uk
Life Centre Manager Mrs Janet Arbery (e-mail: janet.arbery@bridgend.gov.uk)

Reference and Information Centre, Coed Parc, Park Street, Bridgend CF31 4BA
☎(01656) 754810
Fax (01656) 645719
e-mail: blis@bridgend.gov.uk
url: www.bridgend.gov.uk/libraries
Reference Librarian Mrs Lesley A Milne BA MCLIP (e-mail:
lesley.milne@bridgend.gov.uk)

CAERPHILLY
Authority: Caerphilly County Borough Council

Lifelong Learning and Leisure, Penallta House, Tredomen Park, Ystrad Mynach, Hengoed, Caerphilly CF82 7PG
☎(01443) 864033
Fax (01443) 866655
e-mail: libraries@caerphilly.gov.uk

url: www.caerphilly.gov.uk/libraries
Principal Community Education Officer Steve Mason MEd
Assistant Director Peter Gomer

Area libraries

Blackwood Library, 192 High Street, Blackwood, Caerphilly NP12 1AJ
☎(01495) 233000
Fax (01495) 233002
Area Manager: North Mrs Dianne Madhavan MCLIP

Caerphilly Library, Morgan Jones Park, Caerphilly CF8 1AP
☎029 2085 2543
Fax 029 2086 5585
Area Manager: South Mrs Yvonne Harris MCLIP

Lifelong Learning and Leisure, Penallta House, Tredomen Park, Ystrad Mynach, Hengoed,
Caerphilly CF82 7PG
☎(01443) 864062
Fax (01443) 866655
Youth Services Manager Vacant

Risca Library, Park Place, Risca, Caerphilly NP11 6AS
☎(01633) 600920
Fax (01633) 600922
Area Manager: Central Mrs Marion Davies MCLIP

CARDIFF
Authority: Cardiff Council

Cardiff Libraries, 4th Floor, County Hall, Atlantic Wharf, Cardiff CF10 4UW
☎029 2038 2116 (Central Library)
e-mail: centrallibrary@cardiff.gov.uk
url: www.cardiff.gov.uk/libraries
Operational Manager (Libraries) Ms Elspeth Morris BA MCLIP (e-mail:
emorris@cardiff.gov.uk)
Central Library Manager Ms Nicola Richards BA(Hons) DipLib MCLIP (e-mail:
nrichards@cardiff.gov.uk)
Libraries and Information Development Manager Ms Laura Wood (e-mail:
lwood@cardiff.gov.uk)
Branch Libraries Manager Ms Fiona Bailey (e-mail: fiona.bailey@pembrokeshire.gov.uk)
Stock Manager Ms Linda Williams MCLIP (e-mail: lwilliams@cardiff.gov.uk)

CARMARTHENSHIRE
Authority: Carmarthenshire County Council

**Library HQ, Building 2, St David's Parc, Job's Well Road, Carmarthen, Carmarthenshire
SA31 3HB**
☎(01267) 246495
Fax (01267) 246529
url: www.libraries.carmarthenshire.gov.uk

Head of Libraries and Heritage Dewi P Thomas BA DipLib MCLIP (e-mail: dpthomas@sirgar.gov.uk)

Area libraries

Ammanford Area Library, 3 Wind Street, Ammanford, Carmarthenshire SA18 3DN
☎(01269) 598150
Fax (01269) 598151
Area Librarian Myrddin Morgan BSc(Econ) DipLib MCLIP (e-mail: mymorgan@sirgar.gov.uk)

Carmarthen Area Library, St Peter's Street, Carmarthen SA31 1LN
☎(01267) 224824
Fax (01267) 221839
Area Librarian William T Phillips BA DipLib MCLIP (e-mail: wtphillips@sirgar.gov.uk)

Llanelli Area Library, Vaughan Street, Llanelli, Carmarthenshire SA15 3AS
☎(01554) 773538
Fax (01554) 750125
Area Librarian Mark Jewell BSc(Econ) (e-mail: mjewell@sirgar.gov.uk)

CEREDIGION
Authority: Ceredigion County Council

Public Library, Corporation Street, Aberystwyth, Ceredigion SY23 2BU
☎(01970) 633703; 633716
Fax (01970) 625059
url: www.ceredigion.gov.uk
Assistant Director (Cultural Services) Dr Rhodri L Morgan
County Libraries Officer W H Howells BA MLib MCLIP (e-mail: williamh@ceredigion.gov.uk)

Branch library

Branch Library, Canolfan Teifi, Pendre, Ceredigion SA43 1JL
☎(01239) 612578
Fax (01239) 612285
e-mail: teifillb@ceredigion.gov.uk
Branch Librarian D G Evans MCLIP

CONWY
Authority: Conwy County Borough Council

Community Development Service, The Old Board School, Lloyd Street, Llandudno, Conwy LL30 2YG
☎(01492) 576139
e-mail: library@conwy.gov.uk
url: www.conwy.gov.uk/library
Head of Community Service Ms Marianne Jackson
Section Head, Culture and Information Ms Rhian G Williams BA DipLib MCLIP (01492 576139; e-mail: rhian.williams@conwy.gov.uk)

Regional/community libraries

Abergele Library, Market Street, Abergele, Conwy LL22 7BP
☎(01492) 577505
Fax (01745) 823376
e-mail: llyfr.lib.abergele@conwy.gov.uk

Colwyn Bay Library, Woodland Road West, Colwyn Bay, Conwy LL29 7DH
☎(01492) 577512
Fax (01492) 534474
e-mail: llyfr.lib.baecolwynbay@conwy.gov.uk

Conwy Library, Civic Hall, Castle Street, Conwy LL32 6AY
☎(01492) 596242
Fax (01492) 582359
e-mail: llyfr.lib.conwy@conwy.gov.uk

Llandudno Library, Mostyn Street, Llandudno, Conwy LL30 2RP
☎(01492) 574010/574020
Fax (01492) 876826
e-mail: llyfr.lib.llandudno@conwy.gov.uk

Llanrwst Library, Plas yn Dre, Station Road, Llanrwst, Conwy LL26 0DF
☎(01492) 577545
e-mail: llyfr.lib.llanrwst@conwy.gov.uk

DENBIGHSHIRE
Authority: Denbighshire County Council

Library Service, Directorate of Lifelong Learning, Yr Hen Garchar, Clwyd Street, Ruthin, Denbighshire LL15 1HP
☎(01824) 708204 (enquiries)
Fax (01824) 708202
url: www.denbighshire.gov.uk/libraries
Head of Libraries and Archives Robat Arwyn Jones BMus MCLIP DipLib (01824 708203; e-mail: arwyn.jones@denbighshire.gov.uk)

Central/largest library

Rhyl Library, Museum and Arts Centre, Church Street, Rhyl, Denbighshire LL18 3AA
☎(01745) 353814
Fax (01745) 331438
e-mail: rhyl.library@denbighshire.gov.uk
Principal Community Librarian Alastair Barber BSc DipLib MCLIP

FLINTSHIRE
Authority: Flintshire County Council

Library and Information Service, Library Headquarters, County Hall, Mold, Flintshire CH7 6NW
☎(01352) 704400
Fax (01352) 753662
e-mail: libraries@flintshire.gov.uk

url: www.flintshire.gov.uk
Head of Libraries, Culture and Heritage Lawrence Rawsthorne MLib FCLIP MIMgt
Principal Librarian, Community Libraries and Arts Mrs Sheila Kirby MCLIP (01352 704402)
Lifelong Learning Librarian Gareth Edwards MCLIP (01352 704405)

Group libraries

Broughton Library, Broughton Hall Road, Broughton, Nr Chester, Flintshire CH4 0QQ
☎(01244) 533727
Community Librarian Miss Kathleen Morris BA DipLib MCLIP

Buckley Library, Museum and Gallery, The Precinct, Buckley, Flintshire CH7 2EF
☎(01244) 549210
Fax (01244) 548850
Community Librarian Mrs Penelope Corbett MLib MCLIP

Connah's Quay Library and Learning Centre, Wepre Drive, Connah's Quay, Deeside, Flintshire CH5 4HA
☎(01244) 830485
Fax (01244) 856672
Community Librarian Mrs Carol A Guy BA MCLIP

Flint Library Learners Centre, Church Street, Flint, Flintshire CH6 5AP
☎(01352) 703737
Fax (01352) 731010
Community Librarian Ms Kate Leonard BLib MCLIP, Mrs Gillian Fraser MCLIP

Holywell Library Learners Centre, North Road, Holywell, Flintshire CH8 7TQ
☎(01352) 713157
Fax (01352) 710744
Community Librarian Mrs Catherine E Barber MCLIP, Mrs Morwenna Wallbank MCLIP

Mold Library and Museum, Earl Road, Mold, Flintshire CH7 1AP
☎(01352) 754791
Fax (01352) 754655
Community Librarian Miss Nia W Jones BLib MCLIP

GWYNEDD
Authority: Gwynedd Council

Council Offices, Caernarfon, Gwynedd LL55 1SH
☎(01286) 679504
Fax (01286) 677347
e-mail: llyfrgell@gwynedd.gov.uk
url: www.gwynedd.gov.uk/library
Principal Librarian Hywel James BA DipLib MCLIP

Central/largest library

Caernarfon Library, Pavilion Hill, Caernarfon, Gwynedd LL55 1AS
☎(01286) 679463
Fax (01286) 671137

e-mail: llyfrgellcaernarfon@gwynedd.gov.uk
Community Services Librarian Mrs Eirlys Thomas MCLIP
User Services Manager Ms Nia Gruffydd MLib MCLIP (e-mail:
NiaGruffydd@gwynedd.gov.uk)
Information Services Manager Alun Hughes Williams BA DipLib MCLIP (e-mail:
AlunHughesWilliams@gwynedd.gov.uk)

Largest libraries

Bangor Library, Ffordd Gwynedd, Bangor, Gwynedd LL57 1DT
☎(01248) 353479
Fax (01248) 370149
e-mail: llyfrgellbangor@gwynedd.gov.uk
Library Services Promoter Ms Rhiannon Clifford Jones MCLIP

Dolgellau Library, Ffordd y Bala, Dolgellau, Gwynedd LL40 2YF
☎(01341) 422771
Fax (01341) 423560
e-mail: lldolgellau@gwynedd.gov.uk
Information Librarian Vacant

Porthmadog Library, Stryd Wesla, Porthmadog, Gwynedd LL49 9BT
☎(01766) 514091
Fax (01766) 513821
e-mail: llporthmadog@gwynedd.gov.uk
South Gwynedd Community Librarian Ms Anna Yardley Jones BA DipLib MCLIP

MERTHYR TYDFIL
Authority: Merthyr Tydfil County Borough Council

Central Library, High Street, Merthyr Tydfil CF47 8AF
☎(01685) 723057
Fax (01685) 370690
e-mail: library.services@merthyr.gov.uk
url: www.merthyr.gov.uk
Head of Libraries Geraint James BA MCLIP

Area libraries

Dowlais Library, Church Street, Merthyr Tydfil CF48 3HS
☎(01685) 723051
Fax (01685) 723051
(Enquiries to Central Library)

Treharris Library, Perrott Street, Treharris, Merthyr Tydfil CF46 5ET
☎(01443) 410517
Fax (01443) 410675
(Enquiries to Central Library)

MONMOUTHSHIRE

Authority: Monmouthshire County Council

Libraries and Information Service, Chepstow Library, Manor Way, Chepstow, Monmouthshire NP16 5HZ
☎(01291) 635731 (enquiries), 01291 635649 (administration)
Fax (01291) 635736
url: http://libraries.monmouthshire.gov.uk
Principal Librarian Ms Ann Jones MLib MCLIP (e-mail:
annjones@monmouthshire.gov.uk)

Area libraries

Bryn-a-Cwm Area

Abergavenny Library, Baker Street, Abergavenny, Monmouthshire NP7 5BD
☎(01873) 735980
Fax (01873) 735985
e-mail: abergavennylibrary@monmouthshire.gov.uk
Library Manager Ms Vivienne Thomas BA BD MCLIP (e-mail:
viviennethomas@monmouthshire.gov.uk)

Central Monmouthshire Area

Monmouth Library, Rolls Hall, Whitecross Street, Monmouth NP25 3BY
☎(01600) 775215
Fax (01600) 775218
e-mail: monmouthlibrary@monmouthshire.gov.uk
Library Managers Ms Julia Greenway MCLIP (e-mail:
juliagreenway@monmouthshire.gov.uk), Ms Sue Wallbank (e-mail:
suewallbank@monmouthshire.gov.uk) (job share)

Lower Wye Area

Chepstow Library, Manor Way, Chepstow, Monmouthshire NP16 5HZ
☎(01291) 635730
Fax (01291) 635736
e-mail: chepstowlibrary@monmouthshire.gov.uk
Library Managers Ms Sue Wallbank (e-mail: suewallbank@monmouthshire.gov.uk),
Ms Sally Bradford (e-mail: sallybradford@monmouthshire.gov.uk) (job share)

Severnside Area

Caldicot Library, Woodstock Way, Caldicot, Monmouthshire NP26 4DB
☎(01291) 426425
Fax (01291) 426426
e-mail: caldicotlibrary@monmouthshire.gov.uk
Library Manager Ms Fiona Ashley BLib MCLIP (e-mail:
fionaashley@monmouthshire.gov.uk)

NEATH PORT TALBOT

Authority: Neath Port Talbot County Borough Council

Library and Information Services, Reginald Street, Velindre, Port Talbot SA13 1YY
☎(01639) 899829
Fax (01639) 899152
e-mail: npt.libhq@npt.gov.uk
url: www.npt.gov.uk
County Librarian Wayne John MCLIP (e-mail: w.john@npt.gov.uk)

Central/largest libraries

Neath Library, Victoria Gardens, Neath, Neath Port Talbot SA11 3BA
☎(01639) 644604/635017
Fax (01639) 641912
e-mail: neath.library@npt.gov.uk

Port Talbot Library, Aberavon Shopping Centre (1st Floor), Port Talbot SA13 1PB
☎(01639) 763490/1
Fax (01639) 763489
e-mail: porttalbot.library@npt.gov.uk

NEWPORT

Authority: Newport City Council

Community Learning and Libraries Service, Central Library, John Frost Square, Newport, Gwent NP20 1PA
☎(01633) 656656 (enquiries and administration)
Fax (01633) 222615
e-mail: central.library@newport.gov.uk
url: www.newport.gov.uk/libraries
Community Learning and Libraries Manager Mrs Gill John MBA MCLIP
Development and Resources Manager Ms Angela Turner
Children and Young People's Services Manager Ms Tracey Paddon BSc(Hons) DipAppSc MCLIP
Operations Manager Alun Prescott BA(Hons) DipILS

PEMBROKESHIRE

Authority: Pembrokeshire County Council

County Library, Dew Street, Haverfordwest, Pembrokeshire SA61 1SU
☎(01437) 775241 (administration, enquiries); (01437) 775244 (Lending Library); (01437) 775248 (Reference Library)
Fax (01437) 767092
url: www.pembrokeshire.gov.uk
Head of Information and Cultural Services Neil Bennett BSc DMS MCLIP (01437 775240; e-mail: neil.bennett@pembrokeshire.gov.uk)
Principal Librarian (Development) Mrs Anita Thomas MCLIP (01437 776059; e-mail: anita.thomas@pembrokeshire.gov.uk)
Principal Librarian (Service, Delivery & Training) Clive Richards MCLIP (01437 776083; e-mail: clive.richards@pembrokeshire.gov.uk)

Information/ICT Development Librarian Ms Sue Armour MCLIP (01437 776098; e-mail: sue.armour@pembrokeshire.gov.uk)
Stock & User Engagement Librarian Ms Gill Gilliland (01437 774692; e-mail: gill.gilliland@pembrokeshire.gov.uk)
Children's & Young People's Librarian Miss Pamela Harry (01437 776089; e-mail: pamela.harry@pembrokeshire.gov.uk)
Outreach, Social Inclusion & Marketing Librarian Mrs Eleri Evans MCLIP (01437 776088; e-mail: eleri.evans@pembrokeshire.gov.uk)
Local & Family History Librarian George Edwards MCLIP (01437 776126; e-mail: george.edwards@pembrokeshire.gov.uk)

Community libraries

County Library, Dew Street, Haverfordwest, Pembrokeshire SA61 1SU
☎(01437) 775244
Librarian in Charge Vacant

Fishguard Library, Fishguard Town Hall, Market Square, Fishguard, Pembrokeshire SA65 9HA
☎(01437) 776638
Fax (01348) 874990
Cultural Managers Ms Wendy Davies MCLIP (e-mail: wendy.davies@pembrokeshire.gov.uk), Ms Fiona Bailey (e-mail: fiona.bailey@pembrokeshire.gov.uk)

Milford Haven Library, Suite 19, Cedar Court, Milford Haven, Pembrokeshire SA73 3LS
☎(01437) 771888
Senior Library Assistant Vacant

Pembroke Dock Library, Water Street, Pembroke Dock, Pembrokeshire SA72 6DW
☎(01437) 775825
Senior Library Assistant Stuart Croxford

Tenby Library, Greenhill Avenue, Tenby, Pembrokeshire SA70 7LB
☎(01834) 843934 (tel/fax)
Senior Library Assistant Mrs Julie Sutcliffe

POWYS
Authority: Powys County Council

County Library HQ, Cefnllys Lane, Llandrindod Wells, Powys LD1 5LD
☎(01597) 826860 (general enquiries)
Fax (01597) 826872
url: www.powys.gov.uk/libraries
County Librarian Miss Tudfil L Adams BA MCLIP

Library HQ, Cefnllys Lane, Llandrindod Wells, Powys LD1 5LD
☎(01597) 826864
Fax (01597) 826872
Principal Librarian (Field Services) Mrs Helen Edwards BLib MCLIP

Children and Schools Library HQ, Cefnllys Lane, Llandrindod Wells, Powys LD1 5LD
☎(01597) 826867

Fax (01597) 826872
Principal Librarian (Education, Schools and Children) Vacant

Main libraries

Brecon Library, Ship Street, Brecon, Powys LD3 9AE
☎(01874) 623346
Fax (01874) 622818
Group Librarian Ms Vicki Workman

Llandrindod Wells Library, Cefnllys Lane, Llandrindod Wells, Powys LD1 5LD
☎(01597) 826870
Fax (01597) 826872
Acting Group Librarian Mrs Janet Holmes

Newtown Library, Park Lane, Newtown, Powys SY16 1EJ
☎(01686) 626934
Fax (01686) 624935
Group Librarian Mrs Mair Dafydd BA MCLIP

RHONDDA CYNON TAF
Authority: Rhondda Cynon Taf County Borough Council

Education and Lifelong Learning, Ty Trevithick, Abercynon, Mountain Ash, Rhondda Cynon Taf CF45 4UQ
☎(01443) 744000
Fax (01443) 744023
url: www.rhondda-cynon-taf.gov.uk
Head of Libraries, Museums, Heritage and Welsh Language Services Ms Gill Evans
BA DipLib MCLIP (01443 744029; e-mail: Gillian.M.Evans@rhondda-cynon-taff.gov.uk)
Area Manager North Mrs Ros Williams MSc MCLIP (01443 778952; e-mail:
Ros.Williams@rhondda-cynon-taff.gov.uk) (based at Treorchy Library)
Area Manager South Mrs Lindsay Morris BA MCLIP (01443 492138; e-mail:
Lindsay.M.Morris@rhondda-cynon-taff.gov.uk) (based at Pontypridd Library)
Children and Youth Services Librarian Ms Ceri Roberts MCLIP DipEd (01443 478463;
e-mail: Ceri.W.Roberts@rhondda-cynon-taff.gov.uk) (based at Mountain Ash Library)
Information Services Librarian Nick E. Kelland BSc(Econ) (01685 880054; e-mail:
Nick.E.Kelland@rhondda-cynon-taff.gov.uk) (based at Aberdare Library)
Senior Librarian, Mobiles and Special Services Ms Catherine Langdon BA DipLib
MCLIP (01685 880061; e-mail: Catherine.A.Langdon@rhondda-cynon-taff.gov.uk) (based
at Aberdare Library)

Largest library

Aberdare Library, Green Street, Aberdare, Rhondda Cynon Taf CF44 7AG
☎(01685) 880050
Fax (01685) 881181
e-mail: Aberdare.Library@rhondda-cynon-taff.gov.uk
Branch Librarian Steven J. Graham (e-mail: Steven.J.Graham@rhondda-cynon-taff.gov.uk)

Regional libraries

Pontypridd Library, Library Road, Pontypridd, Rhondda Cynon Taf CF37 2DY

☎(01443) 486850
Fax (01443) 493258
e-mail: Pontypridd.Library@rhondda-cynon-taff.gov.uk
Branch Librarian Mrs Edwina Smart BA MCLIP

Treorchy Library, Station Road, Treorchy, Rhondda Cynon Taf CF42 6NN
☎(01443) 773204
Fax (01443) 777047
e-mail: Treorchy.Library@rhondda-cynon-taff.gov.uk
Branch Librarian Richard Reed

SWANSEA
Authority: City and County of Swansea

Library HQ, The Civic Centre, Oystermouth Road, Swansea SA1 3SN
☎(01792) 636430
Fax (01792) 636235
e-mail: swansea.libraries@swansea.gov.uk
url: www.swansea.gov.uk/libraries
Strategic Manager: Libraries and Culture Vacant
Library Services Manager Steve Hardman BSc(Econ) (01792 636610; e-mail:
steve.hardman@swansea.gov.uk)
Assistant Head of Libraries Ms Karen Bewen-Chappell MCLIP (01792 636809; e-mail:
karen.bewen-chappell@swansea.gov.uk), Ms Caroline Tomlin BA DipLib MCLIP (01792
636809; e-mail: caroline.tomlin@swansea.gov.uk) (job share)
Principal Librarian: Resources and Reader Services Mrs Julie Clement BLib MCLIP
(01792 636628; e-mail: julie.clement@swansea.gov.uk)
Principal Librarian: Customer Services and Operations Mrs Jayne Trumper BA DipLib
MCLIP (01792 636938; e-mail: jayne.trumper@swansea.gov.uk)
Principal Librarian: Information and Learning Ms Karen Gibbons (01792 636329;
e-mail: karen.gibbons@swansea.gov.uk)
Principal Librarian: Central Library and Development Ms Rebecca Williams BA(Hons)
PGDip (01792 637132; e-mail: rebecca.williams@swansea.gov.uk)

Central/largest library

Swansea Library, The Civic Centre, Oystermouth Road, Swansea SA1 3SN
☎(01792) 636464
Fax (01792) 205327
e-mail: central.library@swansea.gov.uk
Library Manager Ms Kerry Pillai

Branch libraries

Gorseinon Library, 15 West Street, Gorseinon, Swansea SA4 4AA
☎(01792) 516780
Fax (01792) 516772
e-mail: gorseinon.library@swansea.gov.uk
Library Manager Mrs Carole Bonham

Morriston Library, Treharne Road, Morriston, Swansea SA6 7AA
☎(01792) 516770

Fax (01792) 516771
e-mail: morriston.library@swansea.gov.uk
Library Manager Peter Matthews

Oystermouth Library, Dunns Lane, Mumbles, Swansea SA3 4AA
☎(01792) 368380
Fax (01792) 369143
e-mail: oystermouth.library@swansea.gov.uk
Library Manager Ms Chris Skudra

TORFAEN
Authority: Torfaen County Borough Council

Torfaen Libraries HQ, Civic Centre, Pontypool, Torfaen, Gwent NP4 6YB
☎(01633) 628941
Fax (01633) 628935
url: www.torfaen.gov.uk
Strategic Library and Information Manager Mrs Christine George BA DipLib MCLIP

Central/largest library

Cwmbran Library, Gwent House, Cwmbran, Torfaen, Gwent NP44 1XQ
☎(01633) 647676
Fax (01633) 647684
e-mail: cwmbranlibrary@torfaen.gov.uk
Library Manager Mrs Pat Oakley
Information Librarian Robert Price

Group library

Pontypool Library, Hanbury Road, Pontypool, Torfaen, Gwent NP4 6JL
☎(01495) 762820
Fax (01495) 752530
e-mail: pontypoollibrary@torfaen.gov.uk
Senior Librarian Mark Tanner BA DipLib MCLIP

VALE OF GLAMORGAN
Authority: Vale of Glamorgan Council

Directorate of Learning and Development, Ground Floor, Provincial House, Kendrick Road, Barry, Vale of Glamorgan CF62 8UF
☎(01446) 709381
url: www.valeofglamorgan.gov.uk/libraries
Chief Librarian Ms Sian E Jones BSc(Econ) MSc(Econ) MCLIP (e-mail: sjones@valeofglamorgan.gov.uk)
Principal Librarian Christopher Edwards BA DipLib MCLIP (e-mail: cdedwards@valeofglamorgan.gov.uk)

Central/largest library

County Library, King Square, Barry, Vale of Glamorgan CF63 4RW
☎(01446) 709737

Senior Librarian Vacant
Information Librarian Ms Katherine Owen MCLIP (e-mail:
kowen@valeofglamorgan.gov.uk)
Children's Librarian Ms Gillian Southby BA(Hons) PGDipILM (e-mail:
gsouthby@valeofglamorgan.gov.uk)

Main libraries

Cowbridge Library, Old Hall, Cowbridge, Vale of Glamorgan CF71 7AH
☎(01446) 773941
Community Librarian Ms Melanie Weeks (e-mail: mpweeks@valeofglamorgan.gov.uk)

Dinas Powys Library, The Murch, Dinas Powys, Vale of Glamorgan CF64 4QU
☎029 2051 2556
Community Librarian Ms Susan Sawyer (e-mail: ssawyer@valeofglamorgan.gov.uk)

Llantwit Major Library, Boverton Road, Llantwit Major, Vale of Glamorgan CF61 9XZ
☎(01446) 792700
Community Librarian Ms Ronni Allen MCLIP (e-mail: rallen@valeofglamorgan.gov.uk)

Penarth Library, Stanwell Road, Penarth, Vale of Glamorgan CF64 2YT
☎029 2070 8438
Senior Librarian Marcus Payne BA DipLib MCLIP (e-mail:
mmpayne@valeofglamorgan.gov.uk)

WREXHAM
Authority: Wrexham County Borough Council

Library, Leisure and Culture Department, Lambpit Street, Wrexham LL11 1AR
☎(01978) 297430
Fax (01978) 297422
url: www.wrexham.gov.uk
Chief Leisure, Libraries and Culture Officer Alan Watkin BA DipLib FCLIP MIM FRSA
Libraries Officer Dylan Hughes BA DipLib MCLIP (01978 297442)

Central/largest library

Wrexham Library, Rhosddu Road, Wrexham LL11 1AU
☎(01978) 292090
Fax (01978) 292611
e-mail: reference.library@wrexham.gov.uk
Community Librarian Hedd ap Emlyn BA DipLib MCLIP

Group/branch libraries

Brynteg Library, Quarry Road, Brynteg, Wrexham LL11 6AB
☎(01978) 759523
Community Librarian Mrs Marina Thomas MCLIP

Rhosllanerchrugog Library, Princes Road, Rhos, Wrexham LL14 1AB
☎(01978) 840328
Community Librarian Miss Ann Hughes MA MCLIP

CROWN DEPENDENCIES

ALDERNEY
Authority: Alderney

Alderney Library, Church Street, Alderney, Channel Islands GY9 3TE
☎(01481) 824178
e-mail: info@alderneylibrary.org
url: www.alderneylibrary.org
Chairman, Alderney Committee Mrs Joyce Whitehead
Children's Room Ms Joan Banks
(Alderney Library is a voluntary organization)

GUERNSEY
Authority: Guernsey

Guille-Allès Library, Market Street, St Peter Port, Guernsey, Channel Islands GYI IHB
☎(01481) 720392
Fax (01481) 712425
e-mail: ga@library.gg
url: www.library.gg
Chief Librarian Miss Maggie Falla BA MA MLib MCLIP (e-mail: maggiefalla@library.gg)
Head of Services to Education and Young People Mrs Jane Falla BA DipLib MCLIP
(e-mail: jfalla@library.gg)

Priaulx Library, Candle Road, St Peter Port, Guernsey, Channel Islands GYI IUG
☎(01481) 721998
Fax (01481) 713 804
e-mail: priaulx.library@gov.gg
url: www.priaulxlibrary.co.uk
Chief Librarian Ms Amanda Bennett BA(Hons) MA MCLIP
Deputy Chief Librarian Ms Sue Laker DipLib CMS MCLIP
(The Priaulx Library is a reference and lending library specializing in local history and family
history research in the Channel Islands)

ISLE OF MAN
Authority: Isle of Man

**Henry Bloom Noble Library, Douglas Borough Council, 10/12 Victoria Street, Douglas,
Isle of Man IMI 2LH**
☎(01624) 696461
Fax (01624) 696400
e-mail: enquiries@douglas.gov.im
url: www.douglas.gov.im
Borough Librarian Mrs Jan Macartney BA(Hons) MCLIP (e-mail:
jmacartney@douglas.gov.im)

Castletown Library, Castletown Commissioners, Farrants Way, Castletown, Isle of Man IM9 INR
☎(01624) 829355
Fax (01624) 829355
e-mail: library@castletown.org.im
Librarian Ms Pauline Cringle

Family Library and Mobile Library, Isle of Man Department of Education, Nobles Hall, Westmoreland Road, Douglas, Isle of Man IMI IRL
☎(01624) 673123
Fax (01624) 671043
Librarian (Junior Service) Ms Mary Cousins BA(Hons) (e-mail: m.cousins@doe.sch.im)
Mobile Librarian Mrs Sandra Henderson MCLIP (e-mail: s.henderson@doe.sch.im)

George Herdman Library, Port Erin Commissioners, Bridson Street, Port Erin, Isle of Man IM9 6AL
☎(01624) 832365
Librarian Miss Angela Dryland BSc (e-mail: drylandangela@yahoo.co.uk)

Onchan Library, Onchan District Commissioners, Willow House, 61-69 Main Road, Onchan, Isle of Man IM3 IAJ
☎(01624) 621228 (tel/fax)
e-mail: onchan.library@onchan.org.im
url: www.library.onchan.org.im
Librarian Mrs Pam Hand

Ramsey Town Library, Ramsey Town Commissioners, Town Hall, Parliament Square, Ramsey, Isle of Man IM8 IRT
☎(01624) 810146
e-mail: ramsey.library@rtc.gov.im
Librarian Paul Boulton BA

Ward Library, Peel Town Commissoners, 38 Castle Street, Peel, Isle of Man IM5 IAL
☎(01624) 843533
e-mail: ward_library@hotmail.com
Librarian Mrs Carol Horton

JERSEY
Authority: Jersey

Jersey Library, Halkett Place, St Helier, Jersey, Channel Islands JE2 4WH
☎(01534) 448700 (enquiries), (01534) 448701 (reference), (01534) 448714 (administration)
Fax (01534) 448730
e-mail: je.library@gov.je
url: www.gov.je/library
Chief Librarian Mrs Pat Davis MCLIP

Public Libraries in the
Republic of Ireland

CARLOW

Authority: Carlow County Council
Carlow Central Library, Tullow Street, Carlow, Republic of Ireland
☎(00 353 59) 917 0094
Fax (00 353 59) 914 0548
e-mail: library@carlowcoco.ie
url: www.carlow.ie
Acting County Librarian Ms Deirdre Condron BComm DipLib
Executive Librarian Ms Carmel Flahavan BA(Open) DipLib
Executive Librarian John Shortall BA MSc(Econ)

CAVAN

Authority: Cavan County Council
Johnston Central Library, Farnham Street, Cavan, Republic of Ireland
☎(00 353 49) 437 8500/8501
Fax (00 353 49) 432 6987
e-mail: library@cavancoco.ie
url: www.cavancoco.ie
County Librarian Ms Josephine Brady BA DLIS
Executive Librarian Tom Sullivan DLIS MSSc
Assistant Librarians Mrs Teresa Treacy BA DLIS, Ms Emma Clancy BA DLIS
ICT Officer Brian Connolly

CLARE

Authority: Clare County Council
Clare County Library HQ, Mill Road, Ennis, Co Clare, Republic of Ireland
☎(00 353 65) 684 6350/682 1616
Fax (00 353 65) 684 2462
e-mail: mailbox@clarelibrary.ie
url: www.clarelibrary.ie
County Librarian Ms Helen Walsh BSc DLIS LAI

Central/largest library

De Valera Branch Library, Ennis, Co Clare, Republic of Ireland
☎(00 353 65) 684 6353

Area libraries

Corofin Library, Corofin, Co Clare, Republic of Ireland
☎(00 353 65) 683 7219

Kildysart Library, St John Bosco's Community College, Kildysart, Co Clare, Republic of Ireland
☎(00 353 65) 683 2113

Kilfinaghty Library, Church Street, Sixmile Bridge, Co Clare, Republic of Ireland
☎(00 353 61) 369678

Kilmihil Library, St Michael's Community Centre, Church Street, Kilmihil, Co Clare, Republic of Ireland
☎(00 353 65) 905 0528

Kilrush Library, Kilrush, Co Clare, Republic of Ireland
☎(00 353 65) 905 1504

The Library, Kilnasoolagh Park, Newmarket-on-Fergus, Co Clare, Republic of Ireland
☎(00 353 61) 368411

The Library, The Lock House, Killaloe, Co Clare, Republic of Ireland
☎(00 353 61) 376062

The Library, Ballard Road, Miltown Malbay, Co Clare, Republic of Ireland
☎(00 353 65) 708 4822

Lisdoonvarna Library, Kincora Road, Lisdoonvarna, Co Clare, Republic of Ireland
☎(00 353 65) 707 4029

Local Studies Centre, The Manse, Harmony Row, Ennis, Co Clare, Republic of Ireland
☎(00 353 65) 684 6271

Scariff Library, Mountshannon Road, Scariff, Co Clare, Republic of Ireland
☎(00 353 61) 922893

Sean Lemass Library, Town Centre, Shannon, Co Clare, Republic of Ireland
☎(00 353 61) 364266

Sweeney Memorial Library, O'Connell Street, Kilkee, Co Clare, Republic of Ireland
☎(00 353 65) 905 6034

The Library, The Square, Ennistymon, Co Clare, Republic of Ireland
☎(00 353 65) 7071245

Tulla Library, The Market House, Tulla, Co Clare, Republic of Ireland
☎(00 353 65) 683 5919

CORK CITY

Authority: Cork City Council
Cork City Libraries, 57–61 Grand Parade, Cork, Republic of Ireland
☎(00 353 21) 492 4900
Fax (00 353 21) 427 5684
e-mail: libraries@corkcity.ie
url: www.corkcitylibraries.ie
City Librarian Liam Ronayne BCL DipLib ALAI
Executive Librarian (Bibliographic Services) Ms Sinead Feely

Branch libraries

Bishopstown Library, Wilton, Cork, Republic of Ireland
☎(00 353 21) 492 4950
Fax (00 353 21) 434 5428
e-mail: bishopstown_library@corkcity.ie

Blackpool Library, Blackpool, Cork, Republic of Ireland

☎(00 353 21) 492 4933
Fax (00 353 21) 427 5684
e-mail: blackpool_library@corkcity.ie

Douglas Library, Douglas, Cork, Republic of Ireland
☎(00 353 21) 492 4932
Fax (00 353 21) 427 5684
e-mail: douglas_library@corkcity.ie

Frank O'Connor Library, Old Youghal Road, Mayfield, Cork, Republic of Ireland
☎(00 353 21) 492 4935
Fax (00 353 21) 427 5684
e-mail: mayfield_library@corkcity.ie

Hollyhill Library, Hollyhill, Cork, Republic of Ireland
☎(00 353 21) 492 4928
Fax (00 353 21) 439 3032
e-mail: hollyhill_library@corkcity.ie

Tory Top Road Library, Ballyphehane, Cork, Republic of Ireland
☎(00 353 21) 492 4934
Fax (00 353 21) 427 5684
e-mail: torytop library@corkcity.ie

Children's and Young People's Services, 57 Grand Parade, Cork, Republic of Ireland
☎(00 353 21) 492 4913
Fax (00 353 21) 427 5684
url: www.corkcitylibraries.ie
Children's Services Librarians Ms Breda Hassett BA DipLIS (e-mail:
breda_hassett@corkcity.ie), Ms Patricia Looney BSoc DipLIS

CORK COUNTY

Authority: Cork County Council
Cork County Library and Arts Service, Carrigrohane Road, Cork, Republic of Ireland
☎(00 353 21) 454 6499
e-mail: corkcountylibrary@corkcoco.ie/library
url: www.corkcoco.ie/library
County Librarian Vacant

DONEGAL

Authority: Donegal County Council
Donegal County Library Admin. Centre, Rosemount, Letterkenny, Co Donegal, Republic of Ireland
☎(00 353 74) 912 1968 (enquiries and administration)
Fax (00 353 74) 912 1740
e-mail: library@donegalcoco.ie
url: www.donegallibrary.ie
County Librarian and Divisional Manager, Cultural Services Ms Eileen Burgess

Central/largest library

Central Library, Oliver Plunkett Road, Letterkenny, Co Donegal, Republic of Ireland
☎(00 353 74) 912 4950
Fax (00 353 74) 912 4950
e-mail: central@donegallibrary.ie
Executive Librarian Ms Ciara Cunnane

DUBLIN

Authority: Dublin City Council
Dublin City Public Libraries, Dublin City Library and Archive, 138–144 Pearse Street, Dublin 2, Republic of Ireland
☎(00 353 1) 674 4800
Fax (00 353 1) 674 4880
e-mail: dublinpubliclibraries@dublincity.ie
url: www.dublincity.ie
City Librarian Ms Margaret Hayes BA DipLib HDipEd ALAI (e-mail: margaret.hayes@dublincity.ie)

Central/largest library

Central Public Library, ILAC Centre, Henry Street, Dublin 1, Republic of Ireland
☎(00 353 1) 873 4333
Fax (00 353 1) 872 1451
e-mail: central.library@dublincity.ie

DÚN LAOGHAIRE–RATHDOWN

Authority: Dún Laoghaire–Rathdown County Council
Public Library Service, 2 Harbour Square, Crofton Road, Dún Laoghaire, Co Dublin, Republic of Ireland
☎(00 353 1) 278 1788
Fax (00 353 1) 278 1792
e-mail: libraries@dlrcoco.ie
url: www.dlrcoco.ie/library
County Librarian Ms Mairead Owens MA DLIS
Senior Executive Librarian, Development of Special Projects Ms Orla Gallagher BSocSc DLT
Senior Executive Librarian, Administration, Staff and Policy Co-ordination Ms Geraldine McHugh MA DLIS ALAI
Senior Executive Librarian (ICT) Vacant
Senior Executive Librarian, Culture and Marketing Ms Donagh Brennan BA DipLIS

Branch libraries

Blackrock Library, Valentine House, Temple Road, Blackrock, Co Dublin, Republic of Ireland
☎(00 353 1) 288 8117
e-mail: blackrocklib@dlrcoco.ie
Senior Librarian Jonathan Duggan

Cabinteely Library, Old Bray Road, Cabinteely, Dublin 18, Republic of Ireland

☎(00 353 1) 285 5363
e-mail: cabinteelylib@dlrcoco.ie
Senior Librarian Ms Patricia Byrne BA DLIS

Dalkey Library, Castle Street, Dalkey, Co Dublin, Republic of Ireland
☎(00 353 1) 285 5277
e-mail: dalkeylib@dlrcoco.ie
Senior Librarian Ms Fiona Doherty BA DLIS

Deansgrange Library, Clonkeen Drive, Deansgrange, Dublin 18, Republic of Ireland
☎(00 353 1) 285 0860
e-mail: deansgrangelib@dlrcoco.ie
Senior Librarian Ms Mary McCaughan BA DLIS

Dún Laoghaire Library, Lower George's Street, Dún Laoghaire, Co Dublin, Republic of Ireland
☎(00 353 1) 280 1147
e-mail: dunlaoghairelib@dlrcoco.ie
Senior Librarian Ms Detta O'Connor BA HDipEd DLIS

Dundrum Library, Upper Churchtown Road, Dublin 14, Republic of Ireland
☎(00 353 1) 298 5000
e-mail: dundrumlib@dlrcoco.ie
Senior Librarian Ms Carmel Kelly

Shankill Library, Library Road, Shankill, Co Dublin, Republic of Ireland
☎(00 353 1) 282 3081
e-mail: shankilllib@dlrcoco.ie
Librarian Ms Mary Reynolds BSocSc LIS

Stillorgan Library, St Laurence's Park, Stillorgan, Co Dublin, Republic of Ireland
☎(00 353 1) 288 9655
e-mail: stillorganlib@dlrcoco.ie
Senior Librarian Ms Anne Millane BA DLIS

FINGAL

Authority: Fingal County Council
Fingal County Libraries, Lower Ground Floor, County Hall, Swords, Co Dublin, Republic of Ireland
☎(00 353 1) 890 5524
Fax (00 353 1) 890 5599
e-mail: libraries@fingalcoco.ie
url: www.fingalcoco.ie/libraries
County Librarian Vacant
Senior Executive Librarian (Admin/Personnel & Finance) Ms Phyllis Carter
Senior Librarian (Personnel & Finance) Ms Ann Byrne
Senior Librarian (Bibliographic Services) Ms Evelyn Conway
Senior Executive Librarian (Projects Development) Ms Yvonne Reilly (e-mail: yvonne.reilly@fingalcoco.ie)
Staff Officer (Development & PR) Ms Yvonne Reilly (e-mail: yvonne.reilly@fingalcoco.ie)

Largest library

Blanchardstown Library, Civic Centre, Blanchardstown Centre, Dublin 15, Republic of Ireland
☎(00 353 1) 890 5560
Fax (00 353 1) 890 5574
e-mail: blanchlib@fingalcoco.ie
Senior Executive Librarian Ms Yvonne Reilly (e-mail: yvonne.reilly@fingalcoco.ie)
Senior Librarians Charlie Quinn, Ms Betty Boardman

Branch libraries

Balbriggan Library, St George's Square, Balbriggan, Co Dublin, Republic of Ireland
☎(00 353 1) 870 4401
Fax (00 353 1) 841 2101
e-mail: balbrigganlibrary@fingalcoco.ie
Senior Librarian Ms Assumpta Hickey

Baldoyle Library, Strand Road, Baldoyle, Dublin 13, Republic of Ireland
☎(00 353 1) 890 6793
Fax (00 353 1) 832 3684
e-mail: baldoylelibrary@fingalcoco.ie
Senior Librarian Ms Catherine Keane

County Archives, Clonmel House, Forster Way, Swords, Co Dublin, Republic of Ireland
☎(00 353 1) 870 4496
e-mail: archives@fingalcoco.ie
Archivist Colm McQuinn

Housebound Services, Unit 34, Coolmine Industrial Estate, Coolmine, Dublin 15, Republic of Ireland
☎(00 353 1) 860 4290
Fax (00 353 1) 822 1568
e-mail: houseboundlibrary@finalcoco.ie
Librarian Ms Lynda Beasley

Howth Library, Main Street, Howth, Co Dublin, Republic of Ireland
☎(00 353 1) 832 2130
Fax (00 353 1) 832 2277
e-mail: howthlibrary@fingalcoco.ie
Librarian Ms Nora Finnegan

Local Studies, Clonmel House, Forster Way, Swords, Co Dublin, Republic of Ireland
☎(00 353 1) 870 4495
e-mail: local.studies@fingalcoco.ie
Senior Librarian Ms Jacinta Judge

Malahide Library, Main Street, Malahide, Co Dublin, Republic of Ireland
☎(00 353 1) 870 4430
Fax (00 353 1) 828 3526
e-mail: malahidelibrary@fingalcoco.ie
Senior Librarian Ms Marjory Sliney

Mobile Library Services, Unit 34, Coolmine Industrial Estate, Coolmine, Dublin 15,
Republic of Ireland
☎(00 353 1) 822 1564
Fax (00 353 1) 822 1568
e-mail: mobilelibraries@fingalcoco.ie
Senior Librarian Dermot Bregazzi

Skerries Library, Strand Street, Skerries, Co Dublin, Republic of Ireland
☎(00 353 1) 849 1900
Fax (00 353 1) 849 5142
e-mail: skerrieslibrary@fingalcoco.ie
Librarian Ms Josephine Knight (e-mail: josephine.knight@fingalcoco.ie)

Swords Library, Swords Shopping Centre, Rathbeale Road, Swords, Co Dublin, Republic of
Ireland
☎(00 353 1) 840 4179
Fax (00 353 1) 840 4417
e-mail: swordslibrary@fingalcoco.ie
Senior Librarian Ms Carmel Turner

GALWAY

Authority: Galway County Council
Galway County Library HQ, Island House, Cathedral Square, Galway, Republic of Ireland
☎(00 353 91) 562471
Fax (00 353 91) 565039
e-mail: info@galwaylibrary.ie
url: www.galwaylibrary.ie
County Librarian Pat McMahon DipLib (e-mail: pmcmahon@galwaycoco.ie)
Senior Executive Librarians Ms Maureen Moran, Mrs Bernadette Kelly BA DipLib,
Peter Rabbitt BA LLB DipLib
Librarian, ICT John Fitzgibbon
Executive Librarian, Schools Mrs Josephine Vahey
Archivist Ms Patricia McWalter BA HDipAS
Librarian, Branch System Ms Catherine Farragher

Central/largest library

Galway City Library, Hynes Building, St Augustine Street, Galway, Republic of Ireland
☎(00 353 91) 561666
Executive Librarian Martin Keating

Branch libraries

Ballinasloe Public Library, Fairgreen, Ballinasloe, Co Galway, Republic of Ireland
☎(00 353 90) 964 3464
Executive Librarian Mrs Mary Dillon

Ballybane Public Library, Castlepark Road, Ballybane, Galway, Republic of Ireland
☎(00 353 91) 380590
Executive Librarian Ms Siobhan Arkins

Carraroe Public Library, Co Galway, Republic of Ireland
☎(00 353 95) 95733
Branch Librarian Ms Margaret Vaughan

Clifden Public Library, Clifden, Co Galway, Republic of Ireland
☎(00 353 95) 21092
Senior Library Assistant Paul Keogh

Loughrea Public Library, Loughrea, Co Galway, Republic of Ireland
☎(00 353 91) 847220
Assistant Librarian Ms Anne Callanan

Oranmore Public Library, Oranmore, Co Galway, Republic of Ireland
☎(00 353 91) 792117
Staff Officer, Libraries John Lawlor

Portumna Public Library, Portumna, Co Galway, Republic of Ireland
☎(00 353 90) 974 1261
Senior Library Assistant Ms Teresa Tierney

Tuam Public Library, Tuam, Co Galway, Republic of Ireland
☎(00 353 93) 24287
Staff Officer, Libraries Ms Emer Donoghue

Westside Library, Seamus Quirke Road, Galway City, Galway, Republic of Ireland
☎(00 353 91) 520616
Executive Librarian Ms Cora Gunther

KERRY

Authority: Kerry County Council
Kerry Library, Moyderwell, Tralee, Co Kerry, Republic of Ireland
☎(00 353 66) 712 1200
Fax (00 353 66) 712 9202
e-mail: info@kerrylibrary.ie
url: www.kerrylibrary.ie
County Librarian Tommy O'Connor

Area libraries

Ballybunion Library, Sandhill Road, Ballybunion, Co Kerry, Republic of Ireland
☎(00 353 68) 27615
e-mail: ballybunion@kerrylibrary.ie

Caherciveen Library, Caherciveen, Co Kerry, Republic of Ireland
☎(00 353 66) 947 2287
e-mail: caherciveen@kerrylibrary.ie

Castleisland Library, Castleisland, Co Kerry, Republic of Ireland
☎(00 353 66) 716 3403
e-mail: castleisland@kerrylibrary.ie

Kenmare Library, Shelbourne Street, Kenmare, Co Kerry, Republic of Ireland
☎(00 353 64) 664 1416
e-mail: kenmare@kerrylibrary.ie

Killarney Library, Rock Road, Killarney, Co Kerry, Republic of Ireland
☎(00 353 64) 663 2655
Fax (00 353 64) 663 6065
e-mail: killarney@kerrylibrary.ie

Killorglin Library, Library Place, Killorglin, Co Kerry, Republic of Ireland
☎(00 353 66) 976 1272
e-mail: killorglin@kerrylibrary.ie

Leabharlann an Daingin, Sráid an Dóirín, An Daingean, Co Kerry, Republic of Ireland
☎(00 353 66) 915 1499
e-mail: dingle@kerrylibrary.ie

Listowel Library, Listowel, Co Kerry, Republic of Ireland
☎(00 353 68) 23044
e-mail: listowel@kerrylibrary.ie

Mobile Library Services
Contact details as HQ above

Local History and Archives Department, Kerry Library, Moyderwell, Tralee, Co Kerry, Republic of Ireland
☎(00 353 66) 712 1200
e-mail: localhistory@kerrylibrary.ie; archivist@kerrylibrary.ie

KILDARE

Authority: Kildare County Council
Kildare County Library Service, Riverbank Library and Arts Centre, Main Street, Newbridge, Co Kildare, Republic of Ireland
☎(00 353 45) 431109/431486 (enquiries)
Fax (00 353 45) 432490
e-mail: colibrary@kildarecoco.ie
url: www.kildare.ie
County Librarian Ms Breda Gleeson

Mobile Library Service, Riverbank Library and Arts Centre, Main Street, Newbridge, Co Kildare, Republic of Ireland
☎(00 353 45) 448304 (enquiries)
Librarian in Charge Ms Catherine Rafferty (e-mail: crafferty@kildarecoco.ie)

Main branch libraries

Athy Library, Emily Square, Athy, Co Kildare, Republic of Ireland
☎(00 353 59) 863 1144
Fax (00 353 59) 863 1809
e-mail: athylib@kildarecoco.ie
Librarian in Charge Pat Lonergan

Celbridge Library, St Patrick's Park, Celbridge, Co Kildare, Republic of Ireland
☎(00 353 1) 6272207
e-mail: celbridgelib@kildarecoco.ie
Librarian in Charge Ms Aisling Donnelly

Leixlip Library, Captain's Hill, Leixlip, Co Kildare, Republic of Ireland
☎(00 353 1) 606 0050
e-mail: leixliplib@kildarecoco.ie
Librarian in charge Ms Gillian Allen

Maynooth Library, Main Street, Maynooth, Co Kildare, Republic of Ireland
☎(00 353 1) 628 5530
e-mail: maynoothlib@kildarecoco.ie
Librarians in charge Ms Lorraine Daly, Ms June Branigan

Naas Community Library, Canal Harbour, Naas, Co Kildare, Republic of Ireland
☎(00 353 45) 879111
e-mail: naaslib@kildarecoco.ie
Librarian in Charge Mark Reid

Newbridge Library, Athgarvan Road, Newbridge, Co Kildare, Republic of Ireland
☎(00 353 45) 448353
e-mail: newbridgelib@kildarecoco.ie
Librarian in Charge Ms Suzanne Brosnan

KILKENNY

Authority: Kilkenny County Council
Kilkenny County Library, John's Green House, John's Green, Kilkenny, Republic of Ireland
☎(00 353 56) 779 4160 (enquiries, local studies, mobile, schools, administration)
Fax (00 353 56) 779 4168
e-mail: info@kilkennylibrary.ie
url: www.kilkennylibrary.ie
Acting County Librarian Ms Josephine Coyne BSc DLIS
Senior Executive Librarian Ms Dorothy O'Reilly DLIS ALAI
Executive Librarian Declan Macauley BSc DLIS
Assistant Librarian Ms Brenda Wood

Central/largest library

Kilkenny City Library, John's Quay, Kilkenny, Republic of Ireland
☎(00 353 56) 779 4174
e-mail: citylibrary@kilkennylibrary.ie
Senior Library Assistant Ms Aisling Kelly

Area libraries

Callan Library, Callan, Co Kilkenny, Republic of Ireland
☎(00 353 56) 779 4183
e-mail: callan@kilkennylibrary.ie
Branch Librarian Ms Helen Phillips

Castlecomer Library, Kilkenny Street, Castlecomer, Co Kilkenny, Republic of Ireland
☎(00 353 56) 444 0561
e-mail: castlecomer@kilkennylibrary.ie
Staff Officer Ms Mary Morrissey

Graiguenamanagh Library, Convent Road, Graiguenamanagh, Co Kilkenny, Republic of Ireland
☎(00 353 56) 779 4178
e-mail: graiguenamanagh@kilkennylibrary.ie
Staff Officer Ms Alicia Dunphy

Loughboy Library, Loughboy Shopping Centre, Kilkenny, Republic of Ireland
☎(00 353 56) 779 4176
e-mail: loughboy@kilkennylibrary.ie
Senior Library Assistant Ms Catriona Kenneally

Thomastown Library, Marshes Street, Thomastown, Co Kilkenny, Republic of Ireland
☎(00 353 56) 779 4331
e-mail: tomlib@eircom.net
Branch Librarian Ms Kay Cody

Urlingford Library, The Courthouse, Urlingford, Co Kilkenny, Republic of Ireland
☎(00 353 56) 779 4182
e-mail: urlingford@kilkennylibrary.ie
Branch Librarians Ms Helen Muldowney, Ms Annette Purcell

LAOIS

Authority: Laois County Council
Laois County Library, Áras An Chontae, JFL Avenue, Portlaoise, Co Laois, Republic of Ireland
☎(00 353 57) 867 4315
Fax (00 353 57) 867 8988
url: www.laois.ie/library
County Librarian Gerry Maher LLB(Hons) DLIS (e-mail: gmaher@laoiscoco.ie)

Central/largest library

Portlaoise Branch Library, Dunamase House, Lyster Square, Portlaoise, Co Laois, Republic of Ireland
☎(00 353 57) 862 2333
Executive Librarian Ms Jackie McIntyre

Branch libraries

Abbeyleix Branch Library, Market House, Abbeyleix, Co Laois, Republic of Ireland
☎(00 353 57) 873 0020
Assistant Librarian Ms Laura Brett

Clonaslee Branch Library, Clonaslee Heritage Centre, Clonaslee, Co Laois, Republic of Ireland
☎(00 353 57) 864 8437
Branch Librarian Ms Maureen Cusack

Mountmellick Branch Library, Irishtown, Mountmellick, Co Laois, Republic of Ireland
☎(00 353 57) 864 4572
Assistant Librarian Ms Breda Connell

Mountrath Branch Library, Shannon Street, Mountrath, Co Laois, Republic of Ireland
☎(00 353 57) 875 6378

Assistant Librarian Ms Triona Kenny

Portarlington Branch Library, Station Road, Portarlington, Co Laois, Republic of Ireland
☎(00 353 57) 864 3751
Branch Librarian Ms Patricia Norton

Rathdowney Branch Library, Mill Street, Rathdowney, Co Laois, Republic of Ireland
☎(00 353 505) 46852
Branch Librarian Mrs Catherine Fitzpatrick

Stradbally Branch Library, Court Square, Stradbally, Co Laois, Republic of Ireland
☎(00 353 57) 862 5005
Branch Librarian Ms Julie Ann Stead

Timahoe Branch Library, Timahoe, Co Laois, Republic of Ireland
☎(00 353 57) 862 7231
Branch Librarian Ms Mairin Scully

LEITRIM (LEABHARLANN CHONTAE LIATROMA)

Authority: Leitrim County Council
Leitrim County Library, Main Street, Ballinamore, Co Leitrim, Republic of Ireland
☎(00 353 71) 964 5582
Fax (00 353 71) 964 5572
e-mail: leitrimlibrary@leitrimcoco.ie
url: www.leitrimlibrary.ie
County Librarian Seán Ó'Suilleabháin DLT FLAI ALAI

LIMERICK CITY

Authority: Limerick City Council
Limerick City Library, The Granary, Michael Street, Limerick, Republic of Ireland
☎(00 353 61) 407510
Fax (00 353 61) 411506
e-mail: citylib@limerickcity.ie
url: www.limerickcity.ie
City Librarian Ms Dolores Doyle BA FLAI ALAI (e-mail: ddoyle@limerickcity.ie)
Senior Executive Librarian Ms Deirdre O'Dea (e-mail: dodea@limerickcity.ie)

LIMERICK COUNTY

Authority: Limerick County Council
Limerick County Library HQ, Lissanalta House, Dooradoyle Road, Limerick, Republic of Ireland
☎(00 353 61) 496526 (enquiries and administration)
Fax (00 353 61) 583135
e-mail: colibrar@limerickcoco.ie
County Librarian Damien Brady BA DLIS
Senior Executive Librarian Ms Anne Bennett BA DLIS
Executive Librarian Ms Brenda Frawley BA DLIS (00 353 61 496538)

Central/largest library

Dooradoyle Branch Library, Crescent Shopping Centre, Dooradoyle Road, Limerick, Republic of Ireland
☎(00 353 61) 301101
Executive Librarian Ms Noreen O'Neill BA DLIS

Branch libraries

Abbeyfeale Branch Library, Bridge Street, Abbeyfeale, Co Limerick, Republic of Ireland
☎(00 353 68) 32488
Senior Library Assistant Mike Sweeney

Adare Branch Library, Adare, Co Limerick, Republic of Ireland
☎(00 353 61) 396822
Assistant Librarian Ms Margaret O'Reilly BA DLIS

Kilmallock Branch Library, Aras Mainchin Seoighe, Millmount, Kilmallock, Co Limerick, Republic of Ireland
☎(00 353 63) 20306
Executive Librarian Ms Brenda Frawley BA DLIS

Newcastlewest Branch Library, Newcastlewest, Co Limerick, Republic of Ireland
☎(00 353 69) 62273
Executive Librarian Ms Aileen Dillane BA DLIS

LONGFORD

Authority: Longford County Council
Longford County Library, Archives and Heritage Services, Town Centre, Co Longford, Republic of Ireland
☎(00 353 43) 40731
Fax (00 353 43) 48576
e-mail: library@longfordcoco.ie
url: www.longfordlibrary.ie
County Librarian Ms Mary Carleton-Reynolds DLIS ALAI

Central/largest library

Longford Library, Town Centre, Longford, Co Longford, Republic of Ireland
☎(00 353 43) 40727
e-mail: longfordbranchlibrary@longfordcoco.ie
Senior Executive Librarian Willie O'Dowd BComm LLB MLIS

Branch libraries

Ballymahon Library, Main Street, Ballymahon, Co Longford, Republic of Ireland
☎(00 353 90) 643 2546
e-mail: ballymahonlibrary@longfordcoco.ie
Branch Librarian Ms Carmel Kelly

Drumlish Library, Drumlish, Co Longford, Republic of Ireland
☎(00 353 43) 24760

e-mail: drumlishlibrary@longfordcoco.ie
Branch Librarian Ms Isabella Mallon

Edgeworthstown Library, Edgeworthstown, Co Longford, Republic of Ireland
☎(00 353 43) 71927
e-mail: edgeworthstownlibrary@longfordcoco.ie
Branch Librarian Ms Sheila Walsh

Granard Library, Granard, Co Longford, Republic of Ireland
☎(00 353 43) 86164
e-mail: granardlibrary@longfordcoco.ie
Branch Librarian Ms Rosemary Gaynor

Lanesboro Library, Main Street, Lanesboro, Co Longford, Republic of Ireland
☎(00 353 43) 21291
e-mail: lanesborolibrary@longfordcoco.ie
Branch Librarian Ms Stella O'Sullivan

LOUTH

Authority: Louth County Council
Louth County Library, Roden Place, Dundalk, Co Louth, Republic of Ireland
☎(00 353 42) 935 3190
Fax (00 353 42) 933 7635
url: www.louthcoco.ie
County Librarian Ms Bernadette Fennell

MAYO

Authority: Mayo County Council
Mayo County Library, Library HQ, John Moore Road, Castlebar, Co Mayo, Republic of Ireland
☎(00 353 94) 904 7922 (enquiries and administration)
Fax (00 353 94) 902 6491
e-mail: librarymayo@mayococo.ie
url: www.mayolibrary.ie
County Librarian Austin Vaughan BA DLIS (e-mail: avaughan@mayococo.ie)

Central/largest library

Mayo Central Library, The Mall, Castlebar, Co Mayo, Republic of Ireland
☎(00 353 94) 904 7925
Fax (00 353 94) 902 6491
Librarian Ms Paula Leavy McCarthy

MEATH

Authority: Meath County Council
Meath County Library, Railway Street, Navan, Co Meath, Republic of Ireland
☎(00 353 46) 902 1134; 902 1451
e-mail: colibrar@meathcoco.ie
url: www.meath.ie/library

County Librarian Ciaran Mangan BA MLIS
Senior Executive Librarians Ms Geraldine Donnelly DLIS, Ms Frances Tallon MA DLIS
Executive Librarians Ms Dympna Herward BA DLIS, Ms Yvonne Morrison BA DLIS,
Tom French BA DLIS (Local Studies Dept), Miss Shauna Henry BA(Hons) DipLib MCLIP

Branch libraries

Ashbourne Library, 1-2 Killegland Court, Ashbourne, Co Meath, Republic of Ireland
☎(00 353 1) 835 8185
Executive Librarian Ms Mary Murphy MSc(LIM) DMS CIM ALAI

Athboy Library, Main Street, Athboy, Co Meath, Republic of Ireland
☎(00 353 46) 943 2539
Senior Library Assistant Mrs Ursula Lynskey

Duleek Library, Main Street, Duleek, Co Meath, Republic of Ireland
☎(00 353 41) 988 0709
Library Assistant David Farnan

Dunboyne Library, Castleview, Dunboyne, Co Meath, Republic of Ireland
☎(00 353 1) 825 1248
Executive Librarian Ms Caroline McLoughlin BA HDipEd DipLIS

Dunshaughlin Library, Main Street, Dunshaughlin, Co Meath, Republic of Ireland
☎(00 353 1) 825 0504
Assistant Librarian Ms Barbara Scally BA DLIS

Kells Library, Maudlin Street, Kells, Co Meath, Republic of Ireland
☎(00 353 46) 924 1592
Branch Librarian Ms Rose Grimes

Navan Library, Railway Street, Navan, Co Meath, Republic of Ireland
☎(00 353 46) 902 1134
Acting Executive Librarian Ms Sharon Flanagan BSc(Econ)

Nobber Library, Nobber, Co Meath, Republic of Ireland
☎(00 353 46) 905 2732
Branch Librarian Ms Imelda Griffin

Oldcastle Library, Millbrook Road, Oldcastle, Co Meath, Republic of Ireland
☎(00 353 49) 854 2084
Senior Library Assistant Ms Anne Price

Rathcairn Library, Rathcairn, Co Meath, Republic of Ireland
☎(00 353 46) 943 0929
Branch Librarian Ms Treasa Uí Mhairtín

Slane Library, Castle Hill, Slane, Co Meath, Republic of Ireland
☎(00 353 41) 982 4955
Branch Librarian Ms Patricia McGrane

Trim Library, High Street, Trim, Co Meath, Republic of Ireland
☎(00 353 46) 943 6014
Executive Librarian Ms Maedhbh Rogan BA DLIS

MONAGHAN

Authority: Monaghan County Council
Monaghan County Library, 98 Avenue, Clones, Co Monaghan, Republic of Ireland
☎(00 353 47) 51143
Fax (00 353 47) 51863
e-mail: moncolib@monaghancoco.ie
url: www.monaghan.ie
Acting County Librarian Ms Catherine Elliott BSocSc

Central/largest library

Monaghan Branch Library, North Road, Monaghan Town, Republic of Ireland
☎(00 353 47) 81830
Fax (00 353 47) 38688
Assistant Librarian Ms Karen McCague (e-mail: kmccague@monaghancoco.ie)

Branch libraries

Ballybay Library, Main Street, Ballybay, Co Monaghan, Republic of Ireland
☎(00 353 42) 974 1256
Branch Librarian Mrs Rosemary McDonnell

Carrickmacross Branch Library, Market Square, Carrickmacross, Co Monaghan, Republic of
Ireland
☎(00 353 42) 966 1148
Senior Library Assistant Ms Breda Moore (e-mail: bpmoore@monaghancoco.ie)

Castleblayney Branch Library, Iontas Resource Centre, Castleblayney, Co Monaghan,
Republic of Ireland
☎(00 353 42) 974 0281
Branch Librarian Ms Pauline Duffy

Clones Branch Library, 98 Avenue, Clones, Co Monaghan, Republic of Ireland
☎(00 353 47) 51143
Fax (00 353 47) 51863
Assistant Librarian Ms Laura Carey (e-mail: lcarey@monaghancoco.ie)

OFFALY

Authority: Offaly County Council
Offaly County Library, O'Connor Square, Tullamore, Co Offaly, Republic of Ireland
☎(00 353 57) 934 6834
Fax (00 353 57) 935 2769
e-mail: colibrar@offalycoco.ie
url: www.offaly.ie
County Librarian Ms Mary Stuart DLIS
Executive Librarian Diarmuid Bracken BA DLIS

Central/largest library

Tullamore Library, O'Connor Square, Tullamore, Co Offaly, Republic of Ireland

☎(00 353 57) 934 6832
e-mail: TullamoreLibrary@offalycoco.ie

ROSCOMMON

Authority: Roscommon County Council
Roscommon County Library, Abbey Street, Roscommon, Republic of Ireland
☎(00 353 90) 663 7272/7274 (enquiries and administration)
Fax (00 353 90) 663 7101
url: www.roscommoncoco.ie/home.htm
County Librarian Richie Farrell BA DLIS (e-mail: rfarrell@roscommoncoco.ie)
Executive Librarian Ms Mary Butler
Assistant Librarian (Children's) Ms Carolyn Tunney

Central/largest library

Roscommon Branch Library, Abbey Street, Roscommon, Republic of Ireland
☎(00 353 90) 663 7277
Fax (00 353 90) 663 7101
e-mail: rosllb@roscommoncoco.le
Senior Library Assistant Ms Caitlin Browne

Branch libraries

Ballaghaderreen Branch Library, Barrack Street, Ballaghaderreen, Co Roscommon, Republic
of Ireland
☎(00 353 94) 987 7044
e-mail: ballaghaderreenlibrary@roscommoncoco.ie
Senior Library Assistant Ms Deirdre Creighton

Boyle Branch Library, The King House, Boyle, Co Roscommon, Republic of Ireland
☎(00 353 71) 966 2800
e-mail: boylelibrary@roscommoncoco.ie
Acting Senior Library Assistant Ms Patricia O'Flaherty

Castlerea Branch Library, Main Street, Castlerea, Co Roscommon, Republic of Ireland
☎(00 353 94) 962 0745
e-mail: castlerealibrary@roscommoncoco.ie
Branch Librarian Ms Maura Carroll

Elphin Branch Library, Main Street, Elphin, Co Roscommon, Republic of Ireland
☎(00 353 71) 963 5775
Branch Librarian Ms Mary Walsh

Strokestown Branch Library, Elphin Street, Strokestown, Co Roscommon, Republic of
Ireland
☎(00 353 71) 963 4027
e-mail: strokestownlibrary@roscommoncoco.ie
Branch Librarian Ms Breege Towey

Mobile Library Service, Library HQ, Abbey Street, Roscommon, Republic of Ireland
☎(00 353 90) 663 7279
Senior Library Assistant Ms Meliosa Moran

Prison Library Services, Library HQ, Abbey Street, Roscommon, Republic of Ireland
☎(00 353 90) 663 7326
Assistant Librarian Matthew Gammon

SLIGO

Authority: Sligo County Council
County Library, Stephen Street, Co Sligo, Republic of Ireland
☎(00 353 71) 911 1850
Fax (00 353 71) 914 6798
e-mail: sligolib@sligococo.ie
url: www.sligolibrary.ie
County Librarian Donal Tinney MA DLIS ALAI
Senior Executive Librarian Ms Pauline Brennan DLIS

Central/largest library

Sligo Central Library, Stephen Street, Sligo, Republic of Ireland
☎(00 353 71) 911 1675
e-mail: sligocentrallibrary@sligococo.ie
url: www.sligolibrary.ie
Executive Librarian Ms Caroline Morgan FLAI

Branch libraries

Local History/Reference Library, The Westward Town Centre, Bridge Street, Sligo,
Republic of Ireland
☎(00 353 71) 911 1850
e-mail: sligolib@sligococo.ie
url: www.sligolibrary.ie
Executive Librarian Ultan McNasser MA DLIS

Tubbercurry Community Library, Teach Laighne, Humbert Street, Tubbercurry, Co Sligo,
Republic of Ireland
☎(00 353 71) 911 1705
e-mail: tubberlibrary@sligococo.ie
url: www.sligolibrary.ie
Senior Library Assistant Ms Grainne Brett-Mahon

SOUTH DUBLIN

Authority: South Dublin County Council
Unit I, The Square Industrial Complex, Tallaght, Dublin 24, Republic of Ireland
☎(00 353 1) 459 7834
Fax (00 353 1) 459 7872
e-mail: library@sdublincoco.ie
url: www.southdublinlibraries.ie
County Librarian Ms Georgina Byrne (e-mail: georginabyrne@sdublincoco.ie)

Central/largest library

County Library, County Hall, Tallaght, Dublin 24, Republic of Ireland

☎(00 353 1) 462 0073
Fax (00 353 1) 414 9207
e-mail: talib@sdublincoco.ie
Senior Executive Librarian Ms Una Phelan

Branch libraries

Ballyroan Library, Orchardstown Avenue, Rathfarnham, Dublin 14, Republic of Ireland
☎(00 353 1) 494 1900
Fax (00 353 1) 494 7083
e-mail: ballyroan@sdublincoco.ie
Senior Librarian Ms Ann Dunne

Castletymon Library, Castletymon Shopping Centre, Tymon Road North, Tallaght, Dublin
24, Republic of Ireland
☎(00 353 1) 452 4888
Fax (00 353 1) 459 7873
e-mail: castletymon@sdublincoco.ie
Acting Senior Librarian Ms Helen Brennan

Clondalkin Library, Monastry Road, Clondalkin, Dublin 22, Republic of Ireland
☎(00 353 1) 459 3315
Fax (00 353 1) 459 5509
e-mail: clondalkin@sdublincoco.ie
Acting Senior Librarian Ms Catherine Gallagher

John J Jennings Library, Stewarts Hospital, Palmerstown, Dublin 20, Republic of Ireland
☎(00 353 1) 626 4444 (ext 1129)
Fax (00 353 1) 626 1707
e-mail: library@stewartshospital.com
Senior Librarian Ms Siobhan McChrystal

Lucan Library, Superquinn Shopping Centre, Newcastle Road, Lucan, Co Dublin, Republic
of Ireland
☎(00 353 1) 621 6422
Fax (00 353 1) 621 6433
e-mail: lucan@sdublincoco.ie
Senior Librarian Henry Morrin

Mobile Library Service, Unit 1, The Square Industrial Complex, Tallaght, Dublin 24,
Republic of Ireland
☎(00 353 1) 459 7834
Fax (00 353 1) 459 7872
e-mail: mobiles@sdublincoco.ie
Senior Librarian Ms Bernie Meenaghan

Whitechurch Library, Taylor's Lane, Rathfarnham, Dublin 16, Republic of Ireland
☎(00 353 1) 493 0199
e-mail: whitechurch@sdublincoco.ie
Branch Librarian Ms Breda Bollard

Children's and Young People's Library Services

South Dublin Libraries, Unit 1, The Square Industrial Complex, Tallaght, Dublin 24,
Republic of Ireland
☎(00 353 1) 459 7834
Fax (00 353 1) 459 7872
e-mail: schools@sdublincoco.ie
Senior Librarians Ms Maria O'Sullivan, Ms Laura Joyce

TIPPERARY

Authority: County Tipperary Joint Libraries Committee
Tipperary County Library, Castle Avenue, Thurles, Co Tipperary, Republic of Ireland
☎(00 353 504) 21555
Fax (00 353 504) 23442
e-mail: info@tipperarylibraries.ie
url: www.tipperarylibraries.ie
County Librarian Martin Maher

Branch libraries

Borrisokane Library, Main Street, Borrisokane, Co Tipperary, Republic of Ireland
☎(00 353 67) 27199
Branch Librarian Ms Noirin Duggan

Cahir Library, The Square, Cahir, Co Tipperary, Republic of Ireland
☎(00 353 52) 744 2075
Branch Librarian Mrs Ann Tuohy

Carrick-on-Suir Library, Fair Green, Carrick-on-Suir, Co Tipperary, Republic of Ireland
☎(00 353 51) 640591 (tel/fax)
Senior Library Assistant Ms Orla O'Connor

Cashel Library, Friar Street, Cashel, Co Tipperary, Republic of Ireland
☎(00 353 62) 63825
Fax (00 353 62) 63948
e-mail: cashel@tipperarylibraries.ie
Staff Officer (Library) Ms Gemma Larkin

Clonmel Library, Emmet Street, Clonmel, Co Tipperary, Republic of Ireland
☎(00 353 52) 612 4545
Fax (00 353 52) 612 7336
e-mail: clonmel@tipperarylibraries.ie
Executive Librarian Mrs Marie Boland

Cloughjordan Library, Main Street, Cloughjordan, Co Tipperary, Republic of Ireland
☎(00 353 505) 42425
Branch Librarian Mrs Marie Brady

Killenaule Library, Slieveardagh Centre, River Street, Killenaule, Co Tipperary, Republic of
Ireland
☎(00 353 52) 915 7906
Branch Librarian Ms Maure Barrett

Nenagh Library, O'Rahilly Street, Nenagh, Co Tipperary, Republic of Ireland
☎(00 353 67) 34404
Fax (00 353 67) 34405
e-mail: nenagh@tipperarylibraries.ie
Executive Librarian Ms Breffni Hannon

Roscrea Library, Birr Road, Roscrea, Co Tipperary, Republic of Ireland
☎(00 353 505) 22032 (tel/fax)
Assistant Librarian Ms Aine Beausang

Templemore Library, Old Mill Court, Templemore, Co Tipperary, Republic of Ireland
☎(00 353 504) 32555/6
Fax (00 353 504) 32545
e-mail: templemore@tipperarylibraries.ie
Staff Officer (Library) Pat Bracken

Thurles Library, The Source, Cathedral Street, Thurles, Co Tipperary, Republic of Ireland
☎(00 353 504) 29720
Fax (00 353 504) 21344
e-mail: thurles@tipperarylibraries.ie
Executive Librarian Ms Ann Marie Brophy

Tipperary Library, Dan Breen House, Tipperary, Republic of Ireland
☎(00 353 62) 51761 (tel/fax)
Branch Librarian Ms Nollaig Butler, Ms Gerardine Hughes

Tipperary Studies, Thurles Library, The Source, Cathedral Street, Thurles, Co Tipperary, Republic of Ireland
☎(00 353 504) 29278
e-mail: studies@tipperarylibraries.ie
Staff Officer (Library) Ms Mary Guinan-Darmody

WATERFORD CITY

Authority: Waterford City Council
Library Headquarters, Waterford City Council Depot, Northern Extension Industrial Estate, Old Kilmeadan Road, Waterford, Republic of Ireland
☎(00 353 51) 849839
Fax (00 353 51) 379595
e-mail: city library@waterfordcity.ie
url: www.waterfordcity.ie/library
City Librarian Ms Jane Cantwell
Senior Executive Librarians Ms Katherine Collins, Ms Melanie Cunningham (Acting)

Central/largest library

Central Library, Lady Lane, Waterford, Republic of Ireland
☎(00 353 51) 849975
Fax (00 353 51) 850031
e-mail: library@waterfordcity.ie
url: www.waterfordcity.ie/library
Executive Librarian Ms Sinéad O'Higgins
Assistant Librarians Ms Debbie Johnson, Ms Niamh Baldwin

Other libraries

Ardkeen Library, Ardkeen Shopping Centre, Dunmore Road, Waterford, Republic of Ireland
☎(00 353 51) 849755
Fax (00 353 51) 874100
e-mail: library@waterfordcity.ie
Acting Executive Librarian Ms Sinéad Cummins

Brown's Road Library, Paddy Brown's Road, Waterford, Republic of Ireland
☎(00 353 51) 860845
e-mail: library@waterfordcity.ie
Acting Executive Librarian Ms Sinéad Cummins

WATERFORD COUNTY

Authority: Waterford County Council
Waterford County Library, Ballyanchor Road, Lismore, Co Waterford, Republic of Ireland
☎(00 353 58) 21370
e-mail: libraryhq@waterfordcoco.ie
url: www.waterfordcountylibrary.ie
Acting County Librarian Ms Jean Webster (e-mail: jwebster@waterfordcoco.ie)

Central/largest library

Dungarvan Branch Library, Davitt's Quay, Dungarvan, Dungarvan, Co Waterford, Republic
of Ireland
☎(00 353 58) 41231
e-mail: dungarvanlibrary@waterfordcoco.ie
Executive Librarian Ger Croughan (e-mail: gcroughan@waterfordcoco.ie)

Area libraries

Cappoquin Branch Library, Cappoquin, Waterford, Republic of Ireland
☎(00 353 58) 52263
e-mail: cappoquinlibrary@waterfordcoco.ie
Branch Librarian Mrs Mary Tobin

Dunmore Branch Library, Dunmore East, Waterford, Republic of Ireland
☎(00 353 51) 383211
e-mail: dunmorelibrary@waterfordcoco.ie
Branch Librarian Ms Claire O Mullain

Kilmacthomas Branch Library, Kilmacthomas, Waterford, Republic of Ireland
☎(00 353 51) 294270
e-mail: kilmacthomaslibrary@waterfordcoco.ie
Branch Librarian Ms Laura Kirwan

Lismore Branch Library, Main Street, Lismore, Waterford, Republic of Ireland
☎(00 353 58) 21377
e-mail: lismorelibrary@waterfordcoco.ie
Executive Librarian Eddie Byrne (e-mail: ebyrne@waterfordcoco.ie)

Portlaw Branch Library, The Square, Portlaw, Waterford, Republic of Ireland
☎(00 353 51) 387402

e-mail: portlawlibrary@waterfordcoco.ie
Librarian Ms Helena Fogarty

Tallow Branch Library, Convent Street, Tallow, Waterford, Republic of Ireland
☎(00 353 58) 56347
e-mail: tallowlibrary@waterfordcoco.ie
Branch Librarian Ms Sheila Curtin

Tramore Branch Library, Market Square, Tramore, Waterford, Republic of Ireland
☎(00 353 51) 381479
e-mail: tramorelibrary@waterfordcoco.ie
Executive Librarian Ms Tracy Mceneaney

WESTMEATH

Authority: Westmeath County Council
Westmeath County Library HQ, Dublin Road, Mullingar, Co Westmeath, Republic of Ireland
☎(00 353 44) 933 2162
Fax (00 353 44) 934 2330
url: www.westmeathcoco.ie
County Librarian Miss Mary Farrell BA HDE DLIS ALAI (e-mail: mfarrell@westmeathcoco.ie)
Senior Executive Librarian Mrs Paula O'Dornan BA(Hons) PGDipLIS (e-mail: podornan@westmeathcoco.ie)

Branch libraries

Aidan Heavey Public Library, Athlone Civic Centre, Church Street, Athlone, Co Westmeath, Republic of Ireland
☎(00 353 90) 644 2157/8/9
e-mail: athlib@westmeathcoco.ie
Senior Executive Librarian Gearoid O'Brien DLIS FLAI ALAI (e-mail: gobrien@westmeathcoco.ie)

Ballynacarrigy Library, 2 Kilmurray's Corner, Main Street, Ballynacarrigy, Co Westmeath, Republic of Ireland
☎(00 353 44) 937 3882
e-mail: bnclib@westmeathcoco.ie
Branch Librarian Ms Cecilia Connolly (e-mail: cconnelly@westmeathcoco.ie)

Castlepollard Library, Civic Offices, Mullingar Road, Castlepollard, Co Westmeath, Republic of Ireland
☎(00 353 44) 933 2199
e-mail: cpdlib@westmeathcoco.ie
Staff Officer Ms Nicola Brennan-Gavin (e-mail: ngavin@westmeathcoco.ie)

Kilbeggan Library, Kilbeggan Civic Offices, The Square, Kilbeggan, Co Westmeath, Republic of Ireland
☎(00 353 57) 933 3148
e-mail: killib@westmeathcoco.ie
Senior Library Assistant Ms Margaret Crentsil

Killucan Library, Rathwire Hall, Killucan, Co Westmeath, Republic of Ireland
☎(00 353 44) 937 4260
e-mail: klnlib@westmeathcoco.ie
Branch Librarian Ms Cecilia Connolly (e-mail: cconnolly@westmeathcoco.ie)

Moate Library, Main Street, Moate, Co Westmeath, Republic of Ireland
☎(00 353 90) 648 1888
Fax (00 353 90) 648 1103
e-mail: moatelib@westmeathcoco.ie
Library Assistant Ms Lorna Farrell

Mullingar Library, County Buildings, Mount Street, Mullingar, Co Westmeath, Republic of
Ireland
☎(00 353 44) 933 2161
e-mail: mgarlib@westmeathcoco.ie
Executive Librarian Ms Cailin Gallagher DLIS (e-mail: cailin.gallagher@westmeathcoco.ie)

WEXFORD

Authority: Wexford County Council
**Library Management Services, 6A Ardcavan Business Park, Ardcavan, Co Wexford,
Republic of Ireland**
☎(00 353 53) 912 4922/912 4928
Fax (00 353 53) 912 1097
e-mail: libraryhq@wexfordcoco.ie
url: www.wexford.ie
County Librarian Ms Fionnuala Hanrahan BA DLIS MLIS MCLIP MCLIPI
Senior Executive Librarian Ms Eileen Morrissey BA DLIS

Central/largest library

Wexford Town Library, Selskar House, McCauley's Carpark, off Redmond Square, Co
Wexford, Republic of Ireland
☎(00 353 53) 912 1637
Fax (00 353 53) 912 1639
e-mail: wexfordlib@wexfordcoco.ie
Executive Librarian Ms Hazel Percival BA DLIS ALAI (e-mail:
hazel.percival@wexfordcoco.ie)

Area libraries

Bunclody Branch Library, Mill Wood, Carrigduff, Bunclody, Co Wexford,
Republic of Ireland
☎(00 353 53) 937 5466
e-mail: bunclodylib@wexfordcoco.ie
Executive Librarian Ms Patricia Keenan BA DLIS (e-mail:
patricia.keenan@wexfordcoco.ie)

Enniscorthy Branch Library, Lymington Road, Enniscorthy, Co Wexford, Republic of Ireland
☎(00 353 53) 923 6055
e-mail: enniscorthylib@wexfordcoco.ie
Executive Librarian Jarlath Glynn BA DipLib (e-mail: jarlath.glynn@wexfordcoco.ie)

New Ross Branch Library, Barrack Lane, New Ross, Co Wexford, Republic of Ireland
☎(00 353 51) 421877
e-mail: newrosslib@wexfordcoco.ie
Executive Librarian Ms Nicola Buckley BSocSci(Info) (e-mail:
nicola.buckley@wexfordcoco.ie)

WICKLOW

Authority: Wicklow County Council
Wicklow County Library, Library HQ, Boghall Road, Bray, Co Wicklow, Republic of Ireland
☎(00 353 1) 286 6566 (enquiries and administration)
Fax (00 353 1) 286 5811
e-mail: wcclhq@eircom.net
url: www.wicklow.ie
County Librarian Brendan Martin BA DLIS
Senior Executive Librarian (Schools and Outreach) Ms Noelle Ringwood BA DLIS
Senior Executive Librarian (Administration) Ms Carmel Moore DLIS
Executive Librarian (IT) Ms Mary O'Driscoll BSocSc DLIS

Largest library

Bray Public Library, Eglinton Road, Bray, Co Wicklow, Republic of Ireland
☎(00 353 1) 286 2600
Executive Librarian Ms Fiona Scannell

Area libraries

Arklow Public Library, St Mary's Road, Arklow, Co Wicklow, Republic of Ireland
☎(00 353 402) 39977
Assistant Librarian Ms Ann Murdiff

Ballywaltrim Public Library, Boghall Road, Bray, Co Wicklow, Republic of Ireland
☎(00 353 1) 272 3205
Assistant Librarian Ms Ciara Brennan

Blessington Public Library, New Town Centre, Blessington, Co Wicklow, Republic of
Ireland
☎(00 353 405) 891740
Assistant Librarian Ms Gillian Misstear BA MA

Greystones Public Library, Church Road, Greystones, Co Wicklow, Republic of Ireland
☎(00 353 1) 287 3548
Executive Librarian Ms Mary Murphy MSc(LIM) DMS CIM ALAI

Wicklow Public Library, Market Square, Co Wicklow, Republic of Ireland
☎(00 353 404) 67025
Assistant Librarian Ms Emer O'Grady

Libraries in Academic Institutions in the United Kingdom

UNIVERSITY OF ABERDEEN

Library, University of Aberdeen, Queen Mother Library, Meston Walk, Aberdeen AB24 3UE
☎(01224) 273403 (enquiries/help desk)
Fax (01224) 273956
e-mail: library@abdn.ac.uk
url: www.abdn.ac.uk/library
Head Librarian Ms Chris Banks
Deputy Librarian and Head of Library Services Laurence W. Bebbington
(e-mail: laurence.bebbington@abdn.ac.uk)

Site libraries

Medical Library, University of Aberdeen, Polwarth Building, Foresterhill, Aberdeen
AB25 2ZD
☎(01224) 681818 ext 52488 (enquiries), ext 52740 (administration)
Fax (01224) 685157
e-mail: medlib@abdn.ac.uk
Site Services Manager Ms Melanie Bickerton BA

Reid Library, University of Aberdeen, Rowett Institute of Nutrition and Health, Greenburn
Road, Bucksburn, Aberdeen AB21 9SB
☎(01224) 712751
e-mail: library@rowett.ac.uk
Librarian Ms Mary Mowat BA MLib MCLIP (e-mail: m.mowat@abdn.ac.uk)

Special Libraries and Archives, University of Aberdeen, King's College, Aberdeen AB24 3SW
☎(01224) 272598 (enquiries)
Fax (01224) 273891
e-mail: speclib@abdn.ac.uk
Head of Special Libraries and Archives Ms Siobhan Convery

Taylor Library and European Documentation Centre, University of Aberdeen, Taylor
Building, Aberdeen AB24 3UB
☎(01224) 272601 (law enquiries), 273334 (European Union enquiries), 273892
(administration)
Fax (01224) 273893
e-mail: lawlib@abdn.ac.uk
Site Services Manager Ms Liz Mackie BA (e-mail: e.a.mackie@abdn.ac.uk)

UNIVERSITY OF ABERTAY DUNDEE

Information Services, University of Abertay Dundee, Bell Street, Dundee DD1 1HG
☎(01382) 308866
Fax (01382) 308877
e-mail: infodesk@abertay.ac.uk
url: http://vlib.abertay.ac.uk/
Head of Information Services Michael Turpie

ABERYSTWYTH UNIVERSITY

Hugh Owen Library, Aberystwyth University, Penglais, Aberystwyth, Ceredigion SY23 3DZ

☎(01970) 622399 (enquiries), (01970) 622391 (administration)
Fax (01970) 622404
e-mail: libinfo@aber.ac.uk
url: www.aber.ac.uk
Director of Information Services Ms Rebecca Davies BLib(Hons)

Site/departmental libraries

Law Library, Aberystwyth University, The Hugh Owen Building, Penglais, Aberystwyth, Ceredigion SY23 3DZ
☎(01970) 622401
e-mail: libinfo@aber.ac.uk
Librarian i/c Mrs Lillian Stevenson LLB DipLib MCLIP

Old College Library, Aberystwyth University, Old College, King Street, Aberystwyth, Ceredigion SY23 2AX
☎(01970) 622130
Librarian i/c Elgan Davies BA DipLib

Physical Sciences Library (Mathematics, Computer Sciences and Physics), Aberystwyth University, 4th Floor, Physical Sciences Building, Penglais, Aberystwyth, Ceredigion SY23 3BZ
☎(01970) 622407
e-mail: libinfo@aber.ac.uk
Librarian i/c Mrs Tegwen Meredith

Thomas Parry Library, Aberystwyth University, Llanbadarn Fawr, Aberystwyth, Ceredigion SY23 3AS
☎(01970) 622412
Fax (01970) 621868
e-mail: parrylib@aber.ac.uk
Librarian i/c Stephen Smith BSc DipLib MCLIP

ANGLIA RUSKIN UNIVERSITY

University Library, Anglia Ruskin University, East Road, Cambridge CB1 1PT
☎0845 196 2301 or (01223) 363271 ext 2301
Fax 0845 196 2234
url: www.anglia.ac.uk/library
University Librarian Ms Nicky Kershaw BA CertEd MCLIP (0845 196 3763; e-mail: nicky.kershaw@anglia.ac.uk)
Assistant Director of Library Services (Academic Services Division) Ms Margaret March BA MA MCLIP (0845 196 4644; e-mail: margaret.march@anglia.ac.uk)
Assistant Director of Library Services (Central Services Division) Graham Howorth BA MSc MCLIP (0845 196 3145; e-mail: graham.howorth@anglia.ac.uk)
Assistant Director of Library Services (Customer Services Division) Roddie Shepherd BA DipLib MCLIP (0845 196 2310; e-mail: roddie.shepherd@anglia.ac.uk)

Chelmsford Library, Anglia Ruskin University, Queens Building, Bishop Hall Lane, Chelmsford, Essex CM1 1SQ
☎(01245) 683757
Fax 0845 196 3149 or (01245) 683149

Fulbourn Library, Anglia Ruskin University, Victoria House, Capital Park, Fulbourn, Cambridge CB1 5XA
☎(01223) 695395

Peterborough Library, Anglia Ruskin University, Education Centre, Peterborough District Hospital, Thorpe Road, Peterborough PE3 6DA
☎(01223) 695570

THE ARTS UNIVERSITY COLLEGE AT BOURNEMOUTH

The Library, The Arts University College at Bournemouth, Wallisdown Road, Poole, Dorset BH12 5HH
☎(01202) 363256
Fax (01202) 537729
e-mail: library@aucb.ac.uk
url: www.aucb.ac.uk
Head of Library and Information Services Ms Julia Waite BSc(Econ) MSc MCLIP FHEA
(e-mail: jwaite@aucb.ac.uk)

ASTON UNIVERSITY

Library & Information Services, Aston University, Aston Triangle, Birmingham B4 7ET
☎0121 204 4525 (enquiries)
Fax 0121 204 4530
e-mail: library@aston.ac.uk
url: www1.aston.ac.uk/lis/
Director Nick Smith BSc MSc PhD MCLIP
Assistant Director (Academic Liaison/Information Resources) Mrs Heather Whitehouse BSc DipInfSc
Assistant Director (Academic Liaison/Public Services) Ms Angela Brady BA DipLIS
Head of Library Systems Mrs Zinat Bennett BSc PGDipLib MA MBA

BANGOR UNIVERSITY

Library and Archives Service, Bangor University, College Road, Bangor, Gwynedd LL57 2DG
☎(01248) 382981 (enquiries), (01248) 383772 (secretary)
Fax (01248) 382979
e-mail: library@bangor.ac.uk; ill@bangor.ac.uk (interlibrary loans)
url: www.bangor.ac.uk/library
Head of Library and Archives Service David Learmont (e-mail: d.learmont@bangor.ac.uk)
Librarians Mairwen Owen BA (e-mail: mairwen.owen@bangor.ac.uk), Marion Poulton BA MEd DipLib MCLIP (e-mail: m.poulton@bangor.ac.uk), Vashti Zarach (e-mail: v.zarach@bangor.ac.uk)
Lending and Access Services Manager Tony Heaton (e-mail: t.heaton@bangor.ac.uk)
Collection Management and Library Systems Manager Mieko Yamaguchi BA MA DipLib (e-mail: m.yamaguchi@bangor.ac.uk)
University Archivist, Welsh and Special Collections Einion Wyn Thomas BA DAA
(e-mail: e.w.thomas@bangor.ac.uk)

Bibliographic Librarian Dr Flora Lewis BSc PhD DipILM (e-mail: f.lewis@bangor.ac.uk)
Electronic Resources Librarian Tracey Randall BA(Hons) MSc (e-mail:
t.randall@bangor.ac.uk)

Site libraries

Education Site Library, Bangor University, Safle'r Normal, Holyhead Road, Bangor,
Gwynedd LL57 2PX
☎(01248) 383048

Healthcare Sciences Library, Bangor University, Archimedes Centre, Technology Park,
Wrexham LL13 7YP
☎(01978) 316370

Healthcare Sciences Library, Bangor University, Fron Heulog, Holyhead Road, Bangor,
Gwynedd LL57 2EF
☎(01248) 383131

Main Library, Bangor University, College Road, Bangor, Gwynedd LL57 2DG
☎(01248) 382983

Science Library, Bangor University, Adeilad Deiniol, Deiniol Road, Bangor, Gwynedd
LL57 2UX
☎(01248) 382984

BATH SPA UNIVERSITY

Newton Park Library, Bath Spa University, Newton Park, Newton St Loe, Bath BA2 9BN
☎(01225) 875490
Fax (01225) 875493
e-mail: libenq@bathspa.ac.uk
url: www.bathspa.ac.uk
Head of Library and Information Services Ms Alison Baud MA DipLib MCLIP (01225
875634; e-mail: a.baud@bathspa.ac.uk)
Head of Library Systems Ms Ann Siswell BA DipLib MCLIP (01225 875678; e-mail:
a.siswell@bathspa.ac.uk)
Information Managers Mrs Barbara Molloy BA MCLIP (01225 875727; e-mail:
b.molloy@bathspa.ac.uk), Richard Taylor MCLIP (01225 875476; e-mail:
r.taylor@bathspa.ac.uk), Matt Durant (01225 875477; e-mail: m.durant@bathspa.ac.uk),
Mark de Fleury (01225 876578; e-mail: m.defleury@bathspa.ac.uk)

Sion Hill Library, Bath Spa University, Sion Road, Bath BA1 5SF
☎(01225) 875648
Fax (01225) 427080
Campus Librarians Ms Helen Rayner BA(Hons) DipInf (01225 875648; e-mail:
h.rayner@bathspa.ac.uk), Ms Nicola Morrison BA(Hons) MCLIP (01225 875648; e-mail:
n.morrison@bathspa.ac.uk)

UNIVERSITY OF BATH

Library, University of Bath, Bath BA2 7AY
☎(01225) 385000 (enquiries), (01225) 386084 (administration)
Fax (01225) 386229

e-mail: library@bath.ac.uk
url: www.bath.ac.uk/library
University Librarian Howard Nicholson MA MCLIP FRSA

UNIVERSITY OF BEDFORDSHIRE

Learning Resources Centre, University of Bedfordshire, Park Square, Luton, Beds LU1 3JU
☎(01582) 743488 (enquiries), (01582) 489398 (administration)
Fax (01582) 489325
e-mail: geraldine.kiernan@beds.ac.uk (administration)
url: www.beds.ac.uk; http://lrweb.beds.ac.uk
Director of Learning Resources Tim Stone MA MCLIP (01582 489310; e-mail: tim.stone@beds.ac.uk)
Deputy Director of Learning Resources and Student Services Marcus Woolley BA MCLIP (01582 489102; e-mail: marcus.woolley@beds.ac.uk)

Site libraries

Library, University of Bedfordshire, Bedford Campus, Polhill Avenue, Bedford MK41 9EA
☎(01234) 793202
Library Manager Ms Sue Csoka

Learning Resources Centre, Buckinghamshire Campus, University of Bedfordshire, Faculty of Health and Social Sciences, Oxford House, Oxford Road, Aylesbury, Bucks HP21 8SZ
☎(01296) 734301
Senior Information Officer David Fulton

Butterfield Park Campus, University of Bedfordshire, Unit 260–270, Butterfield, Great Marlings, Luton, Beds LU2 8DL
☎(01582) 743803
Library Manager Ms Ann Wiggins

BIRMINGHAM CITY UNIVERSITY

Library and Learning Resources, Birmingham City University, Franchise Street, Perry Barr, Birmingham B42 2SU
☎0121 331 5289 (enquiries), 0121 331 6300 (administration)
Fax 0121 356 2875
url: http://library.bcu.ac.uk
Director of Library and Learning Resources Ms Judith Andrews MA DipLib MCLIP (e-mail: judith.andrews@bcu.ac.uk)

UNIVERSITY COLLEGE BIRMINGHAM

Library, University College Birmingham, Summer Row, Birmingham B3 1JB
☎0121 604 1000 (tel/fax)
url: www.ucb.ac.uk
Acting Head of Library Services Miss Deborah Findlay BA(Hons) MCLIP (e-mail: d.findlay@ucb.ac.uk)

Library, University College Birmingham, Richmond House, Newhall Street, Birmingham B3 1DB

☎0121 604 1000 (tel/fax)
Deputy Head of Library Services Miss Deborah Findlay BA(Hons) MCLIP
(e-mail: d.findlay@ucb.ac.uk)

UNIVERSITY OF BIRMINGHAM

Library Services, University of Birmingham, Main Library, Edgbaston, Birmingham B15 2TT
☎0121 414 5828 (enquiries)
Fax 0121 471 4691
url: www.library.bham.ac.uk
Director of Library Services Ms Diane Job MA DipLIS
Head of Academic Liaison & Collection Development Geoffrey Gilbert MA(Hons) MA
InfStu MSocSci Rec & Tourism
Head of Library Customer Support Ms Elizabeth Warner-Davies BSc DipLib
DipHECouns MBACP

Special Collections, University of Birmingham, Cadbury Research Library, Muirhead Tower,
Edgbaston, Birmingham B15 2TT
☎0121 414 5838
e-mail: special-collections@bham.ac.uk
Director of Special Collections Ms Susan Worrall MA(Hons) MArchAd

Site libraries

Barber Fine Art Library, University of Birmingham, Edgbaston, Birmingham B15 2TT
☎0121 414 7334
e-mail: fine-arts-library@bham.ac.uk
Manager Ms Jean Scott BA DipLib

Barber Music Library, University of Birmingham, Barber Institute of Fine Arts, Edgbaston,
Birmingham B15 2TT
☎0121 414 5852
e-mail: music-library@bham.ac.uk
Manager Ms Jean Scott BA DipLib

Barnes Library, University of Birmingham, Medical School, Vincent Drive, Edgbaston,
Birmingham B15 2TT
☎0121 414 3567
e-mail: ba-lib@bham.ac.uk
Manager Ms Jean Scott BA DipLib

Education Library, University of Birmingham, Edgbaston, Birmingham B15 2TT
☎0121 414 4869
e-mail: edlib@bham.ac.uk
Manager Ms Dorothy Vuong BSocSc PGDip

Harding Law Library, University of Birmingham, Law School, Edgbaston, Birmingham B15 2TT
☎0121 414 5865
e-mail: law-lib@bham.ac.uk
Manager Geoff Price MCLIP

Orchard Learning Resource Centre, University of Birmingham, Hamilton Drive, Weoley
Park Road, Selly Oak, Birmingham B29 6QW

☎0121 414 8454
e-mail: olrc@bham.ac.uk
Manager Ms Dorothy Vuong BSocSc PGDip

Ronald Cohen Dental Library, Birmingham Dental Hospital, University of Birmingham,
St Chad's Queensway, Birmingham B4 6NN
☎0121 237 2859
e-mail: dlib@bham.ac.uk
Manager Ms Jean Scott BA DipLib

Shakespeare Institute Library, University of Birmingham, Shakespeare Institute, Church
Street, Stratford upon Avon, Warwicks CV37 6HP
☎0121 414 9525
e-mail: silib@bham.ac.uk
Manager Geoff Price MCLIP

BISHOP GROSSETESTE UNIVERSITY COLLEGE LINCOLN

Sibthorp Library, Bishop Grosseteste University College Lincoln, Lincoln LNI 3DY
☎(01522) 583790
e-mail: library-enquiries@bishopg.ac.uk
url: www.bishopg.ac.uk
Director of Library and Knowledge Services Ms Emma Sansby BA(Hons) MA MCLIP
(01522 583793; e-mail: emma.sansby@bishopg.ac.uk)
Assistant Librarians Ms Nicola Perry BA(Hons) MA AMBCS (01522 583744; e-mail:
nicola.perry@bishopg.ac.uk), Mrs Janice Morris BA(Hons) DipLib MEd MCLIP (01522
583759; e-mail: j.m.morris@bishopg.ac.uk), Mrs Susan Rodda BA MSc(Econ) (01522
583759; e-mail: susan.rodda@bishopg.ac.uk), Ms Charlotte Everitt BA(Hons) DipLib
CertEd MCLIP (01522 583744; e-mail: charlotte.everitt@bishopg.ac.uk)

UNIVERSITY OF BOLTON

Library, University of Bolton, Deane Road, Bolton, Lancashire BL3 5AB
☎(01204) 903094 (enquiries), (01204) 903160 (administration)
Fax (01204) 903166
url: www.bolton.ac.uk/library/
Head of Library Patrick O'Reilly (01204 903160; e-mail: p.oreilly@bolton.ac.uk)
Library Manager Trevor Hodgson BSc(Hons) (01204 903160; e-mail:
t.hodgson@bolton.ac.uk)

BOURNEMOUTH UNIVERSITY

**The Sir Michael Cobham Library, Bournemouth University, Talbot Campus, Fern Barrow,
Poole, Dorset BHI2 5BB**
☎(01202) 965959 (enquiries), (01202) 965044 (administration)
Fax (01202) 965475
e-mail: libsupp@bournemouth.ac.uk
url: www.bournemouth.ac.uk/library
Head of Academic Development Services David Ball MA(Oxon) DipLib MLitt FCLIP
MCMI (e-mail: dball@bournemouth.ac.uk)

Site library

Bournemouth House Library, Bournemouth University, Bournemouth House,
19 Christchurch Road, Bournemouth BH1 3LG
☎(01202) 965959 (enquiries)
Fax (01202) 967298
User Services Manager Ms Jan Hutt (01202 967297)

UNIVERSITY OF BRADFORD

J B Priestley Library, University of Bradford, Bradford BD7 1DP
☎(01274) 233301
Fax (01274) 233398
e-mail: library@bradford.ac.uk
url: www.brad.ac.uk/lss/library/
Director of Learner Support Services Sara Marsh MA MCLIP (01274 233303;
e-mail: s.l.marsh@bradford.ac.uk)
Head of Library Services Ms Grace L Hudson

UNIVERSITY OF BRIGHTON

Information Services, University of Brighton, Cockcroft Building, Lewes Road, Brighton BN2 4GJ
☎(01273) 600900
Fax (01273) 642988
url: www.brighton.ac.uk/libraries
Director of Information Services Terry A Hanson BA DipLib
Assistant Director: Library Services Ms Cath Morgan BEd(Hons) PGDipIS MCLIP
(01273 642760)

Central/largest library

The Aldrich Library, University of Brighton, Cockcroft Building, Lewes Road, Brighton
BN2 4GJ
☎(01273) 642760
Fax (01273) 642988
e-mail: AskAldrich@brighton.ac.uk
Information Services Manager Steve Newman BA DipLib

Site libraries

Falmer Library, University of Brighton, Village Way, Falmer, Brighton BN1 9PH
☎(01273) 643569
Fax (01273) 643560
e-mail: AskFalmer@brighton.ac.uk
Information Services Manager Keith Baxter MBA

Health Sciences Library, University of Brighton, District General Hospital, King's Drive,
Eastbourne, West Sussex BN21 2UD
☎(01323) 417400 ext 4048
e-mail: AskDGH@brighton.ac.uk
Librarian-in-Charge Ms Sue Hardwick BA DipLib MCLIP

Queenwood Library, University of Brighton, Darley Road, Eastbourne, East Sussex
BN20 7UN
☎(01273) 643682
Fax (01273) 643825
e-mail: AskQueenwood@brighton.ac.uk
Information Services Manager Ms Lisa Redlinski BA MSc

St Peter's House Library, University of Brighton, 16-18 Richmond Place, Brighton BN2 8NA
☎(01273) 643221
Fax (01273) 607532
e-mail: AskSPH@brighton.ac.uk
Information Services Manager Mrs Louise Tucker BA

The Library, University of Brighton, University Centre Hastings, Havelock Road, Hastings,
East Sussex TN34 1BE
☎(01273) 644640
Fax (01273) 644627
e-mail: AskUCH@brighton.ac.uk
Information Services Manager Ms Sarah Friend PGDipIS MCLIP

UNIVERSITY OF BRISTOL

**Arts and Social Sciences Library, University of Bristol, Information Services, Tyndall
Avenue, Bristol BS8 1TJ**
☎0117 928 8000, 0117 928 8005 (administration)
Fax 0117 925 5334
e-mail: library-enquiries@bristol.ac.uk
url: www.bris.ac.uk/is
Director of Library Services Ms Cathryn Gallacher BA MSc DMS

Branch libraries

Biological Sciences Library, University of Bristol, Woodland Road, Bristol BS8 1UG
☎0117 928 7943

Chemistry Library, University of Bristol, School of Chemistry, Cantocks Close, Bristol
BS8 1TS
☎0117 928 7947

Dental Library, University of Bristol, Lower Maudlin Street, Bristol BS1 2LY
☎0117 342 4419

Education Library, University of Bristol, 35 Berkeley Square, Bristol BS8 1JA
☎0117 331 4231

Geography Library, University of Bristol, University Road, Bristol BS8 1SS
☎0117 928 8116

Medical Library, University of Bristol, Medical School, University Walk, Bristol BS8 1TD
☎0117 331 1501

Physics Library, University of Bristol, H. H. Wills Physics Laboratory, Tyndall Avenue, Bristol
BS8 1TL
☎0117 928 7960

Queen's Library (Engineering, Mathematics, Computer Science), University of Bristol, Queen's Building, University Walk, Bristol BS8 1TR
☎0117 331 5418

Veterinary Science Library, School of Veterinary Science, University of Bristol, Churchill Building, Langford, Bristol BS40 5DU
☎0117 928 9205

Wills Memorial Library (Law, Earth Sciences, EDC), University of Bristol, Wills Memorial Building, Queen's Road, Bristol BS8 1RJ
☎0117 954 5398

BRUNEL UNIVERSITY

Library, Brunel University, Middlesex UB8 3PH
☎(01895) 266154 (enquiries), (01895) 266177 (administration)
Fax (01895) 269741
e-mail: library@brunel.ac.uk
url: www.brunel.ac.uk/life/study/library
Acting Director of Library Services Mrs Ann Cummings BA MA

UNIVERSITY OF BUCKINGHAM

University Library, University of Buckingham, Hunter Street, Buckingham MK18 1EG
☎(01280) 814080
Fax (01280) 820312
e-mail: library@buckingham.ac.uk
url: www.buckingham.ac.uk

Site libraries

Franciscan Library, University of Buckingham, London Road, Buckingham MK18 1EG
☎(01280) 814080
Fax (01280) 828288
Librarian (Law and Science) Miss Louise Hammond BSc

Hunter Street Library, University of Buckingham, Hunter Street, Buckingham MK18 1EG
☎(01280) 814080
Fax (01280) 820312
Assistant Librarian (Business and Humanities) Mrs Kate Worrall BA MCLIP

BUCKINGHAMSHIRE NEW UNIVERSITY

Learning Resource Centre, Buckinghamshire New University, Queen Alexandra Road, High Wycombe, Bucks HP11 2JZ
☎(01494) 522141 ext 5107 (enquiries), ext 3270 (administration)
Fax (01494) 450774
e-mail: hwlib@bucks.ac.uk
url: www.bucks.ac.uk
Library Services Manager Ms Ursula Crow (ext 3292; e-mail: ursula.crow@bucks.ac.uk)

UNIVERSITY OF CAMBRIDGE

Cambridge University Library, University of Cambridge, West Road, Cambridge CB3 9DR
☎(01223) 333000
Fax (01223) 333160
e-mail: library@lib.cam.ac.uk
url: www.lib.cam.ac.uk
Librarian Mrs Anne Jarvis MA
Deputy Librarian Ms Sue Mehrer

Dependent libraries

Betty and Gordon Moore Library, University of Cambridge, Wilberforce Road, Cambridge
CB3 0WD
☎(01223) 765670
Fax (01223) 765678
e-mail: moore-library@lib.cam.ac.uk
url: www.lib.cam.ac.uk/bgml
Librarian Ms Yvonne Nobis

Central Science Library, University of Cambridge, Benet Street, Cambridge CB2 3PY
☎(01223) 334744
Fax (01223) 334748
e-mail: lib-csl-inquiries@lists.cam.ac.uk
url: www.lib.cam.ac.uk/csl
Librarian Ms Yvonne Nobis

Medical Library, University of Cambridge, Cambridge University Library, Addenbrooke's
Hospital, Hills Road, Cambridge CB2 0SP
☎(01223) 336750
Fax (01223) 331918
e-mail: library@medschl.cam.ac.uk
url: www.medschl.cam.ac.uk
Librarian Peter B Morgan MA MCLIP

Squire Law Library, University of Cambridge, 10 West Road, Cambridge CB3 9DZ
☎(01223) 330077
Fax (01223) 330057
Librarian David F Wills BA MCLIP (e-mail: dfw1003@cam.ac.uk)

College, Institute and Departmental

Cambridge Union Society
Keynes Library, Cambridge Union Society, 9(A) Bridge Street, Cambridge CB2 1UB
☎(01223) 741289
Fax (01223) 566444
e-mail: librarian@cus.org
url: www.cus.org
Librarian Ms Catherine Wise BA (e-mail: librarian@cus.org)
(Members only)

Christ's College
Library, Christ's College, St Andrew's Street, Cambridge CB2 3BU
☎(01223) 334950
Fax (01223) 334967
e-mail: library@christs.cam.ac.uk
url: www.christs.cam.ac.uk/collegelife/library
College Librarian Ms Nazlin Bhimani MA MLS MCLIP

Churchill College
Library, Churchill College, Storey's Way, Cambridge CB3 0DS
☎(01223) 336138
url: www.chu.cam.ac.uk/about/library
Librarian Ms Mary Kendall MA MCLIP (e-mail: librarian@chu.cam.ac.uk)
(NB The Library is available to College Members only)

Clare College
Fellows' Library, Clare College, Cambridge CB2 1TL
☎(01223) 333253/333202
Fax (01223) 765560
url: www.clare.cam.ac.uk/academic/libraries/fellows-library.html
Fellows' Librarian Dr Hubertus F Jahn PhD (e-mail: hfj21@cam.ac.uk)

Forbes Mellon Library, Clare College, Cambridge CB3 9AJ
☎(01223) 333202
Fax (01223) 765560
e-mail: library@clare.cam.ac.uk
url: www.clare.cam.ac.uk/academic/libraries/index.html
Librarian Mrs Anne C Hughes MA

Corpus Christi College
Parker Library, Corpus Christi College, Trumpington Street, Cambridge CB2 1RH
☎(01223) 338025
e-mail: parker-library@corpus.cam.ac.uk
url: www.corpus.cam.ac.uk
Librarian Dr Christopher de Hamel
Sub-Librarians Ms Gill Cannell (e-mail: gc110@cam.ac.uk), Dr Suzanne Paul

Taylor Library, Corpus Christi College, Trumpington Street, Cambridge CB2 1RH
☎(01223) 338052
Fax (01223) 338041
e-mail: butler.library@corpus.cam.ac.uk
url: www.corpus.cam.ac.uk
Taylor Librarian Ms Iwona Krasodomska-Jones (e-mail: ik205@cam.ac.uk)
Library Assistant Liam Austin (e-mail: lpba2@cam.ac.uk)

Darwin College
Library, Darwin College, Silver Street, Cambridge CB3 9EU
☎(01223) 763547
Fax (01223) 335667
e-mail: librarian@dar.cam.ac.uk
url: www.dar.cam.ac.uk

Fellow Librarian Dr Margaret Cone MPhil PhD ADR
Student Librarian Ms Lindsey Friedman

Department of Land Economy Library
Mill Lane Library, Department of Land Economy Library, 8 Mill Lane, Cambridge CB2 1RX
☎(01223) 337110
Fax (01223) 337130
url: www.landecon.cam.ac.uk/library/library.htm
Librarian Ms Wendy Thurley BA ALAA (e-mail: wt10000@cam.ac.uk)
(Mill Lane Library also houses the Centre of Latin American Studies and the Centre of International Studies)

Downing College
The Maitland Robinson Library, Downing College, Regent Street, Cambridge CB2 1DQ
☎(01223) 334829 (enquiries), (01223) 335352 (College Librarian), (01223) 334802
(Library Assistant)
url: www.dow.cam.ac.uk/dow_server/library/index.html
Fellow Librarian Dr Marcus Tomalin PhD
College Librarian Ms Karen Lubarr BA (e-mail: college-librarian@dow.cam.ac.uk)
Archivist Dr Kathryn Thompson (01223 762905; e-mail: archivist@dow.cam.ac.uk)

Emmanuel College
Library, Emmanuel College, Cambridge CB2 3AP
☎(01223) 334233
e-mail: library@emma.cam.ac.uk
url: www.emma.cam.ac.uk
Fellow Librarian Dr A S Bendall MCLIP
College Librarian Dr H C Carron BA MA MPhil PhD MCLIP
Assistant Librarian Mrs C E P Bonfield BA

Faculty of Asian and Middle Eastern Studies
Library, Faculty of Asian and Middle Eastern Studies (formerly Faculty of Oriental Studies),
Sidgwick Avenue, Cambridge CB3 9DA
☎(01223) 335112 (enquiries)
Fax (01223) 335110
e-mail: library@ames.cam.ac.uk
url: www.ames.cam.ac.uk/faclib
Librarian Ms Françoise Simmons MA(Cantab) MA(UCL) (01223 335111)

Faculty of Education
Library and Information Service, Faculty of Education, 184 Hills Road, Cambridge CB2 8PQ
☎(01223) 767700 (enquiries)
Fax (01223) 767602
e-mail: library@educ.cam.ac.uk
url: www.educ.cam.ac.uk/library
Librarian Ms Angela Cutts BA DipLib MCLIP
Deputy Librarian Ms Emma Jane Batchelor BA DipILS MCLIP

Faculty of Music
Pendlebury Library of Music, Faculty of Music, 11 West Road, Cambridge CB3 9DP

☎(01223) 335182
Fax (01223) 335067
url: www.mus.cam.ac.uk/pendlebury
Librarian Ms Anna Pensaert LIC

Fitzwilliam College
Library, Fitzwilliam College, Cambridge CB3 0DG
☎(01223) 332042
Fax (01223) 477976
e-mail: library@fitz.cam.ac.uk
url: www.fitz.cam.ac.uk
Librarian Ms Christine E Roberts Lewis BSc(Econ) CertEd (e-mail: cer34@cam.ac.uk)

Girton College
Library, Girton College, Cambridge CB3 0JG
☎(01223) 338970
Fax (01223) 339890
e-mail: library@girton.cam.ac.uk
url: www-lib.girton.cam.ac.uk
Fellow and Librarian Ms Frances Gandy BA MA MCLIP
Assistant Librarian Mrs Jenny Blackhurst MA MA MCLIP
Archivist Ms Hannah Westall MA(Hons) MA

Gonville and Caius College
Library, Gonville and Caius College, Cambridge CB2 1TA
☎(01223) 332419
e-mail: library@cai.cam.ac.uk
url: www.cai.cam.ac.uk/library
College Librarian M S Statham MA MCLIP
(Upper library open to members of the College only. Lower library open to scholars by appointment. All enquiries should be addressed to the College Librarian)

Homerton College
Library, Homerton College, Mary Allan Building, Hills Road, Cambridge CB2 8PH
☎(01223) 747259/747260
e-mail: library@homerton.cam.ac.uk
url: www.homerton.cam.ac.uk
College Librarian Miss Liz Osman BA(Hons) MA
(Library restricted to use by Homerton College members only. Visits to the library by appointment only)

Institute of Criminology
Radzinowicz Library of Criminology, Institute of Criminology, Sidgwick Avenue, Cambridge CB3 9DA
☎(01223) 335386
Fax (01223) 335356
e-mail: crimlib@hermes.cam.ac.uk
url: www.crim.cam.ac.uk/library
Librarian Mrs Mary Gower MCLIP
Senior Assistant Librarian Stuart Stone MPA BA

Jesus College

Quincentenary Library, Jesus College, Jesus Lane, Cambridge CB5 8BL
☎(01223) 339451
Fax (01223) 324910
e-mail: quincentenary-library@jesus.cam.ac.uk
url: www.jesus.cam.ac.uk/college/infservices/library.html
Quincentenary Librarian Ms Rhona Watson BA(Hons) DipLib MCLIP

The Old Library, Jesus College, Jesus Lane, Cambridge CB5 8BL
☎(01223) 339405
Keeper of the Old Library Prof Stephen Heath
Assistant to the Keeper and Archivist Dr Frances Willmoth (e-mail:
f.willmoth.jesus.cam.ac.uk)
(Apply in writing)

King's College Cambridge

Library, King's College Cambridge, Cambridge CB2 1ST
☎(01223) 331232
Fax (01223) 331891
e-mail: library@kings.cam.ac.uk
url: www.kings.cam.ac.uk/library/
Librarian Peter Jones

Lucy Cavendish College

Library, Lucy Cavendish College, Lady Margaret Road, Cambridge CB3 0BU
☎(01223) 332183
Fax (01223) 332178
e-mail: library@lucy-cav.cam.ac.uk
url: www.lucy-cav.cam.ac.uk
Librarian Ms Catherine Reid BSc MSc MCLIP
Assistant Librarian Ms Joan Harris BA
(The Library is open only to the members of the College)

Magdalene College

College Library, Magdalene College, Magdalene Street, Cambridge CB3 0AG
☎(01223) 332125
e-mail: library@magd.cam.ac.uk
url: www.magd.cam.ac.uk
College Librarian Dr S K F Stoddart MA PhD
Sub-Librarian Ms Phillipa Grimstone
(Open to College members only)

Old Library and College Archives, Magdalene College, Magdalene Street, Cambridge
CB3 0AG
☎(01223) 332125
e-mail: library@magd.cam.ac.uk
Keeper of the Old Library Dr Richard Luckett MA PhD
College Archivist Dr Ronald Hyam LittD
Sub-Librarian Ms Phillipa Grimstone
(Open to scholars by appointment only during term-time, plus July and August)

Pepys Library, Magdalene College, Magdalene Street, Cambridge CB3 0AG
☎(01223) 332125
e-mail: pepyslibrary@magd.cam.ac.uk
url: www.magd.cam.ac.uk/pepys/
Pepys Librarian Dr Richard Luckett MA PhD
Sub-Librarian Ms Phillipa Grimstone
(Open Mon–Sat Oct–Mar: term-time only, 2.30–3.30pm; Apr–Aug 11.30–12.30 and
2.30–3.30pm. Scholars by appointment in the open periods)

Murray Edwards College
Rosemary Murray Library, Murray Edwards College, New Hall, Huntingdon Road,
Cambridge CB3 0DF
☎(01223) 762202
Fax (01223) 763110
e-mail: library@newhall.cam.ac.uk
url: www.murrayedwards.cam.ac.uk/exploring/rosemarymurraylibrary/
rosemarymurraylibrary/
Librarian Ms Kirstie Preest BA DipILM MCLIP
(Admittance to New Hall members only; for special collections, please write to the Librarian)

Newnham College
Library, Newnham College, Sidgwick Avenue, Cambridge CB3 9DF
☎(01223) 335740/335739
url: www.newn.cam.ac.uk/aboutnewnham/library
Librarian Ms Deborah Hodder MA MCLIP (e-mail: librarian@newn.cam.ac.uk)

Pembroke College
Library, Pembroke College, Cambridge CB2 1RF
☎(01223) 338121
Fax (01223) 338163
e-mail: lib@pem.cam.ac.uk
url: www.pem.cam.ac.uk
Fellow Librarian Nick McBride
Librarian Ms Patricia Aske MA

Peterhouse
Ward and Perne Libraries, Peterhouse, Cambridge CB2 1RD
☎(01223) 338218 (Ward Library)
e-mail: lib@pet.cam.ac.uk
url: www.pet.cam.ac.uk
Ward Librarian M S Golding MA
Assistant Librarian Ms E A McDonald BA MA MCLIP
Library Assistant Mrs E Grayton
Perne Librarian S H Mandelbrote MA
(Perne library by appointment only)

Queens' College
Library, Queens' College, Silver Street, Cambridge CB3 9ET
☎(01223) 335549/50, Porter's Lodge (01223) 335500
Fax (01223) 335522

e-mail: library@queens.cam.ac.uk
url: www.queens.cam.ac.uk
College Librarian Mrs Karen E Begg MSc(Econ)
Assistant Librarian Mrs Miriam Leonard BSc(Econ)
Fellow Librarian Dr Ian Patterson

Robinson College
Library, Robinson College, Cambridge CB3 9AN
☎(01223) 339124
url: www.robinson.cam.ac.uk
College Librarian Miss Lesley Read MA BA MCLIP

St Catharine's College
Library, St Catharine's College, Cambridge CB2 1RL
☎(01223) 338343
Fax (01223) 338340
e-mail: librarian@caths.cam.ac.uk
url: www.caths.cam.ac.uk/library
Fellow Librarian Dr R S K Barnes
Librarian Colin Higgins BA(Hons) MPhil

St Edmund's College
Library, St Edmund's College, Mount Pleasant, Cambridge CB3 0BN
☎(01223) 336250 (switchboard)
Fax (01223) 762822
url: www.st-edmunds.cam.ac.uk/life/library
Fellow Librarian Dr Petà Dunstan MA PhD (e-mail: librarian@st-edmunds.cam.ac.uk)
Assistant Librarian Ms Susanne Jennings
(Please write in with enquiries)

St John's College
Library, St John's College, Cambridge CB2 1TP
☎(01223) 338661 (administration), (01223) 338662 (enquiries)
Fax (01223) 337035
e-mail: library@joh.cam.ac.uk
url: www.joh.cam.ac.uk/library
Librarian Dr Mark Nicholls MA PhD

Scott Polar Research Institute
Library, Scott Polar Research Institute, Lensfield Road, Cambridge CB2 1ER
☎(01223) 336552
Fax (01223) 336549
e-mail: library@spri.cam.ac.uk
url: www.spri.cam.ac.uk
Librarian Mrs Heather E Lane MA(Oxon) DipLiS MCLIP (e-mail: hel20@cam.ac.uk)

Selwyn College
Library, Selwyn College, Grange Road, Cambridge CB3 9DQ
☎(01223) 335880
e-mail: lib@sel.cam.ac.uk

url: www.sel.cam.ac.uk/library
College Librarian Mrs Sarah Stamford BA(Hons) MA
Assistant Librarian Michael P Wilson BA(Hons) MA

Sidney Sussex College
Library, Sidney Sussex College, Cambridge CB2 3HU
☎(01223) 338852
Fax (01223) 338884
e-mail: librarian@sid.cam.ac.uk
url: www.sid.cam.ac.uk/life/lib
Librarian Stewart Tiley BA(Hons) MA DipILM MCLIP (e-mail: sdt26@cam.ac.uk)

Section library
Archive and Muniment Room, Sidney Sussex College, Cambridge CB2 3HU
☎(01223) 338824
Fax (01223) 338884
e-mail: archivist@sid.cam.ac.uk
Archivist Nicholas J Rogers MA MLitt FSA (01223 338824; e-mail: njr1002@cam.ac.uk)

Trinity College
Library, Trinity College, Cambridge CB2 1TQ
☎(01223) 338488
Fax (01223) 338532
e-mail: trin-lib@lists.cam.ac.uk
url: www.trin.cam.ac.uk
Librarian Prof D J McKitterick FBA
(Undergraduate Library open to members of the College only. Wren Library: readers by appointment. Visitors: Mon–Fri 12–2pm; Sat 10.30–12.30, full term only)

Trinity Hall
Library, Trinity Hall, Trinity Lane, Cambridge CB2 1TJ
☎(01223) 332546
Fax (01223) 332537
e-mail: library@trinhall.cam.ac.uk
Director of Library Services Ms Dominique E Ruhlmann MA(Oxon) (e-mail: der1002@cam.ac.uk)
Deputy Librarian Ms Helen Murphy MA (e-mail: hem37@cam.ac.uk)

Wolfson College
The Lee Library, Wolfson College, Barton Road, Cambridge CB3 9BB
☎(01223) 335965 (direct), (01223) 335900 (Porters' Lodge)
Fax (01223) 335908
e-mail: library@wolfson.cam.ac.uk
url: www.wolfson.cam.ac.uk/library
Librarian Mrs Anna Jones

CANTERBURY CHRIST CHURCH UNIVERSITY

Library, Canterbury Christ Church University, North Holmes Road, Canterbury, Kent CT1 1QU

☎(01227) 782352 (enquiries)
e-mail: library.enquiries@canterbury.ac.uk
url: www.canterbury.ac.uk/library
Head of Library Services Pete Ryan BA(Hons) MCLIP (e-mail:
pete.ryan@canterbury.ac.uk)

Site libraries

Broadstairs Learning Centre, Canterbury Christ Church University, Northwood Road,
Broadstairs, Kent CT10 2WA
☎(01843) 609103
Fax (01843) 609130
e-mail: broadstairslc@canterbury.ac.uk
Learning Centre Manager Dennis Corn BSc (e-mail: dennis.corn@canterbury.ac.uk)

Salomons Hayloft Library, Canterbury Christ Church University, David Salomons Estate,
Broomhill Road, Southborough, Tunbridge Wells, Kent TN3 0TG
☎(01892 507516
Fax (01892 507501
e-mail: hayloft.library@canterbury.ac.uk
Librarian Ms Andrea Ford BA DipLib MCLIP (e-mail: andrea.ford@canterbury.ac.uk)

Salomons Mansion Library, Canterbury Christ Church University, David Salomons Estate,
Broomhill Road, Southborough, Tunbridge Wells, Kent TN3 0TG
☎(01892) 507717
Fax (01892) 507719
e-mail: mansion.library@canterbury.ac.uk
Site Librarian Mrs Kathy Chaney MCLIP (e-mail: kathy.chaney@canterbury.ac.uk)

St Augustine's Library, Canterbury Christ Church University, Burgate House, The Precincts,
Canterbury, Kent CT1 2EH
☎(01227) 865338

CARDIFF UNIVERSITY

Information Services, Cardiff University, 39-41 Park Place, Cardiff CF10 3BB
☎029 2087 4818
Fax 029 2037 1921
e-mail: library@cardiff.ac.uk
url: www.cardiff.ac.uk/insrv/libraries/index.html
Director of Information Services Martyn Harrow
Director of Libraries and University Librarian Mrs Janet Peters MA MLS MCLIP FHEA
FRSA (029 2087 9362)

Site libraries

Aberconway Library, Cardiff University, PO Box 430, Cardiff CF24 0DE
☎029 2087 4770
Fax 029 2087 6499
e-mail: abcyliby@cardiff.ac.uk
Library Manager Miss Sally Earney

Archie Cochrane Library, Education Centre, Cardiff University, University Hospital Llandough, Penarth, Cardiff CF64 2XX
☎029 2071 5497
Fax 029 2071 6497
e-mail: cochraneliby@cardiff.ac.uk
Hospitals Librarian Mrs Rosemary Soper

Architecture Library, Cardiff University, King Edward VII Avenue, Cardiff CF10 3NB
☎029 2087 5974
Fax 029 2087 4192
e-mail: archliby@cardiff.ac.uk
Site Librarian Bute, Architecture, Senghennydd. Subject Librarian – Mathematics Mrs Helen Staffer

Arts and Social Studies Library, Cardiff University, PO Box 430, Cardiff CF24 0DE
☎029 2087 4818
Fax 029 2037 1921
e-mail: asslliby@cardiff.ac.uk
Site Librarian ASSL. Law Service and Subject Librarian – History and Archaeology Duncan Montgomery

Biomedical Sciences Library, Cardiff University, PO Box 430, Cardiff CF24 0DE
☎029 2087 4090
e-mail: biomedliby@cardiff.ac.uk
Biomedical Scences and Science Librarian Mrs Linda Davies

Brian Cooke Dental Library, Cardiff University, 4th Floor, Dental School, Heath Park, Cardiff CF14 4XY
☎029 2074 2525
Fax 029 2074 3834
e-mail: dentliby@cardiff.ac.uk
Dental Librarian Ms Jan Hooper

Bute Library, Cardiff University, PO Box 430, Cardiff CF24 0DE
☎029 2087 4611
Fax 029 2087 4192
e-mail: buteliby@cardiff.ac.uk
Site Librarian Bute, Architecture, Senghennydd. Subject Librarian – Mathematics Mrs Helen Staffer

Cancer Research Wales Library, Cardiff University, Ground Floor, Cancer Research Wales Building, Velindre Hospital, Velindre Road, Whitchurch, Cardiff CF14 2TL
☎029 2031 6291
Fax 029 2031 6927
e-mail: crwlibrary@wales.nhs.uk
Library Manager Mrs Bernadette Coles

Law Library, Cardiff University, PO Box 430, Cardiff CF24 0DE
☎029 2087 4971
Fax 029 2037 1921
e-mail: lawliby@cardiff.ac.uk
Senior Subject Librarian – Law Dr Peter Clinch
Subject Librarian – Law Matthew Davies

Legal Practice Library, Cardiff University, PO Box 430, Cardiff CF24 0DE
☎029 2087 4942
e-mail: lpl@cardiff.ac.uk
Senior Consultant: Informaton Literacy. Subject Librarian – Law Mrs Cathie Jackson

Music Library, Cardiff University, PO Box 430, Cardiff CF24 0DE
☎029 2087 4387
e-mail: musicliby@cardiff.ac.uk
Subject Librarian – Music Ms Charity Dove

Nursing and Healthcare Studies Library, Cardiff University, 2nd Floor, Ty Dewi Sant, Heath Park, Cardiff CF14 4XN
☎029 2068 7713
Fax 029 2068 7715
e-mail: healthcliby@cardiff.ac.uk
Nursing and Healthcare Studies Librarian Ms Meg Gorman

School of Nursing and Midwifery Library, Cardiff University, Caerleon Education Centre, Grounds of St Cadoc's Hospital, Caerleon, Newport, Gwent NP18 3XR
☎(01633) 430919/436124
Fax (01633) 430717
e-mail: caerleonliby@cardiff.ac.uk
Site Librarian Mrs Angela Bowyer

Science Library, Cardiff University, PO Box 430, Cardiff CF24 0DE
☎029 2087 4085
Fax 029 2087 4995
e-mail: sciliby@cardiff.ac.uk
Biomedical Sciences and Science Librarian Mrs Linda Davies

Senghennydd Library, Cardiff University, PO Box 430, Cardiff CF24 0DE
☎029 2087 4158
e-mail: sengliby@cardiff.ac.uk
Site Librarian Bute, Architecture, Senghennydd. Subject Librarian   Mathematics Mrs Helen Staffer

Sir Herbert Duthie Library, Cardiff University, B2 Wales College of Medicine, Biology, Life and Health Sciences, Heath Park, Cardiff CF14 4XN
☎029 2074 2875
Fax 029 2074 3651
e-mail: duthieliby@cardiff.ac.uk
Medical Librarian Mrs Lindsay Roberts

Trevithick Library, Cardiff University, PO Box 430, Cardiff CF24 0DE
☎029 2087 4286
Fax 029 2087 4209
e-mail: trevliby@cardiff.ac.uk
Trevithick Librarian and Subject Librarian – Computer Sciences and Engineering Mrs Ruth Thornton

UNIVERSITY OF CENTRAL LANCASHIRE

Learning Information Service, University of Central Lancashire, Preston, Lancs PR1 2HE

☎(01772) 895355 (LIS Customer Support)
Fax (01772) 892991
e-mail: liscustomersupport@uclan.ac.uk
url: www.uclan.ac.uk
Director of Learning and Information Services Michael Ahern (01772 892351;
e-mail: mahern@uclan.ac.uk)
Head of Library and Training Services Jeremy Andrew BSc (01772 892264;
e-mail: jsandrew@uclan.ac.uk)
Head of Business Administration Ms Lisa Banks (01772 892674;
e-mail: lbanks2@uclan.ac.uk)
Head of Customer Services Craig Hickson (01772 892357;
e-mail: chickson1@uclan.ac.uk)
Head of Infrastructure Management Graham Lee (01772 892820;
e-mail: gjlee@uclan.ac.uk)

Site libraries

Blackburn Clinical Library, University of Central Lancashire, Learning Centre Library, Royal
Blackburn Hospital, Haslingden Road, Blackburn, Lancs BB2 3HH
☎(01254) 734312/3
Fax (01254) 733546
e-mail: lblackburn1@uclan.ac.uk

Blackpool Clinical Library, University of Central Lancashire, Health Professionals Education
Centre, Blackpool Victoria Hospital, Whinney Heys Road, Blackpool, Lancashire FY3 8NR
☎(01253) 303831
Fax (01253) 303818
e-mail: lblackpool1@uclan.ac.uk

Burnley Clinical Library, University of Central Lancashire, Burnley General Hospital
Education Centre, Casterton Avenue, Burnley, Lancs BB10 2PQ
☎(01282) 474699
Fax (01282) 838916
e-mail: lburnley@uclan.ac.uk

Burnley HE Library, University of Central Lancashire, Burnley Campus, Princess Way,
Burnley, Lancs BB12 0EQ
☎(01772) 895355
Librarian Ms Laura Bewick (01772 896086; e-mail: lfbewick@uclan.ac.uk)

Ormskirk Clinical Library, University of Central Lancashire, Learning Resource Centre,
Southport and Ormskirk District General Hospital, Wigan Road, Ormskirk, Lancs L39 2AZ
☎(01695) 656790
Fax (01695) 656235
e-mail: lormskirk@uclan.ac.uk

Wigan Clinical Library, University of Central Lancashire, Wigan Education Centre, Bernard
Surgeon Suite, RAE Infirmary, Wigan Lane, Wigan WN1 2NN
☎(01942) 822162
Fax (01942) 829583
e-mail: lwigan@uclan.ac.uk

CENTRAL SCHOOL OF SPEECH AND DRAMA

Library Services, Central School of Speech and Drama, Embassy Theatre, 64 Eton Avenue, London NW3 3HY
☎020 7559 3942 (enquiries)
Fax 020 7722 4132
e-mail: library@cssd.ac.uk
url: www.cssd.ac.uk
Head of Library Services Antony Loveland BA MA MCLIP (020 7559 3934; e-mail: antony.loveland@cssd.ac.uk)
Head of IT Services Ms Binta Adesida (020 7449 1590; e-mail: binta.adesida@cssd.ac.uk)
Collections and Services Manager Ms Diana Watt (e-mail: diana.watt@cssd.ac.uk)

UNIVERSITY OF CHESTER

Learning and Information Services, Seaborne Library, University of Chester, Parkgate Road, Chester CH1 4BJ
☎(01244) 511234 (enquiries); (01244) 511000 (switchboard)
e-mail: lis.helpdesk@chester.ac.uk
url: www.chester.ac.uk
Director of Learning and Information Services Brian Fitzpatrick BSc (01244 512025; e-mail: b.fitzpatrick@chester.ac.uk)
Deputy Director and Head of Learning Technology Henry Blackman BSc MBCS CITP MHEA (01244 513374; e-mail: h.blackman@chester.ac.uk)
Deputy Director (Health Libraries, Print and Desktop Services) Mrs Wendy Fiander BSc MA MCLIP FHEA (01244 511193; e-mail: w.fiander@chester.ac.uk)
Deputy Director (Academic and User Services) Mrs Angela Walsh BLib MA MCLIP (01244 513308; e-mail: a.walsh@chester.ac.uk)
Deputy Director (Warrington and Network Services) Nigel Williams MSc (01925 534211; e-mail: nigel.williams@chester.ac.uk)

Broomhead Library, University of Chester, Warrington Campus, Crab Lane, Warrington, Cheshire WA2 0DB
☎(01925) 534284
Fax (01925) 530001
Librarian Mrs Emma Walsh BA MCLIP (e-mail: e.walsh@chester.ac.uk)

Learning and Information Services, University of Chester, Riverside Building, Castle Drive, Chester CH1 1SL
☎(01244) 512345
e-mail: riverside.library@chester.ac.uk
Senior Librarian Ms Claire Norton
Site Librarian Ms Karen Spencer

Faculty of Health and Social Care Education Centre Libraries

Clatterbridge Library, University of Chester, Wirral Campus, Clatterbridge Hospital, Bebington, Wirral, Cheshire CH63 4JY
☎(01925) 534056
Librarian Ms Chris Holley MA (e-mail: c.holley@chester.ac.uk)

JET (Joint Education and Training) Library, University of Chester, Leighton Hospital, Middlewich Road, Crewe, Cheshire CWI 4QJ
☎(01270) 612538
Fax (01270) 252611
Librarian Ms Susan Smith (e-mail: susan.smith@chester.ac.uk)

UNIVERSITY OF CHICHESTER

Learning Resources Centre, University of Chichester, Bishop Otter Campus, College Lane, Chichester, West Sussex POI9 6PE
☎(01243) 816089
Fax (01243) 816096
e-mail: leo@chi.ac.uk
url: www.chi.ac.uk/info/LRC.cfm
Head of Library Services Ms Anna O'Neill (01243 816090; e-mail: a.oneill@chi.ac.uk)

Campus library

Library, University of Chichester, Bognor Regis Campus, Upper Bognor Road, Bognor Regis, West Sussex PO21 IHR
☎(01243) 812099
Fax (01243) 812081
Campus Librarian Ms Rosemary Noble MCLIP (01243 812082; e-mail: r.noble@chi.ac.uk)

CITY UNIVERSITY LONDON

University Library, City University London, Northampton Square, London ECIV OHB
☎020 7040 4061 (enquiries)
Fax 020 7040 8194
e-mail: library@city.ac.uk
url: www.city.ac.uk/library
Information Services Director Ms Maire Lanigan MSc PGDL
Senior Associate Director Ms Liz Harris BA(Hons) MCLIP

Site libraries

Learning Resource Centre, City University London, Cass Business School, 106 Bunhill Row, London ECIY 8TZ
☎020 7040 8787 (enquiries)
e-mail: cklib@city.ac.uk
url: www.cass.city.ac.uk/library
Head of LRC Ms Jacqui Gaul MA MCLIP

Library and Information Services, City University London, City Law School Library, 4 Gray's Inn Place, Gray's Inn, London WCIR 5DX
☎020 7400 3605 (enquiries)
e-mail: clslibrarygip@city.ac.uk
url: www.city.ac.uk/law
Associate Director Paul Banks BA(Hons) DipLib MCLIP

West Smithfield Site Library, City University London, School of Community and Health Sciences, 20 Bartholomew Close, London EC1A 7QN
☎020 7040 5759 (enquiries)
e-mail: schslibraries@city.ac.uk
url: www.city.ac.uk/library
Site Librarian Ms Clare Dowsett

Whitechapel Library, City University London, School of Community and Health Sciences, Philpot Street, London E1 2EA
☎020 7040 5859 (enquiries)
e-mail: schslibraries@city.ac.uk
url: www.city.ac.uk/library

COVENTRY UNIVERSITY

Lanchester Library, Coventry University, Frederick Lanchester Building, Gosford Street, Coventry CV1 5DD
☎024 7688 7575 (enquiries); 024 7688 7515 (administration)
Fax 024 7688 7525
url: www.coventry.ac.uk
University Librarian Ms Caroline Rock BA(Hons) MA MCLIP (e-mail: c.rock@coventry.ac.uk)

CRANFIELD UNIVERSITY

Kings Norton Library, Cranfield University, Cranfield, Beds MK43 0AL
☎(01234) 754444 (general enquiries)
Fax (01234) 752391
e-mail: library@cranfield.ac.uk
url: www.cranfield.ac.uk/library/
University Librarian Dr Hazel Woodward PhD BA MCLIP (e-mail: hazel.woodward@cranfield.ac.uk)

Other libraries

Barrington Library, Defence Academy of Management and Technology, Cranfield University, Shrivenham, Swindon SN6 8LA
☎(01793) 785743 (general enquiries)
Fax (01793) 785555
e-mail: library.barrington@cranfield.ac.uk
url: http://diglib.shrivenham.cranfield.ac.uk
Head of Barrington Library Mrs Lesley Castens LLB(Hons)

Management Information Resource Centre, Cranfield University, Cranfield, Beds MK43 0AL
☎(01234) 754440
Fax (01234) 751806
Head of Information Services John Harrington BA(Hons) MA DipLib MCLIP (e-mail: j.harrington@cranfield.ac.uk)

UNIVERSITY FOR THE CREATIVE ARTS

(formerly University for the Creative Arts at Canterbury, Epsom, Farnham, Maidstone and Rochester)

Director of Academic Services Ms Vanessa Crane MBA MCLIP (based at Maidstone)
Head of Library and Learning Services Ms Rosemary Lynch MA MCLIP (based at Farnham)

Campus libraries

University Library, University for the Creative Arts, Canterbury Campus, New Dover Road, Canterbury, Kent CT1 3AN
☎(01227) 817302
url: www.community.ucreative.ac.uk/library
Library Manager Ms Jane Bryder BA(Hons) DipLIM MCLIP (e-mail: jbryder@ucreative.ac.uk)

University Library, University for the Creative Arts, Epsom Campus, Ashley Road, Epsom, Surrey KT18 5BE
☎(01372) 202461
url: www.community.ucreative.ac.uk/library
Library and Learning Services Customer Services Manager, Library Manager Mrs Christina Lewis BSc PGDip MCLIP (e-mail: clewis3@ucreative.ac.uk)

University Library, University for the Creative Arts, Farnham Campus, Falkner Road, Farnham, Surrey GU9 7DS
☎(01252) 892709
url: www.community.ucreative.ac.uk/library
Head of Library and Learning Services, University Librarian Ms Rosemary Lynch MA MCLIP (e-mail: rlynch@ucreative.ac.uk)
Library Manager Simon Harper (e-mail: sharper2@ucreative.ac.uk)

University Library, University for the Creative Arts, Maidstone Campus, Oakwood Park, Maidstone, Kent ME16 8AG
☎(01622) 620000 (switchboard), (01622) 620120 (library)
Fax (01622) 621100
e-mail: librarymaid@ucreative.ac.uk
url: www.community.ucreative.ac.uk/library
Director of Academic Services Ms Vanessa Crane MBA MCLIP
Planning, Communications and Projects Manager/Library and Learning Centre Manager Nicholas Ross MSc MCLIP (e-mail: nross@ucreative.ac.uk)

University Library, University for the Creative Arts, Rochester Campus, Fort Pitt, Rochester, Kent ME1 1DZ
☎(01634) 888729
url: www.community.ucreative.ac.uk/library
Library Manager Ian Badger BA PGDip MCLIP (e-mail: ibadger@ucreative.ac.uk)

UNIVERSITY OF CUMBRIA

Harold Bridges Library, University of Cumbria, Bowerham Road, Lancaster LA1 3JD
☎(01524) 384238
Fax (01524) 384588

url: www.cumbria.ac.uk/liss
Head of Learning, Information and Student Services Ms Margaret Weaver BA MSc
MCLIP FHEA (01524 384238; e-mail: margaret.weaver@cumbria.ac.uk)

Campus libraries

Charlotte Mason Library, University of Cumbria, Rydal Road, Ambleside, Cumbria LA22 9BB
☎(01539) 430274
Fax (01539) 430371
e-mail: LibAmb@cumbria.ac.uk
Learning Centres Manager Ms Lisa Toner BA DipLib MCLIP (01539 430244; e-mail:
lisa.toner@cumbria.ac.uk)

Harold Bridges Library, University of Cumbria, Bowerham Road, Lancaster LA1 3JD
☎(01524) 374542
Fax (01524) 384588
e-mail: LibLan@cumbria.ac.uk
Learning Centres Manager Ms Lisa Toner BA DipLib MCLIP (01524 384682; e-mail:
lisa.toner@cumbria.ac.uk)

Library, University of Cumbria, Fusehill Street, Carlisle CA1 2HG
☎(01228) 626218
Fax (01228) 616263
e-mail: LibcarFS@cumbria.ac.uk
Learning Centres Manager Ms Clare Daniel BA MA MCLIP (01228 616219; e-mail:
clare.daniel@cumbria.ac.uk)

Library, University of Cumbria, Newton Rigg, Penrith, Cumbria CA11 0AH
☎(01768) 893503
Fax (01768) 893506
e-mail: LibPen@cumbria.ac.uk
Learning Centres Manager Ms Clare Daniel BA MA MCLIP (01768 893503; e-mail:
clare.daniel@cumbria.ac.uk)

DE MONTFORT UNIVERSITY

Kimberlin Library, De Montfort University, The Gateway, Leicester LE1 9BH
☎0116 257 7165
Fax 0116 257 7046
url: www.library.dmu.ac.uk
Director of Library Services Ms Kathryn Arnold BA(Hons) DipLib MCLIP (e-mail:
karnold@dmu.ac.uk)
Head of Academic Services Ms Jo Webb MA MLib MBA MCLIP ILTM FRSA (e-mail:
jwebb@dmu.ac.uk)
Head of Public Services Richard Partridge BA(Hons) PGDipLIS (e-mail:
rpartridge@dmu.ac.uk)
Head of Technical Services Alan Brine BA MSc PhD MCLIP (e-mail: abrine@dmu.ac.uk)
Head of Staffing and Quality Enhancement Ms Jane Mortimer BA(Hons) PGDipLib
DMS PGDipHRM MCLIP AHEA

Campus library

Charles Frears Campus Library, De Montfort University, 266 London Road, Leicester
LE2 1RQ
☎0116 270 0661
Fax 0116 270 9722
Campus Librarian Ms Linda Harrison

UNIVERSITY OF DERBY

**Learning Enhancement and Innovation, University of Derby, Kedleston Road, Derby
DE22 1GB**
☎(01332) 591207 (enquiries); (01332) 591205 (administration)
Fax (01332) 622767
e-mail: enquirydesk@derby.ac.uk
url: https://ulib.derby.ac.uk/library/homelib.php
Dean of Learning Enhancement and Innovation Dr Ruth Ayres
University Librarian Richard Finch MA DipLib DMS MCLIP (e-mail:
r.j.finch@derby.ac.uk)
Head of Centre for Learner Support Ms Pat Johnson MCLIP (e-mail:
p.a.johnson@derby.ac.uk)

Campus library

Devonshire Learning Resource Centre, University of Derby, University of Derby Buxton,
Buxton, Derbyshire SK17 6RY
☎(01332) 594673
Manager/Librarian Ms Maria Carnegie (e-mail: m.a.carnegie@derby.ac.uk)

UNIVERSITY OF DUNDEE

Library and Learning Centre, University of Dundee, Small's Wynd, Dundee DD1 4HN
☎(01382) 384087 (enquiries), (01382) 384084 (administration)
Fax (01382) 386228
e-mail: library@dundee.ac.uk
url: www.dundee.ac.uk/library
Librarian Dr Richard Parsons MSc PhD

Site libraries

Book and Paper Conservation Studio, University of Dundee, Small's Wynd, Dundee DD1 4HN
☎(01382) 384094
Fax (01382) 385614
e-mail: conservation@dundee.ac.uk
Senior Conservators Ms Vanessa Charles BA(Hons), Ms Philippa Sterlini BA(Hons)

Duncan of Jordanstone College Library, University of Dundee, Matthew Building,
13 Perth Road, Dundee DD1 4HT
☎(01382) 385255 (enquiries)
Fax (01382) 229283
e-mail: doj-library@dundee.ac.uk
College Librarian Ms Marie Simmons BA MCLIP

Law Library, University of Dundee, Scrymgeour Building, Park Place, Dundee DD1 4HN
☎(01382) 384100
Fax (01382) 381019
e-mail: law-library@dundee.ac.uk
Librarian Iain Gillespie

Ninewells Medical and Nursing Library, University of Dundee, Ninewells Hospital and
Medical School, Dundee DD1 9SY
☎(01382) 632519
Fax (01382) 556179
e-mail: ninewells-library@dundee.ac.uk
Librarian Dr Andrew Jackson BA(Hons) MCLIP

School of Nursing and Midwifery Library - Kirkcaldy, University of Dundee, Fife School of
Nursing and Midwifery, Forth Avenue, Kirkcaldy, Fife KY2 5YS
☎(01382) 385930
Fax (01382) 385931
e-mail: snm-fife-library@dundee.ac.uk
Librarian Dr Andrew Jackson BA(Hons) MCLIP

DURHAM UNIVERSITY

University Library, Durham University, Stockton Road, Durham DH1 3LY
☎0191 334 2968
Fax 0191 334 2971
e-mail: main.library@durham.ac.uk
url: www.dur.ac.uk/library
Librarian Jon Purcell BA(Hons) MBA DMS DipLib MCLIP

Departmental libraries

Durham Business School Library, Durham University, Mill Hill Lane, Durham DH1 3LB
☎0191 334 5213
Fax 0191 334 5201
Academic Support Liaison Librarian Colin Theakston BA MPhil

Education Library, Durham University, Leazes Road, Durham DH1 1TA
☎0191 334 8137
Fax 0191 334 8311
Site Supervisor Mrs Susan McBreen

Palace Green Library, Durham University, Law, Music, Archives & Special Collections,
Palace Green, Durham DH1 3RN
☎0191 334 2932
Fax 0191 334 2942
Head of Heritage Collections Dr Sheila M Hingley BA MA PhD MCLIP
Site Supervisor Mrs Anne E Farrow MA MCLIP

Queen's Campus Library, Durham University, Queen's Campus Section, University
Boulevard, Stockton-on-Tees, Co Durham TS17 6BH
☎0191 334 0270
Fax 0191 334 0271

e-mail: stockton.library@durham.ac.uk
Queen's Campus Library Manager Ms Jane A Hodgson

UNIVERSITY OF EAST ANGLIA

Library, University of East Anglia, Norwich NR4 7TJ
☎(01603) 592421 (enquiries), (01603) 592407 (administration)
Fax (01603) 591010
e-mail: library@uea.ac.uk
url: www.lib.uea.ac.uk
Library Director Nicholas Lewis BA PGCE MA (e-mail: nicholas.lewis@uea.ac.uk)
Head of Library Academic Services Andrew Barker BA PGDipILM MCLIP (01603 592430; e-mail: andrew.barker@uea.ac.uk)
Head of User Services Mrs Heather Wells BSc MSc MCLIP (01603 593440; e-mail: heather.wells@uea.ac.uk)
Faculty Librarian (Social Sciences) Ms Ellen Paterson BA MSc (e-mail: ellen.paterson@uea.ac.uk)
Faculty Librarian (Sciences) Dr Elizabeth Clarke BSc PhD (01603 591249; e-mail: e.clarke@uea.ac.uk)
Faculty Librarian (Arts and Humanities) Ms Sarah Elsegood BSc MCLIP ILTM
Faculty Librarian (Sciences) Ms Rachel Henderson (01603 592428; e-mail: rachel.henderson@uea.ac.uk)
Faculty Librarian (Health) William Jones BSc DipLib MCLIP (01603 592412; e-mail: w.jones@uea.ac.uk)
Information Policy Officer David Palmer BA LLB MLS (01603 593523; e-mail: david.palmer@uea.ac.uk)
Systems Librarian Alan Exelby BA DipLib (01603 592432; e-mail: a.exelby@uea.ac.uk)
Technical Services Librarian Mrs Anne Baker BA MCLIP (01603 592429; e-mail: a.b.baker@uea.ac.uk)
User Services Points Manager Ms Catherine Baker BA (01603 593507; e-mail: catherine.baker@uea.ac.uk)
Information Skills Librarian Ms Jane Helgesen BA MA MCLIP (01603 592221; e-mail: j.helgesen@uea.ac.uk)

UNIVERSITY OF EAST LONDON

Library and Learning Services, University of East London, 4–6 University Way, London E16 2RD
☎020 8223 3434 (enquiries), 020 8223 2619 (administration)
Fax 020 8223 2804
url: www.uel.ac.uk/lls
Director of Library and Learning Services Prof Andrew McDonald FCLIP (020 8223 2620; e-mail: a.mcdonald@uel.ac.uk)
Associate Director, Services Ms Cathy Walsh MA PGDipLib (020 8223 6460; e-mail: c.walsh@uel.ac.uk)
Associate Director, Systems Ms Gurdish Sandhu BSc PGDip MSc MBA MCLIP (020 8223 6463; e-mail: g.sandhu@uel.ac.uk)
Academic Liaison and Skills Manager Ms Simone Okolo (020 8223 2666; e-mail: s.n.okolo@uel.ac.uk)

Collection Development Manager Ms Libby Homer (020 8223 6467; e-mail: l.homer@uel.ac.uk)
Systems Manager Nick Jarrett (020 8223 2615; e-mail: n.p.jarrett@uel.ac.uk)

Campus library and learning centres

Docklands Library and Learning Centre, University of East London, 4–6 University Way, London E16 2RD
☎020 8223 3434 (enquiries)
Campus Library and Learning Centre Manager Ms Judith Preece BA MCLIP (e-mail: j.a.preece@uel.ac.uk)

Duncan House Library and Learning Centre, University of East London, High Street, Stratford, London E15 2JA
☎020 8223 3346 (enquiries)
Site Library and Learning Centre Manager Ms Maureen Azubike BA MCLIP (e-mail: m.azubike.uel.ac.uk)

Stratford Library and Learning Centre, University of East London, University House, Romford Road, Stratford, London E15 4LZ
☎020 8223 4224 (enquiries)
Campus Library and Learning Centre Manager Paul Chopra MA PGDipLib MCLIP (e-mail: p.chopra@uel.ac.uk)

EDGE HILL UNIVERSITY

Learning Services, Edge Hill University, St Helens Road, Ormskirk, Lancs L39 4QP
☎(01695) 584286 (enquiries), (01695) 584284 (administration)
Fax (01695) 584592
e-mail: lshelpdesk@edgehill.ac.uk
url: www.edgehill.ac.uk/ls/
Dean of Learning Services Ms Alison Mackenzie (01695 584284; e-mail: alison.mackenzie@edgehill.ac.uk)
Academic Support Manager Ms Dawn McLoughlin (01695 584518; e-mail: mcloughd@edgehill.ac.uk)
Assistant Head of Learning Services Ms Maria Mirza (01695 584334; e-mail: maria.mirza@edgehill.ac.uk)

Site libraries

Learning Services, Edge Hill University, Woodlands Campus, Southport Road, Chorley, Lancs PR7 1QR
☎(01257) 517136
LRC Manager Ms Ruth Wilson BA DipLib MCLIP (01257 517137; e-mail: wilsonr@edgehill.ac.uk)

The Library and Information Resource Centre, Edge Hill University, Clinical Sciences Centre, University Hospital Aintree, Longmoor Lane, Liverpool L9 7AL
☎0151 529 5851
LIRC Manager Ms Rachel Bury BA(Hons) MCLIP (0151 529 5857; e-mail: buryr@edgehill.ac.uk)

EDINBURGH COLLEGE OF ART

Library, Edinburgh College of Art, Evolution House, 78 West Port, Edinburgh EHI 2LE
☎0131 221 6180
Fax 0131 221 6293
url: www.lib.eca.ac.uk
Reader Services Librarian/Art & Design Librarian Ms Jane Furness
Technical Services Librarian Gordon Andrew

EDINBURGH NAPIER UNIVERSITY

Craiglockhart Campus Library, Edinburgh Napier University, Craiglockhart Campus, Edinburgh EHI4 IDJ
☎0131 455 4260
Fax 0131 455 4276
url: www.napier.ac.uk/
Director of Learning Information Services Chris Pinder BA MLib DipLib FCLIP (0131 455 4270)
Head of Customer Services and Deputy Director Ms Margaret Lobban MA MSc DipLib DipEdTech MCLIP (0131 455 4272)
Head of Information Services Malcolm Jones BA DipLib MCLIP (0131 455 2693)

Campus libraries

Canaan Lane Library, Edinburgh Napier University, Canaan Lane Campus, Edinburgh EH9 2TB
☎0131 455 5616
Fax 0131 455 5608

Comely Bank Library, Edinburgh Napier University, Comely Bank Campus, Edinburgh EH4 2LD
☎0131 455 5319
Fax 0131 455 5358

Craighouse Library, Edinburgh Napier University, Craighouse Campus, Edinburgh EH10 5LG
☎0131 455 6020
Fax 0131 455 6022

Livingston Library, Edinburgh Napier University, Livingston Campus, West Lothian EH54 6PP
☎(01506) 523966
Fax (01506) 523969

Melrose Library, Edinburgh Napier University, Melrose Campus, Melrose, Scottish Borders TD6 9BS
☎(01896) 661632
Fax (01896) 823869

Merchiston Library, Edinburgh Napier University, Merchiston Campus, Edinburgh EH10 5DT
☎0131 455 2582
Fax 0131 455 2377

UNIVERSITY OF EDINBURGH

Library, University of Edinburgh, George Square, Edinburgh EH8 9LJ
☎0131 650 3409 (Access and Lending Services); 0131 650 8379 (Special Collections)
Fax 0131 651 5041
e-mail: library@ed.ac.uk; libref@ed.ac.uk; eishelp@ed.ac.uk; is.helpdesk@ed.ac.uk
url: Library Online: www.lib.ed.ac.uk/
Director of Library Services Mrs Sheila E Cannell MA MCLIP (e-mail:
s.cannell@ed.ac.uk)

Site libraries

Law & Europa Library, University of Edinburgh, Old College, South Bridge, Edinburgh
EH8 9YL
☎0131 650 2044
Site and Services Supervisor Ms Frances Fullarton (e-mail: f.fullarton@ed.ac.uk)

Medical Libraries, University of Edinburgh, George Square, Edinburgh EH8 9LJ
☎0131 537 2299
Site and Services Supervisor Ms Claire Leach BSc(Hons) PGDipLib (e-mail:
claire.leach@ed.ac.uk)
(Sites also at Western General Hospital, Crewe Road South, Edinburgh EH4 2XU and
Royal Infirmary Library, Chancellor's Building, 49 Little France Crescent, Edinburgh
EH6 4SB)

Moray House Library (Education), University of Edinburgh, Dalhousie Land, St John Street,
Edinburgh EH8 8AQ
☎0131 651 6193
Fax 0131 557 3458
Site and Services Supervisor David Fairgrieve MA DipLib MCLIP (e-mail:
david.fairgrieve@ed.ac.uk)

New College Library (Divinity), University of Edinburgh, Mound Place, Edinburgh EH1 2LU
☎0131 650 8957
Fax 0131 650 7952
Site and Services Supervisor Ms Sheila Dunn BA (e-mail: s.dunn@ed.ac.uk)

Science Libraries, University of Edinburgh, 2 King's Buildings, West Mains Road, Edinburgh
EH9 3JF
☎0131 650 5666
Fax 0131 650 6702
Site and Services Supervisor Ms Judy Melville BA(Hons) (e-mail:
judith.melville@ed.ac.uk)

Veterinary Libraries, University of Edinburgh, Summerhall, Edinburgh EH9 1QH
☎0131 650 6175
Fax 0131 650 6593
Site and Services Supervisor Ms Claire Leach BSc(Hons) PGDipLib (e-mail:
claire.leach@ed.ac.uk)
(Sites also at Easter Bush, Roslin, Midlothian EH25 9RG and Roslin Institute, Roslin
Biocentre, Midlothian EH25 9PS)

UNIVERSITY OF ESSEX

The Albert Sloman Library, University of Essex, Wivenhoe Park, Colchester, Essex CO4 3SQ
☎(01206) 873188
Fax (01206) 872289
url: www.essex.ac.uk
Librarian Robert Butler MSc

UNIVERSITY OF EXETER

University Library, University of Exeter, Stocker Road, Exeter, Devon EX4 4PT
☎(01392) 263867 (enquiries)
Fax (01392) 263871
e-mail: library@exeter.ac.uk
url: www.exeter.ac.uk/library/
Director of Academic Services Ms Michele Shoebridge MA

Departmental libraries

Law Library, University of Exeter, Amory Building, Rennes Drive, Exeter, Devon EX4 4RJ
☎(01392) 263356

Old Library, University of Exeter, Prince of Wales Road, Exeter, Devon EX4 4PT
☎(01392) 264052

St Luke's Campus Library, University of Exeter, Exeter, Devon EX1 2LU
☎(01392) 264785

Arab World Documentation Unit, University of Exeter, IAIS Building, Stocker Road, Exeter, Devon EX4 4ND
☎(01392) 264041

UNIVERSITY COLLEGE FALMOUTH

Learning Resources Centre, University College Falmouth, Tremough Campus, Treliever Road, Penryn, Cornwall TR10 9EZ
☎(01326) 370441
Fax (01326) 370437
e-mail: library@falmouth.ac.uk
url: www.falmouth.ac.uk
Head of Library and Information Services Ms Doreen Pinfold BA(Hons) PGDipLib MCLIP (e-mail: doreen.pinfold@falmouth.ac.uk)
Visual Resources Librarian Ms Rebecca Ball BA(Hons) PGDipLib (e-mail: rebeccab@falmouth.ac.uk)
User Services Librarian Ms Ellen Buck BA(Hons) MA MCLIP (e-mail: ellen.buck@falmouth.ac.uk)
Systems Librarian Steve Pellow BA(Hons) PGCE (e-mail: stevep@falmouth.ac.uk)
Technical Services Librarian Stephen Atkinson BSc DipLib MCLIP (e-mail: stephena@falmouth.ac.uk)

(Tremough Campus LRC also serves University of Exeter in Cornwall)

Library and Information Services, University College Falmouth, Woodlane Campus Library, Falmouth, Cornwall TR11 4RA
☎(01326) 213815
Fax (01326) 211205
e-mail: library@falmouth.ac.uk
url: www.falmouth.ac.uk
Art and Design Librarian Ms Dawn Lawrence (e-mail: dawn.lawrence@falmouth.ac.uk)
Campus Librarian Ms Rosalind Tyley MA (e-mail: rosalind.tyley@falmouth.ac.uk), Alan Doherty (e-mail: alan.doherty@falmouth.ac.uk) (job share)

UNIVERSITY OF GLAMORGAN

Learning Resources Centre, University of Glamorgan, Pontypridd, Rhondda Cynon Taf CF37 IDL
☎(01443) 482625 (enquiries)
Fax (01443) 482629
e-mail: lrcenq@glam.ac.uk
url: www.glam.ac.uk/lrc
Director of Learning and Corporate Support Services Jeremy Atkinson BSc MPhil DipLib MCLIP
Head of Learning Resources Steve Morgan BA MEd MBA FCLIP

GLASGOW CALEDONIAN UNIVERSITY

University Library Services, Saltire Centre, Glasgow Caledonian University, Cowcaddens Road, Glasgow G4 0BA
☎0141 273 1000
Fax 0141 273 1183
e-mail: library@gcu.ac.uk
url: www.gcu.ac.uk/library
Director, Library Services Ms Debbi Boden MA BA(Hons) FCLIP FHEA

GLASGOW SCHOOL OF ART

Library, Glasgow School of Art, 167 Renfrew Street, Glasgow G3 6RQ
☎0141 353 4551
Fax 0141 353 4670
url: www2.gsa.ac.uk/library
Head of Learning Resources Ms Catherine Nicholson MA DipLib MCLIP
(e-mail: c.nicholson@gsa.ac.uk)

UNIVERSITY OF GLASGOW

Library, University of Glasgow, Hillhead Street, Glasgow G12 8QE
☎0141 330 6704/5 (enquiries), 0141 330 5634 (administration)
Fax 0141 330 4952
e-mail: library@lib.gla.ac.uk
url: www.lib.gla.ac.uk
University Librarian Ms Helen Durndell MA PGDipLib

Site/departmental libraries

Adam Smith Library, University of Glasgow, Adam Smith Building, Bute Gardens, Hillhead,
Glasgow G12 8RT
☎0141 330 5648
Librarian Kerr Ross

Chemistry Branch, University of Glasgow, Joseph Black Building, Glasgow G12 8QQ
☎0141 330 5502
e-mail: library@lib.gla.ac.uk
Librarian Mrs Denise Currie

James Herriot Library, University of Glasgow, Veterinary School, Garscube Estate,
Bearsden, Glasgow G61 1QH
☎0141 330 5708
e-mail: vetlib@lib.gla.ac.uk
Librarian Mrs Maureen McGovern

James Ireland Memorial Library, University of Glasgow, Dental School and Hospital,
Sauchiehall Street, Glasgow G2 3JZ
☎0141 211 9705
e-mail: library@dental.gla.ac.uk
Librarian Ms Beverley Rankin

UNIVERSITY OF GLOUCESTERSHIRE

**Learning and Information Services, University of Gloucestershire, The Park Campus,
Cheltenham, Glos GL50 2RH**
☎(01242) 714333 (enquiries), (01242) 715442 (administration)
e-mail: lcinfopark@glos.ac.uk
url: www.glos.ac.uk
LIS Transition Manager Scott Jordan BA

Site libraries

Francis Close Hall Learning Centre, University of Gloucestershire, Swindon Road,
Cheltenham, Glos GL50 4AZ
☎(01242) 714600
e-mail: lcinfofch@glos.ac.uk
Learning Centre Manager Ms Sarah Kennedy

Oxstalls Learning Centre, University of Gloucestershire, Oxstalls Lane, Longlevens,
Gloucester GL2 9HW
☎(01242) 175100
e-mail: lcinfoox@glos.ac.uk
Learning Centre Manager Mrs Carole Wrightson BA FHEA MCLIP

Park Learning Centre, University of Gloucestershire, The Park Campus, Cheltenham, Glos
GL50 2RH
☎(01242) 714333
e-mail: lcinfopark@glos.ac.uk
Learning Centre Manager Scott Jordan BA

Pittville Learning Centre, University of Gloucestershire, Albert Road, Cheltenham, Glos GL52 3JG
☎(01242) 714900
e-mail: lcinfopitt@glos.ac.uk
Learning Centre Manager Vacant

GLYNDŴR UNIVERSITY

Library, Glyndŵr University, Plas Coch, Mold Road, Wrexham LL11 2AW
☎(01978) 293250
Fax (01978) 293435
url: www.glyndwr.ac.uk
University Librarian Paul Jeorrett BA MCLIP PGDip (e-mail: p.jeorrett@glyndwr.ac.uk)
Academic Liaison Co-ordinator Nicola Watkinson BSc MCLIP FHEA (e-mail: nicolaw@glyndwr.co.uk)

UNIVERSITY OF GREENWICH

Greenwich Campus Library, University of Greenwich, Old Royal Naval College, Park Row, Greenwich, London SE10 9LS
☎020 8331 8000
url: www.gre.ac.uk/lib
Director of Information and Library Services Ms Maureen E Castens BSc MA MCLIP DMS (020 8331 8160; e-mail: m.castens@gre.ac.uk)
Head of Learning Services Ms Ann Murphy BA DipLib (020 8331 8196; e-mail: a.e.murphy@gre.ac.uk)

Campus libraries

Avery Hill Campus Library, University of Greenwich, Bexley Road, London SE9 2PQ
☎020 8331 8484
Fax 020 8331 9659
Campus Librarian Ms Rosemary Moon BA DipLib (e-mail: r.m.moon@gre.ac.uk)

Dreadnought Library, University of Greenwich, Greenwich Campus, Old Royal Naval College, Park Row, Greenwich, London SE10 9LS
☎020 8331 7788
Fax 020 8331 7775
Campus Librarian Ms Teri Harland BSc MCLIP (e-mail: c.m.harland@gre.ac.uk)

Drill Hall Library, University of Greenwich, North Road, Chatham Maritime, Kent ME4 4TB
☎(01634) 883278
Fax (01634) 883567
Drill Hall Library Manager Ms Virginia Malone (e-mail: v.g.malone@gre.ac.uk)

GUILDHALL SCHOOL OF MUSIC AND DRAMA

Library, Guildhall School of Music and Drama, Silk Street, Barbican, London EC2Y 8DT
☎020 7382 5280 (direct)
e-mail: library@gsmd.ac.uk
url: www.gsmd.ac.uk

Senior Librarian Mrs Kate Eaton BA(Hons) MA MCLIP
Deputy Librarian Adrian Yardley BA(Hons) DipLib MCLIP

HARPER ADAMS UNIVERSITY COLLEGE

Library, Harper Adams University College, Edgmond, Newport, Shropshire TF10 8NB
☎(01952) 820280
e-mail: libhelp@harper-adams.ac.uk
url: www.harper-adams.ac.uk
Librarian Ms Kathryn Greaves BLib(Hons) MCLIP (e-mail: kgreaves@harper-adams.ac.uk)

HERIOT-WATT UNIVERSITY

University Library, Heriot-Watt University, Edinburgh EH14 4AS
☎0131 451 3577
Fax 0131 451 3164
e-mail: libhelp@hw.ac.uk
url: www.hw.ac.uk/library
University Librarian Ms Kirsten Black BA DipISTech

UNIVERSITY OF HERTFORDSHIRE

Learning and Information Services, University of Hertfordshire, College Lane, Hatfield, Herts AL10 9AB
☎(01707) 284678
Fax (01707) 284701
e-mail: lisadmin@herts.ac.uk; helpdesk@herts.ac.uk
url: www.herts.ac.uk
Dean of Learning and Information Services Prof Di Martin MA DipLib MCLIP CertEd MCIPD (e-mail: d.martin@herts.ac.uk)

Learning resources centres

Hatfield College Lane Campus Learning Resources Centre, University of Hertfordshire, College Lane, Hatfield, Herts AL10 9AB
☎(01707) 284678

Hatfield de Havilland Campus Learning Resources Centre, University of Hertfordshire, Hatfield, Herts AL10 9AY
☎(01707) 284678
(post c/o College Lane address above)

UNIVERSITY OF HUDDERSFIELD

Library and Computing Centre, University of Huddersfield, Queensgate, Huddersfield, Yorkshire HD1 3DH
☎(01484) 473930 (enquiries), (01484) 473838 (administration)
Fax (01484) 472385
e-mail: lc@hud.ac.uk
url: www.hud.ac.uk
Director of Computing and Library Services Prof John Lancaster MPhil MCLIP

Head of Library Services Ms Sue White BA(Hons) DipLib MCLIP FHEA
Head of Computing Services Alan Radley MBA

UNIVERSITY OF HULL

The Brynmor Jones Library, University of Hull, Cottingham Road Campus, Cottingham Road, Kingston upon Hull HU6 7RX
☎(01482) 466581
Fax (01482) 466205
e-mail: help@hull.ac.uk
url: www.hull.ac.uk/lib
Director of Academic Services and Librarian Dr Richard Heseltine BA DPhil DipLib

Campus library

Keith Donaldson Library, University of Hull, Scarborough Campus, Filey Road,
Scarborough, North Yorks YO11 3AZ
☎(01723) 357277
Fax (01723) 357328
e-mail: libhelp-scar@hull.ac.uk
Head of Learning Resources (Scarborough) Ms Amanda Withey

IMPERIAL COLLEGE LONDON

Central Library, Imperial College London, South Kensington, London SW7 2AZ
☎020 7594 8820 (enquiries), 020 7594 8816 (administration)
Fax 020 7594 8876
e-mail: library@imperial.ac.uk
url: www.imperial.ac.uk/library
Director of Library Services Ms Deborah Shorley BA FCLIP (020 7594 8880; e-mail:
d.shorley@imperial.ac.uk)
Assistant Director, Faculty Support Services for Learning and Research
Ms Liz Davis BSc MCLIP (020 7594 8877; e-mail: e.davis@imperial.ac.uk)
Assistant Director, Library Support Services Ms Susan Howard BA MSc DipLib MCLIP
(020 7594 8622; e-mail: s.howard@imperial.ac.uk)

Medical libraries

Charing Cross Campus Library, Imperial College London, Charing Cross Campus,
St Dunstan's Road, London W6 8RP
☎020 7594 0755
Fax 020 7594 0851

Chelsea and Westminster Campus Library, Imperial College London, Chelsea and
Westminster Campus, Fulham Road, London SW10 9NH
☎020 8746 8107
Fax 020 8746 8215

Hammersmith Campus Library, Imperial College London, Hammersmith Campus,
Du Cane Road, London W12 0NN
☎020 8383 3246
Fax 020 8383 2195

Royal Brompton Campus Library, Imperial College London, Royal Brompton Campus, Dovehouse Street, London SW3 6LY
☎020 7351 8150
Fax 020 7351 8117

St Mary's Campus Library, Imperial College London, St Mary's Campus, Norfolk Place, London W2 1PG
☎020 7594 3692
Fax 020 7402 3971

Silwood Park Campus Library, Imperial College London, Silwood Park Campus, Buckhurst Road, Ascot, Berks SL5 7TE
☎020 7594 2461

INSTITUTE OF DEVELOPMENT STUDIES

British Library for Development Studies, Institute of Development Studies, University of Sussex, Falmer, Brighton BNI 9RE
☎(01273) 915660
url: blds.ids.ac.uk
Head of Library Ms Julie Brittain BA MA MCLIP
Deputy Librarian Ms Helen Rehin (e-mail: h.rehin@ids.ac.uk)

ISLE OF MAN COLLEGE

Library, Isle of Man College, Homefield Road, Douglas, Isle of Man IM2 6RB
☎(01624) 648207
Fax (01624) 663675
e-mail: libiomc@manx.net
Senior Librarian Miss Carole Graham BA MCLIP MSc (e-mail: Carole.Graham@iomcollege.ac.im)
College Librarian Tim Kenyon BA MCLIP MA (e-mail: Tim.Kenyon@iomcollege.ac.im)

KEELE UNIVERSITY

Library Services, Keele University, Keele, Staffs ST5 5BG
☎(01782) 733535 (enquiries), (01782) 733232 office
Fax (01782) 734502
e-mail: libhelp@lib.keele.ac.uk
url: www.keele.ac.uk/library
University Librarian Paul Reynolds MA MCLIP (e-mail: p.r.reynolds@lib.keele.ac.uk)

Departmental library

Health Library, Keele University, Clinical Education Centre, University Hospital of North Staffordshire, Newcastle Road, Stoke-on-Trent ST4 6QG
☎(01782) 556565
Fax (01782) 556582
e-mail: health.library@keele.ac.uk
Health Library Manager J V P Hutchins MA DipLib (e-mail: j.v.p.hutchins@lib.keele.ac.uk)

UNIVERSITY OF KENT

Templeman Library, University of Kent, Canterbury, Kent CT2 7NU
☎(01227) 823124
Fax (01227) 823984
e-mail: library-enquiry@kent.ac.uk
url: www.kent.ac.uk/library
Director of Information Services John Sotillo BSc
Head of Library Services Ms Carole Pickaver MSc(Econ) BA MCLIP

Site libraries

Drill Hall Library, Universities at Medway, University of Kent, North Road, Chatham
Maritime, Chatham, Kent ME4 4TB
☎(01634) 883278
Fax (01634) 883567
url: http://campus.medway.ac.uk/library
Library Manager Ms Virginia Malone (e-mail: v.g.malone@gre.ac.uk)
Deputy Library Manager Ms Sarah Root (e-mail: s.l.root@gre.ac.uk)
(Shared library with Canterbury Christ Church University and University of Greenwich)

Library, University of Kent Tonbridge Centre, University of Kent, Avebury Avenue,
Tonbridge, Kent TN9 1TG
☎(01732) 368449
e-mail: ton-library@kent.ac.uk
Library Supervisor Mrs Denyse Straker

KINGSTON UNIVERSITY

Library Services, Kingston University, Penrhyn Road, Kingston upon Thames, Surrey KT1 2EE
☎020 8417 2101 (enquiries), 020 8417 2099 (administration)
Fax 020 8417 8115
e-mail: library@kingston.ac.uk
url: www.kingston.ac.uk/library
Director of Information Services Graham Bulpitt MA MCLIP CertEd (020 8417 2099;
e-mail: g.bulpitt@kingston.ac.uk)
Head of Content Development Mrs Elizabeth Malone BA(Hons) DipLib MCLIP
(020 8417 2614; e-mail: e.malone@kingston.ac.uk)
Head of Planning and Resources Simon Mackie (020 8417 2110; e-mail:
s.mackie@kingston.ac.uk)
Head of Learning and Research Support Ms Sandy Leitch BA(Hons) DipLib (020 8417
7785; e-mail: s.leitch@kingston.ac.uk)

Campus libraries

Library Services, Kingston University, Nightingale Centre, Kingston Hill, Kingston upon
Thames, Surrey KT2 7LB
☎020 8417 5380
Fax 020 8417 5312

Library Services, Kingston University, Knights Park, Kingston upon Thames, Surrey KT1 2QJ

☎020 8417 4057
Fax 020 8417 4039

Library Services, Kingston University, Penrhyn Road, Kingston upon Thames, Surrey
KT1 2EE
☎020 8417 2101
Fax 020 8417 8115

Library Services, Kingston University, Sir Sydney Camm Centre, Roehampton Vale, Friars
Avenue, London SW15 3DW
☎020 8417 4903
Fax 020 8417 4891

LANCASTER UNIVERSITY

University Library, Lancaster University, Bailrigg, Lancaster LA1 4YH
☎(01524) 592517 (enquiries), 01524 592535 (administration)
Fax (01524) 65719
e-mail: lbrusrvs@exchange.lancs.ac.uk (Library user services)
url: www.libweb.lancs.ac.uk
University Librarian Ms Clare Powne BMus MA MCLIP (e-mail:
c.powne@lancaster.ac.uk)

LEEDS COLLEGE OF MUSIC

Library, Leeds College of Music, 3 Quarry Hill, Leeds LS2 7PD
☎0113 222 3458 (enquiries), 0113 222 3477 (administration)
e-mail: lcmlibrary@lcm.ac.uk
url: www.lcm.ac.uk
Head of Library Services Ms Jay Glasby BA MCLIP (e-mail: j.glasby@lcm.ac.uk)
Jazz Archivist Ms Claire Marsh BMus MSc MCLIP (e-mail: c.marsh@lcm.ac.uk)

LEEDS METROPOLITAN UNIVERSITY

**City Campus Library, Leeds Metropolitan University, Leslie Silver Building, Civic Quarter,
Leeds LS1 3HE**
☎0113 812 3106
Fax 0113 812 6779
url: www//libraryonline.leedsmet.ac.uk
Director of Libraries and Learning Innovation Ms Jo Norry BA(Hons) MA DipLib
PGDip MCLIP FHEA (0113 812 5966; e-mail: j.norry@leedsmet.ac.uk)
Associate Director of Libraries and Learning Innovation Ms Wendy Luker BA(Hons)
PGDip MCLIP (0113 812 7468; e-mail: w.luker@leedsmet.ac.uk)

Campus libraries

City Campus Library, Leeds Metropolitan University, Leslie Silver Building, Woodhouse
Lane, Leeds LS1 3HE
☎0113 812 3106
Fax 0113 812 3123

Headingley Library, Leeds Metropolitan University, Beckett Park, Leeds LS6 3QS

☎0113 283 3164
Fax 0113 283 3211

LEEDS TRINITY & ALL SAINTS COLLEGE

Library, Leeds Trinity & All Saints College, Brownberrie Lane, Horsforth, Leeds LS18 5HD
☎0113 283 7244
Fax 0113 283 7200
url: www.leedstrinity.ac.uk/services/library
Director of Library and Learning Resources Nick Goodfellow BA MA MCLIP (e-mail: n.goodfelow@leedstrinity.ac.uk)
College Liaison Librarians Ms Rebecca Coombes BA(Hons) MSc (e-mail: r.coombes@leedstrinity.ac.uk), Ms Caroline Parsons (e-mail: c.parsons@leedstrinity.ac.uk), Ms Janice Lavigueur BA(Hons) BSc (e-mail: j.lavigueur@leedstrinity.ac.uk)

UNIVERSITY OF LEEDS

University Library, University of Leeds, Leeds LS2 9JT
☎0113 343 5663
Fax 0113 343 5561
e-mail: library@leeds.ac.uk
url: www.leeds.ac.uk/library
University Librarian/Keeper of the Brotherton Collection Vacant
Deputy Librarian Brian Clifford BA MA HonFCLIP

UNIVERSITY OF LEICESTER

David Wilson Library, University of Leicester, PO Box 248, University Road, Leicester LE1 9QD
☎0116 252 2043 (general enquiries), 0116 252 2031 (Librarian's secretary)
Fax 0116 252 2066
e-mail: library@leicester.ac.uk
url: www.le.ac.uk/library/
University Librarian Mrs Christine Fyfe BA MA MBA
Director of Library Services Ms Louise Jones BA MA MPA (0116 252 2034)

Site libraries

Clinical Sciences Library, University of Leicester, Clinical Sciences Building, Leicester Royal Infirmary, PO Box 65, Leicester LE2 7LX
☎0116 252 3104
Fax 0116 252 3107
e-mail: clinlib@leicester.ac.uk
url: www.le.ac.uk/library/clinical
Clinical Sciences Librarian Miss Joanne E Dunham BA DipLib

UNIVERSITY OF LINCOLN

University Library, University of Lincoln, Brayford Pool, Lincoln LN6 7TS
☎(01522) 886222 (general enquiries), (01522) 886427 (administration)
Fax (01522) 886311

url: www.lincoln.ac.uk/library
University Librarian Ian Snowley BA MBA FCLIP FRSA
Deputy Librarians Ms Philippa Dyson BA MSc PGCE MCLIP ILTM (e-mail: pdyson@lincoln.ac.uk), Ms Lys Ann Reiners (e-mail: lreiners@lincoln.ac.uk)
Customer Services Team Leader Mrs Lesley Thompson (01522 886222; e-mail: lthompson@lincoln.ac.uk)

Campus libraries

Holbeach Campus Library, University of Lincoln, Minerva House, Holbeach Technology Park, Park Road, Holbeach, Spalding, Lincs PE12 7PT
☎(01406) 493007
Fax (01406) 493030
Library Officer Ms Julie Smith

Hull Campus Library, University of Lincoln, The Derek Crothall Building, George Street, Kingston upon Hull HU1 3BW
☎(01482) 311654
Fax (01482) 311656
Team Leader Dave Masterson

Riseholme Campus Library, University of Lincoln, Riseholme Park, Lincoln LN2 2LG
☎(01522) 895310
Fax (01522) 895414
Team Leader Ms Nikki Rogers, Mrs Pam Young (job share)

LIVERPOOL HOPE UNIVERSITY

The Sheppard-Worlock Library, Liverpool Hope University, PO Box 95, Hope Park, Liverpool L16 9LB
☎0151 291 2000 (issue desk), 0151 291 2001 (administration), 0151 291 2041 (enquiries)
Fax 0151 291 2037
e-mail: askalibrarian@hope.ac.uk
url: www.hope.ac.uk/library
Director of Library and Learning Support Mrs Linda J Taylor MEd BA MCLIP ILTM (0151 291 3528; e-mail: taylorl@hope.ac.uk)
Deputy Director Ms Susan Murray MA BSc MCLIP ILTM (0151 291 2002; e-mail: murrays@hope.ac.uk)

LIVERPOOL INSTITUTE FOR PERFORMING ARTS

Learning Services, Liverpool Institute for Performing Arts, Mount Street, Liverpool L1 9HF
☎0151 330 3111
Fax 0151 330 3110
url: www.lipa.ac.uk
Director of Information Services and Technical Support Ken O'Donoghue BA MA DLIS CertEd (0151 330 3250; e-mail: k.odonoghue@lipa.ac.uk)
Learning Services Manager Ms C Holmes BA(Hons) PGDipLib (0151 332 3111; e-mail: c.holmes@lipa.ac.uk)

LIVERPOOL JOHN MOORES UNIVERSITY

Library and Student Support, Liverpool John Moores University, Aldham Robarts Learning Resource Centre, Maryland Street, Liverpool LI 9DE
☎0151 231 3544
Fax 0151 231 3457
url: www.ljmu.ac.uk
Director of Library and Student Support Ms Maxine Melling BA PGDipLib MLib MCLIP (0151 231 3682; e-mail: m.melling@ljmu.ac.uk)
Head of Business and Planning Leo Appleton BA(Hons) MA PGCE MEd (0151 231 3763; e-mail: l.appleton1@ljmu.ac.uk)
Head of Customer Services Mrs Brigid Badger BA DipLib (0151 231 3379; e-mail: b.j.badger@ljmu.ac.uk)
Head of Research and Learner Support Ms Valerie Stevenson BA(Hons) (0151 231 3178; e-mail: v.stevenson@ljmu.ac.uk)
Head of Business and Information Systems Ms Mandy Phillips (0151 231 3246; e-mail: a.phillips@ljmu.ac.uk)
Head of Staffing Ken Graham BA PGDipLib (0151 231 3436; e-mail: k.r.graham@livjm.ac.uk)
Head of Student Administration Ms Claire Breen (0151 231 3120; e-mail: c.l.breen@ljmu.ac.uk)

Site libraries

Aldham Robarts Learning Resource Centre, Liverpool John Moores University, 29 Maryland Street, Liverpool LI 9DE
☎0151 231 3179
Fax 0151 707 1307

Avril Robarts Learning Resource Centre, Liverpool John Moores University, 79 Tithebarn Street, Liverpool L2 2ER
☎0151 231 3179
Fax 0151 231 4479

I M Marsh Learning Resource Centre, Liverpool John Moores University, Barkhill Road, Liverpool L17 6BD
☎0151 231 3179
Fax 0151 231 5378

UNIVERSITY OF LIVERPOOL

University Library, University of Liverpool, Liverpool L69 3DA
☎0151 794 2679 (enquiries), 0151 794 2674 (administration)
Fax 0151 794 2681/5417
url: www.liv.ac.uk/library
University Librarian Phil Sykes BA MCLIP

Site libraries

Continuing Education Library, University of Liverpool, 126 Mount Pleasant, Liverpool L69 3DA
☎0151 794 3285
Continuing Education Librarian Ms Linda Crane BA MCLIP (e-mail: lcrane@liv.ac.uk)

Harold Cohen Library (Science, Medicine, Engineering, Veterinary and Dental Science), University of Liverpool, Ashton Street, Liverpool L69 3DA
☎0151 794 5411
Fax 0151 794 5417
User Services Manager Ms Lesley Butler BA MCLIP (e-mail: l.m.butler@liv.ac.uk)

Sydney Jones Library (Humanities, Social Sciences, Special Collections and Archives), University of Liverpool, Chatham Street, Liverpool L69 3DA
☎0151 794 2679
Fax 0151 794 2681
User Services Manager Ms Laura Dunn BA DipLib MCLIP (e-mail: l.dunn@liv.ac.uk)

LONDON CONTEMPORARY DANCE SCHOOL

Library, London Contemporary Dance School, The Place, 16 Flaxman Terrace, London WC1H 9AT
☎020 7121 1110
e-mail: library@theplace.org.uk
url: www.lcds.ac.uk/91/library/library.html
Librarian Ms Katherine Dike BA(Hons) MSc (e-mail: katherine.dike@theplace.org.uk)

LONDON METROPOLITAN UNIVERSITY

Calcutta House Library, London Metropolitan University, Calcutta House, Old Castle Street, London E1 7NT
☎020 7320 1185
Fax 020 7320 1182
url: www.londonmet.ac.uk
Director of Libraries Ms Julie Howell BSc(SocSci)Hons DipLib (020 7320 1170; e-mail: j.howell@londonmet.ac.uk)
Learning Resources Manager Ms Helen Dalton BSc MCLIP (e-mail: h.dalton@londonmet.ac.uk)

Commercial Road Library, London Metropolitan University, 41–71 Commercial Road, London E1 1LA
☎020 7320 1869
Fax 020 7320 2831
Learning Resources Manager Ms Catherine Phillpotts BA(Hons) MA MCLIP (e-mail: catherine.phillpotts@londonmet.ac.uk)

Holloway Road Library, London Metropolitan University, 236–250 Holloway Road, London N7 6PP
☎020 7133 2100
url: www.londonmet.ac.uk/library
Learning Resources Manager Ms Susie Faulkner BA MCLIP (020 7133 2089; e-mail: s.faulkner@londonmet.ac.uk)
Academic Liaison Manager George Knapp BSc PGDipInf PGDipFilmSt (020 7133 2103; e-mail: g.knapp@londonmet.ac.uk)

Ladbroke House Library, London Metropolitan University, Ladbroke House, 62–66 Highbury Grove, London N5 2AD
☎020 7133 5149

Learning Resources Manager Ms Bridget Shersby BA (020 7133 5148; e-mail: b.shersby@londonmet.ac.uk), Peter Bowbeer BA(Hons) DipInfSci (e-mail: p.bowbeer@londonmet.ac.uk) (job share)

Moorgate Library, London Metropolitan University, 84 Moorgate, London EC2M 6SQ
☎020 7320 1567
Fax 020 7320 1565
Learning Resources Manager Ms Laura Simmons BSc(Hons) MAEd (020 7320 1561; e-mail: l.simmons@londonmet.ac.uk)

Special collections
Head of Special Collections Ms Caroline Ellis BA(Hons) AMA FRSA (e-mail: c.ellis@londonmet.ac.uk)

TUC Library Collections, London Metropolitan University, Holloway Road Library, 236–250 Holloway Road, London N7 6PP
☎020 7133 2260
Fax 020 7133 2529
e-mail: tuclib@londonmet.ac.uk
url: www.londonmet.sc.uk/libraries/tuc; www.unionhistory.info
Librarian Ms Christine Coates MA MCLIP (e-mail: c.coates@londonmet.ac.uk)

The Women's Library, London Metropolitan University, Old Castle Street, London E1 7NT
☎020 7320 2222
Fax 020 7320 2333
e-mail: enquirydesk@thewomenslibrary.ac.uk
url: www.thewomenslibrary.ac.uk
Collections Manager Ms Teresa Doherty

Bibliographical Services, London Metropolitan University, Calcutta House, Old Castle Street, London E1 7NT
☎020 7320 1171
Bibliographical Services Manager Ms Pamela Noble MCLIP (e-mail: p.noble@londonmet.ac.uk)

LONDON SOUTH BANK UNIVERSITY

Perry Library, London South Bank University, 250 Southwark Bridge Road, London SE1 6NJ
☎020 7815 6647
Fax 020 7815 6629
url: www.library.lsbu.ac.uk
Director of Centre for Learning Support and Development Robert Hall BA MA (e-mail: r.hall@lsbu.ac.uk)
Site Manager Alan Doherty (020 7815 6626; e-mail: dohertaa@lsbu.ac.uk)

Site libraries

Harold Wood Education Centre, London South Bank University, Havering Campus, Old Harold Wood Hospital, Gubbins Lane, Harold Wood, Romford, Essex RM3 0BE
☎020 7815 5982
Fax 020 7815 4786
e-mail: lisex@lsbu.ac.uk

Site Manager Ms Patricia Noble MCLIP (e-mail: noblep@lsbu.ac.uk)
Deputy Site Manager Ms Diana Watmough MCLIP CLTHE (e-mail: watmoudj@lsbu.ac.uk)

Library, London South Bank University, Whipps Cross Campus, Whipps Cross Hospital, Leytonstone, London E11 1NR
☎020 7815 4728
Fax 020 7815 4777
e-mail: lisel@lsbu.ac.uk
Site Manager Ms Patricia Noble MCLIP (e-mail: noblep@lsbu.ac.uk)
Deputy Site Manager Ms Diana Watmough MCLIP CLTHE (e-mail: watmoudj@lsbu.ac.uk)

UNIVERSITY OF LONDON

University of London Research Library Services, Senate House Library, University of London, Senate House, Malet Street, London WC1E 7HU
☎020 7862 8461 (enquiries), 020 7862 8432 (administration)
Fax 020 7862 8480 (enquiries), 020 7664 5562 (administration)
e-mail: enquiries@london.ac.uk
url: www.ulrls.lon.ac.uk
Director, University of London Research Library Services Christopher Pressler BA MA MSc FRSA
Director, Technical Services, University of London Research Library Services Paul McLaughlin MA MCLIP (020 7862 8413; e-mail: pmclaughlin@lon.ac.uk)
Director, User Services, University of London Research Library Services Ms Christine Muller BA MCLIP (020 7862 8412; e-mail: cmuller@lon.ac.uk)
Librarian, Institute of Germanic Studies Martin Liebscher (020 7862 8959; e-mail: martin.liebscher@sas.ac.uk)
Librarian, Institute of Commonwealth Studies David Clover DipLib MA (020 7862 8840; e-mail: david.clover@sas.ac.uk)
Librarian, Institute for the Study of the Americas Ms Christine Anderson BAS MCLIP (020 7862 8456; e-mail: christine.anderson@london.ac.uk) (Combines the collections of the former Institute of Latin American Studies and the Institute of United States Studies)

(Includes libraries of the Australian and Canadian High Commissions)

Depository Library, University of London, Spring Rise, Egham, Surrey TW20 9PP
☎(01784) 434560
e-mail: shl.depository@london.ac.uk
Any enquiries relating to the Depository Library should be directed to James Cook (020 7862 8425)

College, Institute and Departmental

Each College listed below is an independent self-governing institution funded, where applicable, by HEFCE, and awarding degrees of the University of London, of which each is a member.

College, Institute and Departmental

Birkbeck
Library, Birkbeck, Malet Street, London WC1E 7HX
☎020 7631 6064 (administration), 020 7631 6063/6239 (enquiries)
Fax 020 7631 6066
e-mail: libhelp@bbk.ac.uk
url: www.bbk.ac.uk/lib/
Librarian Philip Payne BA HonFCLIP MCLIP (020 7631 6250; e-mail: p.payne@bbk.ac.uk)
Deputy Librarian Robert Atkinson MA DipLib MCLIP (020 7631 6366; e-mail:
r.atkinson@bbk.ac.uk)

Courtauld Institute of Art
Library, Courtauld Institute of Art, Somerset House, Strand, London WC2R 0RN
☎020 7848 2701 (enquiries)
Fax 020 7848 2887
url: www.courtauld.ac.uk
Kilfinan Librarian, Head of Book, Witt and Conway Libraries Antony Hopkins
(e-mail: antony.hopkins@courtauld.ac.uk)

Goldsmiths
Library, Goldsmiths, New Cross, London SE14 6NW
☎020 7919 7150 (enquiries), 020 7919 7161 (administration)
Fax 020 7919 7165
e-mail: library@gold.ac.uk
url: www.gold.ac.uk/library
Librarian Ms Mary Nixon BA MA DipLib MCLIP

Heythrop College
Library, Heythrop College, Kensington Square, London W8 5HN
☎020 7795 4250 (enquiries), 020 7795 4251 (administration)
Fax 020 7795 4253
e-mail: library@heythrop.ac.uk
url: www.heythrop.ac.uk
Librarian Christopher J Pedley SJ BA(Econ) BA MTh ThM MA (e-mail:
c.pedley@heythrop.ac.uk)

Institute for the Study of the Americas *see* University of London, Senate House

Institute of Advanced Legal Studies
Library, Institute of Advanced Legal Studies, School of Advanced Study, 17 Russell Square,
London WC1B 5DR
☎020 7862 5800
Fax 020 7862 5770
e-mail: ials@sas.ac.uk
url: www.ials.sas.ac.uk
Librarian Jules R Winterton BA LLB MCLIP
Deputy Librarian and Academic Services Manager David R Gee BA MA MCLIP
Information Systems Manager Steve J Whittle BA MA
Information Resources Manager Ms Lesley Young BA DipLib MCLIP

Institute of Cancer Research

Library, Institute of Cancer Research, Brookes Lawley Building, 15 Cotswold Road, Belmont, Sutton, Surrey SM2 5NG
☎020 8722 4230
Fax 020 8722 4323
e-mail: sutlib@icr.ac.uk
url: www.icr.ac.uk
Librarian Barry Jenkins BA DipLib
Library Information Officer Miss Sue Rogers

Site library

Library, Institute of Cancer Research, Chester Beatty Labs, 237 Fulham Road, London S W3 6JB
☎020 7153 5123
Fax 020 7153 5143
e-mail: fullib@icr.ac.uk
url: www.icr.ac.uk
Librarian Barry Jenkins BA DipLib
Library Assistant Ms June Greenwood

Institute of Classical Studies

Institute of Classical Studies Library and Joint Library of the Hellenic and Roman Societies, Institute of Classical Studies, Senate House, Malet Street, London WC1E 7HU
☎020 7862 8709
Fax 020 7862 8724
url: http://icls.sas.ac.uk/library/home.htm
Librarian Colin H Annis MA MCLIP (e-mail: colin.annis@sas.ac.uk)

Institute of Commonwealth Studies see University of London, Senate House

Institute of Education

Newsam Library and Archives, Institute of Education, 20 Bedford Way, London WC1H 0AL
☎020 7612 6080 (enquiries)
Fax 020 7612 6093
e-mail: lib.enquiries@ioe.ac.uk
url: www.ioe.ac.uk/is
Head of Library Services Stephen Pickles BA (020 7612 6064; e-mail: s.pickles@ioe.ac.uk)

Institute of Germanic Studies see University of London, Senate House

Institute of Historical Research

Library, Institute of Historical Research, School of Advanced Study, Senate House, Malet Street, London WC1E 7HU
☎020 7862 8760
Fax 020 7862 8762
e-mail: IHR.Library@sas.ac.uk
url: www.history.ac.uk/library/; http://catalogue.ulrls.lon.ac.uk
Librarian Ms Jennifer Higham BA(Oxon) MA(UCL)

King's College London

Maughan Library and Information Services Centre, King's College London, Chancery Lane, London WC2A 1LR
☎020 7848 2424
Fax 020 7848 2277
e-mail: issenquiry@kcl.ac.uk
url: www.kcl.ac.uk/iss
Acting Director of Customer Services Mrs Vivien Robertson MA MCLIP (020 7848 2313; e-mail: vivien.robertson@kcl.ac.uk)

Denmark Hill Campus

Information Services Centre, King's College London, Weston Education Centre, Cutcombe Road, London SE5 9RJ
☎020 7848 5541
Fax 020 7848 5550
Information Services Centre Manager Ms Susan Isaac

Guy's Campus

Information Services Centre, King's College London, New Hunt's House, Guy's Campus, London SE1 1UL
☎020 7848 6600
Fax 020 7848 6743
Information Services Centre Manager Ms Janet Hopcroft

Institute of Psychiatry

Institute of Psychiatry Library, King's College London, King's College London, PO18 De Crespigny Park, London SE5 8AF
☎020 7848 0204
e-mail: iop.library@kcl.ac.uk
url: www.iop.kcl.ac.uk/Library
Site Manager Ms Susan Isaac

St Thomas' Campus

Information Services Centre, King's College London, St Thomas' House, St Thomas' Hospital, Lambeth Palace Road, London SE1 7EH
☎020 7188 3740
Fax 020 7188 8358
Information Services Centre Manager Ms Alison Charlesworth BA(Hons) MA

Strand Campus

Maughan Library & Information Services Centre, King's College London, Chancery Lane, London WC2A 1LR
☎020 7848 2424
Fax 020 7848 2277
Information Services Centre Manager Ms Sally Brock BA DipLib MA MCLIP

Waterloo Campus

Information Services Centre, King's College London, Franklin-Wilkins Building, 150 Stamford Street, London SE1 9NH
☎020 7848 4378

Fax 020 7848 4290
Information Services Centre Manager Ms Veronyka Carson (020 7848 4360; e-mail:
veronyka.carson@kcl.ac.uk)

London Business School
Library, London Business School, Regent's Park, London NW1 4SA
☎020 7000 7620
e-mail: library@london.edu
url: www.london.edu/library
Taunton Centre Manager Ms Anne Wilson (020 7000 7675; e-mail:
awilson@london.edu)
Director, Information Systems Richard White

London School of Economics and Political Science
LSE Library (British Library of Political and Economic Science), London School of
Economics and Political Science, 10 Portugal Street, London WC2A 2HD
☎020 7955 7229 (enquiries), 020 7955 7219 (administration)
Fax 020 7955 7454
e-mail: library.enquiries@lse.ac.uk
url: www.library.lse.ac.uk
Chief Information Officer Ms Jean Sykes MBE MA MLitt DipLib MCLIP (020 7955 7218;
e-mail: j.sykes@lse.ac.uk)
Director of Library Services Ms Elizabeth Chapman BA MA DipLib FECert FCLIP (020
7955 7224; e-mail: e.chapman@lse.ac.uk)
Information Services Manager Ms Nicola Wright (020 7955 7217; e-mail:
n.c.wright@lse.ac.uk)
Technical Services Manager Glyn Price BA DipLib MCLIP (020 7955 6755; e-mail:
g.price@lse.ac.uk)
User Services Manager Ms Helen Cocker BA MPhil (020 7955 6336; e-mail:
h.cocker@lse.ac.uk)
Archivist Ms Sue Donnelly BA DipArchiveAdmin (020 7955 7947; e-mail:
document@lse.ac.uk)
Library IT Manager Tim Green DipCompStud (020 7955 6140; e-mail:
t.green@lse.ac.uk)
Communications and Marketing Manager Tariq Aziz (020 7852 3525; e-mail:
t.aziz@lse.ac.uk)
Building Liaison Manager Ms Val Straw BA PGCert(Prof Prac HE Admin) FAUA (020
7955 7238; e-mail: v.straw@lse.ac.uk)

London School of Hygiene & Tropical Medicine
Library, London School of Hygiene & Tropical Medicine, Keppel Street, London WC1E 7HT
☎020 7927 2276 (enquiries), 020 7927 2283 (administration)
Fax 020 7927 2273
e-mail: library@lshtm.ac.uk
url: www.lshtm.ac.uk/library/
Head of Library & Archives Service Ms Caroline Lloyd BA MA MCLIP (e-mail:
caroline.lloyd@lshtm.ac.uk)

London School of Jewish Studies
Library, London School of Jewish Studies, Schaller House, 44A Albert Road, London NW4 2SJ

☎020 8203 6427
Fax 020 8203 6420
url: www.lsjs.ac.uk
Librarian Mrs Erla Zimmels DipLib (e-mail: erla.zimmels@lsjs.ac.uk)

Queen Mary
Library, Queen Mary, 327 Mile End Road, London E1 4NS
☎020 7882 8800
Fax 020 8981 0028
e-mail: library@qmul.ac.uk
url: www.library.qmul.ac.uk/
Director of Library Services Emma Bull BA(Hons) DipInf MCLIP (020 7882 7385;
e-mail: e.j.bull@qmul.ac.uk)
Assistant Director Service Delivery Ms June Hayles BA MCLIP (020 7882 7290; e-mail:
j.m.hayles@qmul.ac.uk)
Assistant Director Business Support Ms Marie Montague BEd MCLIP (020 7882 8804;
e-mail: m.b.montague@qmul.ac.uk)

Site libraries
Medical and Dental Library (Whitechapel), Queen Mary, Barts and the London School,
Newark Street, London E1 2AT
☎020 7882 8800
e-mail: library@qmul.ac.uk

Medical Library (West Smithfield), Queen Mary, St Bartholomew's Hospital, West
Smithfield, London EC1A 7BA
☎020 7882 8800
e-mail: library@qmul.ac.uk

Victoria Park Library, Queen Mary, Education Centre, Bonner Road, London E2 9JX
☎020 7882 8800
e-mail: library@qmul.ac.uk

Royal Holloway
Library, Royal Holloway, University of London, Egham, Surrey TW20 0EX
☎(01784) 443823 (enquiries), 443334 (administration)
Fax (01784) 477670
e-mail: library@rhul.ac.uk
url: www.rhul.ac.uk (College); www.rhul.ac.uk/library
Director of Library Services John Tuck
Associate Director (Planning and Administration) Ms Coral Black BA
Associate Director (Academic Support) Matthew Brooke BA(Hons) MA (e-mail:
m.brooke@rhul.ac.uk)
Associate Director (E-Strategy) Tim Wales BA(Hons) MSc MCLIP FHEA

Royal Veterinary College
Library, Camden Campus, Royal Veterinary College, Royal College Street, London NW1 0TU
☎020 7468 5162
e-mail: library@rvc.ac.uk
url: www.rvc.ac.uk
Customer Services Manager Gwyn Jervis (e-mail: gjervis@rvc.ac.uk)

Library, Hawkshead Campus, Royal Veterinary College, Eclipse Building, Hawkshead Lane, North Mimms, Hatfield, Herts AL9 7TA
☎(01707) 666214
e-mail: library@rvc.ac.uk
url: www.rvc.ac.uk
College Librarian Simon Jackson MA MCLIP (e-mail: sjackson@rvc.ac.uk)
Customer Services Manager Ms Sally Burton (e-mail: sburton@rvc.ac.uk)

St George's, University of London
St George's Library, St George's, University of London, Hunter Wing, Cranmer Terrace, London SW17 0RE
☎020 8725 5466 (direct line)
Fax 020 8725 5377
e-mail: liblearn@sgul.ac.uk
url: www.sgul.ac.uk/services/library/
Library Services Manager Ms Bethan Adams (e-mail: baadams@sgul.ac.uk)

School of Oriental and African Studies
Library, School of Oriental and African Studies, Thornhaugh Street, Russell Square, London WC1H 0XG
☎020 7898 4163 (enquiries), 020 7898 4160 (library office)
Fax 020 7898 4159
e-mail: libenquiry@soas.ac.uk
url: www.soas.ac.uk/library/
Director of Library and Information Services John Robinson
Librarian Vacant

School of Pharmacy
Library, School of Pharmacy, 29–39 Brunswick Square, London WC1N 1AX
☎020 7753 5833
Fax 020 7753 5947
e-mail: library@pharmacy.ac.uk
url: www.pharmacy.ac.uk
Head of Library and Information Services Ms Michelle Wake BA MA MCLIP (e-mail: michelle.wake@pharmacy.ac.uk)

UCL (University College London)
UCL Library Services, UCL (University College London), Gower Street, London WC1E 6BT
☎020 7679 7700 (enquiries), 020 7679 7051 (administration)
Fax 020 7679 7373
e-mail: library@ucl.ac.uk
url: www.ucl.ac.uk/library
Director of UCL Library Services Dr Paul Ayris MA PhD
Group Manager, IT Services Mrs Janet Cropper MSc DipLib (020 7679 7833; e-mail: j.cropper@ucl.ac.uk)
Group Manager, Reader Services Vincent Matthews BSc(Econ) MA MA PhD (020 7679 2607; e-mail: v.matthews@ucl.ac.uk)
Group Manager, Bibliographic Services Ms Diana Mercer MSc DipLib (020 7679 2625; e-mail: d.mercer@ucl.ac.uk)

Site libraries

Library and Information Services, UCL School of Slavonic and East European Studies, UCL (University College London), 16 Taviton Street, London WC1H 0BW
☎020 7679 8701
Fax 020 7679 8710
e-mail: ssees-library@ssees.ucl.ac.uk
url: www.ssees.icl.ac.uk/libarch.htm
Librarian and Director of Information Services Ms Lesley Pitman BA DipLib (e-mail: l.pitman@ssees.ucl.ac.uk)

Library, UCL Eastman Dental Institute, UCL (University College London), 256 Grays Inn Road, London WC1X 8LD
☎020 7915 1045/1262
e-mail: ic@eastman.ucl.ac.uk
url: www.eastman.ucl.ac.uk
Librarian Ms Medwenna Buckland BA (e-mail: medwenna.buckland@ucl.ac.uk)

Rockefeller Medical Library, UCL Institute of Neurology and The National Hospital for Neurology and Neurosurgery, UCL (University College London), Queen Square, London WC1N 3BG
☎020 7829 8709
e-mail: library@ion.ucl.ac.uk
Librarian Ms Louise Shepherd BA (e-mail: l.shepherd@ion.ucl.ac.uk)

Royal Free Medical Library, UCL Library Services, UCL (University College London), Royal Free Hospital, Rowland Hill Street, London NW3 2PF
☎020 7794 0500 ext 33202
Fax 020 7794 3534
e-mail: library@medsch.ucl.ac.uk
Librarian Ms Betsy Anagnostelis BSc(Hons) MSc DipLib (e-mail: b.anagnostelis@medsch.ucl.ac.uk)

UCL Bartlett Built Environment Library, UCL (University College London), Faculty of the Built Environment, Wates House, 22 Gordon Street, London WC1H 0QB
☎020 7679 4900
e-mail: library@ucl.ac.uk
Site Librarians Ms Suzanne Tonkin BA(Hons) MSc (e-mail: suzanne.tonkin@ucl.ac.uk), Ms Caroline Fletcher (e-mail: caroline.fletcher@ucl.ac.uk) (job share)

UCL Cruciform Library, UCL (University College London), Cruciform Building, 90 Gower Street, London WC1E 6BT
☎020 7679 6079
Fax 020 7679 6981
e-mail: clinscilib@ucl.ac.uk
url: www.ucl.ac.uk/Library/crucilib.shtml
Librarian Ms Kate Cheney BA MSc MCLIP (e-mail: k.cheney@ucl.ac.uk)

UCL Ear Institute and RNID Libraries, UCL (University College London), Royal National Throat, Nose and Ear Hospital, 330–336 Gray's Inn Road, London WC1X 8EE
☎020 7915 1445
Fax 020 7915 1443
e-mail: rnidlib@ucl.ac.uk
url: www.ucl.ac.uk/Library/rnidlib.shtml

Librarian Alex Stagg MA (e-mail: a.stagg@ucl.ac.uk)

UCL Institute of Archaeology Library, UCL (University College London), 31–34 Gordon Square, London WC1H 0PY
☎020 7679 4788
Fax 020 7679 7393
e-mail: library@ucl.ac.uk
url: www.ucl.ac.uk/Library/ioalib.shtml
Librarian Robert Kirby MA (e-mail: r.kirby@ucl.ac.uk)

UCL Institute of Child Health Library, UCL (University College London), 30 Guilford Street, London WC1N 1EH
☎020 7242 9789 ext 2424
Fax 020 7831 0488
e-mail: library@ich.ucl.ac.uk
url: www.ich.ucl.ac.uk/library
Librarian John Clarke MA DipLib (e-mail: jclarke@ich.ucl.ac.uk)

UCL Institute of Ophthalmology Library, UCL (University College London), 11–43 Bath Street, London EC1V 9EL
☎020 7608 6814
e-mail: ophthlib@ucl.ac.uk
url: www.ucl.ac.uk/Library/iophth.shtml
Librarian Ms Debbie Heatlie BA (020 7608 6815; e-mail: d.heatlie@ucl.ac.uk)
Deputy Librarian Ms Anna Di Iorio MA (020 7608 6814; e-mail: a.diiorio@ucl.ac.uk)
(Joint library with Moorfields Eye Hospital)

UCL Institute of Orthopaedics Library, UCL (University College London), Sir Herbert Sneddon Teaching Centre, Royal National Orthopaedic Hospital, Brockley Hill, Stanmore, Middlesex HA7 4LP
☎020 8909 5351
Fax 020 8909 5390
e-mail: orthlib@ucl.ac.uk
url: www.ucl.ac.uk/Library/iorthlib.shtml
Librarian Ms Julie Noren MLS (e-mail: j.noren@ucl.ac.uk)

UCL Language and Speech Science Library, UCL (University College London), Chandler House, 2 Wakefield Street, London WC1N 1PF
☎020 7679 4207
Fax 020 7679 4238
e-mail: library@langsci.ucl.ac.uk; library@ucl.ac.uk
url: www.langsci.ucl.ac.uk/Library/index.php
Acting Librarian Ms Breege Whiten MA (e-mail: b.whiten@ucl.ac.uk)
Head of Enquiry Services Ms Debs Furness (e-mail: d.furness@ucl.ac.uk)

UCL Library Special Collections, UCL (University College London), Gower Street, London WC1E 6BT
☎020 7679 5197
Fax 020 7679 5157
e-mail: spec.coll@ucl.ac.uk
url: www.ucl.ac.uk/Library/special-coll/; http://archives.ucl.ac.uk
Head of Special Collections and Archivist Ms Gillian Furlong BA DipArchMan RMSA (020 7679 5155; e-mail: g.furlong@ucl.ac.uk)

Warburg Institute
Library, Warburg Institute, School of Advanced Study, Woburn Square, London WC1H 0AB
☎020 7862 8935/6 (Reading Room)
Fax 020 7862 8939
e-mail: warburg.library@sas.ac.uk
url: http://warburg.sas.ac.uk
telnet (for library): catalogue.ulrls.lon.ac.uk
Librarian Prof Jill Kraye

LOUGHBOROUGH UNIVERSITY

Pilkington Library, Loughborough University, Loughborough, Leics LE11 3TU
☎(01509) 222360 (enquiries), (01509) 222353 (issue desk), (01509) 222341
(administration)
Fax (01509) 223993
e-mail: library@lboro.ac.uk
url: www.lboro.ac.uk/library; Contacts: www.lboro.ac.uk/library/contacts/index.html
University Librarian Ms Ruth Jenkins (01509 222340; e-mail: r.jenkins@lboro.ac.uk)

MANCHESTER METROPOLITAN UNIVERSITY

**Sir Kenneth Green Library, Manchester Metropolitan University, All Saints, Manchester
M15 6BH**
☎0161 247 3096
Fax 0161 247 6349
url: www.library.mmu.ac.uk
Head of Library Services Mrs Gill R Barry BA MSc MCLIP (0161 247 6101; e-mail:
g.r.barry@mmu.ac.uk)

Site libraries

Aytoun Library, Manchester Metropolitan University, Aytoun Street, Manchester M1 3GH
☎0161 247 3093
Library Services Manager David Matthews BA PGDip (0161 247 3091; e-mail:
d.matthews@mmu.ac.uk)

Crewe Library, Manchester Metropolitan University, Crewe Green Road, Crewe, Cheshire
CW1 1DU
☎0161 247 5002
Faculty Librarian Dr Margaret Robinson BA DipLib MCLIP (0161 247 5138; e-mail:
m.g.robinson@mmu.ac.uk)

Didsbury Library, Manchester Metropolitan University, 799 Wilmslow Road, Manchester
M20 8RR
☎0161 247 6126
Library Services Manager Ms Jayne Evans BA MLib (0161 247 6120; e-mail:
j.e.h.evans@mmu.ac.uk)

Elizabeth Gaskell Library, Manchester Metropolitan University, Hathersage Road,
Manchester M13 0JA
☎0161 247 6134
Library Services Manager Ian Harter BSc DipLib (e-mail: i.harter@mmu.ac.uk)

Hollings Library, Manchester Metropolitan University, Old Hall Lane, Manchester M14 6HR
☎0161 247 6119
Library Services Manager Ian Harter BSc DipLib (e-mail: i.harter@mmu.ac.uk)

THE UNIVERSITY OF MANCHESTER

The John Rylands University Library, The University of Manchester, Main Library, Oxford Road, Manchester M13 9PP
☎0161 275 3751 (enquiries); 0161 306 4921 (library office)
Fax 0161 273 7488
url: www.library.manchester.ac.uk
University Librarian and Director of The John Rylands Library Ms Jan Wilkinson BA DipLib DMS FCLIP FRSA (e-mail: jan.wilkinson@manchester.ac.uk)
Deputy University Librarian and Associate Director of The John Rylands Library Dr Stella Butler BSc PhD AMA (e-mail: stella.butler@manchester.ac.uk)
Interim Head of Special Collections Ms Rachel Beckett MA MCLIP (e-mail: rachel.beckett@manchester.ac.uk)
Head of Information Systems Ms Lorraine Beard DipILS MCLIP (e-mail: lorraine.beard@manchester.ac.uk)
Head of Collection Management Ms Sandra Bracegirdle (e-mail: sandra.bracegirdle@manchester.ac.uk)
Head of Finance, Planning and Human Resources John Laidlar (e-mail: john.laidlar@manchester.ac.uk)
Head of Customer Services Ms Katie Woolfenden BA MA (e-mail: katie.woolfenden@manchester.ac.uk)

Site libraries

The Joule Library, The University of Manchester, PO Box 88, Sackville Street, Manchester M60 1QD
☎0161 306 4924
Customer Services Manager – Sites and Customer Relations Mrs Debbie Allan BA DipLib MSc (e-mail: debbie.allan@manchester.ac.uk)

The Eddie Davies Library, Manchester Business School, The University of Manchester, Booth Street West, Manchester M15 6PB
☎0161 275 6507 (enquiries), 0161 275 6500 (administration)
Fax 0161 275 6505
e-mail: libdesk@mbs.ac.uk
url: www.mbs.ac.uk/services/library-services
Librarian Dominic Broadhurst (e-mail: dominic.broadhurst@mbs.ac.uk)

MIDDLESEX UNIVERSITY

Learning Resources, Middlesex University, Sheppard Library, The Burroughs, Hendon, London NW4 4BT
☎020 8411 5234
Fax 020 8411 5163
url: www.lr.mdx.ac.uk
Director of Learning Resources and University Librarian Nick Bevan BSc MSc(Econ) DipLib MSc(InfSc) MCLIP (020 8411 5234; e-mail: n.bevan@mdx.ac.uk)

Deputy Director of Learning Resources Vacant
Assistant Director, Customer Services Vacant
Assistant Director, Technical Support Ms Dilys Hall BA MBA MCLIP (020 8411 5424;
e-mail: d.hall@mdx.ac.uk)
Assistant Director, Academic Support Matthew Lawson BA MA MCLIP (020 8411
4126; e-mail: m.lawson@mdx.ac.uk)

Systems and Bibliographical Services, Middlesex University, Sheppard Library, The
Burroughs, Hendon, London NW4 4BT
☎020 8411 5238 (direct)
e-mail: bibservices@mdx.ac.uk
Technical Manager (Library Services) Alan Hopkinson MA FCLIP MBCS (e-mail:
a.hopkinson@mdx.ac.uk)

Campus libraries

Health Campus Library, Middlesex University, Chase Farm Education Centre, Chase Farm
Hospital, The Ridgeway, Enfield, Middlesex EN2 8JL
☎020 8366 9112
e-mail: libcf1@mdx.ac.uk
Library Manager Ms Sarah Jardine-Willoughby BA(Hons) MCLIP

Library, Middlesex University at Cat Hill, Middlesex University, Barnet, Herts EN4 8HT
☎020 8411 5042 (direct)
e-mail: libch1@mdx.ac.uk

Library, Middlesex University at Hendon, Middlesex University, The Burroughs, London
NW4 4BT
☎020 8411 5852 (direct)
e-mail: libhe1@mdx.ac.uk

Library, Middlesex University at Trent Park, Middlesex University, Bramley Road, London
N14 4YZ
☎020 8411 6181 (direct)
e-mail: libtp1@mdx.ac.uk

(The Health Campus libraries are also served by multidisciplinary libraries at: David
Ferriman Library, North Middlesex Hospital, Sterling Way, London N18 1QX (020 8887
2223; e-mail: libnm1@mdx.ac.uk, libnm2@mdx.ac.uk) and The Archway Healthcare
Library, Holborn Union Building, The Archway Campus, Highgate Hill, London N19 3UA
(020 7288 3567; e-mail: libwh1@mdx.ac.uk, libwh2@mdx.ac.uk)

NEWCASTLE UNIVERSITY

Robinson Library, Newcastle University, Newcastle upon Tyne NE2 4HQ
☎0191 222 7662 (enquiries), 0191 222 7674 (administration)
Fax 0191 222 6235
e-mail: library@newcastle.ac.uk
url: www.ncl.ac.uk/library/
Librarian Wayne Connolly BA DipLib

Divisional libraries

Law Library, Newcastle University, Newcastle Law School, 22-24 Windsor Terrace,
Newcastle upon Tyne NE1 7RU
☎0191 222 7944
Librarian Mrs Linda Kelly BA MCLIP

The Walton Library (Medical and Dental), Newcastle University, The Medical School,
Framlington Place, Newcastle upon Tyne NE2 4HH
☎0191 222 7550
Librarian Ms Erika Gavillet BA(Hons) MA DipLib

NEWMAN UNIVERSITY COLLEGE

Library, Newman University College, Genners Lane, Bartley Green, Birmingham B32 3NT
☎0121 476 1181 ext 2208
e-mail: library@newman.ac.uk
url: www.newman.ac.uk/library
Director of Library and Learning Services Ms Christine Porter BA MLib MCLIP (ext
2327; e-mail: c.porter@newman.ac.uk)
Library Liaison Manager David Crozier BA MSc(Econ) DipMan MCLIP (ext 2339; e-mail:
d.crozier@newman.ac.uk)
Library Operations Manager Ms Loraine Berry MLS (ext 2208; e-mail:
l.m.berry@newman.ac.uk)

UNIVERSITY OF NORTHAMPTON

**Park Campus Library, University of Northampton, Boughton Green Road, Northampton
NN2 7AL**
☎(01604) 735500 ext 2477 (enquiries), ext 2041 (administration)
Fax (01604) 718819
url: www.northampton.ac.uk
Director of Information Services Ms Hilary Johnson BA MA MCLIP (ext 2041; e-mail:
hilary.johnson@northampton.ac.uk)
Deputy Director, Academic Services Chris Powis BA MA MLib PGDipTHE MCLIP
FHEA FRSA (ext 2229; e-mail: chris.powis@northampton.ac.uk)

Avenue Campus Library, University of Northampton, Maidwell Building, St George's
Avenue, Northampton NN2 6JD
☎(01604) 735500 ext 3900
Fax (01604) 719618
Other details as above

NORTHERN SCHOOL OF CONTEMPORARY DANCE

Library, Northern School of Contemporary Dance, 98 Chapeltown Road, Leeds LS7 4BH
☎0113 219 3020
Fax 0113 219 3030
url: www.nscd.ac.uk
Librarian and CDD Athens Administrator Miss Samantha King BA(Hons) MCLIP
(e-mail: sam.king@nscd.ac.uk)

NORTHUMBRIA UNIVERSITY

Library and Learning Services, Northumbria University, Library Building, Sandyford Road, Newcastle upon Tyne NEI 8ST
☎0191 227 4125 (enquiries), 0191 227 4143 (administration)
Fax 0191 227 4563
e-mail: ask4help@northumbria.ac.uk
url: www.northumbria.ac.uk/librarysuccess
Director of Library and Learning Services Prof Jane Core BA MLib MCLIP

Site library

Coach Lane Campus Library, Northumbria University, East Block, Coach Lane, Newcastle upon Tyne NE7 7XA
☎0191 215 6540
Fax 0191 215 6560

NORWICH UNIVERSITY COLLEGE OF THE ARTS

Learning Resource Centre, Norwich University College of the Arts, Francis House, 3–7 Redwell Street, Norwich NR2 4SN
☎(01603) 610561
Fax (01603) 615728
e-mail: library@nuca.ac.uk
url: www.nuca.ac.uk
Librarian Tim Giles BA (e-mail: t.giles@nuca.ac.uk)
Assistant Librarians Ms Jan McLachlan BA(Hons) DipLIS (e-mail: j.mclachlan@nuca.ac.uk), Gordon Burnett MA MCLIP (e-mail: g.burnett@nuca.ac.uk)

NOTTINGHAM TRENT UNIVERSITY

Libraries and Learning Resources, Nottingham Trent University, Goldsmith Street, Nottingham NGI 5LS
☎0115 848 6446
Fax 0115 848 2286
url: www.ntu.ac.uk
Head of Libraries and Learning Resources Vacant
Deputy University Librarian (Customer Services) Mike Berrington BA(Hons) MA DipLib (0115 848 6059; e-mail: mike.berrington@ntu.ac.uk)
Deputy University Librarian (Information Resources) Ms Nuala Devlin BA(Hons) MA MCLIP (0115 848 6056; e-mail: nuala.devlin@ntu.ac.uk)

Site libraries

The Boots Library, Nottingham Trent University, Goldsmith Street, Nottingham NGI 5LS
☎0115 848 2175 (enquiries)
Fax 0115 848 4425

Brackenhurst Campus Library, Nottingham Trent University, Southwell Road, Southwell, Notts NG25 0QF

☎(01636) 817049 (enquiries)
Fax (01636) 817077

Clifton Campus Library, Nottingham Trent University, Clifton Lane, Nottingham NG11 8NS
☎0115 848 3570/6612
Fax 0115 848 6304

UNIVERSITY OF NOTTINGHAM

Information Services, University of Nottingham, University Park, Nottingham NG7 2RD
url: www.nottingham.ac.uk/is
Chief Information Officer Stephen Pinfield MA MA MCLIP (0115 951 5109; e-mail:
stephen.pinfield@nottingham.ac.uk)
Director, Customer Services Graham Moore BA (0115 951 4535; e-mail:
graham.moore@nottingham.ac.uk)
Director, IT Systems Ms Alison Clarke BSc MSc (0115 951 3330; e-mail:
alison.clarke@nottingham.ac.uk)
Director, Research and Learning Resources Christopher Pressler BA MA MSc FRSA
(0115 951 3052)

Library sites

Business Library, University of Nottingham, Business School, Jubilee Campus, Wollaton
Road, Nottingham NG8 1BB
☎0115 846 8069
Fax 0115 846 8064

Denis Arnold Music Library, University of Nottingham, University Park, Nottingham
NG7 2RD
☎0115 951 4596
Fax 0115 951 4558

Derby Medical School Library, University of Nottingham, Derby City General Hospital,
Uttoxeter Road, Derby DE22 3DT
☎(01332) 724650
Fax (01332) 724647

Djanogly LRC (Education, Computer Science), University of Nottingham, Jubilee Campus,
Wollaton Road, Nottingham NG8 1BB
☎0115 846 6700
Fax 0115 846 6705

George Green Library of Science and Engineering, University of Nottingham, University
Park, Nottingham NG7 2RD
☎0115 951 4570
Fax 0115 951 4578

Greenfield Medical Library, University of Nottingham, Queen's Medical Centre,
Nottingham NG7 2UH
☎0115 823 0555
Fax 0115 823 0549

Hallward Library (Arts and Humanities, Law, Social Sciences), University of Nottingham,
University Park, Nottingham NG7 2RD

☎0115 951 4555
Fax 0115 951 4558

James Cameron-Gifford Library (Applied Biosciences, Veterinary Medicine and Science),
University of Nottingham, Sutton Bonington Campus, Sutton Bonington, nr Loughborough,
Leics LE12 5RD
☎0115 951 6390
Fax 0115 951 6389

Manuscripts and Special Collections, University of Nottingham, King's Meadow Campus,
Lenton Lane, Nottingham NG7 2NR
☎0115 951 4565
Fax 0115 846 8651
Keeper D B Johnston BA PhD DipLib (0115 951 4563)

School of Nursing, Midwifery and Physiotherapy Library, Derby, University of Nottingham,
Derby Centre, Derbyshire Royal Infirmary, London Road, Derby DE1 2QY
☎(01332) 347141 ext 2561
Fax (01332) 290321

School of Nursing, Midwifery and Physiotherapy Library, Mansfield, University of
Nottingham, Mansfield Education Centre, Kings Mill Hospital, Mansfield Road,
Sutton-in-Ashfield, Notts NG17 4JL
☎(01623) 465634
Fax (01623) 465601

OPEN UNIVERSITY

**Library and Learning Resources Centre, Open University, Walton Hall, Milton Keynes
MK7 6AA**
☎(01908) 653138
Fax (01908) 653571
e-mail: lib-help@open.ac.uk
url: www.open.ac.uk; http://library.open.ac.uk
Director of Library Services Mrs Nicky Whitsed MSc FCLIP (01908 653254; e-mail:
n.whitsed@open.ac.uk)
Associate Director – Business Performance and Management Ms Ann Davies
BSc(Hons) MSc (01908 652057; e-mail: ann.davies@open.ac.uk)
Associate Director – Academic and Student Services Ms Patricia Heffernan BA(Hons)
DipLib (01908 654850; e-mail: p.a.heffernan@open.ac.uk)
Associate Director – Information Management and Innovation Ms Gill Needham
BA(Hons) DipLib CertMan MSc(Econ) (01908 658369; e-mail: g.needham@open.ac.uk)

OXFORD BROOKES UNIVERSITY

**Headington Library, Oxford Brookes University, Headington Campus, Gipsy Lane,
Headington, Oxford OX3 0BP**
☎(01865) 483156 (enquiries), (01865) 483130 (administration)
Fax (01865) 483998
e-mail: library@brookes.ac.uk
url: www.brookes.ac.uk/library

Director of Learning Resources and University Librarian Dr Helen M Workman PhD MCLIP (e-mail: h.workman@brookes.ac.uk)
Head of Library Services Ms Jan Haines BLib MA DipM MCLIP (e-mail: jan.haines@brookes.ac.uk)

Site libraries

Harcourt Hill Library, Oxford Brookes University, Harcourt Hill Campus, Oxford OX2 9AT
☎(01865) 488222
Fax (01865) 488224
Head of Learning Resources: Harcourt Hill and Wheatley Ms Claire M Jeffery BSc DipLib DMS MCLIP (e-mail: cmjeffery@brookes.ac.uk)

Wheatley Library, Oxford Brookes University, Wheatley Campus, Wheatley, Oxford OX33 1HX
☎(01865) 485869
Fax (01865) 485750
Head of Learning Resources: Harcourt Hill and Wheatley Ms Claire M Jeffery BSc DipLib DMS MCLIP (e-mail: cmjeffery@brookes.ac.uk)

UNIVERSITY OF OXFORD

The Bodleian Libraries

The Bodleian Library, The Bodleian Libraries, Broad Street, Oxford OX1 3BG
☎(01865) 277162
Fax (01865) 277182
e-mail: reader.services@bodleian.ox.ac.uk
url: www.bodleian.ox.ac.uk
Bodley's Librarian Dr Sarah E. Thomas PhD (e-mail: sarah.thomas@bodleian.ox.ac.uk)
Associate Director, Keeper of Special Collections and IT Richard Ovenden MA FRSA FSA (e-mail: richard.ovenden@bodleian.ox.ac.uk)
Director of Administration and Finance Ms Laura How (e-mail: laura.how@bodleian.ox.ac.uk)
Assistant Director, Research and Learning Services Ms JoAnne Sparks (e-mail: joanne.sparks@bodleian.ox.ac.uk)
Assistant Director, Collections and Resource Description Ms Catriona Cannon (e-mail: catriona.cannon@bodleian.ox.ac.uk)
Executive Secretary Mike Heaney (e-mail: mike.heaney@bodleian.ox.ac.uk)

Accessible Resources Acquisition and Creation Unit, The Bodleian Libraries, University of Oxford, Osney One Building, Osney Mead, Oxford OX2 0EW
☎(01865) 283862
Fax (01865) 793731
e-mail: aracu@bodleian.ox.ac.uk
www.bodleian.ox.ac.uk/services/disability
Director/Manager Ms Teresa Pedroso BA(Hons) (01865 283861; e-mail: teresa.pedroso@bodleian.ox.ac.uk)

Alexander Library of Ornithology, University of Oxford, Department of Zoology, Tinbergen Building, South Parks Road, Oxford OX1 3PS

☎(01865) 271143
e-mail: enquiries.zoo@bodleian.ox.ac.uk
url: www.bodleian.ox.ac.uk/science/libraries/zoology
Librarian Ms Sophie Wilcox (e-mail: sophie.wilcox@bodleian.ox.ac.uk)

Bodleian Japanese Library, University of Oxford, 27 Winchester Road, Oxford OX2 6NA
☎(01865) 284506
Fax (01865) 284500
e-mail: japanese@bodleian.ox.ac.uk
url: www.bodleian.ox.ac.uk/dept/oriental/bjl.htm
Librarian Mrs Izumi Tytler MA

Bodleian Law Library, University of Oxford, St Cross Building, Manor Road, Oxford OX1 3UR
☎(01865) 271462
Fax (01865) 271475
e-mail: law.library@bodleian.ox.ac.uk
url: www.bodleian.ox.ac.uk/law
Law Librarian Ms Ruth Bird BA TSTC GradDipLib (e-mail: ruth.bird@bodleian.ox.ac.uk)
Academic Services Librarian Ms Margaret Watson MA DipLib MCLIP (e-mail:
margaret.watson@bodleian.ox.ac.uk)
Information Resources Librarian Ms Helen Garner BA(Hons) DipILM MCLIP (e-mail:
helen.garner@bodleian.ox.ac.uk)

Bodleian Library of Commonwealth and African Studies at Rhodes House, University of
Oxford, Rhodes House, South Parks Road, Oxford OX1 3RG
☎(01865) 270908
Fax (01865) 270912
e-mail: rhodes.house.library@bodleian.ox.ac.uk
url: www.bodleian.ox.ac.uk/rhl
Librarian i/c Ms L McCann

Bodleian Music Faculty Library, University of Oxford, Faculty of Music, St Aldate's, Oxford
OX1 1DB
☎(01865) 276148 (enquiries)
e-mail: music.library@bodleian.ox.ac.uk
url: www.bodleian.ox.ac.uk/music
Librarian Martin Holmes

Continuing Education Library, University of Oxford, Rewley House, 1 Wellington Square,
Oxford OX1 2JA
☎(01865) 270454
Fax (01865) 270309
e-mail: library@conted.ox.ac.uk
url: http://library.conted.ox.ac.uk
Librarian Ms S Pemberton BA DipLib MCLIP

Department of Education Library, University of Oxford, 15 Norham Gardens, Oxford
OX2 6PY
☎(01865) 274028 (library)
Fax (01865) 274027 (department)
e-mail: library@education.ox.ac.uk
url: www.education.ox.ac.uk/library/index.php
Librarian Ms Kate Williams BA(Hons) MSc

Department of Experimental Psychology, Library, University of Oxford, South Parks Road, Oxford OX1 3UD
☎(01865) 271312
Fax (01865) 310447
e-mail: library@psy.ox.ac.uk
url: www.psy.ox.ac.uk/library; www.bodleian.ox.ac.uk/libraries
Librarian Ms Karine Barker

English Faculty Library, University of Oxford, St Cross Building, Manor Road, Oxford OX1 3UQ
☎(01865) 271050
Fax (01865) 271054
e-mail: enquiries@efl.ox.ac.uk
url: www.bodleian.ox.ac.uk/english
English Librarian Ms Sue Usher BA(Hons) DipLib MCLIP

Foreign Cataloguing, University of Oxford, Bodleian Libraries, Broad Street, Oxford OX1 3BG
☎(01865) 277027
Principal Library Assistant Mrs Nathalie Chaddock-Thomas (e-mail: nathalie.thomas@ouls.ox.ac.uk)

History Faculty Library, University of Oxford, Broad Street, Oxford OX1 3BD
☎(01865) 277262
e-mail: library@history.ox.ac.uk
url: www.history.ox.ac.uk
Librarian Ms Isabel Holowaty BA(Hons) MSc (e-mail: isabel.holowaty@ouls.ox.ac.uk)
Deputy Librarian Ms Valerie Lawrence BA(Hons) DipLib (e-mail: valerie.lawrence@ouls.ox.ac.uk)

Indian Institute Library, University of Oxford, New Bodleian Library, Broad Street, Oxford OX1 3BG
☎(01865) 287300
Fax (01865) 277182
e-mail: indian.institute@bodleian.ox.ac.uk
url: www.bodleian.ox.ac.uk/bodleian/library/rooms/iirr
Librarian Dr Gillian Evison MA MPhil DPhil

Institute for Chinese Studies Library, University of Oxford, Walton Street, Oxford OX1 2HG
☎(01865) 280430
Fax (01865) 280431
e-mail: chinese.studies.library@bodleian.ox.ac.uk
url: www.bodleian.ox.ac.uk/dept/oriental/csl.htm
Librarian Minh Chung MA

Latin American Centre, St Antony's College, University of Oxford, 1 Church Walk, Oxford OX2 6JF
☎(01865) 274483 (tel/fax)
e-mail: laclib@bodleian.ox.ac.uk
url: www.bodleian.ox.ac.uk/lac
Librarian in charge Mrs Nathalie Chaddock-Thomas (e-mail: nathalie.thomas@ouls.ox.ac.uk)

Library, Taylor Institution, University of Oxford, St Giles, Oxford OX1 3NA
☎(01865) 278154 (office), 278158/278161 (main desk)
Fax (01865) 278165
e-mail: enquiries@taylib.ox.ac.uk
url: www.taylib.ox.ac.uk
Librarian Ms Amanda Peters MA DipLib
(The Taylor Institution Modern Languages Faculty Library can also be found at this location;
the Taylor Bodleian, Slavonic and Greek Library can be found at 47 Wellington Square,
Oxford OX1 2JF; tel: 01865 270464)

Oriental Institute Library, University of Oxford, Pusey Lane, Oxford OX1 2LE
☎(01865) 278202
Fax (01865) 278204
e-mail: library@orinst.ox.ac.uk
url: www.bodleian.ox.ac.uk/oil
Librarian i/c Ms Diane Bergman

Philosophy Faculty Library, University of Oxford, 10 Merton Street, Oxford OX1 4JJ
☎(01865) 276927
Fax (01865) 276932
e-mail: philosophy.library@bodleian.ox.ac.uk
url: www.bodlelan.ac.uk/philosophy
Librarian Dr Hilla A Wait MA DPhil

Radcliffe Science Library, University of Oxford, Parks Road, Oxford OX1 3QP
☎(01865) 272800
Fax (01865) 272821
e-mail: rsl@bodleian.ox.ac.uk
url: www.bodleian.ox.ac.uk/rsl
Keeper of Scientific Books Ms Alena Ptak-Danchak

Refugee Studies Centre Library, University of Oxford, Queen Elizabeth House,
3 Worcester Street, Oxford OX1 2BX
☎(01865) 270298
Fax (01865) 270721
e-mail: rsclib@qeh.ox.ac.uk
url: www.rsc.ox.ac.uk
Librarian Ms Sarah Rhodes BA DipLib MA (e-mail: sarah.rhodes@qeh.ox.ac.uk)
(Postal address: 3 Mansfield Road, Oxford OX1 3TB)

Sackler Library, University of Oxford, 1 St John Street, Oxford OX1 2LG
☎(01865) 278092
Fax (01865) 278098
e-mail: enquiries@saclib.ox.ac.uk; librarian@saclib.ox.ac.uk
url: www.saclib.ox.ac.uk
Librarian Dr Graham Piddock PhD (e-mail: graham.piddock@ouls.ox.ac.uk)
(Access to the Library is limited to members of Oxford University and holders of Bodleian
Library reader's tickets)

Sainsbury Library, University of Oxford, Park End Street, Oxford OX1 1HP
☎(01865) 288880
Fax (01865) 288805
e-mail: library@sbs.ox.ac.uk

url: www.sbs.ox.ac.uk
Bodleian Business Librarian Ms Chris Flegg

Social Sciences Library, University of Oxford, Manor Road Building, Manor Road, Oxford
OX1 3UQ
☎(01865) 278709 (Librarian), (01865) 271093 (Library)
Fax (01865) 271072
e-mail: library@ssl.ox.ac.uk
url: www.ssl.ox.ac.uk
Librarian Ms Louise Clarke (e-mail: louise.clarke@bodleian.ox.ac.uk)

Theology Faculty Library, University of Oxford, 41 St Giles, Oxford OX1 3LW
☎(01865) 270731
e-mail: library@theology.ox.ac.uk
url: www.theology.ox.ac.uk
Librarian Dr Hilla A Wait MA DPhil

Vere Harmsworth Library (Rothermere American Institute), University of Oxford,
1A South Parks Road, Oxford OX1 3UB
☎(01865) 282700
Fax (01865) 282709
e-mail: vhl@bodleian.ox.ac.uk
url: www.bodleian.ox.ac.uk/vhl
Librarian Ms Margaret Robb BS MA MLS MCLIP
Librarian i/c Ms Jane Rawson MA MA (e-mail: jane.rawson@ouls.ox.ac.uk)

Bodleian Health Care Libraries

Cairns Library, University of Oxford, Oxford Radcliffe Hospitals NHS Trust, The John
Radcliffe Hospital, Headley Way, Headington, Oxford OX3 9DU
☎(01865) 221936
Fax (01865) 221941
e-mail: library@hcl.ox.ac.uk
url: www.bodleian.ox.ac.uk/medicine
Head of Health Care Libraries Donald M Mackay MA(Hons) MA MCLIP

College, Institute and Departmental

All Souls College
Codrington Library, All Souls College, Oxford OX1 4AL
☎(01865) 279318
Fax (01865) 279299
e-mail: codrington.library@all-souls.ox.ac.uk
url: www.asc.ox.ac.uk
Fellow Librarian Prof Ian Maclean FBA
Librarian Dr Norma Aubertin-Potter BA PhD MCLIP

Balliol College
Library, Balliol College, Oxford OX1 3BJ
☎(01865) 277709
Fax (01865) 277803
e-mail: library@balliol.ox.ac.uk

url: www.balliol.ox.ac.uk
Fellow Librarian Vacant
Acting Librarian Jeremy Hinchliff

Brasenose College
Library, Brasenose College, Radcliffe Square, Oxford OX1 4AJ
☎(01865) 277827
Fax (01865) 277831
e-mail: library@bnc.ox.ac.uk
url: www.bnc.ox.ac.uk
Fellow Librarian Dr Simon Palfrey
College Librarian Ms Liz Kay

Campion Hall
Library, Campion Hall, Brewer Street, Oxford OX1 1QS
☎(01865) 286100
url: www.campion.ox.ac.uk
Librarian Revd Peter Edmonds BA STL LSS (01865 286106)
Assistant Librarian Laurence Weeks MA

Christ Church
Library, Christ Church, Oxford OX1 1DP
☎(01865) 276169
e-mail: library@chch.ox.ac.uk
url: www.chch.ox.ac.uk
Assistant Librarians Mrs J E McMullin MA MCLIP, Ms C M Neagu DPhil MCLIP

Corpus Christi College
Library, Corpus Christi College, Merton Street, Oxford OX1 4JF
☎(01865) 276744
Fax (01865) 276767
e-mail: library.staff@ccc.ox.ac.uk
url: www.ccc.ox.ac.uk/p/Library-and-Archives
Librarian Miss Joanna Snelling MA MCLIP (e-mail: joanna.snelling@ccc.ox.ac.uk)

Exeter College
Library, Exeter College, Turl Street, Oxford OX1 3DP
☎(01865) 279600 (switchboard), (01865) 279657 (direct)
Fax (01865) 279630
e-mail: library@exeter.ox.ac.uk
url: www.exeter.ox.ac.uk
Fellow Librarian Dr Helen Spencer DPhil
Sub-Librarian Ms Juliet Chadwick
Assistant Librarian Ms Christine Ellis

Green Templeton College
Library, Green Templeton College, Radcliffe Observatory, Woodstock Road, Oxford
OX2 6HG
☎(01865) 274788
Fax (01865) 274796

e-mail: library@gtc.ox.ac.uk
url: www.gtc.ox.ac.uk
Fellow Librarian Dr Christopher Bulstrode
Librarian Ms Gill Edwards BSc (e-mail: gill.edwards@gtc.ox.ac.uk)

Harris Manchester College
Library, Harris Manchester College, Mansfield Road, Oxford OX1 3TD
☎(01865) 271016 (library), (01865) 281472 (office)
Fax (01865) 271012
e-mail: librarian@hmc.ox.ac.uk
url: www.hmc.ox.ac.uk
Fellow Librarian Ms Sue Killoran BA MA(Oxon) PGDipLib MCLIP (e-mail:
susan.killoran@hmc.ox.ac.uk)
Library Assistant Ms Katrina Malone

Hertford College
Library, Hertford College, Catte Street, Oxford OX1 3BW
☎(01865) 279409
Fax (01865) 279466
e-mail: library@hertford.ox.ac.uk
url: www.hertford.ox.ac.uk
Fellow Librarian and Archivist Dr Toby Barnard (e-mail:
toby.barnard@hertford.ox.ac.uk)
Librarian Mrs Susan Griffin BA DipLib (e-mail: susan.griffin@hertford.ox.ac.uk)

Jesus College
Library, Jesus College, Turl Street, Oxford OX1 3DW
☎(01865) 279704
Fax (01865) 279687 (attn. Librarian)
e-mail: library@jesus.ox.ac.uk
url: www.jesus.ox.ac.uk
Fellow Librarian Prof T M O Charles-Edwards
College Librarian Owen McKnight MMath MA
Archivist Christopher Jeens BA DipArchAdmin (01865 279761; e-mail:
archivist@jesus.ox.ac.uk)
(Visits by bona fide scholars are available only by prior appointment with the College
Librarian or Archivist as appropriate)

Keble College
Library, Keble College, Oxford OX1 3PG
☎(01865) 272797
e-mail: library@keble.ox.ac.uk
url: www.keble.ox.ac.uk/about/library
Fellow Librarian Ms Alena Ptak-Danchak
Librarian Ms Yvonne Murphy BA(Hons) MSSc (e-mail: librarian@keble.ox.ac.uk)

Lady Margaret Hall
Library, Lady Margaret Hall, Norham Gardens, Oxford OX2 6QA
☎(01865) 274361
Fax (01865) 511069

e-mail: library.admin@lmh.ox.ac.uk
url: www.lmh.ox.ac.uk
Fellow Librarian Dr Clive Holmes
Librarian Miss Roberta Staples BA (e-mail: roberta.staples@lmh.ox.ac.uk)
Archivist Oliver Mahony (e-mail: oliver.mahony@mansfield.ox.ac.uk)
(The library is for the use of members of college only, though bona fide researchers may be allowed access to books by arrangement with the Librarian)

Linacre College
Library, Linacre College, St Cross Road, Oxford OX1 3JA
☎(01865) 271661
Fax (01865) 271668
e-mail: library@linacre.ox.ac.uk
url: www.linacre.ox.ac.uk
Fellow Librarian Ms Margaret Robb BS MA MLS MCLIP
Assistant Librarian Mrs Emma Huber BA(Hons) (e-mail: emma.huber@linacre.ox.ac.uk)

Lincoln College
Library, Lincoln College, Turl Street, Oxford OX1 3DR
☎(01865) 279831
e-mail: library@lincoln.ox.ac.uk
url: www.lincoln.ox.ac.uk
Librarian Mrs Fiona Piddock BA DipLib

Magdalen College
Library, Magdalen College, Oxford OX1 4AU
☎(01865) 276045 (direct)
Fax (01865) 276057
e-mail: library@magd.ox.ac.uk
url: www.magd.ox.ac.uk
Fellow Librarian Dr C Y Ferdinand BA MA MA MA DPhil
Deputy Librarian Mrs Hilary Pattison MA MA
Assistant Librarian Dr Tabitha Tuckett BA DPhil

Mansfield College
Library, Mansfield College, Mansfield Road, Oxford OX1 3TF
☎(01865) 270975
Fax (01865) 270970
url: www.mansfield.ox.ac.uk
Fellow Librarian Dr Kathryn Gleadle PhD (e-mail: kathryn.gleadle@mansfield.ox.ac.uk)
Assistant Librarian Oliver Mahony (e-mail: oliver.mahony@mansfield.ox.ac.uk)
Librarian Ms Alma Jenner (e-mail: alma.jenner@mansfield.ox.ac.uk)

Merton College
Library, Merton College, Oxford OX1 4JD
☎(01865) 276380
Fax (01865) 276361
e-mail: library@merton.ox.ac.uk
url: www.merton.ox.ac.uk
Fellow and Librarian Ms Julia Walworth BA MA PhD (01865 276308; e-mail:

julia.walworth@merton.ox.ac.uk)
Assistant Librarian Mrs Catherine Lewis BA DipLib MCLIP
Archivist Julian Reid (e-mail: julian.reid@merton.ox.ac.uk)

New College
Library, New College, Oxford OX1 3BN
☎(01865) 279580 (enquiries and administration)
Fax (01865) 279590
url: www.new.ox.ac.uk/the_library
Librarian Mrs Naomi van Loo MA BA MCLIP (e-mail: naomi.vanloo@new.ox.ac.uk)

Nuffield College
Library, Nuffield College, New Road, Oxford OX1 1NF
☎(01865) 278550
Fax (01865) 278621
e-mail: library-enquiries@nuffield.ox.ac.uk
url: www.nuffield.ox.ac.uk/library
Librarian Ms Elizabeth Martin DipLib MA MCLIP (e-mail: librarian@nuffield.ox.ac.uk)

Oriel College
Library, Oriel College, Oxford OX1 4EW
☎(01865) 276558 (direct)
e-mail: library@oriel.ox.ac.uk
url: www.oriel.ox.ac.uk
Librarian Mrs Marjory Szurko BA MRes DipLib MCLIP

Pembroke College
McGowin Library, Pembroke College, St Aldate's, Oxford OX1 1DW
☎(01865) 276409 (direct)
Fax (01865) 276418
e-mail: library@pmb.ox.ac.uk
url: www.pmb.ox.ac.uk
Librarian Mrs Lucie Walker MA BA BSc
Archivist Ms Amanda Ingram (e-mail: archivist@pmb.ox.ac.uk)

The Queen's College
Library, The Queen's College, Oxford OX1 4AW
☎(01865) 279130
Fax (01865) 790819
e-mail: library@queens.ox.ac.uk
url: www.queens.ox.ac.uk/library
Librarian Ms Amanda Saville MA MCLIP (01865 279213)
Reader Services Librarian Ms Tessa Shaw BA DipLib
Technical Services Librarian Ms Lynette Dobson MA MCLIP
Historic Collections Assistant Mrs Veronika Vernier BA

Regent's Park College
Library, Regent's Park College, Pusey Street, Oxford OX1 2LB
☎(01865) 288120 (College); (01865) 288142 (Library direct line)
Fax (01865) 288121

e-mail: library@regents.ox.ac.uk
url: www.rpc.ox.ac.uk
College Librarian Revd Emma Walsh (e-mail: emma.walsh@regents.ox.ac.uk)
(General College Library open to members of College only. The Angus Library, a research
library for Baptist history, which also incorporates the former libraries of the Baptist Union
of Great Britain and the Baptist Historical Society, and the archives of the Baptist
Missionary Society on deposit, available by appointment.)

St Anne's College
Library, St Anne's College, Woodstock Road, Oxford OX2 6HS
☎(01865) 274810
Fax (01865) 274899
e-mail: library@st-annes.ox.ac.uk
url: www.st-annes.ox.ac.uk/study/undergraduate/library.html
Librarian Dr David Smith MA DPhil MCLIP (e-mail: david.smith@st-annes.ox.ac.uk)

St Antony's College
Library, St Antony's College, 62 Woodstock Road, Oxford OX2 6JF
☎(01865) 274480
Fax (01865) 274526
url: www.sant.ox.ac.uk
The Librarian

St Benet's Hall
Library, St Benet's Hall, 38 St Giles, Oxford OX1 3LN
☎(01865) 280556
url: www.st-benets.ox.ac.uk
Master Rev J. Felix Stephens OSB MA
Librarian Father Michael Phillips OSB (e-mail: michael.phillips@stv.ox.ac.uk)

St Catherine's College
Library, St Catherine's College, Manor Road, Oxford OX1 3UJ
☎(01865) 271707
e-mail: library@stcatz.ox.ac.uk
url: www.stcatz.ox.ac.uk
Fellow Librarian Dr Gervase Rosser MA PhD
Assistant Librarian Ms Sally Jones, Ms Ludmila Gromova

St Cross College
Library, St Cross College, St Giles, Oxford OX1 3LZ
☎(01865) 278481
Fax (01865) 279484
e-mail: librarian@stx.ox.ac.uk
url: www.stx.ox.ac.uk
Librarian Mrs Sheila Allcock BSc

St Edmund Hall
Library, St Edmund Hall, Queen's Lane, Oxford OX1 4AR
☎(01865) 279062
url: www.seh.ox.ac.uk

Librarian Ms Blanca Martin BA Dip (e-mail: blanca.martin@seh.ox.ac.uk)
(The Library is for the use of members of St Edmund Hall only.)

St Hilda's College
Kathleen Major Library, St Hilda's College, Cowley Place, Oxford OX4 1DY
☎(01865) 276849 (general enquiries)
Fax (01865) 276816
e-mail: library@st-hildas.ox.ac.uk
url: www.st-hildas.ox.ac.uk
Librarian Miss Maria Croghan MA (e-mail: maria.croghan@st-hildas.ox.ac.uk)

St Hugh's College
Library, St Hugh's College, St Margaret's Road, Oxford OX2 6LE
☎(01865) 274938
Fax (01865) 274912
e-mail: library@st-hughs.ox.ac.uk
url: www.st-hughs.ox.ac.uk/library
Librarian Ms Laura Wilkinson (e-mail: laura.wilkinson@st-hughs.ox.ac.uk)

St John's College
Library, St John's College, St Giles, Oxford OX1 3JP
☎(01865) 277300 (main lodge), (01865) 277330/1 (direct to library)
Fax (01865) 277435 (College office)
e-mail: library@sjc.ox.ac.uk
url: www.sjc.ox.ac.uk
Fellow Librarian Dr Alastair Wright
Librarian Stewart Tiley BA(Hons) MA DipLIM MCLIP
Library Administrator Mrs Ruth Ogden BA DipLib (e-mail: ruth.ogden@sjc.ox.ac.uk)

St Peter's College
Library, St Peter's College, New Inn Hall Street, Oxford OX1 2DL
☎(01865) 278882
Fax (01865) 278855
e-mail: library@spc.ox.ac.uk
url: www.spc.ox.ac.uk
Librarian Dr David Johnson MA(Lond) DPhil(Oxon) (e-mail: david.johnson@spc.ox.ac.uk)
Assistant Librarian Mrs Janet Foot (e-mail: janet.foot@spc.ox.ac.uk)

Somerville College
Library, Somerville College, Woodstock Road, Oxford OX2 6HD
☎(01865) 270694
Fax (01865) 270620
e-mail: library@some.ox.ac.uk
url: www.some.ox.ac.uk
Librarian Dr Anne Manuel MA MSc MEd PhD MCLIP
Assistant Librarian Miss Susan Purver MA DipLIS (01865 270694)

Trinity College
Library, Trinity College, Broad Street, Oxford OX1 3BH
☎(01865) 279863 (enquiries and administration)

Fax (01865) 279902
url: www.trinity.ox.ac.uk/college/library/
Librarian Ms Sharon Cure (e-mail: sharon.cure@trinity.ox.ac.uk)

University College
Library, University College, High Street, Oxford OX1 4BH
☎(01865) 276621
Fax (01865) 276987
e-mail: library@univ.ox.ac.uk
url: www.univ.ox.ac.uk
Fellow Librarian Dr Bill Child MA BPhil DPhil(Oxon)
College Librarian Miss Christine M Ritchie MA(Aber) MA(Lond) MCLIP

Wadham College
Library, Wadham College, Parks Road, Oxford OX1 3PN
☎(01865) 277900 (College); (01865) 277914 (direct)
Fax (01865) 277937
e-mail: library@wadh.ox.ac.uk
url: www.wadham.ox.ac.uk
Librarian Tim Kirtley
Fellow Librarian Prof Robin Fiddian

Wolfson College
The Library, Wolfson College, Oxford OX2 6UD
☎(01865) 274076
e-mail: library@wolfson.ox.ac.uk
url: www.wolfson.ox.ac.uk/library/
Librarian Ms Fiona E Wilkes BA MA DipLib MCLIP
(Open to members of College and Common Room only)

Worcester College
Library, Worcester College, Walton Street, Oxford OX1 2HB
☎(01865) 278354/278370 (library); (01865) 278300 (porter's lodge)
Fax (01865) 278387
e-mail: library@worc.ox.ac.uk
url: www.worc.ox.ac.uk
Librarian Dr Joanna Parker MA DPhil (e-mail: joanna.parker@worc.ox.ac.uk)

UNIVERSITY COLLEGE PLYMOUTH ST MARK AND ST JOHN

Library, University College Plymouth St Mark and St John, Derriford Road, Plymouth PL6 8BH
☎(01752) 636845 (enquiries), (01752) 636700 ext 4206 (administration)
Fax (01752) 636820
e-mail: libraryenquiries@marjon.ac.uk
url: www.ucpmarjon.ac.uk
Head of Library Mrs Wendy Evans BA(Hons) ILTA MCLIP (01752 636700 ext 4206; e-mail: wevans@marjon.ac.uk)

UNIVERSITY OF PLYMOUTH

Charles Seale-Hayne Library, University of Plymouth, Drake Circus, Plymouth PL4 8AA
☎(01752) 232323/588588 (enquiries); (01752) 587100 (administration)
Fax (01752) 587101
url: www.plymouth.ac.uk/library
Director of Information and Learning Services Ms Penny Holland BA DipLib MCLIP
(e-mail: penny.holland@plymouth.ac.uk)
Head of Learning and Research Support Ms Jane Gosling BSc DipLib MCLIP (e-mail:
jane.gosling@plymouth.ac.uk)
Head of Customer Services Mike Pesterfield (e-mail: mike.pesterfield@plymouth.ac.uk)

UNIVERSITY OF PORTSMOUTH

University Library, University of Portsmouth, Cambridge Road, Portsmouth PO1 2ST
☎023 9284 3228/9 (enquiries), 023 9284 3222 (administration)
Fax 023 9284 3233
e-mail: library@port.ac.uk
url: www.port.ac.uk
University Librarian Ms Roisin Gwyer

QUEEN MARGARET UNIVERSITY, EDINBURGH

**Learning Resource Centre, Queen Margaret University, Edinburgh, Queen Margaret
University Drive, Musselburgh, East Lothian EH21 6UU**
☎0131 474 0000
Fax 0131 474 0001
e-mail: lrchelp@qmu.ac.uk
url: www.qmu.ac.uk/lb
Director of IS and the LRC Fraser Muir
Head of Library Services Mrs Jo Rowley BA(Hons) MSc MCLIP

QUEEN'S UNIVERSITY OF BELFAST

Information Services Directorate, Queen's University of Belfast, McClay Library, 10 College
Park, Belfast BT7 1LP
☎028 9097 6346
url: www.qub.ac.uk/lib/
Director of Information Services John Gormley (e-mail: j.gormley@qub.ac.uk)
Assistant Director (Library Services and Research Support) Ms Elizabeth Traynor BA
MA MCLIP (e-mail: e.traynor@qub.ac.uk)

RAVENSBOURNE
(formerly Ravensbourne College of Design and Communication)

Library, Ravensbourne, Penrose Way, Peninsula Square, London SE10 0EW
☎020 3040 3500
Fax 020 8325 8320
url: www.rave.ac.uk
Director of Information Services Stephen A Bowman BA(Hons) MA FCLIP FHEA
(e-mail: s.bowman@rave.ac.uk)

Media Services Officer Paul Rogers (e-mail: p.rogers@rave.ac.uk)
Library Services Officer Ms Rachel Todd BA MA (e-mail: r.todd@rave.ac.uk)

UNIVERSITY OF READING

University Library and Collections Services, University of Reading, Whiteknights, PO Box 223, Reading RG6 6AE
☎0118 378 8770 (enquiries), 0118 378 8773 (administration)
Fax 0118 378 6636
e-mail: library@reading.ac.uk
url: www.reading.ac.uk/library
Head of University Library and Collections Services and University Librarian Mrs Julia Munro BSc MSc MBA MCLIP (0118 378 8774; e-mail: j.h.munro@reading.ac.uk)
Head of Collections Rupert Wood BPhil MA DipLib ILTM (0118 378 6784; e-mail: r.j.m.wood@reading.ac.uk)
Head of Systems and Services Miss Celia A Ayres BSc DipInfSc MCLIP (0118 378 8781; e-mail: c.a.ayres@reading.ac.uk)
Support Services Manager Ian Burn BA (0118 378 8775; e-mail: i.j.burn@reading.ac.uk)

THE ROBERT GORDON UNIVERSITY

The Georgina Scott Sutherland Library, The Robert Gordon University, Garthdee Road, Aberdeen AB10 7QE
☎(01224) 263450
Fax (01224) 263455
e-mail: library@rgu.ac.uk
url: www.rgu.ac.uk/library
Director of Knowledge and Information Services Ms Michelle Anderson BA(Hons) MA PGDip
Associate Director, Operational Services Ms Judith Moynagh MA MCLIP (e-mail: j.moynagh@rgu.ac.uk)
Associate Director, Client Services Miss Margaret Buchan MA MCLIP (e-mail: m.buchan@rgu.ac.uk)
Associate Director, Technology Services Grant McDougall BA(Hons) DipIT MCLIP (e-mail: g.i.mcdougall@rgu.ac.uk)

Site library

St Andrew Street Library, The Robert Gordon University, St Andrew Street, Aberdeen AB25 1HG
☎(01224) 262888
Fax (01224) 262889
e-mail: saslibrary@rgu.ac.uk
url: www.rgu.ac.uk/library

ROEHAMPTON UNIVERSITY

Library and Learning Services Department, Roehampton University, The University Library, Roehampton Lane, London SW15 5SZ
☎020 8392 3770 (enquiries), 020 8392 3666 (administration)

Fax 020 8392 3026
e-mail: enquiry.desk@roehampton.ac.uk
url: www.roehampton.ac.uk/library
University Librarian and Director of Learning Services Ms Sue Clegg BA MBA MCLIP
(020 8392 3501; e-mail: s.clegg@roehampton.ac.uk)
Head of Library Academic Liaison Services Phil Cheeseman (020 8392 3874; e-mail:
p.cheeseman@roehampton.ac.uk)
Head of Library and IT Facilities and Business Services Ms Michela Wilkins (020 8392
3211; e-mail: m.wilkins@roehampton.ac.uk)
Head of Library User Services Ms Faye Jackson (020 8392 3351; e-mail:
f.jackson@roehampton.ac.uk)
Bibliographic and Technical Services Manager Chris Foreman (020 8392 3352; e-mail:
c.foreman@roehampton.ac.uk)
The Archivist Ms Kornelia Cepok (020 8392 3323; e-mail: k.cepok@roehampton.ac.uk)

ROSE BRUFORD COLLEGE OF THEATRE AND PERFORMANCE

**Learning Resources Centre, Rose Bruford College of Theatre and Performance, Lamorbey
Park, Burnt Oak Lane, Sidcup, Kent DAI5 9DF**
☎020 8308 2626
Fax 020 8308 0542
url: www.bruford.ac.uk
College Librarian Ms Catherine Beach BD(Hons) MA (e-mail:
catherine.beach@bruford.ac.uk)
Assistant Librarian Terence Connolly BA(Hons) PGDipILS (e-mail:
terry.connolly@bruford.ac.uk)

ROYAL ACADEMY OF DRAMATIC ART

RADA Library, Royal Academy of Dramatic Art, I8 Chenies Street, London WCIE 7PA
☎020 7636 7076 (ask for Library)
e-mail: library@rada.ac.uk
url: www.rada.org
Library Manager James Thornton
Senior Library Assistant Ms Jean Madden
Researcher/Assistant Ms Mara Lockowandt

ROYAL ACADEMY OF MUSIC

Library, Royal Academy of Music, Marylebone Road, London NWI 5HT
☎020 7873 7323 (enquiries and administration)
Fax 020 7873 7322
e-mail: library@ram.ac.uk
url: www.ram.ac.uk
Librarian Ms Kathryn Adamson BA MA DipLib HonARAM

ROYAL AGRICULTURAL COLLEGE

Library, Royal Agricultural College, Stroud Road, Cirencester, Glos GL7 6JS
☎(01285) 652531 ext 2274
Fax (01285) 889844
e-mail: library@rac.ac.uk
url: www.rac.ac.uk/library
Head of Library Services Peter Brooks BA MA PGCE MCLIP (01285 655214 ext 2276)

ROYAL COLLEGE OF ART

College Library, Royal College of Art, Kensington Gore, London SW7 2EU
☎020 7590 4224 (enquiries)
Fax 020 7590 4217
e-mail: library@rca.ac.uk
url: www.rca.ac.uk
Head of Information and Learning Services Peter Hassell MCLIP (e-mail:
peter.hassell@rca.ac.uk)
Library Manager Ms Darlene Maxwell (e-mail: darlene.maxwell@rca.ac.uk)
Special Collections and Services Manager Neil Parkinson (e-mail:
neil.parkinson@rca.ac.uk)

ROYAL COLLEGE OF MUSIC

Library, Royal College of Music, Prince Consort Road, London SW7 2BS
☎020 7591 4325
Fax 020 7591 4326
e-mail: library@rcm.ac.uk
url: www.rcm.ac.uk
Chief Librarian Ms Pamela Thompson BA (020 7591 4323; e-mail:
pthompson@rcm.ac.uk)
Reference Librarian Dr Peter Horton MA DipLib MCLIP (020 7591 4324; e-mail:
phorton@rcm.ac.uk)

ROYAL COLLEGE OF NURSING OF THE UNITED KINGDOM

Library and Information Services, Royal College of Nursing of the United Kingdom,
20 Cavendish Square, London WIG ORN
☎020 7647 3610
Fax 020 7647 3420
e-mail: rcn.library@rcn.org.uk
url: www.rcn.org.uk/development/library
Learning and Development Manager – Information and Knowledge Management
Ms Jackie Cheeseborough BA(Hons) DipLib MCLIP FCLIP
(Access for non-members is by appointment)

ROYAL NORTHERN COLLEGE OF MUSIC

Library, Royal Northern College of Music, 124 Oxford Road, Manchester MI3 9RD

☎0161 907 5243
Fax 0161 273 7611
e-mail: library@rncm.ac.uk
url: www.rncm.ac.uk
Librarian Mrs Anna Wright BA MA MCLIP HonRNCM
Deputy Librarian Geoffrey Thomason MusB MusM ARCM LTCL DipLib

ROYAL SCOTTISH ACADEMY OF MUSIC AND DRAMA

Whittaker Library, Royal Scottish Academy of Music and Drama, 100 Renfrew Street, Glasgow G2 3DB
☎0141 270 8268
Fax 0141 270 8353
e-mail: library@rsamd.ac.uk
url: www.rsamd.ac.uk/library
Head of Information Services Ms Caroline Cochrane (0141 270 8269; e-mail: c.cochrane@rsamd.ac.uk)

ROYAL WELSH COLLEGE OF MUSIC AND DRAMA

Library, Royal Welsh College of Music and Drama, Castle Grounds, Cathays Park, Cardiff CFI0 3ER
☎029 2034 2854
Fax 029 2039 1304
url: library.rwcmd.ac.uk
Librarian Mrs Judith Agus BA BMus MCLIP (029 2039 1330; e-mail: judith.agus@rwcmd.ac.uk)

RUSKIN COLLEGE

Library, Ruskin College, Walton Street, Oxford OXI 2HE
☎(01865) 554331
Fax (01865) 554372
e-mail: library@ruskin.ac.uk
url: www.ruskin.ac.uk
Director of Library and Learning Resources Ms Valerie Moyses BA(Hons) MCLIP DipLib
(Admission by appointment only)

UNIVERSITY OF ST ANDREWS

Library, University of St Andrews, University Library, North Street, St Andrews, Fife KYI6 9TR
☎(01334 462281 (enquiries and administration), 01334 462301 (Director's Office)
Fax (01334) 462282
e-mail: library@st-andrews.ac.uk
url: www.st-andrews.ac.uk/library
Acting Director of Library Services and Head of Collections Jeremy Upton MA DipLib BMus(Hons)
Head of Special Collections Norman Reid MA PhD

ST MARY'S UNIVERSITY COLLEGE TWICKENHAM

Learning Resources Centre, St Mary's University College Twickenham, Waldegrave Road, Strawberry Hill, Twickenham, Middlesex TW1 4SX
☎020 8240 4097
Fax 020 8240 4270
e-mail: enquiry@smuc.ac.uk
url: http://portal.smuc.ac.uk/information.html
Acting Director of Information Services and Systems Martin Scarrott BA DipLib MCLIP FHEA

UNIVERSITY OF SALFORD

The Library, University of Salford, Clifford Whitworth Building, Salford, Manchester M5 4WT
☎0161 295 2444 (enquiries to Service Desk)
e-mail: library@salford.ac.uk
url: www.library.salford.ac.uk
Acting Director Ms Julie Berry BA DMS MCLIP
Head of Customer and Learning Services Satish Patel BSc(Hons)
Head of Learning and Research Support (Acting) Ms Sue Hodges BA MA MCLIP

Campus libraries

Adelphi Library, University of Salford, Adelphi Building, Peru Street, Salford, Manchester M3 6EQ
☎0161 295 2444
Fax 0161 295 6083

Allerton Library, University of Salford, Allerton Building, Frederick Road, Salford, Manchester M6 6PU
☎0161 295 2444
Fax 0161 295 2437

Clifford Whitworth Library, University of Salford, Salford, Manchester M5 4WT
☎0161 295 2444
Fax 0161 295 6624

SCOTTISH AGRICULTURAL COLLEGE

The Agriculture Library, Scottish Agricultural College, Peter Wilson Building, King's Buildings, West Mains Road, Edinburgh EH9 3JG
☎0131 535 4117 (enquiries), 0131 535 4116 (administration)
Fax 0131 667 2601
e-mail: libraryed@sac.ac.uk
url: www.sac.ac.uk
Site Librarian Ms Dawn McQuillan MA(Hons) PGDip MCLIP (e-mail: dawn.mcquillan@sac.ac.uk)

Campus libraries

SAC Aberdeen Library, Scottish Agricultural College, Ferguson Building, Craibstone Estate, Aberdeen AB21 9YA
☎(01224) 711057
Fax (01224) 711291
e-mail: libraryab@sac.ac.uk
url: www.sac.ac.uk
Head Librarian Mrs Elizabeth Buchan BA(Hons) (e-mail: elizabeth.buchan@sac.ac.uk)

SAC Auchincruive Library, Scottish Agricultural College, Donald Hendrie Building, Ayr, Ayrshire KA6 5HW
☎(01292) 525209
Fax (01292) 525211
e-mail: libraryau@sac.ac.uk
url: www.sac.ac.uk
Site Librarian Ms Elaine P Muir MA PGDipLib MCLIP (e-mail: elaine.muir@sac.ac.uk)

SHEFFIELD HALLAM UNIVERSITY

Student and Learning Services, Sheffield Hallam University, City Campus, Sheffield S1 1WB
☎0114 225 3333
Fax 0114 225 3859
e-mail: learning.centre@shu.ac.uk
url: www.shu.ac.uk/services/sls/learning/library.html
Assistant Director, Learning and Academic Services Edward Oyston BA MSc MCLIP
Academic Services Manager Ms Alison Ward BA MA MCLIP (e-mail: a.ward@shu.ac.uk)
Information Resources Manager Ms Ann Betterton (e-mail: a.betterton@shu.ac.uk)
Advisory and Operations Maurice Teasdale

Campus Learning Centres

Adsetts Centre, Sheffield Hallam University, Student and Learning Services, City Campus, Sheffield S1 1WB
☎0114 225 3333
Fax 0114 225 3859

Collegiate Learning Centre, Sheffield Hallam University, Student and Learning Services, Collegiate Crescent Campus, Sheffield S10 2BP
☎0114 225 3333
Fax 0114 225 2476

THE UNIVERSITY OF SHEFFIELD

Western Bank Library, The University of Sheffield, Western Bank, Sheffield S10 2TN
☎0114 222 7200 (general enquiries); 0114 222 7224 library (administration)
Fax 0114 222 7290
e-mail: library@sheffield.ac.uk
url: www.shef.ac.uk/library
Director of Library Services and University Librarian Martin J Lewis MA DipLib MCLIP

Major libraries

Health Sciences Library, The University of Sheffield, Royal Hallamshire Hospital, Sheffield
S10 2JF
☎0114 271 2030
Fax 0114 278 0923
e-mail: hsl.rhh@sheffield.ac.uk

Health Sciences Library, The University of Sheffield, Northern General Hospital, Sheffield
S5 7AU
☎0114 226 6800
Fax 0114 226 6804
e-mail: hsl.ngh@sheffield.ac.uk

Information Commons, The University of Sheffield, 44 Leavygreave Road, Sheffield S3 7RD
☎0114 222 9999
e-mail: infocommons@sheffield.ac.uk

St George's Library (Engineering & Management), The University of Sheffield, Mappin
Street, Sheffield S1 4DT
☎0114 222 7301
Fax 0114 279 6406
e-mail: sgl@sheffield.ac.uk

SOUTHAMPTON SOLENT UNIVERSITY

Mountbatten Library, Southampton Solent University, Southampton SO14 ORJ
☎023 8031 9681 (enquiries), 023 8031 9248 (administration)
Fax 023 8031 9672
url: www.solent.ac.uk/library/
Head of Library and Learning Services Steve Rose BA(Hons) DipLib MSc (023 8031
9342; e-mail: steve.rose@solent.ac.uk)
Deputy University Librarian (Customer Services and Operations) Graeme Barber
MSc BA(Hons) DipLib MCLIP (023 8031 9867; e-mail: graeme.barber@solent.ac.uk)
Dean, Learning and Information Service Ms Elizabeth Selby BA DMS MCLIP (023 8031
9679; e-mail: elizabeth.selby@solent.ac.uk)

Site library

Warsash Library, Southampton Solent University, Newtown Road, Warsash, Southampton
SO31 9ZL
☎(01489) 556269

UNIVERSITY OF SOUTHAMPTON

Hartley Library, University of Southampton, Highfield, Southampton SO17 1BJ
☎023 8059 2180 (enquiries), 023 8059 3450 (administration)
Fax 023 8059 5451
e-mail: library@soton.ac.uk
url: www.soton.ac.uk/library
University Librarian Mark Brown MA PhD DipLib DipMgmt MCLIP (023 8059 2677;
e-mail: mlb@soton.ac.uk)

Deputy Librarian Richard Wake MA MA CertMgmt MCLIP (023 8059 2371; e-mail: rlw1@soton.ac.uk)
Head of Archives and Special Collections Christopher Woolgar BA PhD DipArchAdmin FSA FRHistS (023 8059 2721; e-mail: cmw@soton.ac.uk)

Site libraries

Health Services Library MP 883, University of Southampton, Level A, South Academic Block, Southampton General Hospital, Tremona Road, Southampton SO16 6YD
☎023 8079 6547
Fax 023 8079 8939
e-mail: hslib@soton.ac.uk
url: www.soton.ac.uk/library/about/hsl
Head of MHLS Library Services Ms Christine Fowler BSc(Hons) MA MCLIP (e-mail: c.a.fowler@soton.ac.uk)

Library, University of Southampton, Winchester School of Art, Park Avenue, Winchester, Hants SO23 8DL
☎023 8059 6986
e-mail: wsaenqs@soton.ac.uk
url: www.soton.ac.uk/library/about/wsal
Head of Library and Information Services Ms Linda Newington BA(Hons) PGDip MCLIP (e-mail: lan1@soton.ac.uk)

National Oceanographic Library, University of Southampton, Southampton Oceanography Centre, Waterfront Campus, European Way, Southampton SO14 3ZH
☎023 8059 6111 (Marine Information and Advisory Service), 023 8059 6116 (general)
Fax 023 8059 6115
e-mail: mias@noc.soton.ac.uk (marine inf/adv serv); nol@noc.soton.ac.uk (general)
url: www.soton.ac.uk/library/about/nol
Head of Information Services Mrs Jane Stephenson BLib MCLIP (e-mail: js8@soton.ac.uk)

SPURGEON'S COLLEGE

Library, Spurgeon's College, 189 South Norwood Hill, London SE25 6DJ
☎020 8653 0850
Fax 020 8771 0959
e-mail: library@spurgeons.ac.uk
url: www.spurgeons.ac.uk
Librarian Mrs J C Powles BA MCLIP (e-mail: j.powles@spurgeons.ac.uk)

STAFFORDSHIRE UNIVERSITY

Information Services, Staffordshire University, College Road, Stoke-on-Trent ST4 2DE
☎(01782) 295770 (enquiries); (01782) 294443 (administration)
Fax (01782) 295799
e-mail: library@staffs.ac.uk
url: www.staffs.ac.uk
Director of Information Services Bernard Shaw (e-mail: b.shaw@staffs.ac.uk)
Associate Director of Learning, Technology and Information Services David Parkes BA(Hons) MSc MA MCLIP (01782 294369; e-mail: d.parkes@staffs.ac.uk)

Site libraries

Law Library, Staffordshire University, Leek Road, Stoke-on-Trent, Staffs ST4 2DF
☎(01782) 294307
e-mail: libraryhelpdesk@staffs.ac.uk
Law and Business Librarian Ms Alison Pope

Nelson Library, Staffordshire University, PO Box 368, Beaconside, Stafford ST18 0DP
☎(01785) 353236
e-mail: libraryhelpdesk@staffs.ac.uk
Customer Services and Operations Manager Mrs Lynda Hawkins

Shrewsbury Health Library, Staffordshire University, School of Health, Royal Shrewsbury
Hospital, Mytton Oak Road, Shrewsbury SY3 8XQ
☎(01743) 261440
Fax (01743) 261061
Subject and Learning Support Librarian Mrs Shirley Kennedy

Thompson Library, Staffordshire University, PO Box 664, College Road, Stoke-on-Trent
ST4 2DE
☎(01782) 295750 (helpdesk); (01782) 294443 (administration)
Fax (01782) 295799
e-mail: libraryhelpdesk@staffs.ac.uk
Customer Services and Site Liaison Manager Mrs Janice Broad

UNIVERSITY OF STIRLING

University Library, University of Stirling, Stirling FK9 4LA
☎(01786) 467250 (Information Centre), (01786) 467227 (administration)
Fax (01786) 466866
e-mail: isoffice@stir.ac.uk
url: www.is.stir.ac.uk
Director of Information Services Mark Toole MA(Cantab) (e-mail:
mark.toole@stir.ac.uk)

Campus library

Highland Health Sciences Library, University of Stirling, Centre for Health Science,
Old Perth Road, Inverness IV2 3JH
☎(01463) 255600
Librarian Mrs Anne Gillespie BA DipLibStud MCLIP (e-mail: ag5@stir.ac.uk)

UNIVERSITY OF STRATHCLYDE

**Andersonian Library, University of Strathclyde, Curran Building, 101 St James' Road,
Glasgow G4 0NS**
☎0141 548 3701 (enquiries), ext 4621 (administration)
Fax 0141 552 3304
e-mail: library@strath.ac.uk
url: www.lib.strath.ac.uk
Acting Director of Library Services Michael Roberts MA MA MCLIP (0141 548 4619;
e-mail: m.roberts@strath.ac.uk)

Constituent libraries

Jordanhill Library, University of Strathclyde, 76 Southbrae Drive, Glasgow G13 1PP
☎0141 950 3300
Fax 0141 950 3150
e-mail: jordanhill.library@strath.ac.uk
Librarian David Alcock BA MA MCLIP (e-mail: d.alcock@strath.ac.uk)

UNIVERSITY OF SUNDERLAND

Student and Learning Support, University of Sunderland, Chester Road, Sunderland SR1 3SD
☎0191 515 2230
Fax 0191 515 2904
url: www.sunderland.ac.uk/sls
Director of Student and Learning Support Ms Kirsten Black BA DipISTech (0191 515 3904)
Assistant Directors Oliver Pritchard BA MA MA MCLIP (0191 515 2903; e-mail: oliver.pritchard@sunderland.ac.uk), Dave Webster BSc (0191 515 2990; e-mail: dave.webster@sunderland.ac.uk)

Site libraries

Ashburne Library, University of Sunderland, Sunderland SR2 7EG
☎0191 515 2119
Fax 0191 515 3166
Site Librarian Ms J Dodshon BA(Hons) DipLib (0191 515 2120; e-mail: jan.dodshon@sunderland.ac.uk)

The Murray Library, University of Sunderland, Chester Road, Sunderland SR1 3SD
☎0191 515 3149
Fax 0191 515 2904
Site Librarian Ms J Archer BA (0191 515 3272; e-mail: julie.archer@sunderland.ac.uk)

St Peter's Library, University of Sunderland, Prospect Building, St Peter's Riverside Campus, St Peter's Way, Sunderland SR6 0DD
☎0191 515 3318
Fax 0191 515 3061
Site Librarian Mrs E Astan BA MCLIP (e-mail: elizabeth.astan@sunderland.ac.uk)

UNIVERSITY OF SURREY

University Library, University of Surrey, George Edwards Building, Guildford, Surrey GU2 7XH
☎(01483) 683325 (enquiries), 01483 689232 (administration)
Fax (01483) 689500
e-mail: library-enquiries@surrey.ac.uk
url: http://portal.surrey.ac.uk/library
Director of Library and Learning Support Services Ms Jane Savidge MA MCLIP

UNIVERSITY OF SUSSEX

University Library, University of Sussex, Falmer, Brighton BNI 9QL
☎(01273) 678163 (enquiries), (01273) 877097 (administration)
Fax (01273) 678441
e-mail: library@sussex.ac.uk
url: www.sussex.ac.uk/library/
University Librarian Ms Kitty Inglis
Head of Research Services and Special Collections Ms Jane Harvell
Head of Technical Services Adrian Hale
Head of Library Administration Ms Sally Faith

SPRU (Science and Technology Policy Research) – The Keith Pavitt Library, University of
Sussex, The Freeman Centre, Falmer, Brighton BNI 9QE
☎(01273) 678066 (enquiries)
Fax (01273) 685865
e-mail: spru_library@sussex.ac.uk
url: www.sussex.ac.uk/spru/research/kplib; SPRU Library Catalogue:
http://sprulib2.central.sussex.ac.uk/heritage
Resources Assistant Ms Kate Beavis

SWANSEA METROPOLITAN UNIVERSITY

Owen Library, Swansea Metropolitan University, Mount Pleasant, Swansea SAI 6ED
☎(01792) 481141
Fax (01792) 644076
Head of Library and Learning Resources Ms Anne Harvey LLB DipLib (e-mail:
anne.harvey@smu.ac.uk)

Site libraries

Dynevor Library, Swansea Metropolitan University, Dynevor Centre for Art, Design and
Media, De La Beche Street, Swansea SAI 3EU
☎(01792) 481030
Deputy Head of Library and Learning Resources Mrs Alison Scanlon BA MCLIP
(e-mail: alison.scanlon@smu.ac.uk)

Townhill Campus Library, Swansea Metropolitan University, Townhill Road, Swansea SA2 0UT
☎(01792) 482113
url: www.smu.ac.uk/library
Deputy Head of Library and Learning Resources Ms Mari Thomas BA DipLib MCLIP
(e-mail: mari.thomas@smu.ac.uk)

SWANSEA UNIVERSITY

Library and Information Centre, Swansea University, Singleton Park, Swansea SA2 8PP
☎(01792) 295697 (enquiries), (01792) 295175 (administration)
Fax (01792) 295851
e-mail: library@swansea.ac.uk
url: www.swan.ac.uk/lis/index.htm
Director of Library and Information Services Christopher West MA BA MCLIP

Site library

South Wales Miners' Library, Swansea University, Hendrefoelan Campus, Gower Road, Swansea SA2 7NB
☎(01792) 518603
e-mail: miners@swansea.ac.uk
Branch Librarian Ms Siân F Williams BSc MCLIP

TEESSIDE UNIVERSITY

Library and Information Services, Teesside University, Middlesbrough TS1 3BA
☎(01642) 342100 (enquiries), (01642) 342103 (administration)
Fax (01642) 342190
e-mail: lisenquiries@tees.ac.uk
url: www.lis.tees.ac.uk
Director of Library & Information Services Liz Jolly BA(Hons) DipILS FCLIP FRSA
(e-mail: liz.jolly@tees.ac.uk)

THAMES VALLEY UNIVERSITY

Library Services, Thames Valley University, St Mary's Road, Ealing, London W5 5RF
☎020 8231 2405/2248
Fax 020 8231 2402
url: http://library.tvu.ac.uk
Head of Learning and Research Support Ms Elizabeth Powis (020 8231 2631; e-mail: elizabeth.powis@tvu.ac.uk)

Libraries

Paragon House Library, Thames Valley University, 2nd Floor, Paragon House, Boston Manor Road, Brentford, Middlesex TW8 9GA
☎020 8209 4043
Fax 020 8209 4045
Library Manager John Wolstenholme BA (020 8209 4047; e-mail: john.wolstenholme@tvu.ac.uk)

Paul Hamlyn Library, Thames Valley University, Wellington Street, Slough SL1 1YG
☎(01753) 697536 (enquiries)
Fax (01753) 697538
Acting Library Manager John Wolstenholme BA (01753 697525; e-mail: john.wolstenholme@tvu.ac.uk)

St Mary's Road Library, Thames Valley University, Ealing, London W5 5RF
☎020 8231 2405/2248
Fax 020 8231 2631
Library Manager Ms Gillian Briggs (020 8231 2041; e-mail: gillian.briggs@tvu.ac.uk)

TRINITY LABAN

Jerwood Library of the Performing Arts, Trinity Laban, Trinity College of Music, King Charles Court, Old Royal Naval College, Greenwich, London SE10 9JF
☎020 8305 3950 (enquiries)

Fax 020 8305 9444
e-mail: library@tcm.ac.uk
url: www.tcm.ac.uk
Head Librarian Miss Claire Kidwell BA(Hons) MA (e-mail: ckidwell@tcm.ac.uk)
Collection Manager (Mander and Mitcheson Theatre Collection) Ms Kristy Davis
(e-mail: kdavis@tcm.ac.uk)
(Houses the Mander and Mitchenson Theatre Collection)

Library, Laban, Trinity Laban, Creekside, London SE8 3DZ
☎020 8691 8600 (switchboard)
Fax 020 8691 8400
e-mail: library@laban.co.uk
url: www.laban.org
Head of Library and Archives Ralph Cox

UHI MILLENNIUM INSTITUTE

UHI Library Services, UHI Millennium Institute, Executive Office, Ness Walk, Inverness IV3 5SQ
☎(01463) 279000
Fax (01463) 279001
url: www.uhi.ac.uk
UHI Librarian Ms Gillian Anderson BA MCLIP (e-mail: gillian.anderson@uhi.ac.uk)

Academic Partner libraries

Argyll College UHI, UHI Millennium Institute, Stewart Road, Campbeltown, Argyll
PA28 6AT
☎(01631) 559673
Fax (01631) 559671
Learning Resources Contact Ms Liz Richardson

Highland Theological College, UHI Millennium Institute, High Street, Dingwall, Ross shire
IV15 9HA
☎(01349) 780215
Fax (01349) 780001
Learning Resources Contacts Martin Cameron BA DipLib MCLIP(Librarian)

Inverness College UHI, UHI Millennium Institute, 3 Longman Road, Longman Road South,
Inverness IV1 1SA
☎(01463) 273248
Fax (01463) 711977
Learning Resources Contact Ms Carol Hart DipLIS MCLIP

Lews Castle College UHI, UHI Millennium Institute, Stornoway, Isle of Lewis, Hebrides
HS2 0XR
☎(01851) 770408
Fax (01851) 770001
Acting Learning Resources Contact Dave Matheson

Lochaber College UHI, UHI Millennium Institute, An Aird, Fort William, Lochaber,
Inverness-shire PH33 6AN
☎(01397) 874277

Fax (01397) 874001
Learning Resources Contact Ms Louise Penny

Moray College UHI, UHI Millennium Institute, Moray Street, Elgin, Moray IV30 1JJ
☎(01343) 576206
Fax (01343) 576001
Learning Resources Contact Mrs Angie Mackenzie BA DipLib DipEdTech MCLIP

NAFC Marine Centre UHI, UHI Millennium Institute, North Atlantic Fisheries College,
Port Arthur, Scalloway, Shetland ZE1 0UN
☎(01595) 772000
Fax (01595) 772001
e-mail: library@nafc.uhi.ac.uk
url: www.nafc.ac.uk
Learning Resources Contact Ms Ruth Priest BA DipLib MCLIP (e-mail:
ruth.priest@shetland.uhi.ac.uk)

North Highland College UHI, UHI Millennium Institute, Ormlie Road, Thurso, Caithness
KW14 7EE
☎(01847) 889294
Fax (01847) 889001
Learning Resources Contact Ms Rhona Mason BA MLib MCLIP

Orkney College UHI, UHI Millennium Institute, East Road, Kirkwall, Orkney
KW15 1LX
☎(01856) 569000
Fax (01856) 569001
Librarian Ms Anette Andersen (01856 569272)

Perth College Library UHI, UHI Millennium Institute, Crieff Road, Perth PH1 2NX
☎(01738) 877721
Fax (01738) 631364
e-mail: library@perth.uhi.ac.uk
url: www.perth/support/library/Pages/default.aspx
Learning Resources Contact Richard Hughes BA(Hons) MSc ILS MCLIP (01738 877707;
e-mail: richard.hughes@perth.uhi.ac.uk)

Sabhal Mòr Ostaig, UHI Millennium Institute, Colaiste Ghàidhlig na h-Alba, An Teanga,
Slèite, An t-Eilean Sgitheanach IV44 8RQ
☎(01471) 888431
Fax (01471) 888001
e-mail: sm00ll@uhi.ac.uk
url: www.smo.uhi.ac.uk/
College Librarian Ms Cairistìona Cain MA(Hons) MSc DipPsych

Scottish Marine Institute, UHI Millennium Institute, Oban, Argyll PA37 1QA
☎(01631) 559000
Fax (01631) 559001
Learning Resources Contact Ms Olga Kimmins BA(Hons) (e-mail:
olga.kimmins@sams.ac.uk)

Shetland College UHI, UHI Millennium Institute, Gremista, Lerwick, Shetland ZE1 0PX
☎(01595) 771000
Fax (01595) 694830

Learning Resources Contact Ms Ruth Priest BA DipLib MCLIP (e-mail: ruth.priest@shetland.uhi.ac.uk)

UNIVERSITY OF ULSTER

Library, University of Ulster, Coleraine Campus, Cromore Road, Co Londonderry BT52 ISA
☎028 7032 3128
Fax 028 7032 4928
url: www.library.ulster.ac.uk
Assistant Director, Library Mrs Elaine Urquhart MA DipLibInfoStud MCLIP
(028 7032 3343; e-mail: ee.urquhart@ulster.ac.uk)

Campus libraries

LRC, Belfast Campus, University of Ulster, York Street, Belfast BT15 1ED
☎028 9026 7268
Fax 028 9026 7278
LRC Manager Mrs Marion Khorshidian BA DipLIS MCLIP (e-mail: m.khorshidian@ulster.ac.uk)

LRC, Coleraine Campus, University of Ulster, Cromore Road, Coleraine, Co Londonderry BT52 ISA
☎028 7032 4345
Fax 028 7032 4928
LRC Manager Mrs Stephanie McLaughlin BA LibStud (e-mail: sa.mclaughlin@ulster.ac.uk)

LRC, Jordanstown Campus, University of Ulster, Shore Road, Newtownabbey, Co Antrim BT37 0QB
☎028 9036 6399
Fax 028 9036 6849
LRC Manager Ms Laura Mills (e-mail: lj.mills@ulster.ac.uk)

LRC, Magee Campus, University of Ulster, Northland Road, Co Londonderry BT48 7JL
☎028 7137 5264
Fax 028 7137 5626
LRC Manager Ciaran Cregan (e-mail: cr.cregan@ulster.ac.uk)

UNIVERSITY OF THE ARTS LONDON

Information Services, University of the Arts London, 272 High Holborn, London WC1V 7EY
☎020 7514 6000 (switchboard)
url: www.arts.ac.uk/library
Director of Information Services Ms Pat Christie BA MCLIP (020 7514 8072; e-mail: p.christie@arts.ac.uk)

College/site libraries

Camberwell College of Arts
Library Services, Camberwell College of Arts, 43-45 Peckham Road, London SE5 8UF
☎020 7514 6349
Fax 020 7514 6324

Learning Resources Manager Peter Jennett MA MCLIP (e-mail:
p.jennett@wimbledon.arts.ac.uk)
Assistant Learning Resources Manager Ms Evelyn O'Callaghan
Librarians Ms Jane Holt, Ms Jan Morgan, Ms Jane Mann, Gustavo Grandal Montero MA
MCLIP

Central St Martins College of Art and Design
Library and Learning Resources, Central St Martins College of Art and Design,
Southampton Row, London WC1B 4AP
☎020 7514 7037
Fax 020 7514 7033
url: www.csm.arts.ac.uk
Learning Resources Manager Ms Sarah Gilmour (e-mail: s.gilmour@csm.arts.ac.uk)

Library and Learning Resources, Central Saint Martins College of Art and Design, 107
Charing Cross Road, London WC2H 0DU
☎020 7514 7190
Fax 020 7514 7189
Assistant Learning Resources Manager Kenneth Dick (e-mail: k.dick@csm.arts.ac.uk)

Chelsea College of Art and Design
Library and Learning Resources, Chelsea College of Art and Design, 16 John Islip Street,
London SW1P 4JU
☎020 7514 7773/4
Fax 020 7514 7785
url: www.arts.ac.uk/library
Learning Resources Manager Peter Jennett MA MCLIP (e-mail:
p.jennett@wimbledon.arts.ac.uk)
Assistant Learning Resources Manager Ms Tania Olsson
Librarians Gustavo Grandal Montero MA MCLIP, Ms Heather Sneddon MSc, Leo Clarey
MA MCLIP, Ms Alessia Borri

London College of Communication
Library and Learning Resources, London College of Communication, Elephant and Castle,
London SE1 6SB
☎020 7514 8026 (enquiries), 020 7514 6587 (administration)
Fax 020 7514 6597
e-mail: libraryenquiries@lcc.arts.ac.uk
url: www.arts.ac.uk/library
Learning Resources Manager Ms Regina Everitt (e-mail: r.everitt@lcc.arts.ac.uk)

London College of Fashion
Library and Learning Resources, London College of Fashion, 20 John Princes Street,
Oxford Circus, London W1G 0BJ
☎020 7514 7455/7543
Fax 020 7514 7580
Learning Resources Manager Ms Diane Mansbridge BA MA MCLIP (e-mail:
d.mansbridge@fashion.arts.ac.uk)

Wimbledon College of Art
Library and Learning Resources, Wimbledon College of Art, Merton Hall Road, London
SW19 3QA
☎020 7514 9690 (enquiries)
Fax 020 7514 9642
url: www.wimbledon.arts.ac.uk; www.arts.ac.uk/library.htm
Learning Resources Manager Peter Jennett MA MCLIP (e-mail:
p.jennett@wimbledon.arts.ac.uk)
Assistant Learning Resources Manager Helen Davies BA(Hons) MCLIP (e-mail:
h.j.davies@wimbledon.arts.ac.uk)
Librarians Peter Crollie BA(Hons) (e-mail: p.crollie@wimbledon.arts.ac.uk), Lorna Scott
BA MCLIP (e-mail: l.a.scott@wimbledon.arts.ac.uk), Alice Bloom BA (e-mail:
a.bloom@wimbledon.arts.ac.uk)

UNIVERSITY OF WALES INSTITUTE, CARDIFF

Library Division, University of Wales Institute, Cardiff, Llandaff Campus, Western Avenue,
Cardiff CF5 2YB
☎029 2041 6240
Fax 029 2041 6908
url: www.uwic.ac.uk/library
Head of Library Division Paul Riley BA(Hons) MSc (029 2041 6240; e-mail:
priley@uwic.ac.uk)

UNIVERSITY OF WALES, NEWPORT

Learning and Information Services, University of Wales, Newport, Caerleon Campus,
Lodge Road, Caerleon, Newport, Gwent NP18 3QT
☎(01633) 432842
Fax (01633) 432920
e-mail: lis@newport.ac.uk
url: http://lis.newport.ac.uk
Director of Learning and Information Services Tony Rucinski (e-mail:
tony.rucinski@newport.ac.uk)

Campus libraries

Caerleon Campus, University of Wales, Newport, Newport, Gwent NP18 3QT
☎(01633) 432101
Head of Library Services Mrs Lesley May BA DipLib MCLIP PGCE FHEA (01633
432103; e-mail: lesley.may@newport.ac.uk)

Allt-yr-yn Campus, University of Wales, Newport, Allt-yr-yn Road, Newport, Gwent
NP20 5PA
☎(01633) 432101
Quality Manager Ms Dawne Leatherdale MBA MCLIP (01633 432349; e-mail:
dawne.leatherdale@newport.ac.uk)

UNIVERSITY OF WALES TRINITY ST DAVID

(University of Wales Lampeter has merged with Trinity University College to form University of Wales Trinity St David)

The Library, University of Wales Trinity St David, Learning Resources Centre, Lampeter Campus, College Street, Lampeter, Ceredigion SA48 7ED
☎(01570 424798 (enquiries/Librarian)
Fax (01570) 424997
e-mail: lrc@trinitysaintdavid.ac.uk
url: www.trinitysaintdavid.ac.uk/en/lrc
Head of Learning Resources Ms Sally Wilkinson BA DipLib MCLIP

The Library, University of Wales Trinity Saint David, Learning Resources Centre, Carmarthen Campus, College Road, Carmarthen SA31 3EP
☎(01267) 676780
Fax (01267) 676766
e-mail: lrc@trinitysaintdavid.ac.uk
url: www.trinitysaintdavid.ac.uk/en/lrc
Head of Learning Resources Ms Sally Wilkinson BA DipLib MCLIP

UNIVERSITY OF WARWICK

Library, University of Warwick, Gibbet Hill Road, Coventry CV4 7AL
☎024 7652 2026
Fax 024 7652 4211
e-mail: library@warwick.ac.uk
url: www2.warwick.ac.uk/services/library
Librarian Ms Anne Bell BA MA MCLIP

UNIVERSITY OF THE WEST OF ENGLAND, BRISTOL

Library Services, University of the West of England, Bristol, Frenchay Campus, Coldharbour Lane, Bristol BS16 1QY
☎0117 328 2277 (enquiries), 0117 328 2404 (administration)
Fax 0117 328 2407
url: www.uwe.ac.uk/library
Head of Library Services Mrs Cathy Rex BSc DMS MAML MCLIP

UNIVERSITY OF THE WEST OF SCOTLAND

Library, University of the West of Scotland, High Street, Paisley, Renfrewshire PA1 2BE
☎0141 848 3758 (enquiries), 0141 848 3751 (administration)
Fax 0141 848 3761
e-mail: library@uws.ac.uk
url: www.uws.ac.uk/library
University Librarian Gordon Hunt MA (e-mail: gordon.hunt@uws.ac.uk)
Campus Librarian (Paisley) Ms Philomena Millar (e-mail: philomena.millar@uws.ac.uk)

Site Libraries

Ayr Campus Library, University of the West of Scotland, Beech Grove, Ayr KA8 0SR

☎(01292) 886345
Fax (01292) 886288
e-mail: libraryayr@uws.ac.uk
Campus Librarian (Ayr) Neal Buchanan (e-mail: neal.buchanan@uws.ac.uk)

Dumfries Campus Crichton Library, University of the West of Scotland, Dumfries Campus, Dumfries DG1 4UQ
☎(01387) 734323
Campus Librarian (Dumfries) Ms Avril Goodwin (e-mail: avril.goodwin@uws.ac.uk)

Hamilton Campus Library, University of the West of Scotland, Almada Street, Hamilton, Lanarkshire ML3 0JB
☎(01698) 894424
Fax (01698) 286856
Campus Librarian (Hamilton) John Burke (e-mail: john.burke@uws.ac.uk)

UNIVERSITY OF WESTMINSTER

Information Systems and Library Services, University of Westminster, Cavendish House, 101 New Cavendish Street, London W1W 6XH
☎020 7911 5095
url: www.westminster.ac.uk
Director of Information Systems and Library Services (ISLS) Ms Suzanne Enright BA DipLib MCLIP (e-mail: s.enright@westminster.ac.uk)
Associate Director ISLS (Learning & Research Support) Ms Carole Satchwell BA MCLIP (e-mail: c.satchwell@westminster.ac.uk)
Associate Director ISLS (Resources & Planning) Vacant
Library Services Manager Ms Elaine Salter BA MLib FCLIP (e-mail: e.salter@westminster.ac.uk)
Academic Liaison Manager Ms Fiona O'Brien MA MCLIP FRSA (e-mail: f.obrien@westminster.ac.uk)
Collections Manager Mrs Ann Sainsbury BA MCLIP (e-mail: a.sainsbury@wmin.ac.uk)

Libraries

Archive Services, University of Westminster, Regent Campus, 4–12 Little Titchfield Street, London W1W 7UW
☎020 7911 5000 ext 2524
Fax 020 7911 5158
University Archivist Ms Elaine Penn MA RMSA (e-mail: e.s.penn@westminster.ac.uk)

Cavendish Library, University of Westminster, 115 New Cavendish Street, London W1W 6UW
☎020 7911 5000 ext 3613
Fax 020 7911 5093
Library Services Site Manager Ms Adjoa Boateng BA MSc MCLIP (e-mail: a.k.boateng@westminster.ac.uk)

Harrow LRC, University of Westminster, Watford Road, Northwick Park, Harrow, Middlesex HA1 3TP
☎020 7911 5000 ext 4006
Fax 020 7911 5952

Library Services Site Manager Ms Sally Bannard BA PGCDipHistArt (e-mail:
s.bannard@westminster.ac.uk)

Marylebone Library, University of Westminster, 35 Marylebone Road, London NWI 5LS
☎020 7911 5000 ext 3212
Fax 020 7911 5058
Library Services Site Manager Ms Nikki Trigg (e-mail: n.trigg@westminster.ac.uk)

Regent Library, University of Westminster, 4–12 Little Titchfield Street, London WIW 7UW
☎020 7911 5000 ext 2524
Fax 020 7911 5846
Library Services Site Manager Ms Adjoa Boateng BA MSc MCLIP (e-mail:
a.k.boateng@westminster.ac.uk)

UNIVERSITY OF WINCHESTER

Library, University of Winchester, Sparkford Road, Winchester, Hants SO22 4NR
☎(01962) 827306
Fax (01962) 827443
url: www.winchester.ac.uk/library
Librarian David Farley BA(Hons) CertMan(OU) MCLIP (01962 827306; e-mail:
david.farley@winchester.ac.uk)
Deputy Librarian Ms Sarah Bulger BA(Hons) MA (01962 827306; e-mail:
sarah.bulger@winchester.ac.uk)

UNIVERSITY OF WOLVERHAMPTON

**Harrison Learning Centre, University of Wolverhampton, Wulfruna Street,
Wolverhampton WVI IRH**
☎(01902) 322300 (enquiries), 01902 322302 (administration)
Fax (01902) 322668
e-mail: msteamemails@wlv.ac.uk
url: www.wlv.ac.uk
Director of Learning and Information Services Ms Fiona Parsons BA MLib PGCE
(01902 322302)
Assistant Director of Learning and Information Services Mrs Trish Fouracres
BA(Hons) MA MCLIP

Site libraries

Compton Learning Centre, University of Wolverhampton, Compton Road West,
Wolverhampton WV3 9DX
☎(01902) 323648
Fax (01902) 323702
Learning Centre Manager Mrs Linda Thomas MCLIP

Harrison Learning Centre, University of Wolverhampton, Wulfruna Street, Wolverhampton
WVI IRH
☎(01902) 322535
Fax (01902) 322194
Learning Centre Manager Ian Keepins BA(Hons) PGDipLib PGCert(Management)

Telford Learning Centre, University of Wolverhampton, Old Shifnal Road, Priorslee, Telford, Shropshire TF2 9NT
☎(01902) 323983
Fax (01902) 323985
Learning Centre Manager David W Clare BA MCLIP

Walsall Learning Centre, University of Wolverhampton, Gorway, Walsall, West Midlands WS1 3BD
☎(01902) 323158
Fax (01902) 323079
Learning Centre Manager Ian Keepins BA(Hons) PGDipLib PGCert(Management)

School of Health site library

Burton Learning Centre, University of Wolverhampton, Burton Nurse Education Centre, Belvedere Road, Burton upon Trent, Staffs DE13 0RB
☎(01283) 566333 ext 2217/2237
Fax (01283) 515978
Site Librarian Ms Liz Watson BA PGDipLib MCLIP

UNIVERSITY OF WORCESTER

Information and Learning Services, University of Worcester, Peirson Building, Henwick Grove, Worcester WR2 6AJ
☎(01905) 855341
Fax (01905) 855197
e-mail: askalibrarian@worc.ac.uk
url: www.worcester.ac.uk/ils
Director of Information and Learning Services Ms Anne Hannaford BA(Hons) DipLib (e-mail: a.hannaford@worc.ac.uk)
Team Leader, Customer Services and Partnerships Ms Ann Craig BLib MSc MCLI (e-mail: a.craig@worc.ac.uk)
Issue Desk Manager Ms Lissa O'Grady (e-mail: l.ogrady@worc.ac.uk)

WRITTLE COLLEGE

Library, Writtle College, Chelmsford, Essex CM1 3RR
☎(01245) 424245
Fax (01245) 420456
e-mail: thelibrary@writtle.ac.uk
url: www.writtle.ac.uk
Head of Learning Information Services Mrs R M Hewings BSc(Econ) DMS DipLib FCLIP FHEA (ext 26009; e-mail: rachel.hewings@writtle.ac.uk)
Subject Librarian, Science and Sustainable Environments Ms Christina Harbour BA MA (ext 26008; e-mail: christina.harbour@writtle.ac.uk)
Subject Librarian, Horticulture and Design Ms Tina Hohmann DipJng MLIS MCLIP (ext 26008; e-mail: tina.hohmann@writtle.ac.uk)

YORK ST JOHN UNIVERSITY

Library and Information Services, York St John University, Fountains Learning Centre, Lord Mayor's Walk, York YO3I 7EX
☎(01904) 876700
Fax (01904) 876324
e-mail: library@yorksj.ac.uk
url: www.yorksj.ac.uk/library/index.aspx
University Librarian Tony Chalcraft BA MA (01904 876701; e-mail: a.chalcraft@yorksj.ac.uk)
Deputy University Librarian Ms Helen Westmancoat BA MCLIP (e-mail: h.westmancoat@yorksj.ac.uk)
Academic Liaison Librarians Ms Jane Munks BA MCLIP (e-mail: j.munks@yorksj.ac.uk)
Ms Victoria Watt MA (e-mail: v.watt@yorksj.ac.uk)
Ms Lottie Alexander BA (e-mail: l.alexander@yorksj.ac.uk)
Ms Clare McCluskey BA MCLIP (e-mail: c.mccluskey@yorksj.ac.uk)
Acquisitions Librarian Bryan Jones BA (e-mail: b.jones@yorksj.ac.uk)
Database Librarian Ms Ruth Mardall BA MA (e-mail: r.mardall2@yorksj.ac.uk)

UNIVERSITY OF YORK

J B Morrell and Raymond Burton Libraries, University of York, Heslington, York YOIO 5DD
☎(01904) 433873 (enquiries)
Fax (01904) 433866
e-mail: lib-enquiry@york.ac.uk
url: www.york.ac.uk/library/
Director of Information Stephen Town MA DipLib FCLIP

Branch/department library

King's Manor Library, University of York, The King's Manor, York YOI 7EP
☎(01904) 433969

Selected Government, National and Special Libraries in the United Kingdom

ADVOCATES LIBRARY

Advocates Library, Parliament House, Edinburgh EHI IRF
☎0131 260 5683 (enquiries), 0131 260 5637 (Librarian)
Fax 0131 260 5663 (9am–5pm weekdays)
e-mail: inqdesk@advocates.org.uk
url: www.advocates.org.uk
Senior Librarian Ms Andrea Longson BSc DipLib MBA (e-mail: andrea.longson@advocates.org.uk)
(Open to members only. Non-members may access stock at the National Library of Scotland.)

Specialism(s): Law

ALDERSHOT MILITARY MUSEUM

Military Museum and Archive, Aldershot Military Museum, Evelyn Woods Road, Queens Avenue, Aldershot, Hants GUII 2LG
☎(01252) 314598
Fax (01252) 342942
url: www.hants.gov.uk/aldershot-museum
Curator Ms Sally Day BA MCLIP (e-mail: sally.1.day@hants.gov.uk)
(Accessible to enquirers by appointment)

Specialism(s): Military and local history relating to Aldershot and Farnborough

AMBLESS SOCIETY LIBRARY

Ambless Society Library, Shalom House, Lower Celtic Park, Enniskillen, Co Fermanagh BT74 6HP
☎028 6632 0320; Ambless Accident Supportline: 028 6632 0321
(tel/fax/smstext/voicemail/RBS)
Fax 028 6632 0320
url: www.ukselfhelp.info.ambless
Librarian John Wood

Specialism(s): Private research library working closely with the charity Ambless, which offers care and support to accident sufferers and their families

AMERICAN MUSEUM IN BRITAIN

Library, American Museum in Britain, Claverton Manor, Bath BA2 7BD
☎(01225) 823016
Fax (01225) 469160
e-mail: info@americanmuseum.org; library@americanmuseum.org (by appointment only)
url: www.americanmuseum.org
Librarian Dr Cathryn Spence (e-mail: cathryn.spence@americanmuseum.org)

Specialism(s): American history and decorative arts; Religions, e.g. Shakers; North American Indians

AMGUEDDFA CYMRU – NATIONAL MUSEUM WALES

Library, Amgueddfa Cymru – National Museum Wales, Cathays Park, Cardiff CFI0 3NP
☎029 2057 3202
e-mail: library@museumwales.ac.uk
url: www.museumwales.ac.uk
Librarian John R Kenyon BA MCLIP FSA FRHistS FSA(Scot)

Specialism(s): Archaeology; Fine and decorative arts; Botany; Geology; Zoology; Architecture; Welsh history and topography

THE ARMITT MUSEUM AND LIBRARY

Library, The Armitt Museum and Library, Rydal Road, Ambleside, Cumbria LA22 9BL
☎(01539) 431212
e-mail: info@armitt.com
url: www.armitt.com
Museum Manager Ms Clara Li-Dunne

Specialism(s): Specialist Lake District collection (literature, topography, natural history); Cumbria; Mountaineering; Kurt Schwitters; Beatrix Potter, Brunskill and Abraham Brothers (Photographic glass plates), Herbert Bell (Photography), Harriet Martineau, William Green

ARTS AND HUMANITIES RESEARCH COUNCIL (AHRC) see RESEARCH COUNCILS UK

ASSOCIATION OF COMMONWEALTH UNIVERSITIES

Reference Library, Association of Commonwealth Universities, Woburn House, 20–24 Tavistock Square, London WCIH 9HF
☎020 7380 6700
Fax 020 7387 2655
e-mail: info@acu.ac.uk
url: www.acu.ac.uk
Librarian Nicholas Mulhern MA MA DipLIS MCLIP

Specialism(s): Higher Education in the Commonwealth

BABRAHAM INSTITUTE

Library, The Babraham Institute, Babraham Research Campus, Cambridge CB22 3AT
☎(01223) 496214 (enquiries)
Fax (01223) 496027
e-mail: babraham.library@bbsrc.ac.uk
url: www.babraham.ac.uk
Librarian Miss Jennifer R Maddock BA DipLib MCLIP (01223 496235; e-mail: jennifer.maddock@bbsrc.ac.uk)
Library Assistants Ms Suzanne Morley BA MA, Mrs Arwen E Spicer BA

Specialism(s): Electronic resources supporting biomedical research, especially relating to cell signalling and epigenetics

BANK OF ENGLAND

Information Centre, Bank of England, Threadneedle Street, London EC2R 8AH
☎020 7601 4715 (enquiries), 020 7601 4668 (administration)
Fax 020 7601 4356
e-mail: informationcentre@bankofengland.co.uk
url: www.bankofengland.co.uk
Information Centre Manager Ms Penny Hope BA MA MSc DipLib MCLIP

Specialism(s): Economics; Central banking

BERR (DEPARTMENT FOR BUSINESS, ENTERPRISE AND REGULATORY REFORM) *see* DEPARTMENT FOR BUSINESS, INNOVATION AND SKILLS (BIS)

BG GROUP PLC

Information Centre, BG Group plc, Faraday Building 2, 100 Thames Valley Park Drive, Reading RG6 IPT
☎(0118) 929 2496 (enquiries and administration)
Fax (0118) 929 2414
url: www.bg-group.com
Information Analysts Padraig Cronin (0118 929 2496; e-mail:
padraig.cronin@bg-group.com), D Freemantle (0118 929 2497; e-mail:
david.freemantle@bg-group.com)

Specialism(s): Reference collection, mainly energy industry

BIRMINGHAM AND MIDLAND INSTITUTE

The Birmingham Library, Birmingham and Midland Institute, 9 Margaret Street, Birmingham B3 3BS
☎0121 236 3591
Fax 0121 212 4577
e-mail: admin@bmi.org.uk
url: www.bmi.org.uk
Librarian Vacant
(Private members' library)

Specialism(s): History; Literature; Natural history; Science; Travel; Fiction; Biography; Music

BISHOPSGATE INSTITUTE

Bishopsgate Library, Bishopsgate Institute, 230 Bishopsgate, London EC2M 4QH
☎020 7392 9270
Fax 020 7392 9275
e-mail: library@bishopsgate.org.uk
url: www.bishopsgate.org.uk
Library and Archives Manager Stefan Dickers
Deputy Library Manager Edward Weech

Specialism(s): London history and topography; Labour history; 19thC trades union history; Co-operative movement; Freethought movement; Humanism

BRITANNIA ROYAL NAVAL COLLEGE

College Library, Britannia Royal Naval College, Dartmouth, Devon TQ6 0HJ
☎(01803) 677278
Fax (01803) 677015
url: www.royal-navy.mod.uk
College Librarian Ms Gill Smith (e-mail: brnc-lib1@nrta.mod.uk)
(Prior appointment necessary)

Specialism(s): Strategic studies; Naval history; Marine environment; Leadership

BRITISH ANTARCTIC SURVEY

Library, British Antarctic Survey, High Cross, Madingley Road, Cambridge CB3 0ET
☎(01223) 221400
Fax (01223) 362616
e-mail: baslib@bas.ac.uk
url: www.antarctica.ac.uk
Librarian Ms Jo Milton BA(Hons) (e-mail: jolt@bas.ac.uk)

Specialism(s): Geology; Geophysics; Glaciology; Climatology; Upper atmosphere physics; Marine and terrestrial biology (all with accent on Antarctic region)

BRITISH BROADCASTING CORPORATION

BBC Information and Archives, British Broadcasting Corporation, BC3 D6 Broadcast Centre, White City, 201 Wood Lane, London W12 7TP
☎020 8008 2288
e-mail: customerservice@bbc.co.uk
url: www.bbc.co.uk
Head of Media Asset Management Ms Sarah Hayes (020 8008 2250; e-mail: sarah.hayes@bbc.co.uk)

BRITISH COUNCIL

Information Centre, British Council, Bridgewater House, 58 Whitworth Street, Manchester M1 6BB
☎0161 957 7755
Fax 0161 957 7762
e-mail: general.enquiries@britishcouncil.org
url: www.britishcouncil.org
Manager Ms Tanya Dunne (0161 957 7933; e-mail: tanya.dunne@britishcouncil.org)
(For details of British Council information services in 110 countries and territories see website: www.britishcouncil.org.)

BRITISH DENTAL ASSOCIATION

BDA Information Centre, British Dental Association, 64 Wimpole Street, London W1G 8YS

☎020 7563 4545
Fax 020 7935 6492
e-mail: infocentre@bda.org
url: www.bda.org.uk
Head of Library and Knowledge Services R Farbey BA DipLib FCLIP (e-mail:
r.farbey@bda.org)

BRITISH EMPIRE AND COMMONWEALTH MUSEUM

**British Empire and Commonwealth Museum, Archives, Clock Tower Yard, Temple Meads,
Bristol BSI 6QH**
☎0117 925 4980
Fax 0117 925 4983
e-mail: admin@empiremuseum.co.uk
url: www.empiremuseum.co.uk/museumarchives.htm; www.imagesofempire.com
Director Dr Gareth Griffiths
Exhibition Floor Manager Ms Anne Lineen

Specialism(s): Commonwealth literature, archives and resources; Colonial and Empire history

Note: the Museum closed October 2008, and will be moving to London at a future date to
be decided. For progress check the website as above. In the meantime the Museum is not
open to visitors; please e-mail as above.

BRITISH FILM INSTITUTE

BFI National Library, British Film Institute, 21 Stephen Street, London WIT ILN
☎020 7255 1444 (information enquiry service), ext 4752 (administration)
Fax 020 7436 2338
e-mail: library@bfi.org.uk
url: www.bfi.org.uk/filmtvinfo/library
Head Librarian David Sharp BA MCLIP
(Incorporates Independent Television Commission Library collections)

Specialism(s): The moving image (national film and television collection and archives)

BRITISH GEOLOGICAL SURVEY

**Research Knowledge Services, British Geological Survey, Kingsley Dunham Centre,
Keyworth, Nottingham NGI2 5GG**
☎0115 936 3205
Fax 0115 936 3200
e-mail: libuser@bgs.ac.uk
url: www.bgs.org.uk
Head of Research Knowledge Services Ken Hollywood BA MSc DipLib MCLIP (e-mail:
ken.hollywood@nerc.ac.uk)

Branch libraries
Library, British Geological Survey, Scottish Regional Office, Murchison House, West Mains
Road, Edinburgh EH9 3LA
☎0131 650 0322

Fax 0131 668 2683
e-mail: mhlib@bgs.ac.uk
Site Librarian Ms Gail Gray BSc PGDipLIS

London Information Office, British Geological Survey, Natural History Museum, Cromwell Road, South Kensington, London SW7 5BD
☎020 7589 4090
Fax 020 7589 4090
e-mail: bgslondon@bgs.ac.uk
Officer-in-Charge Ms Clare Tombleson (e-mail: cto@bgs.ac.uk)

BRITISH HOROLOGICAL INSTITUTE

Library, British Horological Institute, Upton Hall, Upton, Newark, Notts NG23 5TE
☎(01636) 813795 (switchboard); 817602 (Library)
Fax (01636) 812258
e-mail: clocks@bhi.co.uk
url: www.bhi.co.uk
Librarian and Curator Viscount Alan Midleton FBHI
(Library open to members only; research available to non-members on request)

BRITISH LIBRARY

British Library, British Library, 96 Euston Road, London NW1 2DB
☎020 7412 7332 (general and visitor enquiries), 0843 208 1144 (switchboard)
url: www.bl.uk
Chairman Sir Colin Lucas
Chief Executive Mrs Lynne Brindley MA FCLIP
Director of Human Resources Ms Mary Canavan
Director of Finance and Corporate Resources Steve Morris
Director of Scholarship and Collections Phil Spence
Director of Strategic Marketing and Communications Ms Frances Brindle
Director of e-Strategy and Information Systems Richard Boulderstone
Associate Directors: Operations and Services Ms Caroline Brazier, Patrick Fleming

Enquiry points
The following are based at 96 Euston Road, London NW1 2DB. Admission to the Library's London reading rooms is by pass only. Most of the Library's catalogues are available on its website, www.bl.uk. For general enquiries about the collection, reader services and advance reservations, tel: 020 7412 7676, e-mail: reader-services-enquiries@bl.uk.

Other useful numbers/e-mail addresses
Reader Registration (advice on who may use the Library and how to apply for a reader's pass)
☎020 7412 7676, e-mail: Reader-Registration@bl.uk
Visitor Services (for general enquiries and details of exhibitions, events)
☎020 7412 7332, e-mail: Visitor-Services@bl.uk

Northern Site, British Library, Boston Spa, Wetherby, West Yorks LS23 7BQ
☎01937 546060
e-mail: customer-services@bl.uk

St Pancras Reading Rooms
Librarianship and Information Science Service (LIS)
☎020 7412 7676; e-mail: lis@bl.uk
Maps
☎020 7412 7702; e-mail: maps@bl.uk
Music Collections
☎020 7412 7772; e-mail: music-collections@bl.uk
Sound Archive
☎020 7412 7440; e-mail: sound-archive@bl.uk
Asia, Pacific and Africa Collections (formerly Oriental and India Office Collections)
☎020 7412 7873; e-mail: apac-enquiries@bl.uk
Philatelic
☎020 7412 7635; e-mail: philatelic@bl.uk
Rare Book Collections
☎020 7412 7676; e-mail: rare-books@bl.uk
Science, Technology and Medicine Information
☎020 7412 7676; e-mail: scitech@bl.uk
Manuscripts
☎020 7412 7513; e-mail: mss@bl.uk

Other Reading Rooms
British Library Newspapers, Colindale Avenue, London NW9 5HE
☎020 7412 7353; e-mail: newspaper@bl.uk

For material via Document Supply (BLDSC)
British Library Document Supply Centre, Boston Spa, Wetherby, West Yorks LS23 7BQ
☎(01937) 546060; e-mail: customer-services@bl.uk

BRITISH MEDICAL ASSOCIATION

BMA Library, British Medical Association, BMA House, Tavistock Square, London WC1H 9JP
☎020 7383 6625
Fax 020 7388 2544
e-mail: bma-library@bma.org.uk
url: www.bma.org.uk/library
Librarian Ms Jacky Berry BA(Hons) MBA MCLIP

BRITISH MUSEUM

Anthropology Library, Centre for Anthropology, Department of AOA, British Museum, Great Russell Street, London WC1B 3DG
☎020 7323 8031
Fax 020 7323 8049
e-mail: anthropologylibrary@thebritishmuseum.ac.uk
Senior Librarian Mrs Jan Ayres (020 7323 8069; e-mail: jayres@thebritishmuseum.ac.uk)
(The Anthropology Library in the British Museum is a major anthropological collection. It incorporates the stock of the former library of the Royal Anthropological Institute. It covers every aspect of anthropology – cultural anthropology (with emphasis on material culture), archaeology, biological anthropology, linguistics and such related fields as history,

sociology, description and travel. It also houses a Pictorial Collection. The Library is open to researchers and the general public (proof of identity will be required).

Paul Hamlyn Library, British Museum, Great Russell Street, London WC1B 3DG
☎020 7323 8838
e-mail: collectionenquiries@thebritishmuseum.org
url: www.thebritishmuseum.org
Paul Hamlyn Library Supervisor Charles Hoare (020 7323 8381; e-mail: choare@thebritishmuseum.org)
(The Paul Hamlyn Library is an open access public reference library on subjects relating to the Museum's collections, e.g. ancient history, archaeology, art history, museology. The Library is freely open to the public without any membership or prior appointment.)

The library collections of the British Museum provide an invaluable research resource that supports the study of the rich history of human cultures represented by the Museum's object collection. The British Museum Library catalogue includes material held in all ten of the Museum's libraries: Ancient Egypt and Sudan, Anthropology (the Library of the Department of Africa, Oceania and the Americas), Asia Department, Coins and Medals, Conservation and Scientific Research, Greece and Rome, Middle East, the Paul Hamlyn Library (the Museum's public library), Prehistory and Europe, and Prints and Drawings. These libraries have different levels of accessibility. The Anthropology Library and the Paul Hamlyn Library are accessible to all visitors during opening hours, while the other departmental libraries have restricted access.

BRITISH PSYCHOLOGICAL SOCIETY

Psychology Library, British Psychological Society, Senate House Library, University of London, Malet Street, London WC1E 7HU
☎020 7862 8461
Fax 020 7862 8480
e-mail: enquiries@shl.lon.ac.uk
url: www.shl.lon.ac.uk
Psychology Librarian, Senate House Library, University of London Mrs Mura Ghosh MLS MBA (e-mail: mura.ghosh@london.ac.uk)
(The BPS collection of periodicals is held at the Psychology Library and amalgamated with the University of London Library collection of psychology periodicals.)

BRITISH STANDARDS INSTITUTION

Knowledge Centre, British Standards Institution, 389 Chiswick High Road, London W4 4AL
☎020 8996 7004
Fax 020 8996 7005
e-mail: knowledgecentre@bsigroup.com
url: www.bsigroup.com
Knowledge Centre Manager Ms Lucy Ahmed BA(Hons) PGDipILM
(The Library may be used for reference free of charge by members and students. For non-members there is a charge. Please contact us in advance to arrange a visit.)

Specialism(s): Standards

BRITISH UNIVERSITIES FILM & VIDEO COUNCIL

Information Service, British Universities Film & Video Council, 77 Wells Street, London WIT 3QJ
☎020 7393 1500 (switchboard); 020 7393 1506 (direct)
Fax 020 7393 1555
e-mail: ask@bufvc.ac.uk
url: www.bufvc.ac.uk
Information & Publications Executive Sergio Angelini

Specialism(s): Film; Television; Radio

THE BRITTEN-PEARS FOUNDATION

Library, The Britten-Pears Foundation, The Red House, Golf Lane, Aldeburgh, Suffolk IPI5 5PZ
☎(01728) 451700
Fax (01728) 453076
e-mail: library@brittenpears.org; enquiries@brittenpears.org
url: www.brittenpears.org
Director of Collections and Heritage Dr Christopher Grogan BMus PhD DipLIS (01728 451707)
Librarian Nicholas Clark DipILS (01728 451702)

BROMLEY HOUSE LIBRARY

Bromley House Library, Bromley House, Angel Row, Nottingham NGI 6HL
☎0115 947 3134
e-mail: enquiries@bromleyhouse.org
Librarian Mrs Carol Barstow BSc DipLib MA MCLIP
(Subscription library also available to the public for reference purposes only, by prior appointment)

CANCER RESEARCH UK

Library and Information Services, Cancer Research UK, 44 Lincoln's Inn Fields, London WC2A 3LY
☎020 7269 3206
Fax 020 7269 3084
e-mail: lib.info@cancer.org.uk
url: www.cancerresearchuk.org
LIS Resources Manager Ms Ann Brew (e-mail: ann.brew@cancer.org.uk)
(Note: this is a workplace/research library not open to the public, but it is open to enquiries from other libraries)

CANTERBURY CATHEDRAL

Cathedral Library, Canterbury Cathedral, The Precincts, Canterbury, Kent CTI 2EH
☎(01227) 865287
e-mail: library@canterbury-cathedral.org
url: www.canterbury-cathedral.org/library.html

Acting Librarian Ms Karen Brayshaw BA(Hons) MA (e-mail: brayshawk@canterbury-cathedral.org)

Specialism(s): Theology; Liturgy; Church history; Local (Kentish) history; Anti-slavery movement; Catholic and anti-Catholic history; Natural history

CENTRE FOR ECOLOGY AND HYDROLOGY

Library, Centre for Ecology and Hydrology, Centre for Ecology and Hydrology Edinburgh, Bush Estate, Penicuik, Midlothian EH26 0QB
☎0131 445 4343
Fax 0131 445 3943
url: http://library.ceh.ac.uk
Librarian and Head of CEH Library Service Steve Prince BSc DipLib MCLIP (e-mail: sjpr@ceh.ac.uk)

Research station libraries
Library, Centre for Ecology and Hydrology Bangor, Centre for Ecology and Hydrology, Environment Centre for Wales, University of Wales, Deiniol Road, Bangor, Gwynedd LL57 2UP
☎(01248) 374505
Fax (01248) 355365
Librarian Ms Jackie Cooper (e-mail: jrco@ceh.ac.uk)

Library, Centre for Ecology and Hydrology Lancaster, Centre for Ecology and Hydrology, Lancaster Environment Centre, Library Avenue, Bailrigg, Lancaster LA1 4AP
☎(01524) 595800
Fax (01524) 61536
Librarian Ms Jeanette Coward (e-mail: jcowa@ceh.ac.uk)

Library, Centre for Ecology and Hydrology Oxford, Centre for Ecology and Hydrology, Mansfield Road, Oxford OX1 3SR
☎(01865) 281630
Fax (01865) 281696

Library, Centre for Ecology and Hydrology Wallingford, Centre for Ecology and Hydrology, Maclean Building, Crowmarsh Gifford, Wallingford, Oxon OX10 8BB
☎(01491) 838800
Fax (01491) 692424
Librarian Adrian Smith BSc AIMgt MCLIP (e-mail: wllibrary@ceh.ac.uk)

Specialism(s): Environment (esp. terrestrial and freshwater sciences), Hydrology

CENTRE FOR POLICY ON AGEING

Library, Centre for Policy on Ageing, 25–31 Ironmonger Row, London EC1V 3QP
☎020 7553 6500
Fax 020 7553 6501
e-mail: cpa@cpa.org.uk
url: www.cpa.org.uk
Director Ms Gillian Crosby BA MCLIP (e-mail: gcrosby@cpa.org.uk)
Librarian Ms Ruth Hayes BA MCLIP
Information Officer/Assistant Librarian Ms Kate Jones BA MCLIP

THE CHARTERED INSTITUTE OF LOGISTICS AND TRANSPORT IN THE UK

Knowledge Centre, The Chartered Institute of Logistics and Transport in the UK, Earlstrees Court, Earlstrees Road, Corby, Northants NNI7 4AX
☎(01536) 740123 or 740139 (library), (01536) 740100 (reception)
Fax (01536) 740102 (FAO Knowledge Centre Manager)
url: www.ciltuk.org.uk
Knowledge Centre Manager Peter Huggins MA (e-mail: peter.huggins@ciltuk.org.uk)
Knowledge Centre and Webshop Senior Executive Ms Lynn Mentiply (e-mail: lynn.mentiply@ciltuk.org.uk)
Knowledge Centre and Webshop Administrator Ms Nicola Keane (e-mail: nicola.keane@ciltuk.org.uk)
(Access: free to Institute members and full-time students; a charge is made for non-member use.

Specialism(s): Logistics; Supply-chain; Passenger transport

CHARTERED INSTITUTE OF PERSONNEL AND DEVELOPMENT

Library and Information Services, Chartered Institute of Personnel and Development, ISI The Broadway, London SWI9 IJQ
☎020 8612 6210 (enquiries), 020 8612 6641 (administration)
Fax 020 8612 6232
e-mail: lis@cipd.co.uk
url: www.cipd.co.uk
Head of Library and Information Services Ms Barbara Salmon BA DipLib MCLIP

CHARTERED INSURANCE INSTITUTE

CII Knowledge Services, Chartered Insurance Institute, 20 Aldermanbury, London EC2V 7HY
☎020 7417 4415/4416
e-mail: knowledge@cii.co.uk
url: www.cii.co.uk/knowledge
Knowledge Services Co-ordinator Ms Hannah West BA(Hons) MA MSc

Specialism(s): Insurance, risk and related financial services

CHARTERED MANAGEMENT INSTITUTE

KnowledgeDirect, Chartered Management Institute, Management House, Cottingham Road, Corby, Northants NNI7 ITT
☎(01536) 204222 (switchboard), (01536) 207400 (enquiries)
Fax (01536) 401013
e-mail: mic.enquiries@managers.org.uk
url: www.managers.org.uk

Member Services Manager Kevin Saunders
(Information services, principally to Institute members)

Specialism(s): Management theory, practice and techniques

CHETHAM'S LIBRARY

Chetham's Library, Long Millgate, Manchester M3 ISB
☎0161 834 7961
Fax 0161 839 5797
e-mail: librarian@chethams.org.uk
url: www.chethams.org.uk
Chetham's Librarian Michael Powell BD PhD

Specialism(s): Rare books; Local history

CILIP: THE CHARTERED INSTITUTE OF LIBRARY AND INFORMATION PROFESSIONALS

Information and Advice Team, CILIP: the Chartered Institute of Library and Information Professionals, 7 Ridgmount Street, London WCIE 7AE
☎020 7255 0620
Fax 020 7255 0501
e-mail: info@cilip.org.uk
url: www.cilip.org.uk/info
Textphone 020 7255 0505
Team Leader, Information and Advice Ms Jill Duffin MCLIP

Specialism(s): Library and information management

CILT, THE NATIONAL CENTRE FOR LANGUAGES

CILT Resources Library, CILT, the National Centre for Languages, 3rd Floor, III Westminster Bridge Road, London SEI 7HR
☎0845 612 5885
e-mail: library@cilt.org.uk
url: www.cilt.org.uk; www.cilt.org.uk/libcat (library catalogue)
Acting Librarian and Senior Information Officer Louis Greenstock

Specialism(s): Language teaching methodology and materials, linguistics

CIVIL AVIATION AUTHORITY

Information Management Department, Civil Aviation Authority, Aviation House, Gatwick Airport South, West Sussex RH6 0YR
☎(01293) 573781
Fax (01293) 573181
e-mail: infoservices@caa.co.uk
url: www.caa.co.uk
Information Resources Manager Vagn Pedersen MA MCLIP (01293 573966)

Specialism(s): UK aviation and aviation safety

COLLEGE OF OCCUPATIONAL THERAPISTS

Library, College of Occupational Therapists, 106–114 Borough High Street, Southwark, London SEI ILB
☎020 7450 2303/2320/2316
Fax 020 7450 2364
e-mail: library@cot.co.uk
url: www.cot.org.uk
Librarian Ms Anne Jenkins
Deputy Librarian Ms Lorna Rutherford BA(Hons) PGDip
Assistant Librarian Andy Hughes BA(Hons) MA

COMMONWEALTH SECRETARIAT

Library, Commonwealth Secretariat, Marlborough House, Pall Mall, London SWIY 5HX
☎020 7747 6164
Fax 020 7747 6168
e-mail: library@commonwealth.int
url: www.thecommonwealth.org
Librarian Mrs Catherine Hume BA DipLib MSc FCLIP (e-mail: c.hume@commonwealth.int)

Specialism(s): The Commonwealth (politics, economics, health, education, science and gender)

COMPETITION COMMISSION

Information Centre, Competition Commission, Victoria House, Southampton Row, London WCIB 4AD
☎020 7271 0261
Fax 020 7271 0367
e-mail: info@cc.gsi.gov.uk
url: www.competition-commission.org.uk
Information Centre Manager Miss L J Fisher MA MCLIP
Press and Publicity Officer R Taylor
(Open to government libraries by appointment. Not open to the public, but deals with public written enquiries.)

CONSERVATIVE PARTY ARCHIVE
(formerly Conservative Research Department)

Conservative Party Archive, Conservative Party, 30 Millbank, London SWIP 4DP
☎020 7222 9000 (main)
Fax 020 7984 8273
url: www.conservatives.com
Researcher Sheridan Westlake MA(Oxon) MSc MPhil
(Not open to the public)

Conservative Party Archive, c/o Bodleian Library, Broad Street, Oxford OXI 3BG
☎(01865) 277046
e-mail: modern.papers@bodleian.ox.ac.uk
url: www.cparchive.org.uk; bodley.ox.ac.uk/dept/scwmss/cpa

Archivist Jeremy McIlwaine MArAd (01865 277181; e-mail:
jeremy.mcilwaine@bodleian.ox.ac.uk)
(Open to the public – subject to Bodleian access conditions)

CORUS UK LTD *see* TATA STEEL

COUNTRYSIDE COUNCIL FOR WALES (CYNGOR CEFN GWLAD CYMRU)

Llyfrgell Library, Countryside Council for Wales (Cyngor Cefn Gwlad Cymru), Maes y
Ffynnon, Penrhosgarnedd, Bangor, Gwynedd LL57 2DW
☎(01248) 385522
Fax (01248) 385510
e-mail: library@ccw.gov.uk
url: www.ccw.gov.uk
Librarian Ms Dwynwen Lloyd BA MCLIP

CPRE (CAMPAIGN TO PROTECT RURAL ENGLAND)

Library and Information Unit, CPRE (Campaign to Protect Rural England), 128 Southwark
Street, London SE1 0SW
☎020 7981 2800 (switchboard); 020 7981 2809 (direct)
Fax 020 7981 2899
url: www.cpre.org.uk
Library and Information Services Officer Oliver Hilliam BA (e-mail:
oliverh@cpre.org.uk)

Specialism(s): Planning; Environment; Transport

CROWN PROSECUTION SERVICE

Library Information Services, Crown Prosecution Service, Rose Court, 2 Southwark Bridge
Road, London SE1 9HS
☎020 3357 0915 (direct); 020 3357 0000 (switchboard)
e-mail: cps.libraryinformationservices@cps.gsi.gov.uk
url: www.cps.gov.uk
CPS Librarian Robert Brall BA DipLib MCLIP (e-mail: robert.brall@cps.gsi.gov.uk)

CROWTHER CENTRE FOR MISSION EDUCATION

Library, Crowther Centre for Mission Education, Church Mission Society, Watlington Road,
Cowley, Oxford OX4 6BZ
☎(01865) 787552
Fax (01865) 776375
url: www.cms-uk.org/heritage
Librarian Ken Osborne (e-mail: ken.osborne@cms-uk.org)

Specialism(s): History and theology of mission of the Anglican Church

DEPARTMENT FOR BUSINESS, INNOVATION AND SKILLS (BIS)
(formerly the Department for Business, Enterprise and Regulatory Reform (BERR))

Information Services, Department for Business, Innovation and Skills (BIS), I Victoria Street, London SWIH OET
☎020 7215 5000 (switchboard)
Fax 020 7215 0105
minicom: 020 7215 6740
e-mail: enquiries@bis.gsi.gov.uk
url: www.bis.gov.uk
Director, Information Strategy and Services (CIO) Ms Karen Pile
Information Services Manager Ms Diane Rowland BLib(Hons) MSc MCLIP
(Limited public access to departmental publications, by prior appointment only)

InfoSource, Department for Business, Innovation and Skills (BIS), I Victoria Street, London
SWIH 0ET
☎020 7215 5006 (enquiries)
Fax 020 7215 5713
e-mail: infosource@bsi.gsi.gov.uk
Head of InfoSource Miss Rosemary Zolynski BA(Hons) DipLib MCLIP

Department of Energy and Climate Change (DECC) (3 Whitehall Place, London SWIA 2AW, www.decc.gov.uk)
Shares the library services of Department for Business, Innovation and Skills (BIS)

DEPARTMENT FOR CHILDREN, SCHOOLS AND FAMILIES (DCSF) *see* DEPARTMENT FOR EDUCATON (DFE)

DEPARTMENT FOR COMMUNITIES AND LOCAL GOVERNMENT (DCLG)

Communities and Local Government Information Centre, Department for Communities and Local Government (DCLG), Ground Floor, Eland House, Bressenden Place, London SWIE 5DU
☎0303 444 0000 (switchboard)
e-mail: contactus@communities.gov.uk
url: www.communities.gov.uk
Knowledge Management Policy, Library and Information Services Branch Head
Ms Maewyn Cumming

Specialism(s): Housing; Local Government; Planning

DEPARTMENT FOR CULTURE, MEDIA AND SPORT (DCMS)

Library Policy Team, Department for Culture, Media and Sport (DCMS), 2-4 Cockspur Street, London SWIY 5DH
☎020 7211 6000 (enquiries)

e-mail: enquiries@culture.gsi.gov.uk
url: www.culture.gov.uk
Head, Library Policy Team Ms Abigail Smith (020 7211 6124; e-mail:
abigail.smith@culture.gsi.gov.uk)
(There is no library at DCMS, but the Library Policy Team deals with national library policy
issues)

DEPARTMENT FOR EDUCATION (DFE)
(formerly Department for Children, Schools and Families (DCSF))

**Library, Department for Education (DFE), 5th Floor Sanctuary Buildings, Great Smith
Street, London SWIP 3BT**
☎0870 000 2288
url: www.education.gov.uk
Chief Librarian Ms Gill Baker BSc MSc MCLIP (e-mail: gill.baker@education.gsi.gov.uk)

Departmental Public Communications Unit
☎0870 000 2288
url: www.education.gov.uk

Specialism(s): Education theory and policy

DEPARTMENT FOR ENVIRONMENT, FOOD AND RURAL AFFAIRS (DEFRA)

**Information Resource Centre, Department for Environment, Food and Rural Affairs
(Defra), Lower Ground Floor, Ergon House, c/o Nobel House, 17 Smith Square, London
SWIP 3JR**
☎020 7238 6575
Fax 020 7238 6609
e-mail: defra.library@defra.gsi.gov.uk
url: www.defra.gov.uk
Head of Library and Translations Service and Chief Librarian Kevin Jackson BSc MCLIP
(Visitors must give 24 hours' notice)

*Specialism(s): Environment; Farming; Food; Rural issues; Agriculture; Climate change and
sustainable development*

DEPARTMENT FOR INTERNATIONAL DEVELOPMENT (DFID)

**eLibrary, Knowledge and Information Management Unit, Department for International
Development (DFID), 1 Palace Street, London SWIE 5HE**
☎020 7023 0574
Fax 020 7023 0016
e-mail: library@dfid.gov.uk
url: www.dfid.gov.uk
Business Information Specialist Ms Sharon Skelton BA(Hons)
(Note: eLibrary services only; no visiting.)

DEPARTMENT FOR REGIONAL DEVELOPMENT

Library, Department for Regional Development, Room G-40, Clarence Court, 10–18 Adelaide Street, Belfast BT2 8GB
☎028 9054 1045/6
Fax 028 9054 1081
e-mail: library@drdni.gov.uk
url: www.drdni.gov.uk
Librarian Ms Fiona Sawey BA(Hons)
Assistant Librarian Ms Gillian Potter MA(Hons) MA

DEPARTMENT FOR TRANSPORT (DFT)

Communities and Local Government Information Centre, Department for Transport (DfT), Ground Floor, Eland House, Bressenden Place, London SW1E 5DU
☎0303 444 0000 (switchboard); 0300 330 3000 (DfT helpdesk)
e-mail: fax9643@dft.gsi.gov.uk
url: www.dft.gov.uk
Knowledge Management Policy, Library and Information Services Branch Head
Ms Maewyn Cumming
(Note: shared library service with Department for Communities and Local Government)

DEPARTMENT FOR WORK AND PENSIONS (DWP)

Adelphi Library and Information Centre, Department for Work and Pensions (DWP), Room 114, The Adelphi, 1–11 John Adam Street, London WC2N 6HT
☎020 7712 2500
Fax 020 7962 8491
e-mail: library@dwp.gsi.gov.uk
url: www.dwp.gov.uk
Head of Library and Information Services Graham Monk BA(Hons) MCLIP
Deputy Head of Library and Information Services Ms Melanie Harris BA(Hons) DipLib MCLIP
Information Centre Manager Mrs Anoja Fernando BSc(Hons) MCLIP

DWP Library, Steel City Sheffield, Department for Work and Pensions (DWP), Upper Ground Floor, Steel City House, 12–18 West Street, Sheffield S1 2DQ
☎0114 294 3598
Fax 0114 294 3599
Information Centre Manager Ms Karen Gommersall BA MCLIP

Legal Information Centre, Department for Work and Pensions (DWP), 1st Floor, The Adelphi, 1-11 John Adam Street, London WC2N 6HT
☎020 7962 8882
Fax 020 7962 8491
Information Centre Manager Ms Andria Lannon BA(Hons) MA DipLib MCLIP

Corporate Information Team

Library, Department for Work and Pensions (DWP), Room 114, The Adelphi, 1-11 John Adam Street, London WC2N 6HT
☎020 7912 2863

Fax 020 7962 8491
Senior Librarian Ms Helen Skelton BA(Hons)Lib MSc
Archivist Ms Angela Tailby BA(Hons)
Information Manager Ms Helen Nolan BA(Hons) MSc MSc

DEPARTMENT OF ENERGY AND CLIMATE CHANGE (DECC) *see* DEPARTMENT FOR BUSINESS, INNOVATION AND SKILLS (BIS)

DEPARTMENT OF HEALTH (DH)

Library, Department of Health (DH), Quarry House, Quarry Hill, Leeds LS2 7UE
☎0113 254 5080
Fax 0113 254 5084
e-mail: library.enquiries@dh.gsi.gov.uk
url: www.dh.gov.uk
Head of Library Antony Osborne MSc BA(Hons) MCLIP FHEA LTCL
Senior Librarian (Customer Services) Mrs Natalie Gudgeon BSc(Hons)

Specialism(s): Public health, health services, health services policy and management, medicine, hospitals, social care

DEPARTMENT OF JUSTICE

Records and Information Management Branch, Department of Justice, Annex A, Dundonald House, Stormont Estate, Belfast BT4 3SU
☎(0)28 905 25196
Senior Records & Information Manager Ms Zoe A Smyth (e-mail: Zoe.Smyth@dojni.x.gsi.gov.uk)

ENERGY INSTITUTE

Library and Information Service, Energy Institute, 61 New Cavendish Street, London WIG 7AR
☎020 7467 7114/5 (enquiries), 020 7467 7111 (administration)
Fax 020 7255 1472
e-mail: lis@energyinst.org
url: www.energyinst.org
Library and Information Service Manager Mrs Catherine M Cosgrove BSc(Hons) BA MCLIP FEI
Senior Information Officer Chris L Baker BA(Hons) MEI
Information Officer Miss Emily Heath BA MA MEI

ENGLISH FOLK DANCE AND SONG SOCIETY

Vaughan Williams Memorial Library, English Folk Dance and Song Society, Cecil Sharp House, 2 Regent's Park Road, London NWI 7AY
☎020 7485 2206 exts 29/33
Fax 020 7284 0523

e-mail: library@efdss.org
url: http://library.efdss.org; www.efdss.org
Library Director Malcolm Taylor BA(Lib) MCLIP OBE
Assistant Librarians Ms Peta Webb BA, Ms Rebecca Hughes MA MSt
Archivist Ms Alice Measom BA
Cataloguer Ms Elaine Bradtke PhD

Specialism(s): Traditional music and folk culture

ENGLISH HERITAGE

Library, English Heritage, National Monuments Record Centre, Kemble Drive, Swindon SN2 2GZ
☎(01793) 414632
Fax (01793) 414801
e-mail: library@english-heritage.org.uk
url: www.english-heritage.org.uk
Senior Librarian Ms Felicity Gilmour MA(Hons) DipLib MCLIP

Specialism(s): English archaeology and architecture

ENGLISH-SPEAKING UNION

Page Memorial Library, English-Speaking Union, Dartmouth House, 37 Charles Street, London WIJ 5ED
☎020 7529 1587
e-mail: library@esu.org
url: www.esu.org
Librarian/Information Officer Ms Gill Hale MEd MCLIP. Ms Jeanne Huse MCLIP

Specialism(s): Specialist collection on the USA (politics, sociology, history and literature (including fiction))

EQUALITY AND HUMAN RIGHTS COMMISSION (EHRC)

Library and Information Services, Equality and Human Rights Commission (EHRC), 2nd Floor, Arndale House, Arndale Centre, Manchester M4 3AQ
☎0161 829 8308
Fax 0161 829 8110
url: www.equalityhumanrights.com
Library and Information Services Manager David Sparrow BA(Hons) MA MCLIP
(e-mail: david.sparrow@equalityhumanrights.com)

Specialism(s): Information relating to all equality strands: age, disability, gender, human rights, race, religion and belief, and sexual orientation. EHRC's mission is to reduce inequality, eliminate discrimination, strengthen good relations between people, and protect human rights.

EUROPEAN COMMISSION REPRESENTATION IN THE UNITED KINGDOM

Library, The European Commission Representation in the United Kingdom, 8 Storey's Gate, London SWIP 3AT

☎020 7973 1992
Fax 020 7973 1900
url: http://ec.europa.eu/unitedkingdom
Librarian Mrs Marguerite-Marie Brenchley (e-mail:
marguerite-marie.brenchley@ec.europa.eu)
(Enquiries may only be referred to this library via a recognized EPIC (European Public
Information Centre, formerly known as PiR). For details of your nearest centre please
contact your local library or check on the website)

Specialism(s): All EU legislation and information

FOOD STANDARDS AGENCY

**Information Management Services, Food Standards Agency, Aviation House, 125 Kingsway,
London WC2B 6NH**
☎020 7276 8181
Fax 020 7276 8289
e-mail: infocentre@foodstandards.gsi.gov.uk
url: www.food.gov.uk
Head of Information Section Ms Lorna Goodey BA(Hons)
Information Centre Manager Tony Timmons BA(Hons) DipLIS MCLIP
(Public access by appointment only)

Specialism(s): Food safety; Food science and nutrition.

FOREIGN AND COMMONWEALTH OFFICE

**Legal Library, Foreign and Commonwealth Office, Room K168, King Charles Street,
London SW1A 2AH**
☎020 7008 3050
Fax 020 7008 2280
e-mail: legallibrary@fco.gov.uk
Legal Librarian Ms Caroline Mack BA(Hons) DiP (e-mail: caroline.mack@fco.gov.uk)

Specialism(s): International relations; International law; Diplomacy and politics

FORESTRY COMMISSION

**Library, Forestry Commission, Forest Research Station, Alice Holt Lodge, Wrecclesham,
Farnham, Surrey GU10 4LH**
☎(01420) 22255, (01420) 526216 (direct line)
Fax (01420) 23653
e-mail: library@forestry.gsi.gov.uk
url: www.forestry.gov.uk; www.forestry.gov.uk/forestresearch
Librarian Miss Catherine Oldham BA MA DipLib MCLIP (e-mail:
catherine.oldham@forestry.gsi.gov.uk)

Specialism(s): Forestry; Arboriculture; Plant sciences; Ecology

FRANCIS SKARYNA BELARUSIAN LIBRARY AND MUSEUM

Francis Skaryna Belarusian Library and Museum, 37 Holden Road, London N12 8HS

☎020 8445 5358
Fax 020 8445 5358
e-mail: library@skaryna.org
url: www.skaryna.org
Librarian Mgr Alexander Nadson

Specialism(s): Books, periodicals and archives relating to Belarus

FRESHWATER BIOLOGICAL ASSOCIATION

Library, Freshwater Biological Association, The Ferry Landing, Far Sawrey, Ambleside, Cumbria LA22 0LP
☎(01539) 442468
Fax (01539) 446914
e-mail: lis@fba.org.uk
url: www.fba.org.uk
Librarian Hardy Schwamm MA (e-mail: h.schwamm@fba.org.uk)

Specialism(s): Freshwater biology; Water chemistry; Algology; Ichthyology

GEOLOGICAL SOCIETY OF LONDON

Library, Geological Society of London, Burlington House, Piccadilly, London W1J 0BG
☎020 7432 0999
Fax 020 7439 3470
e-mail: library@geolsoc.org.uk
url: www.geolsoc.org.uk
Librarian Miss Sheila Meredith

GERMAN HISTORICAL INSTITUTE LONDON

Library, German Historical Institute London, 17 Bloomsbury Square, London WC1A 2NJ
☎020 7309 2019/2022 (enquiries)
Fax 020 7309 2069/2072
e-mail: library@ghil.ac.uk
url: www.ghil.ac.uk
Head Librarian Dr Michael Schaich
Librarians Ms A-M Klauk, Ms J Schumann, Dr C Swinbank, Ms J Gambus

GLADSTONE'S LIBRARY (formerly St Deiniol's Residential Library)

Gladstone's Library, Church Lane, Hawarden, Flintshire CH5 3DF
☎(01244) 532350
Fax (01244) 520643
e-mail: enquiries@gladlib.org.uk
url: www.gladstoneslibrary.org
Warden The Very Revd Peter B Francis MTheol
Librarian Miss Patsy Williams BA DipLib (e-mail: patsy.williams@gladlib.org.uk)

Specialism(s): This is a residential library specializing in theology, history and Victorian studies. The collection of over 250,000 volumes includes W E Gladstone's personal library. (Modern residential accommodation is available at modest charges. Day readers welcome. Testimonial required.)

GOETHE-INSTITUT LONDON

Library, Goethe-Institut London, 50 Princes Gate, Exhibition Road, London SW7 2PH
☎020 7596 4040 (lending), 020 7596 4044 (information service)
Fax 020 7594 0230
e-mail: library@london.goethe.org
url: www.goethe.de/london
Head Librarian Mrs Elisabeth Pyroth (e-mail: elisabeth.pyroth@london.goethe.org)

Specialism(s): Contemporary German culture, literature and language

GREATER LONDON AUTHORITY

Information Services, Greater London Authority, City Hall, The Queen's Walk, London SE1 2AA
☎020 7983 4000 (GLA switchboard), 020 7983 4455 (library enquiries)
Fax 020 7983 4674
e-mail: isinfo@london.gov.uk
Information Services Manager Ms Liz Osborne BA(Hons) PGCE:FE MA MCLIP

GUILDFORD INSTITUTE

Library, Guildford Institute, Ward Street, Guildford, Surrey GU1 4LH
☎(01483) 562142
Fax (01483) 451034
e-mail: library@guildford-institute.org.uk
url: www.guildford-institute.org.uk
Librarian Volunteer
(Lending service to members. Research enquiries welcomed by appointment.)

Specialism(s): General collection of literature, humanities and science work dating from late Victorian period to present; Local history collections of Surrey and Guildford.

HEALTH AND SAFETY EXECUTIVE

Information Management Unit, Health and Safety Executive, I.G. Redgrave Court, Merton Road, Bootle, Merseyside L20 7HS
☎0151 951 4382
Fax 0151 951 3674
url: www.hse.gov.uk
Head of Information Management Unit Martin Davies (e-mail: martin.davies@hse.gsi.gov.uk)
Head of Information Services Ms Sue King BA(Hons) MCLIP FRSA (e-mail: sue.king@hse.gsi.gov.uk)

Knowledge Centre

Health and Safety Executive, Knowledge Centre, I.G. Redgrave Court, Merton Road, Bootle, Merseyside L20 7HS

☎0151 951 4382
Fax 0151 951 3674
Site Manager Ms Sue Cornmell BA(Hons) PGDipLib LLB(Hons) MCLIP

(General requests for information on health and safety at work to the HSE Infoline Tel: 0845 345 0055; Minicom: 0845 408 9577. Written enquiries to HSE Infoline, Caerphilly Business Park, Caerphilly CF83 3GG; e-mail: hse.infoline@connaught.plc.uk; Fax: 0845 408 9566)

HEALTH MANAGEMENT LIBRARY

Health Management Library, Scottish Health Service Centre, Crewe Road South, Edinburgh EH4 2LF
☎0131 275 7760
Fax 0131 315 2369
e-mail: nss.hmilibrary@nhs.net
url: www.healthmanagementonline.co.uk
Library Services Manager Mrs Gill Earl BA(Hons) MCLIP
Librarian Mrs Alison Bogle MA DipLib MCLIP

Specialism(s): Health care management

HEALTH PROTECTION AGENCY

Library, Health Protection Agency, Colindale Library, 61 Colindale Avenue, London NW9 5EQ
☎020 8327 7616 (enquiries)
Fax 020 8200 7875
e-mail: colindale.library@hpa.org.uk
url: www.hpa.org.uk
Library Manager Vacant (serving Centre for Infections, Regional Microbiology Network, and Local and Regional Services)

Library, Health Protection Agency, Centre for Emergency Preparedness and Response (CEPR), Porton Down, Salisbury, Wilts SP4 0JG
☎(01980) 612100 (switchboard)
Fax (01980) 612818
e-mail: porton.library@hpa.org.uk
url: www.hpa.org.uk
Librarian Ms Sue Goddard BLib (01980 612711; e-mail: sue.goddard@hpa.org.uk)

Library, Health Protection Agency, Centre for Radiation, Chemical and Environmental Hazards (CRCE), Chilton, Didcot, Oxon OX11 0RQ
☎(01235) 831600 (switchboard)
Fax (01235) 833891
e-mail: chiltonlibrary@hpa.org.uk
url: www.hpa.org.uk
Librarian Vacant
Senior Library Assistant Ms Sue Rose

Information Services, National Institute for Biological Standards and Controls, Health Protection Agency, Blanche Lane, South Mimms, Potters Bar, Herts EN6 3QG

☎(01707) 641000 (Switchboard)
Fax (01707) 641050 (General)
e-mail: library@nibsc.hpa.org.uk
Information Services Manager Ms Anita Brewer (01707 641326; e-mail:
Anita.Brewer@nibsc.hpa.org.uk)

*Specialism(s): (1) CFI: disease surveillance, reference microbiology, microbial epidemiology;
LARS: communicable disease, infection control, emergency planning; RMN: diagnostic and public
health microbiology; (2) CEPR: healthcare emergencies; (3) CRCE: radiation, chemical hazards,
poisons; (4) NIBSC: biological medicines quality*

HEREFORD CATHEDRAL

Library, Hereford Cathedral, The Cathedral, Hereford HR1 2NG
☎(01432) 374225/6
Fax (01432) 374220
e-mail: library@herefordcathedral.org
url: www.herefordcathedral.org
Canon Librarian Revd Canon Chris Pullin
(Open to the public)

HIGH COMMISSION OF INDIA

Library, High Commission of India, India House, Aldwych, London WC2B 4NA
☎020 7632 3166 (Direct Line)
Fax 020 7632 3204
e-mail: info@hcilondon.net
url: www.hcilondon.net
Librarian Sanjay Kumar Bihani
Hon Librarian Miss M S Travis
(Staff library only. Collection is for reference only; no interlibrary lending; visiting at the
discretion of Head of Press and Information Department)

HIGHGATE LITERARY AND SCIENTIFIC INSTITUTION

**Library, Highgate Literary and Scientific Institution, 11 South Grove, Highgate, London
N6 6BS**
☎020 8340 3343
Fax 020 8340 5632
e-mail: librarian@hlsi.net
url: www.hlsi.net
Librarian Ms Margaret Mackay DipLib BEd(Hons) MCLIP
(Public access allowed for reference)

Specialism(s): Biography; Fiction; London/local history; Samuel Taylor Coleridge; John Betjeman

HISPANIC AND LUSO-BRAZILIAN COUNCIL

**Canning House Library, Hispanic and Luso-Brazilian Council, 2 Belgrave Square, London
SW1X 8PJ**
☎020 7235 2303 ext 208

Fax 020 7838 9258
e-mail: library@canninghouse.org
url: www.canninghouse.org
Library and Information Services Manager Alan Biggins BSc DipLib MCLIP (e-mail:
abiggins@canninghouse.com)

*Specialism(s): Latin America, Spain, Portugal (history, archaeology, literature, art, music, cinema,
language, culture, travel, sociology, anthropology, politics, religion, economics)*

HISTORIC SCOTLAND

Library, Historic Scotland, G.55, Longmore House, Salisbury Place, Edinburgh EH9 1SH
☎0131 668 8652
Fax 0131 668 8749
e-mail: hs.library@scotland.gsi.gov.uk
url: www.historic-scotland.gov.uk
Library and Records Manager Mrs Paulette Hill (e-mail:
paulette.hill@scotland.gsi.gov.uk)
Deputy Library Manager Jason Pirie (e-mail: jason.pirie@scotland.gsi.gov.uk)
Library Officer Ms Carolyn Nicol (e-mail: carolyn.nicol@scotland.gsi.gov.uk)

Image Library, Historic Scotland, G55, Longmore House, Salisbury Place, Edinburgh EH9 1SH
☎0131 668 8785
Fax 0131 668 8907
e-mail: hs.photolibrary@scotland.gsi.gov.uk
url: www.historic-scotland.gov.uk
Image Librarian Miss Michelle Andersson (e-mail:
michelle.andersson@scotland.gsi.gov.uk)
Assistant Image Librarian Sean Conlon (e-mail: sean.conlon@scotland.gsi.gov.uk)

*Specialism(s): Built heritage (archaeology, architecture); History; Traditional building materials;
Conservation science; Paintings, stone, textiles conservation*

HM REVENUE AND CUSTOMS

**Library Services, HM Revenue and Customs, 4W Ralli Quays, Stanley Street, Salford,
Manchester M60 9LA**
☎0161 827 0465
Fax 0161 827 0491
e-mail: libraryenquiries@hmrc.gsi.gov.uk
url: www.hmrc.gov.uk
Head of Library Service Ms Lorna Bankes BA(Hons) MCLIP

Department library

Library, HM Revenue and Customs, LG75, 100 Parliament Street, London SW1A 2BQ
☎020 7147 2193
Fax 020 7147 0232
e-mail: libraryenquiries@hmrc.gsi.gov.uk
url: www.hmrc.gov.uk
Senior Information Manager Mrs Marita Ewins

HM TREASURY AND CABINET OFFICE

Research and Library Service, HM Treasury and Cabinet Office, I Horse Guards Road, London SWIA 2HQ
☎020 7270 5290 (enquiries)
Fax 020 7270 4407
e-mail: library@hm-treasury.gov.uk
url: www.hm-treasury.gov.uk
Head of Information Management Ms Nicola Last
Library Services Manager Ms Mary Susan Barry BA DipLib MCLIP (020 7270 4963)
(Note: not open to the public. For all general enquiries contact the Correspondence and Enquiries Unit, tel: 020 7270 4558; e-mail: public.enquiries@hm-treasury.gov.uk)

Specialism(s): Economics and finance; Public administration; Parliamentary material

HMS SULTAN

Library, HMS Sultan, Military Road, Gosport, Hants POI2 3BY
☎023 9254 2678
Fax 023 9254 2682
url: www.royal-navy.mod.uk
Librarian Jim Quibell BA MCLIP (e-mail: jquibell.dcmt@nd.da.mod.uk)
(Visits by arrangement)

Specialism(s): Mechanical, electrical, marine and aeronautical engineering; Naval science, technology and history

HOME OFFICE

Information Management Services, Home Office, Shared Services Directorate, Fourth Floor, Seacole Building, 2 Marsham Street, London SWIP 4DF
☎020 7035 6699
Fax 0870 336 9266
e-mail: informationservicescentre@homeoffice.gsi.gov.uk
url: www.homeoffice.gov.uk
Information Team Manager Ms Susan Payne
Information and Library Manager (Provision) William Mead
Information and Library Manager (Resources) Ms Karen Richardson BA(Hons)

HOUSE OF COMMONS

Department of Information Services, House of Commons, Information Office, London SWIA 0AA
☎020 7219 4272
Fax 020 7219 5839
e-mail: hcinfo@parliament.uk
url: www.parliament.uk
Librarian of the House of Commons John Pullinger (e-mail: pullingerj@parliament.uk)
Head of the Information Office Stephen McGinness (e-mail: mcginnesss@parliament.uk)
(There are specialist sections which deal with enquiries from Members of Parliament only. Outside enquirers should approach the Department's public interface, the House of Commons Information Office (contact details as above).)

HOUSE OF LORDS

Library, House of Lords, London SWIA OPW
☎020 7219 5242 (enquiries), 020 7219 3240 (administration)
Fax 020 7219 6396
e-mail: hllibrary@parliament.uk
url: www.parliament.uk/lords/index.cfm
Director of Information Services and Librarian Dr Elizabeth Hallam Smith PhD FSA FRSA FRHistS
Director of Library Services Dr Isolde Victory PhD

HULTON/ARCHIVE – GETTY IMAGES

Hulton/Archive – Getty Images, Unique House, 21–31 Woodfield Road, London W9 2BA
☎020 7266 6900 (Research), 020 7579 5700 (Reception)
Fax 020 7266 3154
e-mail: archiveresearch@gettyimages.com
url: www.gettyimages.com
Picture Research Manager Ms Caroline Theakstone
Curator Ms Sarah McDonald

Specialism(s): Social history; Personalities; Entertainment; Sport; War, Royalty; Events up to 1980s

IBERS (INSTITUTE OF BIOLOGICAL, ENVIRONMENTAL AND RURAL SCIENCES)

Stapledon Library and Information Service, IBERS (Institute of Biological, Environmental and Rural Sciences), Aberystwyth University, Plas Gogerddan, Ceredigion SY23 3EB
☎(01970) 823053 (library desk)
Fax (01970) 828357
e-mail: gogstaff@aber.ac.uk
url: www.aber.ac.uk/ibers/
Site Librarian/Gogerddan Librarian Steve Smith BSc DipLib MCLIP (e-mail: stephen.smith@bbsrc.ac.uk)

Specialism(s): Grasses; Plant genetics, physiology and breeding; Livestock; Animal nutrition; Cell biology; Ecology

IMPERIAL WAR MUSEUM

Department of Printed Books, Imperial War Museum, Lambeth Road, London SE1 6HZ
☎020 7416 5342
e-mail: collections@iwm.org.uk
url: http://collections.iwm.org.uk
Keeper of Printed Books Richard Golland BA DipLib MCLIP
(Services: Research Room (appointment required) Mon–Fri 10–5; telephone enquiry service Mon–Fri.) Please note: In addition to our Research Room, we now also offer gallery visitors the Explore History Centre where, without an appointment, visitors can make reference enquiries, ask about family history research and browse digitized sound, image and archival collections. Explore History is open seven days a week.

Specialism(s): Conflicts since 1914 involving Great Britain and Commonwealth countries – military, civilian and social historical aspects. NB Research Room access now includes IWM Sound Archive listening facilities

INSTITUT FRANÇAIS D'ÉCOSSE (FRENCH INSTITUTE)

Library, Institut français d'Écosse (French Institute), 13 Randolph Crescent, Edinburgh EH3 7TT
☎0131 225 5366
Fax 0131 220 0648
e-mail: library@ifecosse.org.uk
url: www.ifecosse.org.uk
Librarian Ms Pascale Scott

Specialism(s): French language and culture

INSTITUT FRANÇAIS DU ROYAUME-UNI

The Multimedia Library, Institut français du Royaume-Uni, 17 Queensberry Place, London SW7 2DT
☎020 7073 1350
Fax 020 7073 1363
e-mail: library@ambafrance.org.uk
url: www.institut-francais.org.uk
Head Librarian Mme Anne-Elisabeth Buxtorf

Children's Library, Institut français du Royaume-Uni, 32 Harrington Road, London SW7 3HD
☎020 7073 1350

Specialism(s): Multimedia library on contemporary France (books, audio-books, press-cuttings, DVD, magazines). Free French Archives; CampusFrance: information desk for Studies in France. Children's section. Interlibrary loans. Contributes to joint catalogue COPAC. Culturethèque: digital platform: e-books and documentaries online.

INSTITUTE FOR ANIMAL HEALTH

Library, Institute for Animal Health, Compton Laboratory, Compton, Newbury, Berks RG20 7NN
☎(01635) 577256
e-mail: compton.library@bbsrc.ac.uk
url: www.iah.ac.uk
IAH Libraries Manager Mrs Chris Gibbons (e-mail: chris.gibbons@bbsrc.ac.uk)

Site library

Pirbright Library, Institute for Animal Health, Ash Road, Pirbright, Woking, Surrey GU24 0NF
☎(01483) 232441
e-mail: pirbright.library@bbsrc.ac.uk
Library Assistant Mrs Gail Van der Merwe (e-mail: gail.vandermerwe@bbsrc.ac.uk)

INSTITUTE OF ACTUARIES

Library, Institute of Actuaries, Napier House, 4 Worcester Street, Oxford OXI 2AW
☎(01865) 268206/7
Fax (01865) 268211
e-mail: libraries@actuaries.org.uk
url: www.actuaries.org.uk
Information Manager Ms Sally Grover MA MCLIP
Deputy Librarian Ms Fo Krabben

Specialism(s): Actuarial science; Pensions; Insurance; Finance and investment; Demography

INSTITUTE OF CHARTERED ACCOUNTANTS IN ENGLAND AND WALES

Library and Information Service, Institute of Chartered Accountants in England and Wales, Chartered Accountants' Hall, PO Box 433, Moorgate Place, London EC2P 2BJ
☎020 7920 8620
Fax 020 7920 8621
e-mail: library@icaew.com
url: www.icaew.com/library
Head of Library and Information Services Ms S P Moore BA(Hons)Lib MCLIP
Business Process Manager N Williams BA(Hons)Lib MCLIP
Resource Development Manager Ms J Dixon BA(Hons) MSc
Customer Services Manager Mrs R Mann BA(Hons) MPhil DipInfStud
(The Library is located in the Business Centre within Chartered Accountants' Hall and is for members of the ICAEW and ICAEW-registered students; ACT and IFA members and non-members by arrangement and paying a daily or weekly fee for access. E-mail: businesscentre.reception@icaew.com)

Specialism(s): Accountancy; Auditing; Taxation; Law; Company information; Finance; Management; IT

INSTITUTE OF CHARTERED SECRETARIES AND ADMINISTRATORS

Information Centre, Institute of Chartered Secretaries and Administrators, 16 Park Crescent, London WIB IAH
☎020 7580 4741*
e-mail: informationcentre@icsa.co.uk
url: www.icsa.org.uk
Policy Manager Ms Sheila Doyle
(*Technical enquiries should be sent by e-mail)

Specialism(s): Company law; Corporate governance; Company secretarial practice; Charity law

INSTITUTE OF CLINICAL RESEARCH

Resource Centre, Institute of Clinical Research, Institute House, Boston Drive, Bourne End, Bucks SL8 5YS
☎0845 521 0056 (switchboard)

Fax (01628) 530641
e-mail: info@icr-global.org
url: www.icr-global.org
Head of Media Andrew Smith (e-mail: asmith@icr-global.org)
(Note: Members only professional library; not open to the public)

Specialism(s): Specialist subjects relate to nature of clinical research; Regulations; Ethical issues, the clinical trial process and the personal development of professionals involved in clinical research; Course materials, job descriptions and resource lists

INSTITUTE OF CONSERVATION

Institute of Conservation, 1st Floor, Downstream Building, 1 London Bridge, London SE1 9BG
☎020 7785 3805
Fax 020 7785 3806
e-mail: info@icon.org.uk
url: www.icon.org.uk
Chief Executive Officer Ms Alison Richmond

Chantry Library, Institute of Conservation, Grove Cottage, St Cross Road, Oxford OX1 3TX
☎(01865) 251303
e-mail: chantrylibrary@icon.org.uk
url: www.icon.org.uk
Librarian Ms Ros Buck BA(Hons) DipLIS

Specialism(s): Book and paper conservation including bookbinding, book history, aspects of collection care such as general preservation, disaster mitigation, environmental control, exhibitions, pest management, security and storage. Note: The Chantry Library is administered by the Institute of Conservation. Information on the collection is available at the University of Oxford's online system OLIS (Oxford Libraries Information System).

INSTITUTE OF DIRECTORS

IOD Information Centre, Institute of Directors, 123 Pall Mall, London SW1Y 5ED
☎020 7451 3100
Fax 020 7321 0145
e-mail: businessinfo@iod.com
url: www.iod.com/informationcentre
Head of Information and Advisory Services Mrs A Burmajster MA MCLIP

Specialism(s): Corporate governance; Directorship; Boardroom practice

INSTITUTE OF MATERIALS, MINERALS AND MINING

David West Library, Institute of Materials, Minerals and Mining, 1 Carlton House Terrace, London SW1Y 5DB
☎020 7451 7300 (switchboard)
Fax 020 7451 7406
url: www.iom3.org
Information and Library Co-ordinator Ms Hilda Kaune BA(Hons) DipLib (020 7451

7360 (direct); e-mail: hilda.kaune@iom3.org)
Information Officer Mrs Frances Perry BA (020 7451 7324 (direct); e-mail:
frances.perry@iom3.org)

*Specialism(s): Materials; Metals; Polymers; Ceramics; Composites; Packaging; Clay; Minerals
and Mining; Materials Science; Wood*

INSTITUTE OF OCCUPATIONAL MEDICINE

**Library, Institute of Occupational Medicine, Research Avenue North, Riccarton, Edinburgh
EH14 4AP**
☎0131 449 8000
Fax 0131 449 8084
e-mail: info@iom-world.org
url: www.iom-world.org
Scientific Information Officer Ken Dixon MA(Hons) MA MCLIP

Specialism(s): Occupational medicine and environmental issues

INSTITUTE OF PSYCHOANALYSIS

Library, Institute of Psychoanalysis, 112a Shirland Road, Maida Vale, London W9 2EQ
☎020 7563 5008
Fax 020 7563 5001
e-mail: library@iopa.org.uk
url: www.psychoanalysis.org.uk
Librarian (Mr) Saven Morris
Assistant Librarian Ms Hélène Martin

INSTITUTION OF CIVIL ENGINEERS

**Library, Institution of Civil Engineers, One Great George Street, Westminster, London
SWIP 3AA**
☎020 7665 2251
Fax 020 7976 7610
e-mail: library@ice.org.uk
url: www.ice.org.uk
Head of Knowledge Transfer Michael Chrimes BA MLS MCLIP

THE INSTITUTION OF ENGINEERING AND TECHNOLOGY

Library, The Institution of Engineering and Technology, 2 Savoy Place, London WC2R 0BL
☎020 7240 1871; 020 7344 5461 (general library enquiries)
Fax 020 7344 8467
url: www.theiet.org
Manager of Library and Archives Services John Coupland BA MCLIP (020 7344 5451;
e-mail: jcoupland@theiet.org)

*Specialism(s): Electrical, electronic, control and manufacturing engineering;
Telecommunications, computing and information technology*

INSTITUTION OF MECHANICAL ENGINEERS

Information and Library Service, Institution of Mechanical Engineers, I Birdcage Walk, London SWIH 9JJ
☎020 7973 1274
Fax 020 7222 8762
e-mail: library@imeche.org
url: www.imeche.org.uk/library
Head of Library Service Ms Sarah Rogers MA MCLIP
Information Officers Adrian Clement MA MCLIP, Ms Laura Lipner MA
Archivists Ms Fenella Philpot MA MCLIP, Ms Laura Gardner MA

INSTITUTION OF OCCUPATIONAL SAFETY AND HEALTH

Technical Enquiry and Information Service, The Institution of Occupational Safety and Health, The Grange, Highfield Drive, Wigston, Leicester LEI8 INN
☎0116 257 3199; 0116 257 3100 (switchboard)
Fax 0116 257 3101
e-mail: techinfo@iosh.co.uk
url: www.iosh.co.uk
Information Service Co-ordinator Miss Anne Wells (e-mail: anne.wells@iosh.co.uk)

INSTITUTO CERVANTES

Library, Instituto Cervantes, 102 Eaton Square, London SWIW 9AN
☎020 7201 0757
Fax 020 7235 0329
e-mail: biblon@cervantes.es
url: www.cervantes.es; http://londres.cervantes.es
Chief Librarian Ms Mayte Azoran

Site library

Library, Instituto Cervantes, 326–330 Deansgate, Campfield Avenue Arcade, Manchester M3 4FN
☎0161 661 4210 (direct)
Fax 0161 661 4203
e-mail: bibman@cervantes.es
Librarian Manuel Lafuente Ángel

Specialism(s): Spanish culture, history, literature, language and teaching. A further site library (located in Dublin) can be found in the Academic, National and Special Libraries in the Republic of Ireland section.

THE INTERNATIONAL INSTITUTE FOR STRATEGIC STUDIES (IISS)

Library and Information Department, The International Institute for Strategic Studies (IISS), Arundel House, 13–15 Arundel Street, London WC2R 3DX
☎020 7395 9122 (library enquiries) or 020 7379 7676 (main switchboard)
Fax 020 7836 3108

e-mail: library@iiss.org
url: www.iiss.org/about-us/library
Chief Librarian Mrs Ellena Jamie MA(Oxon) MSc
Deputy Librarian Ms Catherine Micklethwaite BSc(Econ) MA
Assistant Librarian Miss Beth Sockett BA MA

Specialism(s): International relations; War studies

INTERNATIONAL MARITIME ORGANIZATION

Maritime Knowledge Centre, International Maritime Organization, 4 Albert Embankment, London SE1 7SR
☎020 7735 7611 ext 3164
e-mail: maritimeknowledgecentre@imo.org
url: www.imo.org
Head, Maritime Knowledge Centre Mrs Marianne Harvey

Specialism(s): Maritime safety; Prevention of pollution from ships; Ship design; Navigation; Technical co-operation; Liability and compensation

ISLE OF MAN FAMILY HISTORY SOCIETY

Library, Isle of Man Family History Society, Derby Lodge, Derby Road, Peel, Isle of Man IM5 1HH
☎(01624) 843105
e-mail: iomfhs@manx.net
url: www.isle-of-man.com/community/geneaology/iomfhs
Librarian Mrs Doreen Quayle
(Open Tuesdays, Wednesdays and Saturday afternoons, 2–5pm)

ISLE OF MAN PARLIAMENT/LEGISLATURE OF THE ISLE OF MAN

Tynwald Library, Isle of Man Parliament/Legislature of the Isle of Man, Legislative Buildings, Douglas, Isle of Man IM1 3PW
☎(01624) 685520
Fax (01624) 685522
e-mail: library@tynwald.org.im
url: www.tynwald.org.im
Head of Tynwald Information Service Ms Jo Corkish
Librarian Geoffrey Clucas Haywood MCLIP
Research Officer and Deputy Librarian Ms Trudi Thompson BA
Information Executive Graeme Jones

Specialism(s): Manx Parliamentary and Isle of Man Government publications and Isle of Man laws

ITALIAN CULTURAL INSTITUTE (ISTITUTO ITALIANO DI CULTURA)

Eugenio Montale Library, Italian Cultural Institute (Istituto Italiano di Cultura), 39 Belgrave Square, London SW1X 8NX

☎020 7235 1461 (switchboard), 020 7235 1461 ext 203, 020 7396 4425 (library direct line)
Fax 020 7235 4618
e-mail: library.icilondon@esteri.it
url: www.icilondon.esteri.it
Librarian in charge Ms Maria Riccobono Reidy
(Note: Visits by appointment)

Specialism(s): Italian culture and language; Literature and visual arts; Collection of DVDs on Italian cinema

JOINT SERVICES COMMAND AND STAFF COLLEGE

Library, Joint Services Command and Staff College, Faringdon Road, Watchfield, Swindon SN6 8TS
☎(01793) 788236
Fax (01793) 788281
e-mail: library.jscsc@defenceacademy.mod.uk
Head of Library Services C M Hobson MCLIP MBE

Specialism(s): Defence studies; International affairs; Military history

THE KENNEL CLUB

The Kennel Club Library & Art Gallery, The Kennel Club, 1–5 Clarges Street, London W1J 8AB
☎020 7518 1009
Fax 020 7518 1045
e-mail: library@thekennelclub.org.uk
url: www.thekennelclub.org.uk/library
Library and Collections Manager Ms Ciara Farrell BA HDipLIS
(Open Mondays to Fridays, 9.30 am–4.30 pm by appointment)

Specialism(s): Canine literature, registrations and show catalogues, canine art

THE KING'S FUND

Information and Library Service, The King's Fund, 11–13 Cavendish Square, London W1G 0AN
☎020 7307 2568/9 (enquiries)
Fax 020 7307 2805
e-mail: library@kingsfund.org.uk
url: www.kingsfund.org.uk/library
Head of Information Services Development Ray Phillips DipIM MCLIP

Specialism(s): Health and social care policy/management

LABOUR PARTY

Communications Unit, Labour Party, Eldon House, Regents Centre, Newcastle upon Tyne NE3 3PW
☎08705 900200
Fax 0191 246 5136

url: www.labour.org.uk/contact
Communications Unit Manager Jim Harvey

Specialism(s): Labour Party and Government policy

LAMBETH PALACE LIBRARY

Lambeth Palace Library, Lambeth Palace, London SEI 7JU
☎020 7898 1400
Fax 020 7928 7932
e-mail: lpl.staff@c-of-e.org.uk
url: www.lambethpalacelibrary.org; www.churchplansonline.org
Director of Libraries, Archives and Information Services Declan Kelly MSc MCLIP
(e-mail: declan.kelly@c-of-e.org.uk)
Librarian and Archivist Giles Mandelbrote MA FSA

Related libraries

Church of England Record Centre, Lambeth Palace Library, I5 Galleywall Road, Bermondsey, London SEI6 3PB
☎020 7898 1030
Fax 020 7898 1043
e-mail: archivist@c-of-e.org.uk
url: www.cofe.anglican.org/about/librariesandarchives
Records Manager Ms Rebecca Florence
(Reading room access via Lambeth Palace Library.)

Specialism(s): Archives of the central organization of the Church of England, in particular the Church Commissioners; The Archbishops' Council; the General Synod.

Cathedral and Church Buildings Library, Lambeth Palace Library, Church House, Great Smith Street, London SWIP 3AZ
☎020 7898 1884 (Tuesdays & Wednesdays)
Fax 020 7898 1881
e-mail: enquiries@ccc.c-of-e.org.uk
url: www.cofe.anglican.org/about/librariesandarchives
Hon. Librarian Vaughan Whibley MA FRSA MCMI FCLIP

Specialism(s): Ecclesiastical architecture and archaeology; Church fittings and furnishings; Stained glass, organs, bells, monuments

LAW COMMISSION

Library, Law Commission, Steel House, II Tothill Street, London SWIH 9LJ
☎020 3334 0220/I (direct)
Fax 020 3334 0201
e-mail: library@lawcommission.gsi.gov.uk
url: www.lawcom.gov.uk
Librarian Keith Tree BA

THE LAW SOCIETY

Library, The Law Society, 113 Chancery Lane, London WC2A 1PL
☎0870 606 2511
Fax 020 7831 1687
e-mail: library@lawsociety.org.uk; document delivery service: lawdocs@lawsociety.org.uk
url: www.lawsociety.org.uk/library
Online catalogue: www.lawsociety.org.uk/libraryonline
Librarian and Head of Information Services Chris Holland BA MCLIP

Specialism(s): Law; Parliamentary material; Historical legal material

THE LIBRARY AND MUSEUM OF FREEMASONRY

The Library and Museum of Freemasonry, Freemasons' Hall, Great Queen Street, London WC2B 5AZ
☎020 7395 9257
Fax 020 7404 7418
e-mail: libmus@freemasonry.london.museum
url: www.freemasonry.london.museum
Director Ms Diane Clements
Librarian Martin Cherry BSc BA(Hons)
Curator Mark Dennis
Archivist Ms Susan Snell

LIBRARY FOR IRANIAN STUDIES

Library for Iranian Studies, The Woodlands Hall, Crown Street, London W3 8SA
☎020 8993 6384
Fax 020 8752 1300
e-mail: info@iranianlibrary.org.uk
url: www.iranianlibrary.org.uk
Head of Library Dr Mashaallah Ajoudani

LINCOLN CATHEDRAL

Library, Lincoln Cathedral, Minster Yard, Lincoln LN2 1PX
☎(01522) 561640
Fax (01522) 561641
e-mail: librarian@lincolncathedral.com
url: www.lincolncathedral.com
Librarian Dr Nicholas Bennett (e-mail: librarian@lincolncathedral.com)

LINEN HALL LIBRARY

The Linen Hall Library, 17 Donegall Square North, Belfast BT1 5GB
☎028 9032 1707
Fax 028 9043 8586
e-mail: info@linenhall.com
url: www.linenhall.com

Librarian John Killen MA MLS

Specialism(s): Irish history and culture

LINNEAN SOCIETY OF LONDON

Library, Linnean Society of London, Burlington House, Piccadilly, London W1J OBF
☎020 7434 4479
Fax 020 7287 9364
e-mail: library@linnean.org
url: www.linnean.org
Librarian Mrs Lynda Brooks BA DipLib MCLIP FLS (e-mail: lynda@linnean.org)
Deputy Librarian Ben Sherwood MA (e-mail: ben@linnean.org)

Specialism(s): Natural history; Taxonomy; Evolutionary ecology; History of natural history; Conservation and environment

LITERARY AND PHILOSOPHICAL SOCIETY OF NEWCASTLE UPON TYNE

The Lit and Phil Library, Literary and Philosophical Society of Newcastle upon Tyne, 23 Westgate Road, Newcastle upon Tyne NE1 1SE
☎0191 232 0192
Fax 0191 261 4494
e-mail: library@litandphil.org.uk
url: www.litandphil.org.uk
Librarian Ms Kay Easson MA DipLib MCLIP

Specialism(s): Humanities

LONDON CHAMBER OF COMMERCE AND INDUSTRY

Information Centre, London Chamber of Commerce and Industry, 33 Queen Street, London EC4R 1AP
☎020 7248 4444 (switchboard); 020 7203 1866 (direct)
Fax 020 7203 1812
e-mail: info@londonchamber.co.uk
url: www.londonchamber.co.uk
Information Officer Ms Anne Cheng BA(Hons)
(Note: this is a member service)

Specialism(s): General business information

LONDON LIBRARY

London Library, 14 St James's Square, London SW1Y 4LG
☎020 7930 7705
Fax 020 7766 4766
e-mail: membership@londonlibrary.co.uk
url: www.londonlibrary.co.uk
Librarian Miss Inez T P A Lynn BA MLitt MCLIP

Deputy Librarian Ms Jane Oldfield BSc MA MCLIP

Specialism(s): History; Literature; The arts; Related subjects in major European languages

LONDON METROPOLITAN ARCHIVES

Library, London Metropolitan Archives, 40 Northampton Road, London ECIR OHB
☎020 7332 3820
Fax 020 7833 9136
e-mail: ask.lma@cityoflondon.gov.uk
url: www.cityoflondon.gov.uk
Principal Archivist – Public Services E Scudder

Specialism(s): London (local government history; social history)

LONDON TRANSPORT MUSEUM

Information Desk and Library, London Transport Museum, 39 Wellington Street, Covent Garden, London WC2E 7BB
☎020 7565 7280
Fax 020 7565 7252
e-mail: enquiry@ltmuseum.co.uk
url: www.ltmuseum.co.uk
Information Services Manager Ms Caroline Warhurst BA MCLIP, Ms Helen Grove MA
(Visitors by appointment. Opening hours: Mon–Thurs 10am–5pm; Fri 11am–5pm)

Specialism(s): History and development of London's transport past, present and future; information about Transport for London, London Transport and predecessor companies; special emphasis on the development of art, architecture and design in London Transport

MACMILLAN CANCER SUPPORT

Corporate Library, Macmillan Cancer Support, 89 Albert Embankment, London SEI 7UQ
☎020 7840 7840
Fax 020 7840 7841
e-mail: library@macmillan.org.uk
url: www.macmillan.org.uk
Library and Information Specialist (Corporate Library) Chris Wilson (e-mail: cwilson@macmillan.orguk)

Cancer Specialist Library, Macmillan Cancer Support, 89 Albert Embankment, London SEI 7UQ
☎020 7840 7840
Fax 020 7840 7841
e-mail: library@macmillan.org.uk
url: www.macmillan.org.uk
Library and Information Specialist (Cancer Specialist Library) Edward Wallace
(e-mail: ewallace@macmillan.org)

MANX NATIONAL HERITAGE

National Library and Archives, Manx National Heritage, Manx Museum, Douglas, Isle of Man IMI 3LY
☎(01624) 648000; (01624) 648040
Fax (01624) 648001
e-mail: library@mnh.gov.im
url: www.gov.im/mnh/heritage/library/nationallibrary.xml
Library and Archive Services Officer Paul Weatherall BSc MCLIP (e-mail: paul.weatherall.gov.im)
Librarian Alan G Franklin MA MCLIP (e-mail: alan.franklin@mnh.gov.im)
Archivist Ms Wendy Thirkettle BA DipAS (e-mail: wendy.thirkettle@mnh.gov.im)

Specialism(s): History and development of the Isle of Man; Combined local studies, Archive and diocesan record office and place of deposit for public records.

MARINE BIOLOGICAL ASSOCIATION

National Marine Biological Library, Marine Biological Association, Citadel Hill, Plymouth PLI 2PB
☎(01752) 633266
Fax (01752) 633102
e-mail: nmbl@mba.ac.uk
url: www.mba.ac.uk/nmbl/
Head of Library and Information Services Miss Linda Noble BSc MCLIP (01752 633270; e-mail: lno@mba.ac.uk)

Specialism(s): Marine sciences including marine biology, pollution, oceanography and chemistry, fisheries; dating back to 19th century

MARX MEMORIAL LIBRARY

Marx Memorial Library, 37A Clerkenwell Green, London ECIR 0DU
☎020 7253 1485
Fax 020 7251 6039
e-mail: info@marx-memorial-library.org
url: www.marx-memorial-library.org
Librarian Dr John Callow

MARYLEBONE CRICKET CLUB

MCC Library, Marylebone Cricket Club, Lord's Ground, St John's Wood, London NW8 8QN
☎020 7616 8657
Fax 020 7616 8659
e-mail: mcclibrary@mcc.org.uk
url: www.lordsorg/history/mcc-library
Curator Adam Chadwick (020 7616 8655)
Research Officer Neil Robinson (020 7616 8559)

MEDICAL RESEARCH COUNCIL (MRC)

Medical Research Council (MRC), 20 Park Crescent, London WIB IAL
☎020 7636 5422
Fax 020 7436 6179
url: www.mrc.ac.uk
Senior Press Officer Ms Catherine Beveridge (020 7670 5138; e-mail:
catherine.beveridge@headoffice.mrc.ac.uk)
(See also National Institute for Medical Research)

MET OFFICE

National Meterological Library, Met Office, FitzRoy Road, Exeter, Devon EXI 3PB
☎(01392) 884838 (enquiries)
e-mail: metlib@metoffice.gov.uk
url: www.metoffice.gov.uk
Library and Archive Manager Ms Sarah Pankiewicz
(Open to the public)

National Meteorological Archive, Met Office, Great Moor House, Bittern Road, Sowton,
Exeter, Devon EX2 7NL
☎(01392) 360987
e-mail: metlib@metoffice.gov.uk
url: www.metoffice.gov.uk
Assistant Archivist Glyn Hughes
(Open to the public by appointment)

MINISTRY OF DEFENCE

**MOD Information Services, Ministry of Defence, Ground Floor, Zone D, Main Building,
Whitehall, London SWIA 2HB**
☎020 7218 4445 (general enquiries), 020 7218 4184 (administration)
Fax 020 7218 5413
e-mail: info-svcslibrary-office@mod.uk
url: www.mod.uk
Chief Librarian Patrick Ryan BA MBA MCLIP (020 7218 0266; fax: 020 7218 5430;
e-mail: patrick.ryan893@mod.uk)

Site library

Library, Ministry of Defence, Room 1410, Kentigern House, 65 Brown Street, Glasgow
G2 8EX
☎0141 224 2500/1
Fax 0141 224 2257
e-mail: library@khinf.demon.co.uk
Librarian Ms Margaret Gair BA(Hons) DipLib MCLIP

MINISTRY OF JUSTICE

Library, Ministry of Justice, 102 Petty France, London SWIH 9AJ
☎020 3334 3000

Fax 020 3334 4198
e-mail: moj.library@justice.gsi.gov.uk
url: www.justice.gov.uk
Librarian Ms Rachel Robbins BA, Miss Kathy Turner BSc MSc

MORRAB LIBRARY

Morrab Library, Morrab Gardens, Penzance, Cornwall TR18 4DA
☎(01736) 364474
e-mail: morrablibrary@hotmail.co.uk
url: www.morrablibrary.org.uk
Librarian Mrs Annabelle Read
(Available on payment of an annual subscription or a daily fee)

Specialism(s): Cornish literature and history; Napoleonic collection

MUSEUM OF LONDON

Library, Museum of London, London Wall, London EC2Y 5HN
☎020 7001 9844
Fax 020 7600 1058
e-mail: info@museumoflondon.org.uk
url: www.museumoflondon.org.uk
Librarian Ms Sally Brooks MA MCLIP
(Readers by appointment only)

NATIONAL AEROSPACE LIBRARY

National Aerospace Library – Farnborough, National Aerospace Library, The Hub, Fowler Avenue, IQ Farnborough, Hants GU14 7JP
☎(01252) 701038/701060
e-mail: hublibrary@aerosociety.org.uk
url: www.aerosociety.com
Librarian Brian Riddle ((01252 701060; e-mail: brian.riddle@aerosociety.com)

Specialism(s): Extensive collection of material relating to the development and recent technical advances in aeronautics, aviation and aerospace technology. Includes collections of the Royal Aeronautical Society.

THE NATIONAL ARCHIVES

Library, The National Archives, Kew, Richmond, Surrey TW9 4DU
☎020 8876 3444
Fax 020 8487 9207
e-mail: library@nationalarchives.gov.uk
url: www.nationalarchives.gov.uk
Acting Chief Executive Oliver Morley
Director Operations and Services Jeff James
Head of Advice and Records Knowledge Ms Jackie Marfleet

NATIONAL ARMY MUSEUM

Templer Study Centre, National Army Museum, Royal Hospital Road, London SW3 4HT
☎020 7730 0717
Fax 020 7823 6573
e-mail: tsc@national-army-museum.ac.uk
url: www.national-army-museum.ac.uk
Head of Department of Printed Books Michael Ball MA AMA
Head of Archives, Photographs, Film and Sound Alastair Massie MA DPhil
Head of Fine and Decorative Art Miss Jenny Spencer-Smith MA AMA
(Open Wednesday, Thursday and Friday 10am–5pm and 1st and 3rd Saturdays of each
month 10am–5pm, except Bank Holiday weekends)

Specialism(s): Military history; British army; Indian and Commonwealth armies

NATIONAL ART LIBRARY

**Word and Image Department, National Art Library, Victoria and Albert Museum,
Cromwell Road, South Kensington, London SW7 2RL**
☎020 7942 2400 (enquiries)
Fax 020 7942 2410
e-mail: nal.enquiries@vam.ac.uk
url: www.vam.ac.uk/nal
Librarian John Meriton BA BA(Hons) MA DipLib FCLIP FRSA

Site library

Archive of Art and Design, National Art Library, Blythe House, 23 Blythe Road, West
Kensington, London W14 0QF
☎020 7603 1514
Fax 020 7602 0980
e-mail: archive@vam.ac.uk
Archivist Ms Alexia Kirk

NATIONAL ASSEMBLY FOR WALES

Members' Library, National Assembly for Wales, Cardiff Bay, Cardiff CF99 1NA
☎029 2089 8629
url: www.assemblywales.org
Head of Members' Library Mrs Stephanie Wilson (e-mail:
stephanie.wilson@wales.gov.uk)

*Specialism(s): Information resources to support the work of Assembly Members, also the
Members' Research Service, which provides a confidential research and information service to
individual Assembly Members and the Assembly's Committees*

NATIONAL CHILDREN'S BUREAU

**Library and Information Service, National Children's Bureau, 8 Wakley Street, London
EC1V 7QE**
☎020 7843 6008 (enquiry line)
Fax 020 7843 6007

e-mail: library@ncb.org.uk
url: www.ncb.org.uk/library
Head of Library & Information Ms Nicola Hilliard BA MCLIP
(Telephone hours: Mon–Fri 10am–12pm; 2pm–4pm. Ring for appointment to visit)

NATIONAL COAL MINING MUSEUM FOR ENGLAND

Library, National Coal Mining Museum for England, Caphouse Colliery, New Road, Overton, West Yorks WF4 4RH
☎(01924) 848806
Fax (01924) 840694
e-mail: info@ncm.org.uk
url: www.ncm.org.uk
Librarian Mrs Anisha Christison BSc(Hons) MSc MCLIP (e-mail:
curatorial.librarian@ncm.org.uk), Mrs Judith Dennis BA MSc MCLIP (e-mail:
curatorial.librarian@ncm.org.uk) (job share)

NATIONAL GALLERY

Libraries and Archive, The National Gallery, Trafalgar Square, London WC2N 5DN
☎020 7747 2542
Fax 020 7747 2892
e-mail: lad@ng-london.org.uk
url: www.nationalgallery.org.uk
Head of Libraries and Archive Ms Elspeth Hector MA MCLIP (020 7747 2830; e-mail:
elspeth.hector@ng-london.org.uk)
Archivist Alan Crookham (020 7747 2831; e-mail: alan.crookham@ng-london.org.uk)
(Readers by appointment only)

Specialism(s): Western European painting 1200–1900

NATIONAL HERITAGE LIBRARY

National Heritage Library, 313–315 Caledonian Road, London N1 1DR
☎020 7609 9639
url: www.nationalheritagelibrary.org.uk
Founder Director Ms Marg McNiel (e-mail: marg_mcniel@O2.co.uk)
(A comprehensive reference collection covering every aspect of the landscape and culture of the British Isles: open by appointment only)

Specialism(s): The arts; Environmental, historical, industrial and transport sites

NATIONAL INSTITUTE FOR HEALTH AND CLINICAL EXCELLENCE (NICE)

Information Services, National Institute for Health and Clinical Excellence (NICE), Clinical and Public Health Directorate, MidCity Place, 71 High Holborn, London WC1V 6NA
☎0845 003 7780
Fax 0845 003 7784
e-mail: nice@nice.org.uk

url: www.nice.org.uk
Associate Director for Information Services Dr Sarah Cumbers (e-mail: sarah.cumbers@nice.org.uk)

Specialism(s): Evidence-based healthcare; Health technology evaluation; Clinical guidelines; Evidence-based public health

NATIONAL INSTITUTE FOR MEDICAL RESEARCH (MEDICAL RESEARCH COUNCIL)

Library, National Institute for Medical Research (Medical Research Council), The Ridgeway, Mill Hill, London NW7 IAA
☎020 8816 2228
Fax 020 8816 2230
e-mail: library@nimr.mrc.ac.uk
url: www.nimr.mrc.ac.uk/library
Librarian Frank Norman BSc DipLib MCLIP

Specialism(s): Physiology; Neuroscience; Immunology; Microbiology; Molecular biology; Cell biology; Biochemistry; Structural biology; Developmental biology

NATIONAL INSTITUTE OF ECONOMIC AND SOCIAL RESEARCH

Library, National Institute of Economic and Social Research, 2 Dean Trench Street, Smith Square, London SWIP 3HE
☎020 7222 7665
Fax 020 7654 1900
e-mail: library@niesr.ac.uk
url: www.niesr.ac.uk
Librarian Ms Patricia Oliver BA MCLIP (020 7654 1907; e-mail: poliver@niesr.ac.uk)

NATIONAL LIBRARY OF SCOTLAND

National Library of Scotland, George IV Bridge, Edinburgh EHI IEW
☎0131 623 3700
Fax 0131 623 3701
e-mail: enquiries@nls.uk
url: www.nls.uk
National Librarian and Chief Executive Martyn Wade MA MLib MCLIP

Branch/regional libraries

Document Supply Team, Reference Services, National Library of Scotland, George IV Bridge, Edinburgh EHI IEW
☎0131 623 3907/3908
Fax 0131 623 3830
e-mail: ils@nls.uk

Map Collections, National Library of Scotland, 33 Salisbury Place, Edinburgh EH9 ISL
☎0131 623 3970

Fax 0131 623 3971
e-mail: maps@nls.uk

Scottish Screen Archive, National Library of Scotland, 39–41 Montrose Avenue, Hillington
Park, Glasgow G52 4LA
☎(0845) 366 4600
Fax (0845) 366 4601
e-mail: ssaenquiries@nls.uk

Specialism(s): Scottish history and culture

NATIONAL LIBRARY OF WALES: LLYFRGELL GENEDLAETHOL CYMRU

**National Library of Wales: Llyfrgell Genedlaethol Cymru, Aberystwyth, Ceredigion
SY23 3BU**
☎(01970) 632800
Fax (01970) 615709
e-mail: holi@llgc.org.uk
url: www.llgc.org.uk
Librarian Andrew Green MA DipLib MCLIP

*Specialism(s): Legal deposit library housing books, mss, maps, photographs, paintings,
audiovisual and electronic materials; important digitization and exhibitions programmes*

NATIONAL MARITIME MUSEUM

Caird Library, National Maritime Museum, Greenwich, London SE10 9NF
☎020 8312 6516
Fax 020 8312 6599
e-mail: library@nmm.ac.uk; manuscripts@nmm.ac.uk
url: www.nmm.ac.uk
Head of Archive and Library Ms Eleanor Gawne BA(Hons) MA(RCA) RMARA
Reader Services Librarian Gareth Bellis MA
Digital Resources Librarian Ms Renée Orr BA MA MLIS
Archives and Manuscripts Manager Ms Hannah Dunmow MA MArAd

Specialism(s): Maritime history; Horology; Astronomy; Shipbuilding; Navigation

NATIONAL MEDIA MUSEUM

**Royal Photographic Society Collection, National Media Museum, Pictureville, Bradford
BD1 1NQ**
☎0870 7010 200; 0844 856 3797 (box office)
Fax (01274) 772325
e-mail: enquiries@nationalmediamuseum.org.uk
url: www.nationalmediamuseum.org.uk
Curator of Photographs Greg Hobson (01274 203324; e-mail:
greg.hobson@nationalmediamuseum.org.uk)
Curator of Collections Access Brian Liddy (01274 203376; e-mail:
brian.liddy@nationalmediamuseum.org.uk)
(Prior appointment essential for members and non-members)

Science and Society Picture Library, Science Museum, Exhibition Road, South Kensington, London SW7 2DD
☎020 7942 4400
Fax 020 7942 4401
e-mail: piclib@nmsi.ac.uk
url: www.scienceandsociety.co.uk

NATIONAL MUSEUMS SCOTLAND

Library, National Museums Scotland, Chambers Street, Edinburgh EHI IJF
☎0131 247 4137 (enquiries)
Fax 0131 220 4819
e-mail: library@nms.ac.uk
url: www.nms.ac.uk
Head of Information Services Ms Evelyn Simpson (e-mail: e.simpson@nms.ac.uk)

Branch library

Library, National Museums Scotland, National War Museum of Scotland, The Castle, Edinburgh EHI 2NG
☎0131 247 4409

Specialism(s): Decorative arts; Archaeology; Ethnography; History of science and technology; Natural sciences; Museology; Military history

NATIONAL OCEANOGRAPHY CENTRE
(formerly Proudman Oceanographic Laboratory)

Library, National Oceanography Centre, Joseph Proudman Building, 6 Brownlow Street, Liverpool L3 5DA
☎0151 795 4800
Fax 0151 795 4801
url: www.pol.ac.uk
Information and Records Manager Ms Nadina McShane BA MCLIP (e-mail: nm@pol.ac.uk)
Library Manager Andrew J Kennedy BA MPhil MA MCLIP

Specialism(s): Oceanography and marine science

NATIONAL PHYSICAL LABORATORY

Library, National Physical Laboratory, Hampton Road, Teddington, Middlesex TWII OLW
☎020 8943 6417
Fax 020 8614 0424
e-mail: library@npl.co.uk
url: www.npl.co.uk
Library Manager Ian O'Leary MA DLIS (020 8943 6809)

Specialism(s): Physics; Material science; Mathematics; Metrology

NATIONAL POLICING IMPROVEMENT AGENCY

National Police Library, National Policing Improvement Agency, Bramshill, Hook, Hants RG27 0JW
☎(01256) 602650 (enquiries), (01256) 602100 (main switchboard)
Fax (01256) 602285
e-mail: library@npia.pnn.police.uk
url: www.npia.police.uk
Chief Librarian Ms Jill Mussell BA(Hons) DipLib MCLIP (e-mail:
jill.mussell@npia.pnn.police.uk)

NATIONAL PORTRAIT GALLERY

Heinz Archive and Library, National Portrait Gallery, 2 St Martin's Place, London WC2H 0HE
☎020 7321 6617
Fax 020 7306 0056
e-mail: archiveenquiry@npg.org.uk
url: www.npg.org.uk
Head of Archive and Library Robin K Francis BSc(Hons) MA MCLIP
Librarian Joseph Ripp BA MSLS
(Readers by appointment only)

Specialism(s): British portraiture

NATIONAL RAILWAY MUSEUM

Search Engine, National Railway Museum, Leeman Road, York YO26 4XJ
☎(08448) 153139 (all enquiries)
e-mail: search.engine@nrm.org.uk
url: www.nrm.org.uk
Librarian Ms Karen Baker BA MA MCLIP (01904 685745; e-mail:
karen.baker@nrm.org.uk)

Science and Society Picture Library, Science Museum, Exhibition Road, South Kensington, London SW7 2DD
☎020 7942 4400
Fax 020 7942 4401
e-mail: piclib@nmsi.ac.uk
url: www.scienceandsociety.co.uk

NATIONAL STEM CENTRE

National STEM Centre, University of York, Heslington, York, North Yorks YO10 5DD
☎(01904) 328314
Fax (01904) 328328
url: www.nationalstemcentre.org.uk
Resources Co-ordinator Andrew Jones (e-mail: a.jones@nationalstemcentre.org)

Specialism(s): A national collection and archive of Science, Maths, Technology and Engineering (STEM) education resources, including full-text digital resources

NATIONAL UNION OF TEACHERS

Library and Information Unit, National Union of Teachers, Hamilton House, Mabledon Place, London WCIH 9BD
☎020 7380 4713
Fax 020 7387 8458
url: www.teachers.org.uk
Information Officer Ms Janet Friedlander BA MCLIP (e-mail: j.friedlander@nut.org.uk)
Information Assistant Mrs Kate Burry BA MCLIP (e-mail: k.burry@nut.org.uk)

NATURAL ENGLAND

Information and Library Services, Natural England, Touthill House, City Road, Peterborough PEI IXN
☎0845 600 3078 (switchboard)
e-mail: library@naturalengland.org.uk
url: www.naturalengland.org.uk
Legal Adviser, Knowledge and Information Management Ms Brigid Newland BA(Hons) (0300 060 1156)

Specialism(s): Sustainable use and management of the natural environment: biodiversity; wildlife; landscapes; access and recreation; conservation of marine and coastal environments

NATURAL HISTORY MUSEUM

Library, Natural History Museum, Cromwell Road, London SW7 5BD
☎020 7942 5460 (general enquiries)
Fax 020 7942 5559
e-mail: library@nhm.ac.uk
url: www.nhm.ac.uk/library
Head of Library and Information Services Graham Higley BSc
The Library is divided into four specialist sections at South Kensington: General & Zoology (020 7942 5460); Botany (020 7942 5685); Entomology (020 7942 5460) and Earth Sciences (020 7942 5460).

Site library

Ornithology and Rothschild Library, Natural History Museum Tring, Akeman Street, Tring, Herts HP23 6AP
☎020 7942 6156
Fax 020 7942 6150
e-mail: ornlib@nhm.ac.uk
url: www.nhm.ac.uk/tring
Assistant Librarian Ms Alison Harding MA MSc MCLIP

NETWORK RAIL INFRASTRUCTURE LTD

Network Rail Library, Network Rail Infrastructure Ltd, 2nd Floor Library, 40 Melton Street, London NWI 2EE
☎020 7557 8062
Fax 020 7557 9150

url: www.networkrail.co.uk
Librarian Ms Sue Peters (e-mail: sue.peters@networkrail.co.uk)
(Not open to the public but queries welcomed from professional organizations and researchers.)

Specialism(s): UK railway history, legislation, engineering, health and safety

NHS HEALTH SCOTLAND

Library, NHS Health Scotland, The Priory, Canaan Lane, Edinburgh EHIO 4SG
☎0131 536 5581
Fax 0131 536 5502
e-mail: nhs.healthscotland-library@nhs.net
url: www.healthscotland.com/library
Library Services Manager Ms Julia Green BA DipLib MSc
Librarian Ms Julie Arnot

Specialism(s): Public health; Health promotion and education

NHS NATIONAL SERVICES SCOTLAND

Information Services Division, NHS National Services Scotland, Gyle Square, I South Gyle Crescent, Edinburgh EHI2 9EB
☎0131 275 6423
e-mail: NSS.isdlibrary@nhs.net
url: www.isdscotland.org
Manager, ISD Library Services Alan Jamieson MA DipLib MCLIP (e-mail: alan.jamicson@nhs.net)

Specialism(s): Health statistics; Official circulars; Media monitoring

NORTHERN IRELAND ASSEMBLY

Library, Northern Ireland Assembly, Parliament Buildings, Balymiscaw, Stormont, Belfast BT4 3XX
☎028 9052 1250
Fax 028 9052 1922
e-mail: issuedesk.library@niassembly.gov.uk
url: www.ni-assembly.gov.uk
Resource Team Librarian George D Woodman BA DipLib MCLIP (028 9052 1250; e-mail: george.woodman@niassembly.gov.uk)

Specialism(s): Legislation and official publications relating especially to N Ireland, government, politics and Irish history

NORTHERN IRELAND OFFICE

Library, Northern Ireland Office, II Millbank, London SWIP 4PN
☎020 7210 0253
Fax 020 7210 0212
url: www.nio.gov.uk
Records Officer Ms Claire O'Neill (e-mail: claire.o'neill@nio.x.gsi.gov.uk)

OFFICE FOR NATIONAL STATISTICS

Library and Information Service, Office for National Statistics, Room I.063, Government Buildings, Cardiff Road, Newport, Gwent NT10 8XG
☎(01633) 456582
e-mail: library.enquiries@ons.gsi.gov.uk
url: www.statistics.gov.uk
Chief Librarian Ian W Bushnell BA MCLIP (01633 456580; e-mail: ian.bushnell@ons.gsi.gov.uk)
(The library is open to the public by appointment only)

OFFICE OF FAIR TRADING

Information and Advisory Centre, Office of Fair Trading, Lower Ground Floor, Fleetbank House, 2-6 Salisbury Square, London EC4Y 8JX
☎020 7211 8582/8944. For general OFT enquiries 0845 722 4499; OFT Publications orderline 0800 389 3158
e-mail: enquiries@oft.gsi.gov.uk
url: www.oft.gov.uk
Head of Information and Advisory Centre Ms Lyn Burden BA
(Primarily an internal information service)

OFFICE OF RAIL REGULATION

Information Centre, Office of Rail Regulation, I Kemble Street, London WC2B 4AN
☎020 7282 2001
Fax 020 7282 2040
e-mail: info.centre@orr.gsi.gov.uk
url: www.rail-reg.gov.uk
Information Manager Ms Sue MacSwan BA MSc

OFFICE OF THE PARLIAMENTARY AND HEALTH SERVICE OMBUDSMAN (OFFICE OF THE PARLIAMENTARY COMMISSIONER FOR ADMINISTRATION AND HEALTH SERVICE COMMISSIONER FOR ENGLAND)

Learning and Resource Centre, Office of the Parliamentary and Health Service Ombudsman (Office of the Parliamentary Commissioner for Administration and Health Service Commissioner for England), 15th Floor, Millbank Tower, Millbank, London SW1P 4QP
☎0300 061 4104
Fax 0300 061 4940
e-mail: lrc@ombudsman.org.uk
url: www.ombudsman.org.uk
Librarian Ms Deanne Mitchell BA DipLib MCLIP

Specialism(s): Ombudsman issues; Maladministration

OFGEM (OFFICE OF GAS AND ELECTRICITY MARKETS)

Research and Information Centre, OFGEM (Office of Gas and Electricity Markets), 9 Millbank, London SW1P 3GE
☎020 7901 7003
Fax 020 7901 7378
e-mail: library@ofgem.gov.uk
url: www.ofgem.gov.uk
Librarian Keith Smith
Assistant Librarian Ms Emma Davis
(Open 10am–4pm Monday to Friday. By appointment only: 24 hours notice required.)

OMNIBUS SOCIETY

The John F Parke Memorial Library, The Omnibus Society, 100 Sandwell Street, Walsall, West Midlands WS1 3EB
☎(01922) 629358
url: www.omnibussoc.org
Librarian Alan Mills (01922 631867 (tel/fax); e-mail: alanavrilmills@hotmail.com)
(Manned by volunteers, the Library is currently open to casual callers on Wednesdays (09.15–16.15), although other appointments can be made by prior arrangement.)

Specialism(s): Road passenger transport; Unique collection of timetables

PIRA INTERNATIONAL

Information Centre, PIRA International, Cleeve Road, Leatherhead, Surrey KT22 7RU
☎(01372) 802050 (enquiries)
Fax (01372) 802239
e-mail: infocentre@pira-international.com
url: www.pira-international.com
Head of Information Adam Page

Specialism(s): Papermaking; Printing; Packaging; Publishing

PLUNKETT FOUNDATION

Library, Plunkett Foundation, The Quadrangle, Woodstock, Oxon OX20 1LH
☎(01993) 810730
Fax (01993) 810849
e-mail: info@plunkett.co.uk
url: www.plunkett.co.uk
Head of Information and Communications Mike Perry

Specialism(s): Focus on history and practice of cooperatives and rural enterprise; Agriculture

PLYMOUTH PROPRIETARY LIBRARY

Plymouth Proprietary Library, Alton Terrace, 111 North Hill, Plymouth PL4 8JY
☎(01752) 660515
Librarian Ms Shirley Lamerton

Specialism(s): 19th- and early 20th-century classical fiction (available to members only)

POETRY LIBRARY

Saison Poetry Library, Poetry Library, Level 5, Royal Festival Hall, South Bank Centre, London SE1 8XX
☎020 7921 0943/0664
Fax 020 7921 0607
e-mail: info@poetrylibrary.org.uk
url: www.poetrylibrary.org.uk; www.poetrymagazines.org.uk
Librarians Miriam Valencia BA(Hons) MA MCLIP, Chris McCabe

POLISH LIBRARY

Polish Library, 238-246 King Street, London W6 0RF
☎020 8741 0474
Fax 020 8741 7724
e-mail: library@polishlibrary.co.uk; ccl@polishlibrary.co.uk
url: www.posk.org
Acting Librarian Grzegorz Pisarski

PORTICO LIBRARY AND GALLERY

The Portico Library and Gallery, 57 Mosley Street, Manchester M2 3HY
☎0161 236 6785
Fax 0161 236 6785
url: www.theportico.org.uk
Librarian Miss Emma Marigliano BA(Hons) (e-mail: librarian@theportico.org.uk)
(Tours by arrangement. Nineteenth-century stock available for scholarly research and for members. Gallery open to the public.)

PROUDMAN OCEANOGRAPHIC LABORATORY *see* NATIONAL OCEANOGRAPHY CENTRE

QINETIQ

Insight Team, Qinetiq, Dorset Green, Building A33, Dorchester, Dorset DT2 8XJ
☎(01305) 212218
url: www.qinetiq.com
Information Specialist Ms Wendy Gubbels BA (e-mail: wrgubbels@qinetiq.com)

Specialism(s): Sonar and oceanography

RELIGIOUS SOCIETY OF FRIENDS IN BRITAIN (QUAKERS)

Library, Religious Society of Friends in Britain (Quakers), Friends House, 173–177 Euston Road, London NW1 2BJ
☎020 7663 1135
Fax 020 7663 1001

e-mail: library@quaker.org.uk
url: www.quaker.org.uk/library
Head of Library and Archives Ms Beverley Kemp

Specialism(s): Quakerism (17th century to the present); Peace and pacifism; Anti-slavery; Prison reform and penal affairs; Humanitarian assistance; Temperance

RESEARCH COUNCILS UK

Strategy Unit, Research Councils UK, Polaris House, North Star Avenue, Swindon, Wilts SN2 1ET
☎(01793) 444000
url: www.rcuk.ac.uk
Team Leader Peter Rigby (e-mail: peter.rigby@rcuk.ac.uk)
The following research councils have information services on this site. See also separate entries for Medical Research Council (MRC); and Science and Technology Facilities Council (STFC).

AHRC (Arts and Humanities Research Council), Research Councils UK, Polaris House, North Star Avenue, Swindon, Wilts SN2 1FL
☎(01793) 416000
Fax (01793) 416001
e-mail: enquiries@ahrc.ac.uk
Communications Manager Jake Gilmore (01793 416021; e-mail: j.gilmore@ahrc.ac.uk)

Biotechnology and Biological Sciences Research Council (BBSRC), Research Councils UK, Polaris House, North Star Avenue, Swindon, Wilts SN2 1UH
url: www.bbsrc.ac.uk
Information Officer Ms Caroline Dow (01793 414679; e-mail: caroline.dow@bbsrc.ac.uk)

Economic and Social Research Council (ESRC), Research Councils UK, Polaris House, North Star Avenue, Swindon, Wilts SN2 1UJ
url: www.esrc.ac.uk
Information Officer Ms Debbie Stalker (01793 444490; e-mail: debbie.stalker@esrc.ac.uk)

Engineering and Physical Sciences Research Council (EPSRC), Research Councils UK, Polaris House, North Star Avenue, Swindon, Wilts SN2 1ET
☎(01793) 444100 (helpline)
e-mail: infoline@epsrc.ac.uk
url: www.epsrc.ac.uk
Information Officer Russell Cox (01793 413328; e-mail: russell.cox@epsrc.ac.uk)

Natural Environment Research Council (NERC), Research Councils UK, Polaris House, North Star Avenue, Swindon, Wilts SN2 1EU
url: www.nerc.ac.uk
Head, NERC Research Library Service Ken Hollywood BA MSc DipLib MCLIP (01793 411782; e-mail: ken.hollywood@nerc.ac.uk)
Information Officer Mrs Luki Chahal

RNIB NATIONAL LIBRARY SERVICE

**RNIB National Library Service, Far Cromwell Road, Bredbury, Stockport, Cheshire
SK6 2SG**
☎0303 123 9999
Fax 0161 355 2098
e-mail: cservices@rnib.org.uk
url: www.rnib.org.uk/reading
Head Ms Helen Brazier MA MCLIP (0161 355 2004; e-mail: helen.brazier@rnib.org.uk)
Manager Ms Pat Beech MCLIP (0161 355 2005)
(RNIB National Library Service offers a comprehensive range of books and accessible
information for adults and children with sight loss. Books are posted free of charge using
the Articles for the Blind service.)

*Specialism(s): Talking Books: the UK's largest collection (15,000) titles of unabridged audio
books on CD, both fiction and non-fiction; Braille and Moon books: Europe's largest collection of
touch-reading material including maps; books in large print (16pt type) and giant print (24pt
type); Braille Music Library: 14,000 Braille music scores (the largest collection outside the USA)
plus books about music and music theory; online reference services: free access to online
accessible reference materials including dictionaries, encyclopedias, journals and newspapers;
Online catalogues, e-mail discussion group and web message boards for book lovers; reader
magazines and help with choosing books; RNIB Research Library: the most comprehensive UK
collection of print material relating to sight loss (tel: 020 7391 2052)*

RNID LIBRARY

**RNID Library, UCL Ear Institute and RNID Libraries at the Royal National Throat, Nose
and Ear Hospital, 330–332 Gray's Inn Road, London WC1X 8EE**
☎020 7915 1553 (also for Minicom); 020 7915 1445
Fax 020 7915 1443
e-mail: rnidlib@ucl.ac.uk
url: www.ucl.ac.uk/library/rnidlib.shtml
Librarian Alex Stagg MA (e-mail: a.stagg@ucl.ac.uk)

Specialism(s): Audiology; Deaf studies

ROTHAMSTED LIBRARY – ROTHAMSTED RESEARCH

Rothamsted Library – Rothamsted Research, Harpenden, Herts AL5 2JQ
☎(01582) 763133
Fax (01582) 760981
e-mail: res.library@bbsrc.ac.uk
url: www.rothamsted.bbsrc.ac.uk/resources/library/
Librarian Mrs S E Allsopp BA DipLib (e-mail: liz.allsopp@bbsrc.ac.uk)

Specialism(s): Arable crops research; Sustainable land development

ROYAL ACADEMY OF ARTS

Library, Royal Academy of Arts, Burlington House, Piccadilly, London W1J 0BD
☎020 7300 5737 (enquiries), 020 7300 5740 (administration)
Fax 020 7300 5765

e-mail: library@royalacademy.org.uk
url: www.royalacademy.org.uk
Head of Library Services Adam Waterton
Assistant Librarian Ms Miranda Stead BA(Hons) LipLIS, Ms Yamuna Ravindran (job share)

Specialism(s): British art and artists from 18th century to present; History of the Academy since 1768

ROYAL AERONAUTICAL SOCIETY *see* NATIONAL AEROSPACE LIBRARY

ROYAL AIR FORCE COLLEGE

College Library, Royal Air Force College, Cranwell, Sleaford, Lincs NG34 8HB
☎(01400) 266219
Fax (01400) 262532
e-mail: chom.library@btconnect.com
College Librarian & Archivist Ms Mary Guy BA(Hons) DipLib MCLIP (e-mail: collegelibrarian@cranwell.raf.mod.uk)

ROYAL AIR FORCE MUSEUM

Royal Air Force Museum, Grahame Park Way, Hendon, London NW9 5LL
☎020 8205 2266 ext 4873
Fax 020 8200 1751
e-mail: research@rafmuseum.org
url: www.rafmuseum.org
Senior Keeper P J V Elliott MA BSc MCLIP
(Prior appointment necessary)

Specialism(s): Military aviation

ROYAL ASTRONOMICAL SOCIETY

Library, Royal Astronomical Society, Burlington House, Piccadilly, London W1J 0BQ
☎020 7734 3307/4582
Fax 020 7494 0166
e-mail: info@ras.org.uk
url: www.ras.org.uk; www.sciencephotolibrary.com
Librarian Peter D Hingley BA MCLIP RD (e-mail: pdh@ras.org.uk)
(Enquiries in writing or by e-mail preferred, access by appointment)

Specialism(s): Extensive archive and rare book collection covering astronomy and geophysics

ROYAL AUTOMOBILE CLUB

Library, Royal Automobile Club, 89 Pall Mall, London SW1Y 5HS
☎020 7747 3398
Fax 0870 460 6285
e-mail: library@royalautomobileclub.co.uk

url: www.royalautomobileclub.co.uk/guestarea/rac.asp?s=FA&ss=LI
Librarian Trevor G Dunmore BA(Hons) DipLib

Specialism(s): History of motoring and motor sport

ROYAL BOTANIC GARDEN, EDINBURGH

Library, Royal Botanic Garden, Edinburgh, 20A Inverleith Row, Edinburgh EH3 5LR
☎0131 248 2853 (enquiries), 0131 248 2850 (administration)
Fax 0131 248 2901
e-mail: library@rbge.ac.uk
url: www.rbge.org.uk
Head of Library Mrs Jane Hutcheon BSc MCLIP (e-mail: j.hutcheon@rbge.ac.uk)

Specialism(s): Botany; Horticulture; Garden history and botanical art

ROYAL BOTANIC GARDENS, KEW

Library, Art & Archives, Royal Botanic Gardens, Kew, Richmond, Surrey TW9 3AE
☎020 8332 5414
Fax 020 8332 5430
e-mail: library@kew.org
url: www.kew.org
Head of Library, Art and Archives Christopher Mills BA MA DipLib MCLIP (020 8332 5412; e-mail: c.mills@kew.org.uk)

ROYAL COLLEGE OF PHYSICIANS AND SURGEONS OF GLASGOW

Library, Royal College of Physicians and Surgeons of Glasgow, 232–242 St Vincent Street, Glasgow G2 5RJ
☎0141 227 3241 (enquiries), 0141 221 6072 (administration)
Fax 0141 221 1804
e-mail: library@rcpsg.ac.uk
url: www.rcpsg.ac.uk
Library and Heritage Manager Mrs Carol Parry BA(Hons) DAA (e-mail: carol.parry@rcpsg.ac.uk)
Assistant Librarian Mrs Valerie McClure MA(Hons) MSc LIS (e-mail: valerie.mcclure@rcpsg.ac.uk)
Modern Resources Officer Ms Clare Harrison BA MSc (e-mail: claire.harrison@rcpsg.ac.uk)

Specialism(s): History of medicine

ROYAL COLLEGE OF PHYSICIANS OF EDINBURGH

Sibbald Library, Royal College of Physicians of Edinburgh, 9 Queen Street, Edinburgh EH2 1JQ
☎0131 225 7324
Fax 0131 220 3939
e-mail: library@rcpe.ac.uk

url: www.rcpe.ac.uk
Sibbald Librarian Iain A Milne MLib MCLIP

ROYAL COLLEGE OF PHYSICIANS OF LONDON

Library, Royal College of Physicians of London, II St Andrews Place, Regent's Park, London NWI 4LE
☎020 3075 1539
Fax 020 7486 3729
e-mail: infocentre@rcplondon.ac.uk
url: www.rcplondon.ac.uk
Minicom 020 7486 5687
Knowledge Services Manager Mrs Julie Beckwith BA MSc MCLIP (020 3075 1317; e-mail: julie.beckwith@rcplondon.ac.uk)

Specialism(s): UK health policy; Public health; History of medicine; Medical biography; separately managed Jerwood Medical Education Resource Centre

ROYAL COLLEGE OF PSYCHIATRISTS

Library and Information Service, Royal College of Psychiatrists, I7 Belgrave Square, London SWIX 8PG
☎020 7235 2351 ext 138/152
Fax 020 7259 6303
e-mail: infoservices@rcpsych.ac.uk
url: www.rcpsych.ac.uk
Library and Information Manager Ms Sally Blake

Specialism(s): Antiquarian psychiatry textbooks dating from 15th century

ROYAL COLLEGE OF SURGEONS OF ENGLAND

Library and Lumley Study Centre, Royal College of Surgeons of England, 35–43 Lincoln's Inn Fields, London WC2A 3PE
☎020 7869 6555/6556 (enquiries), 020 7405 3474 (College switchboard)
Fax 020 7405 4438
e-mail: library@rcseng.ac.uk; archives@rcseng.ac.uk
url: www.rcseng.ac.uk
Head of Library and Information Services Mrs Thalia Knight MA MA DipLib MCLIP
Information Services Manager Tom Bishop BA(Hons) MA
Records and Archives Manager Ms Beth Astridge BA(Hons) MA RMARA

ROYAL COLLEGE OF VETERINARY SURGEONS

RCVS Trust Library, Royal College of Veterinary Surgeons, Belgravia House, 62–64 Horseferry Road, London SWIP 2AF
☎020 7202 0752
Fax 020 7202 0751
e-mail: library@rcvstrust.org.uk
url: www.rcvslibrary.org.uk
Librarian Ms Clare Boulton

ROYAL COMMISSION ON THE ANCIENT AND HISTORICAL MONUMENTS OF WALES

Library and Enquiries Service, Royal Commission on the Ancient and Historical Monuments of Wales, Crown Building, Plas Crug, Aberystwyth, Ceredigion SY23 INJ
☎(01970) 621200
Fax (01970) 627701
e-mail: nmr.wales@rcahmw.gov.uk
url: www.rcahmw.gov.uk
Secretary Dr Peter Wakelin
Librarian and Enquiry Services Manager Ms Patricia Moore BA MCLIP

Specialism(s): Archaeology; Architectural history and heritage of Wales

ROYAL COURTS OF JUSTICE

Library, Royal Courts of Justice, Ministry of Justice, Strand, London WC2A 2LL
☎020 7947 6587 (enquiries), 020 7947 7582 (administration)
Fax 020 7947 6661
url: www.hmcourts-service.gov.uk; www.justice.gov.uk
Librarian Ms Stephanie Curran BA GradDipLibStudies MIT (e-mail: stephanie.curran@justice.gsi.gov.uk)
(Note: not open to the public)

ROYAL ENGINEERS MUSEUM, ARCHIVES AND LIBRARY

Royal Engineers Museum, Archives and Library, Ravelin Building, Brompton Barracks, Chatham, Kent ME4 4UG
☎(01634) 822221
Fax (01634) 822419
url: www.remuseum.org.uk
Documentation Officer Andrew Davis

ROYAL ENTOMOLOGICAL SOCIETY

Library, Royal Entomological Society, The Mansion House, Chiswell Green Lane, St Albans, Herts AL2 3NZ
☎(01727) 899387
Fax (01727) 894797
e-mail: lib@royensoc.co.uk
url: www.royensoc.co.uk
Librarian Mrs Val McAtear BA(Hons)Lib

ROYAL GEOGRAPHICAL SOCIETY (WITH THE INSTITUTE OF BRITISH GEOGRAPHERS)

Foyle Reading Room, Royal Geographical Society (with the Institute of British Geographers), 1 Kensington Gore, London SW7 2AR
☎020 7591 3044

Fax 020 7591 3001
e-mail: enquiries@rgs.org
url: www.rgs.org
Principal Librarian Eugene Rae MA DipLIS
Deputy Librarian Miss Janet Turner BA(Hons)
Map Librarian David McNeill BA

Specialism(s): Geography; Travel; Exploration

ROYAL HORTICULTURAL SOCIETY

Lindley Library London, Royal Horticultural Society, 80 Vincent Square, London SWIP 2PE
☎020 7821 3050
e-mail: library.london@rhs.org.uk
url: www.rhs.org.uk/Learning/Library
Head of Libraries Ms Barbara Collecott

Lindley Library Wisley, Royal Horticultural Society, RHS Garden Wisley, Woking, Surrey GU23 6QB
☎(01483) 212428
Fax (01483) 479727
e-mail: library.wisley@rhs.org.uk
url: www.rhs.org.uk/Learning/Library

ROYAL INSTITUTE OF BRITISH ARCHITECTS

British Architectural Library, Royal Institute of British Architects, 66 Portland Place, London WIB IAD
☎020 7580 5533 (switchboard); Public information line (calls 50p per min): 0906 302 0400
Fax 020 7631 1802
e-mail: info@inst.riba.org
url: www.architecture.com
Director Dr Irena Murray

Branch library

British Architectural Library Drawings and Archives Collection, Royal Institute of British Architects, Henry Cole Wing, Victoria and Albert Museum, Exhibition Road, London SW7 2RL
☎020 7307 3708 (Study Room)
e-mail: drawings&archives@inst.riba.org
Associate Director and Curator of Drawings Charles Hind

ROYAL INSTITUTE OF INTERNATIONAL AFFAIRS

Library, Royal Institute of International Affairs, Chatham House, 10 St James's Square, London SWIY 4LE
☎020 7957 5723 (enquiries)
Fax 020 7957 5710
e-mail: libenquire@chathamhouse.org.uk
url: www.chathamhouse.org.uk

Librarian Ms Sara Pink (020 7314 3610; e-mail: spink@chathamhouse.org.uk)

Specialism(s): International affairs; Politics; Economics; Security; Environment

ROYAL INSTITUTE OF NAVIGATION

The Cundall Library, Royal Institute of Navigation, I Kensington Gore, London SW7 2AT
☎020 7591 3133
Fax 020 7591 3131
e-mail: editor@rin.org.uk
url: www.rin.org.uk
Librarian Tony Fyler
(The library is free to members and open to the public on an appointment-only basis.)

Specialism(s): Land, sea and air navigation

ROYAL INSTITUTION OF CHARTERED SURVEYORS

Library and Information Services, Royal Institution of Chartered Surveyors, Parliament Square, London SWIP 3AD
☎0870 333 1600 ext 3714; 020 7334 3714
Fax 020 7334 3784
e-mail: library@rics.org
url: www.rics.org
Head of Library and Information Services Ms Cathy Linacre BA DipLib MCLIP
(020 7334 3748; e-mail: clinacre@rics.org)

ROYAL INSTITUTION OF GREAT BRITAIN

Library, Royal Institution of Great Britain, 21 Albemarle Street, London WIS 4BS
☎020 7670 2939
Fax 020 7670 2920
e-mail: ril@ri.ac.uk
url: www.rigb.org
Head of Collections and Heritage Prof Frank James (020 7670 2924; e-mail: fjames@ri.ac.uk)

ROYAL INSTITUTION OF NAVAL ARCHITECTS

Library, Royal Institution of Naval Architects, 10 Upper Belgrave Street, London SWIX 8BQ
☎020 7235 4622
Fax 020 7259 5912
e-mail: hq@rina.org.uk
url: www.rina.org.uk
Information Manager Graeme Mitchell

ROYAL MILITARY ACADEMY SANDHURST

Central Library, Royal Military Academy Sandhurst, Camberley, Surrey GUI5 4PQ
☎(01276) 412367
Fax (01276) 412538

url: www.sandhurst.mod.uk
Senior Librarian Andrew Orgill MA DipLib MCLIP (e-mail: senlibrarian@rmas.mod.uk)

Specialism(s): Military history and international affairs

ROYAL PHARMACEUTICAL SOCIETY OF GREAT BRITAIN

Library, Royal Pharmaceutical Society of Great Britain, I Lambeth High Street, London SEI 7JN
☎020 7735 9141 (switchboard); 020 7572 2300 (direct)
Fax 020 7572 2499
e-mail: library@rpsgb.org
url: www.rpsgb.org; library catalogue: http://olib.rpsgb.org
Information Access and Resource Manager (Librarian) Ms Martha Krumbach (e-mail: martha.krumbach@rpsgb.org)

Specialism(s): Pharmacy; Medicines; Therapeutics; Pharmaceutical science

ROYAL SOCIETY

Library, Royal Society, 6–9 Carlton House Terrace, London SWIY 5AG
☎020 7451 2606
Fax 020 7930 2170
e-mail: library@royalsociety.org
url: www.royalsociety.org
Head of Library and Information Services Keith Moore MA

ROYAL SOCIETY FOR THE PREVENTION OF ACCIDENTS

Information Centre, Royal Society for the Prevention of Accidents, Edgbaston Park, 353 Bristol Road, Birmingham B5 7ST
☎0121 248 2063/6
Fax 0121 248 2001
e-mail: infocentre@rospa.com
url: www.rospa.com
Information Services Manager Dr Ibidapo Oketunji PhD (0121 248 2063; e-mail: ioketunji@rospa.com)

ROYAL SOCIETY OF CHEMISTRY

Library and Information Centre, Royal Society of Chemistry, Burlington House, Piccadilly, London WIJ OBA
☎020 7440 3373 (direct)
Fax 020 7437 8883
e-mail: library@rsc.org
url: www.rsc.org/library
Manager, Library and Archival Services Vacant

ROYAL SOCIETY OF MEDICINE

Library, Royal Society of Medicine, I Wimpole Street, London WIG OAE

☎020 7290 2940/2941 (enquiries), 020 7290 2931 (administration)
Fax 020 7290 2939
e-mail: library@rsm.ac.uk
url: www.rsm.ac.uk
Director of Library Services Wayne Sime BSc(Econ) MCLIP

ROYAL STATISTICAL SOCIETY

Library, Royal Statistical Society, 12 Errol Street, London EC1Y 8LX
☎020 7638 8998
url: www.rss.org.uk
Archives Consultant Ms Janet Foster (e-mail: j.foster@rss.org.uk)
(Historical book collection and Society archives. Viewing by appointment only)

Albert Sloman Library, Royal Statistical Society, University of Essex, Wivenhoe Park,
Colchester, Essex CO4 3SQ
☎(01206) 873181/873172 (enquiries)
Deputy Librarian Nigel Cochrane (e-mail: nigelc@essex.ac.uk)
Assistant Librarian Ms Sandy Macmillen (e-mail: amacmi@essex.ac.uk)
(Houses the Library of the RSS)

Specialism(s): Statistics; Social history

ROYAL TOWN PLANNING INSTITUTE

Library, Royal Town Planning Institute, 41 Botolph Lane, London EC3R 8DL
☎020 7929 9452
Fax 020 7929 8197
e-mail: library@rtpi.org.uk
url: www.rtpi.org.uk
Librarian and Information Manager Vacant
(Visits by appointment only)

RSA

Library, RSA, 8 John Adam Street, London WC2N 6EZ
☎020 7451 6847
e-mail: library@rsa.org.uk
url: www.thersa.org/fellowship/fellows-facilities/library
Head of Archive and Library Rob Baker

Archive, RSA, 8 John Adam Street, London WC2N 6EZ
☎020 7451 6847
e-mail: archive@rsa.org.uk
url: www.thersa.org/about-us/history-and-archive
Archivist Rob Baker
(Access by appointment)

ST DEINIOL'S RESIDENTIAL LIBRARY *see* GLADSTONE'S LIBRARY

ST FAGANS: NATIONAL HISTORY MUSEUM

Library, St Fagans: National History Museum, St Fagans, Cardiff CF5 6XB
☎029 2057 3446
Fax 029 2057 3490
url: www.museumwales.ac.uk/St Fagans
Library Assistant Richard Edwards (e-mail: richard.edwards@museumwales.ac.uk)

Specialism(s): Material, social and cultural history of Wales

SCIENCE AND TECHNOLOGY FACILITIES COUNCIL

Head Office, Science and Technology Facilities Council, Polaris House, North Star Avenue, Swindon SN2 1SZ
☎(01793) 442000
Fax (01793) 442002
e-mail: enquiries@stfc.ac.uk
Information Officer Ms Julia Maddock (01793 442094; e-mail: julia.maddock@stfc.ac.uk)

Chadwick Library, Science and Technology Facilities Council, Daresbury Laboratory, Daresbury Science and Innovation Campus, Warrington, Cheshire WA4 4AD
☎(01925) 603397
Fax (01925) 603779
e-mail: library@dl.ac.uk
url: www.e-science.stfc.ac.uk/services/library
Library Services Development Manager Mrs Debbie Franks BSc MCLIP (01925 603189)

Library, Science and Technology Facilities Council, Rutherford Appleton Laboratory, Harwell Science and Innovation Campus, Didcot, Oxon OX11 0QX
☎(01235) 445384 (general enquiries)
Fax (01235) 446403
e-mail: library@stfc.ac.uk
url: www.e-science.stfc.ac.uk/services/library
Site Librarian Mrs Linda Gilbert BSc(Econ) MCLIP (01235 446151)

SCIENCE FICTION FOUNDATION COLLECTION

Science Fiction Foundation Collection, University of Liverpool Library, PO Box 123, Liverpool L69 3DA
☎0151 794 2696 (library)
Fax 0151 794 2681
url: www.sfhub.ac.uk
Librarian/Administrator Andy Sawyer MPhil MCLIP (0151 794 3142; e-mail: a.sawyer@liverpool.ac.uk)

SCIENCE MUSEUM LIBRARY

Science Museum Library, Imperial College Road, London SW7 5NH
☎020 7942 4242
Fax 020 7942 4243
e-mail: smlinfo@sciencemuseum.org.uk

url: www.sciencemuseum.org.uk/library
Head of Library & Archives Rupert N Williams BA(Hons) MA MCLIP (e-mail: rupert.williams@sciencemuseum.org.uk)
Library Manager Nicholas J Wyatt (e-mail: nick.wyatt@sciencemuseum.org.uk)

Site library

Science Museum Library & Archives, Science Museum Library, Science Museum at Wroughton, Hackpen Lane, Wroughton, Swindon SN4 9NS
☎(01793) 846222
Fax (01793) 815413
e-mail: smlwroughton@sciencemuseum.org.uk

(Open free to the public for reference; by advance appoinment at Swindon)

Science and Society Picture Library, Science Museum, Exhibition Road, South Kensington, London SW7 2DD
☎020 7942 4400
Fax 020 7942 4401

Specialism(s): A national library for the history and public understanding of science and technology.

SCOTTISH ENTERPRISE

Economic Research, Scottish Enterprise, Atrium Court, 50 Waterloo Street, Glasgow G2 6HQ
☎0141 248 2700 (main), 0141 228 2268 (direct line)
Fax 0141 248 1600
url: www.scottish-enterprise.com
Manager of Economic Research Mrs Gail Rogers MA DipLib (e-mail: gail.rogers@scotent.co.uk)

Specialism(s): Business information

SCOTTISH GOVERNMENT

ISIS Information Management Unit, Scottish Government, Library Services, F Spur, Saughton House, Broomhouse Drive, Edinburgh EH11 3XD
☎0131 244 4556
Fax 0131 244 4545
e-mail: SGLibrary@scotland.gsi.gov.uk
Chief Librarian Vacant

Specialism(s): Scottish Government and official publications

SCOTTISH NATURAL HERITAGE

Library Services, Scottish Natural Heritage, Great Glen House, Leachkin Road, Inverness IV3 8NW
☎(01463) 725290 (enquiries); (01463) 725291 (library management)
Fax (01463) 725067

e-mail: library@snh.gov.uk
url: www.snh.org.uk
Library Manager Paul Longbottom MCLIP (e-mail: paul.longbottom@snh.gov.uk)

SCOTTISH PARLIAMENT

Scottish Parliament Information Centre (SPICe), Scottish Parliament, Edinburgh EH99 ISP
☎0131 348 5300
Fax 0131 348 5378
e-mail: spice@scottish.parliament.uk
url: www.scottish.parliament.uk
Head of Research and Information Services and Reporting Group
Ms Henrietta Hales
Head of Information Services Ms Susan Mansfield

SIGNET LIBRARY

Signet Library, Parliament Square, Edinburgh EHI IRF
☎0131 225 4923
Fax 0131 220 4016
e-mail: library@wssociety.co.uk
url: www.wssociety.co.uk
Information Services Manager Vacant

Specialism(s): Scottish law

SOCIÉTÉ JERSIAISE

**Lord Coutanche Library, Société Jersiaise, 7 Pier Road, St Helier, Jersey, Channel Islands
JE2 4XW**
☎(01534) 730538 (enquiries), (01534) 633392 (administration)
Fax (01534) 888262
e-mail: library@societe-jersiaise.org
url: www.societe-jersiaise.org
Librarian Vacant
Library Assistant Ms Anna Baghiani (e-mail: anna.baghiani@societe-jersiaise.org)

Specialism(s): Local studies; Local and family history; Maps, prints, newspapers and ephemera

SOCIETY FOR COOPERATION IN RUSSIAN AND SOVIET STUDIES

**Library, Society for Cooperation in Russian and Soviet Studies, 320 Brixton Road, London
SW9 6AB**
☎020 7274 2282
Fax 020 7274 3230
e-mail: ruslibrary@scrss.org.uk
url: www.scrss.org.uk
Hon Librarian John Cunningham

Specialism(s): Literature, arts and history of Russia/Soviet Union in the 20th century

SOCIETY OF ANTIQUARIES OF LONDON

Library, Society of Antiquaries of London, Burlington House, Piccadilly, London WIJ OBE
☎020 7479 7084
Fax 020 7287 6967
e-mail: library@sal.org.uk
url: www.sal.org.uk
Head of Library and Collections Ms Heather Rowland BA MCLIP

Specialism(s): Archaeology; Antiquities and historic monuments in Britain and Europe

SOCIETY OF GENEALOGISTS

Library, Society of Genealogists, 14 Charterhouse Buildings, Goswell Road, London ECIM 7BA
☎020 7251 8799
Fax 020 7250 1800
e-mail: library@sog.org.uk
url: www.sog.org.uk; online catalogue at www.sog.org.uk/sogcat
Head of Library Services Tim Lawrence (020 7702 5484; e-mail: librarian@sog.org.uk)

Specialism(s): Family, local and national history; Topography; Biography; Heraldry; Demography; Material on most countries worldwide

TATA STEEL, RESEARCH, DEVELOPMENT AND TECHNOLOGY
(formerly Corus UK Ltd, Research, Development and Technology)

Knowledge and Library Services, Tata Steel, Research, Development and Technology, Swinden Technology Centre, Moorgate, Rotherham, South Yorks S60 3AR
☎(01709) 820166
Fax (01709) 825337
e-mail: stc.library@corusgroup.com
url: www.corusgroup.com
Manager, Customised Information Services Ms Carol Patton (located at site library below)

Site library

Knowledge and Library Services, Tata Steel, Research, Development and Technology, Teesside Technology Centre, PO Box 11, Eston Road, Grangetown, Middlesbrough, Cleveland TS6 6US
☎(01642) 382000
Fax (01642) 460321

Specialism(s): Steel engineering and manufacturing

TATE LIBRARY AND ARCHIVE

Hyman Kreitman Reading Rooms, Tate Library and Archive, Tate Britain, Millbank, London SWIP 4RG
☎020 7887 8838

e-mail: reading.rooms@tate.org.uk
url: www.tate.org.uk/research/researchservices/readingrooms
Head of Library, Archive and Collections Access Ms Jane Bramwell
Library Collections Manager Ms Maxine Miller BA(Hons) DipLib MCLIP
Archivist Adrian Glew
Gallery Records Manager Miss Jane Kennedy
Reader Services and Systems Manager Andrew Gent
Opening hours: Library 10am–5.45pm; Archive, Library Special Collection and Gallery
Records: 11am–5pm (appointments required)

*Specialism(s): Library: British art and international modern art – over 150,000 exhibition
catalogues and 50,000 monographs; artists books. Archive: Archive of British Art since 1900:
unpublished and semi-published documentation about fine artists in all media including
commercial galleries and dealers, critics, societies and institutions. Gallery Records: Tate's
official records.*

TAVISTOCK AND PORTMAN NHS FOUNDATION TRUST

**Library, Tavistock and Portman NHS Foundation Trust, 120 Belsize Lane, London
NW3 5BA**
☎020 7435 7111 (switchboard); 020 8938 2520 (direct line)
Fax 020 7447 3734
e-mail: library@tavi-port.org
url: www.tavi-port.org/library
Head of Library Services Ms Angela Douglas MCLIP BSc MA (e-mail:
angeladouglas@tavi-port.org)

Specialism(s): Psychoanalysis; Psychotherapy; Educational psychology

TPS CONSULT LTD

The Information Centre, TPS Consult Ltd, Centre Tower, Whitgift Centre, Croydon CR9 0AU
☎020 8256 4110
Fax 0844 244 0591
e-mail: info@tpsconsult.co.uk
url: www.tpsconsult.co.uk
Marketing and Information Services Manager Gursel Ziynettin (e-mail:
ziynettin.gursel@tpsconsult.co.uk)

Specialism(s): Construction and design

TRADES UNION CONGRESS

**TUC Library Collections, Trades Union Congress, Holloway Road Learning Centre, London
Metropolitan University, 236–250 Holloway Road, London N7 6PP**
☎020 7133 3726
Fax 020 7133 2529
e-mail: tuclib@londonmet.ac.uk
url: www.londonmet.ac.uk/libraries/tuc; www.unionhistory.info
Librarian Ms Christine Coates MA MCLIP (e-mail: c.coates@londonmet.ac.uk)

Specialism(s): Trade unions; Industrial relations; Politics; Economic history; International affairs

UNITED STATES EMBASSY

Information Resource Center, United States Embassy, 24 Grosvenor Square, London WIA IAE
☎020 7894 0925 (10am–12 noon (public enquiries)), 020 7499 9000 ext 2643 (administration)
Fax 020 7629 8288
e-mail: reflond@state.gov
url: http://london.usembassy.gov
Director Ms Anna Girvan

Specialism(s): US government and foreign policy; Current affairs

V&A THEATRE AND PERFORMANCE DEPARTMENT

Research Collections, V&A Theatre and Performance Department, Blythe House, 23 Blythe Road, London WI4 0QX
☎020 7942 2697 (enquiries); 020 7942 2698 (reading room)
Fax 020 7471 9864
e-mail: tmenquiries@vam.ac.uk
url: www.vam.ac.uk/theatre
Head of Collections Management Ms Claire Hudson BA MCLIP

Specialism(s): Performing arts; Stage design

VETERINARY LABORATORIES AGENCY

Library, Veterinary Laboratories Agency, New Haw, Addlestone, Surrey KTI5 3NB
☎(01932) 357314 (enquiries), (01932) 357603 (administration)
Fax (01932) 357608
e-mail: enquiries@vla.defra.gsi.gov.uk
url: www.vla.gov.uk
Librarian and Agency Records Officer Mrs Heather Hulse BA(Hons)
Library Services Manager Mrs Sonja van Montfort BA(Hons) (e-mail: s.vanmontfort@vla.defra.gsi.gov.uk)

Specialism(s): Veterinary science and medicine; Animal husbandry; Diseases of commercial farm animals

WATER SERVICES REGULATION AUTHORITY (OFWAT)

Information Services, Water Services Regulation Authority (OFWAT), Centre City Tower, 7 Hill Street, Birmingham B5 4UA
☎0121 644 7599 (general enquiries); 0121 644 7500 (switchboard)
Fax 0121 625 1400
e-mail: enquiries@ofwat.gsi.gov.uk
url: www.ofwat.gov.uk
Head of Knowledge Management Ms Isabel Merrifield

WELLCOME LIBRARY

Wellcome Library, 183 Euston Road, London NWI 2BE

☎020 7611 8722
Fax 020 7611 8369
e-mail: library@wellcome.ac.uk
url: http://library.wellcome.ac.uk
Head of Library Dr Simon Chaplin
Library Administrator Ms Tracy Tillotson

Wellcome Images
☎020 7611 8348
Fax 020 7611 8577
e-mail: images@wellcome.ac.uk

Moving Image and Sound Collections
☎020 7611 8766
Fax 020 7611 8765
e-mail: misc@wellcome.ac.uk

Specialism(s): History of medicine and allied science subjects

WELSH ASSEMBLY GOVERNMENT

Assembly Library & Publications Service, Welsh Assembly Government, Department of the First Minister and Cabinet, Cathays Park, Cardiff CFI0 3NQ
☎029 2082 5449
e-mail: assemblylibraryservice1@wales.gsi.gov.uk
url: www.wales.gov.uk
Head of the Assembly Library & Publications Service Mrs Helen Staffer (e-mail: helen.staffer@wales.gsi.gov.uk)

Specialism(s): Welsh government publications

WESTMINSTER ABBEY

Muniment Room and Library, Westminster Abbey, London SWIP 3PA
☎020 7654 4830
Fax 020 7654 4827
e-mail: library@westminster-abbey.org
url: www.westminster-abbey.org
Librarian Dr Tony Trowles MA DPhil (e-mail: tony.trowles@westminster-abbey.org)

Specialism(s): History of Westminster Abbey; Coronations; Theology (pre-1800)

WIENER LIBRARY INSTITUTE OF CONTEMPORARY HISTORY

Wiener Library Institute of Contemporary History, 4 Devonshire Street, London WIW 5BH
☎020 7636 7247
Fax 020 7436 6428
e-mail: library@wienerlibrary.co.uk
url: www.wienerlibrary.co.uk
Librarian Ms Katharina Hübschmann

Director Ben Barkow

Specialism(s): Holocaust; Third Reich; Fascism; Modern German–Jewish history; Anti-semitism

WILLIAM SALT LIBRARY

William Salt Library, 19 Eastgate Street, Stafford ST16 2LZ
☎(01785) 278372
Fax (01785) 278414
e-mail: william.salt.library@staffordshire.gov.uk
url: www.staffordshire.gov.uk/salt
Librarian Mrs Thea Randall BA DAS

Specialism(s): Staffordshire local history

DR WILLIAMS'S LIBRARY

Dr Williams's Library, 14 Gordon Square, London WC1H 0AR
☎020 7387 3727
e-mail: enquiries@dwlib.co.uk
url: www.dwlib.co.uk
Director of Dr Williams's Trust and Library D L Wykes BSc PhD FRHistS
Principal Librarian Ms Alice Ford-Smith MA
(The Congregational Library at 15 Gordon Square is administered by Dr Williams's Library, to which any application should be made. Other details are the same)

Specialism(s): History and theology of religious dissent

THE WOMEN'S LIBRARY

The Women's Library, London Metropolitan University, Old Castle Street, London E1 7NT
☎020 7320 2222
Fax 020 7320 2333
e-mail: enquirydesk@thewomenslibrary.ac.uk
url: www.thewomenslibrary.ac.uk
Collections Manager Ms Teresa Doherty

Specialism(s): Women's history; Women's studies

WORKING CLASS MOVEMENT LIBRARY

Working Class Movement Library, Jubilee House, 51 The Crescent, Salford, Manchester M5 4WX
☎0161 736 3601
Fax 0161 737 4115
e-mail: enquiries@wcml.org.uk
url: www.wcml.org.uk
Library Manager Ms Lynette Cawthra MA DipLib MCLIP
Library Assistant Michael Weaver

Specialism(s): Labour history; Trade Unions; Communism; Socialism; Labour Party; Independent Labour Party; Anarchism; Working class autobiography

YORK MINSTER

The York Minster Library, York Minster, The Old Palace, Dean's Park, York YOI 7JQ
☎0844 939 0021 ext 2500
e-mail: library@yorkminster.org.uk
url: www.yorkminster.org; http://aleph.york.ac.uk (online library catalogue)
Librarian Mrs Sarah Griffin (e-mail: sarahg@yorkminster.org)
Archivist Peter Young MA (e-mail: petery@yorkminster.org)
(Library and Archive open to the public Mon–Fri 9am–5pm)

Specialism(s): History; Theology; Church history; Early printed books; Yorkshire history; Stained glass; York Minster archives

ZOOLOGICAL SOCIETY OF LONDON

Library, Zoological Society of London, Regent's Park, London NWI 4RY
☎020 7449 6293
Fax 020 7586 5743
e-mail: library@zsl.org
url: www.zsl.org; http://library.zsl.org (library catalogue)
Librarian Ms A Sylph MSc MCLIP

Specialism(s): Zoology; Animal conservation

Selected Academic, National and Special Libraries in the Republic of Ireland

ARCHBISHOP MARSH'S LIBRARY

Archbishop Marsh's Library, St Patrick's Close, Dublin 8, Republic of Ireland
☎(00 353 1) 454 3511 (enquiries and administration)
Fax (00 353 1) 454 3511
url: www.marshlibrary.ie
Keeper Dr Muriel McCarthy MA LLD (e-mail: keeper@marshlibrary.ie)
(Archbishop Marsh's Library is a 300-year-old research library with a magnificent collection
of 16th and 17th century books. The library also has a book conservation bindery, which
includes a flat paper conservation service.)

CDVEC CURRICULUM DEVELOPMENT UNIT

**Library/Resource Centre, CDVEC Curriculum Development Unit, Captain's Road, Crumlin,
Dublin 12, Republic of Ireland**
☎(00 353 1) 453 5487
Fax (00 353 1) 453 7659
url: www.curriculum.ie
Librarian Ms Eva Hornung DiplBibl MLIS ALAI MCLIP (e-mail:
eva.hornung@cdu.cdvec.ie)

CENTRAL CATHOLIC LIBRARY

Central Catholic Library, 74 Merrion Square, Dublin 2, Republic of Ireland
☎(00 353 1) 676 1264 (enquiries and administration)
e-mail: catholiclibrary@imagine.ie
url: www.catholiclibrary.ie
Librarian Ms Teresa Whitington MA DLIS PhD

CHESTER BEATTY LIBRARY

Chester Beatty Library, Dublin Castle, Dublin 2, Republic of Ireland
☎(00 353 1) 407 0750
Fax (00 353 1) 407 0760
e-mail: info@cbl.ie
url: www.cbl.ie
Director and Librarian Dr Michael Ryan (e-mail: mryan@cbl.ie)
Reference Librarian Ms Celine Ward BA MLIS (e-mail: cward@cbl.ie)

AN CHOMHAIRLE LEABHARLANNA (THE LIBRARY COUNCIL)

**Research Library, An Chomhairle Leabharlanna (The Library Council), 53-54 Upper Mount
Street, Dublin 2, Republic of Ireland**
☎(00 353 1) 678 4900/676 1167
Fax (00 353 1) 676 6721
e-mail: info@librarycouncil.ie
url: www.librarycouncil.ie
Research & Information Officer Alun Bevan MLib (00 353 1 678 4905; e-mail:
abevan@librarycouncil.ie)

DUBLIN BUSINESS SCHOOL

Undergraduate Library, Dublin Business School, 13/14 Aungier Street, Dublin 2 Republic of Ireland
☎(00 353 1) 417 7572
Fax (00 353 1) 417 7543
e-mail: library@dbs.ie
url: http://library.dbs-students.com/
Head Librarian Ms Marie O'Neill BA GradDipBS GradDipLIS (00 353 1 417 7571; e-mail: marie.oneill@dbs.ie)
Systems Librarian David Hughes BSc MSc MLIS (00 353 1 417 8744; e-mail: david.hughes@dbs.ie)
Reader Services Librarian Ms Emilie Jost Licence Maitrise MLIS (00 353 1 417 7594; e-mail: emilie.jost@dbs.ie)
Acquisitions Ms Marie O'Dwyer BEng (00 353 1 417 7508; e-mail: marie.odwyer@dbs.ie)
Information Literacy Librarian Ms Maria Rogers BA MLIS (00 353 1 417 7543; e-mail: maria.rogers@dbs.ie)
Institutional Repository Librarian Alex Kouker BA MLIS (00 353 1 417 7543; e-mail: alexander.kouker@dbs.ie)

Postgraduate and Law Library, Dublin Business School, 19/22 Dame Street, Dublin 2 Republic of Ireland
☎(00 353 1) 417 8745 (Information Desk), (00 353 1) 417 7582 (Librarian's Office)
Deputy Librarian Ms Jane Buggle BA GradDipLIS MLIS (00 353 1 417 7582; e-mail: jane.buggle@dbs.ie)
Assistant Librarian Law Ms Joan Colvin DipLIS (00 353 1 417 8745; e-mail: joan.colvin@dbs.ie)

DUBLIN CITY UNIVERSITY

Library, Dublin City University, Dublin 9, Republic of Ireland
☎(00 353 1) 700 5418 (enquiries); (00 353 1) 700 5212 (administration)
Fax (00 353 1) 700 5010
url: www.dcu.ie/~library/
Director of Library Services Paul Sheehan (e-mail: paul.sheehan@dcu.ie)

DUBLIN INSTITUTE OF TECHNOLOGY

Central Services Unit, Dublin Institute of Technology, Rathmines Road, Dublin 6, Republic of Ireland
☎(00 353 1) 402 7800 (enquiries), 7801 (administration)
Fax (00 353 1) 402 7802
e-mail: csu.library@dit.ie
url: www.dit.ie/library
Head of Library Services Dr Philip Cohen BA MSc PhD DipLib MCLIP (e-mail: philip.cohen@dit.ie)
Sub Librarian, Collection Development Ms Ann McSweeney BA DLIS MLIS (00 353 1 402 7804; e-mail: ann.mcsweeney@dit.ie)
Sub Librarian, Systems Development Ms Ursula Gavin BA DLIS MLIS (00 353 1 402 7805; e-mail: ursula.gavin@dit.ie)

College Librarian Ms Yvonne Desmond BA DLIS (00 353 1 402 7807; e-mail: yvonne.desmond@dit.ie)

Library, Dublin Institute of Technology, Bolton Street, Dublin 1, Republic of Ireland
☎(00 353 1) 402 3681
Fax (00 353 1) 402 3995
e-mail: bst.library@dit.ie
College Librarian Brian Gillespie BA DipLib (00 353 1 402 3682; e-mail: brian.gillespie@dit.ie)

Library, Dublin Institute of Technology, Kevin Street, Dublin 8, Republic of Ireland
☎(00 353 1) 402 4894 (general enquiries)
Fax (00 353 1) 402 4651
e-mail: kst.library@dit.ie
College Librarian Brendan Devlin BA DLIS MLIS MA (00 353 1 402 4631; e-mail: brendan.devlin@dit.ie)

Library, Dublin Institute of Technology, Cathal Brugha Street, Dublin 1, Republic of Ireland
☎(00 353 1) 402 4423/4 (enquiries and administration)
Fax (00 353 1) 402 4499
e-mail: cbs.library@dit.ie
College Librarian Ms Ann Wrigley BA DLIS (00 353 1 402 4128; e-mail. ann.wrigley@dit.ie)

Library, Dublin Institute of Technology, 40-45 Mountjoy Square, Dublin 1, Republic of Ireland
☎(00 353 1) 402 4108
Fax (00 353 1) 402 4290
e-mail: mjs.library@dit.ie
College Librarian Ms Ann Wrigley BA DLIS (00 353 1 402 4128; e-mail: ann.wrigley@dit.ie)

Library, Dublin Institute of Technology, Aungier Street, Dublin 2, Republic of Ireland
☎(00 353 1) 402 3068/9
Fax (00 353 1) 402 3289
e-mail: ast.library@dit.ie
College Librarian Ms Anne Ambrose BA DLIS (00 353 1 402 3067; e-mail: anne.ambrose@dit.ie)

Music and Drama Library, Dublin Institute of Technology, Lower Rathmines Road, Dublin 6, Republic of Ireland
☎(00 353 1) 402 3461
Fax (00 353 1) 402 7854
e-mail: rmh.library@dit.ie
College Librarian Ms Ann Wrigley BA DLIS (00 353 1 402 4128; e-mail: ann.wrigley@dit.ie)

ECONOMIC AND SOCIAL RESEARCH INSTITUTE

Library, Economic and Social Research Institute, Whitaker Square, Sir John Rogerson's Quay, Dublin 2, Republic of Ireland
☎(00 353 1) 863 2000
Fax (00 353 1) 863 2100

url: www.esri.ie
Librarian Ms Sarah Burns BSocSc (e-mail: sarah.burns@esri.ie)

ENTERPRISE IRELAND

Client Knowledge Services, Enterprise Ireland, The Plaza, East Point Business Park, Dublin 3, Republic of Ireland
☎(00 353 1) 727 2325
e-mail: infocentre@enterprise-ireland.com
url: www.enterprise-ireland.com
Head of Department Gerry McMahon
Librarian in Charge Ms Sandra King BA (00 353 1 727 2380; e-mail: sandra.king@enterprise-ireland.com)

INSTITUTO CERVANTES

Library, Instituto Cervantes, Lincoln House, Lincoln Place, Dublin 2, Republic of Ireland
☎(00 353 1) 631 1515
Fax (00 353 1) 631 1599
e-mail: bibdub@cervantes.es
url: http://dublin.cervantes.es
Chief Librarian David Carrion

NATIONAL ARCHIVES

National Archives, Bishop Street, Dublin 8, Republic of Ireland
☎(00 353 1) 407 2300
Fax (00 353 1) 407 2333
e-mail: mail@nationalarchives.ie
url: www.nationalarchives.ie
Director Dr David Craig
(Formed by the amalgamation of the Public Record Office of Ireland and the State Paper Office.)

NATIONAL COLLEGE OF ART AND DESIGN

Library, National College of Art and Design, 100 Thomas Street, Dublin 8, Republic of Ireland
☎(00 353 1) 636 4357
Fax (00 353 1) 636 4387
url: www.ncad.ie/library
Librarian Edward Murphy BA DipLib MLIS (e-mail: murphye@ncad.ie)

NATIONAL GALLERY OF IRELAND

Centre for the Study of Irish Art, National Gallery of Ireland, Merrion Square West, Dublin 2, Republic of Ireland
☎(00 353 1) 632 5517
Fax (00 353 1) 661 5372
e-mail: csia@ngi.ie

url: www.nationalgallery.ie
Administrator Donal Maguire
(By appointment)

Fine Art Library, National Gallery of Ireland, Merrion Square West, Dublin 2, Republic of Ireland
☎(00 353 1) 663 3546 (direct)
Fax (00 353 1) 661 5372
e-mail: library@ngi.ie
url: www.nationalgallery.ie
Librarian Ms Andrea Lydon MA DLIS
Assistant Librarian Ms Catherine Sheridan BA HDipCompSci MLIS
(Opening hours 10–5 Mon–Fri. No appointment necessary)

NGI Archive, National Gallery of Ireland, Merrion Square West, Dublin 2, Republic of Ireland
☎(00 353 1) 663 3508 (direct)
Fax (00 353 1) 661 5372
url: www.nationalgallery.ie
Archivist Ms Leah Benson BA HDipArch (e-mail: lbenson@ngi.ie)
(By appointment)

Yeats Archive, National Gallery of Ireland, Merrion Square West, Dublin 2, Republic of Ireland
☎(00 353 1) 632 3508
Fax (00 353 1) 661 5372
e-mail: yeats@ngi.ie
url: www.nationalgallery.ie
(By appointment)

NATIONAL LIBRARY OF IRELAND

National Library of Ireland, Kildare Street, Dublin 2, Republic of Ireland
☎(00 353 1) 603 0200
Fax (00 353 1) 676 6690
e-mail: info@nli.ie
url: www.nli.ie
Director Ms Fiona A. Ross
Keeper (Administration) Ms Colette Byrne BA
Keeper (Genealogical Office and Manuscripts) Ms Colette O'Flaherty BA DipArchiv
Keeper (Outreach and External Relations) Ms Katherine McSharry
Keeper (Research, Preservation and Conservation) Ms Catherine Fahy BA DipLIS
Keeper (Printed Books and Visual Collections) Brian McKenna BA

National Photographic Archive

National Photographic Archive, Meeting House Square, Temple Bar, Dublin 2, Republic of Ireland
☎(00 353 1) 603 0374
Fax (00 353 1) 677 7451
e-mail: npaoffice@nli.ie
url: www.nli.ie
Curator Ms Elizabeth M. Kirwan

NATIONAL UNIVERSITY OF IRELAND, GALWAY

James Hardiman Library, National University of Ireland, Galway, University Road, Galway, Republic of Ireland
☎(00 353 91) 492540 (administration), 493005 (information point)
Fax (00 353 91) 522394; 494528 (interlibrary loans)
e-mail: library@nuigalway.ie
url: www.library.nuigalway.ie
University Librarian John Cox MA DipLib (00 353 91 493159; e-mail: john.cox@nuigalway.ie)
Head of Organisational Development and Performance Peter Corrigan BA DipLIS (00 353 91 492497; e-mail: peter.corrigan@nuigalway.ie)
Head of Information Access and Learning Services Ms Monica Crump BA MLIS (00 353 91 493765; e-mail: monica.crump@nuigalway.ie)
Head of Customer Focus and Research Services Niall McSweeney BA HDipinEd DipLib (00 353 91 493915; e-mail: niall.mcsweeney@nuigalway.ie)
Head of Staff Development and Service Environment Ms Ann Mitchell BA HDipEd DipLIS (00 353 91 492738; e-mail: ann.mitchell@nuigalway.ie)

Branch library

Medical Library, National University of Ireland, Galway, Clinical Sciences Institute, University Road, Galway, Republic of Ireland
☎(00 353 91) 493601
Fax (00 353 91) 494517
Assistant Librarian Ms Jane Mulligan BA(Hons) (00 353 91 492791)

NATIONAL UNIVERSITY OF IRELAND, MAYNOOTH

The Library, National University of Ireland, Maynooth, Co Kildare, Republic of Ireland
☎(00 353 1) 708 3884
Fax (00 353 1) 628 6008
e-mail: library.information@nuim.ie
url: http://library.nuim.ie
Librarian Cathal McCauley BA MLIS DipFM
Deputy Librarian Ms Helen Fallon MA DLIS
Sub-Librarian Ms Valerie Seymour BA(Mod) MCLIP

OIREACHTAS LIBRARY & RESEARCH SERVICE

Oireachtas Library & Research Service, Houses of the Oireachtas, Leinster House, Kildare Street, Dublin 2, Republic of Ireland
☎(00 353 1) 618 3000 (switchboard), (00 353 1) 618 4701/4702 (enquiries)
Fax (00 353 1) 618 4109
e-mail: lib@oireachtas.ie
url: www.oireachtas.ie
Head of Library and Research Services Ms Madelaine Dennison BSocSc MCLIP (00 353 1 618 4735; e-mail: madelaine.dennison@oireachtas.ie)
Head of Research Ms Maria Fitzsimons (00 353 1 618 4734; e-mail: maria.fitzsimons@oireachtas.ie)

Head of Collections John McDonough (00 353 1 618 4733; e-mail: john.mcdonough@oireachtas.ie)

REPRESENTATIVE CHURCH BODY

Library, Representative Church Body, Braemor Park, Churchtown, Dublin 14, Republic of Ireland
☎(00 353 1) 492 3979
Fax (00 353 1) 492 4770
e-mail: library@ireland.anglican.org
url: www.ireland.anglican.org/
Librarian & Archivist Dr Raymond Refaussé BA PhD (e-mail: raymond.refausse@rcbdub.org)

ROYAL COLLEGE OF SURGEONS IN IRELAND

The Mercer Library, Royal College of Surgeons in Ireland, Mercer Street Lower, Dublin 2, Republic of Ireland
☎(00 353 1) 402 2407 (enquiries); 402 2411 (administration)
Fax (00 353 1) 402 2457
e-mail: library@rcsi.ie
url: www.rcsi.ie/library
Librarian Mrs Kate Kelly MSc DLIS AHIP (e-mail: katekelly@rcsi.ie))

Branch library

RCSI Library, Royal College of Surgeons in Ireland, Beaumont Hospital, Beaumont Road, Dublin 9, Republic of Ireland
☎(00 353 1) 809 2531
Fax (00 353 1) 836 7396
e-mail: bhlibrary@rcsi.ie
Librarian Ms Breffni Smith MPhil DLIS (e-mail: breffnismith@rcsi.ie)

ROYAL DUBLIN SOCIETY

Library, Royal Dublin Society, Merrion Road, Ballsbridge, Dublin 4, Republic of Ireland
☎(00 353 1) 240 7274
Fax (00 353 1) 660 4014
e-mail: library@rds.ie
url: www.rds.ie/library
Library Director Ms Joanna Quinn BA(Mod) DBS DLIS MA (00 353 1 240 7299; e-mail: joanna.quinn@rds.ie)

ROYAL IRISH ACADEMY

Library, Royal Irish Academy, 19 Dawson Street, Dublin 2, Republic of Ireland
☎(00 353 1) 676 2570/676 4222
Fax (00 353 1) 676 2346
e-mail: library@ria.ie
url: www.ria.ie

Librarian Ms Siobhán Fitzpatrick BA HDipEd DLIS (e-mail: s.fitzpatrick@ria.ie)
Deputy Librarian Dr Bernadette Cunningham MA DipLib PhD (e-mail:
b.cunningham@ria.ie)
Deputy Librarian Ms Petra Schnabel MA (e-mail: p.schnabel@ria.ie)

TEAGASC (AGRICULTURE AND FOOD DEVELOPMENT AUTHORITY)

Library, TEAGASC (Agriculture and Food Development Authority), Ashtown Food Research Centre, Ashtown, Dublin 15, Republic of Ireland
☎(00 353 1) 805 9577
Fax (00 353 1) 805 9550
url: www.teagasc.ie
Head Librarian Ms Maire Caffrey BSc DipLIS (e-mail: maire.caffrey@teagasc.ie)

Research libraries

Library, TEAGASC (Agriculture and Food Development Authority), Moorepark Food Research Centre (dairy production, dairy products, cheese production), Fermoy, Co Cork, Republic of Ireland
☎(00 353 25) 42222
Fax (00 353 25) 42340
Librarian Ms Siobhan Keating (e-mail: siobhan.keating@teagasc.ie)

Library, TEAGASC (Agriculture and Food Development Authority), Johnstown Castle Agricultural Research Centre (environment), Wexford, Republic of Ireland
☎(00 353 53) 917 1200
Fax (00 353 53) 914 2213
Clerical Administrator Ms Eleanor Spillane (e-mail: eleanor.spillane@teagasc.ie)

Library, TEAGASC (Agriculture and Food Development Authority), Oak Park Research Centre (crops production), Carlow, Republic of Ireland
☎(00 353 59) 917 0200
Fax (00 353 59) 914 2423
Librarian Ms Cheryl Austin

Library, TEAGASC (Agriculture and Food Development Authority), Grange Research Centre (beef production), Dunsany, Co Meath, Republic of Ireland
☎(00 353 46) 906 1100 (switchboard); (00 353 46) 906 1151 (library)
Fax (00 353 46) 902 6154
Librarian Ms Ann Gilsenan (e-mail: ann.gilsenan@teagasc.ie)

TRINITY COLLEGE DUBLIN

Library, Trinity College Dublin, College Street, Dublin 2, Republic of Ireland
☎(00 353 1) 896 1127 (general enquiries); (00 353 1) 896 1661 (Librarian's office)
Fax (00 353 1) 896 3774
e-mail: librarian@tcd.ie
url: www.tcd.ie/library/
Librarian and College Archivist Robin Adams MA BA DipLib (e-mail: radams@tcd.ie)
Deputy Librarian Ms Jessie Kurtz BA BEd MLS (e-mail: jessie.kurtz@tcd.ie)

Departmental libraries

John Stearne Medical Library, Trinity College Dublin, St James's Hospital, James's Street, Dublin 8, Republic of Ireland
☎(00 353 1) 896 2109
Fax (00 353 1) 453 6087
Medical Librarian David Mockler BSc DLIS (e-mail: mocklerd@tcd.ie)

Science and Engineering Library, Trinity College Dublin, College Street, Dublin 2, Republic of Ireland
☎(00 353 1) 896 1805
Fax (00 353 1) 896 3774
Site Librarian Ms Arlene Healy MA BA MLIS (e-mail: arlene.healy@tcd.ie)

UNIVERSITY COLLEGE CORK

The Boole Library, University College Cork, College Road, Cork, Republic of Ireland
☎(00 353 21) 490 2794
Fax (00 353 21) 427 3428
e-mail: library@ucc.ie
url: www.ucc.ie
Librarian John FitzGerald BA MPhil DLIS (00 353 21 490 2281/2851; fax: 00 353 21 490 3119; e-mail: j.fitzgerald@ucc.ie)

Branch/department libraries

Boston Scientific Health Sciences Library, University College Cork, Brookfield Health Sciences Complex, College Road, Cork, Republic of Ireland
☎(00 353 21) 490 1523
Fax (00 353 21) 490 1522
e-mail: brookfieldlibrary@ucc.ie
Nursing Librarian Cathal Kerrigan (e-mail: c.kerrigan@ucc.ie)

Cork University Hospital Library, University College Cork, Cork University Hospital, Wilton Road, Cork, Republic of Ireland
☎(00 353 21) 490 2976
Fax (00 353 21) 434 5826
e-mail: CUH.Library@ucc.ie
Hospital Librarian Ms Una Ni Chonghaile (e-mail: u.nichonghaile@ucc.ie)

UNIVERSITY COLLEGE DUBLIN

UCD James Joyce Library, University College Dublin, Belfield, Dublin 4, Republic of Ireland
☎(00 353 1) 716 7583 (enquiries); (00 353 1) 716 7694 (administration)
Fax (00 353 1) 283 7667
e-mail: library@ucd.ie
url: www.ucd.ie/library/
Librarian Dr John Howard (e-mail: john.b.howard@ucd.ie)
Associate Librarians Ms Marie Burke (e-mail: marie.burke@ucd.ie), Ms Carmel O'Sullivan (e-mail: cosullivan@ucd.ie)

Site libraries

UCD Library, University College Dublin, Health Sciences Building, Belfield, Dublin 4, Republic of Ireland
☎(00 353 1) 716 6572
Fax (00 353 1) 716 6451
Librarian i/c Ms Kathryn Smith (e-mail: kathryn.smith@ucd.ie)

UCD Library, University College Dublin, Veterinary Sciences Centre, Belfield, Dublin 4, Republic of Ireland
☎(00 353 1) 716 6208
Fax (00 353 1) 716 6267
Librarian i/c Ms Kathryn Smith (e-mail: kathryn.smith@ucd.ie)

UCD Library, University College Dublin, Smurfit Graduate School of Business, Blackrock, Co Dublin, Republic of Ireland
☎(00 353 1) 716 8069
Fax (00 353 1) 716 8011
Librarian i/c Ms Valerie Kendlin (e-mail: valerie.kendlin@ucd.ie)

UCD Richview Library, University College Dublin, Richview, Clonskeagh, Dublin 14, Republic of Ireland
☎(00 353 1) 716 2741
Fax (00 353 1) 283 0329
Librarian i/c Ms Julia Barrett BMus DipLib (e-mail: julia.barrett@ucd.ie)

UNIVERSITY OF LIMERICK

Library and Information Services, University of Limerick, Limerick, Republic of Ireland
☎(00 353 61) 202166 (enquiries); 202156 (administration)
Fax (00 353 61) 213090
e-mail: libinfo@ul.ie
url: www.ul.ie
Director, Library and Information Services Ms Gobnait O'Riordan MA DLIS

Schools and Departments of Information and Library Studies in the United Kingdom and the Republic of Ireland

This information is subject to change.
For a list of institutions that offer currently accredited courses, please visit the CILIP website, www.cilip.org.uk.

ABERYSTWYTH UNIVERSITY

Department of Information Studies, Aberystwyth University, Llanbadarn Fawr, Aberystwyth, Ceredigion SY23 3AS
☎(01970) 622188
Fax (01970) 622190
e-mail: dis-dept@aber.ac.uk
url: www.dis.aber.ac.uk
Head of Department Dr Gayner Eyre BA PhD MCLIP AALIA

UNIVERSITY OF BRIGHTON

Division of Information Management, The School of Computing, Mathematical and Information Sciences, University of Brighton, Watts Building, Lewes Road, Moulsecoomb, Brighton BN2 4GJ
☎(01273) 643500 (switchboard); (01273) 642428
Fax (01273) 642405
url: www.cmis.brighton.ac.uk
Head of School Dr John Taylor BSc PhD CMath FIMA (e-mail: john.taylor@brighton.ac.uk)
Head of Research Prof John Howse (e-mail: john.howse@brighton.ac.uk)
Head of Division of Information Management Dr Martin de Saulles BA(Hons) MSc DPhil (e-mail: m.r.d.saulles@brighton.ac.uk)

CITY UNIVERSITY LONDON

Department of Information Science, School of Informatics, City University London, Northampton Square, London EC1V 0HB
☎020 7040 8381
Fax 020 7040 8584
e-mail: dis@soi.city.ac.uk
url: www.soi.city.ac.uk
Head of Department Dr Vesna Brujic-Okretic (020 7040 8551; e-mail: vesna@soi.city.ac.uk)
Course Director, Information Science and Technology Masters Scheme Dr Andrew MacFarlane BSc MSc PhD MBCS CEng CITP (020 7040 8386; e-mail: andym@soi.city.ac.uk)
Course Director, Information Studies Masters Scheme Dr Lyn Robinson (020 7040 8390; e-mail: lyn@soi.city.ac.uk)

UNIVERSITY COLLEGE DUBLIN

UCD School of Information and Library Studies, University College Dublin, Belfield, Dublin 4, Republic of Ireland
☎(00 353 1) 716 7055
Fax (00 353 1) 716 1161
e-mail: sils@ucd.ie
url: www.ucd.ie/sils
Head of School Prof Diane H. Sonnenwald (e-mail: diane.sonnenwald@ucd.ie)

UNIVERSITY OF GLASGOW

Humanities Advanced Technologies & Information Institute (HATII), University of Glasgow, George Service House, II University Gardens, Glasgow GI2 8QQ
☎0141 330 5512
Fax 0141 330 3788
url: www.hatii.arts.gla.ac.uk
Programme Director Prof Michael Moss (e-mail: M.Moss@hatii.arts.gla.ac.uk)

LIVERPOOL JOHN MOORES UNIVERSITY

Information Strategy Group, Liverpool Business School, Liverpool John Moores University, The John Foster Building, 98 Mount Pleasant, Liverpool L3 5UZ
☎0151 231 3596/3425
Fax 0151 707 0423
url: www.ljmu.ac.uk
Principal Lecturer and Programme Leader for Information Strategy Ms Janet Farrow MA BA MCLIP (0151 231 3596; e-mail: a.j.farrow@ljmu.ac.uk)

LONDON METROPOLITAN UNIVERSITY

Media, Information and Communications, Department of Applied Social Sciences, London Metropolitan University, London North Campus, Ladbroke House, 62-66 Highbury Grove, London N5 2AD
☎020 7423 0000 (main switchboard), 020 7133 5129 (postgraduate office)
Fax 020 7133 5203
url: www.londonmet.ac.uk
Head of Department Prof John Gabriel (e-mail: j.gabriel@londonmet.ac.uk)
Academic contact for Information Management Ms Sue Batley BA PhD (020 7133 5160; e-mail: s.batley@londonmet.ac.uk)

UNIVERSITY COLLEGE LONDON

Department of Information Studies, University College London, Gower Street, London WCIE 6BT
☎020 7679 7204
Fax 020 7383 0557
e-mail: infostudies-enquiries@ucl.ac.uk
url: www.infostudies.ucl.ac.uk
Director of Information Studies Prof David Nicholas MPhil PhD MCLIP

LOUGHBOROUGH UNIVERSITY

Department of Information Science, Loughborough University, Ashby Road, Loughborough, Leics LEII 3TU
☎(01509) 223051/2
Fax (01509) 223053
e-mail: dis@lboro.ac.uk
url: www.lboro.ac.uk/departments/dis/
Professor of Information Management Prof Graham Matthews BA DipLib PhD MCLIP

(e-mail: g.matthews@lboro.ac.uk)
Director of LISU (Library & Information Statistics Unit) Ms Claire Creaser BSc CStat
(e-mail: c.creaser@lboro.ac.uk)

MANCHESTER METROPOLITAN UNIVERSITY

Department of Information and Communications, Manchester Metropolitan University, Geoffrey Manton Building, Rosamond Street West, off Oxford Road, Manchester M15 6LL
☎0161 247 6144
Fax 0161 247 6351
e-mail: infcomms-hums@mmu.ac.uk
url: www.hlss.mmu.ac.uk/infocomms
Acting Head of Department Jonathan Willson BA MA FHEA
Professor of Information and Communications Prof Jenny Rowley BA MSc MSc DMS PhD FCLIP MBCS CEng MCMI

NORTHUMBRIA UNIVERSITY

Information and Communication Management, School of Computing, Engineering and Information Sciences, Northumbria University, Pandon Building, Camden Street, Newcastle upon Tyne NE2 IXE
☎0191 227 3702
Fax 0191 243 7630
url: http://northumbria.ac.uk/sd/academic/ceis/ifa/ceissubjects/icm/
Dean Prof Alistair Sambell
Head of Information and Communication Management Dr Alison Pickard (e-mail: alison.pickard@northumbria.ac.uk)

ROBERT GORDON UNIVERSITY

Department of Information Management, Robert Gordon University, Garthdee Road, Aberdeen AB10 7QE
☎(01224) 262000 (University switchboard); (01224) 263800 (School Reception)
Fax (01224) 263838
e-mail: imopen@rgu.ac.uk
url: www.rgu.ac.uk/abs
Dean, Aberdeen Business School Prof Rita C Marcella MA DipEd DipLib PhD FCMI FCLIP (e-mail: r.c.marcella@rgu.ac.uk)
Associate Dean (Postgraduate Programmes), Aberdeen Business School Prof Robert Newton MA PGDipLib PhD MCLIP (e-mail: r.newton@rgu.ac.uk)
Director of Research Institute, Aberdeen Business School Prof Dorothy A Williams BSc PGDipLib PhD (e-mail: d.williams@rgu.ac.uk)
Head of Department, Department of Information Management Prof Peter H Reid BA PhD (e-mail: p.reid@rgu.ac.uk)
Research Co-ordinator, Department of Information Management Dr Simon Burnett (e-mail: s.burnett@rgu.ac.uk)

THE UNIVERSITY OF SHEFFIELD

The Information School, The University of Sheffield, Regent Court, 2II Portobello Street, Sheffield SI 4DP
☎0114 222 2630 (dept/administration)
Fax 0114 278 0300
e-mail: is@shef.ac.uk
url: www.shef.ac.uk/is
Head of School and Professor of Higher Education Development Prof Philippa Levy BA(Hons) MA MA PhD FHEA (0114 222 2638; e-mail: p.levy@sheffield.ac.uk)

STRATHCLYDE UNIVERSITY

Department of Computer and Information Sciences, Strathclyde University, Livingstone Tower, 26 Richmond Street, Glasgow GI IXH
☎0141 548 3700/2934 (direct); 0141 552 4400 (switchboard)
Fax 0141 548 4523
e-mail: ils-enquiries@cis.strath.ac.uk
url: www.cis.strath.ac.uk
Head of Department Prof Maria Fox BA(Hons) MSc PhD
Course Director David McMenemy BA MSc MCLIP FHEA

THAMES VALLEY UNIVERSITY

Information Management, Faculty of Professional Studies, Thames Valley University, St Mary's Road, Ealing, London W5 5RF
☎020 8231 2314 (faculty)
url: www.tvu.ac.uk
Programme Leaders, MA Library and Information Management Dr Tony Olden BA MLS PhD FCLIP (e-mail: tony.olden@tvu.ac.uk), Dr Stephen Roberts MA MA PhD MCLIP (e-mail: stephen.roberts@tvu.ac.uk)

UNIVERSITY OF ULSTER

Library and Information Management, School of Education, University of Ulster, Cromore Road, Coleraine, Northern Ireland BT52 ISA
☎028 7032 4719
Fax 028 7032 4918
url: www.socsci.ulster.ac.uk/education/library.html
Course Director Dr Jessica Bates (e-mail: j.bates@ulster.ac.uk)

UNIVERSITY OF THE WEST OF ENGLAND, BRISTOL

Department of Information Science and Digital Media, Bristol Institute of Technology, University of the West of England, Bristol, Frenchay Campus, Coldharbour Lane, Bristol BSI6 IQY
☎0117 328 4242
Fax 0117 328 3680
e-mail: bitgraduateschool@uwe.ac.uk
url: www.uwe.ac.uk/bit

Head of Department of Information Science and Digital Media Morris Williams
(0117 328 3037)
Programme Leader Paul Matthews (0117 328 3353)

The Regions of England

Public library authorities are arranged within the nine Government regions in England. (Upper Norwood Joint Library is included. This is not a public library authority but a service jointly managed by the London Boroughs of Croydon and Lambeth. However it has a separate entry). Full entries for these public library authorities will be found in the English Public Libraries section.

East
Bedford
Cambridgeshire
Central Bedfordshire
Essex
Hertfordshire
Luton
Norfolk
Peterborough
Southend on Sea
Suffolk
Thurrock

East Midlands
Derby
Derbyshire
Leicester
Leicestershire
Lincolnshire
Northamptonshire
Nottingham
Nottinghamshire
Rutland

London
Barking and Dagenham
Barnet
Bexley
Brent
Bromley
Camden
City of London
Croydon
Ealing
Enfield
Greenwich
Hackney
Hammersmith and Fulham
Haringey
Harrow
Havering
Hillingdon
Hounslow
Islington
Kensington and Chelsea
Kingston upon Thames
Lambeth
Lewisham
Merton
Newham
Redbridge
Richmond upon Thames
Southwark
Sutton
Tower Hamlets
Upper Norwood Joint Library
Waltham Forest
Wandsworth
Westminster

North East
Darlington
Durham
Gateshead
Hartlepool
Middlesbrough
Newcastle upon Tyne
North Tyneside
Northumberland
Redcar and Cleveland
South Tyneside
Stockton-on-Tees
Sunderland

North West and Merseyside
Blackburn with Darwen
Blackpool
Bolton
Bury
Cheshire East
Cheshire West and Chester
Cumbria
Halton
Knowsley
Lancashire
Liverpool
Manchester

Oldham
Rochdale
St Helens
Salford
Sefton
Stockport
Tameside
Trafford
Warrington
Wigan
Wirral

South East

Bracknell Forest
Brighton and Hove
Buckinghamshire
East Sussex
Hampshire
Isle of Wight
Kent
Medway
Milton Keynes
Oxfordshire
Portsmouth
Reading
Slough
Southampton
Surrey
West Berkshire
West Sussex
Windsor and Maidenhead
Wokingham

South West

Bath and North East Somerset
Bournemouth
Bristol
Cornwall
Devon
Dorset
Gloucestershire

North Somerset
Plymouth
Poole
Somerset
South Gloucestershire
Swindon
Torbay
Wiltshire

West Midlands

Birmingham
Coventry
Dudley
Herefordshire
Sandwell
Shropshire
Solihull
Staffordshire
Stoke-on-Trent
Telford and Wrekin
Walsall
Warwickshire
Wolverhampton
Worcestershire

Yorkshire and The Humber

Barnsley
Bradford
Calderdale
Doncaster
East Riding of Yorkshire
Kingston upon Hull
Kirklees
Leeds
North East Lincolnshire
North Lincolnshire
North Yorkshire
Rotherham
Sheffield
Wakefield
York

Name and place index

All page numbers from 3 to 215 refer to public libraries or public library authorities; page numbers from 219 to 409 refer to academic institutions and special libraries.

A K Bell, Perth and Kinross 160
Abbeyfeale, Limerick County 203
Abbeyleix, Laois 201
Aberconwy, Cardiff University 237
Aberdare, Rhondda Cynon Taf 182
Aberdeen 131
Aberdeen University 219
Aberdeenshire 131 see also Aberdeen
Aberfeldy, Perth and Kinross 161
Abergavenny, Monmouthshire 179
Abergele, Conwy 176
Abertay Dundee University 219
Abertillery, Blaenau Gwent 172
Aberystwyth University 219, 405
Aberystwyth, Ceredigion 175
Access and Inclusion, Camden 18
Accessible Resources, Oxford University 282
Accrington, Lancashire 59
Achiltibuie, Highland 152
Acton, Ealing 33
Adam Smith, Glasgow University 254
Adare, Limerick County 203
Additional Services, Oxfordshire 83
Addlestone, Surrey 106
Adelphi Campus, Salford University 299
Adelphi Library, Department for Work and Pensions 335
Adsetts Centre, Sheffield Hallam University 300
Advocates Library 319
Agriculture and Food Development Authority (TEAGASC) 400
Agriculture Library, Scottish Agricultural College 299
AHRC (Arts and Humanities Research Council) 371
Aidan Heavey, Westmeath 213
Ainsworth, Bury 15
Albert Sloman Library, Essex University 252
Albert Sloman Library, Royal Statistical Society 380
Alderman Lacey, Portsmouth 81
Aldermoor Farm, Coventry 23
Alderney 187
Aldersbrook, Redbridge 84

Aldershot Military Museum 319
Aldham Robarts LRC, Liverpool John Moores University 263
Aldrich, Brighton University 226
Aldridge, Walsall 113
Alexander Library of Ornithology, Oxford University 282
All Souls College, Oxford University 286
Allerton Campus, Salford University 299
Allerton, Liverpool 65
Allesley Park, Coventry 24
Alloa, Clackmannanshire 133
Allt-yr-yn Campus, University of Wales, Newport 311
Almondbank, West Lothian 168
Alness, Highland 152
Alnwick, Northumberland 76
Altrincham, Trafford 112
Alva, Clackmannanshire 133
Alyth, Perth and Kinross 161
Ambless Society Library 319
American Museum in Britain 319
Amersham, Buckinghamshire 13
Amgueddfa Cymru see National Museum Wales
Amgueddfa Werin Cymru (Museum of Welsh Life) see St Fagans: National History Museum
Amlwch, Isle of Anglesey 171
Ammanford, Carmarthenshire 175
An Daingean, Kerry 199
Andersonian Library, Strathclyde University 303
Anglesey, Isle of 171
Anglia Ruskin University 220
Angus 131
Angus Library, Regent's Park College 290
Anlaby Park, Kingston upon Hull 53
Annan, Dumfries and Galloway 135
Anniesland, Glasgow 149
Anthropology Library, Centre for Anthropology, British Museum 325
Arab World Documentation Unit, Exeter University 252
Aragon, Merton 67
Arbroath, Angus 132

Archbishop Marsh's Library 393
Archie Cochrane, Llandough Hospital,
    Cardiff University 238
Architecture Library, Cardiff University 238
Archive and Muniment Room, Sidney
    Sussex, Cambridge 236
Archive Centre, Dumfries and Galloway
    135
Archive of Art and Design, National Art
    Library 360
Archive Services, Westminster University
    313
Archives and Local History, Dudley 32
Archives Centre, Westminster 121
Archives, Isle of Anglesey 171
Archway, Islington 49
Ardcavan, Wexford 214
Ardersier, Highland 154
Ardkeen, Waterford City 212
Ardler, Dundee 138
Ardnamurchan, Highland 155
Ardrossan, North Ayrshire 158
Arena Park, Coventry 23
Argyll and Bute 132
Argyll College, UHI Millennium Institute
    307
Arklow, Wicklow 215
Armadale, West Lothian 168
Armitt Collection, The 320
Arnold, Nottinghamshire 77
Arthurstone, Dundee 138
Arts and Humanities Research Council
    (AHRC) 371
Arts and Social Sciences Library, Bristol
    University 227
Arts and Social Sciences, Cardiff University
    238
Arts London, University of the 309
Arts University College at Bournemouth
    221
Ascot Durning, Windsor and Maidenhead
    122
Ashbourne, Meath 205
Ashburne Library, Sunderland University
    304
Ashburton, Croydon 25
Ashford, Kent 51
Ashford, Surrey 106
Ashington, Northumberland 76
Ashmore Park, Wolverhampton 124

Ashton-under-Lyne, Tameside 108
Ashtown Food Research Centre, TEAGASC
    400
Askew Road, Hammersmith and Fulham 42
Association of Commonwealth Universities
    320
Aston University 221
Athboy, Meath 205
Atherstone, Warwickshire 118
Athlone, Westmeath 213
Athy, Kildare 199
Auchterarder, Perth and Kinross 160
Australian High Commission Library,
    London University 266
Avenue Campus, Northampton University
    278
Avenues, Kingston upon Hull 53
Avery Hill Campus, Greenwich University
    255
Aviemore, Highland 155
Avril Robarts LRC, Liverpool John Moores
    University 263
Aylesbury, Buckinghamshire 13
Ayr Campus Library, University of the West
    of Scotland 312
Ayr, South Ayrshire 166
Ayrshire see East Ayrshire, North Ayrshire,
    South Ayrshire
Aytoun Library, Manchester Metropolitan
    University 275

Babraham Institute 320
Badenoch, Highland 155
Baillieston, Glasgow 149
Balbriggan, Fingal 196
Baldoyle, Fingal 196
Balerno, Edinburgh 145
Balgreen, Edinburgh 145
Balham, Wandsworth 116
Ballaghaderreen, Roscommon 207
Ballinamore, Leitrim 202
Ballinasloe, Galway 197
Balliol College, Oxford University 286
Ballybane, Galway 197
Ballybay, Monaghan 206
Ballybunion, Kerry 198
Ballymahon, Longford 203
Ballynacarrigy, Westmeath 213
Ballyroan, South Dublin 209
Ballywaltrim, Wicklow 215

Banbury, Oxfordshire 79
Bancroft Library, Tower Hamlets 111
Banffshire see Moray
Bangor University 221
Bangor, Centre for Ecology and Hydrology 328
Bangor, Gwynedd 178
Bank of England 321
Banstead, Surrey 106
Baptist Union of Great Britain 291
Barber Fine Art Library, Birmingham University 224
Barber Music Library, Birmingham University 224
Barbican, London, City of 64
Barham Park, Brent 11
Barking and Dagenham 3
Barking, Barking and Dagenham 3
Barmulloch, Glasgow 149
Barnes Library, Birmingham University 224
Barnet 4
Barnsley 6
Barnstaple, Devon 29
Barons Court, Hammersmith and Fulham 42
Barrhead, East Renfrewshire 143
Barrington Library, Cranfield University 243
Barrow-in-Furness, Cumbria 26
Barry, Vale of Glamorgan 184
Bartlett Built Environment Library, UCL, London University 273
Bath and North East Somerset 6
Bath Spa University 222
Bath University 222
Bath, Bath and North East Somerset 6
Bathgate, West Lothian 168
Battersea, Wandsworth 116
Battle, East Sussex 34
Battle, Reading 82
BBC (British Broadcasting Corporation) 322
BBSRC (Biotechnology and Biological Sciences Research Council) 371
Beaconsfield, Buckinghamshire 13
Beauly, Highland 155
Beavers, Hounslow 47
Bebington, Wirral 123
Beccles, Suffolk 103
Beckenham, Bromley 13
Beckton Globe, Newham 70
Beddow, Portsmouth 81

Bedfont, Hounslow 47
Bedford 7
Bedford Campus, Bedfordshire University 223
Bedfordshire see Bedford, Central Bedfordshire
Bedfordshire University 223
Bedlington, Northumberland 76
Beechdale, Walsall 113
Beeston, Nottinghamshire 77
Belfast, University of Ulster at 309
Bell Green, Coventry 23
Belsize, Camden 17
Bembridge, Isle of Wight 48
Berkshire see Bracknell Forest, Reading, Slough, West Berkshire, Windsor and Maidenhead, Wokingham
BERR (Department for Business, Enterprise & Regulatory Reform) see Department for Business, Innovation and Skills (BIS)
Berwick, Northumberland 76
Berwickshire see Scottish Borders
Bethnal Green, Tower Hamlets 111
Betty and Gordon Moore Library, Cambridge University 229
Bettyhill, Highland 153
Bexhill, East Sussex 34
Bexley, London Borough of 7
Bexleyheath, Bexley 8
BFI (British Film Institute) 323
BG Group 321
Bibliographical Services, East Sussex 36
Bibliographical Services, London Metropolitan University 265
Bideford, Devon 29
Biggleswade, Central Bedfordshire 19
Bilborough, Nottinghamshire 78
Billingham, Stockton-on-Tees 101
Bilston, Wolverhampton 125
Biological Sciences Library, Bristol University 227
Biomedical Sciences, Cardiff University 238
Biotechnology and Biological Sciences Research Council (BBSRC) 371
Birchwood Library, Warrington 116
Birkbeck, London University 267
Birkenhead, Wirral 123
Birmingham 8
Birmingham and Midland Institute 321
Birmingham City University 223

Birmingham University 224
Birmingham University College 223
Birnam, Perth and Kinross 161
BIS (Department for Business, Innovation and Skills) 333
Bishop Grosseteste University College Lincoln 225
Bishop Otter Campus, Chichester University 242
Bishop's Stortford, Hertfordshire 46
Bishopbriggs, East Dunbartonshire 140
Bishopsgate Institute 321
Bishopstown, Cork City 192
Bishopton, Renfrewshire 162
Bitterne, Southampton 97
Blackburn Clinical Library, Central Lancashire University 240
Blackburn with Darwen 8
Blackburn, Blackburn with Darwen 8
Blackburn, West Lothian 168
Blackhall, Edinburgh 145
Blackheath, Greenwich 39
Blackness, Dundee 138
Blackpool 8
Blackpool Clinical Library, Central Lancashire University 240
Blackpool, Cork City 192
Blackridge, West Lothian 168
Blackrock, Dún Laoghaire-Rathdown 194
Blackwood, Caerphilly 174
Blaenau Gwent 171
Blaina, Blaenau Gwent 172
Blairgowrie, Perth and Kinross 160
Blakenall, Walsall 113
Blanchardstown, Fingal 196
Blessington, Wicklow 215
Bletchley, Milton Keynes 69
Bloxwich, Walsall 113
Blue Anchor, Southwark 98
Blyth, Northumberland 76
Bo'ness, Falkirk 147
Bodleian Health Care Libraries, Oxford University 286
Bodleian Japanese Library, Oxford University 283
Bodleian Law Library, Oxford University 283
Bodleian Libraries, Oxford University 282
Bodleian Library of Commonwealth and African Studies at Rhodes House, Oxford University 283

Bodleian Library, Oxford University 282
Bodmin, Cornwall 21
Bognor Regis Campus, Chichester University 242
Bolton 9
Bolton University 225
Bonar Bridge, Highland 153
Bonnybridge, Falkirk 147
Bonnyrigg, Midlothian 157
Book and Paper Conservation Studio, Dundee University 246
Boole Library, University College Cork 401
Bootle, Sefton 89
Boots Library, Nottingham Trent University 279
Borrisokane, Tipperary 210
Boston Scientific Health Sciences Library, University College Cork 401
Bourne Hall, Surrey 105
Bournemouth 9
Bournemouth House Library, Bournemouth University 226
Bournemouth University 225
Bow, Tower Hamlets 111
Boyle, Roscommon 207
Brackenhurst Campus, Nottingham Trent University 279
Bracknell Forest 10
Bracknell, Bracknell Forest 10
Bradford 10
Bradford University 226
Bradley Stoke, South Gloucestershire 95
Bradmore Green, Croydon 25
Brandlesholme, Bury 15
Brandon, Southwark 98
Bransholme, Kingston upon Hull 53
Brasenose College, Oxford University 287
Brassey Institute, East Sussex 35
Bray, Wicklow 215
Brechin, Angus 132
Brecon, Powys 182
Brent 10
Brentford, Hounslow 47
Bretton, Peterborough 79
Brian Cooke Library, Cardiff University 238
Bridge and Learning Centre, Glasgow 150
Bridge of Weir, Renfrewshire 162
Bridgend 172
Bridgeton, Glasgow 149
Bridgnorth, Shropshire 93

Bridgwater, Somerset 95
Brierley Hill, Dudley 31
Brighstone, Isle of Wight 48
Brighton and Hove 12
Brighton University 226, 405
Brighton, Brighton and Hove 12
Bristol 12 see also Bath and North East
    Somerset
Bristol University 227
Britannia Royal Naval College 322
British Antarctic Survey 322
British Architectural Library Drawings and
    Archives Collection, RIBA 377
British Architectural Library, Royal Institute
    of British Architects 377
British Broadcasting Corporation 322
British Council 322
British Dental Association 322
British Empire and Commonwealth
    Museum 323
British Film Institute 323
British Geological Survey 323
British Horological Institute 324
British Library 324
British Library for Development Studies,
    Sussex University 258
British Library of Political and Economic
    Science, London School of Economics
    and Political Science 270
British Medical Association 325
British Museum 325
British Psychological Society 326
British Standards Institution 326
British Universities Film & Video Council
    327
Britten-Pears Foundation 327
Brixham, Torbay 110
Brixton, Lambeth 57
Broad Green, Croydon 25
Broadford, Highland 152
Broadstairs Learning Centre, Canterbury
    Christ Church University College 237
Bromley 12
Bromley House Library 327
Brompton, Kensington and Chelsea 50
Bromsgrove, Worcestershire 126
Brookwood, East Dunbartonshire 140
Broomhead, Chester University 241
Broomhill, Sheffield 90
Brora, Highland 153

Broughton, Flintshire 177
Broughty Ferry, Dundee 138
Brown's Road, Waterford City 212
Brownhills, Walsall 113
Broxburn, West Lothian 168
Brunel University 228
Brynmawr, Blaenau Gwent 172
Brynmor Jones Library, Hull University 257
Brynteg, Wrexham 185
Buckie, Moray 158
Buckingham University 228
Buckingham, Buckinghamshire 13
Buckinghamshire 13 see also Milton Keynes
Buckinghamshire Campus, Bedfordshire
    University 223
Buckinghamshire New University 228
Buckley, Flintshire 177
Bude, Cornwall 21
Bunclody, Wexford 214
Burgess Road, Southampton 97
Burngreave, Sheffield 90
Burnley Campus, Central Lancashire
    University 240
Burnley Clinical Library, Central Lancashire
    University 240
Burnley, Lancashire 59
Burnt Oak, Barnet 4
Burton Nurse Education Centre,
    Wolverhampton University 315
Burton, Staffordshire 99
Burtonwood, Warrington 116
Bury 14
Bury St Edmunds, Suffolk 103
Busby, East Renfrewshire 143
Bushbury, Wolverhampton 125
Business Information, Cheshire East 19, 21
Business Library, Nottingham University
    280
Business School Library, Durham University
    247
Bute, Cardiff University 238
Butterfield Park Campus, Bedfordshire
    University 223
Buxton, Derbyshire 28

C L R James, Hackney 40
Cabinteely, Dún Laoghaire-Rathdown 194
Caerleon Campus, University of Wales,
    Newport 311
Caernarfon, Gwynedd 177

Caerphilly 173, 174
Caherciveen, Kerry 198
Cahir, Tipperary 210
Caird Library, National Maritime Museum 363
Cairns Library, Oxford University 286
Caithness see Highland
Calcutta House, London Metropolitan University 264
Calderdale 15
Caldicot, Monmouthshire 179
Callan, Kilkenny 200
Callington, Cornwall 21
Caludon Castle, Coventry 23
Camberley, Surrey 106
Camberwell College of Arts, University of the Arts London 309
Camberwell, Southwark 98
Camborne, Cornwall 21
Cambridge Union Society, Cambridge University 229
Cambridge University 229
Cambridge, Cambridgeshire 16
Cambridgeshire 16 see also Peterborough 17
Camden 17
Camden Campus, Royal Veterinary College, London University 271
Camden Town, Camden 17
Camelford, Cornwall 21
Camomile Street, London, City of 64
Campaign to Protect Rural England (CPRE) 332
Campbeltown, Argyll and Bute 133
Campion Hall, Oxford University 287
Canaan Lane Library, Edinburgh Napier University 250
Canadian High Commission Library, London University 266
Canary Wharf, Tower Hamlets 111
Cancer Research UK 327
Cancer Research Wales, Cardiff University 238
Cancer Specialist Library, Macmillan Cancer Support 356
Canley, Coventry 24
Canning House Library, Hispanic and Luso-Brazilian Council 342
Canning Town, Newham 70
Cannock, Staffordshire 99
Canterbury Campus, University for the

Creative Arts 244
Canterbury Cathedral 327
Canterbury Christ Church University 236
Canterbury, Kent 51
Caol, Highland 155
Cappoquin, Waterford County 212
Cardiff 174
Cardiff University 237
Cardiff, University of Wales Institute 311
Cardonald, Glasgow 150
Carlisle, Cumbria 26
Carlow 191
Carmarthen Campus, University of Wales Trinity St David 312
Carmarthen, Carmarthenshire 175
Carmarthenshire 174
Carmondean, West Lothian 168
Carnegie, Fife 148
Carnegie, Lambeth 58
Carnegie, Portsmouth 81
Carnegie, South Ayrshire 166
Carnoustie, Angus 132
Carraroe, Galway 198
Carrickmacross, Monaghan 206
Carrick-on-Suir, Tipperary 210
Carshalton, Sutton 107
Cashel, Tipperary 210
Cass Business School, City University London 242
Castelnau, Richmond upon Thames 85
Castle Douglas, Dumfries and Galloway 135
Castle Gates, Shropshire 93
Castle Green, Barking and Dagenham 3
Castle Sport and Leisure, Bury 15
Castlebar, Mayo 204
Castlebay, Comhairle nan Eilean Siar 134
Castleblayney, Monaghan 206
Castlecomer, Kilkenny 200
Castleisland, Kerry 198
Castlemilk, Glasgow 150
Castlepollard, Westmeath 213
Castlerea, Roscommon 207
Castletown, Isle of Man 188
Castletymon, South Dublin 209
Cat Hill, Middlesex University 277
Caterham Valley, Surrey 106
Catford, Lewisham 62
Cathedral and Church Buildings Library, Lambeth Palace Library 353
Cavan 191

Cavendish Library, Westminster University 313

Caversham, Reading 82

CDVEC Curriculum Development Unit 393

Celbridge, Kildare 199

Central Bedfordshire 18

Central Catholic Library 393

Central Lancashire University 239

Central Resources, Hertfordshire 46

Central School of Speech and Drama 241

Central Science Library, Cambridge University 229

Central St Martins College of Art and Design, University of the Arts London 310

Centre for Anthropology, British Museum 325

Centre for Ecology and Hydrology 328

Centre for Emergency Preparedness and Response (CEPR), Health Protection Agency 341

Centre for Infections, Health Protection Agency 341

Centre for Policy on Ageing 328

Centre for Radiation, Chemical and Environmental Hazards (CRCE), Health Protection Agency 341

Centre for the Study of Irish Art, National Gallery of Ireland 396

Centre of International Studies, Cambridge University 231

Centre of Latin American Studies, Cambridge University 231

CEPR (Centre for Emergency Preparedness and Response), Health Protection Agency 341

Ceredigion 175

Chadwell Heath, Redbridge 84

Chadwick Library, Daresbury Laboratory, Science and Technology Facilities Council 381

Chalk Farm, Camden 17

Channel Islands 187 see also Alderney, Guernsey, Jersey

Chantry Library, Institute of Conservation 348

Chapeltown, Sheffield 90

Charing Cross Campus, Imperial College London 257

Charing Cross, Westminster 120

Charles Frears Campus, De Montfort University 246

Charles Seale-Hayne Library, Plymouth University 294

Charleston, Dundee 138

Charlotte Mason, Cumbria University 245

Chartered Institute of Library and Information Professionals (CILIP) 330

Chartered Institute of Logistics and Transport in the UK, The 329

Chartered Institute of Personnel and Development 329

Chartered Insurance Institute 329

Chartered Management Institute 329

Chase Farm Education Centre, Middlesex University 277

Chatham, Medway 66

Cheam, Sutton 107

Chelmsford, Anglia Ruskin University 220

Chelmsford, Essex 37

Chelmsley Wood, Solihull 94

Chelsea and Westminster Campus, Imperial College London 257

Chelsea College of Art and Design, University of the Arts London 310

Chelsea, Kensington and Chelsea 50

Cheltenham, Gloucestershire 38

Chemistry Branch, Glasgow University 254

Chemistry Library, Bristol University 227

Chepstow, Monmouthshire 179

Chesham, Buckinghamshire 13

Cheshire East 19

Cheshire see Cheshire East, Cheshire West and Chester

Cheshire West and Chester 20

Chester Beatty Library 393

Chester Lane Centre and Library, St Helens 87

Chester University 241

Chester, Cheshire West and Chester 20

Chesterfield, Derbyshire 28

Chetham's Library 330

Cheylesmore, Coventry 23

Chichester University 242

Chichester, West Sussex 119

Children and Young People, Cork City 193

Children and Young People, Staffordshire 100

Children's and Young People's Library Service, South Dublin 210

Children's Library, Institut français du
    Royaume-Uni 346
Children's Services, Lambeth 58
Childs Hill, Barnet 4
Childwall Fiveways, Liverpool 63
Chippenham, Wiltshire 122
Chipping Barnet, Barnet 4
Chiswick, Hounslow 47
Chomhairle Leabharlanna, An (The Library
    Council) 393
Chorley, Lancashire 59
Chorlton, Manchester 66
Chrisp Street, Tower Hamlets 111
Christ Church, Oxford University 287
Christ's College, Cambridge University 230
Church End, Barnet 4
Church Mission Society, Crowther Centre
    for Mission Education 332
Church of England Record Centre,
    Lambeth Palace Library 353
Church Street, Westminster 120
Churchill College, Cambridge University
    230
Churston, Torbay 110
CILIP (Chartered Institute of Library and
    Information Professionals) 330
CILT, the National Centre for Languages
    330
Cirencester Bingham, Gloucestershire 38
City Business, London, City of 64
City Campus, Leeds Metropolitan
    University 260
City Campus, Sheffield Hallam University
    300
City Law School Library, City University
    London 242
City University London 242, 405
Civic Quarter, Leeds Metropolitan
    University 260
Civil Aviation Authority 330
Clackmannan, Clackmannanshire 133
Clackmannanshire 133
Clapham, Lambeth 57
Clapton, Hackney 40
Clare 191
Clare College, Cambridge University 230
Clarkston, East Renfrewshire 143
Clatterbridge Library, Chester University
    241
Clayhall, Redbridge 84

Cleckheaton, Kirklees 55
Cleethorpes, North East Lincolnshire 72
Cleveland see Hartlepool, Middlesbrough,
    Redcar and Cleveland
Clifden, Galway 198
Clifford Whitworth, Salford University 299
Clifton Campus, Nottingham Trent
    University 280
Clinical Sciences Centre, Edge Hill
    University 249
Clinical Sciences Library, Leicester
    University 261
Clitheroe, Lancashire 59
Clonaslee, Laois 201
Clondalkin, South Dublin 209
Clones, Monaghan 206
Clonmel, Tipperary 210
Cloughjordan, Tipperary 210
Clydebank, West Dunbartonshire 167
Co Carlow see Carlow
Co Cavan see Cavan
Co Clare see Clare
Co Cork see Cork City
Co Donegal see Donegal
Co Dublin see Dublin, Dún Laoghaire-
    Rathdown, Fingal, South Dublin
Co Durham see Darlington, Durham,
    Gateshead, Stockton-on-Tees
Co Galway see Galway
Co Kerry see Kerry
Co Kildare see Kildare
Co Kilkenny see Kilkenny
Co Laois see Laois
Co Leitrim see Leitrim
Co Limerick see Limerick City, Limerick
    County
Co Longford see Longford
Co Louth see Louth
Co Mayo see Mayo
Co Meath see Meath
Co Monaghan see Monaghan
Co Offaly see Offaly
Co Roscommon see Roscommon
Co Sligo see Sligo
Co Tipperary see Tipperary
Co Waterford see Waterford City,
    Waterford County
Co Westmeath see Westmeath
Co Wexford see Wexford
Co Wicklow see Wicklow

Coach Lane, Northumbria University 279
Coalville, Leicestershire 61
Coatbridge, North Lanarkshire 160
Cobbett Road, Southampton 97
Cockerton, Darlington 27
Codrington Library, All Souls College,
    Oxford University 286
Colchester, Essex 37
Coldside, Dundee 138
Coldstream, Scottish Borders 164
Coleraine, University of Ulster at 309
Colinton, Edinburgh 145
College of Occupational Therapists 331
Collegiate Crescent Campus, Sheffield
    Hallam University 300
Collingwood, Wolverhampton 125
Colwyn Bay, Conwy 176
Comely Bank Library, Edinburgh Napier
    University 250
Comhairle nan Eilean Siar 134
Commercial Road, London Metropolitan
    University 264
Commonwealth Secretariat 331
Community Library Service, Hackney 40
Community Services, Southwark 98
Competition Commission 331
Compton Learning Centre, Wolverhampton
    University 314
Comrie, Perth and Kinross 161
Congleton, Cheshire East 20
Connah's Quay, Flintshire 177
Conservative Party Archive 331
Continuing Education Library, Liverpool
    University 263
Continuing Education, Oxford University
    283
Conwy 175, 176
Cookham, Windsor and Maidenhead 122
Coolmine, Fingal 196, 197
Cork City 192
Cork County 193
Cork, University College 401
Cornish Studies, Cornwall 21
Cornwall 21
Corofin, Clare 191
Corpus Christi College, Cambridge
    University 230
Corpus Christi College, Oxford University
    287
Corstophine, Edinburgh 145

Corus UK Ltd see Tata Steel
Cosham, Portsmouth 81
Cottingham Road Campus, Hull University
    257
Coulsdon, Croydon 25
Coundon, Coventry 24
Countryside Council for Wales (Cyngor
    Cefn Gwlad Cymru) 332
County Archives, Fingal 196
Countywide Information Service,
    Worcestershire 126
Coupar Angus, Perth and Kinross 161
Couper Institute, Glasgow 150
Courtauld Institute of Art, London
    University 267
Coventry 22
Coventry University 243
Cowbridge, Vale of Glamorgan 185
Cowes, Isle of Wight 48
Cox Green, Windsor and Maidenhead
    122
CPRE (Campaign to Protect Rural England)
    332
Craighouse Library, Edinburgh Napier
    University 250
Craiglockhart Campus, Edinburgh Napier
    University 250
Craigmillar, Edinburgh 145
Cramlington, Northumberland 76
Cranfield University 243
Cranford, Hounslow 47
Cranleigh, Surrey 106
Crawley, West Sussex 119
CRCE (Centre for Radiation, Chemical and
    Environmental Hazards), Health
    Protection Agency 341
Creative Arts, University for the 244
Crewe Library, Manchester Metropolitan
    University 275
Crewe, Cheshire East 20
Cricklewood, Brent 11
Crieff, Perth and Kinross 161
Cromarty, Highland 153
Crosby, Sefton 89
Crowborough, East Sussex 34
Crowmarsh Gifford, Centre for Ecology
    and Hydrology 328
Crown Prosecution Service 332
Crowther Centre for Mission Education
    332

Croydon 24
Cruciform Library, UCL, London University
    273
Crumpsall, Manchester 66
Crystal Peaks, Sheffield 90
Cubitt Town, Tower Hamlets 111
Culcheth, Warrington 117
Culloden, Highland 155
Cumbria 26
Cumbria University 244
Cundall Library, Royal Institute of
    Navigation 378
Cupar, Fife 148
Currie, Edinburgh 145
Custom House, Newham 70
Cwm, Blaenau Gwent 172
Cwmbran, Torfaen 184
Cyngor Cefn Gwlad Cymru (Countryside
    Council for Wales) 332

Dalbeattie, Dumfries and Galloway 135
Daliburgh, Comhairle nan Eilean Siar 134
Dalkeith, Midlothian 156
Dalkey, Dún Laoghaire-Rathdown 195
Dalry, Dumfries and Galloway 135
Danderhall, Midlothian 157
Daniel Hay, Cumbria 26
Daresbury Campus, Science and
    Technology Facilities Council 381
Darlaston, Walsall 113
Darlington 27
Darnall, Sheffield 90
Dartford, Kent 51
Darwin College, Cambridge University
    230
Datchet, Windsor and Maidenhead 122
Daventry, Northamptonshire 75
David West Library, Institute of Materials,
    Minerals and Mining 348
David Wilson Library, Leicester University
    261
DCLG (Department for Communities and
    Local Government) 333
DCMS (Department for Culture, Media and
    Sport) 333
DCSF (Department for Children, Schools
    and Families) see Department for
    Education (DFE)
De Montfort University 245
De Valera, Clare 191

Deansgrange, Dún Laoghaire-Rathdown
    194
DECC (Department of Energy and Climate
    Change) 333
Dedworth, Windsor and Maidenhead
    123
Defence Academy of Management and
    Technology, Cranfield University 243
Defra (Department for Environment, Food
    and Rural Affairs) 334
Denbighshire 176
Denmark Hill Campus, King's College
    London 269
Dennis Arnold Music Library, Nottingham
    University 280
Dennistoun, Glasgow 150
Denny, Falkirk 148
Dental Library, Bristol University 227
Department for Business, Enterprise &
    Regulatory Reform (BERR) see
    Department for Business, Innovation
    and Skills (BIS)
Department for Business, Innovation and
    Skills (BIS) 333
Department for Children, Schools and
    Families (DCSF) see Department for
    Education (DFE)
Department for Communities and Local
    Government (DCLG) 333
Department for Culture, Media and Sport
    (DCMS) 333
Department for Education (DFE) 334
Department for Environment, Food and
    Rural Affairs (Defra) 334
Department for International Development
    (DFID) 334
Department for Regional Development
    335
Department for Transport (DfT) 335
Department for Work and Pensions (DWP)
    335
Department of Computer and Information
    Sciences, Strathclyde University 408
Department of Education, Oxford
    University 283
Department of Energy and Climate Change
    (DECC) 333
Department of Experimental Psychology,
    Oxford University 284
Department of Health (DH) 336

Department of Information and Communications, Manchester Metropolitan University 407
Department of Information Management, Robert Gordon University 407
Department of Information Science and Digital Media, University of the West of England, Bristol 408
Department of Information Science, City University 405
Department of Information Science, Loughborough University 406
Department of Information Studies, Aberystwyth University 405
Department of Information Studies, University College London 406
Department of Justice 336
Department of Land Economy Library, Cambridge University 231
Depository Library, London University 266
Derby 27
Derby Centre, Nottingham University 281
Derby Medical School, Nottingham University 280
Derby University 246
Derbyshire 27 see also Derby
Dereham, Norfolk 71
Devon 29 see also Plymouth, Torbay
Devonshire LRC, Derby University 246
Dewsbury, Kirklees 55
Dún Laoghaire, Dún Laoghaire-Rathdown 194
Dún Laoghaire-Rathdown 193
DFE (Department for Education) 334
DFID (Department for International Development) 334
DfT (Department for Transport) 335
DH (Department of Health) 336
Didsbury Library, Manchester Metropolitan University 275
Didsbury, Manchester 66
Dinas Powys, Vale of Glamorgan 185
Dingwall, Highland 153
Ditton, Halton 41
Dittons, Surrey 106
Djanogly LRC, Nottingham University 280
Docklands, East London University 249
Dogsthorpe, Peterborough 80
Dolgellau, Gwynedd 178
Dollar, Clackmannanshire 134

Donald Hope (Colliers Wood), Merton 67
Doncaster 30
Donegal 193
Dooradoyle, Limerick County 203
Dorchester, Dorset 30
Dorking, Surrey 106
Dornoch, Highland 152
Dorset 30 see also Bournemouth, Poole
Dorset, Tower Hamlets 111
Douglas, Cork City 193
Douglas, Dundee 138
Douglas, Isle of Man 187
Dover, Kent 51
Dowlais, Merthyr Tydfil 178
Downend, South Gloucestershire 95
Downham, Lewisham 64
Downing College, Cambridge University 231
Dreadnought Library, Greenwich University 255
Drill Hall Library, Greenwich University 255
Drill Hall, Surrey 105
Drill Hall, University of Kent at Medway 259
Droitwich Library, Worcestershire 126
Drumchapel, Glasgow 150
Drumlish, Longford 203
Dublin 194
Dublin Business School 394
Dublin City University 394
Dublin Institute of Technology 394
Dublin, University College 401, 405
Dudley 31
Duleek, Meath 205
Dulwich, Southwark 98
Dumbarton, West Dunbartonshire 167
Dumfries and Galloway 135
Dumfries Campus, University of the West of Scotland 313
Dumfries, Dumfries and Galloway 135
Dunbar, East Lothian 142
Dunbartonshire see Argyll and Bute, East Dunbartonshire, West Dunbartonshire
Dunboyne, Meath 205
Duncan House, East London University 249
Duncan of Jordanstone, Dundee University 246
Dundalk, Louth 204
Dundee 137
Dundee University 246

Dundrum, Dún Laoghaire-Rathdown 195
Dunfermline, Fife 148
Dungarvan, Waterford County 212
Dunmore, Waterford County 212
Dunoon, Argyll and Bute 133
Duns, Scottish Borders 164
Dunshaughlin, Meath 205
Dunstable, Central Bedfordshire 18
Durham 32
Durham Clayport, Durham 32
Durham University 247
Durning, Lambeth 57
DWP (Department for Work and Pensions) 335
Dynevor, Swansea Metropolitan University 305

Eaglesham, East Renfrewshire 143
Ealing 32
Ealing Road, Brent 11
Earlsdon, Coventry 24
Earlston, Scottish Borders 164
East Anglia University 248
East Ayrshire 139
East Barnet, Barnet 4
East Calder, West Lothian 168
East Cowes, Isle of Wight 48
East Dunbartonshire 140
East Finchley, Barnet 4
East Ham, Newham 70
East Kilbride, South Lanarkshire 166
East Linton, East Lothian 142
East London University 248
East Lothian 141
East Park, Wolverhampton 125
East Renfrewshire 143
East Riding of Yorkshire 33
East Sheen, Richmond upon Thames 85
East Street/Old Kent Road, Southwark 98
East Sussex 33 see also Brighton and Hove
Eastbourne, East Sussex 34
Eastman Dental Institute, UCL, London University 273
Eastriggs, Dumfries and Galloway 135
Ebbw Vale, Blaenau Gwent 172
Eccles, Salford 88
Ecclesall, Sheffield 91
Ecclesfield, Sheffield 91
Economic and Social Research Council (ESRC) 371

Economic and Social Research Institute 395
Eddie Davies, Manchester University 276
Edge Hill University 249
Edgeworthstown, Longford 204
Edgware, Barnet 5
Edinburgh 144
Edinburgh College of Art 250
Edinburgh Napier University 250
Edinburgh University 251
Edinburgh, Centre for Ecology and Hydrology 328
Edmonton Green, Enfield 36
Education Library, Birmingham University 224
Education Library, Bristol University 227
Education Library, Durham University 247
Education Site, Bangor University 222
Education, Culture & Sport Office, Highland 152
Egglescliffe, Stockton-on-Tees 101
Egham, Surrey 106
EHRC (Equality and Human Rights Commission) 337
Elder Park, Glasgow 150
Elgin, Moray 158
Elizabeth Gaskell Library, Manchester Metropolitan University 275
Ellesmere Port, Cheshire East 19
Ellesmere Port, Cheshire West and Chester 20
Elm Grove, Portsmouth 82
Elphin, Roscommon 207
Eltham, Greenwich 39
Ely, Cambridgeshire 16
Emmanuel College, Cambridge University 231
Energy Institute 336
Enfield 36
Engineering and Physical Sciences Research Council (EPSRC) 371
English Faculty, Oxford University 284
English Folk Dance and Song Society 336
English Heritage 337
English-Speaking Union 337
Ennis, Clare 191
Enniscorthy, Wexford 214
Ennistymon, Clare 192
Enquiries Direct, Surrey 105
Enterprise Ireland 396

Epsom Campus, University for the Creative Arts 244
Epsom, Surrey 106
EPSRC (Engineering and Physical Sciences Research Council) 371
Equality and Human Rights Commission (EHRC) 337
Erskine, Renfrewshire 162
Esher, Surrey 106
ESRC (Economic and Social Research Council) 371
Essex 36 see also Barking and Dagenham, Havering, Redbridge, Southend-on-Sea, Thurrock
Essex University 252
Eton Wick, Windsor and Maidenhead 123
Eton, Windsor and Maidenhead 123
Eugenio Montale Library, Istituto Italiano di Cultura 351
European Commission Representation in the United Kingdom 337
Evesham, Worcestershire 126
Ewart, Dumfries and Galloway 136
Ewell, Surrey 106
Exeter College, Oxford University 287
Exeter University 252
Exeter, Devon 29
Exmouth, Devon 29
Eye, Peterborough 80
Eyemouth, Scottish Borders 164

Faculty of Asian and Middle Eastern Studies, Cambridge University 231
Faculty of Education, Cambridge University 231
Faculty of Music, Cambridge University 231
Faculty of Music, Oxford University 283
Faculty of Oriental Studies, Cambridge University see Faculty of Asian and Middle Eastern Studies, Cambridge University
Fairfield, Stockton-on-Tees 101
Falkirk 147
Falmer, Brighton University 226
Falmouth, Cornwall 21
Falmouth, University College 252
Family and Mobile, Douglas, Isle of Man 188
Fanshawe, Barking and Dagenham 3
Farnham Campus, University for the Creative Arts 244
Farnham, Surrey 106
Fauldhouse, West Lothian 168
Felixstowe, Suffolk 103
Fellows' Library, Clare College, Cambridge University 230
Feltham, Hounslow 47
Ferguslie Park, Renfrewshire 162
Fife 148
Fife School of Nursing and Midwifery, Dundee University 247
Finchfield, Wolverhampton 125
Fine Art Library, National Gallery of Ireland 397
Fingal 195
Finham, Coventry 24
Finsbury, Islington 49
Fintry, Dundee 138
Firth Park, Sheffield 91
Fishguard, Pembrokeshire 181
Fitzwilliam College, Cambridge University 232
Fleetwood, Lancashire 59
Flint, Flintshire 177
Flintshire 176 see also Wrexham
Flitwick, Central Bedfordshire 19
Foleshill, Coventry 23
Folkestone, Kent 52
Food Standards Agency 338
Forbes Mellon Library, Clare College, Cambridge University 230
Foreign and Commonwealth Office 338
Foreign Cataloguing Department, Oxford University 284
Forest Row, East Sussex 34
Forestry Commission 338
Forfar, Angus 132
Forres, Moray 158
Fort William, Highland 155
Fortrose, Highland 153
Forum, Manchester 66
Fountainbridge, Edinburgh 145
Fountains Learning Centre, York St John University 316
Fowey, Cornwall 21
Foxbar, Renfrewshire 162
Foyle Reading Room, Royal Geographical Society 376
Francis Close Hall, Gloucestershire University 254

Francis Skaryna Belarusian Library and Museum 338
Franciscan Library, Buckingham University 228
Frank O'Connor, Cork City 193
Frecheville, Sheffield 91
Fred Moore, Kingston upon Hull 53
Freedom, Kingston upon Hull 53
French Institute (Institut français d'Écosse) 346
Frenchay Campus, University of the West of England, Bristol 312
Freshwater Biological Association 339
Freshwater, Isle of Wight 48
Friern Barnet, Barnet 5
Fulbourn, Anglia Ruskin University 221
Fulham, Hammersmith and Fulham 42
Fullwell Cross, Redbridge 84

Gairloch, Highland 153
Galashiels, Scottish Borders 164
Galway 197
Galway City, Galway 197
Gants Hill, Redbridge 84
Gatehouse, Dumfries and Galloway 136
Gateshead 37
Gayton, Harrow 44
Geography Library, Bristol University 227
Geological Society of London 339
George Green Library, Nottingham University 280
George Herdman, Isle of Man 187
Georgetown, Dumfries and Galloway 136
Georgina Scott Sutherland Library, Robert Gordon University 295
German Historical Institute London 339
Giffnock, East Renfrewshire 144
Gillingham, Medway 66
Gilmerton, Edinburgh 145
Gipsyville, Kingston upon Hull 53
Girton College, Cambridge University 232
Gladstone's Library 339
Glamorgan see Bridgend, Merthyr Tydfil, Vale of Glamorgan
Glamorgan University 253, 406
Glasgow 149 see also East Dunbartonshire, South Lanarkshire
Glasgow Caledonian University 253
Glasgow School of Art 253
Glasgow University 253, 406

Gleadless, Sheffield 91
Glenburn, Renfrewshire 162
Glenfield, Leicestershire 61
Glenrothes, Fife 149
Glenurquhart, Highland 155
Glenwood, Fife 149
Gloucester, Gloucestershire 38
Gloucestershire 37 see also South Gloucestershire
Gloucestershire University 254
Glyndŵr University 255
Godalming, Surrey 106
Goethe-Institut London 340
Golders Green, Barnet 5
Goldsmiths, London University 267
Golspie, Highland 153
Goma, Glasgow 150
Gonville and Caius College, Cambridge University 232
Goodmayes, Redbridge 84
Gorbals, Glasgow 150
Gorebridge, Midlothian 157
Gorleston, Norfolk 71
Gorseinon, Swansea 183
Govanhill, Glasgow 150
Grahame Park, Barnet 5
Graiguenamanagh, Kilkenny 201
Granard, Longford 204
Grange Research Centre, TEAGASC 400
Grangemouth, Falkirk 148
Grant Thorold, North East Lincolnshire 72
Granton, Edinburgh 145
Grantown, Highland 155
Grappenhall, Warrington 117
Gravesend, Kent 52
Grays, Thurrock 109
Great Sankey, Warrington 117
Great Yarmouth, Norfolk 71
Greater London Authority 340
Greater Manchester see Bury, Manchester, Rochdale, Trafford
Green Street, Newham 70
Green Templeton College, Oxford University 287
Greenfield Medical Library, Nottingham University 280
Greenford, Ealing 33
Greenhill, Sheffield 91
Greenock, Inverclyde 156
Greenwich 39

Greenwich University 255
Greenwood Avenue, Kingston upon Hull 53
Gretna, Dumfries and Galloway 136
Greystones, Wicklow 215
Grimsby, North East Lincolnshire 72
Grove Vale, Southwark 98
Guernsey 187
Guildford Institute 340
Guildford, Surrey 105
Guildhall School of Music and Drama 255
Guildhall, London, City of 64
Guille-Allès, Guernsey 187
Gullane, East Lothian 142
Guy's Campus, King's College London 269
Gwent see Newport, Torfaen
Gwynedd 177

Hackney 39
Hackney Archives, Hackney 40
Haddington, East Lothian 142
Hadleigh, Suffolk 104
Hailsham, East Sussex 34
Hainault, Redbridge 84
Hale End, Waltham Forest 115
Halesowen, Dudley 31
Halewood, Knowsley 56
Halifax, Calderdale 15
Hallward Library, Nottingham University 280
Halton 41
Halton Lea, Halton 41
Ham, Richmond upon Thames 85
Hamilton Campus, University of the West
   of Scotland 313
Hamilton, South Lanarkshire 166
Hammersmith and Fulham 41
Hammersmith Campus, Imperial College
   London 257
Hammersmith, Hammersmith and Fulham
   42
Hampden Park, East Sussex 34
Hampshire 42 see also Southampton
Hampstead Garden Suburb, Barnet 5
Hampton Hill, Richmond upon Thames 86
Hampton Library, Richmond upon Thames
   86
Hampton, Peterborough 80
Hanley, Stoke-on-Trent 102
Hanworth, Hounslow 47
Harcourt Hill, Oxford Brookes University
   282

Harding Law Library, Birmingham
   University 224
Haringey 43
Harlesden, Brent 11
Harold Bridges, Cumbria University 244
Harold Cohen Library, Liverpool University
   264
Harold Wood Education Centre, London
   South Bank University 265
Harper Adams University College 256
Harris Library, Lancashire 59
Harris Manchester College, Oxford
   University 288
Harrison Learning Centre, Wolverhampton
   University 314
Harrogate, North Yorkshire 74
Harrow 43
Harrow Campus, Westminster University
   313
Harrow Green, Waltham Forest 115
Hartlepool 44
Hartley Library, Southampton University
   301
Harwell Campus, Science and Technology
   Facilities Council 381
Haslemere, Surrey 106
Hastings Children's Library, East Sussex 35
Hastings, East Sussex 34
Hatfield College Lane Campus,
   Hertfordshire University 256
Hatfield de Havilland Campus,
   Hertfordshire University 256
Hatfield, Hertfordshire 46
HATII (Humanities Advanced Technologies
   & Information Institute) 406
Haverfordwest, Pembrokeshire 181
Haverhill, Suffolk 104
Havering 44
Havering Campus, London South Bank
   University 265
Hawick, Scottish Borders 164
Hawkshead Campus, Royal Veterinary
   College, London University 272
Hayle, Cornwall 21
Hazlemere, Buckinghamshire 13
Headingley, Leeds Metropolitan University
   260
Headington Campus, Oxford Brookes
   University 281
Health and Safety Executive 340

Health Campus Libraries, Middlesex University 277
Health Library, Keele University 258
Health Management Library 341
Health Protection Agency 341
Health Sciences Library, Sheffield University 301
Health Sciences, Brighton University 226
Health Sciences, University College Dublin 402
Health Services Library, Southampton University 302
Healthcare Sciences Library, Bangor University 222
Healthpoint, Poole 81
Heath, Camden 17
Heathfield, East Sussex 35
Hebrides see Comhairle nan Eilean Siar
Heinz Archive and Library, National Portrait Gallery 365
Helensburgh, Argyll and Bute 133
Helmsdale, Highland 153
Helston, Cornwall 22
Hendon, Barnet 5
Hendon, Middlesex University 277
Hengoed, Caerphilly 173, 174
Henry Bloom Noble, Isle of Man 187
Hereford Cathedral 342
Hereford, Herefordshire 45
Herefordshire 45
Heriot-Watt University 256
Hertford College, Oxford University 288
Hertfordshire 45 see also Barnet
Hertfordshire University 256
Heston, Hounslow 47
Hexham, Northumberland 76
Heythrop College, London University 267
Heywood, Rochdale 86
High Commission of India 342
High Wycombe, Buckinghamshire 14
Higham Hill, Waltham Forest 115
Highfield, Sheffield 91
Highgate Literary and Scientific Institution 342
Highgate, Camden 17
Highland 152
Highland Health Sciences Library, Stirling University 303

Highland Theological College, UHI Millennium Institute 307
Hillfields, Coventry 23
Hillhead, Glasgow 150
Hillingdon 46
Hillsborough, Sheffield 91
Hinckley, Leicestershire 62
Hispanic and Luso-Brazilian Council 342
Historic Scotland 343
History Faculty, Oxford University 284
HM Revenue and Customs 343
HM Treasury and Cabinet Office 344
HMS Sultan 344
Holbeach Campus, Lincoln University 262
Holborn, Camden 17
Holderness, Kingston upon Hull 53
Hollings Library, Manchester Metropolitan University 275
Hollington, East Sussex 35
Holloway Road, London Metropolitan University 264
Hollyhill, Cork City 193
Holmfirth, Kirklees 55
Holton, Oxfordshire 78
Holyhead, Isle of Anglesey 171
Holywell, Flintshire 177
Home Office 344
Homerton College, Cambridge University 232
Homerton, Hackney 40
Honiton, Devon 29
Hook and Chessington, Kingston upon Thames 54
Horley, Surrey 106
Hornsey, Haringey 43
Hospital Library, University College Cork 401
Houghton Regis, Central Bedfordshire 19
Hounslow 47
House of Commons 344
House of Lords 345
Housebound Services, Fingal 196
Hove, Brighton and Hove 12
Howth, Fingal 196
Hub, Dundee 138
Huddersfield University 256
Huddersfield, Kirklees 55
Hugh Owen Library, University of Wales Aberystwyth 219

Hull Campus, Lincoln University 262
Hull University 257
Hulton/Archive – Getty Images 345
Humanities Advanced Technologies &
    Information Institute (HATII) 406
Humberston, North East Lincolnshire 72
Hunslet, Leeds 60
Hunter Street Library, Buckingham
    University 228
Huntingdon, Cambridgeshire 16
Huyton, Knowsley 56
Hyde, Tameside 109
Hyman Kreitman Research Centre, Tate
    Library and Archive 384

I M Marsh LRC, Liverpool John Moores
    University 263
IBERS (Institute of Biological, Environmental
    and Rural Sciences) 345
Ibrox, Glasgow 150
Idea Store, Bow, Tower Hamlets 111
Idea Store, Canary Wharf, Tower Hamlets
    111
Idea Store, Chrisp Street, Tower Hamlets
    111
Idea Store, Whitechapel, Tower Hamlets
    110
IISS (International Institute for Strategic
    Studies) 350
ILAC Centre, Dublin 194
Ilford, Redbridge 83
Ilkeston, Derbyshire 28
Image Library, Historic Scotland 343
Immingham, North East Lincolnshire 72
Imperial College London 257
Imperial War Museum 345
Inches, Highland 155
Indian Institute Library, Oxford University
    284
Information Commons, Sheffield University
    301
Information Management, Faculty of
    Professional Studies, Thames Valley
    University 408
Information School, The, Sheffield
    University 408
Information Strategy Group, Liverpool John
    Moores University 406
InfoSource, Department for Business,
    Enterprise & Regulatory Reform (BERR)

see Department for Business, Innovation
    and Skills (BIS)
Ingleby Barwick, Stockton-on-Tees 101
Ings, Kingston upon Hull 53
Innerleithen, Scottish Borders 164
Institut français d'Écosse (French Institute)
    346
Institut français du Royaume-Uni 346
Institute for Animal Health 346
Institute for Chinese Studies Library,
    Oxford University 284
Institute for the Study of the Americas,
    London University 266
Institute of Actuaries 347
Institute of Advanced Legal Studies, London
    University 267
Institute of Archaeology, UCL, London
    University 274
Institute of Biological, Environmental and
    Rural Sciences (IBERS) 345
Institute of British Geographers see Royal
    Geographic Society
Institute of Cancer Research, London
    University 268
Institute of Chartered Accountants in
    England and Wales 347
Institute of Chartered Secretaries and
    Administrators 347
Institute of Child Health, UCL, London
    University 274
Institute of Classical Studies, London
    University 268
Institute of Clinical Research 347
Institute of Commonwealth Studies,
    London University 266
Institute of Conservation 348
Institute of Criminology, Cambridge
    University 232
Institute of Development Studies, Sussex
    University 258
Institute of Directors 348
Institute of Education, London University
    268
Institute of Germanic Studies, London
    University 266
Institute of Grassland and Environmental
    Research see Institute of Biological,
    Environmental and Rural Sciences (IBERS)
Institute of Historical Research, London
    University 268

Institute of Latin American Studies, London
    University 266
Institute of Materials, Minerals and Mining
    348
Institute of Neurology, UCL, London
    University 273
Institute of Occupational Medicine 349
Institute of Ophthalmology, UCL, London
    University 274
Institute of Orthopaedics, UCL, London
    University 274
Institute of Psychiatry, London University
    269
Institute of Psychoanalysis 349
Institute of United States Studies, London
    University 266
Institution of Civil Engineers 349
Institution of Engineering and Technology
    349
Institution of Mechanical Engineers 350
Institution of Occupational Safety and
    Health 350
Instituto Cervantes 350
Instituto Cervantes (Dublin) 396
International Institute for Strategic Studies
    (IISS), The 350
International Maritime Organization 351
Inverclyde 156
Invergordon, Highland 153
Inverness College, UHI Millennium Institute
    307
Inverness, Highland 155
Inverness-shire see Highland
Ipswich, Suffolk 103
Irvine, North Ayrshire 159
Isle of Anglesey see Anglesey, Isle of
Isle of Barra, Comhairle nan Eilean Siar 134
Isle of Benbecula, Comhairle nan Eilean Siar
    135
Isle of Harris, Comhairle nan Eilean Siar 135
Isle of Lewis, Comhairle nan Eilean Siar 135
Isle of Man 187
Isle of Man College 258
Isle of Man Family History Society 351
Isle of Man Parliament/Legislature of the Isle
    of Man 351
Isle of Skye 154
Isle of South Uist, Comhairle nan Eilean Siar
    134
Isle of Wight 48

Isleworth, Hounslow 47
Islington 49
Istituto Italiano di Cultura (Italian Cultural
    Institute) 351
Italian Cultural Institute (Istituto Italiano di
    Cultura) 351

J B Morrell and Raymond Burton Libraries,
    York University 316
J B Priestley Library, Bradford University
    226
James Cameron-Gifford, Nottingham
    University 281
James Hardiman Library, National
    University of Ireland, Galway 398
James Herriot Library, Glasgow University
    254
James Ireland Memorial Library, Glasgow
    University 254
James Joyce Library, University College
    Dublin 401
Jedburgh, Scottish Borders 165
Jersey 188
Jerwood Library of the Performing Arts,
    Trinity Laban 307
Jesus College, Cambridge University
    233
Jesus College, Oxford University 288
JET (Joint Education and Training) Library,
    Chester University 242
John Barnes, Islington 49
John F Parke Memorial Library, Omnibus
    Society, The 369
John Harvard, Southwark 98
John J Jennings, South Dublin 209
John Radcliffe Hospital, Oxford University
    286
John Rylands University Library, Manchester
    University 276
John Stearne Medical Library, Trinity
    College Dublin 401
Johnston, Cavan 191
Johnstone, Renfrewshire 163
Johnstown Castle Agricultural Research
    Centre, TEAGASC 400
Joint Services Command and Staff College
    352
Jordanhill Library, Strathclyde University
    304
Jordanstown, University of Ulster at 309

Jordanthorpe, Sheffield 91
Joule Library, Manchester University 276
Jubilee Campus, Nottingham University 280
Jubilee, Brighton 12
Jubilee, Coventry 24

Keble College, Oxford University 288
Keele University 258
Keith Axon Centre, Redbridge 84
Keith Donaldson Library, Hull University 257
Keith Pavitt Library, Sussex University 305
Keith, Moray 158
Kells, Meath 205
Kelso, Scottish Borders 165
Kempston, Bedford 7
Kendal, Cumbria 26
Kenmare, Kerry 198
Kennel Club, The 352
Kensal Rise, Brent 11
Kensington and Chelsea 50
Kent 51 see also Bexley, London Borough of, Bromley, Lewisham, Medway
Kent University 259
Kentish Town, Camden 17
Kerry 198
Kettering, Northamptonshire 75
Ketton, Rutland 87
Keynes Library, Cambridge Union Society, Cambridge University 229
Keynsham, Bath and North East Somerset 6
Kidderminster, Worcestershire 126
Kilbeggan, Westmeath 213
Kilburn, Brent 11
Kilburn, Camden 18
Kildare 199
Kildysart, Clare 191
Kilfinaghty, Clare 191
Kilkee, Clare 192
Kilkenny 200
Kilkenny City, Kilkenny 200
Killaloe, Clare 192
Killarney, Kerry 199
Killarney, Kerry 199
Killenaule, Tipperary 210
Killingworth, North Tyneside 83
Killorglin, Kerry 199
Killucan, Westmeath 214
Kilmacthomas, Waterford County 212
Kilmallock, Limerick County 203

Kilmarnock, East Ayrshire 139
Kilmihil, Clare 192
Kilrush, Clare 192
Kimberlin Library, De Montfort University 245
King's College Cambridge, Cambridge University 233
King's College, London University 269
King's Fund 352
King's Lynn, Norfolk 71
King's Manor Library, York University 316
King's Meadow Campus, Nottingham University 281
Kings Norton Library, Cranfield University 243
Kingsbridge, Devon 29
Kingsbury, Brent 11
Kingston Centre, Staffordshire 100
Kingston University 259
Kingston upon Hull 53
Kingston upon Thames 54
Kingston, Kingston upon Thames 54
Kingswood, South Gloucestershire 95
Kingswood, Southwark 98
Kingussie, Highland 155
Kinlochleven, Highland 156
Kinross, Perth and Kinross 160
Kirkby, Knowsley 56
Kirkcaldy, Fife 149
Kirkconnel, Dumfries and Galloway 136
Kirkcudbright, Dumfries and Galloway 136
Kirkintilloch, East Dunbartonshire 140
Kirklees 55
Kirkliston, Edinburgh 145
Kirkton, Dundee 139
Kirkwall, Orkney 160
Kirriemuir, Angus 132
Knightswood, Glasgow 150
Knowledge Centre, Health and Safety Executive 340
Knowsley 56
Knoydart, Highland 156
Kyle, Highland 153

Labour Party 352
Laceby, North East Lincolnshire 72
Ladbroke House, London Metropolitan University 264
Lady Margaret Hall, Oxford University 288

Lairg, Highland 153
Lambeth 57
Lambeth Archives 57
Lambeth Palace Library 353
Lampeter Campus, University of Wales
    Trinity St David 312
Lampeter, University of Wales see
    University of Wales Trinity St David
Lanarkshire see North Lanarkshire, South
    Lanarkshire
Lancashire 59 see also Blackburn with
    Darwen, Blackpool, Bolton, Bury,
    Oldham, Sefton, Wigan
Lancaster University 260
Lancaster, Centre for Ecology and
    Hydrology 328
Lancaster, Lancashire 59
Lanchester Library, Coventry University
    243
Lanesboro, Longford 204
Langholm, Dumfries and Galloway 136
Langney, East Sussex 35
Langside, Glasgow 150
Language and Speech Science Library, UCL,
    London University 274
Lanthorn, West Lothian 169
Laois 201
Larbert, Falkirk 148
Largs, North Ayrshire 159
Latin American Centre, St Antony's
    College, Oxford University 284
Latin American Studies Institute see
    Institute for the Study of the Americas,
    London University
Launceston, Cornwall 22
Law & Europa Library, Edinburgh University
    251
Law Commission 353
Law Library, Aberystwyth University 220
Law Library, Cardiff University 238
Law Library, Dundee University 247
Law Library, Exeter University 252
Law Library, Newcastle upon Tyne
    University 278
Law Library, Staffordshire University 303
Law Society 354
Lea Bridge, Waltham Forest 115
Leagrave, Luton 65
Leamington Spa, Warwickshire 118
Leatherhead, Surrey 106

Lee Library, Wolfson College, Cambridge
    University 236
Leeds 60
Leeds College of Music 260
Leeds Metropolitan University 260
Leeds Trinity & All Saints College 261
Leeds University 261
Leek, Staffordshire 99
Legal Information Centre, Department for
    Work and Pensions (DWP) 335
Legal Library, Foreign and Commonwealth
    Office 338
Legal Practice, Cardiff University 239
Leicester 60
Leicester University 261
Leicestershire 61 see also Leicester
Leigh, Wigan 121
Leighton Buzzard, Central Bedfordshire 19
Leith, Edinburgh 146
Leitrim 202
Leixlip, Kildare 200
Lennoxtown, East Dunbartonshire 141
Lenzie, East Dunbartonshire 141
Leominster, Herefordshire 45
Lerwick, Shetland Islands 165
Letterkenny, Donegal 194
Leven, Fife 149
Lewes, East Sussex 34
Lewis Carroll, Islington 49
Lewisham 62
Lews Castle College, UHI Millennium
    Institute 307
Lewsey, Luton 65
Leyland, Lancashire 59
Leyton, Waltham Forest 115
Leytonstone, Waltham Forest 115
Libraries NI (Northern Ireland Library
    Authority) 129
Library and Museum of Freemasonry 354
Library Council (An Chomhairle
    Leabharlanna) 393
Library for Iranian Studies 354
Library, Laban, Trinity Laban 307
Library Policy Team, DCMS 333
Library Support Unit, Highland 152
Library @ The Gate, Newham 70
Lichfield, Staffordshire 99
Liden, Swindon 108
Limerick City 202
Limerick County 202

Limerick, University of 402
Limpsfield, Sheffield 91
Linacre College, Oxford University 289
Lincoln Cathedral 354
Lincoln College, Oxford University 289
Lincoln University 261
Lincolnshire 62 see also North East
    Lincolnshire, North Lincolnshire
Lindley Library, Royal Horticultural Society
    377
Linen Hall Library, The 354
Liniclate, Comhairle nan Eilean Siar 135
Linlithgow, West Lothian 169
Linnean Society of London 355
Linwood, Renfrewshire 163
Lisdoonvarna, Clare 192
Liskeard, Cornwall 22
Lismore, Waterford County 212
Listowel, Kerry 199
Literacy Development, Lambeth 58
Literary and Philosophical Society of
    Newcastle upon Tyne 355
Liverpool 63
Liverpool Hope University 262
Liverpool Institute for Performing Arts 262
Liverpool John Moores University 263, 406
Liverpool University 263
Livingston Library, Edinburgh Napier
    University 250
Livingston, West Lothian 169
Llandaff Campus, University of Wales
    Institute, Cardiff 311
Llandrindod Wells, Powys 181,182
Llandudno, Conwy 176
Llanelli, Carmarthenshire 175
Llangefni, Isle of Anglesey 171
Llanrwst, Conwy 176
Llantwit Major, Vale of Glamorgan 185
Llyfrgell Genedlaethol Cymru (National
    Library of Wales) 363
Loanhead, Midlothian 157
Local History and Archives, Kerry 199
Local History Centre, East Lothian 143
Local History Centre, Walsall 113
Local History, Southwark 98
Local History/Reference, Sligo 208
Local Studies and Archives, Camden 18
Local Studies, Clare 192
Local Studies, Fingal 196
Local Studies, Midlothian 157

Local Studies, Scottish Borders 165
Loch Leven, Perth and Kinross 160
Lochaber College, UHI Millennium Institute
    307
Lochcarron, Highland 154
Lochee, Dundee 139
Lochmaben, Dumfries and Galloway 136
Lochside, Dumfries and Galloway 136
Lochthorn, Dumfries and Galloway 136
Lochwinnoch, Renfrewshire 163
Lockerbie, Dumfries and Galloway 136
London Business School, London University
    270
London Chamber of Commerce and
    Industry 355
London College of Communication,
    University of the Arts London 310
London College of Fashion, University of
    the Arts London 310
London Contemporary Dance School 264
London Library 355
London Metropolitan Archives 356
London Metropolitan University 264, 406
London School of Economics and Political
    Science, London University 270
London School of Hygiene & Tropical
    Medicine, London University 270
London School of Jewish Studies, London
    University 270
London see Barnet, Brent, Camden, Ealing,
    Enfield, Greenwich, Hackney,
    Hammersmith and Fulham, Haringey,
    Hounslow, Islington, Kensington and
    Chelsea, Lambeth, Lewisham, London,
    City of, Merton, Newham, Redbridge,
    Richmond upon Thames, Southwark,
    Tower Hamlets, Upper Norwood Joint
    Library, Waltham Forest, Wandsworth,
    Westminster
London South Bank University 265
London Transport Museum 356
London University 266
London, City of 63
London, University College see University
    College London
Long Knowle, Wolverhampton 125
Longford 203
Longhill, Kingston upon Hull 53
Longniddry, East Lothian 142
Longsight, Manchester 66

Looe, Cornwall 22
Lord Coutanche Library, Société Jersiaise 383
Lord Louis, Isle of Wight 48
Lordshill, Southampton 97
Lostwithiel, Cornwall 22
Loughborough University 275, 406
Loughborough, Leicestershire 61
Loughboy, Kilkenny 201
Loughrea, Galway 198
Louth 204
Low Hill, Wolverhampton 125
Lowestoft, Suffolk 103
LSE (London School of Economics and Political Science) 270
Lucan, South Dublin 209
Lucy Cavendish College, Cambridge University 233
Lumley Study Centre, Royal College of Surgeons of England 375
Luton 64
Lymm, Warrington 117

Macclesfield, Cheshire East 20
Macmillan Cancer Support 356
Maesteg, Bridgend 173
Magdalen College, Oxford University 289
Magdalene College, Cambridge University 233
Magee, University of Ulster at 309
Maida Vale, Westminster 120
Maidenhead, Windsor and Maidenhead 122
Maidstone Campus, University for the Creative Arts 244
Maidstone, Kent 52
Maitland Robinson Library, Downing College, Cambridge University 231
Malahide, Fingal 196
Mallaig, Highland 156
Malvern, Worcestershire 127
Management Information Resource Centre, Cranfield University 243
Manchester 65 see also Salford
Manchester Metropolitan University 275, 407
Manchester University 276
Manor Park, Newham 70
Manor, Sheffield 91
Mansfield College, Oxford University 289
Mansfield, Nottinghamshire 77

Manx National Heritage 357
Map Collections, National Library of Scotland 362
March, Cambridgeshire 16
Marcus Garvey, Haringey 43
Marfleet, Kingston upon Hull 53
Marine Biological Association 357
Market Harborough, Leicestershire 62
Marks Gate, Barking and Dagenham 3
Markyate, Barking and Dagenham 3
Marlow, Buckinghamshire 14
Marsh Farm and Home Library Service Unit, Luton 65
Marx Memorial Library 357
Maryhill, Glasgow 151
Marylebone Campus, Westminster University 314
Marylebone Cricket Club 357
Marylebone, Westminster 120
Matlock, Derbyshire 27
Maughan Library, King's College London 269
Mayfair, Westminster 120
Mayfield, Cork City 193
Mayfield, East Sussex 35
Mayfield, Midlothian 157
Maynooth, Kildare 200
Mayo 206
McDonald, Edinburgh 146
McGowin Library, Pembroke College, Oxford University 290
Meadowbank, Falkirk 148
Mearns, East Renfrewshire 144
Meath 204
Media, Information and Communications, Dept of Applied Sciences, London Metropolitan University 406
Medical Libraries, Edinburgh University 251
Medical Library, Aberdeen University 219
Medical Library, Bristol University 227
Medical Library, National University of Ireland, Galway 398
Medical Research Council (MRC) 358
Medway 66
Melrose Campus, Edinburgh Napier University 250
Melrose, Scottish Borders 165
Melton Mowbray, Leicestershire 62
Menai Bridge, Isle of Anglesey 171
Mendip and Sedgemoor, Somerset 95

Menstrie, Clackmannanshire 134
Menzieshill, Dundee 139
Mercer Library, Royal College of Surgeons in Ireland 399
Merchiston Library, Edinburgh Napier University 250
Merseyside see Knowsley, Liverpool, St Helens, Sefton
Merthyr Tydfil 178
Merton 67
Merton College, Oxford University 289
Met Office 358
Middlesbrough 68
Middlesex see Brent, Ealing, Enfield, Harrow, Hillingdon, Hounslow, Richmond upon Thames, Surrey
Middlesex University 276
Middleton, Rochdale 86
Midlothian 156
Midsomer Norton, Bath and North East Somerset 7
Mildenhall, Suffolk 104
Mildmay, Islington 49
Miles Platting, Manchester 66
Milford Haven, Pembrokeshire 181
Mill Hill, Barnet 5
Mill Lane Library, Department of Land Economy, Cambridge University 231
Millbrook, Southampton 97
Millennium, Norfolk 71
Milngavie, East Dunbartonshire 141
Milton Keynes 68
Milton of Campsie, East Dunbartonshire 141
Milton, Glasgow 151
Miltown Malbay, Clare 192
Minet, Lambeth 57
Ministry of Defence 358
Ministry of Justice 358
Mitcham, Merton 67
Mitchell, Glasgow 150
Moate, Westmeath 214
Mobile and Home Service, Walsall 114
Mobile and Housebound Readers Service, Hammersmith and Fulham 42
Mobile Service, Kildare 199
Mobile Service, Roscommon 207
Mobile Service, South Dublin 209
Mobile Services, Fingal 197
Mobile Services, Lincolnshire 63
Mobile Services, Manchester 66
Mobile Services, Reading 82
Mobile Services, Sheffield 91
Mobiles and Home Service, Kirklees 55
Mobiles, Edinburgh 147
Mobiles, Kerry 199
Mobiles, Renfrewshire 163
Moffat, Dumfries and Galloway 136
Mold, Flintshire 177
Molesey, Surrey 106
Monaghan 205
Monifieth, Angus 132
Monmouth, Monmouthshire 179
Monmouthshire 179 see also Blaenau Gwent
Montrose, Angus 132
Moorepark Food Research Centre, TEAGASC 400
Moorfields Eye Hospital, London University 274
Moorgate, London Metropolitan University 265
Moorside Community, Bury 15
Moray 158
Moray College, Elgin, UHI Millennium Institute 308
Moray House Library, Edinburgh University 251
Morden, Merton 67
Morecambe, Lancashire 59
Moredun, Edinburgh 146
Morningside, Edinburgh 146
Morpeth, Northumberland 75
Morrab Library 359
Morriston, Swansea 183
Motherwell, North Lanarkshire 159
Mount Pleasant, Dudley 32
Mountain Ash, Rhondda Cynon Taf 182
Mountbatten Library, Southampton Solent University 301
Mountmellick, Laois 201
Mountrath, Laois 201
Moving Image and Sound Collections, Wellcome Library 387
Moyderwell, Kerry 199
MRC (Medical Research Council) 358
Muir of Ord, Highland 154
Muirhouse, Edinburgh 146
Mullingar, Westmeath 214
Multimedia Library, Institut français du Royaume-Uni 346

Muniment Room and Library, Westminster
    Abbey 387
Murray Edwards College, Cambridge
    University 232
Murray Library, Sunderland University 304
Museum of London 359
Music, Cardiff University 239
Musselburgh, East Lothian 141

N4, Islington 50
Naas, Kildare 200
NAFC Marine Centre, UHI Millennium
    Institute 308
Nairn, Highland 156
Nairnshire see Highland
National Aerospace Library 359
National Archives (Republic of Ireland)
    396
National Archives, The 359
National Army Museum 360
National Art Library 360
National Assembly for Wales 360
National Centre for Languages (CILT) 330
National Children's Bureau 360
National Coal Mining Museum for England
    361
National College of Art and Design 396
National Gallery 361
National Gallery of Ireland 396
National Heritage Library 361
National Institute for Health and Clinical
    Excellence (NICE) 361
National Institute for Medical Research
    (Medical Research Council) 362
National Institute of Economic and Social
    Research 362
National Library of Ireland 397
National Library of Scotland 362
National Library of Wales: Llyfrgell
    Genedlaethol Cymru 363
National Maritime Museum 363
National Media Museum 363
National Meteorological Archive, Met
    Office 358
National Monuments Record Centre,
    English Heritage 337
National Museum Wales (Amgueddfa
    Cymru) 320
National Museums Scotland 364
National Oceanographic Library,

    Southampton University 302
National Oceanography Centre 364
National Photographic Archive, National
    Library of Ireland 397
National Physical Laboratory 364
National Policing Improvement Agency 365
National Portrait Gallery 365
National Railway Museum 365
National STEM Centre 365
National Union of Teachers 366
National University of Ireland, Galway 398
National University of Ireland, Maynooth
    398
National War Museum, National Museums
    Scotland 364
Natural England 366
Natural Environment Research Council
    (NERC) 371
Natural History Museum 366
Navan, Meath 205
Neasden, Brent 11
Neath Port Talbot 180
Neath see Neath Port Talbot
Neath, Neath Port Talbot 180
Neilston, East Renfrewshire 144
Nelson Library, Staffordshire University 303
Nelson, Lancashire 59
Nenagh, Tipperary 211
NERC (Natural Environment Research
    Council) 371
Netherlee, East Renfrewshire 144
Network Rail Infrastructure Ltd 366
New Addington, Croydon 25
New College Library, Edinburgh University
    251
New College, Oxford University 290
New Hall, Cambridge University see
    Murray Edwards College, Cambridge
    University
New Invention, Walsall 114
New Kershaw, Bury 15
New Malden, Kingston upon Thames 54
New Malden, Merton 68
New Ross, Wexford 215
Newark-on-Trent, Nottinghamshire 78
Newbridge, Kildare 200
Newbury, West Berkshire 119
Newcastle University 277
Newcastle upon Tyne 69
Newcastle, Staffordshire 99

Newcastlewest, Limerick County 203
Newfield Green, Sheffield 91
Newham 69
Newhaven, East Sussex 35
Newington, Edinburgh 146
Newington, Southwark 98
Newland, Lincolnshire 62
Newman University College 278
Newmarket, Suffolk 104
Newmarket-on-Fergus, Clare 192
Newnham College, Cambridge University
    234
Newport 180
Newport, Isle of Wight 48
Newport, University of Wales 311
Newquay, Cornwall 22
Newsam Library, Institute of Education,
    London University 268
Newton Abbot, Devon 30
Newton Park Library, Bath Spa University
    222
Newton Stewart, Dumfries and Galloway
    136
Newtongrange, Midlothian 157
Newtown, Powys 182
NHS Health Scotland 367
NHS National Services Scotland 367
NICE (National Institute for Health and
    Clinical Excellence) 361
Nightingale Centre, Kingston University 259
Ninewells, Dundee University 247
Niton, Isle of Wight 48
Nobber, Meath 205
Nobles Hall, Isle of Man 188
Norbury, Croydon 25
Norfolk 70
Norris Green, Liverpool 63
North Ayrshire 158
North Berwick, East Lothian 142
North Chingford, Waltham Forest 115
North East Lincolnshire 72
North End, Portsmouth 82
North Finchley, Barnet 5
North Highland College, UHI Millennium
    Institute 308
North Inch, Perth and Kinross 161
North Kensington, Kensington and Chelsea
    50
North Lanarkshire 159
North Lincolnshire 73

North Shields, North Tyneside 73
North Somerset 73
North Swindon, Swindon 108
North Tyneside 73
North Woolwich, Newham 70
North Yorkshire 74
North, Islington 50
Northallerton, North Yorkshire 74
Northampton University 278
Northampton, Northamptonshire 75
Northamptonshire 75
Northern General Hospital, Sheffield
    University 301
Northern Ireland Assembly 367
Northern Ireland Library Authority 129
Northern Ireland Office 367
Northern School of Contemporary Dance
    278
Northern Site, British Library 324
Northumberland 75 see also Gateshead,
    Newcastle upon Tyne
Northumbria University 279, 407
Northwich, Cheshire West and Chester 21
Norton, Stockton-on-Tees 102
Norwich University College of the Arts 279
Norwich, Norfolk 70
Nottingham 76
Nottingham Trent University 279
Nottingham University 280
Nottinghamshire 77 see also Nottingham
Nuffield College, Oxford University 290
Nuneaton, Warwickshire 118
Nunhead, Southwark 98
Nunsthorpe, North East Lincolnshire 72
Nursing and Healthcare, Cardiff University
    239
Nursing and Midwifery, Cardiff University
    239
Nursing and Midwifery, Fife Campus,
    Dundee University 247

Oak Park Research Centre, TEAGASC 400
Oakham, Rutland 87
Oban, Argyll and Bute 133
Offaly 206
Office for National Statistics 368
Office of Fair Trading 368
Office of Gas and Electricity Markets
    (OFGEM) 369
Office of Rail Regulation 368

Office of the Parliamentary and Health
  Service Ombudsman (Office of the
  Parliamentary Commissioner for
  Administration and Health Service
  Commissioner for England) 368
OFGEM (Office of Gas and Electricity
  Markets) 369
OFWAT (Water Services Regulation
  Authority) 386
Oireachtas Library & Research Service 398
Old College Library, Aberystwyth
  University 220
Old Library and College Archives,
  Magdalene College, Cambridge
  University 233
Old Library, Exeter University 252
Old Library, Jesus College, Cambridge
  University 233
Old Malden, Kingston upon Thames 54
Old Windsor, Windsor and Maidenhead 123
Oldcastle, Meath 205
Oldham 78
Oldmeldrum, Aberdeenshire 131
Omnibus Society, The 369
Omnibus, Surrey 105
Onchan, Isle of Man 188
Open University 281
Opus II, Surrey 105
Oranmore, Galway 198
Orchard Learning Resources Centre,
  Birmingham University 224
Ore, East Sussex 35
Orford, Warrington 117
Oriel College, Oxford University 290
Oriental Institute Library, Oxford University
  285
Orkney 160
Orkney College, UHI Millennium Institute
  308
Orkney Islands see Orkney
Ormiston, East Lothian 142
Ormskirk Clinical Library, Central
  Lancashire University 240
Ornithology and Rothschild Library, Natural
  History Museum 366
Orpington, Bromley 12
Orton, Peterborough 79
Osidge, Barnet 5
Osterley, Hounslow 47
Oswestry, Shropshire 93

Owen Library, Swansea Metropolitan
  University 305
Oxford Brookes University 281
Oxford University 282
Oxford, Centre for Ecology and Hydrology
  328
Oxford, Oxfordshire 79
Oxfordshire 78
Oxgangs, Edinburgh 146
Oxstalls Learning Centre, Gloucestershire
  University 254
Oxted, Surrey 107
Oystermouth, Swansea 183

Paddington, Westminster 120
Padgate, Warrington 117
Padstow, Cornwall 22
Page Memorial Library, English-Speaking
  Union 337
Page Moss, Knowsley 56
Paignton, Torbay 110
Paisley, Renfrewshire 162
Palace Green Section, Durham University
  247
Palmer Park, Reading 85
Palmerstown, South Dublin 209
Par, Cornwall 22
Paragon House LRC, Thames Valley
  University 306
Park Campus, Gloucestershire University
  254
Park Campus, Northampton University 278
Park, Sheffield 92
Parker Library, Corpus Christi College,
  Cambridge University 230
Parkhead, Glasgow 151
Parson Cross, Sheffield 92
Partick, Glasgow 151
Paul Hamlyn Library, British Museum 326
Paul Hamlyn LRC, Thames Valley University
  306
Paulsgrove, Portsmouth 82
Peacehaven, East Sussex 35
Peckham, Southwark 98
Peebles, Scottish Borders 164
Peeblesshire see Scottish Borders
Pelsall, Walsall 114
Pembroke College, Cambridge University
  234
Pembroke College, Oxford University 290

Pembroke Dock, Pembrokeshire 181
Pembrokeshire 180
Pen Lloyd, Leicestershire 62
Penarth, Vale of Glamorgan 185
Pencoed, Bridgend 173
Pendeford, Wolverhampton 125
Pendlebury Library of Music, Cambridge University 231
Pendleton, Salford 88
Pendre, Ceredigion 175
Penicuik, Midlothian 156
Penketh, Warrington 117
Penn, Wolverhampton 125
Penrith, Cumbria 26
Penryn, Cornwall 22
Penzance, Cornwall 22
Pepys Library, Magdalene College, Cambridge University 234
Perranporth, Cornwall 22
Perry Library, London South Bank University 265
Perth and Kinross 160
Perth College, UHI Millennium Institute 308
Perth, Perth and Kinross 160
Perthshire see Highland
Perton, Staffordshire 99
Peterborough 79
Peterborough, Anglia Ruskin University 221
Peterhouse, Cambridge University 234
Pevensey Bay, East Sussex 35
Pheasey, Walsall 114
Philosophy Library, Oxford University 285
Physical Sciences Library, Aberystwyth University 220
Physics Library, Bristol University 227
Piershill, Edinburgh 146
Pilkington Library, Loughborough University 275
Pimlico, Westminster 120
PIRA International 369
Pirbright Library, Institute for Animal Health 346
Pitlochry, Perth and Kinross 161
Pittville Learning Centre, Gloucestershire University 255
Plaistow, Newham 70
Pleck, Walsall 114
Plockton, Highland 154
Plumstead, Greenwich 39
Plunkett Foundation 369

Plymouth 80
Plymouth Proprietary Library 369
Plymouth University 294
Plymouth, University College St Mark and St John 293
Poetry Library 370
Polegate, East Sussex 35
Polish Library 370
Pollards Hill, Merton 67
Pollok, Glasgow 151
Pollokshaws, Glasgow 151
Pollokshields, Glasgow 151
Ponteland, Northumberland 76
Pontypool, Torfaen 184
Pontypridd, Rhondda Cynon Taf 182
Poole 80
Port Seton, East Lothian 142
Port Talbot, Neath Port Talbot 180
Port William, Dumfries and Galloway 136
Portarlington, Laois 202
Porthcawl, Bridgend 173
Porthmadog, Gwynedd 178
Portico Library and Gallery, The 370
Portlaoise, Laois 201
Portlaw, Waterford County 212
Portobello, Edinburgh 146
Portree, Highland 154
Portsea, Portsmouth 82
Portsmouth 81
Portsmouth University 294
Portswood, Southampton 97
Portumna, Galway 198
Possilpark, Glasgow 151
Powys 181
Prescot, Knowsley 56
Preston, Brent 11
Preston, Lancashire 58
Prestonpans, East Lothian 142
Prestwich, Bury 14
Priaulx, Guernsey 187
Prison Library Service, Roscommon 208
Prison Service, Staffordshire 100
Proudman Oceanographic Laboratory see National Oceanography Centre
Prudhoe, Northumberland 76
Pumpherston, West Lothian 169
Purley, Croydon 25
Putney, Wandsworth 116
Putnoe, Bedford 7
Pyle, Bridgend 173

Qinetiq 370
Quakers (Religious Society of Friends) 370
Queen Margaret University, Edinburgh 294
Queen Mary (West Smithfield), London
    University 271
Queen Mary (Whitechapel), London
    University 271
Queen Mary, London University 271
Queen Mother Library, Aberdeen
    University 219
Queen's Campus, Durham University 247
Queen's College, The, Oxford University
    290
Queen's Library, Bristol University 228
Queen's Medical Centre, Nottingham
    University 280
Queen's Park, Westminster 120
Queen's University of Belfast 294
Queens Crescent, Camden 18
Queens' College, Cambridge University
    234
Queenwood, Brighton University 227
Quincentenary College, Jesus College,
    Cambridge University 233

Radcliffe Science Library, Oxford University
    285
Radcliffe, Bury 14
Radford, Coventry 24
Radzinowicz Library of Criminology,
    Cambridge University 232
Ralston, Renfrewshire 163
Ramsbottom, Bury 14
Ramsey, Isle of Man 188
Rathcairn, Meath 205
Rathdowney, Laois 202
Rathfarnham, South Dublin 209
Ratho, Edinburgh 146
Ravensbourne 294
Ravensbourne College of Design and
    Communication see Ravensbourne
Rawtenstall, Lancashire 59
Raynes Park, Merton 68
RCSI Library, Royal College of Surgeons in
    Ireland 399
Reader Development, Lambeth 58
Reading 82
Reading University 295
Rectory, Barking and Dagenham 3
Redbridge 83

Redcar and Cleveland 84
Redcar, Redcar and Cleveland 85
Redditch, Worcestershire 127
Redhill, Surrey 107
Redruth, Cornwall 22
Reference and Information Centre,
    Bridgend 173
Reference Library, Richmond upon Thames
    86
Reference Library, Westminster 120
Refugee Studies Centre, Oxford University
    285
Regent Campus, Westminster University
    314
Regent's Park College, Oxford University
    290
Regents Park, Camden 18
Reid, Aberdeen University 219
Reigate, Surrey 106
Religious Society of Friends in Britain
    (Quakers) 370
Renfrew, Renfrewshire 163
Renfrewshire 162 see also East
    Renfrewshire, Inverclyde
Representative Church Body 399
Research Councils UK 371
Resources and Development, Hartlepool 44
Retford, Nottinghamshire 78
Rhodes House, Oxford University 283
Rhondda Cynon Taf 182
Rhosllanerchrugog, Wrexham 185
Rhyl, Denbighshire 176
Richmond upon Thames 85
Richmond, Richmond upon Thames 85
Richview Library, University College Dublin
    402
Riddrie, Glasgow 151
Ringmer, East Sussex 35
Risca, Caerphilly 174
Riseholme Campus, Lincoln University 262
Riverbank, Kildare 199
RNIB National Library Service 372
RNID 372
Robert Gordon University, Aberdeen 295,
    407
Robert Jeyes, Barking and Dagenham 3
Robinson College, Cambridge University
    235
Robinson Library, Newcastle upon Tyne
    University 277

Rochdale 86

Rochester Campus, University for the
  Creative Arts 244

Rockefeller Medical Library, The National
  Hospital, UCL, London University 273

Roehampton University 295

Romford, Havering 44

Ronald Cohen Dental Library, Birmingham
  Dental Hospital, Birmingham 225

Roscommon 207

Roscrea, Tipperary 211

Rose Bruford College of Theatre and
  Performance 296

Roseberry Billingham, Stockton-on-Tees
  102

Rosemary Murray Library, Murray Edwards
  College, Cambridge University 234

Roseworth, Stockton-on-Tees 102

Roslin, Midlothian 157

ROSPA (Royal Society for the Prevention of
  Accidents) 379

Ross-on-Wye, Herefordshire 45

Rothamsted Library – Rothamsted Research
  372

Rotherham 87

Rotherhithe, Southwark 98

Rothermere American Institute, Oxford
  University 286

Rothesay, Argyll and Bute 133

Roxburghshire see Scottish Borders

Royal Academy of Arts 372

Royal Academy of Dramatic Art 296

Royal Academy of Music 296

Royal Aeronautical Society see National
  Aerospace Library

Royal Agricultural College 297

Royal Air Force College 373

Royal Air Force Museum 373

Royal Astronomical Society 373

Royal Automobile Club 373

Royal Botanic Garden, Edinburgh 374

Royal Botanic Gardens, Kew 374

Royal Brompton Campus, Imperial College
  London 258

Royal College of Art 297

Royal College of Music 297

Royal College of Nursing of the United
  Kingdom 297

Royal College of Physicians and Surgeons of
  Glasgow 374

Royal College of Physicians of Edinburgh
  374

Royal College of Physicians of London
  375

Royal College of Psychiatrists 375

Royal College of Surgeons in Ireland 399

Royal College of Surgeons of England 375

Royal College of Veterinary Surgeons 375

Royal Commission on the Ancient and
  Historical Monuments of Wales 376

Royal Courts of Justice 376

Royal Dublin Society 399

Royal Engineers Museum, Archives and
  Library 376

Royal Entomological Society 376

Royal Free Medical Library, UCL, London
  University 273

Royal Geographical Society (with the
  Institute of British Geographers) 376

Royal Hallamshire Hospital, Sheffield
  University 301

Royal Holloway, London University 271

Royal Horticultural Society 377

Royal Institute of British Architects 377

Royal Institute of International Affairs 377

Royal Institute of Navigation 378

Royal Institution of Chartered Surveyors
  378

Royal Institution of Great Britain 378

Royal Institution of Naval Architects 378

Royal Irish Academy 399

Royal Military Academy Sandhurst 379

Royal National Orthopaedic Hospital, UCL,
  London University 274

Royal National Throat, Nose and Ear
  Hospital, UCL, London University 273

Royal Northern College of Music 297

Royal Pharmaceutical Society of Great
  Britain 379

Royal Photographic Society Collection,
  National Media Museum 363

Royal Scottish Academy of Music and
  Drama 298

Royal Shrewsbury Hospital, Staffordshire
  University 303

Royal Society 379

Royal Society for the Prevention of
  Accidents (ROSPA) 379

Royal Society of Chemistry 379

Royal Society of Medicine 379

Royal Statistical Society 380
Royal Town Planning Institute 380
Royal Veterinary College, London
    University 271
Royal Welsh College of Music and Drama
    298
Royston, Glasgow 151
RSA 380
Rugby, Warwickshire 118
Runcorn, Halton 41
Rush Green, Barking and Dagenham 3
Rushall, Walsall 114
Ruskin College 298
Rutherford Appleton Laboratory, Science
    and Technology Facilities Council 381
Ruthin, Denbighshire 176
Rutland 87
Ryde, Isle of Wight 48
Rye, East Sussex 35
Ryhall, Rutland 87

Sabhal Mòr Ostaig, UHI Millennium
    Institute 308
SAC Aberdeen Library, Scottish Agricultural
    College 300
SAC Auchincruive Library, Scottish
    Agricultural College 300
Sackler Library, Oxford University 285
Sainsbury Library, Oxford University 285
St Agnes, Cornwall 22
St Albans, Hertfordshire 46
St Andrew Street Library, Robert Gordon
    University 295
St Andrews University 298
St Andrews, Fife 149
St Anne's College, Oxford University 291
St Anne's, Lancashire 60
St Antony's College, Oxford University 291
St Augustine's Library, Canterbury Christ
    Church University College 237
St Austell, Cornwall 22
St Benet's Hall, Oxford University 291
St Catharine's College, Cambridge
    University 235
St Catherine's College, Oxford University
    291
St Columb, Cornwall 22
St Cross College, Oxford University 291
St Deiniol's Residential Library see
    Gladstone's Library

St Dennis, Cornwall 22
St Edmund Hall, Oxford University 291
St Edmund's College, Cambridge University
    235
St Fagans: National History Museum 381
St George's Library, Sheffield University
    301
St George's, London University 272
St Helens 87
St Helier, Jersey 188
St Hilda's College, Oxford University 292
St Hugh's College, Oxford University 292
St Ives, Cambridgeshire 16
St Ives, Cornwall 22
St James's, Westminster 120
St John's College, Cambridge University
    235
St John's College, Oxford University 292
St John's Wood, Westminster 120
St Just, Cornwall 22
St Keverne, Cornwall 22
St Luke's Campus, Exeter University 252
St Mary's Campus, Imperial College
    London 258
St Mary's Mill, Scottish Borders 165
St Mary's Road LRC, Thames Valley
    University 306
St Mary's University College Twickenham
    299
St Neots, Cambridgeshire 16
St Pancras, Camden 18
St Peter Port, Guernsey 187
St Peter's College, Oxford University 292
St Peter's House, Brighton University 227
St Peter's Library, Sunderland University
    304
St Thomas, Devon 30
St Thomas' Campus, King's College London
    269
Saison Poetry Library 370
Sale, Trafford 112
Salford 88
Salford University 299
Salisbury, Wiltshire 122
Salomons Hayloft Library, Canterbury
    Christ Church University College 237
Salomons Mansion Library, Canterbury
    Christ Church University College 237
Saltash, Cornwall 22
Saltcoats, North Ayrshire 159

Saltire Centre, Glasgow Caledonian University 253
Sandbach, Cheshire East 19
Sanderstead, Croydon 25
Sandown, Isle of Wight 48
Sands End, Hammersmith and Fulham 42
Sandwell 88
Sanquhar, Dumfries and Galloway 136
Sauchie, Clackmannanshire 134
Scarborough Campus, Hull University 257
Scarborough, North Yorkshire 75
Scariff, Clare 192
Scartho, North East Lincolnshire 72
School Library Service, Staffordshire 100
School of Community and Health Sciences, City University London 243
School of Computing, Engineering and Information Science, Northumbria University 407
School of Computing, Mathematical and Information Sciences, Brighton University 405
School of Education, Ulster University 408
School of Informatics, City University 405
School of Information and Library Studies, University College Dublin 405
School of Oriental and African Studies, London University 272
School of Pharmacy, London University 272
School of Slavonic and East European Studies, UCL, London University 273
Schools Library Service, East Sussex 36
Schools Library Service, Portsmouth 81
Schools of Nursing, Nottingham University 281
Science and Engineering Library, Trinity College Dublin 401
Science and Society Picture Library 364, 365, 382
Science and Technology Facilities Council (STFC) 381
Science Fiction Foundation Collection 381
Science Libraries, Edinburgh University 251
Science Library, Bangor University 222
Science Museum Library 381
Science, Cardiff University 239
Scone, Perth and Kinross 160
Scott Polar Research Institute, Cambridge University 235
Scottish Agricultural College 299

Scottish Borders 163
Scottish Enterprise 382
Scottish Government 382
Scottish Health Service Centre, Health Management Library 341
Scottish Marine Institute, UHI Millennium Institute 313
Scottish Natural Heritage 382
Scottish Parliament 383
Scunthorpe, North Lincolnshire 73
Seaford, East Sussex 35
Sean Lemass, Clare 192
Search Engine, National Railway Museum 365
Sedgeley Park, Bury 15
Sedgley, Dudley 31
Sefton 89
Selkirk, Scottish Borders 165
Selkirkshire see Scottish Borders
Selsdon, Croydon 25
Selwyn College, Cambridge University 235
Senate House Library, London University 266
Senghennydd, Cardiff University 239
Service Development, Glasgow 151
Sevenoaks, Kent 52
Sgitheanach see Isle of Skye
Shakespeare Institute Library, Birmingham University 225
Shankill, Dún Laoghaire-Rathdown 195
Shanklin, Isle of Wight 48
Shannon, Clare 192
Shawbost, Comhairle nan Eilean Siar 135
Sheffield 90
Sheffield Hallam University 300
Sheffield University 300, 408
Shefford, Central Bedfordshire 19
Shepherds Bush, Hammersmith and Fulham 42
Shepley, Kirklees 55
Sheppard Library, Middlesex University 276
Sheppard-Worlock Library, Liverpool Hope University 262
Shepway-Folkestone Library, Kent 52
Shetland College, UHI Millennium Institute 308
Shetland Islands 165
Shetland, Shetland Islands 165
Shettleston, Glasgow 151
Shire Hall, Staffordshire 99

Shirley, Croydon 25
Shirley, Southampton 97
Shoe Lane, London, City of 64
Shoreditch, Hackney 40
Shrewsbury, Shropshire 93
Shropshire 92 see also Telford and Wrekin
Sibbald Library, Royal College of Physicians
    of Edinburgh 374
Sibthorp Library, Bishop Grosseteste
    College 225
Sidcup, Bexley 7
Sidmouth, Devon 30
Sidney Sussex College, Cambridge
    University 236
Sighthill, Edinburgh 146
Signet Library 383
Silwood Park Campus, Imperial College
    London 258
Sion Hill, Bath Spa University 222
Sir E Scott School, Comhairle nan Eilean
    Siar 135
Sir Herbert Duthie, Cardiff University   239
Sir Kenneth Green Library, Manchester
    Metropolitan University 275
Sir Michael Cobham Library, Bournemouth
    University 225
Sir Sydney Camm Centre, Kingston
    University 260
Sittingbourne, Kent 52
Skelmersdale, Lancashire 60
Skerries, Fingal 197
Skirlaugh, East Riding of Yorkshire 33
Slamannan, Falkirk 148
Slane, Meath 205
Sleaford, Lincolnshire 63
Sligo 208
Slough 93
SLS, Camden 18
Smethwick, Sandwell 89
Smurfit Graduate School of Business,
    University College Dublin 402
Social Sciences, Oxford University 286
Société Jersiaise 383
Society for Cooperation in Russian and
    Soviet Studies 383
Society of Antiquaries of London 384
Society of Genealogists 384
Solihull 93
Somerset 94 see also Bath and North East
    Somerset, North Somerset

Somerville College, Oxford University   292
South Ayrshire 166
South Chingford, Waltham Forest 115
South Cross, Bury 15
South Dublin 208
South Friern, Barnet 6
South Gloucestershire 95
South Kensington Campus, Imperial College
    London 257
South Lambeth, Lambeth 57
South Lanarkshire 166
South Norwood, Croydon 25
South Queensferry, Edinburgh 147
South Shields, South Tyneside 96
South Somerset, Somerset 95
South Tyneside 96
South Wales Miners' Library, Swansea
    University 306
South Walsall, Walsall 114
South Woodford, Redbridge 84
South, Islington 50
Southall, Ealing 33
Southampton 96
Southampton Solent University 301
Southampton University 301
Southcote, Reading 83
Southend, Southend on Sea 97
Southend-on-Sea 97
Southey, Sheffield 92
Southport, Sefton 90
Southwark 97
Sowton, Devon 29
Special Collections, Birmingham University
    224
Special Collections, UCL, London
    University 274
Special Libraries and Archives, Aberdeen
    University 219
Spennymoor, Durham 32
SPICe (Scottish Parliament Information
    Centre) 383
Spring Vale, Wolverhampton 125
Springburn, Glasgow 151
Springfield, Kent 51
SPRU (Science and Technology Policy
    Research) – The Keith Pavitt Library,
    Sussex University 305
Spurgeon's College 302
Squire Law Library, Cambridge University
    229

Stadium, Kingston upon Hull 53
Stafford, Staffordshire 99
Staffordshire 98 see also Stoke-on-Trent
Staffordshire University 302
Staines, Surrey 107
Stamford Hill, Hackney 40
Stanground, Peterborough 80
Stannington, Sheffield 92
Stapledon Library and Information Service
    (IBERS) 345
Steel City Sheffield, Department for Work
    and Pensions 335
Stevenage, Hertfordshire 46
STFC (Science and Technology Facilities
    Council) 381
Stillorgan, Dún Laoghaire-Rathdown 195
Stirling 166
Stirling University 303
Stock Services, Lambeth 58
Stockbridge Village, Knowsley 56
Stockbridge, Edinburgh 147
Stockport 100
Stocksbridge, Sheffield 92
Stockton Heath, Warrington 117
Stockton-on-Tees 101
Stoke Newington, Hackney 40
Stoke, Coventry 23
Stoke-on-Trent 102
Stopsley, Luton 65
Stornoway, Comhairle nan Eilean Siar 134
Stourbridge, Dudley 31
Stowmarket, Suffolk 104
Stradbally, Laois 202
Strand Campus, King's College, London
    269
Stranraer, Dumfries and Galloway 136
Stratford, East London University 249
Stratford, Newham 69
Stratford, Warwickshire 118
Strathclyde University 303, 408
Strathearn, Perth and Kinross 161
Streatham, Lambeth 58
Streetly, Walsall 114
Stretford, Trafford 112
Strokestown, Roscommon 207
Strood, Medway 67
Stroud, Gloucestershire 38
Student and Learning Support, Sunderland
    University 304
Sudbury, Brent 11

Sudbury, Suffolk 104
Suffolk 103
Sunderland 104
Sunderland University 304
Sundon Park, Luton 65
Sunninghill, Windsor and Maidenhead 123
Support Services, Lambeth 58
Support Services, Nottinghamshire 78
Surbiton, Kingston upon Thames 54
Surrey 105 see also Croydon, Kingston
    upon Thames, Merton, Richmond upon
    Thames, Sutton
Surrey University 304
Sussex University 305
Sutherland see Highland
Sutton 107
Sutton Bonington Campus, Nottingham
    University 281
Sutton in Ashfield, Nottinghamshire 78
Swale-Sittingbourne, Kent 52
Swansea 184
Swansea Metropolitan University 305
Swansea University 305
Sweeney, Clare 192
Swindon 107
Swinton, Salford 88
Swiss Cottage, Camden 17
Swords, Fingal 197
Sydney Jones Library, Liverpool University
    264

Tain, Highland 154
Talbot Campus, Bournemouth University
    225
Tallaght, South Dublin 208
Tallow, Waterford County 213
Tameside 108
Tamworth, Staffordshire 100
Tarbert, Comhairle nan Eilean Siar 135
Tata Steel 384
Tate Library and Archive 384
Taunton Deane and West Somerset 95
Taunton, Somerset 95
Tavistock and Portman NHS Foundation
    Trust 385
Tavistock, Devon 30
Taylor Institution, Oxford University 285
Taylor Library and European
    Documentation Centre, Aberdeen
    University 219

Taylor Library, Corpus Christi College, Cambridge University 230

TEAGASC (Agriculture and Food Development Authority) 400

Teddington, Richmond upon Thames 86

Teesside Technology Centre, Corus UK Ltd see Tata Steel

Teesside University 306

Teignmouth, Devon 30

Telford and Wrekin 109

Telford Learning Centre, Wolverhampton University 315

Telford, Telford and Wrekin 109

Templeman Library, University of Kent 259

Templemore, Tipperary 211

Templer Study Centre, National Army Museum 360

Tenby, Pembrokeshire 181

Tettenhall, Wolverhampton 125

Tewkesbury, Gloucestershire 38

Thames Valley University 306, 408

Thames View, Barking and Dagenham 3

Thanet-Margate, Kent 52

Theology Faculty, Oxford University 286

Thetford, Norfolk 71

Thomas Parry Library, Aberystwyth University 220

Thomastown, Kilkenny 201

Thompson Library, Staffordshire University 303

Thornaby Westbury, Stockton-on-Tees 102

Thornaby, Stockton-on-Tees 102

Thornbury, South Gloucestershire 95

Thorney, Peterborough 80

Thornhill, Dumfries and Galloway 136

Thornhill, Southampton 97

Thornliebank, East Renfrewshire 144

Thornton Heath, Croydon 25

Thurles, Tipperary 211

Thurrock 109

Thurso, Highland 154

Tile Hill, Coventry 24

Tilehurst, Reading 83

Tillicoultry, Clackmannanshire 134

Timahoe, Laois 202

Tinsley, Sheffield 92

Tipperary 210, 211

Tiverton, Devon 30

Tokyngton, Brent 11

Tolworth, Kingston upon Thames 54

Tonbridge Centre, University of Kent at Tonbridge 259

Tonbridge, Kent 52

Tooting, Wandsworth 116

Topping Fold, Bury 15

Torbay 110

Torfaen 184

Torpoint, Cornwall 22

Torquay, Torbay 110

Tory Top, Cork City 193

Totley, Sheffield 94

Tottington, Bury 14

Tower Hamlets 110

Town Hall, Brent 11

Townhill Campus Library, Swansea Metropolitan University 305

Toy, Renfrewshire 163

TPS Consult Ltd 385

Trades Union Congress 385

Trafford 112

Tralee, Kerry 198

Tramore, Waterford County 213

Tranent, East Lothian 142

Tredegar, Blaenau Gwent 172

Treharris, Merthyr Tydfil 178

Tremough Campus, University College Falmouth 252

Trent Park, Middlesex University 277

Treorchy, Rhondda Cynon Taf 183

Trevithick, Cardiff University 239

Trim, Meath 205

Trinity College Dublin 400

Trinity College, Cambridge University 236

Trinity College, Oxford University 292

Trinity Hall, Cambridge University 236

Trinity Laban 306

Trinity University College see University of Wales Trinity St David

Trowbridge, Wiltshire 121

Truro, Cornwall 22

Tuam, Galway 198

Tubbercurry, Sligo 208

TUC Library Collections, London Metropolitan University 265, 393

Tudor Drive, Kingston upon Thames 54

Tulla, Clare 192

Tullamore, Offaly 206

Tullibody, Clackmannanshire 134

Tunbridge Wells, Kent 52

Twickenham, Richmond upon Thames 86

Tyne and Wear see Gateshead, North Tyneside, South Tyneside, Sunderland
Tynwald Library, Isle of Man Parliament/Legislature of the Isle of Man 351

UCD School of Information and Library Studies, University College Dublin 405
Uckfield, East Sussex 34
UCL (University College London), London University 272, 406
UHI Millennium Institute 307
Ullapool, Highland 154
Ulster University 309, 408
United States Embassy 386
United States Studies Institute see Institute for the Study of the Americas, London University
University College Dublin 401, 405
University College Falmouth 252
University College London (UCL), London University 272, 406
University College, Oxford University 293
University Medical Library, Cambridge University 229
University of . . . see under individual name
University of the Arts London 309
University of Wales Trinity St David 312
Unsworth, Bury 15
Uplawmoor, East Renfrewshire 144
Upper Norwood Joint Library 112
Upperthorpe, Sheffield 92
Uppingham, Rutland 87
Upton Cross, Cornwall 22
Urlingford, Kilkenny 201
Urmston, Trafford 112
Uxbridge, Hillingdon 46

V&A Theatre and Performance Department 386
Vale of Glamorgan 185
Valence, Barking and Dagenham 3
Vaughan Williams Memorial Library, English Folk Dance and Song Society 336
Velindre, Neath Port Talbot 181
Ventnor, Isle of Wight 48
Vere Harmsworth Library (Rothermere American Institute), Oxford University 286
Veterinary Laboratories Agency 386

Veterinary Libraries, Edinburgh University 251
Veterinary Science Library, Bristol University 228
Veterinary Sciences Centre, University College Dublin 402
Victoria and Albert Museum see National Art Library
Victoria Park, Queen Mary, London University 271
Victoria, Westminster 120

Wadebridge, Cornwall 22
Wadham College, Oxford University 293
Wadhurst, East Sussex 35
Wakefield 112
Wales Institute, Cardiff, University of 311
Wales, Newport, University of 311
Wales, University of, Lampeter see University of Wales Trinity St David
Walkden, Salford 88
Walker Street, Kingston upon Hull 53
Walkley, Sheffield 92
Wallasey, Wirral 124
Wallingford, Centre for Ecology and Hydrology 328
Wallington, Sutton 107
Wallsend, North Tyneside 74
Wallyford, East Lothian 143
Walsall 113
Walsall Learning Centre, Wolverhampton University 315
Walsall Wood, Walsall 114
Waltham Forest 114
Waltham, North East Lincolnshire 73
Walthamstow, Waltham Forest 115
Walton Library, Newcastle upon Tyne University 278
Walton, Surrey 107
Wandsworth 116
Wanstead, Redbridge 84
Wantz, Barking and Dagenham 3
Warburg Institute, London University 275
Ward and Perne Libraries, Peterhouse, Cambridge University 234
Ward, Isle of Man 188
Warrington 116
Warsash Library, Southampton Solent University 301
Warstones, Wolverhampton 125

Warwick University 312
Warwick, Warwickshire 117
Warwickshire 117 see also Coventry
Washington, Sunderland 105
Water Services Regulation Authority
    (OFWAT) 386
Waterdale, Doncaster 30
Waterford City 211
Waterford County 212
Waterford, Waterford City 211
Waterfront Campus, Southampton
    University 302
Waterloo Campus, King's College London
    269
Waterloo, Lambeth 57
Watford, Hertfordshire 46
Watney Market, Tower Hamlets 111
Wednesfield, Wolverhampton 125
Wellcome Images, Wellcome Library 387
Wellcome Library 386
Welsh Assembly Government 387
Welwyn Garden City, Hertfordshire 46
Wembley, Brent 10
Werrington, Peterborough 80
West Barnes, Merton 68
West Berkshire 118
West Bridgford, Nottinghamshire 78
West Bromwich, Sandwell 89
West Calder, West Lothian 169
West Dunbartonshire 167
West Hampstead, Camden 18
West Kirby, Wirral 124
West Lothian 167
West Midlands see Birmingham, Dudley,
    Sandwell, Solihull, Walsall,
    Wolverhampton
West Mill Street, Perth and Kinross 161
West Norwood, Lambeth 58
West of England University, Bristol 312, 408
West of Scotland University 313
West Smithfield, City University London
    243
West Sussex 119
West, Islington 50
Westbrook, Warrington 117
Wester Hailes, Edinburgh 147
Western Bank Library, Sheffield University
    300
Western Isles see Chomhairle Nan Eilean
    Siar

Western, Kingston upon Hull 53
Westerton, East Dunbartonshire 141
Westmeath 213
Westminster 119
Westminster Abbey 387
Westminster University 313
Weston, North Somerset 73
Weston, Southampton 97
Weston-super-Mare, North Somerset 73
Westside, Galway 198
Wexford 214
Weybridge, Surrey 106
Wheatley, Oxford Brookes University 282
Wheatsheaf, Rochdale 86
Whipps Cross Campus, London South Bank
    University 266
Whiston, Knowsley 56
Whitburn, West Lothian 169
Whitchurch, Cardiff University 238
Whitechapel, City University London 243
Whitechapel, Tower Hamlets 110
Whitchurch, South Dublin 209
Whitefield, Bury 15
Whiteinch, Glasgow 151
Whitfield, Dundee 139
Whithorn, Dumfries and Galloway 137
Whitley Bay, North Tyneside 74
Whitley, Reading 83
Whitmore Reans, Wolverhampton 125
Whittaker Library, Royal Scottish Academy
    of Music and Drama 298
Whitton Library, Richmond upon Thames
    86
Wick, Highland 154
Wicklow 215
Widnes, Halton 41
Wiener Library Institute of Contemporary
    History 387
Wigan 121
Wigan Clinical Library, Central Lancashire
    University 240
Wigmore, Luton 65
Wigston, Leicestershire 61
Wigtown, Dumfries and Galloway 137
Willenhall, Coventry 24
Willenhall, Walsall 114
Willesden Green, Brent 12
William Patrick, East Dunbartonshire 140
William Salt Library 388
Williams's Library, Dr 388

Willingdon, East Sussex 35
Willows, North East Lincolnshire 73
Wills Memorial Library, Bristol University 228
Wilmslow, Cheshire East 20
Wiltshire 121 see also Swindon
Wimbledon College of Art, University of the Arts London 311
Wimbledon, Merton 67
Winchester School of Art Library, Southampton University 302
Winchester, Hampshire 42
Winchester, University of 314
Windsor and Maidenhead 122
Windsor, Windsor and Maidenhead 123
Wirral 123
Wirral Campus, Chester University 241
Wisbech, Cambridgeshire 16
Woking, Surrey 105
Wokingham 124
Wolfson College, Cambridge University 236
Wolfson College, Oxford University 293
Wolverhampton 124
Wolverhampton University 314
Women's Library, The 388
Women's Library, London Metropolitan University 265
Wood Green, Haringey 43
Wood Street, Waltham Forest 115
Woodberry Down, Hackney 40
Woodbridge, Suffolk 104
Woodburn, Midlothian 157
Woodford Green, Redbridge 84
Woodhouse, Sheffield 92
Woodlands Campus, Edge Hill University 249
Woodlane Campus, University College Falmouth 253

Woodseats, Sheffield 92
Woodside, Glasgow 151
Woodston, Peterborough 80
Woolston, Southampton 97
Woolston, Warrington 117
Woolwich, Greenwich 39
Worcester College, Oxford University 293
Worcester Park, Sutton 107
Worcester University 315
Worcester, Worcestershire 127
Worcestershire 126
Word and Image Department, National Art Library 360
Working Class Movement Library 388
Workington, Cumbria 26
Worthing, West Sussex 119
Wrexham 185
Writtle College 315

Yarm, Stockton-on-Tees 102
Yate, South Gloucestershire 95
Yeats Archive, National Gallery of Ireland 397
Yeovil, Somerset 95
York 127
York Minster 389
York St John University 316
York University 316
Yorkshire see Barnsley, Bradford, Calderdale, Doncaster, East Riding of Yorkshire, Kingston upon Hull, Kirklees, Leeds, North Yorkshire, Rotherham, Sheffield, Wakefield, York

Zoological Society of London 389
Zoology Department, Oxford University 282